Lecture Notes in Computer Scie

T0238588

Commenced Publication in 1973
Founding and Former Series Editors:
Gerhard Goos, Juris Hartmanis, and Jan van Leeuwen

Marco Bernardo   Vittorio Cortellessa
Alfonso Pierantonio (Eds.)

Formal Methods for Model-Driven Engineering

12th International School
on Formal Methods for the Design of Computer,
Communication, and Software Systems, SFM 2012
Bertinoro, Italy, June 18-23, 2012
Advanced Lectures

 Springer

Volume Editors

Marco Bernardo
Università di Urbino "Carlo Bo"
Dipartimento di Scienze di Base e Fondamenti
Piazza della Repubblica 13, 61029 Urbino, Italy
E-mail: marco.bernardo@uniurb.it

Vittorio Cortellessa
Università dell'Aquila
Dipartimento di Informatica
Via Vetoio 1, 67010 Coppito - L'Aquila, Italy
E-mail: vittorio.cortellessa@univaq.it

Alfonso Pierantonio
Università dell'Aquila
Dipartimento di Informatica
Via Vetoio 1, 67010 Coppito - L'Aquila, Italy
E-mail: alfonso.pierantonio@univaq.it

ISSN 0302-9743   e-ISSN 1611-3349
ISBN 978-3-642-30981-6   e-ISBN 978-3-642-30982-3
DOI 10.1007/978-3-642-30982-3
Springer Heidelberg Dordrecht London New York

Library of Congress Control Number: 2012939229

CR Subject Classification (1998): D.2.4, D.2, D.3.1, F.3-4, K.6, C.3

LNCS Sublibrary: SL 2 – Programming and Software Engineering

Typesetting: Camera-ready by author, data conversion by Scientific Publishing Services, Chennai, India

Printed on acid-free paper

Springer is part of Springer Science+Business Media (www.springer.com)

Preface

This volume presents a set of papers accompanying the lectures of the 12th International School on Formal Methods for the Design of Computer, Communication and Software Systems (SFM).

This series of schools addresses the use of formal methods in computer science as a prominent approach to the rigorous design of the above-mentioned systems. The main aim of the SFM series is to offer a good spectrum of current research in foundations as well as applications of formal methods, which can be of help for graduate students and young researchers who intend to approach the field.

SFM 2012 was devoted to model-driven engineering and covered several topics including modeling languages, model transformations, functional and performance modeling and analysis, and model evolution management.

This volume comprises 11 articles. Selic's paper reviews how UML has changed over time and what new features it can provide that support not only informal lightweight sketching in early phases of development, but also full implementation capability. The paper by Andova, Van Den Brand, Engelen, and Verhoeff discusses the basic aspects of model-driven engineering in combination with textual domain-specific languages developed using the language invention pattern. Cabot and Gogolla present a comprehensive view of OCL and its applications including the use for expressing model transformations, well-formedness rules, and code-generation templates. The paper by Di Ruscio, Eramo, and Pierantonio introduces a classification of model-transformation approaches and languages and illustrates the characteristics of the most prominent ones. Giese, Lambers, Becker, Hildebrandt, Neumann, Vogel, and Wätzoldt show that graph transformations can be employed to engineer solutions for model-driven development, dynamic adaptation, and models at run time. The paper by De Caso, Braberman, Garbervetsky, and Uchitel deals with enabledness-preserving abstractions, which are concise representations of the behavior space for software engineering artifacts such as source code and specifications. Petriu, Alhaj, and Tawhid consider quantitative performance analysis of UML software models annotated with performance attributes according to the MARTE profile and describe a model-transformation chain that enables the integration of performance analysis in a UML-based software development process. Becker's paper gives an overview on the process of model-driven quality analyses with a special focus on issues that arise in fully automated approaches. The paper by Cortellessa, Di Marco, and Trubiani addresses the problem of capturing performance problems in the software design process by means of software performance antipatterns. Brosch, Kappel, Langer, Seidl, Wieland, and Wimmer offer an introduction to the foundations of model versioning, the underlying technologies for processing models and their evolution, and the state of the art in the field. Finally, the paper by Vallecillo, Gogolla, Burgueño, Wimmer, and Hamann presents model-transformation specification and testing by discussing and classifying some of the existing approaches and introducing a generalization of model-transformation contracts.

We believe that this book offers a useful view of what has been done and what is going on worldwide in the field of formal methods for model-driven engineering. We wish to thank all the speakers and all the participants for a lively and fruitful school. We also wish to thank the entire staff of the University Residential Center of Bertinoro for the organizational and administrative support.

June 2012

Marco Bernardo
Vittorio Cortellessa
Alfonso Pierantonio

Table of Contents

The Less Well Known UML

A Short User Guide

Bran Selic

Malina Software Corp., Nepean, Ontario, Canada
selic@acm.org

Abstract. The general perception and opinion of the Unified Modeling Language in the minds of many software professionals is colored by its early versions. However, the language has evolved into a qualitatively different tool: one that not only supports informal lightweight sketching in early phases of development, but also full implementation capability, if desired. Unfortunately, these powerful new capabilities and features of the language remain little known and are thus underutilized. In this article, we first review how UML has changed over time and what new value it can provide to practitioners. Next, we focus on and explain one particularly important new modeling capability that is often overlooked or misrepresented and explain briefly what is behind it and how it can be used to advantage.

Keywords: Unified Modeling Language, model-driven development, computer language semantics, architectural description languages.

1   Introduction

Available evidence suggests that the Unified Modeling Language (UML) is the most widely used modeling language in industrial practice [4]. Based on that and the fact that it is taught in most software engineering and information technology curricula around the world, it would be reasonable to expect that it is also a very well understood language, with all its capabilities known and exploited as appropriate. However, it seems that the reality is different. There is much misunderstanding and misinformation about the true nature of UML so that some of its more powerful features are unknown or underexploited.

The reasons behind this are due in large part to the way the language evolved. When it was first launched and then standardized in the mid 1990's, UML was (perhaps rightly) perceived as a mostly commercial initiative rather than a technical contribution. It was promoted as an attempt to consolidate the confusing explosion of diverse object-oriented analysis and design methods and notations that preceded it. While many of these notations were supported by computer-based commercial tools, very few were supported by multiple vendors. This created a problem for practitioners, since they not only had to make the difficult decision of choosing a suitable method and tool, but also had to contend with the potentially risky circumstance of being inextricably bound to a single tool vendor and a single narrowly-specialized method.

M. Bernardo, V. Cortellessa, and A. Pierantonio (Eds.): SFM 2012, LNCS 7320, pp. 1–20, 2012.

Other than its object-oriented base, the original conception of UML was very much in the tradition of earlier software engineering notations: a graphical notation with informal semantics intended primarily to assist in early conceptual design of software. In other words, it originated as a *descriptive* tool, in contrast to programming languages, which are formal *prescriptive* tools. Despite subsequent efforts at tightening up the language definition in the original standardized version through the use of meta-modeling and the formal Object Constraint Language (OCL) [17], its primarily descriptive and informal nature remained. Adoption by the Object Management Group (OMG) in 1996 drew a lot of public attention to UML, resulting in the publication of a number of popular UML books intended to provide user friendly guides for practitioners. It is fair to say that these early books and contemporary technical debates reported in various professional publications were formative, leaving lasting impressions and opinions of the language that have mostly persisted in spite of over 15 years of dramatic changes.

The most significant of these changes occurred with the release of the first major revision of the language, UML 2, which was adopted by the OMG in 2005. This was followed by several important standardized increments to the language definition, all of which were designed to provide a more precise specification of both its syntax and semantics. The net result is that UML can now even be used as a programming language, if desired.

Unfortunately, neither the authors of the original best-selling textbooks[1] nor the broader public have taken sufficient note of these important qualitative differences. Consequently, the understanding of current UML is inadequate and many of its important new capabilities remain little known and little used. It is the intent of this article to shed light on some of the lesser known but very useful features and modeling capabilities of UML.

2   The Progressive Formalization of UML

It is probably true that, despite being the most widely used modeling language, UML must also qualify among the most heavily criticized computer languages (e.g., [3] and [6]). As noted above, in its earlier incarnations, UML was intended primarily as an informal tool, to be used for descriptive purposes, providing support for analysis and design and for documentation. Consequently, the semantics of the original language were very weak and highly ambiguous, prompting one recognized language design expert to comment, alluding to UML, that "…bubbles and arrows, as opposed to programs, never crash…"[7]. The original conception of the language by its two primary authors, Grady Booch and Jim Rumbaugh, (joined subsequently by Ivar Jacobson), was as a kind of power-booster facility already widely represented in the previous generation of software design methodologies such as structured analysis and structured design (SASD). These early methodologies typically involved informal

---

[1] More up-to-date UML user textbooks have been published, such as [8], but, unfortunately, the original outdated books still remain as the most frequently used and cited references.

graphical (modeling) languages, and were designed to raise the level of abstraction above that of traditional programming language technology. Their imprecise nature meant that interpretation of the meaning of models depended on users' intuitions, leaving space for much confusion and misinterpretation.

As a result, programmers quickly lost confidence in these informal high-level descriptions of the software, since they often bore little resemblance to what was actually implemented in the programs. The net result is that modeling has a very negative reputation among many experienced practitioners, who perceive it as mostly a waste of time and effort. This view that code is the only trustworthy design artifact, the only one worth bothering with, is still quite prevalent and is echoed by many adherents of present-day agile methods, such as "eXtreme Programming" [1][2].

This line of thinking, of course, denies the value of abstraction as a means of coping with complexity, which is really the essence of what modeling provides. The semantic gap between application domain concepts and programming technology used to implement those concepts is still quite significant, and, with the exception of trivial programs, it presents a major hurdle to the design of reliable software. In other words, we *need* abstract representations of our solutions, since the complexity and technological bias of programs can easily overwhelm us. This holds even for modern object-oriented languages, which do allow the definition of application-domain concepts (i.e., via the class construct) but which, unfortunately, still contain an excess of implementation-level detail that gets in the way of comprehension and reasoning.

It is worth noting that there are actually very sound reasons for high degrees of informality in modeling: until an idea is properly understood and validated, it is inappropriate to burden designers with bureaucratic niggling about low-level syntactical details such as missing punctuation marks. The process of design almost invariably starts with informal and vague notions that are gradually firmed up and made more precise over time. If a seemingly promising idea turns out to be inappropriate once it has been elaborated and understood, the effort expended on specifying such detail will have been wasted. (Alternatively, it may lead to an even worse predicament whereby a bad design is retained because so much effort was vested in constructing a working prototype that there may be an understandable reluctance to discard it.)

But, as design firms up it is necessary to eventually transition from informal sketchy models to fully formal computer implementations. Ideally, to ensure preservation of design intent from inception to implementation, a good computer language should enable a gradual progression through this continuum, as free of error-inducing discontinuities as possible. This notion of enabling a smooth transition from descriptive to prescriptive modeling by using a single language throughout the process was one of the primary motivations for introducing UML 2 and is also the principal characteristic that distinguishes it from its predecessor.

The progression towards a more precise and more formal language definition occurred in four major steps:

---

[2] In the author's view this is a very narrow and somewhat distorted interpretation of agility and not one necessarily intended by the designers of such methods.

1. The first step was the definition of a supplement to the original UML 1 specification: the UML Action Semantics specification. The Action Semantics added the capability to specify fine-grained behavior, such as the sending and receiving of messages, the reading and writing of classifier features, or the creation and destruction of objects. As an integral part of the definition of these actions, a much more precise, albeit still informal, definition of the dynamic semantics of the core of UML was also defined.

2. The definition and adoption of UML 2 [10], which fully incorporated the Action Semantics, and which, in addition to a more precise and more modular language specification, provided a small number of new modeling capabilities[3]. Perhaps most significant was the addition of advanced structural modeling features taken from several widely used architectural description languages. These little known and often misunderstood capabilities are explained in more detail in section 7.2 below.

3. The "Semantics of a Foundational Subset for Executable UML Models" specification [11], which included a fully formal definition of a key subset of the UML 2 actions, using a variant of first-order predicate logic. In addition, it included an operational semantics specification of a UML virtual machine for executing those actions. A more detailed discussion of this specification is provided in section 5.

4. The "Concrete Syntax for a UML Action Language" specification [12], recently adopted by the OMG, which provides a precise textual surface syntax for UML actions,

With the last increment above the progression to a fully-fledged implementation quality language was completed. Note, however, that—in contrast to traditional programming languages—the degree of formality to be used with UML is at the discretion of the modeler. This means that it is possible to use UML both informally for rapid and lightweight "sketching" of early design ideas as well as for implementation—a full-cycle language.

In conclusion, UML is very far from being a "notation without semantics", as it is often characterized by those who are less familiar with it. In fact, when it comes to a mathematically formal specification, UML is ahead of most popular programming languages—at least for its executable subset.

3   UML "versus" Domain-Specific Modeling Languages

Another common criticism directed at UML is that, being a "general-purpose" language, it is (a) too big and unwieldy and (b) too blunt an instrument to adequately cope with the kinds of domain-specific subtleties encountered in highly-specialized software applications. In such discussions UML is often pitted against so-called "domain-specific modeling languages" (DSMLs) [3] [16]. These are typically compact high-level languages designed specifically to address a relatively narrow application domain.

---

[3] To be fair, the current version of UML (UML 2.4 at the time of this writing) still suffers from numerous technical flaws. However, the latest version of the language currently under development, UML 2.5, is designed with the sole objective of eliminating as much as possible remaining ambiguities and imprecision in the language specification.

As is argued below, this particular controversy, like many similar ones in the history of computing, is more a conflict of commercial marketing messages than of technical visions. That is, it should be fairly obvious that a custom domain-specific language will, usually, produce more concise and more direct specifications and, therefore, more effective solutions for problems in its domain than a more general language. Getting closer to the application domain and its concepts, is precisely what is meant by "raising the level of abstraction" when modeling languages are discussed. The real technical issue is to find the most effective method of realizing a DSML.

There are three different ways in which this can be done:

1. A completely new language can be designed from scratch
2. An existing (base) language can be *extended* with domain-specific concepts
3. The concepts of a general existing (base) language can be *refined* (specialized) to represent domain-specific concepts

The latter two methods may seem similar, but they are fundamentally different. Namely, *extending* a language involves adding completely new concepts to the language—concepts that are unlike any of the concepts in the base language—whereas *refining* a language means *narrowing* the definition of existing base language concepts, so that they match application semantics. In principle, the refinement approach provides some important advantages over the other two approaches, but, these are often overlooked in heated theological debates. This is because they are not technical in nature, although they may actually be more important in practical industrial settings.

The primary advantage of the refinement approach to DSMLs is the ability to take advantage of several factors:

1. Reuse of the expertise that went into designing the base language (and, we should point out that, given the absence of a sound and proven theory, modeling language design expertise is still quite scarce),
2. Reuse of the tooling for the base language as well as any training materials.
3. If the base language is standardized and widely taught—as is the case with UML— it should be much easier to find experienced practitioners who are familiar with it and who will more readily absorb the specialized DSML based on it. This also reduces the training cost, which can be a significant for new languages.

Of the above, perhaps the most important is the ability to reuse existing base language tools. Although modern DSML design tools, such as those offered by *itemis AG,*[4] provide the very useful ability to automatically or semi-automatically generate some language-specific tooling directly from the language definition (e.g., model editing tools, code generators), this is usually far from sufficient for more complex applications. Industrial-scale software development needs a very wide variety of tools such as debuggers, model validators of different kinds, simulators, test generators, document generators, version management tools, and the like. The effort required to develop industrial-strength tools of this type that are scalable, usable, and robust is not

---

[4] http://www.itemis.com/

trivial and should never be underestimated (this is why there are commercial development tool vendors). Moreover, tool development is rarely a one-time cost, because tools will typically need to be maintained and upgraded over time. In balance, the impact of these costs may in some cases exceed any technical benefits of having a custom language.

From this perspective, refinement-based approaches have an advantage over the other two, since they offer a lot of opportunity for reuse, particularly for widely-used languages such as UML, for which there already exists a rich choice of tools.

This is not to say that custom DSMLs have no role to play, but it seems that their "sweet spot" lies with smaller highly-specialized stand-alone applications ("small languages for small problems"). The case of complex multi-faceted systems is different, however, even when they can be decomposed into multiple specialized sub-domains. This is because these sub-domains often overlap, so that some parts of the system may be represented in multiple models that are written in different DSMLs. These different views then have to be reconciled, which can be difficult if the individual languages are designed independently of each other (this is sometimes referred to as the "fragmentation problem" of DSMLs). In such situations, the problem is easier to manage if the various overlapping languages share a common semantics foundation. Once again, refinement-based approaches hold the advantage here, since the various DSMLs can all be evolved from the same base language.

But, refinement-based approaches do have one fundamental disadvantage: the domain-specific concepts of a DSML must have a corresponding base concept in the base language. If no suitable base concept can be found, then either an extension-based or a new language alternative must be used. (The former is usually preferred since it is more likely to have more potential for reuse in general than a completely new language.)   This is why a concept-rich general-purpose language may be the best base for DSMLs, paradoxical as this may sound. Moreover, as explained earlier, such a language can also help us deal with the fragmentation problem, since all the derived DSMLs would be sharing the same semantic core.

This brings us back to UML and its ability to serve as a source language for defining refinement-based DSMLs via its *profile* mechanism. A UML profile comprises a set of domain-specific refinements of standard UML language constructs and corresponding constraints. Because such refinements are semantically aligned with their base concepts, existing UML tools may be directly applicable for the DSML defined by the profile[5]. This capability has been used extensively to produce numerous UML-based DSMLs, many of which have been standardized by the OMG as well as other standardization bodies [9].

Unfortunately, the profile mechanism of UML is far from perfect[6]. This is due to the fact that, when the approach was first proposed, there was little practical experience with it. For example, it is not easy to determine with precision whether or not a

---

[5] Needless to say, it is best if the UML tool itself be sensitized to the added domain-specific semantics, which is why many current UML tools are designed to be highly customizable.

[6] Improvements to the profile mechanism are being considered within the OMG at the present time.

particular specialization of a UML concept is semantically aligned with its base concept so that a standard UML tool will treat it correctly. Nevertheless, despite its technical shortcomings, because it is a refinement-based approach to DSML design, it has the advantages that come with that approach. It has proven adequate in practice, although, admittedly, not universally so.

In addition to serving as a mechanism for defining DSMLs, the profile mechanism has one additional and important capability. This is the ability to use profiles as an *annotation mechanism* for re-interpreting UML models or profile-based DSML models. Namely, using stereotypes of a profile, it is possible to attach customized annotations to elements of a UML or DSML model. These annotations are like overlays that do not affect the underlying model in any way and can, therefore, be dynamically applied or removed as required. Such annotations are typically used to provide custom supplementary information not supported in standard UML and which can be exploited by various model analyzers or model transformers. For example, the standardized MARTE profile [13], provides facilities for adding information that is useful for certain types of real-time systems, such as timing information (deadlines, durations, processing times, delays, etc.), which can be used by specialized tools to analyze the timing characteristics of a design.

In summary, UML and the idea of DSMLs are not mutually exclusive as is often suggested. In fact, UML may provide the best solution to supporting a DSML in many practical situations, particularly for more complex systems.

4   The Structure of UML 2

Since it was designed to cover a broad spectrum of application types, UML is, undoubtedly, a large computer language. This makes it difficult to master in its full extent. (Although, it should be noted that the intellectual effort required to master UML pales in comparison to the effort required to master modern programming languages such as Java, which, although relatively compact, is only truly useful if it is combined with numerous standard class libraries and other utilities.) But, is it really "too big" as its critics often like to repeat?

It is probably fair to say that it is "too big", *if the language is approached without a particular purpose in mind*, meaning that one would need to digest all of it in a single sweep. Fortunately, in UML 2, the structure of the language has been modularized so that it is rarely a need master the full language. In fact, UML consists of a set of distinct *sub-languages*, each with its own concrete syntax (notation), but which, fortunately, share a common foundation (Fig. 1[7]). With a few exceptions, these languages are independent of each other and can be used independently or in combination. Thus, one only needs to learn the sub-languages of direct interest and the sub-languages that these depend on, while ignoring the rest. For instance, users interested in capturing event-driven behavior via state machines, need only to know the State Machine language, a subset of the Activities language, and the Foundations they both rest on.

---

[7] Note that this diagram depicts a language user's view of the various sub-languages and their relationships. The actual internal structure of the UML metamodel is somewhat different.

UML 2 consists of the following sub-languages:

- The *Foundations* module contains a *Structural Kernel,* which covers basic structural concepts such as classes, associations, instances, values, etc., and a *Behavioral Kernel*, which in turn depends on the Structural Kernel, and which covers essential behavioral concepts, such as events, messages, and the like. The Structural Kernel alone is sufficient for certain basic forms of software modeling provided via class diagrams. The Foundations provide the common core that is shared by all other sub-languages
- The *Structured Classes* language was added in UML 2 and supports the modeling complex classes representing complex architectural entities. It is a distillation of a number of architectural description languages. It is described in more detail in section 7.2.
- The *Deployment* language is used for capturing the allocation of software modules (e.g., binaries) to underlying hardware or software platforms[8].
- The *Collaborations* language is used to describe complex structural patterns of collaborating objects. Despite its name, this language is used to specify structure and not behavior. However, it is often used to define the structural setting for interactions. It is covered in section 7.1.
- The *Interactions* language serves to model interactions between multiple collaborating entities and the actions that occur as a result. In UML 2, interactions can be specified using three different graphical syntactical forms as well as one tabular one.
- *Actions* are used for specifying fine-grained behavioral elements comparable to traditional programming language instructions. UML actions depend on the Activities language, which provides facilities for combining actions into more complex behavioral fragments as well as to control their order of execution. Note that, except for a generic syntactical form (which does not differentiate between the various types of actions), there is no concrete syntax for representing actions. Instead, behavior at this level can be specified using the ALF language [12], which has a textual concrete syntax reminiscent of conventional programming languages such as Java. (The raw UML Actions can be thought of as a kind of UML assembler, whereas the ALF language is of a higher order.)
- The *Activities* language is used to model complex control or data flow based behaviors, or even combinations of the two. It is inspired by a colored Petri Net formalism and is well-suited to the modeling parallel processes, such as complex business processes.
- The *State Machine* language is used for specifying discrete event-driven behaviors, where the responses to input events are a function of history. In UML 2 a special variant called *protocol state machines* was added to support the specification of interface protocols.

---

[8] This language provides a relatively simple model of deployment that is suitable for some applications. A much more sophisticated deployment modeling capability is provided by the MARTE profile [14].

- The *Use Case* language captures use cases and their relationships, as well as the actors that participate in those use cases.
- The *Information Flow* language serves to capture the type and direction of flow of information between elements of a system at a very abstract level.
- The *Profiles* language, as already explained, is not used for modeling systems but for defining DSMLs based on UML.

In addition to the above set that are part of UML proper, two other languages can be used when modeling with UML:

- The *Object Constraint Language* (OCL), which is used to write formal logic constraints either in user models or in profiles.
- The *Action Language for Foundational UML (ALF)*, a high-level language with a concrete textual syntax used for specifying detailed behaviors in the context of UML Activities. The semantics of ALF constructs are expressed in terms of UML actions and activities and are fully compatible with the dynamic semantics of UML itself. As noted earlier, the combination of UML and ALF (including its libraries) is sufficient to make UML an implementation language.

Naturally, all of these languages can be combined as needed. This is facilitated by the fact that they are all based on the same Foundations, including OCL and ALF.

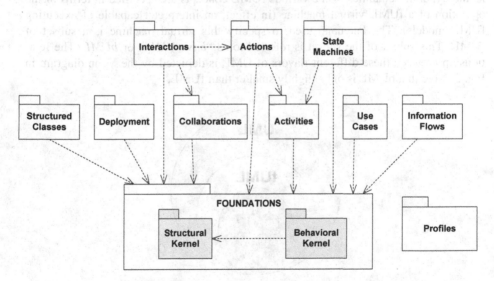

Fig. 1. The UML 2 sub-languages and their relationships

This new modularized architecture of the UML 2 language provides a lot of flexibility, enabling modelers to select an appropriate subset of the language suited to their needs. Combined with the profile mechanism, such a subset can be specialized even further to suit specific application domains.

5   The Specification of UML Semantics

As noted above, the definition of UML semantics, originally expressed almost exclusively in natural language, has been significantly tightened with the adoption of the "Semantics of a Foundational Subset for Executable UML Models" specification [11]. Although it does not cover the full UML language, this specification provides a foundation for the semantic core of UML, upon which the rest of the language rests. The subset of UML covered is referred to as "*foundational UML*" or *fUML* for short. It covers the following four major groupings of UML concepts from Fig. 1:

- The *Structural Kernel of UML* (part of the Foundations package).
- The *Behavioral Kernel of UML* (also part of the Foundations package).
- A major subset of the UML *Activities* sub-language
- A major subset of the UML *Actions*

This subset was carefully chosen because it was deemed sufficient for describing the semantics of the remainder of UML. Note, however, that it is not a minimal set. Instead, a tradeoff was made between minimality and expressiveness, providing for a relatively compact and understandable specification.

The approach taken for defining the semantics of fUML is an *operational* one; that is, the dynamic semantics of the various fUML concepts are specified in terms of the operation of a fUML virtual machine (in effect, an interpreter capable of executing fUML models). The language used to specify this virtual machine is a subset of fUML. This subset of the subset is referred to as "*base UML*", or *bUML*. The relationship between these different flavors of UML is depicted by the Venn diagram in Fig. 2. Note that bUML is only slightly smaller than fUML.

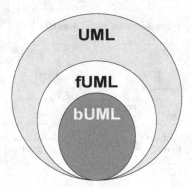

Fig. 2. Relationship between full UML, fUML, and bUML

Of course, to avoid a fully circular definition of the semantics, it is necessary to describe the semantics of bUML using some other formalism, preferably one that is well recognized and well understood. Therefore, a separate *formal* definition of the semantics of bUML is provided in the fUML specification. This definition uses a *declarative* approach, using a special formalism for modeling concurrent systems called

Process Specification Language (PSL), which has been adopted as a standard by the International Standards Organization (ISO) [5]. PSL is based on first-order mathematical logic.

The details of the fUML virtual machine and how PSL is used to capture bUML semantics are outside the scope of this article. However, the following section provides an informal overview of the semantics of UML, which incorporate the semantics of fUML.

6   The Dynamic (Run-Time) Semantics of UML

The run-time semantics of UML, as defined in the general standard and as further refined within fUML, are relatively straightforward. The basic behavioral paradigm is a discrete event driven model.

The prime movers of all behavior in the system are active objects, which interact with each other by sending messages through links. The sending and receiving of messages, result in event occurrences. The reception of an event by an active object may cause the execution of appropriate behaviors associated with the receiving object.

An *active object* in UML is an object that, once created, will commence executing its *classifier behavior* (a specially designated behavior associated with the class of the object). This behavior will run until it either completes or until the object is terminated. In a given system, the classifier behaviors of multiple active objects can be running concurrently. It is sometimes said that an active object "runs on its own thread", but this formulation can be misleading. One problem is that the concept of a "thread" is technology specific and has many different realizations and interpretations in different systems. (It is, of course, preferable if the semantics of UML are defined precisely and independently of any particular technology.) It is also inappropriate, since there can be many such "threads" associated with the behavior of an active object. For example, the composite states of UML state machines may include multiple concurrent regions, or, a UML activity may fork its control or data flows into multiple concurrent flows.

When an active object needs to interact with another active object, it sends a message through a link to the object at the opposite end of the link. The message is a carrier of information and may represent either a synchronous invocation of an *operation* of the target object, or an asynchronous signal corresponding to a *reception*[9]. Once the message arrives at its destination, it is placed in the *event pool* associated with the receiving object. The message will remain in the event pool until it is dispatched according to a scheduling policy. To allow modeling of different kinds of systems, the scheduling and dispatching policies are semantic variation points in fUML, although a default first-come-first-serve policy is supplied.

---

[9] In UML a reception is a behavioural feature similar to an operation, except that it is invoked (by sending a signal) and executed asynchronously. Only active objects can have receptions.

Messages are extracted from the event pool only when the receiving object executes a "receive" action[10]. Which message is selected and dispatched at that point depends on the scheduling policy. Once the message is received, it is processed by the active object according to its classifier behavior.

As part of executing its classifier behavior, an active object may access the features of passive objects. Passive objects are created by active objects and their operations and attributes are accessed synchronously. Note that, unless care is taken, it is possible for conflicts to occur when multiple active objects access the same passive object concurrently.

7   Advanced Structure Modeling in UML 2

Empirical evidence suggests that of all the diagram types provided by UML, class diagrams are by far the most widely used in practice [2], [4]. This is generally a positive outcome, since class diagrams are an excellent example of the power of abstraction and the benefits that it can bring to the design of complex systems. Nevertheless, there is much confusion about the precise meaning of these diagrams (undoubtedly due in part to the imprecise and vague descriptions provided in the standard itself), leading to frequent misuse.

One common mistake is to treat class models as instance models. A class in UML, as in most object-oriented languages, is a specification of what is common to all instances of that class (e.g., the number and types of its features), that is, a set of rules that define what constitutes a valid instance of the class. Using mathematical terminology, we say that a class is an *intentional* specification. (Corresponding to it is an extension represented by the set of all possible instances of that class.) Consequently, a class says nothing about characteristics that are unique to individual instances— those are abstracted out in class models. This level of modeling is sufficient in some types of applications, particularly in databases. In fact, class modeling evolved from standard entity-relationship modeling that originated in database theory.

But, there are many applications where it is necessary to capture instance-specific information. For example, consider the two distinct systems depicted in the two instance diagrams in Fig. 3(a) and Fig. 3(b). That these are two different systems should be clear, since they contain a different number of elements. However, note that they share the same class diagram (Fig. 3(c))[11].

Clearly, class diagrams are not suitable for this purpose and we need something more. In UML, there are two types of structure sub-languages specifically designed to support instance-based modeling: collaborations and structured classes. In contrast to simple instance (object) diagrams, which merely represent snapshots of systems at some point in time, these sub-languages provide a means for specifying rules for what constitutes *valid configurations of instances*. In other words, they do for instances what class modeling does for classes.

---

[10] In case of state machines, this action is implicit and occurs upon the full completion of a transition when a steady state is reached – hence, the term "run-to-completion".

[11] In fact, the class diagram represents a potentially infinite number of different systems.

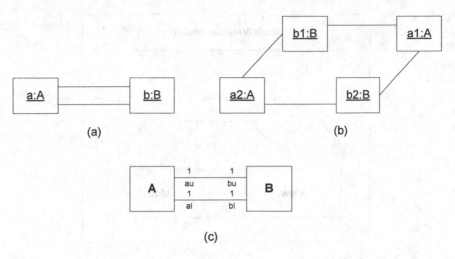

(a)   (b)

(c)

Fig. 3. Class versus instance models

7.1   Collaborations and Collaboration Uses

A common example of an instance-based pattern (configuration of instances) is the well-known Model-View-Controller architectural pattern shown in Fig. 4 [18]. This is a general pattern that can take on many concrete forms. In it, we differentiate the individual participants based their responsibilities, or *roles,* within the pattern rather than by their identities [14]. Thus, we need to represent instances in a structural context while abstracting away their identities. For example, the fact that in some realizations of Model-View-Controller a single object might be filling both the Model and the Controller roles is irrelevant to the specification of the pattern.

When working with roles, we may not be interested in the type of the object playing a particular role, leaving it undefined. However, in UML, we also have the option to specify the type of a role, a constraint which signifies that only instances of the designated type or its compatible subtypes can fill that role.

A role only makes sense in a greater structural context in which interacts with other roles. In UML, the structural context containing roles is called a *collaboration*[12]. UML.

(*Practical tip*: Note the use of the rectangle notation for classifiers in Fig. 4, to represent the collaboration rather than the more widely known dashed oval notation found in most UML textbooks. The rectangle notation is the default UML notation for any kind of classifier, including collaborations. This is usually a much more convenient and efficient form than the enclosing oval, since it provides for more effective use of scarce screen surface area.)

---

[12] This is a rather unfortunate choice of name, since the term "collaboration" has dynamic connotations, although the UML concept is structural in essence. (In fact, in UML 1, collaborations were misclassified as a kind of behavioural modelling.).

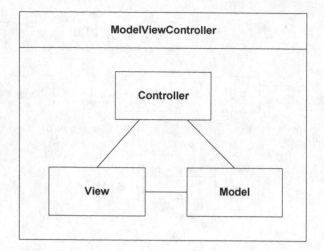

Fig. 4. Model-View-Controller pattern expressed as a collaboration

The roles of a collaboration may be linked to each other via *connectors*, representing communication paths by which the roles interact with each other. Connectors explicitly identify which roles are mutually coupled and which ones are not. Since deciding on the coupling between components of a system is a critical architectural design decision, the presence of connectors provides a concrete manifestation of design intent. Since inter-object communications in UML is accomplished via links, a connector denotes a link instance, in the same way that a role denotes an object instance. Note that it is not necessary to define associations for such implicit links, although it is possible, particularly if all the connected roles are typed.

Standard UML does not define fully the semantics of connectors. Specifically, the communication properties of such links (i.e., whether they are order preserving, non-duplicating, and non-lossy) are left as semantic variation points. If a stronger definition is required, it can be provided through a profile[13].

Collaborations are frequently combined with interactions, providing the structural setting over which message exchange sequences are overlaid. (In fact, it is this combination of two distinct UML sub-languages that gave rise to the term "collaboration".[14]) In those cases, the lifelines of an interaction are associated with the roles of the underlying collaboration. Clearly, messages between two lifelines should only be permitted if the corresponding roles are connected (although standard UML does not enforce this constraint).

(*Practical tip*: In support of this combination of collaborations and structures, UML provides the *communications diagram* notation, which shows what appears to be a collaboration diagram with roles corresponding to the lifelines of the interaction and messages shown as numbered arrows running parallel to the connectors they traverse. While this notational form is widely advertised in many UML textbooks,

---

[13] fUML is more constrained and does assume perfect communication properties for links.
[14] It is only in UML 2 that these two sub-languages were separated.

practical experience has shown that it is not particularly useful due to graphical limitations, and is probably best avoided. In practice, message names are often longer than the space provided between the roles of the graph so that they do not fit in the diagram. Moreover, for anything but trivial message sequences, it is very difficult to follow the flows of messages by keeping track of message sequence numbers, especially when concurrent sequences are involved.)

Collaborations that capture structural patterns, such as Model-View-Controller, can be treated as a kind of macro definition that can be reused whenever a pattern needs to be applied in a given model. In UML this can be achieved through a mechanism called *collaboration use*. Consider, for example, the case where we would like to capture a special variant of the Model-View-Controller pattern such that the Model and the Controller roles are filled by the same object. We can represent this by a new collaboration, shown by the collaboration diagram in Fig. 5.

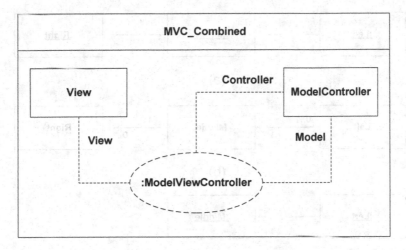

Fig. 5. Collaboration use example

The dashed oval in Fig. 5 is the notation for a collaboration use, and it represents a reference to (i.e., application of) the original ModelViewController pattern. The dashed lines emanating from it represent the roles of the corresponding collaboration (ModelViewController). Of course, in this particular case, we could have done this by simply having a simple collaboration with just two roles, View and ModelController, avoiding the collaboration use. However, that would have obscured the design intent, which was to take advantage of the well-known design pattern. The collaboration use makes that explicit.

Although collaborations have been a part of UML from the very first release of the standard[15], evidence indicates that, in contrast to class diagrams, they are little used by practitioners [4]. This is surprising at first, since one would normally expect instance

---

[15] Although the technical definition of collaborations has changed somewhat between UML 1 and UML 2, the essence has remained unchanged.

based modeling to be the more intuitive form of representing structure to most people. Class modeling requires an extra inductive reasoning step: abstracting from the particular to the general. The most likely explanation is that most software developers trained in object-oriented programming are familiar with the class concept, whereas the notion of a role is less well known and is not supported explicitly in common object-oriented programming languages.

This is unfortunate, since there are many cases where collaborations are the most natural modeling technique. Instead, it often happens that attempts are made to capture instance-specific structures unsuccessfully using class diagrams. For example, Fig. 6 illustrates one of the most common mistakes. In attempting to capture the structure shown in Fig. 6(a) even experienced modelers might define a class diagram like the one in Fig. 6(b). However, this is incorrect since that particular class model supports a variety of different instance patterns, including the one shown in Fig. 6(c).

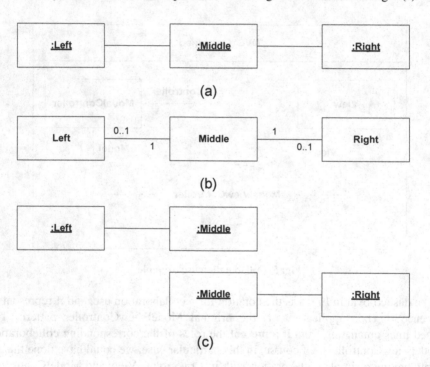

Fig. 6. Inappropriate use of class modeling

7.2   Structured Classes and Components

UML 2 added another form of instance-based modeling via the *structured class* concept. Structured classes were inspired by various architectural description languages used to represent the architectural structure of software systems.

Structured classes are distinguished from "simple" classes by virtue of the following two features:

- The possible presence of one or more communication *ports* on its interface.
- The possible encapsulation of an *internal structure* consisting of a network of collaborating objects.

Ports. Ports are a common feature of most architectural description languages but they are rarely encountered in programming languages. Ports are analogous to the pins of a hardware chip: instead of a single interface, it is possible to have a set of distinct interface points each dedicated to a specific purpose. Ports in UML add two important modeling capabilities:

1. Like any interface, a port provides an explicit and focused *point of interaction* between the object that owns it (i.e., an instance of a structured class) and its environment, thereby isolating each from the other. An important characteristic of ports is that they can be *bi-directional*. This means that a port has (a) an *outward face*, which it presents to its collaborators and which defines the services that the object provides to its collaborators, and (b) an *inward face*, which can be accessed by its internal components and which reflects the services that are expected of the collaborators on the outside. Thus, a port represents a full two-way contract, with the obligations and expectations of each party explicitly spelled out.
2. Since an object can have multiple ports, they allow an object to *distinguish between multiple, possibly concurrent collaborators* by virtue of the port (interface) through which an interaction occurs.

Reflecting the bi-directional nature of ports, in UML a port can be associated with UML Interfaces[16] in two different ways. For its outward face, a port may *provide* zero or more Interfaces, which specify its offered services. For its inward face, a port may *require* zero or more Interfaces, which define what is expected of the party at the opposite end of the port.

(*Practical* tip: It is generally better to associate no more than one provided Interface with a port, to avoid possible conflicts when the definitions of two or more Interfaces overlap (e.g., they provide the same service). If different Interfaces are desired, it is always possible to add a separate port for each Interface.)

Note that it is possible for an object to have multiple ports that provide the same Interface. This allows an object to distinguish between multiple collaborators even though they require the same type of service. This capability is particularly useful when Interfaces have associated protocols, that is, when the interactions between an Interface user and an Interface provider must conform to a particular order. For example, a database class may impose a two-phase commit protocol to be used when data is being written. This usually means that at any given time, an interface (i.e., port) instance may have a state, corresponding to the phase of the protocol that it is in. With multiple ports supporting Interfaces of the same type with each dedicated to a separate client, it is possible for individual ports to be in different states, allowing thus full decoupling of concurrent clients all using the same Interface.

---

[16] To distinguish between the generic notion of "interface" and the specific UML concept with the same name, the latter is capitalized in the text.

The dynamic semantics of UML ports are quite straightforward: whatever messages (operation calls, signals) come from the outside they are simply relayed inwards, and vice versa. In other words, they are simply relay devices and nothing more.

Ports must be connected to something on either face; otherwise, whatever comes in from a connected side will simply be lost. There are two possible ways in which a port can be connected: (a) to the end of a connector or (b) to the classifier behavior of the object that owns the port. In the latter case, the port is called a *behavior port*. It is only when a message arrives at a behavior port that anything actually happens (see section 6 above).

Of course, only compatible ports can be connected through a connector. The specific rules for compatibility are not defined in standard UML (i.e., it is a semantic variation point). But, generally speaking, two ports are compatible if the services required by one are provided by the other and vice versa. If protocols are associated with the ports, compatibility rules are more complex except in the trivial case where the associated protocols are exact precise complements of each other.

The standard UML notation for ports is shown in Fig. 7. Port **Pa** is a non-behavior port, whereas **Pb** is a behavior port (indicated by the small "roundtangle" attached to it). Note that ports do not necessarily have to appear on the boundary of the classifier icon, although that is the usual convention.

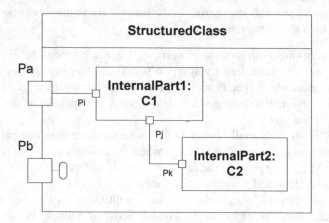

Fig. 7. A structured class with parts and ports

Internal Structure. In a sense, as shown in Fig. 7, the internal structure of a structured class is very much like a collaboration that is contained within the confines of an object. The only difference is that the *parts* comprising the internal structure do not represent roles, but the structural features of the class, such as attributes and ports. (Naturally, some of these parts may be typed by structured classes with their own ports and internal parts, as the example in Fig. 7 illustrates.) The extra modeling capability provided by internal structure is that the parts can be linked via connectors. In other words, in addition to a set of structural features (e.g., attributes), structured classes also own an interconnection topology that shows explicitly how the various parts interact.

The full run-time semantics of structured classes are not fully specified in standard UML (nor are structured classes covered by fUML). Are the parts and connectors automatically created when an instance of the class is created? That would certainly be quite useful, since: (a) then there would be no need to specify the tedious house-keeping code for creating the internal objects and connections, and (b) it would result in more reliable implementations, since the implementation code would be automatically generated from the class definition. Moreover, this would also ensure that only possible couplings between elements of the system would be those that are explicitly specified by the modeler. In fact, a number of UML profiles, such as the UML-RT profile [15], define such semantics.

The addition of concepts such as ports, connectors, and structured classes means that UML can be used as an architectural description language extending the range of UML from the highest levels of a system down to very fine-grained detail (e.g., using ALF).

Components. There a common misconception that in order to take advantage of UML's architectural modeling constructs such as ports, connectors, and internal structures one must use the UML Component construct. As explained above, this is not the case. In fact, the Component construct in UML 2 is merely a specialization of the structured class concept, with a few additional features that are included primarily for backward compatibility with previous versions of UML. Namely, the UML 1 definition of Component attempted to cover a variety of different interpretations of that widely used term with a single concept. Consequently, a component was used to denote both a unit of software reuse (e.g., the source code and binary modules) residing in some design repository as well as an instantiable run-time entity similar to a class. While UML 2 has retained this hybridized concept (to smooth the transition of UML llegacy models to UML 2), it is probably best to avoid it, using instead structured classes which have clear and unambiguous semantics.

8   Summary

UML has evolved a long way from its informal early versions, characterized by ambiguous and imprecise semantics. It has gradually emerged as a full-cycle computer language, equally capable of being used in a highly informal lightweight design sketching mode as well as a fully-fledged implementation language. Unfortunately, this progression from a purely descriptive tool to a prescriptive one, has received little attention so that there is much misunderstanding of its role and capabilities.

In this article, we have briefly summarized the nature of this dramatic evolution, pointing out how the tightening of the semantics of UML has been achieved and what benefits that provides.

In addition, we have focused on an important new capability provided by UML 2, but one which is little known and often misinterpreted: the mechanisms for capturing and enforcing instance-based structural patterns. This adds an important new dimension to UML by providing the standard constructs found in architectural description languages, extending thus the scope of abstractions that can be represented.

References

1. Beck, K.: Extreme Programming Explained. Addison-Wesley, Boston (2000)
2. Dobing, B., Parsons, J.: How UML is Used. Communications of the ACM 49, 109–113 (2006)
3. Greenfield, J., Short, K., et al.: Software Factories. Wiley Publishing, Inc., Indianapolis (2004)
4. Hutchinson, J.: An Empirical Assessment of Model Driven Development in Industry. PhD Thesis, School of Computing and Communications, Lancaster University, UK (2011)
5. International Standards Organization (ISO): Industrial automation systems and integration – Process specification language (Part 1: Overview and basic principles). ISO standard 18629-1:2004 (2004), http://www.iso.org/iso/iso_catalogue/catalogue_tc/catalogue_detail.htm?csnumber=3543
6. Kelly, S., Tolvanen, J.-P.: Domain-Specific Modeling. John Wiley & Sons, Hoboken (2008)
7. Meyer, B.: UML: The Positive Spin (1997), http://archive.eiffel.com/doc/manuals/technology/bmarticles/uml/page.html
8. Milicev, D.: Model-Driven Development with Executable UML. Wiley Publishing Inc., Indianapolis (2009)
9. Object Management Group (OMG): Catalog of UML Profile Specifications, http://www.omg.org/technology/documents/profile_catalog.htm
10. Object Management Group (OMG): OMG Unified Modeling Language (OMG UML) Superstructure. OMG document no. ptc/10-11-14 (2010), http://www.omg.org/spec/UML/2.4.1/Superstructure/PDF/
11. Object Management Group (OMG): Semantics of a Foundational Subset for Executable UML Models (fUML). OMG document no. formal/2011-02-01 (2011), http://www.omg.org/spec/FUML/1.0/PDF/
12. Object Management Group (OMG): Action Language for Foundational UML. OMG document no. ptc/2010-10-05 (2010), http://www.omg.org/spec/ALF/1.0/Beta2/PDF
13. Object Management Group (OMG): UML Profile for MARTE: Modeling and Analysis of Real-Time and Embedded Systems. OMG document no. formal/2011-06-02 (2011), http://www.omg.org/spec/MARTE/1.1/PDF
14. Reenskaug, T., Wold, P., Lehne, A.: Working With Objects. Manning Publications Co., Greenwich (1996)
15. Selic, B., Rumbaugh, J.: Using UML for Modeling Complex Real-Time Systems. IBM developerWorks (1998), http://www.ibm.com/developerworks/rational/library/content/03July/1000/1155/1155_umlmodeling.pdf
16. Völter, M.: From Programming to Modeling—and Back Again. IEEE Software, 20–25 (November/December 2011)
17. Warmer, J., Kleppe, A.: The Object Constraint Language: Getting Your Models Ready for MDA. Addison-Wesley Professional, Reading (2003)
18. Wikipedia, Model-View-Controller, http://en.wikipedia.org/wiki/Model-view-controller

MDE Basics with a DSL Focus

Suzana Andova, Mark G.J. van den Brand, Luc J.P. Engelen, and Tom Verhoeff

Eindhoven University of Technology, Den Dolech 2, NL-5612 AZ Eindhoven
{s.andova,m.g.j.v.d.brand,l.j.p.engelen,t.verhoeff}@tue.nl

Abstract. Small languages are gaining popularity in the software engineering community. The development of MOF and EMF has given the Domain Specific Language community a tremendous boost. In this tutorial the basic aspects of model driven engineering in combination with Domain Specific Languages will be discussed. The focus is on textual Domain Specific Languages developed using the language invention pattern. The notion of abstract syntax will be linked to metamodels as well as the definition of concrete syntax. Defining static and dynamic semantics will be discussed. A small but non trivial Domain Specific Language SLCO will be used to illustrate our ideas.

1 Introduction

Our society has become completely dependent on software. We do our bank transactions via the internet, we book our holiday trips, order books, etc. on line, and we submit our tax forms electronically. Medical information is exchanged electronically between doctors. Software is no longer running only on "traditional computers", but is incorporated into products that we use in daily life like mobile phones, personal organizers, game computers, personal care equipment, and even cars. A modern car contains about 10 million lines of code; a wafer stepper is run by over 30 million lines of code. Apart from this code explosion, people put more trust in software. In fact, we have become software dependent, *all* modern devices are software based.

The software engineering community is facing two main challenges; how to produce and maintain this huge amount of software written in a broad variety of (programming) languages and how to guarantee the correctness of the resulting software. Increasing the level of abstraction seems to be a logical solution. This is in line with the development of programming languages over time, see Section 1.1. In the last decade (graphical) models have become popular when developing software and new formalisms such as the Unified Modeling Language (UML) have been defined, see Section 1.2. These new formalisms have created a new field within software engineering: *model driven (software) engineering* (MDSE) which may be a solution but it may also be the next "no silver bullet" [24]. The use of high level models offers also the possibility to perform model analysis and verification of properties. This is beneficial for any sort of systems but is crucial for safety critical systems.

M. Bernardo, V. Cortellessa, and A. Pierantonio (Eds.): SFM 2012, LNCS 7320, pp. 21–57, 2012.
© Springer-Verlag Berlin Heidelberg 2012

1.1   From Low Level to High Level Programming Languages

In the middle of the previous century, computers where introduced to perform calculations for ballistic missiles. Soon after this, the first commercial software applications were developed [27]. In 1951, Grace Hopper wrote the first compiler, A-0, see [94]. She was also involved in the development of the first compiler-based programming languages, including ARITH-MATIC, MATH-MATIC and FLOW-MATIC. A compiler is a program that transforms high-level statements in a programming language into low-level computer instructions. Since the programmer is working at a higher level of abstraction, more can be expressed in fewer lines of code. Programming has evolved enormously since then. The development can be characterized by indeed making programming easier, by introducing, for instance, high-level language constructs, and by increasing the level of abstraction, by introducing procedures and classes. The introduction of high-level control flow constructs, such as, conditionals, loops and exceptions (which replace low-level constructs like GOTOs, see [31]) has improved the quality of the software. Increasing the level of abstraction does not only lead to an improvement in productivity but also to better quality of the code.

Models raise programming to the next level of abstraction. They are in general used to design both hardware and software. Often the models are manually translated into other more detailed design documents and/or code. However, that route offers no guarantee for consistency between model, design and the resulting code and should be improved.

1.2   From Informal to Formal Modeling

Models have become important when designing software. People used to make informal drawings of the (structure of the) software when designing software. However, these informal drawings are not machine processable, and have to be converted into (source) code manually. One can observe more than once that developers take pictures of the black board to recreate the models in Visio or some other modeling tool. These informal models lack any form of semantics, or the semantics is only in the head of the designer.

Apart from these informal drawings, others advocate the use of formal methods as much as possible to describe the (behaviour of) software systems. The advantages of formal methods are their rigorousness and software developed using these methods is usually free of errors. They have well defined semantics and can be automatically processed. A number of formal methods allow the interpretation of the models, or even generation of executable code. However, the learning curve of formal methods is steep, whereas the learning curve for drawing diagrams on the black board is very low.

1.3   From UML to MOF

Quite a number of modeling languages have been developed over the years, each dealing with different aspects of software (development). Some of these modeling languages are data oriented, e.g., E/R models; some are structure oriented, e.g., class diagrams; some behaviour oriented, e.g., use cases, state machines, sequence diagrams, activity diagrams, and others are architecture oriented, e.g., package diagrams, component diagrams.

The Object Management Group (OMG) took the initiative of unifying a number of these diagrams, among others class diagrams, state machine diagrams, sequence diagrams, into UML1.x [65]. This was done by James Rumbaugh, Grady Booch and Ivar Jacobson (the Three Amigos) [76]. UML combines Rumbaugh's Object-Modeling Technique (OMT), for Object-Oriented Analysis (OOA), and Booch method, for Object-Oriented Design (OOD), with the work of Jacobson, the Object-Oriented Software Engineering (OOSE) method.

UML, via the UML profiles, offers an extensibility mechanism that can be used to develop domain specific modeling languages [81]. The lecture on "MDE Basics with a UML Focus" by Bran Selic discussed this approach in more detail. The development of UML has also lead to the creation of the Meta Object Facility (MOF) [46], also by OMG. MOF is used to define the various modeling formalisms of UML in a uniform way. The Meta Object Facility has a four-layered architecture:

M3. The **Meta-Meta-Model Layer** contains the MOF language, which is used to describe the structure of metadata (and, also, of MOF itself). It provides a meta-metamodel at the top layer.

M2. The **Meta-Model Layer** contains definitions for the structure of metadata. The M3-model is used to build metamodels on level M2. The most prominent example is the UML metamodel, the model that describes the UML itself.

M1. The **Model Layer** contains definitions of data in the information layer. The metamodels of level M2 describe the structure of elements of the M1-layer, for example, models written in UML.

M0. The **Model Layer** contains objects or data in the information layer.

MOF is an alternative for developing domain specific (modeling) languages. Although MOF is the official standard, there are only a few implementations [78], the most popular of which is the Eclipse Modeling Framework (EMF) [25,83]. EMF has become very popular for developing Domain Specific Languages (DSLs). An entire range of Eclipse plugins have been developed to deal with the various aspects of DSL development. In this tutorial, we address the design of DSLs, and EMF among others is used as the main implementation medium, although the presentation will be as tool independent as possible.

1.4   Outline of Tutorial

The tutorial uses a small but non-trivial language called "Simple Language of Communicating Objects" (SLCO) as a running example. All aspects of designing and implementing a DSL will be demonstrated using this language. In Section 2, background information on DSLs in general is given. This section gives some definitions of DSLs and a rough classification of DSLs. In Section 3, the notions of abstract syntax and metamodels are introduced. Section 4 describes the static and dynamics of a DSL. We provide some background information on static semantics and what we understand by it. The second half of this section is devoted to the formalization of the dynamic semantics. Section 5 presents ways of defining the concrete syntax of a DSL. The focus in this section is mainly on the context-free syntax and less on the lexical part. We conclude this tutorial, Section 6, by discussing the way we use SLCO in our research. We will also sketch a number of research directions for the DSL community.

2   Domain Specific Languages

It is hard to give a very precise definition of Domain Specific Languages or little languages [29]. In general, a language is a symbolic system for communication. More formally, a language is a collection of sentences or expressions, constructed according to certain grammatical rules, where the language elements refer to real-world entities. In this sense, a DSL is a formal, processable language targeting a specific aspect of an information-processing system or task, for instance building user interfaces, performing database queries, building web pages, exchanging data, generating scanners and parsers. There is no requirement that a DSL should be Turing complete, in contrast to a general purpose language. Its semantics, flexibility and notation are designed to support working with these aspects as efficiently as possible. Yet another definition of DSLs can be found in the annotated bibliography [30]: "A language that offers, through appropriate notations and abstractions, expressive power focused on, and usually restricted to, a particular problem domain".

2.1   Forms of Domain Specific Languages

Given these definitions we know DSLs are not general purpose languages but rather languages used to address problems in a restricted domain. The next question is what do DSLs look like? Mernik et.al. [62] give a detailed description of the various domain specific design patterns. The classification given in this tutorial is from a user perspective instead of a developer perspective. DSLs differ a lot in their external appearance. It all depends on which viewpoint is taken.

In a number of cases, (built-in) libraries that come with an integrated development environment or a programming language, such as the Swing library of Java, can be considered as a DSL. It contains the vocabulary of concepts that are needed to deal with specific tasks. The programs written to solve these tasks use these libraries. Adapting the DSL reduces to changing the libraries.

Another approaches is to embed a DSL in an existing language. Hagl [93] is an example of such an embedding in Haskell [49]. This way of developing DSLs is very efficient. The embedded language has the flavour of the host language and reuses the underlying parser and type system, at least in case of Haskell.

The difference with the first approach, the library approach, is not very obvious from a user perspective. Both approach can be considered as internal DSLs.

Yet another way is to add extensions to existing languages to increase the expressive power of the language. This can be considered as a partly external DSL. TOM [63] is an example of such a domain specific extension, that adds a pattern matching facility to the host language. The language constructs of the "extension" are translated to the host language Java in case of TOM. Such extensions involve quite a large implementation effort. The grammar of the host language has to be extended and in many cases a separate static analysis phase has to be developed along with finally a translator. The benefit is added expressive power, combined with the general utility of Java.

The last category are DSLs which are not built on top of, or embedded in, an existing general purpose language, but are independent DSLs. This can be considered as a fully external DSL. In Mernik et.al. [62], these are called *language invention*. This type of DSL is the main focus of this tutorial. The design effort for this type of language is comparable to that for other forms of DSLs, see Section 2.3, but the implementation effort is bigger due to the fact that the language has to be built from scratch.

2.2   Effectiveness of Domain Specific Languages

Before continuing, it is important to summarize the advantages and drawbacks of DSLs, independent of their category. The effort to design, implement, and maintain a DSL is huge, even given the fact that they are "little". Designing a good DSL involves not only writing a syntax definition, but also the definition of a proper semantics, tooling and eventually methodology and documentation. The gain in investing this effort must exceed the costs. Note, however, that not using a DSL also has its costs, especially in the longer run.

First, we enumerate the drawbacks of DSLs.

- The cost of a DSL implementation and the training of its users may be high.
- It may be difficult to identify the right scope of domain specific concepts and to find a good balance between these concepts and general-purpose language constructs. In other words: is the resulting language usable and effective?
- Domain specific languages offer solutions for a limited set of problems. They are not generally applicable. In a few cases, a DSL evolves into a general purpose language.

In contrast to these drawbacks, a number of obvious advantages can be identified.

- The possibility of expressing the solution in terms of domain concepts. This may lead to higher productivity when developing software. Furthermore, the models developed may offer the opportunity of use in a different setting, for documentation purposes or verification purposes.
- Besides the gain in productivity, the reliability, maintainability, and portability may increase. Or, to put it differently, not using a DSL may lead to software that is hard or impossible to maintain and port.

– A DSL captures domain knowledge and thus leads to concise and in many cases self-documenting specifications.

It is up to the reader to decide whether a DSL is an appropriate solution to his or her problem.

2.3   Identification of Domain Concepts

As with software development in general [12,14], the first step when designing a DSL is to capture the domain concepts, since without an understanding of the domain concepts it is impossible to design a DSL that will be practical and usable. The domain concepts have to be captured in appropriate language constructs, for instance in a mechanism to exchange messages between state machines. The language constructs should be at the right abstraction level, they should not be geared towards a specific platform or general purpose programming language. Furthermore, they should have a proper specified semantics, both statically and dynamically.

The identification of domain concepts is closely related to the field of requirements engineering. So, elicitation techniques used there can also be applied to design a domain specific language, see traditional software engineering course books on this topic [92]. However, before starting the elicitation phase, it is important to identify the problem domain: "A problem domain is defined by consensus, and its essence is the shared understanding of some community" [8]. In the design of a DSL for financial products [9], the world of financial transactions has to be well defined and understood, for instance what is the notion of a customer, bank account, interest period? Given the problem domain, the next step is to identify the problem space, for instance the creation of new interest products which may take too long or the software developed to implement the interest products contains too many bugs. The next step is to identify the language concepts. This can be done by studying the existing informal description of the interest products and their implementations. From this it is, for instance, possible to identify the relevant library components. This information can now be used to identify and define the relevant DSL concepts [60]. This process is clearly an iterative and continuing process. It may even be the case that during the implementation phase of the language some steps have to be redone.

Capturing DSL concepts can be done in multiple ways depending on the underlying implementation pattern [62]. The concepts can be implemented in a library, as extension, embedding or as a complete new language. In the latter case, more general purpose language constructs must be added, such as control flow, procedural abstraction or modularity, of course depending on the need for expressiveness.

2.4   Examples of Domain Specific Languages

It is impossible to give an exhaustive list of all domain specific language. In 1966, Landin [57] already predicted an explosion of programming languages.

DSLs have contributed to the growth of languages considerably. Nevertheless it makes sense to mention a few languages which can be seen as DSLs. HyperText Markup Language (HTML) the language for developing web pages is an example of a non-executable DSL. In the area of web pages there is whole range of DSLs. A recent development is WebDSL [40], which is a DSL which captures the concepts of designing web pages but shields of the underlying implementation details. SQL is a very well known and popular language for relational database queries which has evolved into a general purpose language PL/SQL [37]. YACC [47] is a tool, but the corresponding grammar definition formalism is a non-executable DSL for creating parsers. LEX [59] is the language for defining regular expressions for specifying lexers. In this area SDF (Syntax Definition Language) [44] is a DSL to describe grammars in a declarative and modular way. GraphViz [39] is a software package used for graph layout and DOT is the corresponding language to describe the graphs. BOX [23] is a small non-executable language to describe the formatting of computer programs. LaTeX [56] is a language for formatting texts.

We shall now study a small DSL in detail.

2.5   Simple Language of Communicating Objects

The *Simple Language of Communicating Objects* (SLCO) provides constructs for specifying systems consisting of objects that operate in parallel and communicate with each other. SLCO has been used to describe the software that controls conveyor belts, even though there are no conveyor belt related concepts or concepts like motors and sensor in the language. Instead, each of these concepts are simply represented by objects that communicate over channels. In Section 3.2 we will present the metamodels of SLCO, but in this section we describe the language and motivate a number of the design decisions.

An SLCO model consists of a number of classes, objects, and channels, see Listing 1.2. Objects are instances of classes and communicate with each other via channels, which are either bidirectional or unidirectional, see Figure 9 for the metamodel of the channels. SLCO offers three types of channels: synchronous channels, asynchronous lossy channels, and asynchronous lossless channels. An example of two objects connected by three channels is shown in Figure 1. The objects p and q, which are instances of classes P and Q, can communicate over channels $p1\_q1$, $q2\_p2$, and $p3\_q3$. The arrows at the ends of the channels denote the direction of communication. Synchronous channels are denoted by plain lines (e.g. $p1\_q1$), asynchronous lossless channels are denoted by dashed lines (e.g. $p3\_q3$), and asynchronous lossy channels are denoted by dotted lines (e.g. $q2\_p2$). A channel can only be used to send and receive signals with a certain signature, indicated by a number of argument types listed between brackets after the name of the channel. Channel $p1\_q1$, for instance, can only be used to send and receive signals with a boolean argument, and channel $q2\_p2$ only allows signals without any arguments.

A class describes the structure and behaviour of its instances, see Figure 6 for the metamodel of classes. A class has ports and variables that define the structure

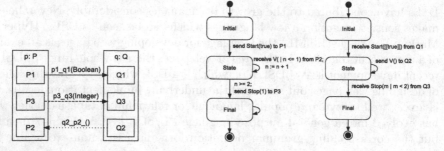

Fig. 1. Objects, ports and channels in SLCO

Fig. 2. Two SLCO state machines

of its instances, and state machines that describe their behaviour. Variables may be initialized. If no initial value is specified, integer variables are initialized to 0, boolean variables are initialized to *true*, and string variables are initialized to the empty string. Ports are used to connect channels to objects. Figure 1 shows that object p has ports $P1$, $P2$, and $P3$, connecting it to channels $p1\_q1$, $q2\_p2$, and $p3\_q3$, and that object q has ports $Q1$, $Q2$, and $Q3$, connecting it to the same channels.

A state machine consists of variables, states, and transitions, see Figure 6 for the metamodel of state machines. SLCO allows for two special types of state: initial states and final states. Each state machine has exactly one initial state, and can contain any number of ordinary and final states. Figure 2 shows an example of an SLCO model consisting of two state machines, whose initial states, Initial, are indicated by a black dot-and-arrow, and whose final states, Final, are indicated by an outgoing arrow to a circled black dot. As explained below, the left state machine specifies the behaviour of object p and the right state machine specifies the behaviour of object q, both already introduced in Figure 1.

A transition has a source and a target state, and a finite number of statements. There are multiple types of statements. Expressions denote statements that must evaluate to true to enable the transition from the source to the target state to be taken. The expression n >= 2 that is part of the transition with the source State and the final state as the target state in the state machine of p is an example of such a statement. A transition with a delay statement is enabled after a specified amount of time has passed since entering its source state. Note that our running example does not have this type of statement. A transition with a signal reception statement is enabled if a signal is received via the port indicated by the statement. When a signal reception statement has a condition, naturally, the condition must hold for the transition to be enabled. It is allowable for the condition to refer to arguments of the signal just being received. Take for instance the transition in q from State to the final state, with signal reception receive Stop($m \mid m$ < 2) from $Q3$. It is only taken if the value of the argument sent with the signal Stop is smaller than 2. Additionally, another form of conditional signal reception is offered. Expressions given as arguments of a signal reception specify that only signals whose argument values are equal to the corresponding expressions are accepted. Thus, q in state `Initial` accepts only signals whose argument equals *true*. SLCO also offers statements for assigning values to variables and for sending signals over channels. The state machines in Figure 2 specify the following communication between p and q, assuming that the variable n is initialized to 0. The two objects first communicate synchronously over channel $p1\_q1$, after which q repeatedly sends signals to p over the lossy channel $q2\_p2$. As soon as p receives 2 of the signals sent by q, it sends a signal over channel $p3\_q3$ and terminates. After receiving this signal, q terminates as well.

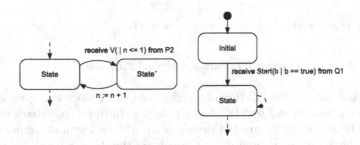

Fig. 3. Parts of an SLCO model without syntactic sugar

The example in Figure 2 contains two transitions that both contain two statements, whereas the metamodel in Figure 7 allows at most one statement per transition. Although multiple statements per transition are not allowed according to the metamodel, we consider models containing such transitions valid SLCO models and regard these models as the syntactically sugared versions of equivalent models that adhere to the stricter metamodel. The leftmost part of Figure 3 shows the unsugared version of one these transitions, that features an auxiliary intermediate state. The rightmost part of this figure shows that expressions given as arguments of signal receptions can also be regarded as a form of syntactic sugar. The conditional signal reception on the transition from `Initial` to `State` in this figure is equivalent to the conditional signal reception on the corresponding transition in Figure 2, assuming that variable b is an auxiliary boolean variable.

In addition to the graphical concrete syntax shown above, SLCO has a textual concrete syntax. Listing 1.1 shows a part of the textual equivalent of the model described above.

3   Defining the Structure of a Domain Specific Language

In the rest of this tutorial we will concentrate on the design of DSLs based on the invention pattern. We assume that the first step in the design of a new DSL, the identification of the domain concepts, has been performed as described in Section 2.3.

```
model M {
  classes
    P {
      variables Integer n
      ports P1 P2 P3
      state machines
        P {
          initial Initial state State final Final
          transitions
            Receive from State to State {
            receive V( | n <= 1) from P2;
            n := n + 1 }
            ...
        }
    }
    ...
  objects p:P q:Q
  channels p1_q1(Boolean) sync from p.P1 to q.Q1
    ...
}
```

Listing 1.1. Part of a textual SLCO model

The design and implementation of an effective DSL is more than just writing a context-free grammar in Xtext [32] and a code generator for some back-end, such as Java. The proper steps are the design of an abstract syntax, semantics and concrete syntax. One can argue about the order of the steps. Kleppe [52] proposes to design the concrete syntax after defining the abstract syntax. Whilst defining the semantics it may turn out that the abstact syntax is not optimal and has to be adapted. This may lead to a modification of the concrete syntax. However, having a concrete syntax may facilitate experimentation and interaction with the users of the language and provide usable feedback. It is obvious these steps must be performed iteratively and continuously, leading to evolutionary design of a DSL [4].

In this section we will explain why a proper abstract syntax is needed as the basis for a DSL. We shall discuss the material on an abstract level and give examples of metamodels in EMF [83], but this tutorial is not an introduction into a specific technology or tool.

In Section 3.1 we will start with introducing the basic concepts of defining abstract syntax. In Section 3.2 we will make this concrete in terms of metamodeling based on EMF.

3.1   Abstract Syntax

The abstract syntax, signature or abstract data type of a language describes the basic structure (skeleton) of a language. It can serve as the starting point for defining a concrete syntax (both textual and graphical), semantics (static and dynamic), and is the basis for tool development. It abstracts from specific details on the concrete level, such as the keywords, priorities between operators, associativities of binary operators, etc. In its basic form an abstract syntax definition is a collection of constructors. Starting with the definition of a language in an abstract syntax notation has the advantage of having a concise overview of the underlying structure of the language.

Unfortunately there is no ISO standard for defining abstract syntax. We will use a signature-like notation to describe the abstract syntax of a language. A signature can be defined as follows:

- A collection of constructors which define sorts and operators.
- A sort represents a nonempty set of terms.
- A term is the application of a k-ary operator to k terms of the appropriate sort.
- A k-ary operator is a constructor function mapping k terms to a term.
- The argument of a k-ary operator may represent zero or more (*) or one or more (+) terms of the same sort.
- A sort can be considered a nonterminal in the abstract syntax.

Listing 1.2 shows a part the abstract syntax of the SLCO language as a signature.

```
"Synchronous"()            -> ChannelType
"AsynchronousLossless"() -> ChannelType
"AsynchronousLossy"()      -> ChannelType

"Integer"()      -> PrimitiveType
"Boolean"()      -> PrimitiveType
"String"()       -> PrimitiveType

"model"(Class*,Object*,Channel*)                      -> Model
"class"(Name,Port*,StateMachine*,Variable*)           -> Class
"object"(Name,Class)                                   -> Object
"channel"(Name,ChannelType,ArgumentType*)             -> Channel
"port"(Name)                                            -> Port
"statemachine"(Name,Variable*,Vertex*,Transition*)    -> StateMachine
"variable"(Name,PrimitiveType)                         -> Variable
"argumenttype"(PrimitiveType)                          -> ArgumentType
"vertex"(Name,Transition*,Transition*)                -> Vertex
"transition"(Name,Vertex,Vertex)                      -> Transition
"transition"(Name,Vertex,Vertex,Statement)            -> Transition
```

Listing 1.2. Signature specification of a part of the abstract syntax of SLCO

Given a signature definition it is possible to generate Application Programming Interfaces (APIs). GOM [73] generates an API for accessing the underlying abstract syntax when developing TOM specifications [63] and ApiGen [50,20] generates, given a signature definition, a type API to access terms in the ATerm libary [19].

3.2 Metamodeling

The next step is to represent the abstract syntax as a metamodel. A metamodel describes the model elements that are available for developing a class of models as well as their attributes and interrelations. A model describes the elements

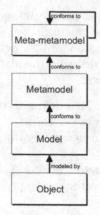

Fig. 4. Four-layer metamodeling architecture

of a real-world object as well as their attributes and the way they interrelate. Therefore, a metamodel can be considered as a model of a class of models [80], or a model of a modeling language [55]. Since a metamodel is itself a model, the concepts and relations that can be used to define them need to be described as well. The metamodel used for this purpose is called a meta-metamodel. A meta-metamodel is typically a reflexive metamodel. This means that it is expressed using the concepts and relations it defines itself. This four-layer metamodeling architecture [66] is schematically depicted in Figure 4.

EMF provides a metamodel (also referred to as Ecore) which is a general model of models from which any model can be defined. It can be used to model classes, attributes, relationships, data types, etc. Figure 5 (taken from [83]) shows a simplified Ecore metamodel:

EClass models classes that
  − are identified by a name,
  − contain zero or more attributes, and
  − contain zero or more references.
EAttribute models attributes that
  − are identified by a name, and
  − have a type.
EDataType represents basic types.
EReference models associations between classes and
  − are identified by a name,
  − have a type which must be an EClass, and
  − a containment attribute indicating whether the EReference is used as "whole-part" relation.

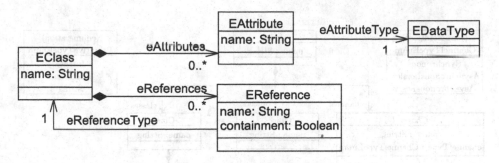

Fig. 5. Simplified Ecore metamodel

In Section 2.5 the SLCO language has been described in great detail, we will now only present the metamodels. Figure 6 shows the main metaclasses of the Ecore metamodel of SLCO, which corresponds to the signature presented in Listing 1.2. Figure 7 gives the details of statements. Figure 8 defines the expressions of SLCO and Figure 9 shows the details of the channels.

4   Semantics

While syntax is concerned with the form of a valid model or program, semantics is about its meaning. Kleppe [52] introduces the term *mogram* in order not to make the distinction between a program and a model. We will consistently use the term *model*, because a program is also a model. We shall consider two different views on defining the semantics of a DSL. The static semantics of a language defines the structural properties of valid models (Section 4.1). The dynamic semantics is concerned with the execution and operation of models (Section 4.2).

4.1   Static Semantics

Static semantics defines properties of models that can be determined without considering either input or execution. Because of this there is always a debate on the status of static semantics. Static semantics can be considered to be part of syntax analysis, because the models need not be executed. We consider static semantics to be a separate phase. We shall distinguish three separate aspects:

- identifier resolution;
- scope resolution; and
- type resolution.

In many languages these aspects are intertwined. If the language supports overloading, type resolution is needed when performing identifier resolution.

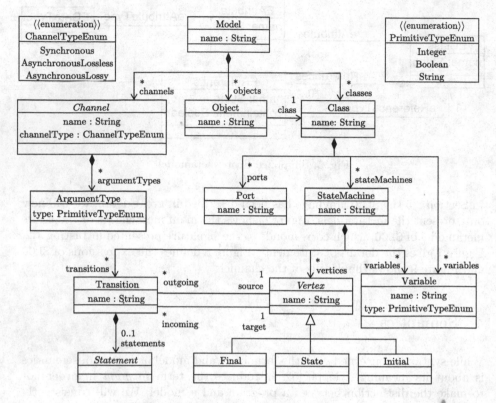

Fig. 6. Main concepts of the SLCO metamodel

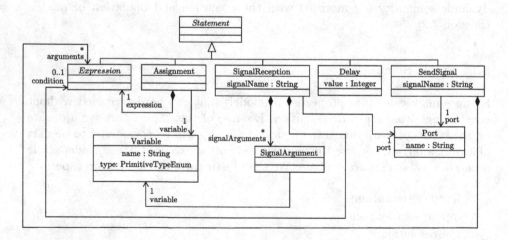

Fig. 7. Statements in the SLCO metamodel

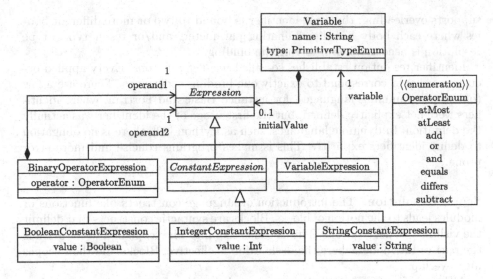

Fig. 8. Expressions in the SLCO metamodel

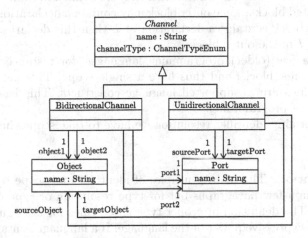

Fig. 9. Channels in the SLCO metamodel

Identifier Resolution. Identifiers are an important notion in (programming) languages. They may represent for instance values, variables, functions, etc. In order to be valid, in many (programming) languages an identifier has to be explicitly declared. In many cases the declaration of an identifier is accompanied by a description of its type, for instance for a value or variable. If the identifier represents a function, procedure or method, the declaration captures the operational behaviour in the body. Furthermore, the parameters (together with their types) and the result parameter have to be specified. A declaration establishes a *binding* of an identifier I to some entity X. An *applied occurrence* is an occurrence of I where X is made available through I. Note that if the language supports overloading, the same identifier is bound to two or more different bodies where each body has discriminating parameters and/or result types, type resolution is needed when resolving the binding.

Identifier resolution establishes so-called *use-def* relations. Every applied occurrence should correspond to exactly one binding occurrence. There are a few (older) programming languages, for instance Basic and Fortran, where identifiers were not explicitly defined, but the first usage of the identifier was actually the definition. In dynamic languages, such as Python [89], there is no obligation to define identifiers explicitly. This is makes programs concise and more error prone.

Scope Resolution. The introduction of language constructs like functions or modules leads to the notion of blocks. Blocks are syntactic constructs that delimit the visibility of declarations. This is called scoping. The scope of a declaration is the part of the model where the declaration is effective. Blocks and their scopes may overlap.

Although for every applied occurrence there should be exactly one binding occurrence, it is possible that an identifier may be defined in multiple blocks. In the case of nested blocks, some outer block may contain a declaration of identifier I. If the inner block contains a declaration of I, then this declaration hides the declaration of I in the outer block.

There are a few (older) programming languages, for instance again Basic, which do not offer blocks and thus have a single scope. This means that (recursive) functions are unsupported language constructs. This leads to a very restricted way of programming.

When performing identifier resolution we have to take scopes into consideration.

Type Resolution. The main principles of identifier and scope resolution can be explained in a few paragraphs but for type resolution or type checking this is impossible. The definition of proper type check rules for a language depends heavily on the expressive power of the language. If a language contains overloading, polymorphism, inheritance, etc. the definition of a type checker is far from trivial, see the book on type checking by Pierce [71] for an elaborate discussion of type checking.

A type system is an important component of the static semantics of a language. Language constructs, for instance expressions and functions, may produce results and some cases these results respresent values. Types represent abstractions of these results. For instance, the evaluation of an expression may yield the values `true` or `false`, the corresponding type is then `boolean`. Expressions use operators to calculate the results and these operators are only valid for a restricted set of types, in many cases only one type. The purpose of a type system is to prevent illegal operations, like multiplication of strings by booleans, which should result in a type error, disambiguation in case of (operator or function) overloading. The process of assigning types is referred to as *typing*.

Until recently not much work has been done on type checking of DSLs developed using EMF. Xtext offers a primitive mechanism to deal with identifier resolution and OCL [67] is used to write simple constraints to do a basic form of type checking. [11] and [22] describe approaches to tackle type checking of DSLs in a more structured way. [26] uses attribute grammar JastAdd [33] to add the semantics to metamodels.

Static Semantics of SLCO. A number of static semantic rules can be defined for the SLCO language. Here are a few of the rules:

- Classes should have a unique name within a model.
- Objects should have a unique name within a model.
- Only classes that have been defined can be instantiated as objects.
- Variables should be declared before they can be used.
- Variables should have a unique name within a class.
- State machines should have a unique name within a class.
- The source and target state of a transition should exist.
- States should have a unique name within a state machine.
- Transitions should have a unique name within a state machine.
- The expressions should be type correct.

Listing 1.3 presents a simplified version for checking the uniques of class names using a rewriting based specification formalism.

4.2   Dynamic Semantics

Defining a DSL by means of its abstract and concrete syntax allows the rapid development of languages and some associated tools, such as editors. We have already seen that static semantics is another important ingredient of a DSL definition. Static semantics defines aspects such as the well-formedness and typing of concrete models in order to make the DSL more usable and the development of models more robust. However, none of these aspects of the DSL definition help to understand the behaviour described by models nor help us to inspect whether the behaviour specified is exactly as intended nor help us to create a proper execution model.

Dynamic semantics (also known as execution semantics) covers these language aspects: it defines the model of computation for the execution behaviour of models. There are many ways of defining dynamic semantics, natural language being one of them. In practice, the dynamic semantics of DSLs are implicitly and informally defined through, either, a software constructor that generates compilable source code, or by an engine/interpreter that directly processes DSL models. In these cases, the quality of the design of a system, due to the lack of a formal definition of the DSL semantics, is usually assessed by manually studying and exploring the created models, and by testing the software before actual delivery. Given the increasing complexity of current systems, this has become an error-prone, time-consuming and costly process, which often results

```
module SLCO-typecheck

signature
  "checkModel"(Model)            -> {Error ","}*
  "checkClasses"(Class*, TNPT)   -> {Error ","}* # TNPT
  "checkClass"(Name, TNPT)       -> {Error ","}* # TNPT

signature
  Table[[Name,PrimitiveType]] -> TNPT

variables
  "vChannel*"       -> Channel*
  "vClass*"         -> Class*
  "vError*"[12]*    -> {Error ","}*
  "vName"           -> Name
  "vObject*"        -> Object*
  "vPort*"          -> Port*
  "vStatemachine*"  -> Statemachine*
  "vTNPT"[123]*     -> TNPT
  "vVariable*"      -> Variable*

equations
[cMdl1] checkModel(model(vClass*, vObject*, vChannel*)) =
          when vError* # vTNPT := checkClasses(vClass*, new-table)

[Clss1] checkClasses(, vTNPT) = # vTNPT
[Clss2] checkClasses(vClass vClass*, vTNPT1) = vError*1, vError*2 # vTNPT3
          when vError*1 # vTNPT2 := checkClasses(vClass*, vTNPT1),
               vError*2 # vTNPT3 := checkCLass(vClass, vTNPT2)

[cCls1] checkCLass(class(vName,   vPort*, vStatemachine*, vVariable*), vTNPT)=
          error("Class redefined: " ++ vName) # vTNPT
          when lookup(vTNPT, vName) != not-in-table

[cCls2] checkCLass(class(vName,   vPort*, vStatemachine*, vVariable*), vTNPT)=
          # insert(vName, vTNPT)
          when lookup(vTNPT, vName) == not-in-table
```

Listing 1.3. Part of specification of the static semantics of SLCO in a rewrite rule style

in software design faults being uncovered only after the system is fully developed and installed.

However, as a result of a significant amount of academic research, different approaches and techniques used to express dynamic semantics of languages in a formal manner have been defined. Furthermore, supporting (semi-)automated tools have been developed for model analysis, which can process models described in a particular formal modeling language. The question of making these formal frameworks available to domain engineers to be used for unambiguous specification and analysis of domain models has been receiving much attention in the last decade, from both the industrial and academic community. In order to make the results useful for industry, it is essential to have precise understanding of the DSL semantics. The lack of well-understood DSL semantics may easily lead to semantic ambiguities or a semantic mismatch between a DSL (the developed models) and modeling languages of analysis tools.

There are various ways to define the dynamic semantics of a language formally. The most common techniques are operational, translational, and denotational semantics. *Operational semantics* specifies the computation a language construct induces when it is executed, thus describing not only the effect of the computation, but also how the computation is produced. Another technique to define the dynamic semantics of a DSL is *translational semantics* which maps language constructs from the initial domain to another language with an already defined formal semantics. Thus, the semantics of the original DSL is defined by the syntactic mapping. *Denotational semantics* is given by a mathematical function which maps the syntax of the language to semantic values – denotations. In that sense denotational semantics corresponds to translational semantics, where the target language is a mathematical formalism.

Both, the operational and translational approach, have advantages and drawbacks. A number of papers report on explicit definitions of the corresponding operational semantics of individual or a family of DSLs and the way they have been directly expressed in other existing environments (see for instance [28,82,16,36,15,75,77]). In this way DSL models can be executed. However, operational semantics is not easy to implement in general, and so far there is no semantic framework that supports an automated and efficient implementation of the operational language semantics allowing for direct DSL model execution. Nevertheless, it is beneficial to have the operational semantics of the DSL explicitly defined, first of all, because it enables rather easy detection of possible inconsistencies between or redundancies of (the semantics of) language constructs. Furthermore, the investment of defining the operational semantics of a DSL eases the effort of anchoring the DSL to different target languages for different purposes. It allows also (due to its modularity) for low-effort adjustments of the semantics needed in case of language evolution or language changes.

Translational semantics saves the effort of defining the semantics of the DSL explicitly. This approach is very appropriate when the initial language and target language are semantically closely correlated, or when semantic reasoning only for particular instances of the DSL models is required. However, establishing syntactic mappings between the two languages requires implicit semantic knowledge of the DSL and an extensive in-depth knowledge of the (semantics of the) target language. Therefore if, due to a lack of a single sufficiently expressive underlying target framework, multiple frameworks are needed, this approach is obviously not appropriate. Furthermore, as the mappings to different target languages and platforms are defined only at the syntactic level, there is no guarantee that the final translation models still adhere to the semantics of the original model. For example, consider a mapping that transforms the source model to executable code, whereas another mapping translates the source model to a model for formal analysis. It is natural to ask whether the model that has been analysed is the one that will be actually executed.

As a last technique to define dynamic semantics of languages we mention *Action Semantics* [64]. Action semantics is based on operational semantics and allows a modular way of defining the semantics of language constructs. The actions defining the semantics of a language can be interpreted and there is an

$$\frac{\langle \mathtt{Class}^*, \mathtt{Object}^*, \mathtt{Channel}^*, S_{\mathrm{OSMS}}, V_{\mathrm{OS}}, V_{\mathrm{OSMS}}, B \rangle \xrightarrow{1}_{\mathrm{OBJECTS}} \langle S'_{\mathrm{OSMS}}, V'_{\mathrm{OS}}, V'_{\mathrm{OSMS}}, B' \rangle}{\begin{array}{c} \langle\ \mathtt{model}(\mathtt{Class}^*, \mathtt{Object}^*, \mathtt{Channel}^*), S_{\mathrm{OSMS}}, V_{\mathrm{OS}}, V_{\mathrm{OSMS}}, B\ \rangle \\ \xrightarrow{1}_{\mathrm{MODEL}} \langle\ \mathtt{model}(\mathtt{Class}^*, \mathtt{Object}^*, \mathtt{Channel}^*), S'_{\mathrm{OSMS}}, V'_{\mathrm{OS}}, V'_{\mathrm{OSMS}}, B'\ \rangle \end{array}}$$

Fig. 10. Deduction rule for models

execution environment [18] for composing semantic definitions, which makes this approach one of the exceptions. In [84] action semantics has been applied in the context of model driven engineering and the semantics of a small DSL is defined. This work is very preliminary.

Dynamic Semantics of SLCO. The semantics of SLCO has been formalized in the form of Structural Operational Semantics (SOS) [72]. Using SOS rules, the behaviour of an SLCO model is described in terms of the behaviour of its parts. The behaviour of these parts is in turn specified in terms of the behaviour of their parts, and so on. Figure 10 shows the SOS rule that describes the behaviour of models. A state of a model is referred to as a configuration. A model configuration is determined by: the current states of the state machines of the objects (function S_{OSMS}), the current values of the all local and global variables that appear in the model (functions V_{OS} and V_{OSMS}), and the current contents of the buffers associated to the asynchronous channels (function B). In the rule in Figure 10, one configuration is represented by the functions S_{OSMS}, V_{OS}, V_{OSMS}, and B, and another by the functions S'_{OSMS}, V'_{OS}, V'_{OSMS}, and B' (which essentially represent corresponding updates of the previous functions). The rule specifies that a model can take a step labeled 1 from one configuration to another configuration, if the list of classes (Class*), objects (Object*) and channels (Channel*) that are part of the model can take the same step labeled 1. In short, the behaviour of a model is defined in terms of the behaviour of its objects, classes, and channels.

Figure 11 shows that a list of classes, objects and channels can take a step labeled $\mathtt{bvn} := \mathtt{bc}$ if one of the objects, $\mathtt{object}(\mathtt{oname}, \mathtt{cname})$, is an instance of a class, $\mathtt{class}(\mathtt{cname}, \mathtt{Port}^*, \mathtt{StateMachine}^*, \mathtt{Variable}^*)$, that can take the same step labeled $\mathtt{bvn} := \mathtt{bc}$. This is one of a number of rules that specify the behaviour of lists of objects, classes, and channels in terms of their parts. The other rules define communication between objects over the various types of channels.

$$\frac{\begin{array}{c} \mathtt{Class}^* \equiv \mathtt{Class}_1^*\ \mathtt{class}(\mathtt{cname}, \mathtt{Port}^*, \mathtt{StateMachine}^*, \mathtt{Variable}^*)\ \mathtt{Class}_2^*, \\ \mathtt{Object}^* \equiv \mathtt{Object}_1^*\ \mathtt{object}(\mathtt{oname}, \mathtt{cname})\ \mathtt{Object}_2^*, \\ \langle\ \mathtt{class}(\mathtt{cname}, \mathtt{Port}^*, \mathtt{StateMachine}^*, \mathtt{Variable}^*), \\ S_{\mathrm{OSMS}}(\mathtt{oname}), V_{\mathrm{OS}}(\mathtt{oname}), V_{\mathrm{OSMS}}(\mathtt{oname})\ \rangle \xrightarrow{\mathtt{bvn} := \mathtt{bc}}_{\mathrm{CLASS}} \langle\ S_{\mathrm{SMS}}, V_0, V_{\mathrm{SMS}}\ \rangle, \\ S'_{\mathrm{OSMS}} = S_{\mathrm{OSMS}}[S_{\mathrm{SMS}}/\mathtt{oname}], \quad V'_{\mathrm{OS}} = V_{\mathrm{OS}}[V_0/\mathtt{oname}], \quad V'_{\mathrm{OSMS}} = V_{\mathrm{OSMS}}[V_{\mathrm{SMS}}/\mathtt{oname}] \end{array}}{\begin{array}{c} \langle\ \mathtt{Class}^*, \mathtt{Object}^*, \mathtt{Channel}^*, S_{\mathrm{OSMS}}, V_{\mathrm{OS}}, V_{\mathrm{OSMS}}, B\ \rangle \\ \xrightarrow{\mathtt{bvn} := \mathtt{bc}}_{\mathrm{OBJECTS}} \langle\ S'_{\mathrm{OSMS}}, V'_{\mathrm{OS}}, V'_{\mathrm{OSMS}}, B\ \rangle \end{array}}$$

Fig. 11. Deduction rule for lists of objects concerning assignments

$$\frac{\begin{array}{c}\texttt{StateMachine}^* \equiv \texttt{StateMachine}_1^*\ \texttt{statemachine}\ \texttt{StateMachine}_2^*,\\ \langle\, \texttt{statemachine}, \mathtt{S_{SMS}}, \mathtt{V_O}, \mathtt{V_{SMS}}\,\rangle \xrightarrow{\texttt{l}}_{\mathtt{SM}} \langle\, \mathtt{S'_{SMS}}, \mathtt{V'_O}, \mathtt{V'_{SMS}}\,\rangle\end{array}}{\langle\, \texttt{class(cname, Port}^*\texttt{, StateMachine}^*\texttt{, Variable}^*\texttt{)}, \mathtt{S_{SMS}}, \mathtt{V_O}, \mathtt{V_{SMS}}\,\rangle \xrightarrow{\texttt{l}}_{\mathtt{CLASS}} \langle \mathtt{S'_{SMS}}, \mathtt{V'_O}, \mathtt{V'_{SMS}}\rangle}$$

Fig. 12. Deduction rule for classes

The behaviour of a class is defined in terms of the behaviour of the state machines of that class. Figure 12 shows that a class can take a step labeled `l` if one (`statemachine`) of the state machines (`StateMachine`) that are a part of that class can take that same step.

$$\frac{\begin{array}{c}\texttt{Transition}^* \equiv \texttt{Transition}_1^*\ \texttt{transition}\ \texttt{Transition}_2^*,\\ \langle \texttt{transition}, \mathtt{S_{SMS}(smname)}, \mathtt{V_O}, \mathtt{V_{SMS}(smname)}\rangle \xrightarrow{\texttt{l}}_{\mathtt{TRANS}} \langle \texttt{vertex}', \mathtt{V'_O}, \mathtt{V_{SM}}\rangle,\\ \mathtt{S'_{SMS}} = \mathtt{S_{SMS}}[\texttt{vertex}'/\texttt{smname}], \quad \mathtt{V'_{SMS}} = \mathtt{V_{SMS}}[\mathtt{V_{SM}}/\texttt{smname}]\end{array}}{\begin{array}{c}\langle \texttt{statemachine(smname, Variable}^*\texttt{, Vertex}^*\texttt{, Transition}^*\texttt{)}, \mathtt{S_{SMS}}, \mathtt{V_O}, \mathtt{V_{SMS}}\rangle\\ \xrightarrow{\texttt{l}}_{\mathtt{SM}} \langle \mathtt{S'_{SMS}}, \mathtt{V'_O}, \mathtt{V'_{SMS}}\rangle\end{array}}$$

Fig. 13. Deduction rule for state machines

Figure 13 shows the SOS rule that specifies that the behaviour of a state machine is deduced from the behaviour of the transitions, `Transition`*, that are a part of that state machine. If a transition `transition` from the list of transitions can take a step labeled `l`, then the state machine can also take a step labeled `l`.

$$\frac{\langle \texttt{AssignmentStatement}, \mathtt{V_O}, \mathtt{V_{SM}}\rangle \xRightarrow{\texttt{l}}_{\mathtt{ASSIGN}} \langle \mathtt{V'_O}, \mathtt{V'_{SM}}\rangle}{\begin{array}{c}\langle\, \texttt{transition(tname, vertex, vertex}'\texttt{, AssignmentStatement)}, \texttt{vertex}, \mathtt{V_O}, \mathtt{V_{SM}}\rangle\\ \xrightarrow{\texttt{l}}_{\mathtt{TRANS}} \langle \texttt{vertex}', \mathtt{V'_O}, \mathtt{V'_{SM}}\rangle\end{array}}$$

Fig. 14. Deduction rule for transitions

Figure 14 shows that a transition from `vertex` to `vertex`′ leads to a step labeled `l` if the assignment `AssignmentStatement` leads to a step labeled `l` given valuation functions $\mathtt{V_O}$ and $\mathtt{V_{SM}}$. (Here $\langle \texttt{AssignmentStatement}, \mathtt{V_O}, \mathtt{V_{SM}}\rangle \xRightarrow{\texttt{l}}_{\mathtt{ASSIGN}} \langle \mathtt{V'_O}, \mathtt{V'_{SM}}\rangle$ simply means an update of the valuation functions $\mathtt{V_O}$ and $\mathtt{V_{SM}}$

according to the assignment statement `AssignmentStatement`, which is also defined by a set of rules.) These valuation functions are part of the configuration mentioned above, and are deduced from the model valuation functions V_{OS} and V_{OSMS} as follows. Given an object named `on` and a variable named `vn`, $V_{OS}(on)(vn)$ represents the value of this variable. A valuation function V_0 that maps the global variables of a particular object named `on` to their values is obtained by applying the function V_{OS} to the name `on`. The model valuation function V_{OSMS} has a similar purpose and valuation functions for state machines such as V_{SM} are obtained similarly.

There are rules for transitions with (conditional) signal receptions, expressions, and send signal statements similar to one described.

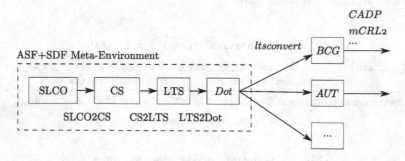

Fig. 15. Languages involved in the executable prototype of the semantics of `SLCO`

To test various alternative semantics for `SLCO`, we first implemented an executable prototype of the semantics before formally defining the semantics on paper [7]. The prototype consists of a number of transformations that transform `SLCO` models to Labeled Transition Systems (LTSs) [72] represented as Dot graphs [39] via a number of intermediate languages. Figure 15 shows the languages and transformations that are involved in this prototype. The boxes in Figure 15 represent (intermediate) languages. The names of existing languages are shown in italics and the names of newly created languages are shown using a plain typeface. The arrows in the figure represent transformations. The names of transformations implemented by existing tools are again shown in italics and the names of newly created transformations are shown using a plain typeface. The transformation *SLCO2CS* transforms an `SLCO` model into a list of configurations and a list of steps, where each step is a pair: configuration and label. The implementation of this transformation uses conditional rewrite rules, which closely resemble the SOS rules described above and the notation used to specify the static semantics. This simplifies the process of formalizing the semantics after the prototype reached a stable state.

Figure 16 shows the state space of the example model of Section 2.5. It is obtained by transforming the `SLCO` model to an LTS represented as a directed

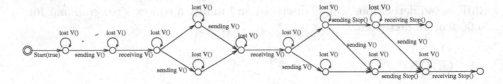

Fig. 16. State space of the example model of Section 2.5

graph in Dot format. The behaviour represented by the LTS matches the informal description of the behaviour in the final paragraph of Section 2.5.

5   Concrete Syntax

Having defined the abstract syntax of a DSL, the next step is the definition of a concrete representation of the DSL. Although it is possible to define a concrete graphical representation of a DSL using the Graphical Modeling Framework (GMF), see for instance Chapter 4 of [41], we will restrict ourselves to the development of textual based DSLs.

In Figure 4, the four-layered architecture of the metamodeling world is presented. For the grammar world, a similar four-layer architecture exists [2,54].

M3. (E)BNF grammar defines structure of the (E)BNF in (E)BNF.

M2. Programming language grammar defines the structure of programming language in (E)BNF.

M1. Program describes the manipulation (algorithm) of data in the data layer.

M0. Data layer where the data we wish to manipulate resides.

Although both worlds seem to be far apart, given the development of Xtext, EMFtext, etc., they are getting closer together [17].

The concrete textual syntax of a (programming or domain specific) language can be described using regular expressions (for the lexical tokens of the language) and context-free grammars (for the (tree) structure of the language). Scanning and parsing have been extensively studied in relation to compilers and interactive development environments. Over the years a broad range of algorithms, see [42], and tools [68] have been developed. The aforementioned tools, like LEX [59] and YACC [47] are results of this research. The formalisms underlying LEX and YACC have been considered as the standard for defining lexical and context-free grammars. In that sense, they are DSLs themselves. Unfortunately there is no ISO standard for defining context-free grammars; every tool comes with their own formalism.

We will first present some context-free grammar terminology and discuss recent developments with respect to modular grammar specification formalisms, which is relevant because of the modularity of metamodels. Then ANTLR and

EMF based derivations will be discussed and finally a context-free grammar for SLCO will be presented.

5.1   (E)BNF

The fact that there is no standard notation for grammars makes it ackward to present concepts and ideas. Formally, a context-free grammar is a 4-tuple $G = (N, \Sigma, P, S)$ where:

- N is the set of nonterminals;
- Σ is the set of terminals (disjoint from N);
- P is a subset of $N \times (N \cup \Sigma)^*$, where an element $(A, \alpha) \in P$ is called a production, usually written as $A ::= \alpha$;
- $S \in N$ is the start symbol; and
- sets N, Σ, and P are finite.

A context-free grammar can be considered a simple rewrite system: $\alpha A \beta \Rightarrow \alpha \gamma \beta$ if $A ::= \gamma \in P$ where $\alpha, \beta, \gamma \in (N \cup \Sigma)^*, A \in N$.

A full example of a context-free grammar is:

$$N = \{\text{E}\}$$
$$\Sigma = \{\text{+, *, (,), -, a}\}$$
$$S = \text{E}$$
$$P = \{\text{E ::= E + E, E ::= E * E, E ::= (E), E ::= - E, E ::= a}\}$$

When writing grammar definitions, the nonterminals and terminals are usually implicitly defined and only the start symbol and the production rules are defined explicitly. If the production rules have the form as presented in the example, the grammar is in Backus Normal Form (BNF). If the grammar definition formalism offers operators like *, +, and ?, the grammar is in Extended BNF (EBNF). Xtext [32] and EMFtext use variations of EBNF.

The language $L(G)$ generated/recognized by the context-free grammar $G = (N, \Sigma, P, S)$ is defined by $L(G) = \{w \in \Sigma^* | S \Rightarrow^* w\}$. A sentential form α is a string of terminals and nonterminals which can be derived from S: $S \Rightarrow^* \alpha$ with $\alpha \in (N \cup \Sigma)^*$. A sentence in $L(G)$ is a sentential form in which no nonterminals occur.

There a number of aspects one has to take care of when writing context-free grammars:

1. *The grammar may be left recursive.*
   A grammar G is left recursive if one or more of the production rules has the form $A ::= A\alpha$, so called direct left recursion. This means that after one or more steps in a derivation an occurrence of A reduces again to an occurrence of A without recognizing anything in the input sentence. Or there is a collection of production rules, for instance $A ::= B\alpha$ and $B ::= A\beta$, such

that $A \Rightarrow^* A\gamma$, so called indirect left recursion. It is relatively easy to remove (in)direct left recursion from a grammar. However, removing left recursion introduces new nonterminals and changes the structure of the grammar. In a conventional top-down parser or recursive descent parser, left recursion leads to non-termination. However, Frost et.al. [38] have developed a recursive descent parser using parser combinators, that can deal with left recursion. The GLL algorithm [79] can also handle it without modifying the grammar.

2. *The grammar may be non-left factored.*
A grammar G is non-left factored if one or more of the production rules has at least 2 alternatives that derive strings with the same prefix that is non-empty, for instance $A ::= \alpha\beta_1|\alpha\beta_2|\ldots$. This case is relatively easy to left factor, but again new nonterminals are introduced and the structure of the grammar is changed. However, $A ::= X\beta_1|Y\beta_2|\ldots$, where $X ::= 'x'$ and $Y ::= 'x'$, requires a *First* calculation; see [1] for details. In a top-down parser or recursive descent parser, arbitrary look ahead may be needed to decide which of these alternatives to choose.

3. *The grammar may contain cycles.*
A grammar G is cyclic if in one or more derivation steps A produces A without recognizing any token from the input: $A \Rightarrow^* A$. This can be considered a bug in the grammar specification. Both top-down (LL) and bottom-up ((LA)LR) parsers will have trouble with grammars containing cycles; both types of parsers will not terminate.

4. *The grammar may be ambiguous.*
A grammar G is *ambiguous* if a word $w \in L(G)$ has two or more derivations. This may happen if there are production rules of the form E ::= E O E without an explicit definition of priorities between binary operators or associativity of the binary operators. The sentence a + a * a can be recognized in two different ways. If a language is inherently ambiguous, no refactorings of production rules will help to solve the problem.

5.2 SDF

The Syntax Definition Formalism (SDF) [44,91] is a modular declarative grammar definition formalism. SDF allows modularization of context-free grammars in order to enable reuse and clarity. Associativity and priorities of binary operators can be defined in a declarative way. The definition of lexical and context-free syntax rules are fully integrated which contributes also to the declarative way of writing grammar definitions. Restricted classes of context-free grammars, such as the classes of LL and LR grammars, are not closed under union, only the largest class of general context-free grammars is closed under union. The underlying implementation of SDF is a generalized LR parsing algorithm (S)GLR [74,90] which can handle this general class. General context-free grammars may be ambiguous; SDF offers multiple various mechanisms to deal with ambiguities [21]. Johnstone et.al. [48] describes the fundamentals of modularity of grammar formalisms. Spoofax/SDF [51] is an Eclipse plugin for developing SDF modular grammar definitions. Rascal [53] offers also a modular grammar definition formalism, it can be considered as a follow up of SDF, Rascal is available as an Eclipse plugin as well.

5.3 ANTLR, Xtext and EMFtext

Recent developments (over the last 10 years) have resulted in a renewed interested in parsing technology. ANTLR [69], GLR [86,74], SGLR [90] and GLL [79] are recent implementations of newly developed algorithms.

ANTLR. ANTLR is the basis of the popular Xtext [32] and EMFtext[88] implementations available for EMF. ANTLR is very popular because of its availability on multiple platforms. ANTLR is based on LL(*) parsing [70] and this is in many cases a serious drawback since it prohibits left recursion in the grammar. ANTLR, in contrast to SDF, does not support grammar modularity.

Xtext. Xtext [32] is popular for defining the concrete syntax of DSLs [34]. It is available as an Eclipse plugin and is well integrated with EMF. Given a context-free syntax definition, a metamodel can be derived automatically. The nonterminal in the left hand side of a production rule is transformed into an object of that type, and nonterminals in the right hand side are transformed into attributes of this object. You can enforce the creation of a class of a specific type using the **returns** action to create of an object of that specific type. In addition, Xtext offers a mechanism to create cross references. A link can be automatically established to an earlier created object. Actually, this feature breaks the context-freeness of Xtext grammars.

A number of common lexemes are predefined, such as `ID`, `INT`, `STRING`, `WS`, `ML_COMMENT`, `SL_COMMENT`, and `ANY_OTHER`.

Xtext is based on ANTLR, so it has the same characteristics. Xtext is very suited to define the concrete syntax of new DSLs, however for the definition of languages for which an abstract or concrete syntax already exists, Xtext is more tedious.

Grammar rules for `Model` and `CLass` of the Xtext specification of `SLCO` is given in Listing 1.4. Both grammar rules show the use of the Xtext `+:=` operator to concatenate lists. Listing 1.5 shows the grammar rules for `Expression` after removing left recursion. Note, that the binary operators have all become right associative and have the same priority. This listing shows the use of the Xtext `enum` construct when defining `Operator`. In the grammar rules for `TerminalExpression` and `BracketExpression`, the Xtext `returns` operator is used.

EMFtext. EMFtext [88] is tightly integrated with EMF. It enables the definition of a textual concrete syntax for Ecore based metamodels. Similarly to

```
Model :
  'model' name = ID '{'
    ('classes'
      (classes += Class)*
    )?
    ('objects'
      (objects += Object)*
    )?
    ('channels'
      (channels += Channel)*
    )?
  '}';

Class :
  name = ID '{'
    ('variables'
      (variables += Variable)*
    )?
    ('ports'
      (ports += Port)*
    )?
    ('state machines'
      (stateMachines += StateMachine)*
    )?
  '}';
```

Listing 1.4. The Model and Class definition in Xtext

Xtext, it uses ANTLR as its underlying parsing technology. It differs from Xtext in that it assumes an existing set of metamodels for which a concrete syntax has to be defined. EMFtext offers some sort of modularity; it offers an import mechanisms for various metamodels and modularization of the concrete syntax specifications.

EMFtext offers predefined lexical tokens, as well as the option to define the lexical syntax yourself.

EMFtext offers a special annotation (@Operator) to define the operator precedence and associativity of unary and binary operators. This annotation can be used when defining the expression syntax which would otherwise be defined using left recursive rules.

6 Outlook

6.1 Development and Usage of SLCO

The creation of the SLCO language has been, to some extent, motivated by the Falcon project [35,43]. The overall challenge of the project was developing a fully integrated and automated logistics warehouse of the future. One part of the project activities has been centered on investigating the applicability of MDE techniques for modeling of composite system components and for their proper integration with advanced hardware components (like grippers) [6]. The underlying concept was that:

```
Expression :
  TerminalExpression ({BinaryOperatorExpression.operand1 = current}
                      operator = Operator operand2 = Expression)?;

TerminalExpression returns Expression :
  BooleanConstantExpression |
  IntegerConstantExpression |
  StringConstantExpression |
  VariableExpression |
  BracketExpression;

enum Operator :
  atLeast = '>=' | atMost = '<=' | add = '+' | and = '&&' |
  or = '||' | equals = '==' | differs = '!=' | subtract = '-';

BooleanConstantExpression :
  value = BOOLEAN;

IntegerConstantExpression :
  value = INT;

StringConstantExpression :
  value = STRING;

VariableReference :
  name = ID;

VariableExpression :
  variable=VariableReference;

BracketExpression returns Expression:
  "(" Expression ")";
```

Listing 1.5. The Xtext specification of SLCO Expressions

- Warehouse control software is usually a collection of interacting components, which have the same (or very similar) functionality.
- All components' activities are triggered by the reception of messages/signals from other components.
- All system components have the same interfaces.
- The overall system behaviour is determined by the communication of the system components.

Having these aspects in mind as the main guidelines and taking a rather abstract and simplified view at the warehouse software control design issue, SLCO has been developed to describe the software that controls conveyor belts. In order to do simple experiments we have built a simple conveyor belt system using Lego Mindstorms [58]. By shifting the problem domain towards the communication between components, we could abstract even further away from conveyor belt related concepts and concepts like motors and sensors. Besides developing a language, the driving idea was to develop an environment which, among other things, allows automated generation of various refined models for different purposes from a *single* abstract SLCO model:

- automated generation of models for model (simulation) analysis and
- variants of executable code for different platforms.

Before we go in some more detail on the SLCO development process, we stress once again that these two aspects are very important for a DSL to be properly used in practice. First, using one single (abstract) DSL source model, from which various (refined) models are generated, guarantees that the requirements modeled in the original model and validated by simulation or checked by formal analysis are also preserved in the code to be executed, under the assumption of the correctness of the used model transformations. Second, the DSL modeling should be independent from the platform on which the system is going to be implemented. In the simple case of SLCO and control software for Lego Mindstorms conveyor belts, an abstract SLCO model capturing communication between controllers, should not contain details about the number of controllers in the implemented system. These details are very likely irrelevant also for simulation or verification of the abstract model, and they can easily increase the model complexity, and thus make the analysis more difficult. Therefore, such platform details should be added at some later stage, when the control software execution code is generated: starting from a single abstract model, various well-defined model transformations shall generate platform-dependent code for the various platforms used.

Simultaneously with the development of the SLCO, a number of model transformations to other formalisms has been defined and implemented: one for simulation, one for execution, and one for formal verification. These model transformations were developed consecutively. First, a model transformation was implemented to enable simulation of the models using POOSL [85]. In this way, models developed using an intuitive, graphical syntax can be simulated without the need for modelers to learn the syntax and semantics of a formalism for simulation. Second, a model transformation was implemented to generate NQC [10] models for execution on the Lego Mindstorms platform [58]. Executing the code generated from a model revealed bugs in the model that originated from unforeseen interleavings of concurrent objects. These bugs were not encountered during simulation. To detect these kinds of problems, a third model transformation was implemented to the Promela formalism for formal verification using the model checker SPIN [45]. All three of the aforementioned formalisms have semantic properties that are different from the semantic properties of SLCO. To enable model transformations from SLCO to each of these platforms, several semantic gaps needed to be bridged [5].

Each of these gaps is bridged by one or more *endogenous* model transformations that transform a given SLCO model to different but equivalent models, also specified in SLCO. The resulting model is semantically better aligned with the target platform. Endogenous model transformations are model transformations where the input and output model adhere to the same metamodel [61].

To be able to use endogenous transformations for this purpose, we needed to extend SLCO with constructs to specify systems on a lower level of abstraction too. In other words, the transformations add implementation details to the original SLCO model, resulting in a refined SLCO model that is closer to one of the target formalisms. This approach has as advantage that the *exogenous*

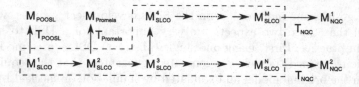

Fig. 17. Sequences of fine-grained model transformations for three target formalisms

transformations to the different platforms are simplified to purely syntactic transformations. Exogenous model transformations are model transformations where the input and output model adhere to the different metamodels [61].

Figure 17 depicts a number of composed model transformations that transform an SLCO model to the three target formalisms. The arrows inside the dashed shape depict endogenous model transformations that transform SLCO models into more refined SLCO models. The arrows across the border of the dashed shape depict exogenous model transformations. Because the semantic gaps between SLCO and the target formalisms are bridged completely by the endogenous model transformations, these exogenous transformations are straightforward translations of SLCO constructs into equivalent constructs in the target formalisms.

Using the prototype semantics we have been able to inspect the relation between original and transformed SLCO models, for a number of model instances. For each of the endogenous transformations, we conjectured that applying such a transformation leads to a model with observationally equivalent behaviour. Although experiments supported the established conjecture for a given number of input models, a more generic approach has been required to establish a relation between an arbitrary input and the output models of an SLCO model transformation.

For this purpose, we needed a general formal framework for the SLCO language allowing us to reason about and to compare model behaviours. For this purpose, we used the SOS definition of SLCO semantics. It generates a labeled transition system (LTS) representation of the dynamics of an SLCO model. In this way, the relation between SLCO models boils down to establishing an appropriate (behavioural) equivalence relation between LTSs.

Here, additional benefits of fine-grained transformations (see [3]) are evident, since they allow for rather straightforward proofs. For the constraints that were required on the input models for some of the transformations, which we detected earlier during our experimental work, it can now be formally shown that these are necessary for the correctness of the transformations as well. Thus, we formally proved that the sequences of transformations used to generate code are well composed.

6.2   How to Get Started

One way to develop experience in model driven software engineering is to dive in and apply it to your own problem domain. Other ways are to explore examples and case studies, such as SLCO, or to do your own case studies on familiar domains. We briefly describe a few of such domains here. The Eclipse Modelling Framework can be downloaded for free, and provides all the tools you need to get started.

Puzzles and games make for interesting case studies, since their domains are small and well defined, and their semantics are often not trivial but still well contained. More specifically, the reader can try to model sliding block puzzles, like *Rush Hour* [95]. For Rush Hour, the metamodel (abstract syntax) will define the puzzle elements, in particular, the board, the various types of cars and trucks, and how they can be positioned on the board, without overlapping. A concrete syntax provides a language in which one can express specific instances of the Rush Hour puzzle. The dynamic (behavioural) semantics defines the concept of a solution, in particular, the allowed moves and the puzzle's objective, viz. 'liberating' the red car. Finally, model transformations can be used to generate code to visualize and interactively simulate Rush Hour puzzles, or to generate input for a tool (such as a state space explorer) to solve these puzzles. A bigger challenge is to generalise the DSL so as to cover a larger range of sliding block puzzles.

In [60], the domain of traffic light control is used as a case study in DSL design. The main concepts to be modelled in the abstract syntax are: time, traffic participants, junctions consisting of multiple, possibly intersecting, traffic flows, traffic lights, and sensors. The dynamic semantics concerns *state changes* in the traffic flows (as detected by sensors) and in the traffic lights, and the notions of *safety* and *fairness*. Of course, one can start with simplified situations first, e.g., two intersecting traffic flows with a sensor for one flow.

An extensive modelling effort for the railway domain is presented in [13,87]. Again, one can start small, e.g., with railway infrastructure, consisting of railway lines and stations, where railway lines are built from units such as linear segments, switches, simple crossovers, and switchable crossovers. Later, one can add light signals and secured railroad crossings. The DSL can describe specific railway nets. By adding dynamic semantics, one can address the configuration of routes, by appropriate switch and crossover settings. The models can be used to generate code for animation, or to generate input for analysis tools.

Finally, elevator control is an accessible domain. The metamodel defines concepts such as passengers, elevator shafts, elevator cages, floors, doors (in the cage and on the floors), request buttons with controllable lights, and optionally sensors. The elevator control DSL can describe specific elevator systems. The dynamic semantics concerns the movement of passengers, doors, and cages, and the making and handling of passenger requests. The models can be used in ways similar to those for railway nets.

6.3   Future Developments

Model driven software engineering is a promising development with the potential to raise software development to a higher level and to disclose formal methods in disguise to the (embedded) software industry. The formalization of static and dynamic semantics of DSLs is a must, especially if proofs of correctness are required.

The fact that Eclipse is used as the default implementation platform has led and will lead to bottom-up standardization of formalisms for defining metamodels and model transformations. Xtext and EMFtext are promising tools, but more powerful and declarative grammar formalisms in the context of EMF are still needed. Also, metamodel refactoring with model co-evolution and (meta)-model modularity need better support for large-scale industrial application. Furthermore, a boost for the development of more standardized formalisms to describe static and dynamic semantics is still needed. Some (promising) initial work is done, but more work is needed.

There are some risks; the Eclipse framework may become too heavy and transform into a technological "Tower of Babel". Metamodels, concrete grammars, model transformations, etc. have become mature software artifacts that have to be versioned, maintained and analyzed. Some preliminary work in this area has been performed and will be presented at SFM-2012, but more research needs still to be performed.

The development of DSLs may become easier thanks to better tool support, but the intellectual challenge will remain. The tutorial "DSL Design for Dummies" is still to be written.

Acknowledgment. We would like to thank Arjan van der Meer for proof reading the section on static semantics. We would to thank Adrian Johnstone and Elizabeth Scott of Royal Holloway University London for reviewing this tutorial several times. The second author was on sabbatical in their group and wrote this tutorial during this period and had very fruitful discussions on the various topics addressed in this tutorial.

References

1. Aho, A.V., Sethi, R., Ullman, J.D.: Compilers: principles, techniques, and tools. Addison-Wesley Longman Publishing Co., Boston (1986)
2. Alanen, M., Porres, I.: A Relation between Context-Free Grammars and Meta Object Facility Metamodels. Technical Report 606, TUCS (2004)
3. van Amstel, M.F., van den Brand, M.G.J., Engelen, L.: Using a DSL and Fine-Grained Model Transformations to Explore the Boundaries of Model Verification. In: Proc. ICSTW 2011, pp. 63–66. IEEE Computer Society (2011)
4. van Amstel, M.F., van den Brand, M.G.J., Engelen, L.J.P.: An Exercise in Iterative Domain-Specific Language Design. In: Proceedings of the Joint ERCIM Workshop on Software Evolution (EVOL) and International Workshop on Principles of Software Evolution (IWPSE), Antwerp, Belgium, pp. 48–57. ACM Press (September 2010)
5. van Amstel, M.F., van den Brand, M.G.J., Protić, Z., Verhoeff, T.: Transforming Process Algebra Models into UML State Machines: Bridging a Semantic Gap? In: Vallecillo, A., Gray, J., Pierantonio, A. (eds.) ICMT 2008. LNCS, vol. 5063, pp. 61–75. Springer, Heidelberg (2008)

6. van Amstel, M.F., van den Brand, M.G.J., Protić, Z., Verhoeff, T.: Model-driven software engineering. In: Hamberg, R., Verriet, J. (eds.) Automation in Warehouse Development, pp. 45–58. Springer, London (2011)
7. Andova, S., van den Brand, M.G.J., Engelen, L.: Prototyping the Semantics of a DSL using ASF+SDF: Link to Formal Verification of DSL Models. In: Proceedings of the Second International Workshop on Algebraic Methods in Model-based Software Engineering, AMMSE 2011 (2011)
8. Arango, G.: Domain analysis: from art form to engineering discipline. SIGSOFT Softw. Eng. Notes 14, 152–159 (1989)
9. Arnold, B.R.T., van Deursen, A., Res, M.: An algebraic specification of a language for describing financial products. In: Wirsing, M. (ed.) ICSE-17 Workshop on Formal Methods Application in Software Engineering, pp. 6–13. IEEE (April 1995)
10. Baum, D.: NQC Programmer's Guide (2003)
11. Bettini, L.: A DSL for writing type systems for Xtext languages. In: Proceedings of the 9th International Conference on Principles and Practice of Programming in Java, PPPJ 2011, pp. 31–40. ACM, New York (2011)
12. Bjørner, D.: Rôle of Domain Engineering in Software Development—Why Current Requirements Engineering Is Flawed ! In: Pnueli, A., Virbitskaite, I., Voronkov, A. (eds.) PSI 2009. LNCS, vol. 5947, pp. 2–34. Springer, Heidelberg (2010)
13. Bjørner, D.: Train: The Railway Domain. In: Jacquart, R. (ed.) Building the Information Society. IFIP, vol. 156, pp. 607–611. Springer, Boston (2004)
14. Bjørner, D.: Domain Engineering. In: Boca, P., Bowen, J.P., Siddiqi, J. (eds.) Formal Methods: State of the Art and New Directions, pp. 1–41. Springer, London (2010), doi:10.1007/978-1-84882-736-3_1
15. Bodeveix, J.-P., Filali, M., Lawall, J., Muller, G.: Formal Methods Meet Domain Specific Languages. In: Romijn, J., Smith, G., van de Pol, J. (eds.) IFM 2005. LNCS, vol. 3771, pp. 187–206. Springer, Heidelberg (2005)
16. Bozzano, M., Cimatti, A., Katoen, J.-P., Nguyen, V., Noll, T., Roveri, M.: Safety, Dependability and Performance Analysis of Extended AADL Models. Comput. J. 54(5), 754–775 (2011)
17. van den Brand, M.G.J.: Model-Driven Engineering Meets Generic Language Technology. In: Gašević, D., Lämmel, R., Van Wyk, E. (eds.) SLE 2008. LNCS, vol. 5452, pp. 8–15. Springer, Heidelberg (2009)
18. van den Brand, M.G.J., Iversen, J., Mosses, P.D.: An Action Environment. Science of Computer Programming 61(3), 245–264 (2006)
19. van den Brand, M.G.J., de Jong, H.A., Klint, P., Olivier, P.A.: Efficient annotated terms. Software: Practice & Experience 30(3), 259–291 (2000)
20. van den Brand, M.G.J., Moreau, P.E., Vinju, J.J.: A generator of efficient strongly typed abstract syntax trees in Java. IEE Proceedings Software 152(2), 70–78 (2005)
21. den van Brand, M.G.J., Scheerder, J., Vinju, J.J., Visser, E.: Disambiguation Filters for Scannerless Generalized LR Parsers. In: CC 2002. LNCS, vol. 2304, pp. 143–158. Springer, Heidelberg (2002)
22. van den Brand, M.G.J., van der Meer, A.P., Serebrenik, A., Hofkamp, A.T.: Formally specified type checkers for domain specific languages: experience report. In: Proceedings of the Tenth Workshop on Language Descriptions, Tools and Applications, LDTA 2010, pp. 12:1–12:7. ACM, New York (2010)
23. van den Brand, M.G.J., Visser, E.: Generation of formatters for context-free languages. ACM Transactions on Software Engineering and Methodology 5(1), 1–41 (1996)

24. Brooks Jr., F.P.: No silver bullet essence and accidents of software engineering. Computer 20, 10–19 (1987)
25. Budinsky, F., Brodsky, S.A., Merks, E.: Eclipse Modeling Framework. Pearson Education (2003)
26. Bürger, C., Karol, S., Wende, C.: Applying attribute grammars for metamodel semantics. In: Proceedings of the International Workshop on Formalization of Modeling Languages, FML 2010, pp. 1:1–1:5. ACM, New York (2010)
27. Campbell-Kelly, M.: From airline reservations to Sonic the Hedgehog: a history of the software industry. History of computing. MIT Press (2003)
28. Combemale, B., Crégut, X., Garoche, P.-L., Thirioux, X.: Essay on semantics definition in MDE - an instrumented approach for model verification. JSW 4(9), 943–958 (2009)
29. van Deursen, A., Klint, P.: Little languages: little maintenance. Journal of Software Maintenance 10, 75–92 (1998)
30. van Deursen, A., Klint, P., Visser, J.: Domain-specific languages: an annotated bibliography. SIGPLAN Not. 35, 26–36 (2000)
31. Dijkstra, E.W.: Letters to the editor: go to statement considered harmful. Commun. ACM 11, 147–148 (1968)
32. Eclipse. Xtext (2012), http://www.eclipse.org/Xtext (accessed February 20, 2012)
33. Ekman, T., Hedin, G.: The JastAdd extensible Java compiler. ACM SIGPLAN Notices 42(10), 1–18 (2007)
34. Eysholdt, M., Behrens, H.: Xtext: implement your language faster than the quick and dirty way. In: Proceedings of the ACM International Conference Companion on Object Oriented Programming Systems Languages and Applications Companion, SPLASH 2010, pp. 307–309. ACM, New York (2010)
35. FALCON. Falcon project – "System-of-systems" performance and reliability in logistics (2012), http://www.esi.nl/research/applied-research/ current-projects/falcon/index.dot (accessed February 21, 2012)
36. Farail, P., Gaufillet, P., Canals, A., Camus, C.L., Sciamma, D., Michel, P., Crégut, X., Pantel, M.: The TOPCASED project: a Toolkit in OPen source for Critical Aeronautic SystEms Design. In: Embedded Real Time Software – ERTS 2006, SIA, SEE, AAAF (2006)
37. Feuerstein, S., Pribyl, B.: Oracle PL/SQL Programming, 4th edn. O'Reilly Media, Inc. (2005)
38. Frost, R.A., Hafiz, R., Callaghan, P.: Parser Combinators for Ambiguous Left-Recursive Grammars. In: Hudak, P., Warren, D.S. (eds.) PADL 2008. LNCS, vol. 4902, pp. 167–181. Springer, Heidelberg (2008)
39. Gansner, E.R., North, S.C.: An open graph visualization system and its applications to software engineering. Software: Practice & Experience 30(11), 1203–1233 (2000)
40. Groenewegen, D.M., Hemel, Z., Kats, L.C.L., Visser, E.: WebDSL: A domain-specific language for dynamic web applications. In: Mielke, N., Zimmermann, O. (eds.) Companion to the 23rd ACM SIGPLAN Conference on Object-Oriented Programing, Systems, Languages, and Applications (OOPSLA 2008), pp. 779–780. ACM, New York (2008) (poster)
41. Gronback, R.C.: Eclipse Modeling Project: A Domain-Specific Language (DSL) Toolkit, 1st edn. Addison-Wesley Professional (2009)
42. Grune, D.: Parsing Techniques: A Practical Guide, 2nd edn. Springer Publishing Company, Incorporated (2010)

43. Hamberg, R., Verriet, J.: Automation in Warehouse Development. Springer (2011)
44. Heering, J., Hendriks, P.R.H., Klint, P., Rekers, J.: The Syntax Definition Formalism SDF — reference manual. ACM SIGPLAN Notices 24, 43–75 (1989)
45. Holzmann, G.J.: The SPIN Model Checker: Primer and Reference Manual. Addison-Wesley (2003)
46. ISO. ISO/IEC 19502:2005 information technology – Meta Object Facility (MOF) (2005)
47. Johnson, S.C.: YACC—yet another compiler-compiler. Technical Report CS-32, AT & T Bell Laboratories, Murray Hill, N.J. (1975)
48. Johnstone, A., Scott, E., van den Brand, M.G.J.: LDT: a language definition technique. In: Proceedings of the Eleventh Workshop on Language Descriptions, Tools and Applications, LDTA 2011, pp. 9:1–9:8. ACM, New York (2011)
49. Jones, S.P. (ed.): Haskell 98 Language and Libraries: The Revised Report (September 2002), http://haskell.org/
50. de Jong, H.A., Olivier, P.A.: Generation of abstract programming interfaces from syntax definitions. Journal of Logic and Algebraic Programming 59(1-2), 35–61 (2004)
51. Kats, L.C., Visser, E.: The spoofax language workbench: rules for declarative specification of languages and ides. SIGPLAN Not. 45, 444–463 (2010)
52. Kleppe, A.: Software Language Engineering: Creating Domain-specific Languages Using Metamodels. Addison-Wesley (2009)
53. Klint, P., van der Storm, T., Vinju, J.: EASY Meta-programming with Rascal. In: Fernandes, J.M., Lämmel, R., Visser, J., Saraiva, J. (eds.) GTTSE 2009. LNCS, vol. 6491, pp. 222–289. Springer, Heidelberg (2011)
54. Kunert, A.: Semi-automatic generation of metamodels and models from grammars and programs. Electron. Notes Theor. Comput. Sci. 211, 111–119 (2008)
55. Kurtev, I.: Adaptability of Model Transformations. PhD thesis, University of Twente, Enschede, The Netherlands (2005)
56. Lamport, L.: Latex: a document preparation system. Addison-Wesley Longman Publishing Co., Inc., Boston (1986)
57. Landin, P.J.: The next 700 programming languages. Commun. ACM 9, 157–166 (1966)
58. LEGO. Lego Mindstorms (2012), http://www.lego.com/eng/education/mindstorms/ (accessed February 21, 2012)
59. Lesk, M.E., Schmidt, E.: Lex–a lexical analyzer generator, pp. 375–387. W.B. Saunders Company, Philadelphia (1990)
60. Mauw, S., Wiersma, W., Willemse, T.: Language-driven system design. International Journal of Software Engineering and Knowledge Engineering 14(6), 625–664 (2002)
61. Mens, T., Van Gorp, P.: A taxonomy of model transformation. Electron. Notes Theor. Comput. Sci. 152, 125–142 (2006)
62. Mernik, M., Heering, J., Sloane, A.M.: When and how to develop domain-specific languages. ACM Computing Surveys 37(4), 316–344 (2005)
63. Moreau, P.-E., Ringeissen, C., Vittek, M.: A Pattern Matching Compiler for Multiple Target Languages. In: Hedin, G. (ed.) CC 2003. LNCS, vol. 2622, pp. 61–76. Springer, Heidelberg (2003)
64. Mosses, P.D.: Action semantics. Cambridge University Press, New York (1992)
65. OMG. Unified Modeling Language specification, version 1.3 (2001), http://www.omg.org/spec/UML/1.3/PDF/index.htm (accessed February 21, 2012)
66. OMG. Meta Object Facility specification. Technical Report 2002-04-03, Object Management Group (2004)

67. OMG. OCL (2012),
    http://en.wikipedia.org/wiki/Object_Constraint_Language
    (accessed February 22, 2012)
68. Open Directory Project. Links for lexer and parser generators,
    http://www.dmoz.org/Computers/Programming/
    Compilers/Lexer_and_Parser_Generators/ (accessed on February 22, 2012)
69. Parr, T.: The Definitive ANTLR Reference: Building Domain-Specific Languages.
    Pragmatic Bookshelf (2007)
70. Parr, T., Fisher, K.: LL(*): the foundation of the ANTLR parser generator. SIG-
    PLAN Not. 46, 425–436 (2011)
71. Pierce, B.C.: Types and programming languages. MIT Press, Cambridge (2002)
72. Plotkin, G.: A Structual Approach to Operational Semantics. Journal of Logic and
    Algebraic Programming (2004)
73. Reilles, A.: Canonical Abstract Syntax Trees. In: 6th International Workshop on
    Rewriting Logic and Applications, WRLA 2006, Vienna, Autriche. Carolyn Talcott
    and Grit Denker (2006)
74. Rekers, J.: Parser Generation for Interactive Environments. PhD thesis, University
    of Amsterdam, Amsterdam, The Netherlands (January 1992)
75. Rivera, J., Durán, F., Vallecillo, A.: Formal specification and analysis of domain
    specific models using Maude. Simulation 85(11-12), 778–792 (2009)
76. Rumbaugh, J., Jacobson, I., Booch, G. (eds.): The Unified Modeling Language
    reference manual. Addison-Wesley Longman Ltd., Essex (1999)
77. Rusu, V., Lucanu, D.: A 𝕂-Based Formal Framework for Domain-Specific Mod-
    elling Languages. In: Proc. of 2nd International Conference on Formal Verification
    of Object-Oriented Systems (FoVeOOS 2011), Torino, Italy, pp. 306–323. Springer
    (2011)
78. Scheidgen, M.: CMOF-model semantics and language mapping for MOF 2.0 imple-
    mentations. In: Proceedings of the Fourth Workshop on Model-Based Development
    of Computer-Based Systems and Third International Workshop on Model-Based
    Methodologies for Pervasive and Embedded Software, pp. 84–93. IEEE Computer
    Society, Washington, DC (2006)
79. Scott, E., Johnstone, A.: GLL Parsing. Electronic Notes in Theoretical Computer
    Science 253(7), 177–189 (2010)
80. Seidewitz, E.: What Models Mean. IEEE Software 20(5), 26–32 (2003)
81. Selic, B.: A systematic approach to domain-specific language design using uml. In:
    IEEE International Symposium on Object-Oriented Real-Time Distributed Com-
    puting, pp. 2–9 (2007)
82. Stappers, F.P.M., Weber, S., Reniers, M.A., Andova, S., Nagy, I.: Formalizing a
    Domain Specific Language Using SOS: An Industrial Case Study. In: Aßmann, U.
    (ed.) SLE 2011. LNCS, vol. 6940, pp. 223–242. Springer, Heidelberg (2012)
83. Steinberg, D., Budinsky, F., Paternostro, M., Merks, E.: EMF: Eclipse Modeling
    Framework 2.0, 2nd edn. Addison-Wesley Professional (2009)
84. Stuurman, G.: Action Semantics applied to Model Driven Engineering. Master's
    thesis, University of Twente, The Netherlands (2010)
85. Theelen, B.D., Florescu, O., Geilen, M.C.W., Huang, J., van der Putten, P.H.A.,
    Voeten, J.P.M.: Software/hardware engineering with the parallel object-oriented
    specification language. In: Proceedings of the 5th IEEE/ACM International Con-
    ference on Formal Methods and Models for Codesign, MEMOCODE 2007, pp.
    139–148. IEEE Computer Society, Washington, DC (2007)

86. Tomita, M.: An efficient context-free parsing algorithm for natural languages. In: Proceedings of the 9th International Joint Conference on Artificial Intelligence, vol. 2, pp. 756–764. Morgan Kaufmann Publishers Inc., San Francisco (1985)
87. TRain. Train – The Railway Domain (2012), http://www.railwaydomain.org/ (accessed February 25, 2012)
88. TUDresden. EMFtext (2012), http://www.emftext.org/ (accessed February 20, 2012)
89. van Rossum, G.: An Introduction to Python for Unix/C Programmers. In: Proc. of the NLUUG Najaarsconferentie. Dutch UNIX users group (1993)
90. Visser, E.: Scannerless Generalized-LR Parsing. Technical Report P9707, Programming Research Group, University of Amsterdam (July 1997)
91. Visser, E.: Syntax Definition for Language Prototyping. PhD thesis, University of Amsterdam (1997)
92. van Vliet, H.: Software Engineering: Principles and Practice, 3rd edn. Wiley Publishing (2008)
93. Walkingshaw, E., Erwig, M.: A domain-specific language for experimental game theory. J. Funct. Program. 19, 645–661 (2009)
94. Wikipedia. Grace hopper — Wikipedia, the free encyclopedia (2012), http://en.wikipedia.org/wiki/Grace_Hopper (accessed February 18, 2012)
95. Wikipedia. Rush hour — Wikipedia, the free encyclopedia (2012), http://en.wikipedia.org/wiki/Rush_Hour_board_game (accessed February 25, 2012)

Object Constraint Language (OCL):
A Definitive Guide

Jordi Cabot[1] and Martin Gogolla[2]

[1] INRIA / École des Mines de Nantes, France
jordi.cabot@inria.fr
[2] University of Bremen, Germany
gogolla@informatik.uni-bremen.de

Abstract. The Object Constraint Language (OCL) started as a complement of the UML notation with the goal to overcome the limitations of UML (and in general, any graphical notation) in terms of precisely specifying detailed aspects of a system design. Since then, OCL has become a key component of any model-driven engineering (MDE) technique as the default language for expressing all kinds of (meta)model query, manipulation and specification requirements. Among many other applications, OCL is frequently used to express model transformations (as part of the source and target patterns of transformation rules), well-formedness rules (as part of the definition of new domain-specific languages), or code-generation templates (as a way to express the generation patterns and rules).

This chapter pretends to provide a comprehensive view of this language, its many applications and available tool support as well as the latest research developments and open challenges around it.

1 Introduction

The Object Constraint Language (OCL) appeared as an effort to overcome the limitations of UML when it comes to precisely specifying detailed aspects of a system design. OCL was first developed in 1995 inside IBM as an evolution of an expression language in the Syntropy method [26]. The work on OCL was part of a joint proposal with ObjectTime Limited presented as a response to the RFP for a standard object-oriented analysis and design language issued by the Object Management Group (OMG) [26]. That standard came to be what we now know as UML and OCL became integrated in it in 1997.

Initially, OCL was only used as a constraint language for UML but quickly expanded its scope and now OCL has become a key component of any model-driven engineering (MDE) technique as the default language for expressing all kinds of (meta)model query, manipulation and specification requirements. Among many other applications, OCL is frequently used to express model transformations (as part of the source and target patterns of transformation rules), well-formedness rules (as part of the definition of new domain-specific languages, or code generation templates (as a way to express the generation patterns and rules).

M. Bernardo, V. Cortellessa, and A. Pierantonio (Eds.): SFM 2012, LNCS 7320, pp. 58–90, 2012.

To adapt the language to these new applications, several new (sub)versions of the language have been released. At the moment of writing this chapter, the current version of the OCL language is version 2.3.1 [20].

This chapter pretends to provide a comprehensive view of this language, its many applications and available tool support as well as the latest research developments and open challenges around it. The rest of this chapter is structured as follows. Section 2 motivates the need for OCL. Section 3 gives a brief overview of the language, while Section 4 provides a more precise language description. Then, Section 5 classifies existings OCL tools. Finally, Section 6 outlines a possible research agenda for OCL and Section 7 provides some final conclusions.

2 Motivation·

Graphical modeling languages are the preferred choice for many designers when it comes to define the structural aspects of a domain (i.e., its main concepts, their properties and the relationships between them). The most typical example of a graphical notation is UML [21], specially its class diagram which is by far the most used UML diagram [13].

Nevertheless, this facility of use comes with a price. In order to keep the number of notational elements manageable, language designers must limit the expressiveness of the language. This means that graphical notations can only express a limited subset of all the relevant information of a domain. This is where OCL (and in general, any other textual language) comes into play. They are a necessary complement of the UML (or other graphical languages) notation in order to be able to precisely specify all detailed aspects of a system design.

As an example, take a look at the class diagram of Figure 1 that will be used as running example throughout the chapter. This diagram is an excerpt of the EU-Rent Car Rentals Specification [14], an in-depth specification of the EU-Rent case study, which is a widely known case study being promoted as a basis for demonstration of product capabilities. EU-Rent presents a car rental company with branches in several countries that provides typical rental services. EU-Rent was originally developed by Model Systems, Ltd.

This excerpt contains information about the rentals of the company (*Rental* class), the company branches (*Branch* class), the rented cars (*Car*), the category to which they belong (*CarGroup*) and the customers (*Customer*) that at some point in time may become blacklisted (*BlackListed*) due to delayed car returns, unpaid rentals, etc. Each rented car has one or more registered drivers and a pickup and drop off branch assigned.

This may look like a quite complete definition of the problem but in reality it is just the tip of the iceberg. Many important details cannot be defined just using the notation available for UML class diagrams. Just to mention some aspects that the UML diagram does not answer:

1. Can blacklisted people rent new cars? (common sense may suggest answering no to this question but in fact this is not specified anywhere in the diagram so different people may assume different answers)

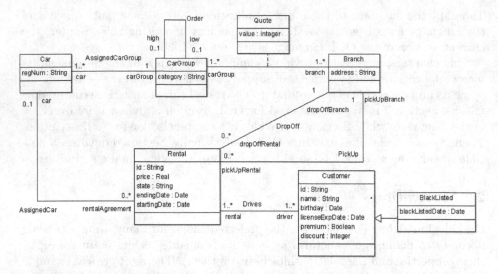

Fig. 1. Running Example - Partial Class Diagram of the EU-Rent company

2. How is the price of a rental calculated?
3. What are the conditions to be able to extend an existing rental?
4. Should the driving license of all drivers be valid throughout the full rental period? Is there a minimum driving seniority required? Can the same driver have two active rentals?
5. Can the pickup and drop off branches differ?
6. Can I choose a car already assigned to another rental?

The next section will show how OCL can be used to express all these additional concerns.

3   OCL in a Nutshell

The goal of this section is to give you an informal short description of the OCL and show its usefulness by exemplifying how it can be used to solve the open questions left at the end of the last section.

OCL is a general-purpose (textual) formal[1] language adopted as a standard by the OMG (see the current version of the OCL specification [20]) used to define several kinds of expressions that complement the information of (UML) models.

OCL is a typed, declarative and side-effect free specification language. *Typed* means that each OCL expression evaluates to a type (either one of the predefined OCL types or a type in the model where the OCL expression is used) and must conform to the rules and operations of that type. *Side-effect free* implies that OCL expressions can query or constrain the state of the system but not modify

---

[1] The degree of formality of OCL is under discussion but we could agree that at least it can be considered a semi-formal language.

it. *Declarative* means that OCL does not include imperative constructs like assignments. And finally, *specification* refers to the fact that the language definition does not include any implementation details nor implementation guidelines.

Among the many applications of OCL, it can be used to define the following kinds of expressions[2]:

- Invariants to state all necessary condition that must be satisfied in each possible instantiation of the model.
- Initialization of class properties.
- Derivation rules that express how the value of derived model elements must be computed.
- Query operations
- Operation contracts (i.e., set of operation pre- and postconditions)

In the following we briefly introduce each expression type and explain some basic OCL constructs along the way. The next section will present the full details of the language.

3.1   Invariants

Integrity constraints in OCL are represented as invariants defined in the context of a specific type, named the *context type* of the constraint. Its body, the boolean condition to be checked, must be satisfied by all instances of the context type.

Invariants are without a doubt the most common OCL expression since they allow designers to easily specify all kinds of conditions that the system must comply with.

Invariants can restrict the value of single objects, like the following *QuoteOverZero*:

```
context Quote inv QuoteOverZero: self.value > 0
```

stating that all quotes must have a positive value. Note that the *self* variable represents an arbitrary instance of the *Quote* class and the dot notation is used to access the properties of the *self* object (as the *value* attribute in the example). As stated above, all instances of *Quote* (the context type of the constraint in this case) must evaluate this condition to true.

Nevertheless, many invariants express more complex conditions limiting the possible relationships between different objects in the system, usually related through association links. For instance, this *NoRentalsBlackListed* constraint forbids BlackListed people of renting cars:

```
context BlackListed inv NoRentalsBlackListed:
    self.rental->forAll(r | r.startDate < self.blackListedDate)
```

---

[2] For the sake of simplicity, we focus on the kinds of expressions useful for class diagrams; e.g., OCL can also be used to define guards in state machines.

where we first retrieve all rentals linked to a blacklisted person and then we make sure that all of them were created before the person was blacklisted. This is done by iterating on all related rentals and evaluating the date condition on each of them; the *forAll* iterator returns true iff all elements of the input collection evaluate the condition to true.

3.2   Initialization Expressions

OCL can be used to specify the initial value that the properties of an object must take upon the object creation. Obviously, the type of the expression must conform to the type of the initialized property (this must also take into account cases where the property to be initialized is a collection).

For instance, the following OCL expression initializes to false the value of the *premium* attribute of Customers (we are assuming that customers can only promote to the premium status after renting several cars).

```
context Customer::premium: boolean init: false
```

3.3   Derived Elements

Derived elements are elements whose value/population can be inferred from the value/population of other model elements as defined in the element's derivation rule. OCL is a popular choice for specifying these derivation rules.

OCL derivation rules follow the same structure as init expressions (see above) although their interpretation is different. An *init* expression must be true when the object is created but the restricted property may change its value afterwards (i.e., customers start as non-premium but may evolve to premium during their time in the system). Instead, derivation rules constrain the value of a derived element throughout all its life-span. Note that this does not imply that the value of a derived element cannot change, it only means that it will always change according to the evaluation of its derivation rule.

As an example, consider the following rule for the derived element *discount* in class *Customer*, stating that premium members get a 30% discount while non-premium members get 15% if they have at least rented high category cars five times while the rest of the customers get no discount at all.

```
context Customer::discount: integer
derive:
  if not self.premium then
    if self.rental.car.carGroup->
        select(c|c.category='high')->size()>=5
    then 15
    else 0 endif
  else 30 endif
```

The *select* iterator in the expression returns the subcollection of elements from the input collection that satisfy the condition. Then, the *size* collection operator returns the cardinality of the output subcollection and this value is compared with the '5' threshold. Note that in this example, the input collection (self.rental.car.carGroup) is not a set but a bag (i.e., a collection with repeated elements) since a user may have rented the same car twice in different rentals or two cars belonging to the same car group.

3.4 Query Operations

As the name indicates, query operations are a *wrapped* OCL expression that queries the system data and returns the information to the user.

As an example, the following query operation returns true if the car on which the operation is executed is the most popular in the rental system.

```
context Car::mostPopular(): boolean
body: Car::allInstances()->forAll(c1|c1<>self implies
      c1.rentalAgreement->size()<=self.rentalAgreement->size())
```

3.5 Operation Contracts

There are two different approaches for specifying an operation effect: the *imperative* and the *declarative* approach [27]. In an imperative specification, the designer explicitly defines the set of structural events (inserts/updates/deletes) to be applied when executing the operation. Instead, in a declarative specification, a contract for each operation must be provided. The contract consists of a set of pre- and postconditions. A precondition defines a set of conditions on the operation input and the system state that must hold when the operation is issued while postconditions state the set of conditions that must be satisfied by the system state at the end of the operation. OCL is usually the language of choice to express pre- and postconditions for operation contracts at the modeling level.

As an example, the following newRental operation describes (part of) the business logic behind the creation of a new rental in the EU-rent system:

```
context Rental::newRental(id:Integer, price:Real, startingDate:Date,
                endingDate:Date, customer:Customer, carRegNum:String,
                pickupBranch: Branch, dropOffBranch: Branch)
pre: customer.licenseExpDate>endingDate
post: Rental.allInstances->one(r |
        r.oclIsNew() and r.oclIsTypeOf(Rental) and
        r.endingDate=endingDate and r.startingDate=startingDate and
        r.driver=customer and r.pickupBranch=pickupBranch and
        r.dropOffBranch=dropOffBranch and
        r.car=Car.allInstances()->any(c | c.regNum=carRegNum))
```

The precondition checks that the customer has a valid license for the duration of the rental[3] while the postcondition states that by the end of the operation a new object r of type *Rental* must have been created and initialized with the set of values passed as parameters[4].

4 Language Description

Figure 2 gives an overview on the OCL type system in form of a feature model. Using a tree-like description[5], feature models allow to describe mandatory and optional features of a subject, and they allow to specify alternative features as well as conjunctive features. In particular, the figure pictures the different kinds of available types. Before explaining the type system in a systematic way, let us discuss OCL example types which are already known or which can be deduced from the class diagram of our running example in Fig. 3. Attributes types, as for example in `Car::regNum:String`, are *predefined basic, atomic* types. Classes which are defined by the class diagram are *atomic, user-defined class* types. If we already have an expression `cg` of type `CarGroup`, then the OCL expression `cg.car` has the type `Set(Car)` due to the multiplicity `1..*`. The type `Set(Car)` is a *flat, concrete collection* type. `Set(Car)` is a reification of the *parametrized collection* type `Set(T)` where `T` denotes an arbitrary type parameter which can be stubstituted. The type `Sequence(Set(Car))` is a *nested* collection type being a reification of the parametrized, nested collection type `Sequence(Set(T))`. If `cg:CarGroup` is given, then the expression `Tuple{cat:cg.category, cars:cg.car}` has type `Tuple(cat:String, cars:Set(Car))` which is a *tuple* type.

4.1 OCL Types

Let us now consider the types in Fig. 2 in a systematic way. An OCL type is either an atomic type or a template type. Atomic types are either predefined basic types or user-defined types. Predefined basic types are `Integer`, `Real`, `String`, and `Boolean`. User-defined types are either class types (e.g., `Customer`) or enumeration types (e.g., `BranchKind=#airport, #downtown, #onTheRoad`). A template type is a type which uses at least one of the six predefined type constructors: `Set`, `Bag`, `Sequence`, `OrderedSet`, `Collection`, and `Tuple`. A parametrized template type has one or more parameters (e.g., `Bag(T)` or `Tuple(part1:T1, part2:T2)`)

---

[3] There are several styles when writing preconditions, some people choose to include in the preconditions the verification of all integrity constraints that may be affected by the operation while others consider this redundant.

[4] Note that postconditions are underspecifications, i.e., they only specify part of the system state at the end of the execution which leads to the frame problem [4] and other similar issues; this problem is not OCL-specific and thus it is outside of the scope of this chapter.

[5] The actual structure of the feature model is a dag (directed, acyclic graph).

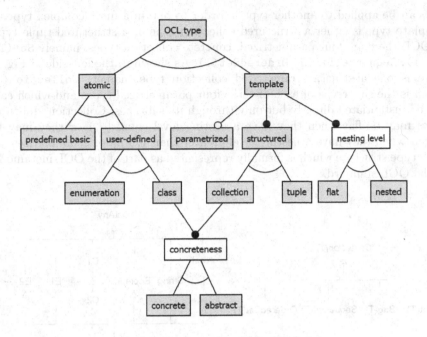

Fig. 2. OCL Types as a Feature Model

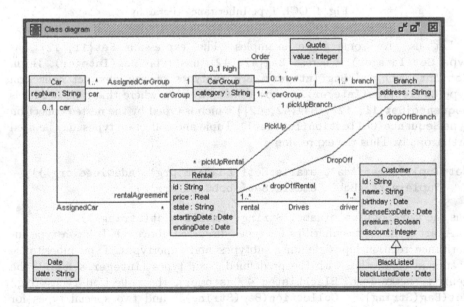

Fig. 3. Example Class Diagram modeled with the USE tool

and can be applied to another type in order to obtain a more complex type. A template type is either a structured collection type or a structured tuple type. In OCL there are four parametrized, concrete collection types, namely `Set(T)`, `Bag(T)`, `Sequence(T)`, and `OrderedSet(T)`. As shown in the left side of Fig. 4, there is one abstract, parametrized collection type, namely `Collection(T)` which is the supertype of each of these four parametrized types and which cannot be instantiated directly but only through its subtypes. Collection and tuple types may be flat when they have a nesting level equal to 1 or they may be nested when they have a nesting level greater than 1. Figure 2 summarizes the OCL type structure which is formally represented as part of the OCL metamodel in the OCL standard.

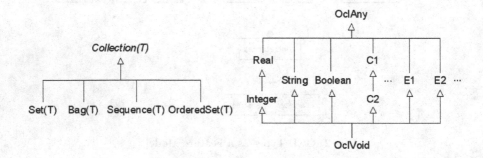

Fig. 4. OCL Type Inheritance Hierarchy

Let us give some more examples. The expression `Set{11, 12}` has type `Set(Integer)`, whereas `Bag{42, 42}` has type `Bag(Integer)`. Both, `Set(Integer)` and `Bag(Integer)`, are subtypes of the abstract collection type `Collection(Integer)`. An example expression where this type occurs is `Sequence{Set{11, 12}, Bag{42, 42}}` which is typed by the nested collection type `Sequence(Collection(Integer))`. Tuple and collection types may be used orthogonally. Thus the expression

```
Set{Tuple{name:'Ada', emails:Set{'ada@acm.org','ada@ieee.org'}},
    Tuple{name:'Bob', emails:Set{'bob@acm.org'}}}
```

has the type `Set(Tuple(name: String, emails: Set(String)))`.

Apart from the peculiarities for types discussed above, OCL has a type inheritance relationship < defining subtypes and supertypes. Type inheritance occurs in connection with the predefined basic types (`Integer < Real`), the defined classes (e.g., `BlackListed < Customer`), the collection types (e.g., `Set(Bag(String)) < Collection(Bag(String))`) and two special types for the top and the bottom of the type hierarchy, namely `OclAny` for the top type and `OclVoid` for the bottom type. A general overview is shown in Fig. 4. On the right side, the subtypes of `OclAny` being at the same time the supertypes of OclVoid are displayed. The subtypes can be categorized into the predefined basic types, the class types, and the enumeration types. Please note that neither Collection(T) nor any of its reifications (e.g., Set(String)) is a subtype of OclAny. However, any type from the right side may be substituted for the type parameter T in the left side, and any subtyping relationship is carried over from the right side to the left side, e.g., C2 < C1 induces Bag(C2) < Bag(C1) and Set(C2) < Collection(C2) < Collection(C1).

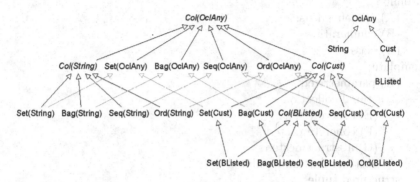

Fig. 5. OCL Example Types and Induced Collection Types

For our running example, we obtain Set(Integer) < Collection(Real) or Bag(BlackListed) < Collection(Customer). Please also be aware of the fact, that, for example, Set(OclAny) is a valid type and, therefore, the expression Set{42, true, 'ABBA', @Car42} including an Integer constant, a Boolean constant, a String constant, and an object of class Car is a valid OCL expression of type Set(OclAny). However, a construct like Set{42,Sequence{42}} is invalid, because the types Integer and Sequence(Integer) do not have a common supertype. The upper right part of Fig. 5 shows a subset of the example types and its induced first level collection types where the collections are applied only once and therefore no nested collection types arise. We have used the abbreviations Seq[uence], Ord[eredSet], Col[lection], Cust[omer], B[lack]Listed in the Figure, and we will use the shortcuts of the collections also further down, if we need it. Please note, that, for example, Set(BListed) has five supertypes: Set(Cust), Col(BListed), Set(OclAny), Col(Cust), Col(OclAny). The type relationships would become even richer when all example types (e.g., Integer and Branch) would have been used. In principle, there is an infinite number of induced collection types, because the nesting level may be arbitrarily deep, but the used maximal nesting level is always finite: every class model and every OCL term will use only a finite fraction of all possible types.

4.2   OCL Values

As you see from the feature model, the OCL type system is involved, but for an introductory paper, we want to offer to the reader a way through all possible combinations by means of a clear, manageable number of categories. The OCL type feature model gives rise to nine different categories of available types. We label the categories with letters from (A) to (I) and show examples for OCL expressions representing values in each of the nine categories.

- atomic
  - (A) predefined basic
  - (B) enumeration
  - (C) class
- template
  - (D) parametrized
  - structured collection
    — (E) concrete flat
    — (F) concrete nested
    — (G) abstract nested
    — abstract flat: unpopulated
  - structured tuple
    — (H) flat
    — (I) nested

We will first go through the categories (A) to (I), explain each single category and show positive examples. Afterwards, we will explain why we consider the category *abstract, flat structured collection* as being unpopulated.

The OCL expressions for category (A) are straight forward and need not be explained. The enumeration values in category (B) show that an enumeration literal can be introduced by the hash sign as required in early OCL versions and that they can be written down preceeding their type name and separated by double colons in later OCL versions. As shown in category (C), a literal for an object can be any allowed identifier. Often the literal indicates somehow the class type for the object, but this is not a requirement. For small examples often well choosen object literals (like `ibm,sun:Company`) support intuition about the use of the object. In category (D), the parametrized types always possess at least one type parameter. Parametrized types can be nested arbitrarily deep, but the nesting in each type is always finite. The six keywords `Set`, `Bag`, `Sequence`, `OrderedSet`, `Collection`, and `Tuple` occur in connection with parametrized types.

```
(A) 42 : Integer
    43.44 : Real
    'fortytwo' : String
    false : Boolean
```

```
(B) #airport, #downtown, #onTheRoad : BranchKind
    BranchKind::airport : BranchKind

(C) car42, Herbie, OFP857 : Car
    branch42, SunsetStrip77 : Branch

(D) Set(T)
    Sequence(T)
    Tuple(part1:T1,part2:T2)
    Sequence(OrderedSet(T))
    Sequence(Collection(T))
```

Category (E) contains values for flat, concrete collections, category (F) displays nested, concrete collections, and category (G) involves nested, abstract collections. As the examples point out, values for collection types can be built with constructor operations denoted by Set, Bag, Sequence and OrderedSet. A type is considered to be *abstract* if its type expression involves Collection or an abstract class type from the underlying class diagram. Note that collections may contain different values which have different least types, but in any case the values inside a single collection must have a common supertype. For example, the last expression in category (E) Set{car42,'fortytwo'} involves values of type Car and String. The example for ordered sets shows that ordered sets are not neccessarily sorted. Please note that the top-most example set in category (F) contains three elements which are pairwise distinct. The last example in category (G) shows a degree of flexibilty gained through the possibility of having abstract collections: A collection of email adresses can be a set or a sequence of strings, depending on whether a priority for email adresses is required to be stated or not.

```
(E) Set{42,43} : Set(Integer)
    Bag{42,42,43} : Bag(Integer)
    Sequence{43,42,44,42} : Sequence(Integer)
    OrderedSet{43,42,44} : OrderedSet(Integer)
    Sequence{'Steve','Jobs'} : Sequence(String)
    Bag{backlisted42,blacklisted43} : Bag(BlackListed)
    Set{42,43.44} : Set(Real)
    Sequence{blacklisted42,customer43} : Sequence(Customer)
    Set{car42,'fortytwo'} : Set(OclAny)

(F) Sequence{Bag{42,42},Bag{42,43}} : Sequence(Bag(Integer))
    Set{Sequence{Set{7},Set{8}},
        Sequence{Set{8},Set{7}},
        Sequence{Set{7,8}}} : Set(Sequence(Set(Integer)))

(G) Sequence{Set{7,8},Bag{7,7}} : Sequence(Collection(Integer))
    Set{Set{Set{7}},Bag{Bag{7}}} : Set(Collection(Collection(Integer)))
    Set{Tuple{name:'Ada',emails:Set{'ada@acm','ada@ibm'}},
        Tuple{name:'Bob',emails:Sequence{'bob@omg','bob@sun'}}} :
      Set(Tuple(emails:Collection(String),name:String))
```

Categories (H) shows flat tuples and category (I) nested tuples. Tuples can
be constructed with the keyword Tuple and by additionally specifying part
names and part values. In category (H), the first two examples explain that
tuple parts may be assigned by using the colon or alternatively by the equality symbol. Tuples may contain parts of arbitrary types, e.g., class types and
predefined types as in the third example. The order of tuple parts does not matter in OCL. Thus we have for example Tuple{first:'Steve',last:'Jobs'} =
Tuple{last:'Jobs',first:'Steve'}. The tool employed here (USE) [17] sorts
the tuple parts by their names, and therefore the shown type to the right of
the colon may exhibit a different part order than the input expression. In category (I), four tuple values are presented. The first one is a nested tuple with
two parts having a tuple type. The second one is a tuple with two parts having
type String and Set(String), respectively. The third one is an OCL representation of a simple relational database state in first normal form. The fourth one
represents the same state information in a non-first normal form style in which
the second relation has a set-valued, non-atomic part type.

```
(H)  Tuple{first:'Steve',last:'Jobs'} : Tuple(first:String,last:String)
     Tuple{first='Steve',last='Jobs'} : Tuple(first:String,last:String)
     Tuple{carRef:Herbie,year:1963,manufRef:VW} :
         Tuple{carRef:Car,manufRef:Company,year:Integer}


(I)  Tuple{name:Tuple{first:'Steve',last:'Jobs'},
             adr:Tuple{street:'Infinite Loop',no:1}} :
     Tuple(adr:Tuple(no:Integer,street:String),
           name:Tuple(first:String,last:String))


     Tuple{name:'Ada',emails:Set{'ada@acm','ada@ibm'}} :
       Tuple{emails:Set(String),name:String}


     Tuple{Customers:Set{Tuple{name:'Ada',birth:1962},
                         Tuple{name:'Bob',birth:1962}},
         Rentals:Set{Tuple{name:'Ada',start:'2012-01-01'},
                     Tuple{name:'Ada',start:'2002-01-01'},
                     Tuple{name:'Cyd',start:'2002-01-01'}}} :
       Tuple(Customers:Set(Tuple(birth:Integer,name:String)),
             Rentals:Set(Tuple(name:String,start:String)))


     Customers | name  | birth    Rentals | name  | start
     ----------+-------+-------  ---------+-------+--------------
               | 'Ada' | 1962             | 'Ada' | '2012-01-01'
               | 'Bob' | 1962             | 'Ada' | '2002-01-01'
                                          | 'Cyd' | '2002-01-01'


     Tuple{Customers:Set{Tuple{name:'Ada',birth:1962},
                         Tuple{name:'Bob',birth:1962}},
         Rentals:Set{Tuple{name:'Ada',
                           starts:Set{'2012-01-01','2002-01-01'}},
                     Tuple{name:'Cyd',starts:Set{'2002-01-01'}}}} :
```

```
Tuple(Customers:Set(Tuple(birth:Integer,name:String)),
      Rentals:Set(Tuple(name:String,starts:Set(String))))
```

The category *abstract, flat structured collection* cannot be populated because, for example, you cannot build a value for `Collection(Integer)` which is not also a value for `Set(Integer)` or `Bag(Integer)` or `Sequence(Integer)` or `OrderedSet(Integer)`. Of course we have: `Set{42}`: `Set(Integer)` and `Set{42}`: `Collection(Integer)` because `Set(Integer) < Set(Collection)`. But there is no *proper* value in `Collection(Integer)` which is only in that type and not also in one its subtypes. The statement can be expressed formally as follows.

```
VALUES[Collection(Integer)]  - VALUES[Set(Integer)]
                             - VALUES[Bag(Integer)]
                             - VALUES[Sequence(Integer)]
                             - VALUES[OrderedSet(Integer)]  = EMPTY
```

This is different for the combination *abstract and nested*. For example, we have `Sequence{Set{42},Bag{42}}` has type `Sequence(Collection(Integer))`. Note however, that all abstract types, which have `Collection` as its top type and are arbitrarily nested, but concrete type as its inner type, cannot be (in the above sense) *properly* populated. For example, we have `Set{Sequence{42}}` has type `Set(Sequence(Integer))` and as a consequence `Set{Sequence{42}}` has type `Collection(Sequence(Integer))`. And we have `Bag{Sequence{42}}` has type `Bag(Sequence(Integer))` and as a consequence `Bag{Sequence{42}}` has type `Collection(Sequence(Integer))`. But there are no values in `Collection(Sequence(Integer))` which are at the same time not in `Set(Sequence(Integer))` or `Bag(Sequence(Integer))` or `Sequence(Sequence(Integer))` or `OrderedSet(Sequence(Integer))`.

4.3   OCL Collection Properties

OCL denotes equality and inequality with the operations = und <>, respectively. Let us consider equality and inequality on collection values in more detail. This will also lead us to an explanation of the similarities and the differences between the four different collection kinds.[6]

```
  Set{7,8}  =  Set{8,7}     OrderedSet{7,8}  <>  OrderedSet{8,7}
        \     /                          \      /
         =   =                            =    <>
        \     /                          \      /
        Set{7,8,7}                     OrderedSet{7,8,7}
```

---

[6] Collection kind VS collection type: In our view each collection kind is manifested by many collection types. For example, the collection kind set is manifested by `Set(String)` or `Set(Sequence(Integer))`.

```
Bag{7,8}  =  Bag{8,7}        Sequence{7,8}  <>  Sequence{8,7}
     \      /                        \          /
     <>    <>                        <>        <>
       \  /                            \      /
     Bag{7,8,7}                    Sequence{7,8,7}
```

Above we have displayed twelve different collection expressions: three sets, three ordered sets, three bags, and three sequences. There are three element insertion orders: (A) first 7 and second 8, (B) first 8 and second 7, and (C) first 7, second 8, third 7. We have also displayed whether the respective collection expressions are equal or inequal. The four collection kinds can be distinguished by their equal-inequal pattern: sets show (=,=,=), ordered sets display (<>,=,<>), bags give (=,<>,<>), and sequences have (<>,<>,<>). Using these examples one can also check general properties which collections may possess: insensibility to element insertion order and insensibility to element insertion frequency. The four collection kinds can be distinguished nicely on the basis of these two criteria.

```
                                |    insertion order
                                | insensible |  sensible
--------------------------------+------------+------------
insertion frequency insensible |    Set     | OrderedSet
                    sensible |    Bag     | Sequence
```

Both criteria can formally be defined in an OCL-like style with predicates as stated below. Here, we already use three operations on collections which will be explained later. The operation forAll checks whether a boolean expression evaluates to true on all collection elements. The operation including inserts an element into a collection and (possibly) constructs a new collection. The operation includes checks whether an item is part of a collection.

```
orderInsensible(c:Collection(OclAny),witness:Bag(OclAny)):Boolean=
  witness->forAll(e,f |
    c->including(e)->including(f)=c->including(f)->including(e))
frequencyInsensible(c:Collection(OclAny),witness:Bag(OclAny)):Boolean=
  witness->forAll(e |
    c->includes(e) implies c->including(e)=c)
```

The operation orderInsensible checks whether for a parameter collection the order in the addition of two further elements does not matter. The operation frequencyInsensible checks whether the addition of an already present collection element does not matter. Both operations have an additional parameter determining a collection of test witnesses with which the respective property is checked. The actual OCL definitions are a bit more complicated because the operation including does not work on collections, but on the concrete subtypes only. We do not show them here. Using these two operations we can build the following OCL evaluations which demonstrate the distinctive features of the four different OCL collections. The OCL construct let allows us to define a name for an expression which can be used later.

```
? let C=Set{7} in let W=Bag{7,8,9} in
    Sequence{orderInsensible(C,W),frequencyInsensible(C,W)}
> Sequence{true,true} : Sequence(Boolean)

? let C=OrderedSet{7} in let W=Bag{7,8,9} in
    Sequence{orderInsensible(C,W),frequencyInsensible(C,W)}
> Sequence{false,true} : Sequence(Boolean)

? let C=Bag{7} in let W=Bag{7,8,9} in
    Sequence{orderInsensible(C,W),frequencyInsensible(C,W)}
> Sequence{true,false} : Sequence(Boolean)

? let C=Sequence{7} in let W=Bag{7,8,9} in
    Sequence{orderInsensible(C,W),frequencyInsensible(C,W)}
> Sequence{false,false} : Sequence(Boolean)
```

The OCL evaluations emphasize what was presented in the above table: Sets are order insensible and frequency insensible; bags are order insensible but frequency sensible; sequences are order sensible and frequency sensible; ordered sets are order sensible but frequency insensible.

We must mention some further details concerning equality and inequality on collections. We have seen that equality and inequality can be checked between two expressions possessing the same collection kind, e.g., we obtain (Set{7,8} = Set{8,7,7}) = true. But equality and inequality can also be applied between expressions of different collection kinds. For example, we obtain (Set{7,8} = Bag{7,8}) = false and (OrderedSet{8,9} <> Sequence{8,9}) = true. Note that although left and right-hand side of the collection comparisions contain the same values (even in the same order) the collections are different because their types are different. In particular, although bags possess the potential to contain one element twice, they are not forced to do so. In ordered sets, the first insertion of an element dominates over following insertions, e.g., we obtain (OrderedSet{7,8,8} = OrderedSet{7,8,7}) = true and (OrderedSet{7,8,8} <> OrderedSet{8,7,8}) = true. And, ordered sets are not *sorted*: (OrderedSet{7,9,8} <> OrderedSet{9,7,8}) = true

4.4   OCL null Value

As we have seen before, the OCL type system knows a top type, namely OclAny, which includes all atomic values (but not the structured values). We have mentioned also a bottom type, namely OclVoid. This type is populated by one extra value denoted by null. As in the database language SQL, this value can be used to express that some particular information is not available. Because, OclVoid is a subtype of any other atomic type, the value null is present in all atomic types and can be used in collections and tuples. The literal null was introduced in a newer OCL version. Formerly, there was the check oclIsUndefined on OclAny with which it is still possible to test for this value. Let us consider some uses of null.

```
ada.discount=null : Boolean
branch42.address=null : Boolean
1/0=null : Boolean
Tuple{name:'Jobs, Steve',telno:null} : Tuple(name:String,telno:String)
(1/0).oclIsUndefined=true : Boolean
42.oclIsUndefined=false : Boolean
Set{'800-275-2273','800-694-7466',null} : Set(String)
```

The first two example express that the discount of customer ada and the address
of branch branch42 are currently undefined. In the third example null is used
to express the partiality of a function. The fourth example shows a tuple whose
part telno is undefined. The last example shows the null value in a collection.
As in SQL, the value null is an exceptional value distinct from all ordinary
values. For example, in OCL we have that the following propositions are true:
0<>null, ''<>null, 'null'<>null, 'NULL'<>null, and 'Null'<>null.

4.5   Navigation in OCL

Given an object diagram, i.e., a system state, OCL allows us to access objects and
their properties, e.g., attributes, and to navigate between them by using opposite
side role names from associations. This navigation is syntactically denoted by
a dot. Consider the object diagram in Fig. 6 which shows a valid system state
where all classes and associations are instantiated through objects and links and
where all association multiplicities are satisfied. Then the following attribute
accesses and navigation possibilities exist.

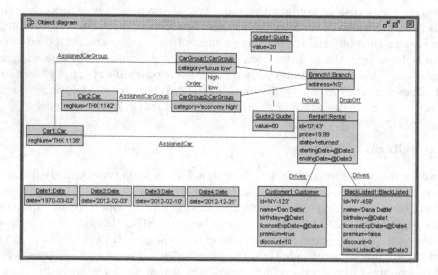

Fig. 6. Example Object Diagram

```
? Car1
> @Car1 : Car

? Car2.regNum
> 'THX 1142' : String

? Car2.carGroup
> @CarGroup2 : CarGroup

? Car2.carGroup.category
> 'economy high' : String

? Branch1.carGroup
> Set{@CarGroup1,@CarGroup2} : Set(CarGroup)

? Branch1.carGroup.car
> Bag{@Car1,@Car2} : Bag(Car)

? Rental1.driver
> Set{@BlackListed1,@Customer1} : Set(Customer)

? Rental1.driver.birthday
> Bag{@Date1,@Date1} : Bag(Date)

? CarGroup2.high
> @CarGroup1 : CarGroup

? CarGroup2.high.low
> @CarGroup2 : CarGroup

? CarGroup2.high.high
> null : OclVoid

? Car2.rentalAgreement
> Set{} : Set(Rental)
```

Navigation from one object with an opposite side role name results either in a single-valued return type (as in Car2.carGroup : CarGroup) or in a set-valued return type (as in Branch1.carGroup : Set(CarGroup)) depending on the multiplicity of the role name (here, 0..1 VS 1..*). The multiplicities 0..1 and 1 yield single-valued return types whereas other multiplicities, for example 0..* and 1..*, give set-valued return types. In the set-valued case, the result is empty (as in Car2.rentalAgreement) if no object connection exists, whereas in the single-valued case the result is null (as in CarGroup2.high.high) if no object connection exists. Further navigation through a second dot is possible in a single expression and can yield a bag-valued result (as in Rental1.driver.birthday = Bag{@Date1,@Date1}). In this example, the preservation of duplicates with a bag-valued result reflects the fact that the two different objects in Rental1.driver evaluate identical with respect

to the second navigation birthday. A flat bag will also be the result in the case
of two succesive set-valued navigations (as in codeBranch1.carGroup.car).

4.6   Logic-Related Operations in OCL

Because OCL has the null value and Boolean is a predefined type, the null
value is also a Boolean value. This leads to a three-valued logic. Apart from the
standard Boolean operations and, or, and not, OCL knows a (binary) exclusive
xor and the implication implies. The truth tables for these operation are shown
in the tables below. Of course, all Boolean operations coincide with the standard
two-valued interpretation if one leaves out the null value.

```
b       | not(b)
------+-------
null  | null
false | true
true  | false
```

```
           |      b2                        |      b2
b1 or b2 | null  false true      b1 and b2 | null  false true
---------+-----------------      ----------+------------------
    null | null  null  true          null | null  false null
b1 false | null  false true      b1 false | false false false
    true | true  true  true          true | null  false true
```

```
           |      b2                        |      b2
b1 xor b2 | null  false true   b1 implies b2 | null  false true
----------+------------------   --------------+------------------
    null | null  null  null          null | null  null  true
b1 false | null  false true      b1 false | true  true  true
    true | null  true  false         true | null  false true
```

```
           |      b2                        |      b2
b1 = b2  | null  false true      b1 <> b2 | null  false true
---------+------------------      ---------+------------------
    null | true  false false         null | false true  true
b1 false | false true  false     b1 false | true  false true
    true | false false true          true | true  true  false
```

With respect to equality and inequality, the null value is treated like any other
value. Equality and inequality do not return null as a result and operate as
equality and inequality on Set{null, false, true}.

Apart from the usual, above discussed Boolean connectives, OCL has a universal quantifier forAll and an existial quantifier exists, both in the spirit of
first order logic. However, both quantifiers range over finite collections only and
cannot be used, for example, on all instances of the type Integer or String. We
show examples for using the quantifiers. We here employ the not yet mentioned
OCL feature to define collections of integers with range expressions taking the
form low..high.

```
? Set{1,2,3,4,5,6,7,8,9,10,11,12}=Set{1..12}
> true : Boolean

? Set{1..12}->exists(n|n.mod(2)=0 and n.mod(3)=0)
> true : Boolean

? Bag{1..12}->exists(n|n.mod(3)=0 and n.mod(7)=0)
> false : Boolean

? Sequence{1..12}->forAll(n|0<=n*n and n*n<=255)
> true : Boolean

? OrderedSet{1..12}->forAll(n|0<=n*n and n*n<=127)
> false : Boolean

? Set{}->exists(n|n.mod(2)=0 and n.mod(3)=0)
> false : Boolean

? Bag{}->exists(n|n.mod(3)=0 and n.mod(7)=0)
> false : Boolean

? Sequence{}->forAll(n|0<=n*n and n*n<=255)
> true : Boolean

? OrderedSet{}->forAll(n|0<=n*n and n*n<=127)
> true : Boolean

? not(Set{1..12}->forAll(n|not(n.mod(2)=0 and n.mod(3)=0)))
> true : Boolean

? not(OrderedSet{1..12}->exists(n|not(0<=n*n and n*n<=127)))
> false : Boolean
```

4.7   OCL Collection Operations

The basic OCL operations for collection construction are the already mentioned constructor operations Set, Bag, Sequence and OrderedSet. In addition, OCL knows the constructor including which (possibly) adds an element to a collection. The strongly related, but not inverse operation is excluding that removes *all* occurrences of an element from the collection. Note that a law like c = c->including(e)->excluding(e) does not hold in OCL for all collections c and all elements e. We will observe the following evaluations.

```
? Set{7,8}=Set{}->including(8)->including(7)
> true : Boolean

? Bag{7,8,7}=Bag{8}->including(7)->including(7)
> true : Boolean
```

```
? Sequence{7,8,7}=Sequence{7,8}->including(7)
> true : Boolean

? OrderedSet{7,8}=OrderedSet{7}->including(8)->including(7)
> true : Boolean

? Set{7,8}->excluding(8)=Set{7}
> true : Boolean

? Bag{7,8,7}->excluding(7)=Bag{8}
> true : Boolean

? Sequence{7,8,7}->excluding(7)=Sequence{8}
> true : Boolean

? OrderedSet{9,6,7,8,6,7}->excluding(6)=OrderedSet{9,7,8}
> true : Boolean
```

In order to test membership in collections the operations `includes` and `excludes` testing on single elements as well as `includesAll` and `excludesAll` for testing element collections are available. The following examples explain the use of the operations.

```
? Set{7,8}->includes(9)
> false : Boolean

? Bag{7,8}->excludes(9)
> true : Boolean

? Sequence{7,9,8,7}->includesAll(Sequence{7,8,8})
> true : Boolean

? OrderedSet{7,9,8,7}->excludesAll(OrderedSet{3,2,4,2})
> true : Boolean
```

The operations `isEmpty`, `notEmpty` and `size` check for the existence of elements and determine the number of elements in the collection, respectively.

```
? Set{7}->excluding(7)->isEmpty()
> true : Boolean

? Bag{7}->excluding(8)->notEmpty()
> true : Boolean

? Set{7,8,7,8,9}->size()
> 3 : Integer

? Bag{7,8,7,8,9}->size()
> 5 : Integer
```

```
? Sequence{7,8,7,9}->size()
> 4 : Integer
```

```
? OrderedSet{7,8,7,9}->size()
> 3 : Integer
```

In order to filter collection elements the operations `select` and `reject` apply and in order to construct new collections from existing ones the operations `collect` and `collectNested` can be employed. Please note that `collect` applied to a set has to return a bag, because the functional term inside the collect may map two different source elements to the same target value. An analogous mechanism applies to ordered sets when a `collect` is used, because then the result will be a sequence. When applying `collect`, a possibly nested result is automatically converted into a flat collection. When you want to obtain the nested result you have to use `collectNested`. The following examples use a conditional `if then else endif` which is available in OCL on all types.

```
? Set{7,8,9}->select(i|i.mod(2)=1)
> Set{7,9} : Set(Integer)
```

```
? Bag{7,8,7,9}->reject(i|i.mod(2)=1)
> Bag{8} : Bag(Integer)
```

```
? Sequence{7,8,9}->collect(i|i*i)
> Sequence{49,64,91} : Sequence(Integer)
```

```
? Set{-1,0,+1}->collect(i|i*i)
> Bag{0,1,1} : Bag(Integer)
```

```
? OrderedSet{-1,0,+1}->collect(i|i*i)
> Sequence{1,0,1} : Sequence(Integer)
```

```
? Set{7,8,9}->collect(i|if i.mod(2)=0 then 'Even' else 'Odd' endif)
> Bag{'Even','Odd','Odd'} : Bag(String)
```

```
? Set{7,8}->collectNested(i|Sequence{i,i*i})
> Bag{Sequence{7,49},Sequence{8,64}} : Bag(Sequence(Integer))
```

```
? Set{7,8,9}->collect(i|Sequence{i,i*i})
> Bag{7,8,9,49,64,81} : Bag(Integer)
```

Another group of OCL collection operations are the operations `one`, `any`, `isUnique`, and `sortedBy`. `one` is a variation of the `exists` quantifier which yields true if exactly one element in the collection meets the specified predicate. `any` is a non-deterministic choice from the collection elements which satisfy the specified predicate. A deterministic use of this operation is when it is applied to a collection with exactly one value. Such a call realizes a coercion from the collection type `Collection(T)` to the parameter type `T`. `isUnique` checks whether the mapping achieved by applying the functional inner expression to each collection element is a one-to-one mapping. sortedBy converts a collection into a sequence using the specified collection element properties. union builds the union of the two specified collections. For sequences and ordered sets, it results in the concatenation.

```
? Set{7,8,9}->one(i|i.mod(2)=0)
> true : Boolean

? Set{7,8,9}->one(i|i.mod(2)=1)
> false : Boolean

? Set{7,8,9}->any(true)
> 7 : Integer -- implementor's decision
> 8 : Integer -- also allowed
> 9 : Integer -- also allowed

? Set{7,8,9}->any(i|i.mod(2)=0)
> 8 : Integer

? let C=Set{7} in if C->size()=1 then C->any(true) else null endif
> 7 : Integer

? let C=Set{7,8,7} in if C->size()=1 then C->any(true) else null endif
> null : OclVoid

? Set{7,8,9}->isUnique(i|i*i)
> true : Boolean

? Set{7,8,9}->isUnique(i|i.mod(2)=0)
> false : Boolean

? Bag{8,7,8,9}->sortedBy(i|i)
> Sequence{7,8,8,9} : Sequence(Integer)

? Set{7,8,9}->sortedBy(i|if i.mod(2)=0 then 'Even' else 'Odd' endif)=
> Sequence{8,7,9} : Sequence(Integer)

? Sequence{-8,9,-7}->sortedBy(i|i.abs)
> Sequence{-7,-8,9} : Sequence(Integer)

? Set{7,8}->union(Set{9,8})
> Set{7,8,9} : Set(Integer)

? Bag{7,8}->union(Bag{9,8})
> Bag{7,8,8,9} : Bag(Integer)

? Sequence{7,8}->union(Sequence{9,8})
> Sequence{7,8,9,8} : Sequence(Integer)
```

```
? OrderedSet{7,8}->union(OrderedSet{9,8})
> OrderedSet{7,8,9} : OrderedSet(Integer)
```

OCL offers the possiblity to convert one collection kind into any of the other three collection kinds by means of the operations asSet, asBag, asSequence, and asOrderedSet. Please be aware of the fact that some these conversions must make an implementation dependent decision, for example, the conversion that takes sets and returns sequences. In order to flatten a nested collection the operation flatten can be used to obtain a flat collection having the same elements as the source nested collection. Thus the operation collect can be seen as a shortcut for collectNested and a following flatten. flatten returns the top-most collection kind of the source expression. flatten also must make implementation dependent decisions. Such decisions must be taken, if the conversion goes from an order insensible collection kind to an order sensible collection kind.

```
? Sequence{8,7,7,8}->asSet()
> Set{7,8} : Set(Integer)

? Sequence{8,7,7,8}->asBag()
> Bag{7,7,8,8} : Bag(Integer)

? Set{8,7,7,8}->asSequence()
> Sequence{7,8} : Sequence(Integer) -- implementor's decision
> Sequence{8,7} : Sequence(Integer) -- also allowed

? Sequence{8,7,7,8}->asOrderedSet()
> OrderedSet{8,7} : OrderedSet(Integer)

? Set{8,7,9}->asSequence()
> Sequence{7,8,9} : Sequence(Integer) -- implementor's decision
> Sequence{9,8,7} : Sequence(Integer) -- also allowed
> Sequence{7,9,8} : Sequence(Integer) -- also allowed

? Set{7,8}->collectNested(i|Sequence{i,i*i})->flatten()
> Bag{7,8,49,64} : Bag(Integer)

? Sequence{Set{7,8},Set{8,9}}->flatten()
> Sequence{7,8,9,8} : Sequence(Integer) -- implementor's decision

? Set{Bag{7,8},Bag{8,9}}->flatten()
> Set{7,8,9} : Set(Integer)

? OrderedSet{Bag{7,9},Bag{8,7}}->flatten()
> OrderedSet{7,9,8} : OrderedSet(Integer)

? OrderedSet{Set{7,8,9}}->flatten()
> OrderedSet{7,9,8} : OrderedSet(Integer) -- implementor's decision
> OrderedSet{9,7,8} : OrderedSet(Integer) -- also allowed
> OrderedSet{7,9,8} : OrderedSet(Integer) -- also allowed
```

Concerning the above decision which the implementor has to take, one might argue that the order on type `Integer` is pretty well determined. But please recall that ordered sets are not sorted sets. And, there is not natural *single* order on object collections for user-defined class types: one natural order on objects is determined by their object identity often being an identifier, and a second natural order is the order in which the objects are created.

4.8   OCL Collection Operation `iterate`

The last collection operation `iterate` is the most complicated one, but also the most powerful collection operation, because, basically, all other collection operation are special cases of `iterate`. The syntax of the basic form of an iterate expression is represented as follows.

```
COLEXPR->iterate(ELEMVAR:ELEMTYPE; RESVAR:RESTYPE=INITEXPR | ITEREXPR)
```

An iterate expression is based on other expressions, on variables and on types: a collection expression `COLEXPR` for the argument collection, an element variable `ELEMVAR` for an iteration variable, an element type `ELEMTYPE`, a result variable `RESVAR`, a result type `RESTYPE`, an initialization expression `INITEXPR` for the result variable, and an iteration expression `ITEREXPR` for the result variable. The iterate expression is applied to an argument collection `COLEXPR`. Within a loop, each argument collection element having the type `ELEMTYPE` is considered once with the variable `ELEMVAR`. Thus the number of steps in the loop is equal to the number of elements in the argument collection. The result of the iterate expression is of type `RESTYPE` and fixed by the variable `RESVAR` which is initialized with the expression `INITEXPR` before the loop is entered. Within the loop, the expression `ITEREXPR` is evaluated for each element of the argument collection once and the intermediate result is again assigned to `RESVAR`. `ITEREXPR` may use `ELEMVAR` and `RESVAR` as free variables, but `ITEREXPR` is not forced to do so. The overall result of the iterate expression is determined by the last value of `RESVAR`.

We consider the following examples for `iterate`. These examples will use the relational database state which we have expressed above as a nested tuple value. The OCL examples will use the abbreviations C and R, for all customer and rental tuples, respectively. For the respective example, we will show also its SQL counterpart and a formulation without `iterate`.

(A) Show names in Customers together with names in Rentals. Two `iterate` expressions are employed: one over the `Customer` relation, one over the `Renatls` relation. The formulation without `iterate` employs two `collect` enpressions.

```
let dbs=Tuple{Customers:Set{Tuple{name:'Ada',birth:1962},
                            Tuple{name:'Bob',birth:1962}},
              Rentals:Set{Tuple{name:'Ada',start:'2012-01-01'},
                          Tuple{name:'Ada',start:'2002-01-01'},
                          Tuple{name:'Cyd',start:'2002-01-01'}}} in
let C=dbs.Customers in let R=dbs.Rentals in
C->iterate(c;R1:Bag(String)=Bag{}|R1->including(c.name))->union(
```

```
R->iterate(r;R2:Bag(String)=Bag{}|R2->including(r.name)))
```

```
Bag{'Ada','Ada','Ada','Bob','Cyd'} : Bag(String)
```

```
SELECT name FROM Customers UNION SELECT name FROM Rentals
```

```
C->collect(c|c.name)->union(R->collect(r|r.name))
```

(B) Retrieve the earliest rentals. The formulation with iterate uses two nested iterate expression with different result types. The outer iterate corresponds to a select call, the inner iterate to a universal quatification.

```
R->iterate(r1;R1:Set(Tuple(name:String,start:String))=Set{}|
    if R->iterate(r2;R2:Boolean=true|R2 and r1.start<=r2.start)
        then R1->including(r1) else R1 endif)
```

```
Set{Tuple{name='Ada',start='2002-01-01'},
    Tuple{name='Cyd',start='2002-01-01'}} :
    Set(Tuple(name:String,start:String))
```

```
SELECT * FROM Rentals WHERE start <= ALL (SELECT start FROM RENTALS)
```

```
R->select(r1|R->forAll(r2|r1.start<=r2.start))
```

(C) Show names in Rentals from year 2002. This OCL expression uses the operation substring which is applied to a String value with two parameters indicating the first and the last position of the substring to be retrieved. Note that the same effect in the two calls to select and collect in the second formulation is achieved in the first formulation with a single iterate call.

```
R->iterate(r;R1:Bag(String)=Bag{}| if r.start.substring(1,4)='2002'
    then R1->including(r.name) else R1 endif)
```

```
Bag{'Ada','Cyd'} : Bag(String)
```

```
SELECT name FROM Rentals WHERE start.substring(1,4)='2002'
```

```
R->select(r|r.start.substring(1,4)='2002')->collect(r|r.name)
```

5   Tool Support

Though still limited, OCL tool support has been considerably growing in the last years. The goal of this section is to present a sorted (non-exhaustive) list of tools that can help in your OCL learning process. Other reports of OCL tools are [10] and [12].

5.1   OCL Parsers and IDEs

The two main OCL Parsers available today are MDT/OCL[7] and Dresden OCL[8].

MDT/OCL is part of the official Model Development tools Eclipse project whose goal is to provide an implementation of industry standard metamodels and to provide exemplary tools for developing models based on those metamodels. MDT/OCL provides a set of APIs for parsing and evaluating OCL constraints and queries on Ecore or UML models, support for serializing parsed OCL expressions (avoiding the need for reparsing them every time we load the model), and a visitor API for the abstract syntaxt tree to allow their transformation.

DresdenOCL provides a set of tools to parse and evaluate OCL constraints on various types of models thanks to its Pivot Model strategy [18]. The pivot model decouples the OCL parser and interpreter from a specific metamodel and thus enables connecting the tool to every meta-model supporting basic object-oriented concepts. DresdenOCL can be executed as an independent tool or integrated in the EMF Eclipse framework.

Due to the relevance of OCL in other areas, we can also find OCL parsers embedded in other kinds of MDE components. This is specially true in the case of model transformations where each transformation engine (e.g., the ATL[9] one) comes with its own OCL parser. This is not an ideal situation since each differs on the kind of OCL expressions supported (and even worse, sometimes also on how they interpret them). In this sense, SimpleOCL[10] looks like a step in the right direction for MDE tools that do not need/want to integrate the full OCL language. SimpleOCL is intended as an embeddable OCL implementation for inclusion in transformation languages.

5.2   UML Tools with OCL Support

Unfortunately only a handful of UML modeling tools are equipped with OCL support. By "OCL support" we mean that the UML tool is able to at least understand (i.e., parse) the OCL expressions attached to the model and not treat them just as plain text strings (same as they were just natural language).

Some exceptions are:

- ArgoUML[11] provides syntax and type checking of OCL expressions thanks to the integration of DresdenOCL
- Rational Rose thanks to the OClarity plug-in[12] offers syntax,type and some semantic checkings for OCL Expressions (e.g., detecting that a non-navigable association is traversed as part of the expression)
- Enterprise Architect[13] allows users to add and validate OCL constraints

---

[7] http://www.eclipse.org/modeling/mdt/?project=ocl
[8] http://www.dresden-ocl.org/index.php/DresdenOCL
[9] http://www.eclipse.org/atl/
[10] http://soft.vub.ac.be/soft/research/mdd/simpleocl
[11] http://argouml.tigris.org/
[12] http://www.empowertec.de/products/rational-rose-ocl/
[13] http://www.sparxsystems.com/

- MagicDraw[14] includes an OCL execution engine that can be used to write, validate (models vs metamodels, instances vs models) and execute (e.g., querying) OCL expressions
- Borland Together[15] offers syntax highlighting and checking of OCL expressions
- Several UML tools in Eclipse like Papyrus[16] integrate the MDT/OCL component introduced in the previous section.

We believe that the increasing quality and availability of OCL parsers and evaluators ready to be embedded in other tools will help to improve this situation in the near future.

5.3   Verification and Validation Tools for OCL

OCL is a very expressive language that allows designer to write complex constraint, derivation rules, pre/postconditions,etc. Therefore, it is easy to make mistakes while writing OCL expressions. Tools mentioned in the previous section take care of the syntactic errors (i.e., they make sure that the expressions are "grammatically" correct). Nevertheless, syntactic correctness is not enough. This section introduces some tools to validate and verify OCL expressions. With these tools designers may check that the expressions are a valid representation of the domain and that there are no inconsistencies, redundancies, ... among them.

The tool USE (UML-based Specification Environment) [16,19] can be employed to validate and partly to verify a model. System states (snapshots of a running system) can be created semi-automatically and manipulated. For each snapshot the OCL constraints are automatically checked and the results are given to the designer using graphical or textual views. This simulation of the system allows designers to identify if the model is overconstrained (i.e., some valid situations in the domain are not allowed by the specification) or underconstrained (some invalid scenarios are evaluated as correct in the specification). With USE properties like constraint consistency or independency [17] can be checked. USE supports UML class, object, sequence and statechart diagrams.

Advanced correctness properties may require a more complete reasoning on the expressions and the system states that each constraint restricts. At least, we must ensure that the constraints are *satisfiable*, i.e., there are finite and non-empty system states that evaluate to true all model constraints at the same time (obiously, if the model constraints are unsatisfiable, the model is useless since users will never be able to create valid instantiations of it). Unfortunately, reasoning on OCL is undecidable in general. Therefore, current verification tools either require user interaction with the verification procedure (e.g., HOL-OCL [6], based on the Isabelle theorem prover), restrict the OCL constructs that can be used when writing OCL expressions (e.g., [23], based on query containment checking techniques) or follow a bounded verification approach, where the

---

[14] https://www.magicdraw.com/

[15] http://www.borland.com/us/products/together/index.aspx

[16] http://www.eclipse.org/modeling/mdt/papyrus/Papyrus

search space is finite in order to guarantee termination. The bounds in the verification are set by limiting the number of instances and restricting the attribute domains to explore during the verification. Examples of tools in this category are UML2Alloy [1] (based on a translation of the UML/OCL models into Alloy), [24] (OCL constraints reexpressed as a boolean satisfiability problem) and UMLtoCSP [8] and EMFtoCSP[17](UML/OCL and EMF models, respectively, are reexpressed as a Constraint Satisfaction Problem (CSP)).

Other correctness properties can be defined in terms of this basic satisfiability property.

5.4   Code Generation from OCL Expressions

Constraints at the model level state conditions that the "data" ot the system must satisfy at runtime. Therefore, the implementation of a system must guarantee that all operations that modify the system state will leave the data in a consistent state (by consistent we mean a state that evaluates to true all model invariants). Clearly, the best way to achieve this goal (and to reuse the effort put by the designers when precisely specifying the models) is by providing code-generation techniques that take the OCL constraints and produce the appropriate checking code in the target platform where the system is going to be executed.

Typically, OCL expressions are translated into code either as database triggers or as part of the method bodies in the classes corresponding to the constraint context types. Roughly, in the database strategy each invariant is translated as a SQL SELECT expression (or a view) that returns a value if the data does not satisfy that given constraint (usually, this value returned by the SELECT is the set of rows that are inconsistent). This SELECT expression is called inside the body of a trigger so that if the SELECT returns a non-empty value then the trigger raises an exception. Triggers are fired after every change on the data to make sure that the system is always in a consistent state. When implementing the constraints as part of an object-oriented language, constraints are usually embedded in the method bodies of the classes. There are several ways to embed them. For instance, we could add them as if-then conditions at the beginning of the method or, if the language offers this possibility, as assertion expressions.

In both scenarios, the efficiency of the integrity checking process can be improved a lot if we follow an incremental checking strategy [11]. The idea is to minimize the amount of data that must be reevaluated after every update on the system state by determining at design-time, when and how each constraint must be checked at runtime to avoid irrelevant verifications. Clearly, the *NoRentals-BlackListed* invariant can become violated when adding a rental to a BlackListed person but not when changing the name of that person, nor when we remove one of his rentals or change its rental price. Therefore, instead of checking this constraint after each state change we can just check it (and only for the affected pieces of data) after assignments of new rentals, a blacklisting of a Customer or

---

[17] http://code.google.com/a/eclipselabs.org/p/emftocsp/

changes on the involved dates and forget about it for all the other events. This "knowledge" can be used to decide which triggers must call the SELECT expression corresponding to this constraint or on which method bodies the if-then condition for the constraint must be added.

Despite the usefulness of these code-generation techniques for OCL, most MDD tools do not include them as part of their code-generation features (in fact, for this particular aspect the survey in [10] is still valid nowadays). Some prefer to provide more limited (in terms of expressiveness) DSLs that allow users to define simple validation rules to be implemented in the interface layer (as part of form validation conditions).

6   Research Agenda for OCL

This section hints at some research lines we belive are important challenges for the evolution and continued success of OCL.

6.1   Modularization and Extensibility

OCL is a very expressive language with an extensive standard library. In fact, the large number of operators in the library and their overlappings (many expressions can be written using alternative combinations of operators) may be confusing for users only interested in writing simple expressions.

On the other hand, the library is missing some relevant operators, like basic statistical functions [9] that make cumbersome using OCL in some domains.

Therefore, we believe there is a clear need of adding modularization constructs to the language that enable users to select the exact set of OCL *modules* they need, including, when necessary, the import of external OCL libraries created by OCL experts to extend the language.

The need of OCL libraries has also been raised by other researchers [2], [28] but it is still an open problem with many issues to be solved: how to make the libraries available?, who validates them?, strategies to solve conflicts when importing several libraries?, how are the libraries defined?, how to express the semantic of each individual operation?, etc.

6.2   Language Improvements

Even if OCL is already in its version 2.3 the language itself offers plenty of opportunities for improvement both at the concrete and abstract syntax levels.

At the concrete level, users still have problems with some notational aspects like the overlapping of the dot notation and the arrow notation for collections with a single element. Besides, OCL expressions involving iterators become quite verbose quickly so a few shortcuts have been proposed[18]. Moreover, at the abstract syntax level, several issues regarding the OCL type system (e.g., [7]) and undefinedness semantics [5] have been detected. Not to mention that OCL is still missing a complete definition of its formal semantics.

---

[18] http://eclipsemde.blogspot.com/2010/05/acceleo-ocl-made-simple.html

6.3   Efficient Reasoning on OCL Expressions

The application of MDE to more complex problems (like model-driven reverse engineering where very large models are automatically obtained from source code) requires efficient evaluation and reasoning techniques for OCL. Right now, OCL analysis techniques exhibit scalability issues when dealing with large models (e.g., when verifying them or when identifying matching submodels as part of a model transformation).

Some initial results in the area have focused on the incremental [11,3] or lazy evaluation of OCL expressions [25]. In the former, we aim to minimize the number of instances that are accessed every time we evaluate the expression while in the latter we delay the evaluation of the OCL expressions to the last possible moment, i.e., only when the user wants to access an element that it is computed by an OCL expression (e.g., a target element in a model transformation), that expression is evaluated.

Nevertheless much work needs to be done. One area worth exploring is the use of a cloud computing environment as an execution infrastructure for OCL-related analysis services. The model to be evaluated could be sliced and processed in parallel in a network of virtual nodes in the cloud.

6.4   Establishing an OCL Community

One aspect hindering the adoption (and as a consequence the evolution) of OCL is the lack of an established community of OCL practitioners that pushes the language forward.

The *OCL and Textual Modeling Languages Workshop*[19] is the most important (and basically the only) annual meeting point for researchers. Even though the organizers (among them the authors of this chapter) always try to bring industrial practitioners, the success is limited.

The OMG OCL RTF (Revision Task Force) who maintains the OCL specification could lead the creation of a professional community around OCL but given the *closed*[20] nature of the OMG, its impact is rather limited. For instance, it has been proven very difficult for researchers to influence the evolution of the OCL standard (of course, this is not only OMG's fault but also due to the nature of the research work; researchers have very limited time and resources to actively participate in standardization committees).

Some online forums, like the Eclipse OCL community forum[21] facilitate a joint discussion between researchres and practitioners but they focus on specific tools. The OCL Portal[22] was born with the goal of collecting all information about OCL but unfortunately the activity level is low. OCL is also a topic discussed in the Modeling Languages portal[23].

---

[19] See `http://gres.uoc.edu/OCL2011/` for information on its latest edition
[20] The results of the task force are public but participation for non-OMG members is restricted.
[21] `http://www.eclipse.org/forums/index.php?t=thread&frm_id=26`
[22] `http://st.inf.tu-dresden.de/ocl/`
[23] `http://modeling-languages.com`

We hope that with the increasing adoption of OCL, the number of practitioncer reaches the critical mass needed to create a real community around the language where researchres and practitioners work and discuss together.

7 Conclusions

This chaper has provided a broad overview of the OCL language including its main usage scenarios, a precise overview of the language constructs and the current tool support available to those interested in using OCL in their new software development projects.

Of course, OCL is far from perfect. We have identified several research challenges that the community must address in order to facilitate the adoption of OCL among practitioners. We hope by now you are convinced that, given the important role of OCL in the model-driven engineering paradigm, these challenges are worth pursuing.

References

1. Anastasakis, K., Bordbar, B., Georg, G., Ray, I.: UML2Alloy: A Challenging Model Transformation. In: Engels, G., Opdyke, B., Schmidt, D.C., Weil, F. (eds.) MoD-ELS 2007. LNCS, vol. 4735, pp. 436–450. Springer, Heidelberg (2007)
2. Baar, T.: On the need of user-defined libraries in OCL. ECEASST 36 (2010)
3. Bergmann, G., Horváth, Á., Ráth, I., Varró, D., Balogh, A., Balogh, Z., Ökrös, A.: Incremental Evaluation of Model Queries over EMF Models. In: Petriu, D.C., Rouquette, N., Haugen, Ø. (eds.) MoDELS 2010, Part I. LNCS, vol. 6394, pp. 76–90. Springer, Heidelberg (2010)
4. Borgida, A., Mylopoulos, J., Reiter, R.: On the frame problem in procedure specifications. IEEE Trans. Software Eng. 21(10), 785–798 (1995)
5. Brucker, A.D., Krieger, M.P., Wolff, B.: Extending OCL with null-references. In: Ghosh [15], pp. 261–275
6. Brucker, A.D., Wolff, B.: The HOL-OCL book. Technical Report 525, ETH Zurich (2006)
7. Büttner, F., Gogolla, M., Hamann, L., Kuhlmann, M., Lindow, A.: On better understanding OCL collections *or* an OCL ordered set is not an OCL set. In: Ghosh [15], pp. 276–290
8. Cabot, J., Clarisó, R., Riera, D.: UMLtoCSP: a tool for the formal verification of UML/OCL models using constraint programming. In: ASE, pp. 547–548. ACM (2007)
9. Cabot, J., Mazón, J.-N., Pardillo, J., Trujillo, J.: Specifying aggregation functions in multidimensional models with OCL. In: Parsons, et al. [22], pp. 419–432
10. Cabot, J., Teniente, E.: Constraint Support in MDA Tools: A Survey. In: Rensink, A., Warmer, J. (eds.) ECMDA-FA 2006. LNCS, vol. 4066, pp. 256–267. Springer, Heidelberg (2006)
11. Cabot, J., Teniente, E.: Incremental integrity checking of UML/OCL conceptual schemas. Journal of Systems and Software 82(9), 1459–1478 (2009)
12. Chimiak-Opoka, J.D., Demuth, B., Awenius, A., Chiorean, D., Gabel, S., Hamann, L., Willink, E.D.: OCL tools report based on the ide4OCL feature model. ECE-ASST 44 (2011)

13. Dobing, B., Parsons, J.: How UML is used. Commun. ACM 49, 109–113 (2006)
14. Frias, L., Queralt, A., Olivé, A.: Eu-rent car rentals specification. Technical Report LSI Research Report. LSI-03-59-R, UPC (2003)
15. Ghosh, S. (ed.): MoDELS 2009. LNCS, vol. 6002. Springer, Heidelberg (2010)
16. Gogolla, M., Bohling, J., Richters, M.: Validating UML and OCL Models in USE by Automatic Snapshot Generation. Journal on Software and System Modeling 4(4), 386–398 (2005)
17. Gogolla, M., Büttner, F., Richters, M.: Use: A UML-based specification environment for validating UML and OCL. Sci. Comput. Program. 69(1-3), 27–34 (2007)
18. Heidenreich, F., Wende, C., Demuth, B.: A framework for generating query language code from OCL invariants. ECEASST 9 (2008)
19. Kuhlmann, M., Hamann, L., Gogolla, M.: Extensive Validation of OCL Models by Integrating SAT Solving into USE. In: Bishop, J., Vallecillo, A. (eds.) TOOLS 2011. LNCS, vol. 6705, pp. 290–306. Springer, Heidelberg (2011)
20. Object Management Group. OCL 2.3.1 Specification (2010)
21. Object Management Group. UML 2.4.1 Superstructure Specification (2011)
22. Parsons, J., Saeki, M., Shoval, P., Woo, C.C., Wand, Y. (eds.): ER 2010. LNCS, vol. 6412. Springer, Heidelberg (2010)
23. Queralt, A., Rull, G., Teniente, E., Farré, C., Urpí, T.: Aurus: Automated reasoning on UML/OCL schemas. In: Parsons, et al. [22], pp. 438–444
24. Soeken, M., Wille, R., Kuhlmann, M., Gogolla, M., Drechsler, R.: Verifying UML/OCL models using boolean satisfiability. In: DATE, pp. 1341–1344. IEEE (2010)
25. Tisi, M., Martínez, S., Jouault, F., Cabot, J.: Lazy Execution of Model-to-Model Transformations. In: Whittle, J., Clark, T., Kühne, T. (eds.) MoDELS 2011. LNCS, vol. 6981, pp. 32–46. Springer, Heidelberg (2011)
26. Warmer, J., Kleppe, A.: The Object Constraint Language: Getting Your Models Ready for MDA. Addison-Wesley (2003)
27. Wieringa, R.: A survey of structured and object-oriented software specification methods and techniques. ACM Comput. Surv. 30(4), 459–527 (1998)
28. Willink, E.D.: Modeling the OCL standard library. ECEASST 44 (2011)

Model Transformations

Davide Di Ruscio, Romina Eramo, and Alfonso Pierantonio

Dipartimento di Informatica
Università degli Studi dell'Aquila
I-67100 L'Aquila, Italy
name.surname@univaq.it

Abstract. In recent years, Model-Driven Engineering has taken a leading role in advancing a new paradigm shift in software development. Leveraging models to a first-class status is at the core of this methodology. Shifting the focus of software development from coding to modeling permits programs to transform models in order to generate other models which are amenable for a wide range of purposes, including code generation. This paper introduces a classification of model transformation approaches and languages, illustrating the characteristics of the most prominent ones. Moreover, two specific application scenarios are proposed to highlight *bidirectionality* and *higher-order transformations* in the change propagation and coupled evolution domains, respectively.

1 Introduction

In recent years, Model-Driven Engineering [1] (MDE) has taken a leading role in advancing a new paradigm shift in software development. Leveraging models to a *first-class* status is at the core of this methodology. In particular, MDE proposes to extend the formal use of modelling languages in several interesting ways by adhering to the "everything is a model" principle [2]. Domains are analysed and engineered by means of metamodels, i.e., coherent sets of interrelated concepts. A model is said to conform to a metamodel, or in other words it is expressed in terms of the concepts formalized in the metamodel, constraints are expressed at the metalevel, and model transformations occur to produce target models out of source ones. Summarizing, these constitute a body of inter-related entities pursuing a common scope as in an ecosystem [3]. In this respect, model transformations represent the major gluing mechanism of the ecosystem by bridging different abstraction layers and/or views of a system. To this end, they require *"specialized support in several aspects in order to realize the full potential, for both the end-user and transformation developer"* [4].

In 2002 OMG issued the Query/View/Transformation Request For Proposal [5] in an attempt to define a standard transformation language. Although a final specification has been adopted at the end of 2005, the area of model transformation can still be considered in its infancy and further research is necessary

a) to investigate intrinsic characteristics of model transformation languages, such as bidirectionality, change propagation, and genericity;

b) to examine and devise transformation semantics, strategies and tools for testing and automatically verifying transformations; finally

M. Bernardo, V. Cortellessa, and A. Pierantonio (Eds.): SFM 2012, LNCS 7320, pp. 91–136, 2012.

c) to extend the scope of model transformation by assessing its full potential for new applications.

Interestingly, while *a)* and *b)* are analogous to what has been done in traditional programming research, *c)* is dealing with problems and needs which emerged over the last years during the adoption and deployment of MDE in industry. Since the beginning, model transformations have always been conceived as the essential mean to mainly transform models in order to generate artifacts considered very close to the final system (e.g., see [6–9] for the Web domain). However, lately specialized languages and techniques have been introduced to address more complex problems such as the coupled evolution which typically emerges during an MDE ecosystem life-cycle (e.g., [10–12]), or to manage simulation and fault detection in software systems (e.g., [13]).

In this paper, we summarize a classification of model transformation approaches and illustrate the main characteristics of prominent languages falling in this classification. Then, change propagation and coupled evolution are considered to illustrate complex application scenarios assessing the potential and significance of model transformations as described in the following.

Change Propagation. Change propagation and bidirectionality are relevant aspects in model transformations: often it is assumed that during development only the source model of a transformation undergoes modifications, however in practice it is necessary for developers to modify both the source and the target models of a transformation and propagate changes in both directions [14, 15]. There are two main approaches for realizing bidirectional transformations and supporting change propagation: by programming forward and backward transformations in any convenient unidirectional language and manually ensuring they are consistent; or by using a bidirectional transformation language where every program describes both a forward and a backward transformation simultaneously. A major advantage of the latter approach is that the consistency of the transformations can be guaranteed by construction.

Metamodel/Model Coupled Evolution. Evolution is an inevitable aspect which affects the whole life-cycle of software systems [16]. In general, artefacts can be subject to many kinds of changes, which range from requirements through architecture and design, to source code, documentation and test suites. Similarly to other software artefacts, metamodels can evolve over time too [17]. Accordingly, models need to be *co-adapted*[1] in order to remain compliant to the metamodel and not become eventually invalid. When manually operated the adaptation is error-prone and can give place to inconsistencies between the metamodel and the related artefacts. Such issue becomes very relevant when dealing with enterprise applications, since in general system models encompass a large population of instances which need to be appropriately adapted, hence inconsistencies can possibly lead to irremediable information erosion [18].

Outline. The structure of the paper is as follows. In Section 2 we review the basic concepts of Model-Driven Engineering, i.e., models, metamodels, and transformations.

---

[1] The terms (co-)adaptation, (co-)evolution, and coupled evolution will be used as synonyms throughout the paper, although in some approached the term coupled evolution denoted the parallel and coordinated evolution of two classes of artifacts.

Next section illustrates a number of approaches to model transformations and their characteristics, also prominent languages are outlined. Section 4 presents the Janus Transformation Language (JTL), a declarative model transformation language specifically tailored to support bidirectionality and change propagation. Section 5 proposes an approach based on higher-order model transformations (HOTs) to model coupled evolution. In particular, HOTs take a difference model formalizing the metamodel modifications and generate a model transformation able to adapt and recovery the validity of the compromised models. Section 6 draws some conclusions.

2   Model Driven Engineering

Model-Driven Engineering (MDE) refers to the systematic use of models as first-class entities throughout the software engineering life cycle. Model-driven approaches shift development focus from traditional programming language codes to models expressed in proper domain specific modeling languages. The objective is to increase productivity and reduce time to market by enabling the development of complex systems by means of models defined with concepts that are much less bound to the underlying implementation technology and are much closer to the problem domain. This makes the models easier to specify, understand, and maintain [19] helping the understanding of complex problems and their potential solutions through abstractions.

The concept of Model Driven Engineering emerged as a generalization of the Model Driven Architecture (MDA) proposed by OMG in 2001 [20]. Kent [21] defines MDE on the base of MDA by adding the notion of software development process and modeling space for organizing models. Favre [22] proposes a vision of MDE where MDA is just one possible instance of MDE implemented by means of a set of technologies defined by OMG (MOF [23], UML [24], XMI [25], etc.) which provided a conceptual framework and a set of standards to express models, metamodels, and model transformations.

Even though MDA and MDE rely on *models* that are considered "first class citizens", there is no common agreement about what is a model. In [26] a model is defined as "a set of a statements about a system under study". Bézivin and Gerbé in [27] define a model as "a simplification of a system built with an intended goal in mind. The model should be able to answer questions in place of the actual system". According to Mellor et al. [28] a model "is a coherent set of formal elements describing something (e.g. a system, bank, phone, or train) built for some purpose that is amenable to a particular form of analysis" such as communication of ideas between people and machines, test case generation, transformation into an implementation etc. The MDA guide [20] defines a model of a system as "a description or specification of that system and its environment for some certain purpose. A model is often presented as a combination of drawings and text. The text may be in a modeling language or in a natural language".

In MDE models are not considered as merely documentation but precise artifacts that can be understood by computers and can be automatically manipulated. In this scenario *metamodeling* plays a key role. It is intended as a common technique for defining the abstract syntax of models and the interrelationships between model elements. metamodeling can be seen as the construction of a collection of "concepts" (things, terms, etc.) within a certain domain. A model is an abstraction of phenomena in the

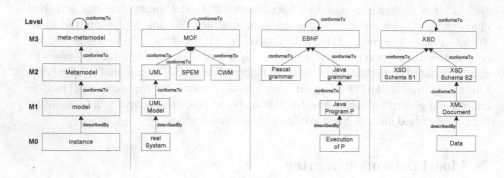

Fig. 1. The four layer metamodeling architecture

real world, and a metamodel is yet another abstraction, highlighting properties of the model itself. A model is said to *conform to* its *metamodel* like a program conforms to the grammar of the programming language in which it is written [2]. In this respect, OMG has introduced the four-level architecture shown in Fig. 1. At the bottom level, the M0 layer is the real system. A model represents this system at level M1. This model conforms to its metamodel defined at level M2 and the metamodel itself conforms to the metametamodel at level M3. The metametamodel conforms to itself. OMG has proposed MOF [23] as a standard for specifying metamodels. For example, the UML metamodel is defined in terms of MOF. A supporting standard of MOF is XMI [25], which defines an XML-based exchange format for models on the M3, M2, or M1 layer. In EMF [29], Ecore is the provided language for specifying metamodels. This metamodeling archi-tecture is common to other technological spaces as discussed by Kurtev et al. in [30]. For example, the organization of programming languages and the relationships between XML documents and XML schemas follows the same principles described above (see Fig. 1).

In addition to metamodeling, *model transformation* is also a central operation in MDE. While technologies such as MOF [23] and EMF [29] are well-established foun-dations on which to build metamodels, there is as yet no well-established foundation on which to rely in describing how we take a model and transform it to produce a target one. In the next section more insights about model transformations are given and after a brief discussion about the general approaches, the attention focuses on some of the today's available languages.

3   Model Transformations

The MDA guide [20] defines a model transformation as "the process of converting one model to another model of the same system". Kleppe et al. [31] defines a *transformation* as the automatic generation of a target model from a source model, according to a transformation definition. A *transformation definition* is a set of transformation rules that together describe how a model in the source language can be transformed to a model in the target language. A *transformation rule* is a description of how one or more

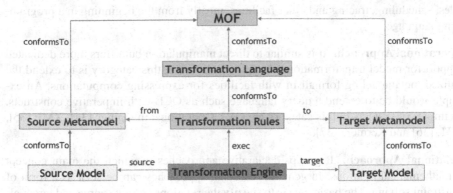

Fig. 2. Basic Concepts of Model Transformation

constructs in the source language can be transformed to one or more constructs in the target language.

Rephrasing these definitions by considering Fig. 2, a model transformation program takes as input a model conforming to a given source metamodel and produces as output another model conforming to a target metamodel. The transformation program, composed of a set of rules, should itself considered as a model. As a consequence, it is based on a corresponding metamodel, that is an abstract definition of the used transformation language.

Many languages and tools have been proposed to specify and execute transformation programs. In 2002 OMG issued the Query/View/Transformation request for proposal [5] to define a standard transformation language. Even though a final specification has been adopted at the end of 2005, the area of model transformation continues to be a subject of intense research. Over the last years, in parallel to the OMG process a number of model transformation approaches have been proposed both from academia and industry. The paradigms, constructs, modeling approaches, tool support distinguish the proposals each of them with a certain suitability for a certain set of problems.

In the following, a classification of the today's model transformation approaches is briefly reported, then some of the available model transformation languages are separately described. The classification is mainly based upon [32] and [33].

3.1 Classification

At top level, model transformation approaches can be distinguished between *model-to-model* and *model-to-text*. The distinction is that, while a model-to-model transformation creates its target as a model which conforms to the target metamodel, the target of a model-to-text transformation essentially consists of strings. In the following some classifications of model-to-model transformation languages discussed in [32] are described.

Direct Manipulation Approach. It offers an internal model representation and some APIs to manipulate it. It is usually implemented as an object oriented framework, which may also provide some minimal infrastructure. Users have to implement transformation rules, scheduling, tracing and other facilities, mostly from the beginning in a programming language.

Operational Approach. It is similar to direct manipulation but offers more dedicated support for model transformations. A typical solution in this category is to extend the utilized metamodeling formalism with facilities for expressing computations. An example would be to extend a query language such as OCL with imperative constructs. Examples of systems in this category are QVT Operational mappings [34], XMF [35], MTL [36] and Kermeta [37].

Relational Approach. It groups declarative approaches in which the main concept is mathematical relations. In general, relational approaches can be seen as a form of constraint solving. The basic idea is to specify the relations among source and target element types using constraints that in general are non-executable. However, declarative constraints can be given executable semantics, such as in logic programming where predicates can be used to describe the relations. All of the relational approaches are side-effect free and, in contrast to the imperative direct manipulation approaches, create target elements implicitly. Relational approaches can naturally support multidirectional rules. They sometimes also provide backtracking. Most relational approaches require strict separation between source and target models, that is, they do not allow in-place update. Example of relational approaches are QVT Relations [34] and those enabling the specification of weaving models (like AMW [38]), which aim at defining rigorous and explicit correspondences between the artifacts produced during a system development [39]. Moreover, in [40] the application of logic programming has been explored for the purpose. Finally, in [41] we have investigated the application of the Answer Set Programming [42] for specifying relational and bidirectional transformations.

Hybrid Approach. It combines different techniques from the previous categories, like ATL [43] and ETL [44] that wrap imperative bodies inside declarative statements.

Graph-Transformation Based Approach. It draws on the theoretical work on graph tranformations. Describing a model transformation by graph transformation, the source and target models have to be given as graphs. Performing model transformation by graph transformation means to take the abstract syntax graph of a model, and to transform it according to certain transformation rules. The result is the syntax graph of the target model. Being more precise, graph transformation rules have an *LHS* and an *RHS* graph pattern. The *LHS* pattern is matched in the model being transformed and replaced by the *RHS* pattern in place. In particular, *LHR* represents the pre-condition of the given rule, while *RHS* describes the post-conditions. $LHR \cap RHS$ defines a part which has to exist to apply the rule, but which is not changed. $LHS - LHS \cap RHS$ defines the part which shall be deleted, and $RHS - LHS \cap RHS$ defines the part to be created. AGG [45] and AToM3 [46] are systems directly implementing the theoretical approach to attributed graphs and transformations on such graphs. They have built-in fixpoint scheduling with non-deterministic rule selection and concurrent application to all matching locations, and the rely on implicit scheduling by the user. The transformation rules are unidirectional and in-place. Systems such as VIATRA2 [47] and GReAT [48] extend the basic functionality of AGG and AToM3 by adding explicit scheduling. VIATRA2 users can build state machines to schedule transformation rules whereas GReAT relies on data-flow graphs. Another interesting mean for transforming models is given by triple graph grammars (TGGs), which have been introduced by Schürr[49]. TGGs are a technique for defining the correspondence between two different types of models in a declarative way. The power of TGGs comes from the fact that the relation between the two models cannot only be defined, but the definition can be made operational so that one model can be transformed into the other in either direction; even more, TGGs can be used to synchronize and to maintain the correspondence of the two models, even if both of them are changed independently of each other; i.e., TGGs work incrementally. The main tool support for TGGs is Fujaba[2], which provided the foundation for MOFLON[3].

Rule Based Approach. Rule based approaches allow one to define multiple independent rules of the form *guard* => *action*. During the execution, rules are activated according to their guard not, as in more traditional languages, based on direct invocation [4]. When more than one rule is fired, more or less explicit management of such conflicting situation is provided, for instance in certain language a runtime error is raised. Besides the advantage of having an implicit matching algorithm, such approaches permit to encapsulate fragments of transformation logic within the rules which are self-contained units with crispy boundaries. This form of encapsulation is preparatory to any form of transformation composition [50].

3.2 Languages

In this section some of the languages referred above are singularly described. The purpose of the description is to provide the reader with an overiew of some existing model transformation languages.

QVT. In 2002 OMG issued the QVT RFP [5] describing the requirements of a standard language for the specification of model queries, views, and transformations according to the following definitions:

– A *query* is an expression that is evaluated over a model. The result of a query is one or more instances of types defined in the source model, or defined by the query language. Object Constraint Language (OCL 2.0) [51] is the query language used in QVT;
– A *view* is a model which is completely derived from a base model. A view cannot be modified separately from the model from which it is derived and changes to the base model cause corresponding changes to the view. If changes are permitted to the view then they modify the source model directly. The metamodel of the view is typically not the same as the metamodel of the source. A query is a restricted kind of view. Finally, views are generated via transformations;
– A *transformation* generates a target model from a source one. If the source and target metamodels are identical the transformation is called *endogeneous*. If they are different the transformation is called *exogeneous*. A model transformation may

---

[2] http://www.fujaba.de
[3] http://www.moflon.org

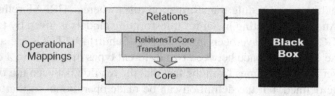

Fig. 3. QVT Architecture

also have several source models and several target models. A view is a restricted kind of transformation in which the target model cannot be modified independently from the source model. If a view is editable, the corresponding transformation must be bidirectional in order to reflect the changes back to the source model.

A number of research groups have been involved in the definition of QVT whose final specification has been reached at the end of November 2005 [34]. The abstract syntax of QVT is defined in terms of MOF 2.0 metamodel. This metamodel defines three sub-languages for transforming models. OCL 2.0 is used for querying models. Creation of views on models is not addressed in the proposal.

The QVT specification has a hybrid declarative/imperative nature, with the declarative that forms the framework for the execution semantics of the imperative part. By referring to Fig. 3, the layers of the declarative part are the following:

- A user-friendly *Relations* metamodel which supports the definition of complex object pattern matching and object template creation;
- A *Core* metamodel defined using minimal extensions to EMOF and OCL.

By referring to [34], a relation is a declarative specification of the relationships between MOF models. The *Relations* language supports complex object pattern matching, and implicitly creates trace classes and their instances to record what occurred during a transformation execution. Relations can assert that other relations also hold between particular model elements matched by their patterns. Finally, *Relations* language has a graphical syntax.

Concerning the *Core* it is a small model/language which only supports pattern matching over a flat set of variables by evaluating conditions over those variables against a set of models. It treats all of the model elements of source, target and trace models symmetrically. It is equally powerful to the *Relations* language, and because of its relative simplicity, its semantics can be defined more simply, although transformation descriptions described using the *Core* are therefore more verbose. In addition, the trace models must be explicitly defined, and are not deduced from the transformation description, as is the case with *Relations*. The core model may be implemented directly, or simply used as a reference for the semantics of *Relations*, which are mapped to the Core, using the transformation language itself.

To better clarify the conceptual link between *Relations* and *Core* languages, an analogy can be drawn with the Java architecture, where the Core language is like Java Byte Code and the Core semantics is like the behavior specification for the Java Virtual Machine. The Relations language plays the role of the Java language, and the standard transformation from Relations to Core is like the specification of a Java Compiler which produces Byte Code.

Sometimes it is difficult to provide a complete declarative solution to a given transformation problem. To address this issue QVT proposes two mechanisms for extending the declarative languages *Relations* and *Core*: a third language called *Operational Mappings* and a mechanism for invoking transformation functionality implemented in an arbitrary language (*Black Box*).

The *Operational Mappings* language is specified as a standard way of providing imperative implementations. It provides OCL extensions with side effects that allow a more procedural style, and a concrete syntax that looks familiar to imperative programmers. A transformation entirely written using Operation Mappings is called an "operational transformation".

The *Black Box* mechanism makes possible to "plug-in" and execute external code. This permits to implement complex algorithms in any programming language, and reuse already available libraries.

AGG. AGG [45] is a development environment for attributed graph transformation systems supporting an algebraic approach to graph transformation. It aims at specifying and rapid prototyping applications with complex, graph structured data. AGG supports typed graph transformations including type inheritance and multiplicities. It may be used (implicitly in "code") as a general purpose graph transformation engine in high-level JAVA applications employing graph transformation methods. The source, target, and common metamodels are represented by typed graphs. Graphs may additionally be attributed using Java code. Model transformations are specified by graph rewriting rules that are applied non-deterministically until none of them can be applied anymore. If an explicit application order is required, rules can be grouped in ordered layers. AGG features rules with negative application conditions to specify patterns that prevent rule executions. Finally, AGG offers validation support that is consistency checking of graphs and graph transformation systems according to graph constraints, critical pair analysis to find conflicts between rules (that could lead to a non-deterministic result) and checking of termination criteria for graph transformation systems. An available tool support provides graphical editors for graphs and rules and an integrated textual editor for Java expressions. Visual interpretation and validation of transformations are also supported.

ATL. ATL (ATLAS Transformation Language) [43] is a hybrid model transformation language containing a mixture of declarative and imperative constructs. The former allows to deal with simple model transformations, while the imperative part helps in coping with transformation of higher complexity. ATL transformations are unidirectional, operating on read-only source models and producing write-only target models. During the execution of a transformation source models may be navigated but changes are not allowed. Target models cannot be navigated.

ATL transformations are specified in terms of *modules*. A module contains a mandatory *header* section, *import* section, and a number of *helpers* and *transformation rules*. Header section gives the name of a transformation module and declares the source and target models (e.g., see lines 1-2 in Fig. 4). The source and target models are typed by their metamodels. The keyword `create` indicates the target model, whereas the keyword `from` indicates the source model. In the example of Fig. 4 the target model bound

```
1 module PetriNet2PNML;
2 create OUT : PNML from IN : PetriNet;
3 ...
4 rule Place {
5       from
6               e : PetriNet!Place
7               --(guard)
8       to
9               n : PNML!Place
10              (
11                      name <- e.name,
12                      id <- e.name,
13                      location <- e.location
14              ),
15              name : PNML!Name
16              (
17                      labels <- label
18              ),
19              label : PNML!Label
20              (
21                      text <- e.name
22              )
23 }
```

Fig. 4. Fragment of a declarative ATL transformation

to the variable OUT is created from the source model IN. The source and target meta-models, to which the source and target model conform, are PetriNet and PNML [52], respectively.

Helpers and transformation rules are the constructs used to specify the transformation functionality. Declarative ATL rules are called *matched rules*. They specify relations between *source patterns* and *target patterns*. The name of a rule is given after the keyword rule. The source pattern of a rule (lines 5-7, Fig. 4) specifies a set of *source types* and an optional *guard* given as a Boolean expression in OCL. A source pattern is evaluated on a set of matches in the source models. The target pattern (lines 8-22, Fig. 4) is composed of a set of *elements*. Each of these elements (e.g., the one at lines 9-14, Fig. 4) specifies a *target type* from the target metamodel (e.g., the type Place from the PNML metamodel) and a set of *bindings*. A binding refers to a feature of the type (i.e. an attribute, a reference or an association end) and specifies an expression whose value is used to initialize that feature. In some cases complex transformation algorithms may be required and it may be difficult to specify them in a pure declarative way. For this issue ATL provides two imperative constructs: *called rules*, and *action blocks*. A called rule is a rule called by other ones like a procedure. An action block is a sequence of imperative instructions that can be used in either matched or called rules. The imperative statements in ATL are the well-known constructs for specifying control flow such as conditions, loops, assignments, etc.

ETL. Similarly to ATL, ETL [44] (Epsilon Transformation Language) is a hybrid model transformation language that has been developed atop the infrastructure provided by the Epsilon model management platform [53]. By building on Epsilon, ETL achieves syntactic and semantic consistency and enhanced interoperability with a number of additional languages, also been built atop Epsilon, and which target tasks such as model-to-text transformation, model comparison, validation, merging and unit testing.

ETL enables the specification of transformations that can transform an arbitrary number of source models into an arbitrary number of target models. ETL transformations are given in terms of modules. An ETL module can import a number of other ETL modules. In this case, the importing ETL module inherits all the rules and pre/post blocks specified in the modules it imports (recursively).

GReAT. GReAT [48] (Graph Rewriting and Transformation Language) is a graph-transformation language that supports the high-level specification of complex model transformation programs. In this language, one describes the transformations as sequenced graph rewriting rules that operate on the input models and construct an output model. The rules specify complex rewriting operations in the form of a matching pattern and a subgraph to be created as the result of the application of the rule. The rules *i)* always operate in a context that is a specific subgraph of the input, and *ii)* are explicitly sequenced for efficient execution. The rules are specified visually using a graphical model builder tool. GReAT can be divided into three distinct parts:

- *Pattern specification language.* This language is used to express complex patterns that are matched to select elements in the current graph. The pattern specification language uses a notion of cardinality on each pattern vertex and each edge;
- *Graph transformation language.* It is a rewriting language that uses the pattern language described above. It treats the source model, the target model and temporary objects as a single graph that conforms to a unified metamodel. Each pattern object's type conforms to this metamodel and only transformations that do not violate the metamodel are allowed. At the end of the transformation, the temporary objects are removed and the two models conform exactly to their respective metamodels. Guards to manage the rule applications can be specified as boolean C++ expressions;
- *Control flow language.* It is a high-level control flow language that can control the application of the productions and allow users to manage the complexity of the transformations. In particular, the language supports a number of features: *(i)* *Sequencing*, rules can be sequenced to fire one after another, *(ii)* *Non-Determinism*, rules can be specified to be executed "in parallel", where the order of firing of the parallel rules is non deterministic, *(iii)* *Hierarchy*, compound rules can contain other compound rules or primitive rules, *(iv)* *Recursion*, a high level rule can call itself, *(v)* *Test/Case*, a conditional branching construct that can be used to choose between different control flow paths.

VIATRA2. VIATRA2 [47] is an Eclipse-based general-purpose model transformation engineering framework intended to support the entire life-cycle for the specification, design, execution, validation and maintenance of transformations within and between various modelling languages and domains.

Its rule specification language is a unidirectional transformation language based mainly on graph transformation techniques that combines the graph transformation and Abstract State Machines [54] into a single paradigm. Being more precise, in VIATRA2 the basic concept to define model transformations is the (graph) pattern. A pattern is a collection of model elements arranged into a certain structure fulfilling additional constraints (as defined by attribute conditions or other patterns). Patterns can be matched on certain model instances, and upon successful pattern matching, elementary model manipulation is specified by graph transformation rules. There is no predefined order of execution of the transformation rules. Graph transformation rules are assembled into complex model transformations by abstract state machine rules, which provide a set of commonly used imperative control structures with precise semantics. This permits to collocate VIATRA2 as a hybrid language since the transformation rule language is declarative but the rules cannot be executed without an execution strategy specified in an imperative manner.

Important specification features of VIATRA2 include recursive (graph) patterns, negative patterns with arbitrary depth of negation, and generic and meta-transformations (type parameters, rules manipulating other rules) for providing reuse of transformations [55].

4   Application Scenario 1: Change Propagation with JTL

Bidirectionality and change propagation are relevant aspects in model transformations: often it is assumed that during development only the source model of a transformation undergoes modifications, however in practice it is necessary for developers to modify both the source and the target models of a transformation and propagate changes in both directions [14, 15]. There are two main approaches for realizing bidirectional transformations: by programming forward and backward transformations in any convenient unidirectional language and manually ensuring they are consistent; or by using a bidirectional transformation language where every program describes both a forward and a backward transformation simultaneously. A major advantage of the latter approach is that the consistency of the transformations can be guaranteed by construction. Moreover, source and target roles are not fixed since the transformation direction entails them. Therefore, considerations made about the mapping executed in one direction are completely equivalent to the opposite one.

The relevance of bidirectionality in model transformations has been acknowledged already in 2005 by the Object Management Group (OMG) by including a bidirectional language in their Query View Transformation (QVT) [56]. Unfortunately, as pointed out by Perdita Stevens in [57] the language definition is affected by several weaknesses. Therefore, while MDE requirements demand enough expressiveness to write non-bijective transformations [58], the QVT standard does not clarify how to deal with corresponding issues, leaving their resolution to tool implementations. Moreover, a number of approaches and languages have been proposed due to the intrinsic complexity of bidirectionality. Each language is characterized by a set of specific properties pertaining to a particular applicative domain [32].

This section outlines the Janus Transformation Language (JTL), a declarative model transformation language specifically tailored to support bidirectionality and change propagation. In particular, the distinctive characteristics of JTL are

- *non-bijectivity*, non-bijective bidirectional transformations are capable of mapping a model into a set of models, as for instance when a single change in a target model might semantically correspond to a family of related changes in more than one source model. JTL provides support to non-bijectivity and its semantics assures

that all the models are computed at once independently whether they represent the outcome of the backward or forward execution of the bidirectional transformation;
- *model approximation*, generally transformations are not total which means that target models can be manually modified in such a way they are not reachable anymore by any forward transformation, then traceability information are employed to back propagate the changes from the modified targets by inferring the *closest* model that approximates the ideal source one at best.

The language expressiveness and applicability have been validated by implementing a number of model transformations. In this section we focus on the *Collapse/Expand State Diagrams* benchmark which have been defined in the *GRACE International Meeting on Bidirectional Transformations* [59] to compare and assess different bidirectional approaches. The JTL semantics is defined in terms of the Answer Set Programming (ASP) [42], a form of declarative programming oriented towards difficult (primarily NP-hard) search problems and based on the stable model (answer set) semantics of logic programming. Bidirectional transformations are translated via semantic anchoring [60] into search problems which are reduced to computing stable models, and the DLV solver [61] is used to perform search.

4.1 Motivating Scenario

Let us consider the *Collapse/Expand State Diagrams* benchmark defined in [59]: starting from a hierarchical state diagram (involving some one-level nesting) as the one reported in Fig. 5.a, a flat view has to be provided as in Fig. 5.b. Furthermore, any manual modifications on the (target) flat view should be back propagated and eventually reflected in the (source) hierarchical view. For instance, let us suppose the designer modifies the flat view by changing the name of the initial state from Begin Installation to Start Install shield (see Δ_1 change in Figure 6). Then, in order to persist such a refinement to new executions of the transformation, the hierarchical state machine has to be consistently updated by modifying its initial state as illustrated in Fig. 7.

The flattening is a non-injective operation requiring specific support to back propagate modifications operated on the flattened state machine to the nested one. For instance, the flattened view reported in Fig. 5 can be extended by adding the alternative try again from the state Disk Error to Install software (see Δ_2 changes in Fig. 6). This gives place to an interesting situation: the new transition can be equally mapped to each one of the nested states within Install Software as well as to the container state itself. Consequently, more than one source model propagating the changes exists[4]. Intuitively, each time hierarchies are flattened there is a loss of information which causes ambiguities when trying to map back corresponding target revisions. Some of these problems can be alleviated by managing traceability information of the transformation executions which can be exploited later on to trace back the changes: like this each generated element can be linked with the corresponding source and contribute to the resolution of some of the ambiguities. Nonetheless, traceability is a necessary

---

[4] It is worth noting that the case study and examples have been kept deliberately simple since they suffice to show the relevant issues related to non-bijectivity.

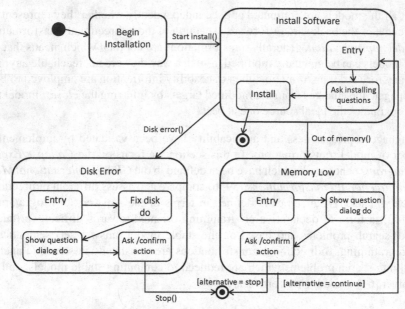

a) A sample Hierarchical State Machine (HSM).

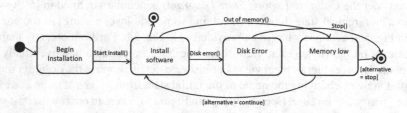

b) The corresponding Non-Hierarchical State Machine (NHSM).

Fig. 5. Sample models for the *Collapse/Expand State Diagrams* benchmark

but not sufficient condition to support bidirectionality, since for instance elements discarded by the mapping may not appear in the traces, as well as new elements added on the target side. For instance, the generated flattened view in Fig. 5.b can be additionally manipulated through the Δ_3 revisions which consist of adding some extra-functional information for the `Install Software` state and the transition between from `Memory low` and `Install Software` states. Because of the limited expressive power of the hierarchical state machine metamodel which does not support extra-functional annotations, the Δ_3 revisions do not have counterparts in the state machine in Fig. 7.

Current declarative bidirectional languages, such as QVT relations (QVT-R), are often ambivalent when discussing non-bijective transformations as already pointed out in [57]. Other approaches, notably hybrid or graph-based transformation techniques, even if claiming to support bidirectionality, are able to deal only with (partially) bijective mappings [14]. As a consequence, there is not a clear understanding of what

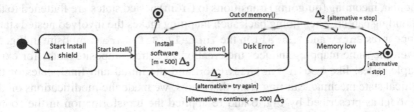

Fig. 6. A revision of the generated non-hierarchical state machine

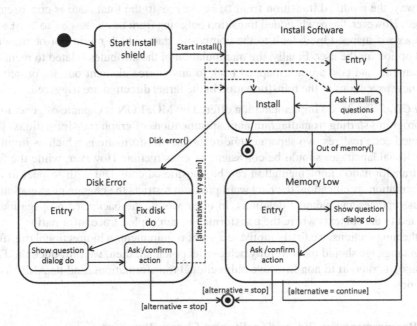

Fig. 7. The source hierarchical state machine synchronised with the target changes

non-bijectivity implies causing language implementors to adopt design decisions which differ from an implementation to another.

In order to better understand how the different languages deal with non-bijectivity, we have specified the hierarchical to non-hierarchical state machines transformation (HSM2NHSM) by means of the Medini[5] and MOFLON[6] systems. The former is an implementation of the QVT-R transformation language, whereas the latter is a framework which bases on Triple Graph Grammars (TGGs) [49]: our experience with them is outlined in the following

Medini. When trying to map the generated target model back to the source without any modification, a new source model is generated which differs from the original one[7].

---

[5] http://projects.ikv.de/qvt/
[6] http://www.moflon.org
[7] The interested reader can access the full implementation of both the attempts at the following address http://www.mrtc.mdh.se/~acicchetti/HSM2NHSM.php

In particular, incoming (outgoing) transitions to (from) nested states are flattened to the corresponding parent: when going back such mapping makes the involved nested states to disappear (as `Entry` and `Install` in the `Install Software` composite in Fig. 5). Moreover, the same mapping induces the creation of extra composite states for existing simple states, like `Begin Installation` and the initial and final states of the hierarchical state machine. Starting from this status, we made the modifications on the target model as prescribed by Fig. 6 and re-applied the transformation in the source direction, i.e. backward. In this case, the `Start Install shield` state is correctly mapped back by renaming the existing `Begin Installation` in the source. In the same way, the modified transition from `Disk Error` to the final state is consistently updated. However, the newly added transition outgoing from `Disk Error` to `Install software` is mapped by default to the composite state, which might not be the preferred option for the user. Finally, the manipulation of the attributes related to memory requirements and cost are not mapped back to any source element but are preserved when new executions of the transformation in the target direction are triggered.

MOFLON. The TGGs implementation offered by MOFLON is capable of generating Java programs starting from diagrammatic specifications of graph transformations. The generated code realizes two separate unidirectional transformations which as in other bidirectional languages should be consistent by construction. However, while the forward transformation implementation can be considered complete with respect to the transformation specification, the backward program restricts the change propagation to attribute updates and element deletions. In other words, the backward propagation is restricted to the contexts where the transformation can exploit trace information.

In the next sections, we firstly motivate a set of requirements a bidirectional transformation language should meet to fully achieve its potential; then, we introduce the JTL language, its support to non-bijective bidirectional transformations, and its ASP-based semantics.

4.2 Requirements for Bidirectionality and Change Propagation

This section refines the definition of bidirectional model transformations as proposed in [57] by explicitly considering non-bijective cases. Even if some of the existing bidirectional approaches enable the definition of non-bijective mappings [57, 15], their validity is guaranteed only on bijective sub-portions of the problem. As a consequence, the forward transformation can be supposed to be an injective function, and the backward transformation its corresponding inverse; unfortunately, such requirement excludes most of the cases [62]. In general, a bidirectional transformation R between two classes of models, say M and N, and M more expressive than N, is characterized by two unidirectional transformations

$$\overrightarrow{R} : M \times N \to N$$
$$\overleftarrow{R} : M \times N \to M^*$$

where $\overrightarrow{R}$ takes a pair of models *(m, n)* and works out how to modify n so as to enforce the relation $\overrightarrow{R}$. In a similar way, $\overleftarrow{R}$ propagates changes in the opposite direction: $\overleftarrow{R}$ is a non-bijective function able to map the target model in a set of corresponding source models conforming to M^8. Furthermore, since transformations are not total in general, bidirectionality has to be provided even in the case the generated model has been manually modified in such a way it is not reachable anymore by the considered transformation. Traceability information is employed to back propagate the changes from the modified targets by inferring the *closest*[9] model that approximates the ideal source one at best. More formally the backward transformation $\overleftarrow{R}$ is a function such that:

(i) if R(m,n) is a non-bijective consistency relation, $\overleftarrow{R}$ generates all the resulting models according to R;

(ii) if R(m,n) is a non-total consistency relation, $\overleftarrow{R}$ is able to generate a result model which approximates the ideal one.

This definition alone does not constrain much on the behavior of the reverse transformation and additional requirements are necessary in order to ensure that the propagation of changes behaves as expected.

Reachability. In case a generated model has been manually modified (n'), the backward transformation $\overleftarrow{R}$ generates models (m^*) which are exact, meaning that the original target may be reached by each of them via the transformation without additional side effects. Formally:

$$\overleftarrow{R}(m, n') = m^* \in M^*$$

$$\overrightarrow{R}(m', n') = n' \in N \text{ for each } m' \in m^*$$

Choice preservation. Let n' be the target model generated from an arbitrary model m' in m^* as above: when the user selects m' as the appropriate source pertaining to n' the backward transformation has to generate exactly m' from n' disregarding the other possible alternatives $t \in m^*$ such that $t \neq m'$. In other words, a valid round-trip process has to be guaranteed even when multiple sources are available [63]:

$$\overleftarrow{R}(m', \overrightarrow{R}(m', n')) = m' \text{ for each } m' \in m^*$$

Clearly, the above requirement in order to be met demands for adequate traceability information management.

In the rest of the paper, the proposed language is introduced and shown to satisfy the above requirements. The details of the language and its supporting development environment are presented in Section 4.3, whereas in Section 4.4 the usage of the language is demonstrated by means of the benchmark case.

---

[8] For the sake of readability, we consider a non-bijective backward transformation assuming that only M contains elements not represented in N. However, the reasoning is completely analogous for the forward transformation and can be done by exchanging the roles of M and N.

[9] This concept is clarified in Sect. 4.3, where the transformation engine and its derivation mechanism are discussed.

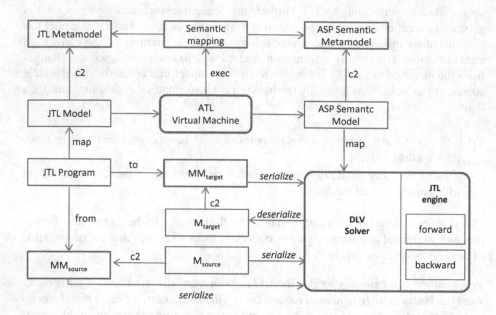

Fig. 8. Architecture overview of the JTL environment

4.3   The Janus Transformation Language

The Janus Transformation Language (JTL) is a declarative model transformation language specifically tailored to support bidirectionality and change propagation. The implementation of the language relies on the Answer Set Programming (ASP) [42]. This is a form of declarative programming oriented towards difficult (primarily NP-hard) search problems and based on the stable model (answer set) semantics of logic programming. Being more precise model transformations specified in JTL are transformed into ASP programs (search problems), then an ASP solver is executed to find all the possible stable models that are sets of atoms which are consistent with the rules of the considered program and supported by a deductive process.

The overall architecture of the environment supporting the execution of JTL transformations is reported in Fig. 8. The *JTL engine* is written in the ASP language and makes use of the *DLV solver* [61] to execute transformations in both forward and backward directions. The engine executes JTL transformations which have been written in a QVT-like syntax, and then automatically transformed into ASP programs. Such a semantic anchoring has been implemented in terms of an ATL [43] transformation defined on the JTL and ASP metamodels. Also the source and target metamodels of the considered transformation (MM_{source}, MM_{target}) are automatically encoded in ASP and managed by the engine during the execution of the considered transformation and to generate the output models.

The overall architecture has been implemented as a set of plug-ins of the Eclipse framework and mainly exploits the Eclipse Modelling Framework (EMF) [29] and the

ATLAS Model Management Architecture (AMMA) [64]. Moreover, the DLV solver has been wrapped and integrated in the overall environment. In the rest of the section all the components of the architecture previously outlined are presented in detail.

The Janus Transformation Engine. As previously said the Janus transformation engine is based on a relational and declarative approach implemented using the ASP language to specify bidirectional transformations. The approach exploits the benefits of logic programming that enables the specification of relations between source and target types by means of predicates, and intrinsically supports bidirectionality [32] in terms of unification-based matching, searching, and backtracking facilities.

Starting from the encoding of the involved metamodels and the source model (see the *serialize* arrows in the Fig. 8), the representation of the target one is generated according to the JTL specification. The computational process is performed by the JTL engine (as depicted in Figure 8) which is based on an ASP bidirectional transformation program executed by means of an ASP solver called DLV [61].

Encoding of Models and Metamodels. In the proposed approach, models and meta-models are defined in a declarative manner by means of a set of logic assertions. In particular, they are considered as graphs composed of nodes, edges and properties that qualify them. The metamodel encoding is based on a set of *terms* each characterized by the predicate symbols metanode, metaedge, and metaprop, respectively. A fragment of the hierarchical state machine metamodel considered in Section 4.1 is encoded in Listing 1.1. For instance, the metanode(HSM, state) in line 1 encodes the metaclass state belonging to the metamodel HSM. The metaprop(HSM, name, state) in line 3 encodes the attribute named name of the metaclass state belonging to the metamodel HSM. Finally, the metaedge(HSM, association, source, transition, state) in line 6 encodes the association between the metaclasses transition and state, typed association, named source and belonging to the metamodel HSM. The terms induced by a certain metamodel are exploited for encoding models conforming to it. In particular, models are sets of entities (represented through the predicate symbol node), each characterized by properties (specified by means of prop) and related together by relations (represented by edge). For instance, the state machine model in Fig. 5 is encoded in the Listing 1.2. In particular, the node(HSM, "s1", state) in line 1 encodes the instance identified with "s1" of the class state belonging to the meta-model HSM. The prop(HSM, "s1", name, "start") in line 4 encodes the attribute

```
1 metanode(HSM, state).
2 metanode(HSM, transition).
3 metaprop(HSM, name, state).
4 metaprop(HSM, trigger, transition).
5 metaprop(HSM, effect, transition).
6 metaedge(HSM, association, source, transition, state).
7 metaedge(HSM, association, target, transition, state).
8 [...]
```

Listing 1.1. Fragment of the State Machine metamodel

```
1 node(HSM, "s1", state).
2 node(HSM, "s2", state).
3 node(HSM, "t1", transition).
4 prop(HSM,"s1.1","s1",name,"begin_installation").
5 prop(HSM,"s2.1","s2",name,"install_software").
6 prop(HSM,"t1.1","t1",trigger,"install_software").
7 prop(HSM,"t1.2","t1",effect,"start_install").
8 edge(HSM,"tr1",association,source, "s1","t1").
9 edge(HSM,"tr1",association,target, "s2","t1").
10 [...]
```

Listing 1.2. Fragment of the State Machine model in Figure 5

name of the class "s1" with value "start" belonging to the metamodel HSM. Finally, the edge(HSM,"tr1",association,source,"s1","t1") in line 7 encodes the instance "tr1" of the association between the state "s1" and the transition "t1" belonging to the metamodel HSM.

Model Transformation Execution. After the encoding phase, the deduction of the target model is performed according to the rules defined in the ASP program. The transformation engine is composed of *i) relations* which describe correspondences among element types of the source and target metamodels, *ii) constraints* which specify restrictions on the given relations that must be satisfied in order to execute the corresponding mappings, and an *iii) execution engine* (described in the rest of the section) consisting of bidirectional rules implementing the specified relations as executable mappings. Relations and constraints are obtained from the given JTL specification, whereas the execution engine is always the same and represents the bidirectional engine able to interpret the correspondences among elements and execute the transformation. The transformation process logically consists of the following steps:

(i) given the input (meta)models, the execution engine induces all the possible solution candidates according to the specified relations;
(ii) the set of candidates is refined by means of constraints.

Listing 1.3 contains a fragment of the ASP code implementing relations and constraints of the HSM2NHSM transformation discussed in Section 4.1. In particular, the terms in lines 1-2 define the relation called "r1" between the metaclass State machine belonging to the HSM metamodel and the metaclass State machine belonging to the NHSM metamodel. An ASP constraint expresses an invalid condition: for example, the constraints in line 3-4 impose that each time a state machine occurs in the source model it has to be generated also in the target model. In fact, if each atoms in its body is true then the correspondent solution candidate is eliminated. Similarly, the relation between the metaclasses State of the involved metamodels is encoded in line 6-7. In this case, constraints in line 8-11 impose that each time a state occurs in the HSM model, the correspondent one in the NHSM model is generated only if the source element is not a sub-state, vice versa, each state in the NHSM model is mapped into the HSM model. Finally, the relation between the metaclasses Composite state and State is encoded

```
1 relation ("r1",  HSM, stateMachine).
2 relation ("r1", NHSM, stateMachine).
3 :- node(HSM, "sm1", stateMachine), not node'(HSM, "sm1", stateMachine).
4 :- node(NHSM, "sm1", stateMachine), not node'(NHSM, "sm1", stateMachine).
5
6 relation ("r2", HSM, state).
7 relation ("r2", NHSM, state).
8 :- node(HSM, "s1", state), not edge(HSM, "ow1", owningCompositeState, "s1", "cs1
      "), not node'(NHSM, "s1", state).
9 :- node(HSM, "s1", state), edge(HSM, "ow1", owningCompositeState, "s1", "cs1"),
      node(HSM, "cs1", compositeState), node'(NHSM, "s1", state).
10 :- node(NHSM, "s1", state), not trace_node(HSM, "s1", compositeState), not node
      '(HSM, "s1", state).
11 :- node(NHSM, "s1", state), trace_node(HSM, "s1", compositeState), node'(HSM, "
      s1", state).
12
13 relation ("r3", HSM, compositeState).
14 relation ("r3", NHSM, state).
15 :- node(HSM, "s1", compositeState), not node'(NHSM, "s1", state).
16 :- node(NHSM, "s1", state), trace_node(HSM, "s1", compositeState), not node'(HSM
      , "s1", compositeState).
17 [...]
```

Listing 1.3. Fragment of the HSM2NHSM transformation

in line 13-14. Constraints in line 15-16 impose that each time a composite state occurs in the HSM model a correspondent state in the NHSM model is generated, and vice versa. Missing sub-states in a NHSM model can be generated again in the HSM model by means of trace information (see line 10-11 and 16). Trace elements are automatically generated each time a model element is discarded by the mapping and need to be stored in order to be regenerated during the backward transformation.

Note that the specification order of the relations is not relevant as their execution is bottom-up; i.e., the final answer set is always deduced starting from the more nested facts.

Execution Engine. The specified transformations are executed by a generic engine which is (partially) reported in Listing 1.4. The main goal of the transformation execution is the generation of target elements as the *node'* elements in line 11 of Listing 1.4. As previously said transformation rules may produce more than one target models, which are all the possible combinations of elements that the program is able to create. In particular, by referring to Listing 1.4 target node elements with the form node'(MM,ID,MC) are created if the following conditions are satisfied:

- the considered element is declared in the input source model. The lines 1-2 contain the rules for the source conformance checking related to node terms. In particular, the term is_source_metamodel_conform(MM,ID,MC) is true if the terms node(MM,ID,MC) and metanode(MM,MC) exist. Therefore, the term bad_source is true if the corresponding is_source_metamodel_con- form(MM,ID,MC) is valued to false with respect to the node(MM,ID,MC) source element;
- at least a relation exists between a source element and the candidate target element. In particular, the term mapping(MM,ID,MC) in line 3 is true if there exists a relation which involves elements referring to MC and MC2 metaclasses and an element node(MM2,ID,MC2). In other words, a mapping can be executed each time it is

```
1 is_source_metamodel_conform(MM,ID,MC) :- node(MM,ID,MC), metanode(MM,MC).
2 bad_source :- node(MM,ID,MC), not is_source_metamodel_conform(MM,ID,MC).
3 mapping(MM,ID,MC) :- relation(R,MM,MC), relation(R,MM2,MC2), node(MM2,ID,MC2),
     MM!=MM2.
4 is_target_metamodel_conform(MM,MC) :- metanode(MM,MC).
5 {is_generable(MM,ID,MC)} :- not bad_source, mapping(MM,ID,MC),
     is_target_metamodel_conform(MM,MC), MM=mmt.
6 node'(MM,ID,MC) :- is_generable(MM,ID,MC), mapping(MM,ID,MC), MM=mmt.
```

Listing 1.4. Fragment of the *Execution engine*

specified between a source and a target, and there exists the appropriate source to compute the target;

- the candidate target element conforms to the target metamodel. In particular, the term is_target_metamodel_conform(MM,MC) in line 6 is true if the MC metaclass exists in the MM metamodel (i.e. the target metamodel);
- finally, any constraint defined in the *relations* in Listing 1.3 is valued to false.

The invertibility of transformations is obtained by means of trace information that connect source and target elements; in this way, during the transformation process, the relationships between models that are created by the transformation executions can be stored to preserve mapping information in a permanent way. Furthermore, all the source elements lost during the forward transformation execution (for example, due to the different expressive power of the metamodels) are stored in order to be generated again in the backward transformation execution.

Specifying Model Transformation with Janus. Due to the reduced usability of the ASP language, we have decided to provide support for specifying transformations by means of a more human readable syntax inspired by QVT-R. In Listing 1.5 we report a fragment of the HSM2NHSM transformation specified in JTL and it transforms hierarchical state machines into flat state machines and the other way round. The forward transformation is clearly non-injective as many different hierarchical machines can be flattened to the same model and consequently transforming back a modified flat machine can give place to more than one hierarchical machine. Such a transformation consists of several relations like *StateMachine2StateMachine*, *State2State* and *CompositeState2State* which are specified in Listing 1.5. They define correspondences between *a)* state machines in the two different metamodels *b)* atomic states in the two different metamodels and *c)* composite states in hierarchical machines and atomic states in flat machines. The relation in lines 11-20 of Listing 1.5 is constrained by means of the *when* clause such that only atomic states are considered. Similarly to QVT, the *checkonly* and *enforce* constructs are also provided: the former is used to check if the domain where it is applied exists in the considered model; the latter induces the modifications of those models which do not contain the domain specified as *enforce*. A JTL relation is considered bidirectional when both the contained domains are specified with the construct *enforce*.

```
 1 transformation hsm2nhsm(source : HSM, target : NHSM) {
 2
 3 top relation StateMachine2StateMachine {
 4
 5    enforce domain source sSM : HSM::StateMachine;
 6    enforce domain target tSM : NHSM::StateMachine;
 7
 8 }
 9
10 top relation State2State {
11
12    enforce domain source sourceState : HSM::State;
13    enforce domain target targetState : NHSM::State;
14
15    when {
16      sourceState.owningCompositeState.oclIsUndefined();
17    }
18
19 }
20
21 top relation CompositeState2State {
22
23    enforce domain source sourceState : HSM::CompositeState;
24    enforce domain target targetState : NHSM::State;
25
26 }
27 }
```

Listing 1.5. A non-injective JTL program

The JTL transformations specified in the QVT-like syntax are mapped to the correspondent ASP program by means of a semantic anchoring operation as described in the next section.

ASP Semantic Anchoring. According to the proposed approach, the designer task is limited to specifying relational model transformations in JTL syntax and to applying them on models and metamodels defined as EMF entities within the Eclipse framework.

Designers can take advantage of ASP and of the transformation properties previously discussed in a transparent manner since only the JTL syntax is used. In fact, ASP programs are automatically obtained from JTL specifications by means of an ATL transformations as depicted in the upper part of Fig. 8. Such a transformation is able to generate ASP predicates for each relation specified with JTL. For instance, the relation *State2State* in Listing 1.5 gives place to the *relation* predicates in lines 6-7 in Listing 1.3.

The JTL *when* clause is also managed and it induces the generation of further ASP constraints. For instance, the JTL clause in line 16 of Listing 1.5 gives place to a couple of ASP constraints defined on the *owningCompositeState* feature of the state machine metamodels (see lines 8-9 in Listing 1.3). Such constraints are able to filter the states and consider only those which are not nested.

To support the backward application of the specified transformation, for each JTL relation additional ASP constraints are generated in order to support the management of trace links. For instance, the *State2State* relation in Listing 1.5 induces the generation of the constraints in lines 10-11 of Listing 1.3 to deal with the non-bijectivity of the transformation. In particular, when the transformation is backward applied on a *State* element of the target model, trace links are considered to check if such a state has been previously generated from a source *CompositeState* or *State* element. If such trace information is missing all the possible alternatives are generated.

4.4   JTL in Practice

In this section we show the application of the proposed approach to the *Collapse/Expand State Diagrams* case study presented in Section 4.1. The objective is to illustrate the use of JTL in practice by exploiting the developed environment, and in particular to show how the approach is able to propagate changes dealing with non-bijective and non-total scenarios.

Modelling State Machines. According to the scenario described in Section 4.1, we assume that in the software development lifecycle, the designer is interested to have a behavioral description of the system by means of hierarchical state machine, whereas a test expert produces non-hierarchical state machine models. The hierarchical and non-hierarchical state machine matamodels (respectively HSM and NHSM) are given by means of their Ecore representation within the EMF framework. Then a hierarchical state machine model conforming to the HSM metamodel can be specified as the model reported in the left-hand side of Fig. 9. Models can be specified with graphical and/or concrete syntaxes depending on the tool availability for the considered modeling language. In our case, the adopted syntaxes for specifying models do not affect the overall transformation approach since models are manipulated by considering their abstract syntaxes.

Specifying and Applying the HSM2NHSM Model Transformation. Starting from the definition of the involved metamodels, the JTL transformation is specified according to the QVT-like syntax described in Section 4.3 (see Listing 1.5). By referring to Fig. 8, the *JTL program*, the *source* and *target metamodels* and the *source model* have been created and need to be translated in their ASP encoding in order to be executed from the transformation engine. The corresponding ASP encodings are automatically produced by the mechanism illustrated in Section 4.3. In particular, the ASP encoding of both source model and source and target metamodels is generated according to the Listing 1.2 and 1.1, while the JTL program is translated to the corresponding ASP program (see Listing 1.3).

After this phase, the application of the HSM2NHSM transformation on *sampleHSM* generates the corresponding *sampleNHSM* model as depicted in the right part of Fig. 8. Note that, by re-applying the transformation in the backward direction it is possible to obtain again the *sampleHSM* source model. The missing sub-states and the transitions involving them are restored by means of trace information.

Propagating Changes. Suppose that in a refinement step the designer needs to manually modify the generated target by the changes described in Section 4.1 (see Δ changes depicted in Fig. 6), that is:

1. renaming the initial state from `Begin Installation` to `Start Install shield`;

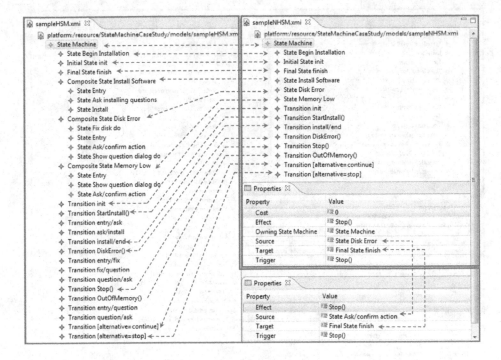

Fig. 9. HSM source model and the correspondent NHSM target model

2. adding the alternative `try again` to the state `Disk Error` to come back to `Install software`;
3. changing the attributes related to memory requirements (m=500) in the state `Install software` and cost (c=200) of the transition from `Memory low` to `Install software`.

The target model including such changes (*sampleNHSM'*) is shown in the left part of the Fig. 10. If the transformation HSM2NHSM is applied on it, we expect changes to be propagated back to the source model. However, due to the different expressive power of the involved metamodels, target changes may be propagated in a number of different ways, thus making the application of the reverse transformation to propose more solutions. The generated sources, namely *sampleHSM'_1/2/3/4* can be inspected through Figure 10: the change (1) has been propagated renaming the state to `Start Install shield`; the change (2) gives place to a non-bijective mapping and for this reason more than one model is generated. As previously said, the new transition can be equally targeted to each one of the nested states within `Install Software` as well as to the super state itself (see the properties *sampleHSM'_1/2/3/4* in Figure 10). For example, as visible in the property of the transition, *sampleHSM'_1* represents the case in which the transition is targeted to the composite state `Install Software`; finally, the change (3) is out of the domain of the transformation. In this case, the new values for memory and cost are not propagated on the generated source models.

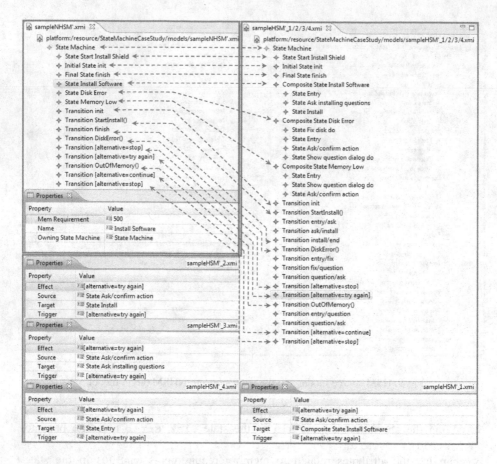

Fig. 10. The modified NHSM target model and the correspondent HSM source models

Even in this case, if the transformation is applied on one of the derived *sampleHSM'*
models, the appropriate *sampleNHSM'* models including all the changes are generated.
However, this time the target will preserve information about the chosen *sampleHSM'*
source model, thus causing future applications of the backward transformation to generate only *sampleHSM'*.

With regard to the performances of our approach, we performed no formal study on
its complexity yet, since that goes beyond the scope of this work; however, our observations showed that the time required to execute each transformation in the illustrated
case study is more than acceptable since it always took less than one second. In the
general case, when there are a lot of target alternative models the overall performance
of the approach may degrade.

5 Application Scenario 2: Metamodel/Model Coupled Evolution

Metamodels can be considered one of the constituting concepts of MDE, since they
are the formal definition of well-formed models, or in other words they constitute the

languages by which a given reality can be described in some abstract sense [2]. Meta-models are expected to evolve during their life-cycle, thus causing possible problems to existing models which conform to the old version of the metamodel and do not conform to the new version anymore. The problem is due to the incompatibility between the metamodel revisions and a possible solution is the adoption of mechanisms of model co-evolution, i.e. models need to be migrated in new instances according to the changes of the corresponding metamodel. Unfortunately, model co-evolution is not always simple and presents intrinsic difficulties which are related to the kind of evolution the meta-model has been subject to. Going into more details, metamodels may evolve in different ways: some changes may be additive and independent from the other elements, thus requiring no or little instance revision. In other cases metamodel manipulations introduce incompatibilities and inconsistencies which can not be easily (and automatically) resolved.

This section proposes an approach based on higher-order model transformations (HOTs) to model coupled evolution [65]. In particular, HOTs take a difference model formalizing the metamodel modifications and generate a model transformation able to adapt and recovery the validity of the compromised models. The approach has been applied successfully in different application domains, e.g., to manage the evolution of Web applications [66].

5.1 Metamodel Differences

In Fig. 11 it is depicted an example of the evolution of a (simplified) Petri Net metamodel, which takes inspiration from the work in [18]. The initial Petri Net (MM_0) consists of Places and Transitions; moreover, places can have source and/or destination transitions, whereas transitions must link source and destination places (src and dst association roles, respectively). In the new metamodel MM_1, each Net has at least one Place and one Transition. Besides, arcs between places and transitions are made explicit by extracting PTArc and TPArc metaclasses. This refinement permits to add further properties to relationships between places and transitions. For example, the Petri Net formalism can be extended by annotating arcs with weights. As PTArc and TPArc both represent arcs, they can be generalized by a superclass, and a new integer metaproperty can be added in it. Therefore, an abstract class Arc encompassing the integer metaproperty weight has been added in MM_2 revision of the metamodel. Finally, Net has been renamed into PetriNet. The metamodels in Fig. 11 will be exploited as the running example throughout this section. They have been kept deliberately simple because of space limitations, even though they are suitable to present all the insights of the co-adaptation mechanisms as already demonstrated in [18].

The revisions illustrated so far can invalidate existing instances; therefore, each version needs to be analysed to comprehend the various kind of updates it has been subject to and, eventually, to elicit the necessary adaptations of corresponding models. Meta-model manipulations can be classified by their corrupting or non-corrupting effects on existing instances [67]:

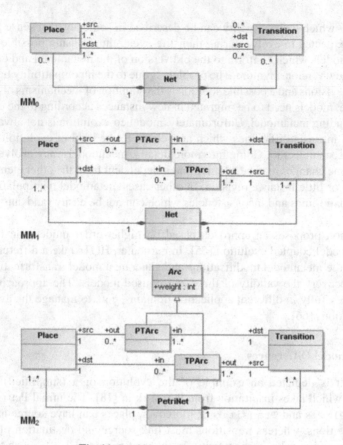

Fig. 11. Petri Net metamodel evolution

- *non-breaking changes*: changes which do not break the conformance of models to the corresponding metamodel;
- *breaking and resolvable changes*: changes which break the conformance of models even though they can be automatically co-adapted;
- *breaking and unresolvable changes*: changes which break the conformance of models which can not automatically co-evolved and user intervention is required.

In other words, *non-breaking changes* consist of additions of new elements in a metamodel MM leading to MM' without compromising models which conform to MM and thus, in turn, conform to MM'. For instance, in the metamodel MM_2 illustrated in Fig. 11 the abstract metaclass Arc has been added as a generalization of the PTArc and TPArc metaclasses (without considering the new attribute weight). After such a modification, models conforming to MM_1 still conform to MM_2 and co-evolution is not necessary. Unfortunately, this is not always the case since in general changes may break models even though sometimes automatic resolution can be performed, i.e. when facing *breaking and resolvable changes*. For instance, the Petri Net metamodel MM_1 in Fig. 11 is enriched with the new PTArc and TPArc metaclasses. Such a modification breaks the models that conform to MM_0 since according to the new metamodel MM_1, Place and

Transition instances can not be directly related, but PTArc and TPArc elements are required. However, models can be automatically migrated by adding for each couple of Place and Transition entities two additional PTArc and TPArc instances between them.

Often manual interventions are needed to solve breaking changes like, for instance, the addition of the new attribute weight to the class Arc of MM_2 in Fig. 11 which were not specified in MM_1. The models conforming to MM_1 can not be automatically co-evolved since only a human intervention can introduce the missing information related to the weight of the arc being specified, or otherwise default values have to be considered. We refer to such situations as *breaking and unresolvable changes*.

All the scenarios of model co-adaptations can be managed with respect to the possible metamodel modifications which can be distinguished into *additive*, *subtractive*, and *updative*. In particular, with additive changes we refer to metamodel element additions which in turn can be further distinguished as follows:

- *Add metaclass*: introducing new metaclasses is a common practice in metamodel evolution which gives place to metamodel extensions. Adding new metaclasses raises co-evolution issues only if the new elements are mandatory with respect to the specified cardinality. In this case, new instances of the added metaclass have to be accordingly introduced in the existing models;
- *Add metaproperty*: this is similar to the previous case since a new metaproperty may be or not obligatory with respect to the specified cardinality. The existing models maintain the conformance to the considered metamodel if the addition occurs in abstract metaclasses without subclasses; in other cases, human intervention is required to specify the value of the added property in all the involved model elements;
- *Generalize metaproperty*: a metaproperty is generalized when its multiplicity or type are relaxed. For instance, if the cardinality 3..n of a sample metaclass MC is modified in 0..n, no co-evolution actions are required on the corresponding models since the existing instances of MC still conform to the new version of the metaclass;
- *Pull metaproperty*: a metaproperty p is pulled in a superclass A and the old one is removed from a subclass B. As a consequence, the instances of the metaclass A have to be modified by inheriting the value of p from the instances of the metaclass B;
- *Extract superclass*: a superclass is extracted in a hierarchy and a set of properties is pulled on. If the superclass is abstract model instances are preserved, otherwise the effects are referable to metaproperty pulls.

Subtractive changes consist of the deletions of some of the existing metamodel elements as described in the following:

- *Eliminate metaclass*: a metaclass is deleted by giving place to a sub metamodel of the initial one. In general, such a change induces in the corresponding models the deletions of all the metaclass instances. Moreover, if the involved metaclass has subclasses or it is referred by other metaclasses, the elimination causes side effects also to the related entities;

Table 1. Changes classification

Change type	Change
Non-breaking changes	Generalize metaproperty
	Add (non-obligatory) metaclass
	Add (non-obligatory) metaproperty
Breaking and resolvable changes	Extract (abstract) superclass
	Eliminate metaclass
	Eliminate metaproperty
	Push metaproperty
	Flatten hierarchy
	Rename metaelement
	Move metaproperty
	Extract/inline metaclass
Breaking and unresolvable changes	Add obligatory metaclass
	Add obligatory metaproperty
	Pull metaproperty
	Restrict metaproperty
	Extract (non-abstract) superclass

– *Eliminate metaproperty*: a property is eliminated from a metaclass, it has the same effect of the previous modification;
– *Push metaproperty*: pushing a property in subclasses means that it is deleted from an initial superclass A and then cloned in all the subclasses C of A. If A is abstract then such a metamodel modification does not require any model co-adaptation, otherwise all the instances of A and its subclasses need to be accordingly modified;
– *Flatten hierarchy*: to flatten a hierarchy means eliminating a superclass and introducing all its properties into the subclasses. This scenario can be referred to metaproperty pushes;
– *Restrict metaproperty*: a metaproperty is restricted when its multiplicity or type are enforced. It is a complex case where instances need to be co-adapted or restricted. Restricting the upper bound of the multiplicity requires a selection of certain values to be deleted. Increasing the lower bound requires new values to be added for the involved element which usually are manually provided. Restricting the type of a property requires type conversion for each value.

Finally, a new version of the model can consist of some updates of already existing elements leading to updative modifications which can be grouped as follows:

– *Rename metaelement*: renaming is a simple case in which the change needs to be propagated to existing instances and can be performed in an automatic way;
– *Move metaproperty*: it consists of moving a property p from a metaclass A to a metaclass B. This is a resolvable change and the existing models can be easily co-evolved by moving the property p from all the instances of the metaclass A to the instances of B;

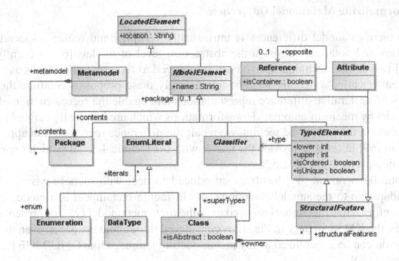

Fig. 12. KM3 metamodel

– *Extract/inline metaclass*: extracting a metaclass means to create a new class and move the relevant fields from the old class into the new one. Vice versa, to inline a metaclass means to move all its features into another class and delete the former. Both metamodel refactorings induce automated model co-evolutions.

The classification illustrated so far is summarized in Tab. 1 and makes evident the fundamental role of evolution representation. At a first glance it seems that the classification does not encompass *references* that are associations amongst metaclasses. However, references can be considered properties of metaclasses at the same level of attributes.

Metamodel evolutions can be precisely categorized by understanding the kind of modifications a metamodel undergone. Moreover, starting from the classification it is possible to adopt adequate countermeasures to co-evolve existing instances. Nonetheless, it is worth noting that the classification summarized in Tab. 1 is based on a clear distinction between the metamodel evolution categories. Unfortunately, in real world experiences the evolution of a metamodel can not be reduced to a sequence of atomic changes, generally several types of changes are operated as affecting multiple elements with different impacts on the co-adaptation. Furthermore, the entities involved in the evolution can be related one another. Therefore, since co-adaptation mechanisms are based on the described change classification, a metamodel adaptation will need to be decomposed in terms of the induced co-evolution categories. The possibility to have a set of dependences among the several parts of the evolution makes the updates not always distinguishable as single atomic steps of the metamodel revision, but requires a further refinement of the classification as introduced in the next section and discussed in details in Sect. 5.3.

5.2 Formalizing Metamodel Differences

The problem of model differences is intrinsically complex and requires specialized algorithms and notations to match the abstraction level of models [68]. Recently, in [69, 70] two similar techniques have been introduced to represent differences as models, hereafter called *difference models*; interestingly these proposals combine the advantages of declarative difference representations and enable the reconstruction of the final model by means of automated transformations which are inherently defined in the approaches. In the rest of the section, we recall the difference representation approach defined in [69] in order to provide the reader with the technical details which underpin the solution proposed in Sect. 5.3.

Despite the work in [69] has been introduced to deal with model revisions, it is easily adaptable to metamodel evolutions too. In fact, a metamodel is a model itself, which conforms to a metamodel referred to as the meta metamodel [2]. For presentation purposes, the KM3 language in Fig. 12 is considered throughout the paper, even though the solution can be generalized to any metamodeling language like OMG/MOF [23] or EMF/Ecore [29].

The overall structure of the change representation mechanism is depicted in Fig. 13: given two *base metamodels* MM_1 and MM_2 which conform to an arbitrary *base meta metamodel* (KM3 in our case), their difference conforms to a *difference metamodel* MMD derived from KM3 by means of an automated transformation MM2MMD. The base meta metamodel, extended as prescribed by such a transformation, consists of new constructs able to represent the possible modifications that can occur on metamodels and which can be grouped as follows:

- *additions*: new elements are added in the initial metamodel; with respect to the classification given in Sect. 5.1, *Add metaclass* and *Extract superclass* involve this kind of change;
- *deletions*: some of the existing elements are deleted as a whole. *Eliminate metaclass* and *Flatten hierarchy* fall in this category of manipulations;
- *changes*: a new version of the metamodel being considered can consist of updates of already existing elements. For instance, *Rename metaelement* and *Restrict metaproperty* require this type of modification. Also the addition and deletion of metaproperty (i.e. *Add metaproperty* and *Eliminate metaproperty*, respectively) are modelled through this construct. In fact, when a metaelement is included in a container the manipulation is represented as a *change* of the container itself.

In order to represent the differences between the Petri Net metamodel revisions, the extended KM3 meta metamodel depicted in Fig. 14 is generated by applying the MM2MMD transformation in Fig. 13 previously mentioned. For each metaclass MC of the KM3 metamodel, the additional metaclasses AddedMC, DeletedMC, and ChangedMC are generated. For instance, the metaclass Class in Fig. 12 induces the generation of the metaclasses AddedClass, DeletedClass, and ChangedClass as depicted in Fig. 14. In the same way, Reference metaclass induces the generation of the metaclasses AddedReference, DeletedReference, and ChangedReference.

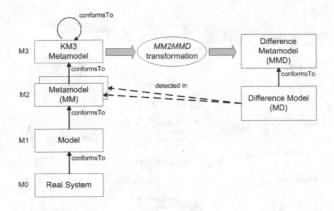

Fig. 13. Overall structure of the model difference representation approach

The generated difference metamodel is able to represent all the differences amongst metamodels which conform to KM3. For instance, the model in Fig. 15 conforms to the generated metamodel in Fig. 14 and represents the differences between the Petri Net metamodels specified in Fig. 11. The differences depicted in such a model can be summarized as follows:

1) the addition of the new class PTArc in the MM_1 revision of the Petri Net metamodel is represented by means of an AddedClass instance, as illustrated by model difference $\Delta_{0,1}$ in Fig. 15. Moreover, the reference between Place and Transition named dst has been updated to link PTArc with name out. Analogously, the reverse reference named src has been manipulated to point PTArc and named as in. Two new references have been added through the corresponding AddedReference instances to realize the reverse links from PTArc to Place and Transition, respectively. Finally, the composition relationship between Net and Place has been updated by prescribing the existence of at least one Place through the lower property which has been updated from 0 to 1. The same enforcement has been done to the composition between Net and Transition;

2) the addition of the new abstract class Arc in MM_2 together with its attribute weight is represented through an instance of the AddedClass and the AddedAttribute metaclasses in the $\Delta_{1,2}$ delta of Fig. 15. In the meanwhile, PTArc and TPArc classes are made specializations of Arc. Finally, Net entity is renamed as PetriNet.

Difference models like the one in Fig. 15 can be obtained by using today's available tools like EMFCompare [71] and SiDiff [72].

The representation mechanism used so far allows to identify changes which occurred in a metamodel revision and satisfies a number of properties, as illustrated in [69]. One of them is the *compositionality*, i.e. the possibility to combine difference models in interesting constructions like the sequential and the parallel compositions, which in turn result in valid difference models themselves. For the sake of simplicity, let us consider only two modifications over the initial model: the sequential composition of such

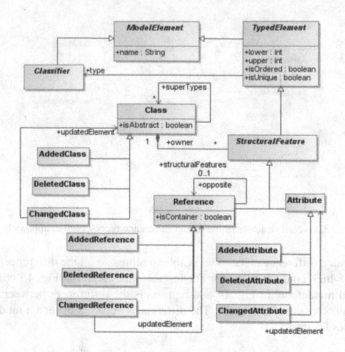

Fig. 14. Generated difference KM3 metamodel

manipulations corresponds to merging the modifications conveyed by the first document and then, in turn, by the second one in a resulting difference model containing a
minimal difference set, i.e., only those modifications which have not been overridden
by subsequent manipulations. Whereas, parallel compositions are exploited to combine modifications operated from the same ancestor in a concurrent way. In case both
manipulations are not affecting the same elements they are said *parallel independent*
and their composition is obtained by merging the difference models by interleaving the
single changes and assimilating it to the sequential composition. Otherwise, they are
referred to as *parallel dependent* and conflict issues can arise which need to be detected
and resolved [73].

Finally, difference documentation can be exploited to re-apply changes to arbitrary
input models (see [69] for further details) and for managing model co-evolution induced by metamodel manipulations. In the latter case, once differences between metamodel versions have been detected and represented, they have to be partitioned in
resolvable and non resolvable scenarios in order to adopt the corresponding resolution
strategy. However, this distinction is not always feasible because of parallel dependent
changes, i.e. situations where multiple changes are mixed and interdependent one another, like when a resolvable change is in some way related with a non-resolvable one,
for instance. In those cases, deltas have to be decomposed in order to isolate the non-
resolvable portion from the resolvable one, as illustrated in the next section.

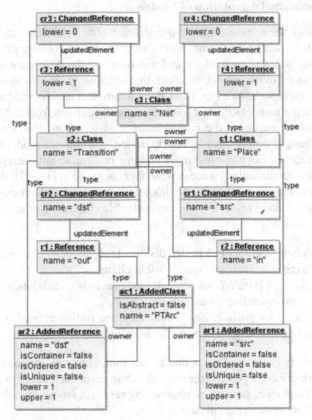

$\Delta_{0,1}$ ($MM_1 - MM_0$)

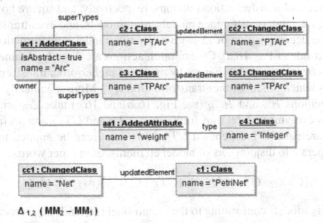

$\Delta_{1,2}$ ($MM_2 - MM_1$)

Fig. 15. Subsequent Petri Net metamodel adaptations

5.3   Transformational Adaptation of Models

This section proposes a transformational approach able to consistently adapt existing models with respect to the modifications occurred in the corresponding metamodels. The proposal is based on model transformation and the difference representation techniques presented in the previous section. In particular, given two versions MM_1 and MM_2 of the same metamodel (see Fig. 16.a), their differences are recorded in a difference model Δ, whose metamodel KM3Diff is automatically derived from KM3 as described in Sect. 5.2. In realistic cases, the modifications consist of an arbitrary combination of the atomic changes summarized in Tab. 1. Hence, a difference model formalizes all kind of modifications, i.e. non-breaking, breaking resolvable and unresolvable ones. This poses additional difficulties since current approaches (e.g. [18, 67]) do not provide any support to co-adaptation when the modifications are given without explicitly distinguishing among breaking resolvable and unresolvable changes. Our approach consists of the following steps:

   i) automatic decomposition of Δ in two disjoint (sub) models, Δ_R and $\Delta_{\neg R}$, which denote breaking resolvable and unresolvable changes;
   ii) if Δ_R and $\Delta_{\neg R}$ are *parallel independent* (see previous section) then we separately generate the corresponding co-evolutions;
   iii) if Δ_R and $\Delta_{\neg R}$ are *parallel dependent*, they are further refined to identify and isolate the interdependencies causing the interferences.

The distinction between *ii)* and *iii)* is due to fact that when two modifications are not independent their effects depend on the order the changes occur leading to non confluent situations. The confluence can still be obtained by removing those modifications which caused the conflicts as described in Sect. 5.3.

The general approach is outlined in Figure 16 where dotted and solid arrows represent conformance and transformation relations, respectively, and square boxes are any kind of models, i.e. models, difference models, metamodels, and even transformations. In particular, the decomposition of Δ is given by two model transformations, T_R and $T_{\neg R}$ (right-hand side of Fig. 16.a). Co-evolution actions are directly obtained as model transformations from metamodel changes by means of higher-order transformations, i.e. transformations which produce other transformations [2]. More specifically, the higher-order transformations $\mathcal{H}_R$ and $\mathcal{H}_{\neg R}$ (see Fig. 16.b and 16.c) take Δ_R and $\Delta_{\neg R}$ and produce the (co-evolving) model transformations CT_R and $CT_{\neg R}$, respectively. Since Δ_R and $\Delta_{\neg R}$ are parallel independent CT_R and $CT_{\neg R}$ can be applied in any order because they operate to disjoint sets of model elements, or in other words

$$(CT_{\neg R} \cdot CT_R)(M_1) = (CT_R \cdot CT_{\neg R})(M_1) = M_2$$

with M_1 and M_2 models conforming to the metamodel MM_1 and MM_2, respectively (see Fig. 16.d).

In the rest of the section we illustrate the approach and its implementation. In particular, we describe the decomposition of Δ and the generation of the co-evolving model transformations for the case of parallel independent breaking resolvable and

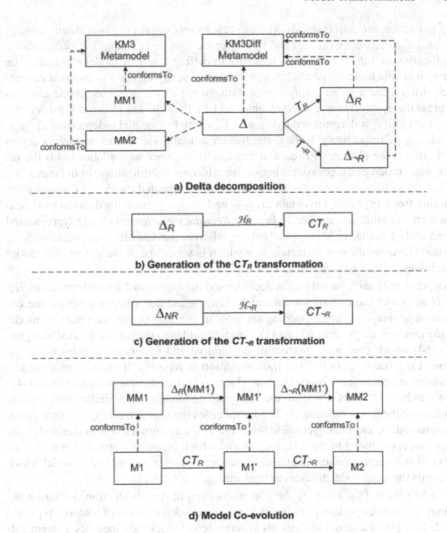

Fig. 16. Overall approach

unresolvable changes. Finally, we outline how to remove interdependencies from parallel dependent changes in order to generalize the solution provided in Sect. 5.3.

Parallel Independent Changes. The generation of the co-evolving model transformations is described in the rest of the section by means of the evolutions the `PetriNet` metamodel has been subject to in Fig. 11. The differences between the subsequent metamodel versions are given in Fig. 15 and have, in turn, to be decomposed to distinguish breaking resolvable and unresolvable modifications.

In particular, the difference $\Delta_{(0,1)}$ from MM_0 to MM_1 consists of two atomic modifications, i.e. an *Extract metaclass* and a *Restrict metaproperty* change (according to the classification in Tab. 1), which are referring to different sets of model elements. The approach is able to detect parallel independence by verifying that the eventual decomposed differences have an empty intersection. Since *a)* the previous atomic changes are breaking resolvable and unresolvable, and *b)* they do not share any model element, then $\Delta_{(0,1)}$ is decomposed by T_R and $T_{\neg R}$ into the parallel independent $\Delta_{R(0,1)}$ and $\Delta_{\neg R(0,1)}$, respectively. In fact, the former contains the extract metaclass action which affects the elements Place and Transition, whereas the latter holds the restrict metaproperty changes consisting of the reference modifications in the metaclass Net. Analogously, the same decomposition can be operated on $\Delta_{(1,2)}$ (denoting the evolution from MM_1 to MM_2) to obtain $\Delta_{R(1,2)}$ and $\Delta_{\neg R(1,2)}$ since the denoted modifications do not conflict one another. In fact, the *Rename metaelement* change (represented by cc1 and c1 in Fig. 15.b) is applied to Net, whereas the *Add obligatory metaproperty* operation involves the new metaclass Arc which is supertype of the PTArc and TPArc metaclasses.

As previously said, once the Δ is decomposed the higher-order transformations $\mathcal{H}_R$ and $\mathcal{H}_{\neg R}$ detect the occurred metamodel changes and accordingly generate the co-evolution to adapt the corresponding models. In the current implementation, model transformations are given in ATL, a QVT compliant language part of the AMMA platform [64] which contains a mixture of declarative and imperative constructs. In the Listing 1.6 a fragment of the $\mathcal{H}_R$ transformation is reported: it consists of a module specification containing a header section (lines 1-2), transformation rules (lines 4-41) and a number of helpers which are used to navigate models and to define complex calculations on them. In particular, the header specifies the source models, the corresponding metamodels, and the target ones. Since the $\mathcal{H}_R$ transformation is higher-order, the target model conforms to the ATL metamodel which essentially specifies the abstract syntax of the transformation language. Moreover, $\mathcal{H}_R$ takes as input the model which represents the metamodel differences conforming to KM3Diff.

The helpers and the rules are the constructs used to specify the transformation behaviour. The source pattern of the rules (e.g. lines 15-20) consists of a source type and a OCL [51] guard stating the elements to be matched. Each rule specifies a target pattern (e.g. lines 21-25) which is composed of a set of elements, each of them (as the one at lines 22-25) specifies a target type from the target metamodel (for instance, the type MatchedRule from the ATL metamodel) and a set of bindings. A binding refers to a feature of the type, i.e. an attribute, a reference or an association end, and specifies an expression whose value initializes the feature. $\mathcal{H}_R$ consists of a set of rules each of them devoted to the management of one of the resolvable metamodel changes reported in Tab. 1. For instance, the Listing 1.6 contains the rules for generating the co-evolution actions corresponding to the *Rename metaelement* and the *Extract metaclass* changes.

```
1 module H_R;
2 create  OUT : ATL  from Delta : KM3Diff;
3 ...
4 rule atlModule {
5     from
6         s: KM3Diff!Metamodel
7     to
8     t : ATL!Module (
9         name <- 'CTR',
10        outModels <- Sequence {tm},
11       inModels <- Sequence {sm},...
12     ),...
13 }
14 rule CreateRenaming {
15   from
16      input : KM3Diff!Class,
17      delta : KM3Diff!ChangedClass
18      ...
19      (not input.isAbstract
20       and input.name <> delta.updatedElement.name...)
21   to
22      matchedRule :  ATL!MatchedRule (
23        name<-input.name + '2' + delta.updatedElement.name,
24        ...
25      ),...
26 }
27 rule CreateExtractMetaClass {
28  from
29      cr1: KM3Diff!ChangedReference, cr2: KM3Diff!ChangedReference, r1 : KM3Diff!
               Reference, r2 : KM3Diff!Reference, c1 : KM3Diff!Class,
30      c2 : KM3Diff!Class,...
31      ( cr1.updatedElement = r2 and cr1.owner = c2
32        and cr1.type = c1 and ...)
33  to
34      -- MatchedRule generation
35      matchedRule_i_c2 :  ATL!MatchedRule (
36        name<-i_c2.name + '2' + i_c2.name,
37        inPattern <- ip_i_c2,
38        outPattern <- op_i_c2,
39        ...
40      ),...
41 }
42 ...
```

Listing 1.6. Fragment of the HOT_R transformation

The application of $\mathcal{H}_R$ to the metamodel MM$_0$ in Fig. 11 and the difference model $\Delta_{R(0,1)}$ in Fig. 15 generates the model transformation reported in the Listing 1.7. In fact, the source pattern of the CreateExtractMetaClass rule (lines 28-32 in the Listing 1.6) matches with the two *Extract metaclass* changes represented in $\Delta_{R(0,1)}$. They consist of the additions of the PTArc and TPArc metaclasses instead of the direct references between the existing elements Place and Transition. Consequently, according to the structural features of the involved elements, the CreateExtractMetaClass rule generates the transformation $CT_{R(0,1)}$ which is able to co-evolve all the models conforming to MM$_0$ by adapting them with respect to the new metamodel MM$_1$ (see line 1-2 of the Listing 1.7). In particular, each element of type Place has to be modified by changing all the references to elements of type Transition with references to new elements of type PTArc (see lines 4-23 in the Listing 1.7). The same modification has to be performed for all the elements of type Transition by creating new elements of type TPArc which have to be added instead of direct references between Transition and Place instances (see lines 24-42).

```
1 module CTR;
2 create OUT : MM1 from IN : MM0;
3 ...
4 rule Place2Place {
5   from
6     s : MM1!Place
7     ...
8   to
9     t : MM2!Place (
10        name <- s.name,
11        net <- s.net,
12        out <- s.dst->collect(e |
13          thisModule.createPTArc(e, t)
14        )
15    )
16 }
17 rule createPTArc(s : OclAny, n : OclAny) {
18   to
19     t : MM2!PTArc (
20        src <- s,
21        dst <- n
22    ), ...
23 }
24 rule Transition2Transition {
25   from
26     s : MM1!Transition
27     ...
28   to
29     t : MM2!Transition (
30        net <- s.net,
31        in <- s.dst->collect(e |
32          thisModule.createTPArc(e, t)
33        )
34    )
35 }
36 rule createTPArc(s : OclAny, n : OclAny) {
37   to
38     t : MM2!PTArc (
39        dst <- s,
40        src <- n
41    ), ...
42 }
43 ...
```

Listing 1.7. Fragment of the generated $CT_{R(0,1)}$ transformation

The management of the breaking and unresolvable modifications is based on the same techniques presented so far for the breaking resolvable case. However, as mentioned in Sect. 5.1, the involved transformations can not automatically co-adapt the models but are limited to default actions which have to be refined by the designer.

Parallel Dependent Changes. As mentioned above, the automatic co-adaptation of models relies on the parallel independence of breaking resolvable and unresolvable modifications, or more formally

$$\Delta_R | \Delta_{\neg R} = \Delta_R; \Delta_{\neg R} + \Delta_{\neg R}; \Delta_R \qquad (1)$$

where $+$ denotes the non-deterministic choice. In essence, their application is not affected by the adopted order since they do not present any interdependencies. In case the modifications in Tab. 1 refer to the same elements then the order in which such modifications take place matters and does not allow the decomposition of a difference model as, for instance, when evolving MM_0 directly to MM_2 (although the sub steps $MM_0 - MM_1$ and $MM_1 - MM_2$ are directly manageable as described in the previous section).

A possible approach, which is only sketched in the following, consists in isolating the interdependencies whenever (1) does not hold. The intention is to define an iterative process consisting in *diminishing* the modifications between two metamodels until the corresponding breaking resolvable and unresolvable differences are parallel independent. In particular, let Δ be a difference between two metamodels, then we denote by $\mathcal{P}(\Delta)$ the *difference powermodel*, that is the (partially ordered) set of all possible valid sub models of Δ (i.e. fragments of the difference model which are still conforming to the difference metamodel)

$$\mathcal{P}(\Delta) = \{\delta_0 = \phi, \cdots, \delta_i, \delta_{i+1}, \cdots, \delta_n = \Delta\}$$

Then, the solution is the smallest k in $\{0, \cdots, n\}$ such that

$$\Delta^{(k)}; \delta_k = \Delta$$

where $\Delta^{(k)}$ is the difference model between Δ and δ_k, and

$$\Delta^{(k)} = \Delta_R^{(k)} | \Delta_{\neg R}^{(k)}$$

with $\Delta_R^{(k)}$ and $\Delta_{\neg R}^{(k)}$ parallel independent. Hence, the problem of parallel dependence is reduced to the following

$$\Delta = (\Delta_R^{(k)} | \Delta_{\neg R}^{(k)}); \delta_k$$

by applying the higher-order transformation introduced in the previous section. For instance, if we consider ($MM_2 - MM_0$) the solution consists in iteratively finding a difference model which maps MM_0 to the intermediate metamodel corresponding to MM_2 without the attribute *weight* of the `Arc` metaclass. Therefore, the remaining δ_k in this example is a non resolvable change, while in general it may demand for further iterations of the decomposition process.

The problem of finding the correct scheduling of the adaptation steps has been solved in [74] which proposes a dependency analysis which underpins a resolution strategy for their correct application. In particular, all the metamodel change dependencies have been considered and for each of them a resolution schema is proposed enabling the complete automation of the adaptation. Interestingly, the technique is independent from the metamodel and its underlying semantics, since it relies only on the definition of the metamodeling language.

6 Conclusions

In this paper, model transformation approaches have been illustrated. They have been grouped according to (macro) characteristics which distinguished their intrinsic features. A number of languages which are prominent in their specificity have been briefly discussed. Finally, two different application scenarios have been presented in order to illustrate complex situations where model transformations have been successfully applied. In the first case, the JTL language has been presented and particularly its capability in dealing with non-bijective transformations which present interesting difficulties when modifications operated on a target model must be back propagated to source models. The second case illustrated an application of higher-order transformations to the problem of the coupled evolution of metamodels and models. In partcicular, the evolution of a metamodel is specified in a difference model that once entered in a given HOT produces other transformations capable of adapting those models which have been invalidated by the metamodel changes.

Model transformations are considered among the most distinguished element of MDE as their constitute the main gluing and composing mechanism within any MDE ecosystem. However, the maturity of this field is still to be assessed as many aspects still need to be further investigated. In general, very important aspects such as bidirectionality and change propagation have been already object of intense debate, as witnessed by the work in [57], while genericity [75] and model typing [76] has been only more recently considered. Other aspects, like transformation semantics, strategies and tools for testing and verifying transformations, are addressed in another course [77] of the SFM-12: MDE Summer School[10] [78].

Acknowledgments. We would like to thank Antonio Cicchetti and Ludovico Iovino for the never ending discussions we had over the last few years about the topics covered by this paper (and mountaineering). Also, we are grateful to many colleagues, including Jean Bézivin, Jeff Gray, Richard Paige, Laurie Tratt, and Antonio Vallecillo, who shared their opinions and visions with us.

References

1. Schmidt, D.: Guest Editor's Introduction: Model-Driven Engineering. Computer 39(2), 25–31 (2006)
2. Bézivin, J.: On the Unification Power of Models. Jour. on Software and Systems Modeling (SoSyM) 4(2), 171–188 (2005)
3. Bosch, J.: From software product lines to software ecosystems. In: Proceedings of the 13th International Software Product Line Conference, SPLC 2009, pp. 111–119. Carnegie Mellon University, Pittsburgh (2009)
4. Tratt, L.: Model transformations and tool integration. Jour. on Software and Systems Modeling (SoSyM) 4(2), 112–122 (2005)
5. Object Management Group (OMG): MOF 2.0 Query/Views/Transformations RFP, OMG document ad/02-04-10 (2002)
6. Visser, E.: WebDSL: A Case Study in Domain-Specific Language Engineering. In: Lämmel, R., Visser, J., Saraiva, J. (eds.) GTTSE 2007. LNCS, vol. 5235, pp. 291–373. Springer, Heidelberg (2008)
7. Ceri, S., Fraternali, P., Bongio, A.: Web Modeling Language (WebML): a Modeling Language for Designing Web sites. Computer Networks 33(1-6), 137–157 (2000)
8. Di Ruscio, D., Muccini, H., Pierantonio, A.: A Data Modeling Approach to Web Application Synthesis. Int. Jour. of Web Engineering and Technology 1(3), 320–337 (2004)

---

[10] http://www.sti.uniurb.it/events/sfm12mde/

9. Cicchetti, A., Di Ruscio, D., Eramo, R., Maccarrone, F., Pierantonio, A.: beContent: A Model-Driven Platform for Designing and Maintaining Web Applications. In: Gaedke, M., Grossniklaus, M., Díaz, O. (eds.) ICWE 2009. LNCS, vol. 5648, pp. 518–522. Springer, Heidelberg (2009)

10. Cicchetti, A., Di Ruscio, D., Eramo, R., Pierantonio, A.: Model Differences for Supporting Model Co-evolution. In: Procs. MoDSE, 2nd Workshop on Model-Driven Software Evolution (2008)

11. Rose, L.M., Kolovos, D.S., Paige, R.F., Polack, F.A.C.: Model Migration with Epsilon Flock. In: Tratt, L., Gogolla, M. (eds.) ICMT 2010. LNCS, vol. 6142, pp. 184–198. Springer, Heidelberg (2010)

12. Herrmannsdoerfer, M., Benz, S., Juergens, E.: Cope - automating coupled evolution of metamodels and models, pp. 52–76 (2009)

13. Di Cosmo, R., Di Ruscio, D., Pelliccione, P., Pierantonio, A., Zacchiroli, S.: Supporting software evolution in component-based foss systems. Technical Report TRCS 003/2010, Computer Science Department, University of L'Aquila (2010)

14. Stevens, P.: A Landscape of Bidirectional Model Transformations. In: Lämmel, R., Visser, J., Saraiva, J. (eds.) GTTSE 2007. LNCS, vol. 5235, pp. 408–424. Springer, Heidelberg (2008)

15. Xiong, Y., Song, H., Hu, Z., Takeichi, M.: Supporting Parallel Updates with Bidirectional Model Transformations. In: Paige, R.F. (ed.) ICMT 2009. LNCS, vol. 5563, pp. 213–228. Springer, Heidelberg (2009)

16. Lehman, M.M., Belady, L.A. (eds.): Program evolution: processes of software change. Academic Press Professional, Inc., San Diego (1985)

17. Favre, J.M.: Meta-Model and Model Co-evolution within the 3D Software Space. In: Procs. of the Int. Workshop on Evolution of Large-scale Industrial Software Applications (ELISA) at ICSM 2003, Amsterdam (September 2003)

18. Wachsmuth, G.: Metamodel Adaptation and Model Co-adaptation. In: Bateni, M. (ed.) ECOOP 2007. LNCS, vol. 4609, pp. 600–624. Springer, Heidelberg (2007)

19. Selic, B.: The Pragmatics of Model-driven Development. IEEE Software 20(5), 19–25 (2003)

20. Object Management Group (OMG): MDA Guide version 1.0.1, OMG Document: omg/2003-06-01 (2003)

21. Kent, S.: Model Driven Engineering. In: Butler, M.J., Petre, L., Sere, K. (eds.) IFM 2002. LNCS, vol. 2335, pp. 286–298. Springer, Heidelberg (2002)

22. Favre, J.M.: Towards a Basic Theory to Model Model Driven Engineering. In: Procs. of the 3rd Int. Workshop in Software Model Engineering (WiSME 2004) (2004)

23. Object Management Group (OMG): Meta Object Facility (MOF) 2.0 Core Specification, OMG Document ptc/03-10-04 (2003),
http://www.omg.org/docs/ptc/03-10-04.pdf

24. Object Management Group (OMG): Unified Modelling Language (UML) V1.4 (2001)

25. Object Management Group (OMG): XMI Specification, v1.2, OMG Document formal/02-01-01 (2002)

26. Seidewitz, E.: What Models Mean. IEEE Software 20(5), 26–32 (2003)

27. Bézivin, J., Gerbé, O.: Towards a Precise Definition of the OMG/MDA Framework. In: Automated Software Engineering (ASE 2001), pp. 273–282. IEEE Computer Society, Los Alamitos (2001)

28. Mellor, S.J., Clark, A.N., Futagami, T.: Guest Editors' Introduction: Model-Driven Development. IEEE Software 20(5), 14–18 (2003)

29. Budinsky, F., Steinberg, D., Merks, E., Ellersick, R., Grose, T.: Eclipse Modeling Framework. Addison Wesley (2003)

30. Aksit, M., Kurtev, I., Bézivin, J.: Technological Spaces: an Initial Appraisal. In: International Federated Conf. (DOA, ODBASE, CoopIS), Industrial Track, Los Angeles (2002)

31. Kleppe, A., Warmer, J.: MDA Explained. The Model Driven Architecture: Practice and Promise. Addison-Wesley (2003)
32. Czarnecki, K., Helsen, S.: Feature-based Survey of Model Transformation Approaches. IBM Systems J. 45(3) (June 2006)
33. Taentzer, G., Ehrig, K., Guerra, E., de Lara, J., Lengyel, L., Levendovszky, T., Prange, U., Varró, D., Varró-Gyapay, S.: Model Transformation by Graph Transformation: A Comparative Study. In: ACM/IEEE 8th International Conference on Model Driven Engineering Languages and Systems, Montego Bay, Jamaica (October 2005)
34. OMG: MOF QVT Final Adopted Specification, OMG Adopted Specification ptc/05-11-01 (2005)
35. Xactium: Xmf-mosaic, http://xactium.com
36. Vojtisek, D., Jézéquel, J.M.: MTL and Umlaut NG: Engine and Framework for Model Transformation, http://www.ercim.org/publication/Ercim_News/enw58/vojtisek.html
37. Muller, P.A., Fleurey, F., Jézéquel, J.M.: Weaving Executability into Object-Oriented Metalanguages. In: ACM/IEEE 8th International Conference on Model Driven Engineering Languages and Systems, Montego Bay, pp. 264–278 (2005)
38. Didonet Del Fabro, M., Bezivin, J., Jouault, F., Breton, E., Gueltas, G.: AMW: A generic Model Weaver. In: Int. Conf. on Software Engineering Research and Practice (SERP 2005) (2005)
39. Cicchetti, A., Di Ruscio, D.: Decoupling Web Application Concerns through Weaving Operations. Science of Computer Programming 70(1), 62–86 (2008)
40. Gerber, A., Lawley, M., Raymond, K., Steel, J., Wood, A.: Transformation: The Missing Link of MDA. In: Corradini, A., Ehrig, H., Kreowski, H.-J., Rozenberg, G. (eds.) ICGT 2002. LNCS, vol. 2505, pp. 90–105. Springer, Heidelberg (2002)
41. Cicchetti, A., Di Ruscio, D., Eramo, R., Pierantonio, A.: JTL: A Bidirectional and Change Propagating Transformation Language. In: Malloy, B., Staab, S., van den Brand, M. (eds.) SLE 2010. LNCS, vol. 6563, pp. 183–202. Springer, Heidelberg (2011)
42. Gelfond, M., Lifschitz, V.: The Stable Model Semantics for Logic Programming. In: Kowalski, R.A., Bowen, K. (eds.) Proceedings of the Fifth Int. Conf. on Logic Programming, pp. 1070–1080. The MIT Press, Cambridge (1988)
43. Jouault, F., Kurtev, I.: Transforming Models with ATL. In: Bruel, J.-M. (ed.) MoDELS 2005. LNCS, vol. 3844, pp. 128–138. Springer, Heidelberg (2006)
44. Kolovos, D.S., Paige, R.F., Polack, F.A.C.: The Epsilon Transformation Language. In: Vallecillo, A., Gray, J., Pierantonio, A. (eds.) ICMT 2008. LNCS, vol. 5063, pp. 46–60. Springer, Heidelberg (2008)
45. Taentzer, G.: AGG: A Graph Transformation Environment for Modeling and Validation of Software. In: Pfaltz, J.L., Nagl, M., Böhlen, B. (eds.) AGTIVE 2003. LNCS, vol. 3062, pp. 446–453. Springer, Heidelberg (2004)
46. de Lara, J., Vangheluwe, H.: AToM^3: A Tool for Multi-formalism and Meta-modelling. In: Kutsche, R.-D., Weber, H. (eds.) FASE 2002. LNCS, vol. 2306, pp. 174–188. Springer, Heidelberg (2002), http://link.springer.de/link/service/series/0558/bibs/2306/23060174.htm
47. Varró, D., Varró, G., Pataricza, A.: Designing the automatic transformation of visual languages. Science of Computer Programming 44(2), 205–227 (2002)
48. Agrawal, A., Karsai, G., Kalmar, Z., Neema, S., Shi, F., Vizhanyo, A.: The Design of a Language for Model Transformations. Journal of Software and System Modeling (2005)
49. Konigs, A., Schurr, A.: Tool Integration with Triple Graph Grammars - A Survey. Electronic Notes in Theoretical Computer Science 148, 113–150 (2006)

50. Wagelaar, D., Tisi, M., Cabot, J., Jouault, F.: Towards a General Composition Semantics for Rule-Based Model Transformation. In: Whittle, J., Clark, T., Kühne, T. (eds.) MoDELS 2011. LNCS, vol. 6981, pp. 623–637. Springer, Heidelberg (2011)
51. Object Management Group (OMG): OCL 2.0 Specification, OMG Document formal/2006-05-01 (2006)
52. Billington, J., Christensen, S., van Hee, K.M., Kindler, E., Kummer, O., Petrucci, L., Post, R., Stehno, C., Weber, M.: The Petri Net Markup Language: Concepts, Technology, and Tools. In: van der Aalst, W.M.P., Best, E. (eds.) ICATPN 2003. LNCS, vol. 2679, pp. 483–505. Springer, Heidelberg (2003)
53. Extensible Platform for Specification of Integrated Languages for mOdel maNagement (Epsilon), http://www.eclipse.org/gmt/epsilon
54. Börger, E., Stärk, R.: Abstract State Machines - A Method for High-Level System Design and Analysis. Springer (2003)
55. Varró, D., Pataricza, A.: Generic and Meta-Transformations for Model Transformation Engineering. In: International Conference on the Unified Modeling Language, pp. 290–304 (2004)
56. Object Management Group (OMG): MOF 2.0 QVT Final Adoptet Specification v1.1, OMG Adopted Specification formal/2011-01-01 (2011)
57. Stevens, P.: Bidirectional model transformations in QVT: semantic issues and open questions. Software and Systems Modeling 8 (2009)
58. Steven Witkop: MDA users' requirements for QVT transformations, OMG document 05-02-04 (2005)
59. Czarnecki, K., Foster, J.N., Hu, Z., Lämmel, R., Schürr, A., Terwilliger, J.F.: Bidirectional Transformations: A Cross-Discipline Perspective—GRACE Meeting Notes, State of the Art, and Outlook. In: Paige, R.F. (ed.) ICMT 2009. LNCS, vol. 5563, pp. 260–283. Springer, Heidelberg (2009)
60. Chen, K., Sztipanovits, J., Abdelwalhed, S., Jackson, E.: Semantic Anchoring with Model Transformations. In: Hartman, A., Kreische, D. (eds.) ECMDA-FA 2005. LNCS, vol. 3748, pp. 115–129. Springer, Heidelberg (2005)
61. Leone, N., Pfeifer, G., Faber, W., Eiter, T., Gottlob, G., Perri, S., Scarcello, F.: The DLV System for Knowledge Representation and Reasoning (2004)
62. Tratt, L.: A change propagating model transformation language. Journal of Object Technology 7(3), 107–126 (2008)
63. Hettel, T., Lawley, M., Raymond, K.: Model Synchronisation: Definitions for Round-Trip Engineering. In: Vallecillo, A., Gray, J., Pierantonio, A. (eds.) ICMT 2008. LNCS, vol. 5063, pp. 31–45. Springer, Heidelberg (2008)
64. Bézivin, J., Jouault, F., Rosenthal, P., Valduriez, P.: Modeling in the Large and Modeling in the Small. In: Aßmann, U., Aksit, M., Rensink, A. (eds.) MDAFA 2003. LNCS, vol. 3599, pp. 33–46. Springer, Heidelberg (2005)
65. Cicchetti, A., Di Ruscio, D., Pierantonio, A.: Managing Model Conflicts in Distributed Development. In: Czarnecki, K., Ober, I., Bruel, J.-M., Uhl, A., Völter, M. (eds.) MoDELS 2008. LNCS, vol. 5301, pp. 311–325. Springer, Heidelberg (2008)
66. Cicchetti, A., Di Ruscio, D., Iovino, L., Pierantonio, A.: Managing the evolution of data-intensive web applications by model-driven techniques. Software and Systems Modeling (2011)
67. Gruschko, B., Kolovos, D., Paige, R.: Towards Synchronizing Models with Evolving Meta-models. In: Proceedings of the Workshop on Model-Driven Software Evolution, MODSE 2007 (2007)
68. Lin, Y., Zhang, J., Gray, J.: Model Comparison: A Key Challenge for Transformation Testing and Version Control in Model Driven Software Development. In: OOPSLA Workshop on Best Practices for Model-Driven Software Development (2004)

69. Cicchetti, A., Di Ruscio, D., Pierantonio, A.: A Metamodel Independent Approach to Difference Representation. Journal of Object Technology 6(9), 165–185 (2007)
70. Rivera, J., Vallecillo, A.: Representing and Operating with Model Differences. In: Objects, Components, Models and Patterns. LNBIP, vol. 11, pp. 141–160. Springer, Heidelberg (2008)
71. Brun, C., Pierantonio, A.: Model Differences in the Eclipse Modeling Framework. Upgrade, Special Issue on Model-Driven Software Development (April-May 2008)
72. Treude, C., Berlik, S., Wenzel, S., Kelter, U.: Difference computation of large models. In: ESEC-FSE 2007: Proceedings of the the 6th Joint Meeting of the European Software Engineering Conference and the ACM SIGSOFT Symposium on the Foundations of Software Engineering, pp. 295–304. ACM, New York (2007)
73. Cicchetti, A.: Difference Representation and Conflict Management in Model-Driven Engineering. PhD thesis, University of L'Aquila, Computer Science Dept. (2008)
74. Cicchetti, A., Di Ruscio, D., Pierantonio, A.: Managing Dependent Changes in Coupled Evolution. In: Paige, R.F. (ed.) ICMT 2009. LNCS, vol. 5563, pp. 35–51. Springer, Heidelberg (2009)
75. Sánchez Cuadrado, J., Guerra, E., de Lara, J.: Generic Model Transformations: *Write Once, Reuse Everywhere*. In: Cabot, J., Visser, E. (eds.) ICMT 2011. LNCS, vol. 6707, pp. 62–77. Springer, Heidelberg (2011)
76. Steel, J., Jézéquel, J.M.: On model typing. Software and System Modeling 6(4), 401–413 (2007)
77. Vallecillo, A., Gogolla, M., Burgueño, L., Wimmer, M., Hamann, L.: Formal Specification and Testing of Model Transformations. In: Bernardo, M., Cortellessa, V., Pierantonio, A. (eds.) SFM 2012. LNCS, vol. 7320, pp. 399–437. Springer, Heidelberg (2012)
78. Bernardo, M., Cortellessa, V., Pierantonio, A. (eds.): SFM 2011. LNCS, vol. 7320. Springer, Heidelberg (2012)

Graph Transformations
for MDE, Adaptation, and Models at Runtime

Holger Giese, Leen Lambers, Basil Becker, Stephan Hildebrandt,
Stefan Neumann, Thomas Vogel, and Sebastian Wätzoldt

System Analysis and Modeling Group,
Hasso Plattner Institute at the University of Potsdam, Germany
`prename.surname@hpi.uni-potsdam.de`

Abstract. Software evolution and the resulting need to continuously
adapt the software is one of the main challenges for software engineering.
The model-driven development movement therefore aims at improving
the longevity of software by keeping the development artifacts more consistent and better changeable by employing models and to a certain degree automated model operations. Another trend are systems that tackle
the challenge at runtime by being able to adapt their structure and behavior to be more flexible and operate in more dynamic environments
(e.g., context-aware software, autonomic computing, self-adaptive software). Finally, models at runtime, where the benefits of model-driven
development are employed at runtime to support adaptation capabilities, today lead towards a unification of both ideas.

In this paper, we present *graph transformations* and show that they
can be employed to engineer solutions for all three outlined cases. Furthermore, we will even be able to demonstrate that graph transformation
based technology has the potential to also unify all three cases in a single scenario where models at runtime and runtime adaptation is linked
with classical MDE. Therefore, we at first provide an introduction in
graph transformations, then present the related techniques of Story Pattern and Triple Graph Grammars, and demonstrate how with the help
of both techniques model transformations, adaptation behavior and runtime model framework work. In addition, we show that due to the formal
underpinning analysis becomes possible and report about a number of
successful examples.

1   Introduction

Software code does in principle not decay as hardware does and thus, it could be
employed forever when the underlying hardware is timely replaced on a regular
basis. However, Lehman [1,2] observed and documented in his *laws of software
evolution* that unless continuously being adapted, the typical software becomes
less and less useful over time. Parnas [3] referred to this phenomena as *software
aging* and identified two sources of the problem. (1) *lack of movement* when a
software is not changed according to changing needs and (2) *ignorant surgery*
which is caused by improper changes that are made to the software. Therefore,

M. Bernardo, V. Cortellessa, and A. Pierantonio (Eds.): SFM 2012, LNCS 7320, pp. 137–191, 2012.

a steady deterioration of the value and quality of the software can be observed unless special action is taken and nowadays software is continuously adapted, which is referred to as *software evolution* [4].

Today, the majority of the costs for software are resulting from *adaptation steps*[1] that happen after the software has been first shipped. In the related *maintenance* [5] effort, versions of the shipped software are adapted in a *construction environment* in parallel to deploying the software in potentially many *runtime environments*. In addition to standard maintenance activities, oftentimes *reengineering* including *reverse engineering* [6] to recover necessary higher level information and *redesign* to improve the inner structure of the software (a popular approach for that is *refactoring* [7]) are employed to counteract the aging. A today often highly automated *distribution* activity then transports the adaptation developed and tested in the construction environment to the different runtime environments.

In addition to the code, software systems today also include configuration data and require a dedicated deployment capturing the mapping of the software components on the available hardware and software platforms in the *runtime environment*. Here, an even stronger demand for continuous adaptation has been observed. As the required adaptation steps have to be handled by the administrators of each individual runtime environment, it does not seem economically feasible in the long run to realize all the required adaptation steps manually and the *autonomic computing* initiative therefore advocates their automation (cf. [8]).

Furthermore, for an increasingly important class of software holds that the required adaptation steps have to happen for each runtime environment and according to the individual context that is only known at runtime. Therefore, the required adaptation steps have to be done in the runtime environment and can only be at most pre-planned in the construction environment (cf. *context-aware computing* [9]). In addition, today's software has to operate in more dynamic organizations and contexts and is often expected to be more versatile, flexible, and resilient. Also it is often envisioned that the software is dependable, robust, continuously available, energy-efficient, recoverable, customizable, self-healing, configurable, or self-optimizing by adapting itself in response to changing requirements and contexts. In all these cases, adaptation steps have to be supported for the runtime environment and have to be initiated by the software itself.

Besides this trend towards context-aware and more versatile software, also the integration of beforehand isolated software islands into extremely complex systems-of-systems, so-called *ultra-large scale systems* [10], leads to a situation where due to their size and complexity such systems are no longer managed by a single central authority. Moreover, for such systems, the structure resp. architecture is subject to changes at runtime and they have to be highly

---

[1] We use *adaptation* here in the broad sense such that it also includes corrective changes such as fixing faults and adding new or modifying existing features and not only making changes in existing software to accommodate it to a changing platform.

context-aware and to adjust themselves accordingly. Furthermore, the adaptation steps that are necessary for such systems can hardly be developed in the construction environment manually upfront but they have to be derived automatically at runtime.

To address this need for support of adaptation steps in the runtime environment, several approaches where the software itself takes care of the adaptation steps [11,12,13,14,15] have been proposed, which all can be united under the term *self-adaptive software* [16,17,18]. In general, self-adaptive software can be built by following the *internal approach* or the *external approach* [18]. The internal approach realizes self-adaptation capabilities by intertwining the adaptation logic and the application logic at the level of programming languages. Therefore, often programming languages features, like reflection [19], are employed. In contrast, the external approach separates the adaptation logic from the application logic by having a dedicated *adaptation engine* that controls the *core function* within the application. Most approaches for software engineering of self-adaptive systems today support the external approach (cf. survey [18]) and operate with a separation at the architectural level with well-defined interfaces between the adaptation engine and the core function. We refer to adaptation due to development or maintenance activities as *classical adaptation* in the following in order to clearly distinguish it form self-adaptation or in general adaptation.

As also emphasized in autonomic computing [8], not only the self-adaptation steps within the software but the complete feedback loops determining such self-adaptation steps in the form of monitor, analyze, plan and execute steps that happen within the runtime environment have to be taken into account when engineering self-adaptive software [20]. Studying the feedback is easier in case of the external approach. However, oftentimes today the feedback loops are not very visible in the architectures, but rather hidden (cf. [20]). Moreover, self-adaptive software often supports more than a single feedback loop. As an example, the reference architecture suggested in [21] distinguishes a *component layer* where the core functionality resides, a *change management layer* on top of that which manages the changes of the component layer, and a *goal management layer* that is responsible for the long term self-adaptation. Each of the two upper layers employs a feedback loop that steers the directly underlying layer.

Any solution that explicitly captures and analyzes the software and its context at a certain level of abstraction has to use runtime representations of them and thus uses runtime models. Otherwise, it can only consist of a simple case by case treatment in form of adaptation rules that immediately react to observed sensor inputs. While several approaches, like [22,23], employ runtime representations based on architecture description languages, a next step is to leverage the benefits of MDE for such runtime representations by means of *models at runtime* (M@RT) that are built on MDE principles as argued in [24].

Thus, we can conclude that in order to address the evolution challenge, a solution is required that supports adaptation steps initiated both in the construction environment (classical adaptation) as well as in the runtime environment (e.g., context-aware software, autonomic computing, self-adaptive software). As pointed out in

[25] the clear boundary between both cases already starts to disappear. Furthermore, as we pointed out already earlier in [26], a solution is required where adaptation steps in the construction environment and in the runtime environment happen in an integrated manner.

To address the adaptation challenge thus an approach is required that is able to cover *model-driven engineering* (MDE) that supports adaptation steps in the construction environment but also has to lay the foundation for later adaptation steps in the runtime environment, *modeling structural dynamics* that is the foundation for advanced adaptation steps in the runtime environment that goes beyond parameter adaptation, and *models at runtime* that support advanced adaptation steps in the runtime environment by providing a means to represent and handle complex information about the context as well as the system itself as a basis for adaptation decisions.

In this paper, we present *graph transformations*. We show that they can be employed to engineer the required class of systems with adaptation in the construction environment and runtime environment. We will be able to demonstrate that graph transformation based technology has the potential to also cover all three areas with a single formalism such that models at runtime and runtime adaptation can be linked straight forward with classical MDE. Furthermore, we show that due to the formal foundation of graph transformation sound analysis techniques such as conflict detection, invariant checking, and model checking can be applied.

In contrast to [27] introducing graph transformation from a more general software engineering perspective and in contrast to [28] that emphasizes the general benefits of graph transformations compared to other formalisms, we focus in this paper on the particular needs when approaching evolution by supporting MDE, modeling structural dynamics, and models at runtime.

Besides graph transformations, we will in particular present the related techniques of Story Patterns and Triple Graph Grammars, and how with the help of both model transformations, adaptation behavior and runtime model framework work. In addition, we show that due to the formal underpinning analysis becomes possible and report about a number of successful examples.

To exemplify the benefits of graph transformations for MDE and modeling adaptation, we will use the following two running examples.

Example 1 (RailCab). RailCab is a research project at the University of Paderborn, Germany addressing autonomously driving shuttles on regular railway tracks. The shuttles operate like cabs on request and not according to timetables. An important feature is the creation of convoys where the shuttles are not mechanically coupled but drive only with a short distance to each other. This reduces drag and thus permits to saves energy (cf. [29]). Networking and software should further ensure the safe operation and high system efficiency. A small test track has been setup to show the existing prototypes.[2]

Example 2 (SDL). The Specification and Description Language (SDL) [30] is a specification language targeted the specification and description of reactive and distributed systems. We restrict our attention here to a simplified version for the block diagrams

---

[2] http://nbp-www.upb.de

of SDL covering mostly structure and communication. A system consists of a number of blocks. Blocks communicate with each other using channels. A block further consists of processes that are the carrier of behavior. The later in this context considered model transformation is a simplified version of a transformation used in the industrial case study on flexible production control systems [31] from SDL block diagrams to UML class diagrams.

The paper explores how graph transformation fulfills the needs of engineering MDE solutions, engineering solutions with adaptation and even engineering solutions that combine both in form of solutions that adapt with the help of models at runtime as follows: At first we introduce graph transformation in Section 2. This introduction intuitively defines how the different forms of graph transformation such as graph transformation systems and graph grammars work together with a definition of their semantics based on set theory. Then, we introduce the concrete graph transformation based languages of Story Patterns, Triple Graph Grammars and a Runtime Model Framework in Section 3. Besides defining their syntax and semantics of the languages based on the beforehand introduced graph transformations, this also includes detailed examples. However, the introduced graph transformations are not only a means for specification and execution. As outlined in Section 4, we can take benefit of available analysis techniques. Finally, we discuss the state-of-the-art for MDE solutions, engineering solutions with adaptation and even engineering solutions that combine both in form of solutions that adapt with the help of models and the benefits graph transformation based techniques offer in Section 5. Afterwards, the paper closes with some final conclusions.

2   Graph Transformations

There are plenty examples where *annotated graphs* are a natural representation of the states of a system. Let us for instance consider the RailCab system of Example 1.

Example 3 (RailCab - Topology). A core element of the RailCab system is its track topology which resides in a 2-dimensional space but is most appropriately represented as a graph that abstracts from the geometric details. Also the shuttles are distributed over a 2-dimensional space, but what again matters is how their position is relative to the track topology. When shuttle build convoys they build new structures which again are best represented at an abstract level using graphs. Fig. 1 summarizes this analogy between a complex RailCab system and graphs and graph transformation systems. As depicted in Fig. 2 we can also further equip the graphs with attributes to store additional information about the available energy in the batteries of the shuttles.

We will see in the following that this analogy does not only hold for the state, but that also the behavior can accordingly be captured using graph transformations that describe which changes to the state represented as a graph will or can happen.

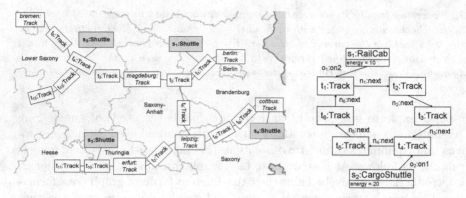

Fig. 1. A simple graph capturing a RailCab topology and the distribution of the shuttles on a map

Fig. 2. An attributed graph for the RailCab topology and shuttles

Graphs, Type Graphs, and Graph Morphisms. As outlined *graphs* can be used to represent a particular state of a system in a formal way. Also the abstract syntax of (visual) models can be captured by graphs. Thereby, graphs occur at two levels: the type level and the instance level. A fixed *type graph* TG serves as a representation of the combination of node types and edge types that may occur in graphs at the instance level. In particular, instance graphs of a type graph are equipped with a structure-preserving mapping (i.e. a *graph morphism*) to the type graph. First, we introduce graphs and graph morphisms with different useful properties in a formal way. Then, we introduce the notion of typed graphs formally.

Definition 1 (graph and graph morphism). *A graph $G = (G_V, G_E, s, t)$ consists of a set G_V of vertices, a set G_E of edges and two total mappings $s, t : G_E \rightarrow G_V$, assigning to each edge $e \in G_E$ a source $s(e) \in G_V$ and target $t(e) \in G_V$. A graph morphism $f : G_1 \rightarrow G_2$ between two graphs $G_i = (G_{i,V}, G_{i,E}, s_i, t_i)$, $(i = 1, 2)$ is a pair $f = (f_V : G_{V,1} \rightarrow G_{V,2}, f_E : G_{E,1} \rightarrow G_{E,2})$ of total mappings, such that $f_V \circ s_1 = s_2 \circ f_E$ and $f_V \circ t_1 = t_2 \circ f_E$.*

Graph morphisms may satisfy different useful properties. A graph morphism that does not map two nodes or two edges to the same node or edge, respectively, satisfies the so-called *injectivity* property. A graph morphism defining a preimage for each node and edge of the target graph satisfies the *surjectivity* property. Two graph morphisms having the same target graph defining for each node and edge of the target graph a preimage in at least one of both source graphs are called *jointly surjective*. In this case, we also say that the target graph is an *overlapping* of both source graphs. A graph morphism being both injective and surjective is also called a *graph isomorphism*. It uniquely maps all nodes and edges of source and target graphs to each other. Consequently, trivially speaking, isomorphic graphs are copies of each other, whereas an injective graph morphism finds a copy of the source graph somewhere in the target graph.

Definition 2 (injective, (jointly) surjective morphisms, graph isomorphism). *A graph morphism* $m : G_1 \to G_2$ *is* injective (resp. surjective) *if* m_V *and* m_E *are injective (resp. surjective) mappings. Two graph morphisms* $m_1 :$ $L_1 \to G$ *and* $m_2 : L_2 \to G$ *are jointly surjective if* $m_{1,V}(L_{1,V}) \cup m_{2,V}(L_{2,V}) =$ G_V *and* $m_{1,E}(L_{1,E}) \cup m_{2,E}(L_{2,E}) = G_E$. *A pair of jointly surjective morphisms* (m_1, m_2) *is also called an* overlapping *of* L_1 *and* L_2. *A graph morphism* m *which is injective and surjective is called a* graph isomorphism. *Two graphs* G_1 *and* G_2 *are* isomorphic *if there exists a graph isomorphism* $m : G_1 \to G_2$.

Definition 3 (typed graph). *A* type graph *is a distinguished graph* $TG =$ $(V_{TG}, E_{TG}, s_{TG}, t_{TG})$. V_{TG} *and* E_{TG} *are called the vertex and the edge type alphabets, respectively. A tuple* $(G, type)$ *of a graph* G *together with a graph morphism* $type : G \to TG$ *is a* graph typed over TG *or* instance graph *of* TG.

Example 4 (RailCab - Typed Graph). Fig. 3 depicts a graph G typed over the type graph TG via the typing morphism $type : G \to TG$. G consists of a set of nodes $G_V =$ $\{s_1, t_1, t_2, t_3\}$ and a set of edges $G_E = \{o_1, n_1, n_2\}$. The source and target mappings s_G and t_G map these edges to the respective source and target nodes as depicted. For example, $s_G(n_1) = t_1$ and $t_G(n_1) = t_2$. The typing morphism $type : G \to TG$ is visualized using dashed arrows. Analogously, TG consists of a set of nodes $TG_V =$ $\{Shuttle, Track\}$ and a set of edges $TG_E = \{on, next\}$ where s_{TG} and t_{TG} map these edges to the respective source and target nodes as depicted. In particular, type is a graph morphism since it is structure-preserving. This means, for example, for edge o_1 that $s_{TG}(type_E(o_1)) = Shuttle = type_V(s_G(o_1))$. Note that this typing morphism type is surjective, since each node and edge in TG has a preimage in G. However type is not injective, since, for example, the nodes t_1, t_2 and t_3 are mapped to the same node Track. Fig. 4 depicts a short-hand notation for a typed graph that we will use in the rest of the paper. The typing morphism between graph and type graph is not explicitly depicted anymore. Instead, each node and edge name is followed by ":" and then the type name of the node type or edge type, the typing morphism assigns the node or edge to.

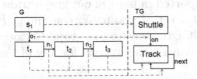

Fig. 3. Typed Graph   **Fig. 4.** Typed Graph (shorthand notation)

Typed graph morphisms formalize the concept of structure-preserving mappings compatible with typing. Therefore, they are a formal means to ensure type correctness later on when performing graph transformations.

Definition 4 (typed graph morphism). *Consider typed graphs* $G_1^T = (G_1,$ $type_1)$ *and* $G_2^T = (G_2, type_2)$, *a typed graph morphism* $f : G_1^T \to G_2^T$ *is a graph morphism* $f : G_1 \to G_2$ *such that* $type_2 \circ f = type_1$.

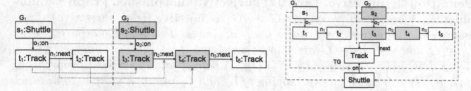

Fig. 5. The example graph morphism f **Fig. 6.** Type-compatibility of f

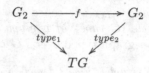

Example 5 (RailCab - Typed Graph Morphism). Fig. 5 depicts an injective typed graph morphism f from $(G_1, type_1)$ to $(G_2, type_2)$. The pointed edges visualize f. Note that the graph morphism f is indeed type-compatible because each node or edge of a specific type is mapped to a node or edge of the same type, respectively. Fig. 6 depicts an extract of the same morphism f and an extract of the typing morphisms $type_1$ and $type_2$ illustrating more formally that according to Def. 4 $type_2 \circ f = type_1$.

Assumption: For the rest of this paper we work with typed graphs and morphisms, although not always explicitly mentioned. This means also that we denote a typed graph $(G, type)$ also simply as G. Moreover, if the edge mapping of graph morphisms is clear from the respective source and target node mappings, then we do not always visualize them completely in the corresponding figures.

Graph Patterns and Graph Properties. Graph patterns describe sample graphs for which matches may exist for given instance graphs. We present a simple pattern concept, which is used and supported in most of our graph transformation tools. It consists of a graph P and a set of graphs N_i containing P (with identical typing). We say that a match for this pattern in graph G exists if a copy of P can be found in G, but at the same time no copy for any of the graphs N_i can be found in G.

Definition 5 (graph pattern). *A graph pattern $\Pi = (P, \{N_i, i \in I\})$ consists of a graph P and a finite set of graphs N_i containing P as a subgraph. As shorthand notation for the graph pattern $(P, \emptyset)$ we simply write P.*

Definition 6 (match). *Given a graph pattern $\Pi = (P, \{N_i, i \in I\})$ and a graph G, then each injective morphism $m : P \to G$ such that there does not exist an injective morphism $q : N_i \to G$ with q being identical to m on P, is called a match of the graph pattern Π in G.*

To visualize N_i we use crossed out dashed boxes and edges. We draw a dashed box around all nodes of $N_i \setminus P$. Also all edges which source and target nodes

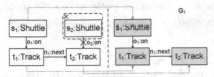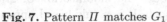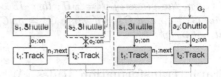

Fig. 7. Pattern Π matches G_1 **Fig. 8.** Pattern Π does not match G_2

are in $N_i \setminus P$ are contained in the box. All edges connecting P and $N \setminus P$ are not contained in the box and in addition crossed out. In the special case that N_i equals a single edge, it is also only crossed out.

Example 6 (RailCab - Graph Pattern). Fig. 7 depicts the pattern $\Pi = (P, \{N\})$. The graph P consists of the nodes s_1, t_1, t_2 and edges o_1, n_1. The graph N consists of P together with the crossed out node s_2 and edge o_2. There exists a match m for Π in G_1, since an injective graph morphism (visualized by pointed lines) exists between P and G_1 and no injective graph morphism exists between N and G_1, since a second node of type Shuttle is not available.

Fig. 8 depicts the same pattern $\Pi = (P, \{N\})$, but a different graph G_2 such that no match exists for Π in G_2. There exists one injective graph morphism from P to G_2, but this graph morphism can be completed to an injective graph morphism from N to G_2, which is not allowed according to Def. 6.

We use graph patterns as basic constructs to define graph properties (also called graph constraints or graph conditions [32,33]). As explained in [32] graph properties may reach the expressiveness of first-order logic, which is not the case here, since we have a more restricted property language.

Definition 7 (graph property, forbidden and required pattern). *A graph pattern $\Pi = (P, \{N_i, i \in I\})$ is a graph property, any combination of two graph properties p and q of the form $p \wedge q$, $p \vee q$, and $\neg q$ is also a graph property. We define satisfaction of graph properties p by a graph G (written $G \models p$), recursively, as follows:*

- *If $p = \Pi$ with $\Pi = (P, \{N_i, i \in I\})$ a graph pattern, then p is satisfied if there exists a match for the graph pattern Π in G,*
- *if $p = p_1 \wedge p_2$, then p is satisfied if $G \models p_1$ and $G \models p_2$,*
- *if $p = p_1 \vee p_2$, then p is satisfied if $G \models p_1$ or $G \models p_2$,*
- *if $p = \neg p_1$, then p is satisfied if $G \not\models p_1$.*

Given a graph property $p = \Pi = (P, \{N_i, i \in I\})$ we say that Π occurs as a required *graph pattern. For a graph property $p = \neg\Pi = \neg(P, \{N_i, i \in I\})$ we further say that Π occurs as a* forbidden *graph pattern.*

Example 7 (RailCab - Graph Properties). Given the property $p = \Pi = (P, \{N\})$ with Π the pattern depicted in Fig. 7, then this pattern occurs as a required graph pattern. $G_1 \models p$ since there exists a match for the required graph pattern Π in G. In Fig. 8, a graph G_2 is depicted which does not satisfy p since a match for the required graph pattern Π does not exist.

Given the property $p' = \neg \Pi$, then Π occurs as a forbidden pattern and $G_1 \not\models p'$ since $G_1 \models p$ and $G_2 \models p'$ since $G_2 \not\models p$. Consequently, G_1 and G_2 both satisfy $p \vee p'$, but not $p \wedge p'$.

Graph Transformation Rules. We can model the modification of graphs by introducing the *graph transformation* approach. It is a rule-based approach, meaning that the way in which a graph can potentially be modified is described by a set of graph transformation rules. By applying these rules to a particular graph, this graph can be transformed. We present a compact, set-theoretical description of graph transformation here and refer to [34,35] for a more comprehensive description with category-theoretical background.

We start with defining the notion of *graph transformation rules*. A rule $r :$ $\langle \Pi_{LHS}, \Pi_{RHS} \rangle$ consists of a left-hand side (LHS) pattern Π_{LHS} describing the pre-condition, and a right-hand side (RHS) pattern Π_{RHS} describing the post-condition of the rule. In simple rules, the patterns Π_{LHS} and Π_{RHS} are just graphs, L and R, denoting required patterns before and after rule application, respectively. As a consequence, before applying the rule to a graph G, at least L should be present in G, which is replaced by R via the rule's application. In particular, the graph part $L \setminus (L \cap R)$ is to be deleted, and the graph part $R \setminus (L \cap R)$ is to be created when applying the rule. Finally, $L \cap R$ describes which part is to be preserved, when applying the rule. Note that the *graph intersection* $L \cap R$ should form a *well-defined* typed graph again. To this extent the source and target mappings in L and R must be identical on edges belonging to $L \cap R$ such that source and target mappings for $L \cap R$ can be inherited from L and R. Moreover, the type mappings for L and R must be identical on nodes and edges in $L \cap R$ such that the type mapping in $L \cap R$ can be inherited from L and R. The LHS pattern of a rule Π_{LHS} can be also a pattern of the form $(L, \{N_i, i \in I\})$ instead of the simple pattern L. Thus the pattern $(L, \{N_i, i \in I\})$ instead of L is required before rule application. In this context, we say that N_i are the *negative application conditions* (NACs) of the rule r, since the rule can only be applied if a copy of L, but no copies of N_i can be found before rule application.

Definition 8 (rule). *A graph transformation rule $r :$ $\langle \Pi_{LHS}, \Pi_{RHS} \rangle$ consists of a rule name r and two patterns $\Pi_{LHS} = (L, \{N_i, i \in I\})$ and $\Pi_{RHS} = R$ with L and R graphs such that the intersection $L \cap R$ of L and R is well-defined. The patterns Π_{LHS} and Π_{RHS} are called the left-hand side (LHS), and the right-hand side (RHS) of r, respectively. We say that $del(r) = L \setminus (L \cap R)$ is the graph part to be deleted and $cre(r) = R \setminus (L \cap R)$ is the graph part to be created by the rule r.*

There are two main *different ways to define rule application* of a rule r to a graph G as soon as a match for the LHS pattern of r in G has been found. One of both rule application approaches can be chosen to perform graph transformation depending on if implicit side-effects are desired or not.

The first main approach *accepts implicit side-effects* such as the deletion of dangling edges. It deletes dangling edges during rule application although this is not explicitly specified within the rule. This approach has been called the single-pushout (SPO) approach for historical reasons. In particular, a rule application (also called direct graph transformation or graph transformation step) can be formalized in a categorical way by a so-called pushout – a categorical concept generalizing the idea of graph gluing constructions – in the category of graphs with partial graph morphisms [34]. Here we reintroduce this rule application approach in a constructive, set-theoretical way and propose to call it the *dangling-edge-collecting approach*.

The second main approach does not put up with implicit side-effects. It simply does not apply a rule – even if a match has been found – if it is not possible to apply the rule without the implicit side-effects that dangling edges are removed. This is ensured by the fact that a match in this approach needs to satisfy in addition the so-called *dangling edge condition* – expressing that nodes marked for deletion by the rule are matched in such a way that all incident edges are marked for deletion by the rule as well. Like this no dangling edges arise during rule application. This more conservative approach to rule application has been called the double-pushout (DPO) approach for historical reasons. In particular, a rule application can be described formally in a categorical way by a construction consisting of two pushouts in the category of graphs with total graph morphisms [35].[3] Here we reintroduce this rule application approach in a constructive, set-theoretical way and propose to call it the *conservative approach* since no implicit side-effect during rule application is allowed.[4]

Definition 9 (dangling edges, dangling edge condition). *Given a rule* $r : \langle \Pi_{LHS}, \Pi_{RHS} \rangle$ *and match* $g : L \to G$ *for the pattern* $\Pi_{LHS} = (L, \{N_i, i \in I\})$ *in* G, *then* $dan(g, r) = \{e | e \in G_E, s(e) \vee t(e) \in g(del(r)), e \notin g(del(r))\}$ *is the* set of dangling edges *in* G *for match* g *and rule* r. *The match* g *fulfills the* dangling edge condition *for rule* r *if* $dan(g, r)$ *is empty.*

Definition 10 (rule applicability). *A rule* $r : \langle \Pi_{LHS}, \Pi_{RHS} \rangle$ *with* $\Pi_{LHS} = (L, \{N_i, i \in I\})$ *and* $\Pi_{RHS} = R$ *is* applicable *to a graph* G *in the* conservative approach *if there exists a match* $g : L \to G$ *for* $(L, \{N_i, i \in I\})$ *in* G *fulfilling the dangling edge condition.*

A rule $r : \langle \Pi_{LHS}, \Pi_{RHS} \rangle$ *with* $\Pi_{LHS} = (L, \{N_i, i \in I\})$ *and* $\Pi_{RHS} = R$ *is* applicable *to a graph* G *in the* dangling-edge-collecting approach *if there exists a match* $g : L \to G$ *for* $(L, \{N_i, i \in I\})$ *in* G.

After having found a match g for the LHS rule pattern of rule r in graph G making the rule applicable, we can define a rule application via rule r to G by

---

[3] The left pushout of a rule application describes the deletion of graph parts, and the right pushout describes the addition of graph parts, marked accordingly by the corresponding rule.

[4] Note that a match of a LHS rule pattern does not have to be, in general, an injective graph morphism. In some application fields, it makes sense to allow non-injective graph morphisms as matches. In this case however, rule application becomes more difficult because a conflict arises when a match maps two graph elements in L, one marked for deletion and the other one marked for creation by the rule, to the same element in G.

a two-step construction such that in the application result the RHS rule pattern is fulfilled: First, the elements in $del(r)$ are deleted from G together with the implicit deletion of possible dangling edges $dan(g, r)$ obtaining an intermediate result D. Secondly, a copy of the RHS pattern graph R is unified with D such that exactly the elements in $cre(r)$ are indeed created. Thereby nodes and edges in $L \cap R$ to be preserved are glued with the already corresponding elements in D matched via g. Therefore this construction is often also called gluing construction.

Definition 11 (rule application). *A rule application $G \overset{r,g}{\Rightarrow} H$ from G to H via an applicable rule $r : \langle \Pi_{LHS}, \Pi_{RHS} \rangle$ with $\Pi_{LHS} = (L, \{N_i, i \in I\})$ and $\Pi_{RHS} = R$ and match $g : L \to G$ is constructed as follows:*

1. *$D = G \setminus (g(del(r)) \cup dan(g, r))$ (delete nodes and edges to be deleted together with possible dangling edges)*
2. *$H = D \cup i(R)$ with $i : R \to i(R)$ a graph isomorphism identical to g on elements of $L \cap R$ and disjoint with D on elements in $cre(r)$ (create nodes and edges to be created).*

Each graph H' isomorphic to H is a valid result of this rule application too.

Note that a rule which is only applicable in the conservative approach will be applied without implicit side-effects, since in this case the set of dangling edges is empty because each match fulfills the dangling edge condition. Moreover, note that because of the fact that dangling edges are deleted, D is a well-defined graph again since source and target mappings can be inherited from G. The application result H is a graph again as well, since source and target mappings in D or $i(R)$ are identical on edges belonging to $D \cap i(R)$. This is because the graph morphisms g and i are identical on $L \cap R$.

We omit r and/or g in $G \overset{r,g}{\Rightarrow} H$ if not relevant. As a last remark, note that the typing of H can be inherited from the typing of elements stemming from G (i.e. being left in D) and the typing of created elements in rule r because of type compatibility of g,i and rule r. This means that by construction rule application ensures *type correctness*.

Example 8 (RailCab - Graph Transformation Rule and Rule Application). Fig. 9 depicts the application of rule r_1 to a graph G_1. It is a simple rule, since the LHS pattern consists of a single graph L. Rule r_1 is applicable in the conservative as well as the dangling-edge-collecting approach, since a match $g : L \to G_1$ can be found, depicted with pointed lines. The rule can be applied in the conservative as well as in the dangling-edge-collecting approach, since the depicted match fulfills the dangling edge condition. In particular, this holds already because no node is deleted. The result of the rule application is therefore the same in both approaches. First, $g(del(r_1))$ consisting of o_3 as image of o_1 in G_1 is deleted from G_1 leading to a graph D. A copy of the RHS graph is then unified in a suitable way with D. This means that the elements s_1, t_1, t_2, n_1 in $L \cap R$ are mapped by an isomorphism i identical to g inducing the gluing of $i(R)$ with D in the elements s_2, t_3, t_4, n_2. Moreover, a copy $o_4 = i(o_2)$ of o_2, belonging to

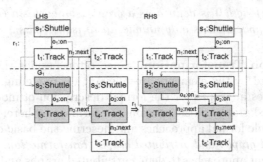

Fig. 9. SimpleMove rule and its application

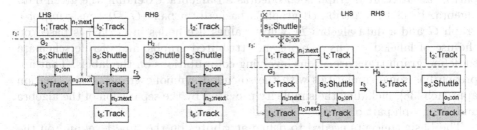

Fig. 10. DeleteTrack rule and its applica- **Fig. 11.** Corrected DeleteTrack rule and its
tion with unwanted dangling edge deletion   proper application

$cre(r_1)$ *is indeed created, since it is added disjointly to* D^5 *and glued with source node* $i(s_1) = g(s_1) = s_2$ *and target node* $i(t_2) = g(t_2) = t_4$.

Fig. 10 depicts the application of the DeleteTrack *rule to a graph G. The rule can only be applied in the dangling-edge-collecting approach, since the depicted match* $g : L \to G_2$ *does not fulfill the dangling edge condition. This is because* $dan(g, r_2) = \{o_2\}$, *since* o_2 *is an edge which is not matched by g, but its target node* t_3 *is matched by g and identified as a node to be deleted. When applying this rule in the dangling-edge-collecting approach, this means that* o_2 *is implicitly deleted together with* t_3 *and* n_2. *This has as a consequence that the node* s_2 *of type* Shuttle *would not be on a track anymore and thus decoupled of the modeled track system. Forbidding the deletion of a* Track *if some* Shuttle *is still* on *a track would make more sense. To this extent, it is possible to add a negative application condition to the LHS rule pattern expressing that it can be applied only if no* Shuttle *is on the* Track. *In this case, only edges of type* next *are implicitly deleted during rule application as can be seen in Fig. 11.*

Besides a single application we are also interested in the effect of multiple rule applications. Therefore, we define graph transformation as the reflexive and transitive closure of separate rule applications.

Definition 12 (Graph Transformation). *A graph transformation, denoted as* $G_0 \overset{*}{\Rightarrow} G_n$, *is a sequence* $G_0 \Rightarrow G_1 \Rightarrow \cdots \Rightarrow G_n$ *of* $n \geq 0$ *rule applications. A*

---

[5] Since another edge called o_2 is present in D, this renaming via $i(o_2) = o_4$ is indeed necessary in this example.

rule application of length 0 *is defined as a graph isomorphism* $G_0 \cong G_0'$ *because the result of rule application is only unique up to isomorphism.*

Attributed Graph Transformation. Since often besides the structure also attributes contained by the elements are relevant for modeling, we need a way to include attributes in graphs for the formal description of models. We do not introduce attributed graph transformation in a formal way here, but give a short overview on available formal approaches and describe the basic concepts needed to define *attributed graphs and attributed graph transformation.*

There are different approaches to define attributed graphs and graph transformation. In [36] attributed graphs are seen as algebras. In particular, the graph part of an attributed graph is encoded as an algebra, extending the given data algebra. In [35] an attributed graph is basically a pair (G, D) consisting of a graph G and a data algebra D, whose values are nodes in G. [37] is based on the use of labeled graphs to represent attributed graphs, and of rule schemata to define graph transformations involving computations on the labels. That approach has some similarities with the so-called symbolic graph transformation approach [38], including the simplicity provided by the separation of the algebra and the graph part of attributed graphs.

The basic concepts needed to define attributes on the type level and on the instance level are described as follows. For each node type (sometimes also edge types) in the type graph TG a *number of attributes* of a certain data type is defined leading to an *attributed type graph ATG.* Each node (or edge) in a graph on the instance level may have the same number of *attributes.* These have *attribute assignments* mapping each attribute to a concrete value of a data type compatible with the attribute definition of the corresponding node type (or edge type) in the attributed type graph ATG. Each graph in a graph pattern may be equipped with an *attribute condition Φ* over attribute labels in this graph constraining the range of possible values for these attributes when matching the pattern to some instance graph. Moreover, attribute assignment mappings in L of a LHS rule pattern may define assignments to variables that are reused within a computation instruction in an attribute assignment mapping for some attribute a of the RHS rule pattern. Matching the LHS pattern leads to a concrete value assignment of such a variable (respecting the attribute conditions) and this value is reused to compute the attribute value of a according to the computation instruction.[6] The attribute condition and assignment mappings need to be compatible with the data types defined in the attributed type graph for each attribute.

Graph Transformation with Inheritance. Another concept often used in modeling is inheritance that leads to generalization upwards in the inheritance relation and specialization downwards leading to attributed graphs and attributed

---

[6] In [38], assignments and attribute conditions in rule patterns are summarized into one attribute formula over the attribute labels in both rule patterns that needs to evaluate to true during rule application.

graph transformations *with inheritance* [39,35,40]. Again, we do not introduce this formally here, but give a short informal idea of the basic concepts needed to define attributed graphs and attributed graph transformation with inheritance.

The concept of generalization, specialization and inheritance can be described in a type graph TG by introducing an *inheritance relation* between nodes in the type graph, visualized by special edges from each type node to its super type node, which we label with is_a, and marking specific type nodes as abstract. Patterns typed over such a type graph with inheritance $ATGI$ consist of graphs that may use these abstract nodes. Moreover, source and target mappings are compatible with the inheritance relation. The created elements in the RHS pattern of a rule should not be abstract because when a rule is applied it should be clear which type of node is to be created on the instance level. Now there are two possibilities to define attributed graph transformation with inheritance according to such a type graph with inheritance $ATGI$ and rules and patterns typed as described briefly above over $ATGI$. (1) The type graph with inheritance $ATGI$ is flattened in a suitable way to an equivalent type graph TG without inheritance relation and abstract nodes. Moreover, the rules and patterns typed over $ATGI$ as described briefly above are *flattened* to an equivalent set of rules and patterns typed over TG. Using these flattened rules and patterns regular typed attributed graph transformation can be applied. (2) The *match notion* for patterns is *extended* to patterns typed over $ATGI$ such that the derived notions of rule application and property satisfaction are equivalent to flattened regular rule application or property satisfaction.

For analysis we usually apply variant (1) and work with flattened properties and rules, since most analysis techniques do not explicitly deal with inheritance yet. For rule application and graph property checking at runtime we usually apply the more efficient variant (2).

Graph Transformation with Priorities. Non-determinism due to several applicable rules can be explicitly reduced by *priorities* over these rules. Given a rule set $\mathcal{R}$ with priorities specified by a function prio : $\mathcal{R} \to \mathbb{N}$ assigning priorities to the rules in $\mathcal{R}$, the notion of rule applicability of Def. 10 defined for a separate rule becomes more severe and has to be defined relative to the complete rule set. We say that the rule is *applicable with priority* if for two rules $r, r' \in \mathcal{R}$ that are both applicable to the same graph if considered separately holds that if they have different priorities only the rule with the highest priority is applicable. Thus applicability with priority requires besides a match and the dangling edge condition in case of the conservative approach also that no rule with a higher priority is applicable as a separate rule. Given a set of rules $\mathcal{R}$ with priority function prio, we write $G \overset{r,g}{\Rightarrow}_{\mathcal{R},\text{prio}} G'$ if for rule $r \in \mathcal{R}$ a match g for G exists, r is applicable with priority, and $G \overset{r,g}{\Rightarrow} G'$. For the reflexive and transitive closure we write $\overset{*}{\Rightarrow}_{\mathcal{R},\text{prio}}$.

Assumption: For the rest of this paper we work with attributed typed graphs with inheritance and rules with priorities where necessary, although not explicitly mentioning it each time. Consequently, we sometimes write $G \stackrel{r,g}{\Rightarrow}_\mathcal{R} G'$ instead of $G \stackrel{r,g}{\Rightarrow}_{\mathcal{R},\text{prio}} G'$ and $\stackrel{*}{\Rightarrow}_\mathcal{R}$ instead of $\stackrel{*}{\Rightarrow}_{\mathcal{R},\text{prio}}$.

*Example 9 (RailCab - Attributes, Inheritance & Priorities). As depicted in Fig. 12 we may equip the type graph of our running example with an attribute **energy** of data type **Int** for the node type **Shuttle**. Moreover we can make the node type **Shuttle** abstract and insert two subtypes **RailCab** and CargoShuttle into the inheritance relation, respectively. An assignment in an attributed instance graph as depicted in Fig. 2 defines a concrete integer value for the attribute **energy** in nodes of node type **RailCab** or **CargoShuttle**. The type graph with inheritance in Fig. 12 can be flattened into a regular type graph as depicted on the right in Fig. 12.*

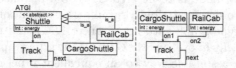

Fig. 12. Attributed Type Graph with Inheritance and Flattening

Fig. 13 depicts a graph pattern with inheritance P_I that can be flattened into four patterns without inheritance on the right. Note that the patterns P_1 and P_2 are isomorphic, so it is sufficient to keep one of these patterns after flattening.

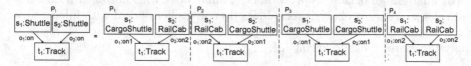

Fig. 13. A graph pattern and the related flattened graph patterns

*Now our running example rule, moving a **Shuttle** from one **Track** to another (see Fig. 9), can be flattened to two different rules by flattening the corresponding LHS and RHS rule patterns. In Fig. 14, the first rule is depicted and we have added an operation on the previously introduced attribute **energy**. The attribute value of the attribute **energy** is constrained such that in the instance graph to which the pattern can be matched to, a value bigger than or equal to 2 should appear. After rule application this attribute value is diminished by 2. In Fig. 15, a similar rule is depicted modeling the movement of a **Railcab** which is less expensive in the sense that the attribute value of **energy** is diminished only by 1, when moving the **Railcab** from one **Track** to another **Track**.*

*In the example so far we do not need priorities. However, let us assume that the rule of Fig. 15 refers to the general case of a **Shuttle** rather than a **RailCab** and thus defines that all shuttles by default require one energy point to move along one **Track**. Then, the rules of Fig. 14 and Fig. 15 could both be applied for **CargoShuttles** with **energy** attribute value higher than 1. To ensure that in case of a **CargoShuttle** always only the more specific rule of Fig. 14 and not the generic one of Fig. 15 is applied, we can then assign the former rule of Fig. 14 a higher priority.*

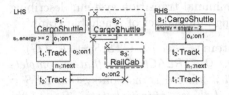

Fig. 14. MoveCargoShuttle rule with attribute condition and side effect

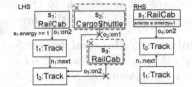

Fig. 15. MoveRailCab rule with attribute condition and side effect

Graph Transformation Systems. A dynamic system can be specified by a so-called graph transformation system. It consists of a set of graph transformation rules describing the dynamics in the system. Each system state is described by a graph and state transitions correspond to rule applications. Initial states of a dynamic system can be described by an initial graph or a set of initial graphs.

Definition 13 (graph transformation system). *A graph transformation system (GTS) $S = (\mathcal{R}, TG)$ consists of a set of rules $\mathcal{R}$ typed over a type graph TG. A graph transformation system may be equipped with an initial graph G_0 or a set of initial graphs I being graphs typed over TG.*

Note that the definition is analogous whatever type of type graph with inheritance and attributes or without is employed. Also, the rule set $\mathcal{R}$ may support priorities, which we do not always explicitly mention as described in the previous assumption.

The set of reachable graphs of a graph transformation system models the set of reachable states of a dynamic system from its initial states. A graph is reachable if a graph transformation via the system rules exists from some initial graph, describing some initial system state, to this graph. Since often in praxis it does not make sense to distinguish isomorphic graphs, we also define a minimal set of reachable graphs, where exactly one representative of the isomorphism class of each reachable graph is contained.

Definition 14 (set of reachable graphs). *For a GTS $S = (\mathcal{R}, TG)$ and a set of initial graphs I the set of reachable graphs $REACH(S, I)$ is defined as $\{G | G_0 \overset{*}{\Rightarrow}_{\mathcal{R}} G, G_0 \in I\}$ consisting of all graphs G such that there exists a graph transformation via rules in $\mathcal{R}$ from some initial graph G_0 to G of arbitrary length. We say that $\mathcal{G} \subseteq REACH(S, I)$ is a complete set of reachable graphs up to isomorphism for a GTS S and I if it contains at least one representative graph of each isomorphism class of graphs in $REACH(S, I)$ and that it is a minimal set of reachable graphs up to isomorphism if it contains exactly one representative graph of each isomorphism class of graphs in $REACH(S, I)$.*

Often, it is not only desired to analyze which system states can be reached, but also how they can be reached. The transition system generated by a graph transformation system and its initial graphs therefore describes the state space of a dynamic system. If a distinction between isomorphic graphs (or states) is not desired, then it is possible to consider a minimal transition system, describing rule applications between the corresponding minimal set of reachable graphs.

Definition 15 (labeled transition system). *Given a GTS $S = (\mathcal{R}, TG)$, a set of initial graphs I, and a set of graphs $\mathcal{G} \subseteq REACH(S, I)$ that is complete up to isomorphism for S and I, the implied labeled transition system $LTS = (\mathcal{G}, I, \mathcal{R} \times \mathcal{M}, \Rightarrow_{\mathcal{R}})$ with $\mathcal{G}$ the set of states, I the set of initial states, $\mathcal{R} \times \mathcal{M}$ the label alphabet with $\mathcal{M}$ the set of injective morphisms, and $\Rightarrow_{\mathcal{R}} \subseteq \mathcal{G} \times (\mathcal{R} \times \mathcal{M}) \times \mathcal{G}$ the transition relation defined as $\{(G, (r, g), H) | G, H \in \mathcal{G} \wedge \exists H' \in REACH(S, I) : G \overset{r,g}{\Rightarrow}_{\mathcal{R}} H' \wedge H' \cong H\}$. LTS is minimal if its set of states $\mathcal{G}$ is a minimal set of reachable graphs up to isomorphism for the GTS S with initial graphs I.*

Example 10 (RailCab - GTS). The rules depicted in Fig. 14 and Fig. 15 typed over the flattened type graph ATG as depicted in Fig. 12 constitute a GTS modeling the structural dynamics and energy consumption of the shuttle system. Given also the attributed graph in Fig. 2 as initial graph, we can consider the corresponding set of reachable graphs and the corresponding transition system. They will have a finite minimal set of reachable graphs and minimal transition system, respectively. Since Shuttle movement goes along with diminishing the energy attribute values of s_1 and s_2, this leads to a terminating system. Moreover, each reachable graph satisfies the property $p = \neg P_i$ with P_i one of the graph patterns depicted in Fig. 13. This property can be checked statically with the invariant checker as explained in Section 4.2 or dynamically by analyzing the state transition system via model checking as explained in Section 4.3.

Graph Grammars. A modeling language L, where the abstract syntax of models is described by graphs, can be specified in a constructive way by an attributed graph grammar. A graph grammar consists of a set of creating[7] attributed graph transformation rules and an attributed start graph. The graph transformation rules describe how valid instances of the modeling language at the level of the abstract syntax can be generated.

Definition 16 (graph grammar, graph language). *A graph grammar (GG) $GR = (\mathcal{P}, S, TG)$ consists of a set of non-deleting rules $\mathcal{P}$ and a start graph S typed over TG. The graph language $\mathcal{L}(GR)$ is defined as $\{G | S \overset{*}{\Rightarrow} G\}$ consisting of all graphs G such that there exists a graph transformation from S to G of arbitrary length.*

Example 11 (SDL - Graph Grammar). As an example for a simple graph grammar we consider the generation of all valid SDL block diagrams. At first, we have to define a related type graph. In this case, we make use of generalization and assume a GTS formalism that is able to cope with it. In Fig. 16, the related type graph with generalization can be seen. Note that flattening the type graph would require adding the name attribute to all nodes that are a specialization of type Element as well as the addition of related edge types for all specializations of Connectable. The start graph and rules (productions)

---

[7] Note that in graph transformation standard literature the rules of a graph grammar are in general not required to be creating or are not restricted to generate a language, but we restrict them here accordingly to be consistent with more widely used notion of grammars.

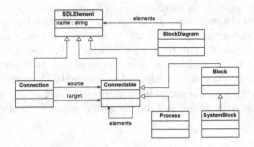

Fig. 16. Type graph for SDL instance graphs

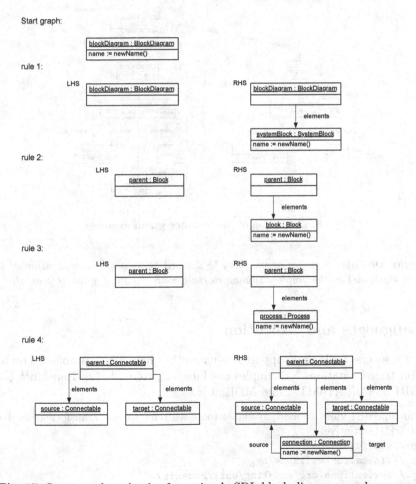

Fig. 17. Start graph and rules for a simple SDL block diagram graph grammar

of the grammar are described in Fig. 17. The start graph creates a BlockDiagram with a new and unique name (described by newName()). The first rule creates a SystemBlock as an element of a BlockDiagram node to which also a new and unique name is assigned. A Block as an element of a Block node to which also a new and unique name is assigned is created by rule 2. The third rule creates a Process as an element of a Block node to which also a new and unique name is assigned. In contrast to a process, the blocks created by rule 2 may have contained connectable elements. Finally, rule 4 describes that between any two Connectable elements that are contained by the same Connectable a Connection with a new and unique name might be created. An example

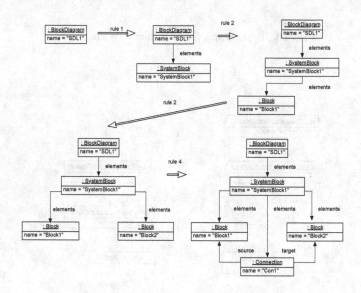

Fig. 18. Derivation of the instance graph example

of how the particular instance graph may be derived by subsequent application of the rules (productions) of the graph grammar starting with the start graph is presented in Fig. 18.

3   Languages and Execution

There are several tools that support languages that have been established on top of graph transformations.[8] Examples are Fujaba[9], AGG[10] [42], Henshin[11] [43], PROGRESS [44], AToM3[12], and MDElab[13].

---

[8] For an updated view on more available tools we refer to the Transformation Tool Contest[41] initiative.

[9] http://www.fujaba.de

[10] http://tfs.cs.tu-berlin.de/agg

[11] http://www.eclipse.org/modeling/emft/henshin/

[12] http://atom3.cs.mcgill.ca/

[13] http://www.mdelab.org

We will in the paper and this section in particular look on the languages supported by MDElab. We will focus on the direct integration of meta-models resp. class diagrams as type graphs presented in Section 3.1, Story Pattern outlined in Section 3.2, Triple Graph Grammars introduced in Section 3.3, and a Runtime Model Framework introduced in Section 3.4. Additionally concepts supported by MDElab omitted for space reasons are Story Diagrams [45] that extend Story Patterns with control flow constructs and Mega Models for model management and traceability in scenarios with multiple models [46].

3.1   Type and Instance Graphs

In the last section we could already observe that type graphs and instance graphs seem quite similar to class diagrams and object diagrams. Another similarity to meta-models and models also became apparent. We will in the following study both relation in more detail using two concrete examples.

Modeling: Structure with Class Diagrams and Object Diagrams. Concerning the similarity between type graphs and instance graphs on the one hand and class diagrams and object diagrams on the other hand holds that node types and their defined attributes relate directly to class definitions and their attributes. Furthermore, simple associations relate to edge types. Undirected associations have to be mapped to directed edges. Thus, the core concepts of class diagrams can be directly mapped. Some other concepts such as association attributes, cardinality constraints, or OCL constraints have to be mapped to additional node types that do not represent classes and sufficiently expressive graph property specification techniques. Analogously, an object diagram is related to an instance graph. It is to be noted that here less differences exist. The common case of binary links can be represented directly in an instance graph and only non binary links require a indirect encoding. An example for such a mapping only for the class diagram is explained in the following Example 12.

Example 12 (RailCab - Class Diagram). A class diagram used for modeling the collision avoidance for the RailCab Example 1 is shown in Fig. 19(a). The class diagram defines the classes Shuttle, Track and DistanceCoordinationPattern which are connected through associations. A Track may have one successor Track, the annotation "0 . . . 1" expresses the multiplicity of the successor association. A Shuttle is always located at exactly one Track (association one) and can mark further Tracks through the associations next and go. A Track is marked through the go association if the Shuttle is about to go to this Track, the next association models the Shuttle's intent for the following move operation. To avoid collisions, Shuttles can instantiate a DistanceCoordinationPattern collaboration between them. The DistanceCoordinationPattern collaboration employs two roles front and rear which are both modeled through associations.

The similarity to the corresponding type graph can be seen in Figure 19(b), which only differs from Figure 19(a) in the absence of the cardinality constraints, which have to be specified by appropriate graph properties (cf. Definition 7), and undirected associations that are mapped to directed edge types.

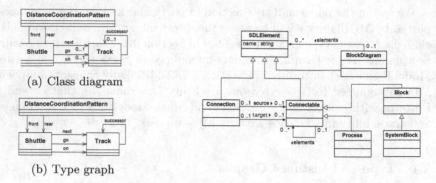

(a) Class diagram

(b) Type graph

Fig. 19. Class diagram and type graph for the collision avoidance model

Fig. 20. A simplified meta-model for SDL block diagrams

Due to the explained mapping of class diagrams on type graphs and object diagrams on graphs, we have a sound foundation and semantics based on typed graphs with attributes and inheritance. This will be exploited later when the complete model of the RailCab example that besides the class diagram also includes a number of Story Patterns and simple graph properties are analyzed in Section 4.2 and 4.3 .

MDE: Meta-Model and Model. The relation observed for the class diagrams and object diagrams also holds for type graphs and instance graphs on the one hand and meta-models and models on the other hand. Node types and their defined attributes relate directly to class definitions in the meta-model and their attributes. We also explain the mapping by the following Example 13. For the syntax we use in the following as usual the notation of UML class diagrams to depict EMF meta-models.

Example 13 (SDL - Meta-Model). The simplified meta-model used in the following for our consideration of the Example 2 is depicted in Fig. 20. It introduces the main concepts Connection and Connectable that are linked via the associations source and target. Furthermore, the concept Connectable can be refined to be a Process or Block, where a Block can be further be refined to be a SystemBlock. The grammar of Example 11 defines in addition that SystemBlocks may only contain Blocks, Blocks may only contain Blocks or Processes and that Processes cannot contain anything. These restrictions are not encoded in this meta-model and additional OCL constraints would have to be added to declaratively exclude all unwanted forms of containment.

Thus, we have seen that the core concepts of meta-models can also be mapped to typed graphs with attributes and inheritance such that we have also a sound foundation and semantics for them. This will be a foundation for the analysis of model transformations later in Section 4.1 and 4.2.

3.2   Story Pattern

We introduce in this section *Story Patterns* (SPs) [47] that are a compact visual notation for graph transformation rules and graph patterns. SPs have been introduced in the context of Story Diagrams. They take advantage of the similarity between UML object diagrams and graph patterns. As in object diagrams, objects have a name and a classifier, separated by a colon. SPs represent a graph transformation rule such that both sides of the rule are combined. Regular elements belong to both sides, elements with a ++ have to be created and belong only to the RHS, elements with a −− belong only to the LHS and have to be removed.

Example 14 (RailCab - SP(1/3)). The SP in Fig. 21 related to the class diagram in Fig. 19(a) deletes the associations of type go and on between Shuttle s1 and Tracks t2 and t1, respectively. Further, the SP creates an association of type on between s1 and t2. The SP can only be applied to an instance situation if no Shuttle is located at Track t2.

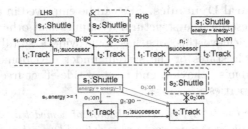

Fig. 21. moveSingle: SP for moving a shuttle to an empty track

The semantics of SP is given via a mapping on GTS rules (cf. Def. 8) assuming a proper mapping from class diagrams (meta-models) to type graphs with attributes and inheritance as described in Section 3.1. For the translations of SPs into GTS rules we have split up SPs into a graph pattern for the LHS and RHS as follows: All elements that have no annotation or a −− become nodes and edges in the graph pattern for the LHS. Note that in particular the NACs are not allowed to carry annotations and thus always become part of the LHS. Given the case that the SP contains NACs, they are directly mapped to NACs in the graph pattern $(L, \{N_i | 1 \le i \le I\})$ (cf. Def. 5) with I being the number of NACs. Elements that have no −− attached and are not part of a NAC become nodes and edges of the RHS. The types of the nodes and edges are set according to the mapping to the type graph. All elements only occurring in the RHS but not in the LHS are obviously those annotated with a ++ and all elements besides the NACs only occurring in the LHS but not in the RHS are obviously those annotated with a −−. A SP is called *side-effect free* if no elements are annotated with ++ or −− and can be used to describe basic graph properties. If the SPs do not delete nodes but at most edges, the conservative and dangling-edge-collecting approach are identical. However, if also nodes are deleted, one of the two options has to be chosen.

Example 15 (RailCab - SP(2/3)). To exemplify the mapping from a SP to a GTS rule, we consider here again the simple rule for the Example 12 of the RailCab system that describes the **Shuttle**'s move operation. The SP for this rule is given in Fig. 21 (lower part) and the corresponding GTS rule is given in Fig. 21 (lower part). The correspondence between nodes and edges in the SP and the GTS rule is indicated through the names. Note that this an improved version of the GTS rule in Fig. 9 (upper part) that excludes collisions by checking that no other **Shuttle** is located on the **Track** the **Shuttle** moves to.

We restrict our discussion here to the main features of SP and refer to [48] for a more complete coverage of features. The Story Diagrams language integrates SPs as basic building blocks and in addition offers the typical control flow concepts of an UML activity diagram to steer when which SP should be applied. An additional activity node foreach in these Story Diagrams permit to also apply a SP to all matches in the considered object graph. More on Story Diagrams can be found also in [48].

Modeling: Structural Dynamics. SPs can be employed in combination with class diagrams to describe the structural dynamics and other behavior of dynamic systems. To achieve this, one has to provide a suitable class diagram describing all possible states of the system under development, a set of SPs that specify the system's behavior, and a set of side-effect free SPs that specify required system properties.

Example 16 (RailCab - SP(3/3)). The behavior of a model of the RailCab system of Example 1 to study the collision avoidance is defined by a set of SPs. The class diagram of the model is depicted in Fig. 19(a) of Example 12. Based on this class diagram the SPs shown in Fig. 21, 22(b), 22(c), and 22(d) describe how a shuttle may move. Fig. 21, 22(c), and 22(d) specify the movement of **Shuttles** under different conditions – i.e. succeeding **Track** is empty, **Shuttle** has the **DistanceCoordinationPattern** protocol established – and Fig. 22(b) specifies the instantiation of the **DistanceCoordinationPattern** protocol. The operational rules are equipped with priorities ensuring that rules specifying the **Shuttles**' movement without an established **DistanceCoordinationPattern** protocol are preempted by rules requiring the **DistanceCoordinationPattern** protocol. The instantiation of the **DistanceCoordinationPattern** protocol has the highest priority and it's removal the lowest.

Besides operational rules, the model also consists of forbidden patterns that identify system states, which are considered unsafe or may lead to an unsafe situation. For the RailCab system these forbidden patterns are depicted in Figure 22(a) and Figure 22(e), which are SP without side-effects and describe situations where the **DistanceCoordination-Pattern** protocol is not established for two **Shuttles** located at succeeding **Tracks** and a collision – i.e. two **Shuttles** at the same **Track** – respectively.

Overall, the complete RailCab system is specified through six rules and 19 forbidden patterns (see [49]). Most of the forbidden patterns are required to encode cardinality constraints. We use the conservative approach for the rule execution for this example, as edges represent meaningful real world concepts that should not be implicitly deleted. Anyway, the rules only delete **DistanceCoordinationPattern** nodes together with its two links to the connected shuttles. Thus, in this case there will be no valid graph where the behavior would differ if the dangling-edge-collecting approach would have been chosen.

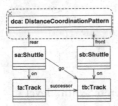

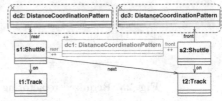

(a) Invariant: No uncoordinated movement of Shuttles in close proximity, which would constitute a hazard

(b) Instantiation rule: creating a Distance-CoordinationPattern

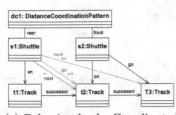

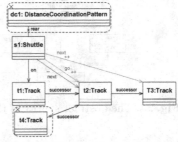

(c) Behavioral rule: Coordinated movement

(d) Behavioral rule: unrestricted movement for a solitary Shuttle

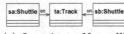

(e) Invariant: No collision accident

Fig. 22. SPs specifying the structural dynamics of the RailCab model

MDE: Refactoring. As outlined in the following example, SPs can be also used in the context of MDE. A first example is the specification and execution of a *refactoring* [50,7]. Based on the meta-model of a source model (in this case the SDL block diagram meta-model), the required refactorings are described by SPs. An in-place transformation of a source model then results in a refactored model.

Example 17 (SDL - Refactoring). We consider here again SDL block diagrams as in Example 11.[14] Assume that we want to develop a refactoring that change improper connections across Block boundaries. In case two Blocks are embedded into different Blocks but are directly connected, this single Connection has to be replaced by three Connections with the same name. One Connection between the outer blocks and two additional Connections linking the inner bocks to their outer block (see Fig. 23). As in case of refactoring deleting all edges to removed elements is rather cumbersome, here the dangling-edge-collecting approach is used.

---

[14] It is to be noted that the case considered here is not covered by the GG example and later TGG examples where for space reasons the rule for connections across the hierarchy are omitted.

Fig. 23. Required refactoring at the concrete syntax level

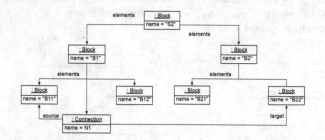

Fig. 24. The abstract syntax of the example model before the refactoring

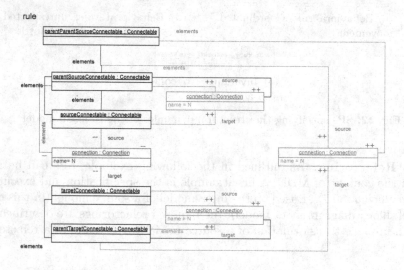

Fig. 25. SP for the refactoring that corrects connections across hierarchy

To capture the SDL block diagrams, we at first need a meta-model as depicted in Fig. 20. Based on this meta-model the example of Fig. 23 can be depicted at the level of the abstract syntax in Fig. 24. With a single SP we can then describe how to manipulate the models by means of in-place model transformations. The required changes for the refactoring are depicted in SP of Fig. 25. The direct **Connection** is removed and instead three new **Connections** with the same name as the removed **Connection** are created that ensure that the **Connections** are always respect the block hierarchy. In Fig. 26 we can see the expected result of refactoring the model of Fig. 24 according to Fig. 25.

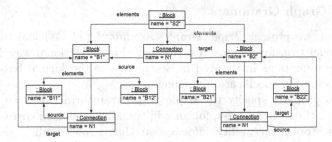

Fig. 26. Result of refactoring the model of Fig. 24 with the SP of Fig. 25

It is to be noted that the SPs can also be used to define complete model transformations in an operational style. However, either we simply identify corresponding elements in the other model using names or complex additional structures have to be maintained explicitly or explicit control structures as supported by Story Diagrams would be required. In the next section, we will instead discuss how the same kind of problem can be addressed with a graph grammar based approach in a more elegant and effective manner by specifying the relation between source and target model declaratively and derive related operational solutions for the model transformation.

Code Generation and Interpreter. Story diagrams can be executed by generating code, which is the approach used in Fujaba and former versions of our tool, and by interpreting them directly [45].

The former code generation required that all conditions are specified as Java conditions such that they can be simply embedded in the generated code. The generated code has a very good performance, but was not very flexible. First, it did not support OCL. Second, the search for a match happened according to fixed order for the nodes of an SP set at compile-time. Third, changes of the SPs and Story Diagrams at runtime were not possible due to the generated code.

To overcome these limitations, an interpreter was developed that supports OCL conditions, adjusts the matching order to the instance graph to decrease the worst-case execution times, and permits to modify the SPs and Story Diagrams at runtime (higher-order transformations). In addition, the SP matcher can start the matching with any initial bindings such that also incremental matching of SPs based on change events could be realized with the interpreter. The tool set is completed by a debugger at modeling level (see [51]).

Note also that SPs and Story Diagrams have already be employed for industrial strength case study such as the MATE project [52] for the enhanced model validation and model transformation of Simulink/Stateflow models. The current and older versions of the SP and Story Diagram Interpreter have been realized based on Eclipse and the Eclipse Modeling Framework. It can be downloaded from our Eclipse update site http://www.mdelab.org/update-site.

3.3   Triple Graph Grammars

In this section, we present *Triple Graph Grammars* (TGGs) [53] that allows specifying model transformations in a rule-based and relational way. In particular, graph grammars as introduced in Section 2 are the formal basis for this model transformation specification language.

In order to properly specify the triple graph transformations, we require a meta-model for the source model, for an additionally supported correspondence model, which stores traceability information that allows finding elements of one model that correspond to an element of the other model, and for the target model. TGG rules are accordingly divided into three domains: The source model domain (left), target model domain (right), and the correspondence model domain (middle).

A TGG consists of an axiom (the grammar's start graph) and several TGG rules that describes how consistent triples of source, correspondence and target models can be generated. TGGs permit to derive three kinds of model transformation directions: Forward, backward, and correspondence transformations. A forward (backward) transformation takes a source (target) model as input and creates the correspondence and target (source) model. A correspondence transformation[15] requires a source and target model and creates only the correspondence model. In addition, also forward or backward model synchronization is possible where only changes are propagated. As in case of TGGs and related operational SPs only bookkeeping edges are deleted, the chosen approach whether conservative or dangling-edge-collecting does not matter.

Example 18 (SDL - TGG Specification). For a transformation from SDL block diagrams to UML class diagrams we require a meta-model for SDL block diagrams (as already depicted in Fig. 20), and a meta-model for UML class diagrams as presented in Fig. 27. There is also a correspondence meta-model as depicted in Fig. 28.

The axiom in Fig. 29 relates the root elements of the source and target models with the axiom correspondence node. The attribute assignments, defined through OCL expressions in our tool environment, state that the names of the block and class diagrams must be equal. Rule 1 creates a Block and a corresponding UMLClass. The BlockDiagram and ClassDiagram must already exist. Rule 2 creates a Block in the block diagram domain and connects it to an already existing parent Block. In the class diagram domain, a class is created and connected to the parent Block's UMLClass with an Association. Rule 3 is analogous to Rule 2, but covers the creation Process in the block diagram domain. Rule 4 creates a Connection and a corresponding UMLAssoc between already corresponding Connectables in the block diagram domain and UMLClasses in the class diagram domain.

Triple Generation. The TGG itself can be used to build the three models in parallel by applying TGG rules successively to extend the axiom. In the resulting graphs, the source and target components (i.e. the source and target models) are consistent to each other according to the TGG. We employ this triple generation, for example, to generate test cases for model transformation

---

[15] The correspondence transformation is also known as mapping or model integration.

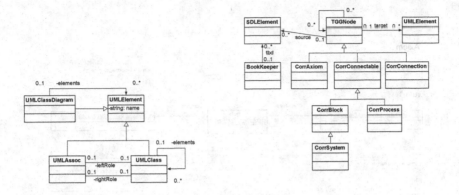

Fig. 27. Simplified meta-model for UML class diagrams

Fig. 28. Correspondence meta-model with extra concept for bookkeeping

implementations that need to adhere to the TGG. Since the TGG is a specific graph grammar (see Section 2), it defines a language of consistent source and target models.

Example 19 (SDL - TGG - Triple Generation). For the SDL block diagram to UML class diagram transformation of Example 18 the triples can be generated by starting with the axiom and then applying the rules directly as if they were simply SPs.

Forward & Backward Transformation. However, to perform model transformations in practice it would be too cumbersome to generate all triples of related size to determine what the output of a transformation should be. Instead, under some well-formedness conditions for the TGG rules an efficient operationalization can be generated, which create target model elements for given source model elements, so that both are consistent to each other. These well-formedness conditions are described in more detail in [54,55] and range from simple syntactical checks to more expensive checks (as discussed, for example, in Section 4.1) that can still be performed at design time.

For each of the aforementioned transformation directions, separate operational rules are derived from the TGG rules. In particular, the elements with ++ in the source domain become regular elements by removing the ++. The parts with ++ of the correspondence domain and target domain remain as they are. The operational rules also have to make sure that a given source model element is only transformed once. This requires a bookkeeping mechanism, which keeps track of those elements that were already transformed, and those that still have to be transformed. Accordingly, an initially set link to a special bookkeeping object is removed when a source element has been translated and its non-existence is tested for all context objects as they should have been translated already.

Example 20 (SDL - TGG - Forward Transformation). For Example 18 the SPs derived from the TGG rules to transform SDL block diagrams into UML class diagrams

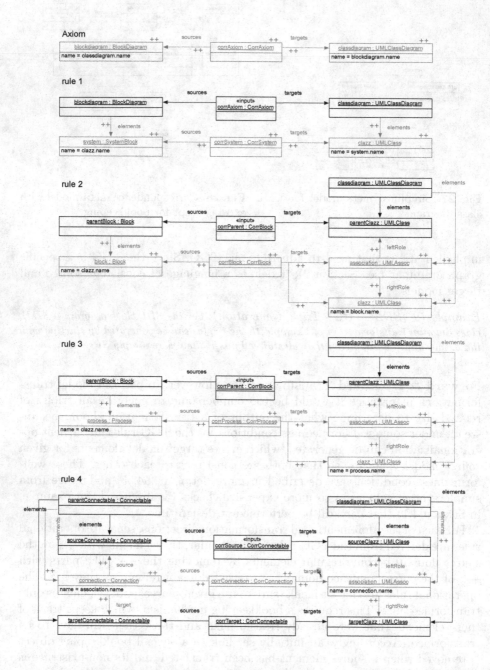

Fig. 29. TGG rules to transform SDL block diagrams into UML class diagrams

are depicted in Fig. 30. While the elements of the source model become additional pre-conditions, the new elements of the TGG rule in the correspondence model and target model are generated. In addition, it is checked if a link to a bookkeeping object is available. It ensures that the translated source elements have not yet been processed (required edge) and that all context elements of the source model have been processed (forbidden edges). The links to the translated elements are deleted by the rules such that subsequent rule applications will not consider the covered elements of the source model.

The steps of a forward transformation with TGGs are depicted in Fig. 31. Dashed lines separate the elements covered by each step for the source model and the generated elements for the correspondence and target model.

Consistency Transformation. TGGs can also be used to derive the correspondence model for a give source and target model. In that case, in each TGG rule all elements of the source and target domain become part of the precondition of the related SP and only the parts of the correspondence domain to be generated become part of the post-condition. In addition, bookkeeping must ensure that only those elements of the source and target model are considered as match for the SP.

Forward & Backward Synchronization. In case of model synchronization, the target and correspondence model are also input for the processing. Next links leading from all referenced correspondence nodes to the newly created correspondence nodes (also created by the model transformation, but omitted there for space reasons) capture the dependencies between different rule applications related to the correspondence nodes. The goal of the forward synchronization is then to propagate only the changes that occur in the source model to the correspondence model and target model but regenerate only the necessary minimum.

Example 21 (SDL - TGG - Model Synchronization). We consider here how to synchronize a SDL block diagram with a UML class diagram, which is related to the transformation considered in Example 18 and 20.

*The considered change in a SDL block diagram is depicted in Fig. 32. A block **Block3** and a contained block **Block4** are moved from the embedding block **Block1** into another block **Block2**. Using model synchronization only the changes are propagated.*

Model Transformation and Synchronization Engine. Our implementation of the *model transformation* takes advantage of the knowledge which correspondence nodes can be a trigger for a TGG rule. It manages a queue of the created correspondence nodes and then only triggers the necessary rules for those nodes. In addition, the bookkeeping is used as an additional side-condition to limit the search space as newly matched elements are always still connected with the bookkeeping object. Both tricks permit to avoid any global search for matches and considerably speedup the transformation.

In case of *model synchronization*, the correspondence model and target model are also input for the processing. In addition, we remember the dependencies

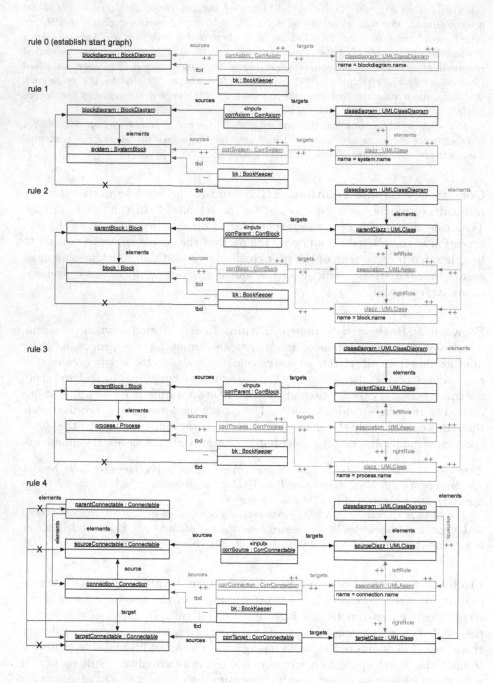

Fig. 30. Derived SPs to transform SDL block diagrams into UML class diagrams

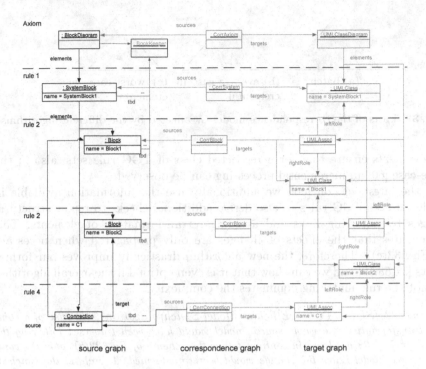

Fig. 31. Derivation of a forward transformation with TGGs

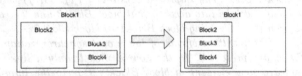

Fig. 32. Considered change in a SDL block diagram

between rule applications in the correspondence model in form of additional next links as defined in Fig. 28 between the newly created correspondence nodes and those in the LHS when transforming as well as synchronizing the models. Therefore, the correspondence model with the next links has further the form of a directed acyclic graph (visualized in Fig. 33 as a tree) and we can exploit this acyclic structure in a number of improvements for the efficient incremental processing of changes for the synchronization (similar to ideas for incremental parsing as outlined in [56]).

In [57,58], we have achieved that in most cases a single change can be processed in the average case with only logarithmic effort concerning the size of the models involved. In [59], we further improved the solution in such a way that even in the case of multiple changes, we can ensure only a slow increase of the efforts and that the effort always remains below or equal to the batch algorithm. Further

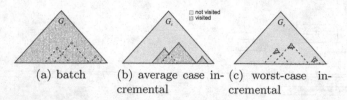

(a) batch   (b) average case in- (c) worst-case in-
                 cremental   cremental

Fig. 33. Parts of the correspondence model G_c affected by the different algorithms

improvements ensure that for a restricted class of TGG rule sets, also in the worse-case [60] an incremental processing can be observed.

In the latest version [60], we additionally use the information available in the declarative TGG rules to also derive additional checks to repair structural changes by adjusting links and avoiding retransformation of elements. This also ensures that the effects of changes are only propagated when necessary (cf. Fig. 33(c)). Therefore, the new algorithm drastically improves our former results [57,58,59] and we can show that it is even optimal if the overall algorithm and not the rule matching dominates the complexity.

Example 22 (SDL - TGG - Efficient Model Synchronization). In case of a complete transformation the whole source model would have been traversed following the scheme in Fig. 33(a). If we in contrast follow the scheme of Fig. 33(b), only the complete source model below the change would be retransformed. Therefore, the synchronization would work as if Block3 and a contained block Block4 embedded into the block Block1 are first deleted and a new Block3 and a contained block Block4 are created located under the block Block2. The improved version of Fig. 33(c)) will instead consider the right scenario and take into account that block Block3 and the contained block Block4 are moved from the embedding block Block1 to block Block2.

Finally, in Fig. 34 the resulting effects of the model synchronization following the scheme of Fig. 33(c) are presented. In the source model, only a link is deleted and block Block3 is added a new element of block Block2. Due to the improved handling the resulting synchronization effects requires that in the correspondence model and the target model the related links are corrected as the algorithm is able to reuse the old correspondence model and target model related to block Block3 and block Block4.

It should be noted that in the considered case the absolute improvement is only moderate while the relative improvement is already considerable. However, if the part of the correspondence model located under the correspondence directly affected by the a change is large, the effort without repair can become as large as transforming the model anew while only a few local changes are required for our synchronization algorithm.

TGGs have already be employed for an industrial strength case study in the context of an automotive tool chain. The task was to transform elements of SysML system models, which refer to the software, into an AUTOSAR software architecture model. Additionally, both models had to be kept synchronized after transformation [61]. The current and older versions of the presented TGG Engines have been realized based on Eclipse and the Eclipse Modeling Framework. The current version can be downloaded from our Eclipse update site http://www.mdelab.org/update-site.

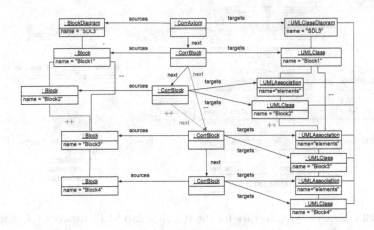

Fig. 34. Effects of the model synchronization following the scheme of Fig. 33(c)

3.4   Runtime Model Framework

In the following, we discuss a framework leveraging runtime models for self-adaptive systems [62,63,64,65]. Having explicit models that represent the running system, MDE techniques based on graph transformations (cf. Section 2) can be applied. The generic architecture of the framework, which extends the control loop concept proposed in [8], is depicted in Fig. 35.

A *Managed System* provides *Sensors* and *Effectors* that are used to observe and change the running system, respectively. These sensors and effectors provide the so-called *Source Model*, which is a runtime representation of the system. This model is *causally connected* to the system, which generally means that any change in the running system is reflected in the source model, and any change in the source model is reflected in the system. Therefore, this model can be directly used by *Autonomic Managers* to perform the feedback loop activities that comprise the monitoring and analysis of the running system, and if changes are required, the planning and execution of adaptation to the system.

However, a source model represents all functionalities and concerns of the sensors and effectors. Therefore, it is usually complex and related to the solution space and platform of a managed system. Thus, a source model provides a view on a system at a low level of abstraction, which could make it laborious to use it as a basis for the feedback loop activities performed by managers.

Therefore, several *Target Models* are derived from a source model at runtime. Each target model abstracts from the source model and it provides a specific view on a managed system required for a certain self-management capability. As an example, a target model might represent the performance state or failures of a system to address self-optimization or self-healing, respectively. A manager concerned with self-optimization will use only the target models relevant for optimizing a system, but not necessarily consider target models addressing other capabilities like self-healing. This and appropriate abstractions of models, reduce

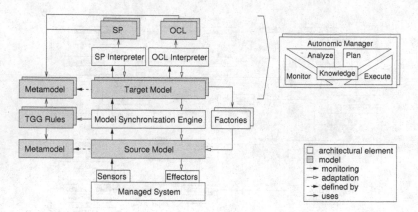

Fig. 35. Generic Architecture for the Runtime Model Framework (cf. [64])

the complexity for individual managers in coping with runtime models and performing their activities.

Thus, target models tend to provide views related to problem spaces of different self-management capabilities and to abstract from the underlying system platform. This supports the reusability of managers that focus on problem spaces shared by different managed systems. Furthermore, as target models can be platform-independent, the kinds of target models used in our approach are primarily defined with the needs of the autonomic managers in mind rather than focusing on the underlying infrastructure.

Therefore, managers preferably use target models than a complex source model to perform the feedback loop activities. This requires that a target model is causally connected to the source model. Thus, changes in the source model are reflected in target models for monitoring, and vice versa for adaptation. To maintain different target models at runtime and to realize causal connections between the models, we use our *Model Synchronization Engine* based on TGGs that incrementally synchronizes models with each other (cf. Section 3.3). To use the engine, source and target models have to be defined by meta-models that are the basis to define *TGG Rules* (cf. Fig. 35). These rules define how a pair of source and target models are synchronized with each other.

However, all concepts in one model need not to be represented in the other model. Especially, concepts in a source model may not be reflected in the target model since target models are at a higher level of abstraction than source models. Hence, synchronizing source model changes reflecting changes in the managed system to a target model for monitoring is not problematic. During synchronization, concepts that are represented in a source model but not in a target model are simply discarded, which causes the intended abstraction. Therefore, changes can be propagated from source to target models without any difficulty. However for adaptation, the opposite direction of propagating target model changes to the source model is problematic since these changes have to be refined in order to be reflected properly in the source model. The abstraction gap between source and target models prevents a bidirectional synchronization using the TGG-based transformation engine. Therefore, this abstraction gap is filled by *Factories* (cf. Fig. 35) that are invoked on target models but they operate on the source model where all required information is provided. Hence, the intended changes are performed by factories on the source model and afterwards they are synchronized to target models by the synchronization engine, which makes them visible for managers. Though factories are currently implemented in *Java*, they could also be specified and realized by graph transformation rules, like SPs (cf. Section 3.2), that perform an in-place transformation of the source model. Further issues concerning adaptations based on target models are discussed in [64].

Overall, this approach leverages abstract runtime models and MDE techniques for adaptive systems. In contrast to a complex source model, an abstract target model provides a more appropriate abstraction for autonomic managers and a more specific view for a self-management capability. Both aspects ease the work of managers. Moreover, target models can abstract from a concrete managed system and platform, which supports the reusability and extensibility of managers being able to operate on these models across different systems.

While the synchronization between source and target models with TGGs as discussed above supports the monitoring and the execution of adaptations, the analysis and planning activities of the feedback loop can be tackled as well by graph transformations. In [65], we discuss the applicability of SPs (cf. Section 3.2) working on runtime (target) models. For analysis, SPs perform checks on a runtime (target) model, while for planning adaptations, a runtime (target) model is transformed in-place by SPs. In addition to SPs, OCL expressions can be used by autonomic managers to perform the feedback loop activities. This is outlined on top of Fig. 35 by an implementation example of an autonomic manager. The analysis and planning activites of this manager are specified by SPs and OCL expressions based on the target meta-models. These SPs and OCL expressions are executed by corresponding interpreters and they operate on target models to analyze the managed system and to plan adaptations.

As sketched in Fig. 35, several runtime models, like SPs, OCL, or target models, and several model operations, i.e., tools like the synchronization engine and different interpreters, are used to implement and execute a feeback loop with its activities. To explicitly specify the interplay between all these models and operations, so-called *megamodels* can be employed [66]. A megamodel is a model that has models as its elements and that captures the relationships between these models in the form of model operations. Thus, a feedback loop and especially its flow of activities implemented by interacting models and model operations can be specified by a megamodel. Moreover, having an interpreter for megamodels, a megamodel can be kept alive at runtime in order to maintain the different runtime models and operations, and to directly execute a feedback loop. Therefore, besides making feedback loops explicit in the design of a self-adaptive system, a megamodel approach together with an interpreter supports the execution, adaptation, and composition of feedback loops [67].

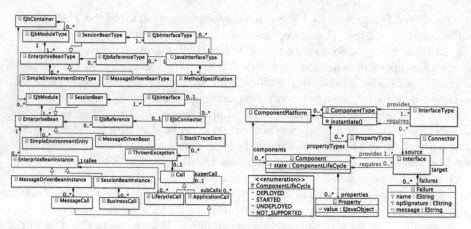

Fig. 36. Simplified source meta-model [64]   **Fig. 37.** Simplified target meta-model [64]

Example 23 (Runtime Model Framework). As an example, we consider managed systems implemented with Enterprise Java Beans 3.0 (EJB) *technology. Fig. 36 shows the simplified*[16] *meta-model for the source model. Based on this meta-model, EJB-based systems can be described at three different layers. The top layer covers components types that correspond to artifacts from the development phase. These types define the configuration space for a system. Concrete configurations of a system are instances of these types that are deployed in a container (server) and they are considered by the middle layer. Finally, the lower layer addresses bean instances and interactions by means of calls among them.*

Since models conforming to this meta-model are complex, very detailed, and platform-specific, we introduce a meta-model for generic component-based software systems, which is used for target models. A simplified version[17] *of this meta-model is depicted in Fig. 37. It generally considers component-based systems and it covers failures that have occurred when using a provided interface.*

Using this generic meta-model, EJB-based systems can be described in a platform-independent and abstract manner, while highlighting the specific concern of failures occurring in the running system. Hence, a target model as an instance of this generic meta-model has to be synchronized at runtime with the source model conforming to the meta-model depicted in Fig. 36.

Overall, eleven TGG rules were required to specify the synchronization between instances of these specific source and target meta-models. One of these rules is depicted in Fig. 38. This rule transforms and synchronizes an EjbInterface *element to an* Interface *element, or vice versa. Model elements on the left refer to the source model, elements in the middle to the correspondence model, and elements on the right to the target model. Thus, for each* EjbInterface *provided by a* SessionBean *that is part of an* EjbModule *in the source model an* Interface *is created in the target model and associated*

---

[16] The meta-model depicted in Fig. 36 is simplified as it does not show any attributes, operations, and enumerations, and it hides some associations. Moreover, elements for concerns like security, transaction, timers, or quiescence are hidden.

[17] The meta-model is simplified as several attributes and three associations to navigate from a Component, Interface, or Property to their corresponding types are hidden.

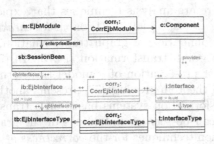  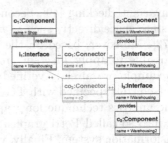

Fig. 38. Example TGG Rule [64]   **Fig. 39.** Example adaptation SP

as a provided interface to the Component that corresponds to the EjbModule. Moreover, a CorrEjbInterface element as part of the correspondence model is created that stores the mapping between the EjbInterface and the Interface. Finally, the Interface is associated to the InterfaceType that corresponds to the EjbInterfaceType to which the EjbInterface is linked. Likewise, if an Interface is created in the target model, it is transformed or synchronized to an EjbInterface in the source model. This rule also shows how attribute values are synchronized. The uid of an Interface is directly derived from the uid of the EjbInterface, and vice versa.

Moreover, this rule exemplifies that not all concepts in one model need to be represented in the other model. A SessionBean in a source model is not reflected in the target model and therefore no correspondence model element exists that is connected to a SessionBean.

As an example for manipulating a target model, Fig. 39 shows a SP specifying one step within a complex architectural adaptation. This pattern works on target models that conform to the meta-model shown in Fig. 37. Considering a web shop as an example system, it changes the binding between components of the system by removing the connector between the Shop and the Warehousing components, and creating a new connector to bind the Shop component to the Warehousing2 component. This architectural adaptation is motivated by a faulty Warehousing component that causes failures at runtime. This requires that requests from the Shop component are routed to the alternative Warehousing2 component. Similar SPs are used for the other adaptation steps, like checking if failures occur at runtime, to deploy and start the alternative component, and to stop and undeploy the faulty component.

The framework has been employed to academic case studies for self-adaptive software systems. The framework's implementation is continuously enhanced and elaborated, and it is available on request. For further information on the research prototype, please contact us at `contact@mdelab.org`.

4 Analysis

For the introduced SP and TGG languages as well as the Runtime Models Framework a number of analysis techniques available for graph transformations can be employed. The formal foundation of graph transformation permits to analyze them in different ways. At first we can use *static analysis techniques* that only analyze the structure of the GTS rule sets such as static conflict detection [68] or invariant checking [49]. Secondly, there are analysis techniques that explore the state space directly such as *model-based testing* [69,70,71] or *model checking* [72,73]. Moreover, based on the formal foundation of graph transformation, it is possible to apply *theorem proving* to graph transformation [74,75]. In [76], for example, we already verified behavior preservation of a model transformation (see [76]) specified with TGGs using theorem proving. [77] presents another static analysis technique for graph transformation systems based on a translation into so-called Petri graphs, which can be seen as unfoldings of the graph transformation system. Finally, verification techniques for the *correctness of so-called graph programs*, equipping graph transformation rules with basic control structures, have been developed in [78], following Dijkstra's approach to program verification, and [79], where a Hoare calculus for graph programs is presented.

We will look in the following into static conflict detection for model transformations with TGGs in Section 4.1, invariant checking for model refactorings with SPs and systems with structural dynamics with SPs in Section 4.2, and model checking for systems with structural dynamics with SPs in Section 4.3.

4.1   Static Conflict Detection

Conflict detection allows for detecting and visualizing conflicts that may occur between rule applications. Conflicts arise, for example, if one rule deletes an element used by the other rule. This is because after applying the first rule and deleting this used element from the other rule, this other rule cannot be applied anymore. Conflicts between rule applications can be computed at design time by analyzing the corresponding graph transformation rules. To this extent, the so-called theory of critical pairs [35,80] can be applied. A critical pair describes a conflict between two rule applications in a minimal context. AGG is a graph transformation tool [42] able to compute the complete set of critical pairs for a given set of graph transformation rules for the conservative approach.[18] Since this set can be computed from the rules (without executing them and generating a corresponding state space), conflict detection is a so-called static analysis technique. In general, computing the complete set of critical pairs for a given pair of rules is exponential in the number of rule elements in the LHSs of these rules. This is because so-called overlaps (jointly surjective morphisms, see Def. 2) of the rules' preconditions need to be built in order to compute all possible minimal contexts of rule applications.

Example 24 (SDL - TGG - Static Conflict Detection).   In [54,55], we perform conflict detection using AGG on the rule-based specification of model transformations in order to find out at design time if each model transformation following this specification can be performed efficiently, i.e. without backtracking at runtime.

For the example transformation rules in Fig. 40, depicting backward transformation rules with bookkeeping from class diagrams to block diagrams derived from a similar

---

[18] Note that we can verify with the invariant checker discussed in Section 4.2 whether for a given rule set the dangling-edge-collecting approach and the conservative approach result in the same behavior.

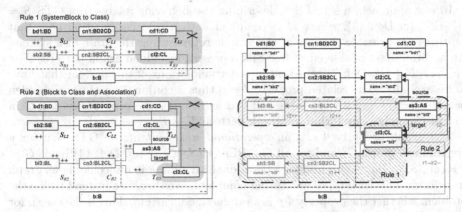

Fig. 40. Backward rules $r1^{BB}$ and $r2^{BB}$ in conflict

Fig. 41. Operational backward rules $r1^{BB}$ and $r2^{BB}$ competing for translating cl3

TGG as presented earlier in this paper, a conflict arises. The LHS of rule 1 is completely contained in the LHS of rule 2 (shaded background). Therefore, both rules can be applied in the same context and compete for the translation of the same Class, namely cl2 in rule 1 and cl3 in rule 2, respectively. Fig. 41 shows the backward transformation of a class diagram model with both alternatives. In particular, cl3 can be translated by rules 1 and 2 but with different results, which are both shown in the figure.[19] Rule 1 creates a second SystemBlock in the block diagram model, rule 2 creates a Block. In particular, we have a delete-use-conflict because if the bookkeeping edge to the instance class cl3 is deleted by rule 1, then it cannot be matched anymore by rule 2 and the other way round. In addition, rule 1 leaves as3 untranslated. After applying rule 1 to translate cl3, the bookkeeping edge to as3 still exists. Therefore, the transformation result is not unique and our TGG model transformation implementation can not perform in a safe way the corresponding model transformation efficiently without backtracking.

4.2   Invariant Checking

Given a set of SPs describing the behavior of a system and required properties in form of side-effect free SPs being forbidden graph patterns, we present here a static verification technique we developed for analyzing the structure of the underlying GTS rules assuming the conservative approach to determine whether the required properties are inductive invariants.[18] Since it is a static analysis technique, it even works when we have arbitrary many or even infinitely many reachable graphs. We will only review here the basic idea [49] and refer the interested reader to [81] for an extension for timed models. For the collaboration building and its structural dynamism, a fully automatic checker for inductive invariants of graph transformation systems [49] presented in Section 4.2 and an extension supporting timed graph transformation systems [81] and an incremental checker [82] have been developed.

---

[19] Thereby, cl2 of rule 1 as well as cl3 of rule 2 are mapped to the instance Class cl3.

In our approach, a set of SPs describing the behavior relates to a GTS $S = (\mathcal{R}, TG)$ (cf Def. 13), where $\mathcal{R}$ is equipped with a priority function prio, that captures the possible changes of the graphs representing the state of a system. An additional set of side-effect free SPs represent forbidden graph patterns $\mathcal{F} = \{F_1, \ldots, F_n\}$ (cf. Def. 7) representing safety-violations of our system that have to be excluded. The related property $\Phi_{\mathcal{F}}$ is thus a conjunction of the forbidden patterns $(\neg F_1) \wedge \cdots \wedge (\neg F_n)$. We call G a *witness* for the property $\neg\Phi_{\mathcal{F}}$ if G in contrast matches any forbidden graph pattern $F \in \mathcal{F}$.

The graph property $\Phi_{\mathcal{F}}$ is an *operational invariant* of the GTS S if for a given initial graph G^0 and for all $G \in \mathsf{REACH}(S, \{G^0\})$ (cf. Def. 14) holds $G \models \Phi_{\mathcal{F}}$ (cf. [83]). However, checking operational invariants is undecidable as graph transformations with types are Turing-complete. We therefore instead tackle the problem whether the property $\Phi_{\mathcal{F}}$ is an *inductive invariant*. This is the case if for all graphs G typed over TG and for all rules $r \in \mathcal{R}$ holds that $G \models \Phi_{\mathcal{F}} \wedge G \overset{r}{\Rightarrow}_{\mathcal{R}} G'$ implies $G' \models \Phi_{\mathcal{F}}$. If we have an inductive invariant and the initial graph G^0 fulfills the graph property, then $\Phi_{\mathcal{F}}$ is also an *operational invariant* as inductive invariants are stronger than their operational counterparts.

We can reformulate the definition of an *inductive invariant* as follows to have a falsifiable form: a graph property $\Phi_{\mathcal{F}}$ is an inductive invariant of a GTS $S = (\mathcal{R}, TG)$ if and only if there exists no pair (G, r) of a graph G and a rule $r \in \mathcal{R}$ such that $G \models \Phi_{\mathcal{F}}$, $G \overset{r}{\Rightarrow}_{\mathcal{R}} G'$ and $G' \not\models \Phi_{\mathcal{F}}$. Such a pair (G, r) which witnesses the violation of graph property $\Phi_{\mathcal{F}}$ by rule r is then a *counterexample* for the initial hypothesis.

The invariant checker proceeds as follows for verifying statically that the absence of *forbidden patterns*[20] is preserved by a set of graph transformation rules with priorities: it is analyzed statically which kind of graph elements may be produced by a rule and then, it is checked how these created graph elements may be overlapped with the forbidden pattern $F \in \mathcal{F}$. In case that overlappings are present, counterexamples can be constructed (by inverse rule application to the overlapping), expressing that if the rule is applied to a graph holding the remaining part of the forbidden pattern (*source pattern*), then after rule application the complete forbidden pattern F will be present (*target pattern*). Thereby, counterexamples may be rejected because of three reasons: (1) the source pattern comprises the precondition for a rule with a higher priority to be applicable (2) the source pattern comprises forbidden elements of one of the NACs of the rule (3) the source pattern comprises a forbidden pattern. In the first case, the rule with the higher priority ensures that the rule with lower priority under verification would not be applicable anyway. In the second case, similarly, the rule under verification would not be applicable because the source pattern comprises one of its NACs. In the latter case, the rule under verification would lead to a state comprising the forbidden pattern, if it is applied to a state which comprises the forbidden pattern already. If no counterexamples exist, it is ensured

---

[20] We explain the algorithm for patterns of the form $(F, \emptyset)$, denoted also as F. For an explanation of invariant checking for patterns of the form $\Pi = (F, \{N_i, i \in I\})$, we refer to [49].

that a set of rules with priorities cannot be applied in such a way that they allow for transitions from states holding no forbidden pattern to states holding some forbidden pattern.

Example 25 (SP - Correct Model Refactorings). *We have applied invariant check-ing in the context of in-place model transformations, in particular, refactorings. In this application context, invariant checking is very useful to investigate at design time if a rule-based refactoring specification could lead to inconsistent refactored models at runtime. We briefly review this approach here and we refer to [84] for a detailed description.*

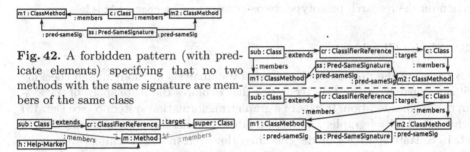

Fig. 42. A forbidden pattern (with predicate elements) specifying that no two methods with the same signature are members of the same class

Fig. 43. Refactoring rule for the "Pull Up **Fig. 44.** Counterexample for the "Pull Up Method" refactoring   Method" refactoring

For example, for the consistency of the refactoring Pull Up Method [50], it is impor-tant that afterwards "no two **Methods** sharing the same signature are contained in one **Class**". This well-formedness constraint is depicted as a forbidden pattern in Fig. 42. The types **Pred-SameSignature** and **Pred-NotSameSignature** mark that two **Methods** have the same or a different signature, respectively. If we run our Invariant Checker with the well-formedness constraint shown in Fig. 42 and the refactoring rule depicted in Fig. 43 the verification result is likely to be a counterexample as the one shown in Fig. 44. The reason that the refactoring rule is unsafe is that the rule completely ig-nores the **Pred-SameSignature** nodes. If we change the rule to require the existence of a **Pred-NotSameSignature** and forbid the existence of a **Pred-SameSignature** node, the rule is safe.

Example 26 (RailCab - Invariant Checking for Structural Dynamics). *A further example successfully applying our Invariant Checker is the Railcab system. Obviously, this system is hard to check using other verification techniques, such as model checking, as the system's potential state space would be very large and it is hard to identify a valid initial state.*

To ensure that the Railcab system is safe, we have to verify that **Shuttles** never collide. A collision can be expressed by a forbidden pattern, as shown in Fig. 22(e). An invariant that is implied in this specification of the Railcab system is that a **Shuttle** will never try to go to a **Track** occupied by another **Shuttle** without making sure the other **Shuttle** is moving (see Fig. 22(a)). Along with several structural constraints restricting cardinalities, these two forbidden patterns form the set $\mathcal{F}$.

The complete set of rules is given through the Story-Pattern shown in Fig. 22(d), 22(b), 21 and 22(c). For a short description of the rules we refer to Example 16. For the

RailCab system to be safe it is required that rules for the creation of the DistanceCoordinationPattern protocol (cf. Fig. 22(b)) preempts all move-rules. Therefore this rule has the highest priority. Due to space limitations we have omitted the rule that destroys the DistanceCoordinationPattern protocol, however the complete example including a more detailed explanation of the rules can be found in [49]. Using the rules mentioned above we have verified in[49] that the RailCab system is collision free.

The Invariant Checker has be employed for several variants of the reported case studies for MDE including the rules of the industrial case study [61] and models with structural dynamics. The current implementation of our Invariant Checker tool is constantly improved and is available on request only. For further information on the research prototype, please contact us at `contact@mdelab.org`.

4.3   Model Checking

In contrast to the previously described static analysis methods model checking [85] is a dynamic verification technique that explores the state space of the system under consideration. In case of a graph transformation system S (see Def. 13) with a set of initial graphs I, a related labeled transition system as specified in Def. 15 as state space for model checking. However, model checking can only be efficiently applied if the state space is finite, which is not necessarily the case for graph transformation systems where nodes and edges can be dynamically created. In addition, such a finite state space can only be build when the initial graph or set of initial graphs is known. If a meaningful criterion to limit the explored state space exists, bounded model checking [86] can be used to investigate only the related finite subset of the overall state space. Other approaches use symbolic representations of the state space to overcome this limitation [87].

A desired property is usually expressed as a condition for all reachable states or in form of a sequence property by some form of temporal-logic. An example of such a temporal-logic is the Computation-Tree-Logic (compare [85]). The state space is analyzed and depending on the given property a counterexample is derived as a witness in the case the property is violated. Accordingly, also for graph transformation systems approaches for model checking exist [72].

In [49] we used the particular tool GROOVE [88,73]. To be able to apply model checking GROOVE requires a GTS according to Def. 13 including an initial graph and supports the dangling-edge-collecting approach[21] (see Def. 10). Moreover, GROOVE allows for generating a minimal labeled transition system in the sense of Def. 15. Atomic properties can be expressed in GROOVE in form of side-effect free rules that are checked for applicability on a given graph state. This conforms to properties as given in Def. 7 consisting of a required pattern, where the pattern consists of the LHS of the side-effect free rule. If the required pattern can be matched (see Def. 6) in a specific graph state, the property

---

[21] Note that given a type graph additional NACs can be derived such that the adjusted rule in the dangling-edge-collecting approach behaves like the original one in the conservative approach. The additional NACs simply ensure that no dangling edges can exist if the rule is applicable.

represented by the rule is fulfilled for that state. These atomic properties can then be used inside a Computation-Tree-Logic (CTL) formula. GROOVE then allows automatically exploring the reachable states via the transition relation of the given GTS as well as automatically evaluating the given CTL formulae. In case an example respectively counterexample in form of a witness can be found, GROOVE provides an alternating sequence of states and rule applications leading to or directly representing the witness.

The Henshin tool [43] also provides model checking capabilities for graph transformation systems. Henshin is based on typed graphs and supports both the dangling-edge-collecting approach and the conservative approach. State spaces generated by Henshin can be checked for given properties. Model checking is supported using external, third party verification tools, such as mCRL2 and CADP.[22] Similarly to the approach implemented in GROOVE, the specification of atomic properties is based on matched graph patterns.

Example 27 (RailCab - SP - Model Checking for Structural Dynamics). In [49] we used the GTS model checker GROOVE [88] and compared the results of GROOVE with those of the approach described in Section 4.2. We have further investigated the complexity of the different analysis methods. To be able to do so the rules describing the application example of the Railcab system depicted in Fig. 22(d), 22(b) and 22(c) beneath others have been imported into GROOVE. We analyzed our model in GROOVE, using the forbidden pattern collision depicted in Fig. 22(e). The outcome of the investigation was that models of moderate size can be effectively analyzed and accordingly we have been able to apply model checking in GROOVE on systems with smaller topologies. However, experiments on a Railcab system with more than 15 tracks turned out to be to complex and leading to a large state space for which it was rarely possible to apply model checking using GROOVE in a efficient way. For more details about the used graph rules, the analyzed properties as well as the evaluation results concerning the complexity of the different approaches compare [49].

5   Discussion

In order to discuss the benefits of graph transformations for MDE, the modeling of structure dynamics, and models at runtime, we will at first look at the options that exist for each of the areas and finally look into their combination.

In MDE, the models are not only a byproduct but become the core carrier of the higher-level knowledge about the software. Model transformation to partially generate subsequent models and code generation result in a situation where, if properly done, the code and the models remain consistent. Thus, required classical adaptation steps can take advantage of the up-to-date higher-level knowledge about the software. Therefore, MDE promises to better support the long-term evolution of the software. Today, the principles of MDE are to employ *meta-models* to define the modeling languages and to use related techniques for model operations such as model transformations or consistency checks (e.g., QVT, ATL,

---

[22] See http://www.mcrl2.org and http://www.inrialpes.fr/vasy/cadp/ for more information about mCRL2 and CADP.

or OCL) that take advantage of an underlying *meta-meta-model* and considerably ease to develop the required model operations. We presented in particular graph transformation based techniques such as SPs for model manipulation and checking models in Section 3.2 and on model transformation and incremental model synchronization based on TGGs in Section 3.3.

Besides the evolution of the software, also the *co-adaptation* resp. *language evolution* is a fact that matters for the long-term evolution (cf. [89,90]). Typically, this leads to a need for transformations to adjust the models but also *higher-order transformations* to adjust model operation (e.g., model transformations). Due to the employed interpreter for SPs [45] presented in Section 3.2 that is also used as a basis for executing the derived TGG rules, our techniques support higher order transformations of the transformation models at runtime.

Today, most existing work on (semi-)automatic correctness verification of model operations only permits to prove that a particular result of a model transformation is correct with respect to the input [91,92]. In our own work partially presented in Section 4 we were in contrast able to derive guarantees that hold for all possible results of a model operation with respect to the input. We presented an approach employing a theorem prover for model transformations with TGGs in [76] that show behavioral equivalence and an automated verification technique for refactorings with SPs [84] that permit to guarantee that required properties are preserved by the refactorings. [93] approach the first problem by comparing two proof techniques with respect to chances of successful mechanization. [94] tackles the problem of verifying required properties for model transformations specified with TGGs by proposing a method to derive OCL invariants from TGGs in order to enable their automated verification and analysis.

Structure dynamics is required to realize complex capabilities such as self-healing, self-configuring etc. on top of related basic capabilities such as self-awareness and context-awareness. A proper combination of the higher level capabilities then finally leads to the capability of self-managing or more general self-adaptive software [12,21,18]. Suggestions for the construction of such system include frameworks like the *Rainbow* approach [22] that addresses the construction of self-adaptive software systems by providing reusable elements for the adaptation engine in order to reduce development efforts. The *MUSIC* approach [95], the context-aware and quality of service aware architectural variability of the core function is specified by models during development. Likewise, in [96] modeling and code generation are employed to simplify the development of self-adaptive software, while any further changes to the generated software requires re-modeling and re-generation steps.

Our own work has resulted in the Mechatronic UML approach [97] for the model-driven development of self-optimizing embedded real-time systems. It employs graph transformation systems and hybrid statecharts to reconfigure hierarchical component-based systems. For the ad hoc formation of collaborations between mechatronic systems (e.g., vehicles that form convoys) or other forms of structural dynamism graph transformation systems are employed [49,81,98] including also first ideas for exchanging models at runtime [99].

A first direction for assurance that is employed for self-adaptive systems is runtime verification [100]. Available techniques for the assurance of self-adaptive systems using model checking either restrict their focus to separate adaptation steps [101,102,103] or assume a decoupling of the adaptation decision from the local functional state [104] in order to achieve scalability. More fundamental work is studying properties of graph transformation systems [105] for characteristics which must hold for self-healing, a special case of self-adaptive behavior.

For our Mechatronic UML approach and and ad hoc real-time collaborations between multiple complex subsystems a compositional verification approach has been developed [106]. For the collaboration building and its structural dynamism, a fully automatic checker for inductive invariants of graph transformation systems [49] presented in Section 4.2 and an extension supporting timed graph transformation [81] has been developed. Finally, the combination of the verification results for inductive invariants for graph transformation models and the compositional verification of the collaboration of multiple roles represented by real-time statecharts has been presented in [98]. These results have also led to studies for self-adaptive software in general and first general results for modeling and verifying them [107]. Furthermore, also an incremental invariant checker [82] has been developed which allows to reduce the effort for performing checks when the behavior has changed at runtime.

There is a lack of work on systematically developing *causal connections* between a runtime model and the running system to reflect changes of the system in the model, and changes of the model in the system. Usually, manually developed solutions are employed, or some work tries to simplify the development by increasing the level of automation for implementing a causal connection [108]. Most approaches focus on having appropriate abstractions (runtime models) of a running system and.on connecting a model and a system. Thereby, monitoring the system and effecting adaptations to the system are supported. However, the approaches do not completely work incrementally, like [109,110,111] that entirely compares two models to identify the changes to be executed. However, the available techniques are often very demanding and thus result in a too high overhead while being not responsive enough (cf. need for an incremental handling at runtime in general as discussed in the sidebar of [24]). In our work [62,63,64], the monitoring [63] and effecting [64] stages of the feedback loop can handle the causal connection including an abstraction step automatically. Furthermore, our own model synchronization techniques [58], that we employ at runtime, works incrementally as outlined in Section 3.2 and thus enable responsive solutions.

Existing approaches address assurances through validation and verification of adaptation mechanisms, like testing conceivable adaptation results at the level of the runtime model before executing it to the running system. First approaches employing certain techniques have been proposed for constraint checking [110,111], simulation [112], and model checking [113]. However, there is a lack of work on assurances for the runtime models themselves as well as for employing incremental MDE techniques working on these models. We think that the in Section 4 presented results provide a solid basis for a more subtantial coverage of this problem.

As we pointed out in [26], a solution is required where adaptation steps in the construction environment and in the runtime environment happen in an integrated manner. Consequently, the integrated co-existence of self-adaptation and classical adaptation including dependencies between them also have to be addressed. In this direction, only few preliminary ideas exist [110] and a more thorough approach towards integrating these ideas is required and we think that due to the in this paper outlined support for the different cases graph transformations are a good candidate as a foundation for such efforts.

6   Conclusion

As outlined in the paper graph transformations provide a solid basis for related techniques such as SP, Story Diagrams and TGGs such that we cannot only address MDE, structural dynamics as well as models at runtime using these techniques but also analyze important properties for the resulting systems. Due to the fact that all the developed techniques share the underlying concepts of graph transformations, they do not only provide basic building blocks for MDE, systems with structural dynamics, and models at runtime, but furthermore provide a basis to integrate these directions into a single coherent approach. Therefore, graph transformations seem to be a good candidate to provide a solid foundation for approaching the evolution challenge.

References

1. Lehman, M.M., Belady, L.A. (eds.): Program evolution: processes of software change. Academic Press Professional, Inc., San Diego (1985)
2. Lehman, M.M.: Laws of Software Evolution Revisited. In: Montangero, C. (ed.) EWSPT 1996. LNCS, vol. 1149, pp. 108–124. Springer, Heidelberg (1996)
3. Parnas, D.L.: Software aging. In: ICSE 1994: Proceedings of the 16th International Conference on Software Engineering, pp. 279–287. IEEE Computer Society Press, Los Alamitos (1994)
4. Mens, T., Demeyer, S.: Software Evolution. Springer (2008)
5. Martin, R., Osborne, W.: Guidance of Software Maintenance. Technical Report NBS Pub. 500-129, U.S. Nat. Bureau of Standards (December 1983)
6. Chikofsky, E.J., Cross II, J.H.: Reverse Engineering and Design Recovery: A Taxonomy. IEEE Software 7(1), 13–17 (1990)
7. Mens, T., Tourwe, T.: A survey of software refactoring. IEEE Transactions on Software Engineering 30(2), 126–139 (2004)
8. Kephart, J.O., Chess, D.: The Vision of Autonomic Computing. Computer 36(1), 41–50 (2003)
9. Brown, P., Bovey, J., Chen, X.: Context-aware applications: from the laboratory to the marketplace. IEEE Personal Communications 4(5), 58–64 (1997)
10. Northrop, L., Feiler, P.H., Gabriel, R.P., Linger, R., Longstaff, T., Kazman, R., Klein, M., Schmidt, D.: Ultra-Large-Scale Systems: The Software Challenge of the Future. Software Engineering Institute, Carnegie Mellon University, Pittsburgh, PA (2006)

11. Sztipanovits, J., Karsai, G., Bapty, T.: Self-adaptive software for signal processing. Commun. ACM 41(5), 66–73 (1998)
12. Oreizy, P., Gorlick, M.M., Taylor, R., Heimbigner, D., Johnson, G., Medvidovic, N., Quilici, A., Rosenblum, D.S., Wolf, A.L.: An Architecture-Based Approach to Self-Adaptive Software. IEEE Intelligent Systems 14(3), 54–62 (1999)
13. Musliner, D.J., Goldman, R.P., Pelican, M.J., Krebsbach, K.D.: Self-Adaptive Software for Hard Real-Time Environments. IEEE Inteligent Systems 14(4) (July 1999)
14. Robertson, P., Shrobe, H.E., Laddaga, R. (eds.): IWSAS 2000. LNCS, vol. 1936. Springer, Heidelberg (2001)
15. Laddaga, R., Shrobe, H.E., Robertson, P. (eds.): IWSAS 2001. LNCS, vol. 2614. Springer, Heidelberg (2003)
16. Cheng, B.H.C., de Lemos, R., Giese, H., Inverardi, P., Magee, J., Andersson, J., Becker, B., Bencomo, N., Brun, Y., Cukic, B., Di Marzo Serugendo, G., Dustdar, S., Finkelstein, A., Gacek, C., Geihs, K., Grassi, V., Karsai, G., Kienle, H.M., Kramer, J., Litoiu, M., Malek, S., Mirandola, R., Müller, H.A., Park, S., Shaw, M., Tichy, M., Tivoli, M., Weyns, D., Whittle, J.: Software Engineering for Self-Adaptive Systems: A Research Roadmap. In: Cheng, B.H.C., de Lemos, R., Giese, H., Inverardi, P., Magee, J. (eds.) Self-Adaptive Systems. LNCS, vol. 5525, pp. 1–26. Springer, Heidelberg (2009)
17. Cheng, B.H.C., de Lemos, R., Giese, H., Inverardi, P., Magee, J. (eds.): Self-Adaptive Systems. LNCS, vol. 5525. Springer, Heidelberg (2009)
18. Salehie, M., Tahvildari, L.: Self-adaptive software: Landscape and research challenges. ACM Trans. Auton. Adapt. Syst. 4(2), 1–42 (2009)
19. Maes, P.: Concepts and experiments in computational reflection. In: Conference Proceedings on Object-Oriented Programming Systems, Languages and Applications, OOPSLA 1987, pp. 147–155. ACM, New York (1987)
20. Brun, Y., Di Marzo Serugendo, G., Gacek, C., Giese, H., Kienle, H., Litoiu, M., Müller, H., Pezzè, M., Shaw, M.: Engineering Self-Adaptive Systems through Feedback Loops. In: Cheng, B.H.C., de Lemos, R., Giese, H., Inverardi, P., Magee, J. (eds.) Self-Adaptive Systems. LNCS, vol. 5525, pp. 48–70. Springer, Heidelberg (2009)
21. Kramer, J., Magee, J.: Self-Managed Systems: an Architectural Challenge. In: FOSE 2007: Future of Software Engineering, pp. 259–268. IEEE Computer Society, Washington, DC (2007)
22. Garlan, D., Cheng, S.W., Huang, A.C., Schmerl, B., Steenkiste, P.: Rainbow: Architecture-Based Self-Adaptation with Reusable Infrastructure. Computer 37(10), 46–54 (2004)
23. Georgas, J.C., Hoek, A., Taylor, R.N.: Using Architectural Models to Manage and Visualize Runtime Adaptation. Computer 42(10), 52–60 (2009)
24. Blair, G., Bencomo, N., France, R.B.: Models@run.time: Guest Editors' Introduction. Computer 42(10), 22–27 (2009)
25. Baresi, L., Ghezzi, C.: The disappearing boundary between development-time and run-time. In: Proceedings of the FSE/SDP Workshop on Future of Software Engineering Research (FoSER 2010), pp. 17–22. ACM, New York (2010)
26. Gacek, C., Giese, H., Hadar, E.: Friends or Foes? – A Conceptual Analysis of Self-Adaptation and IT Change Management. In: Proc. of the ICSE 2008 Workshop on Software Engineering for Adaptive and Self-Managing Systems (SEAMS 2008), Leipzig, Germany. ACM Press (2008)

27. Baresi, L., Heckel, R.: Tutorial Introduction to Graph Transformation: A Software Engineering Perspective. In: Corradini, A., Ehrig, H., Kreowski, H.-J., Rozenberg, G. (eds.) ICGT 2002. LNCS, vol. 2505, pp. 402–429. Springer, Heidelberg (2002)

28. Rensink, A.: The Edge of Graph Transformation — Graphs for Behavioural Specification. In: Engels, G., Lewerentz, C., Schäfer, W., Schürr, A., Westfechtel, B. (eds.) Nagl Festschrift. LNCS, vol. 5765, pp. 6–32. Springer, Heidelberg (2010)

29. Giese, H., Klein, F.: Autonomous Shuttle System Case Study. In: Leue, S., Systä, T.J. (eds.) Scenarios. LNCS, vol. 3466, pp. 90–94. Springer, Heidelberg (2005)

30. International Telecommunication Union, I.: ITU-T Recommendation Z.100: Specification and Description Language (SDL) (2002)

31. Schäfer, W., Wagner, R., Gausemeier, J., Eckes, R.: An Engineer's Workstation to Support Integrated Development of Flexible Production Control Systems. In: Ehrig, H., Damm, W., Desel, J., Große-Rhode, M., Reif, W., Schnieder, E., Westkämper, E. (eds.) INT 2004. LNCS, vol. 3147, pp. 48–68. Springer, Heidelberg (2004)

32. Habel, A., Pennemann, K.H.: Correctness of high-level transformation systems relative to nested conditions. Mathematical Structures in Computer Science 19, 1–52 (2009)

33. Ehrig, H., Habel, A., Lambers, L., Orejas, F., Golas, U.: Local Confluence for Rules with Nested Application Conditions. In: Ehrig, H., Rensink, A., Rozenberg, G., Schürr, A. (eds.) ICGT 2010. LNCS, vol. 6372, pp. 330–345. Springer, Heidelberg (2010)

34. Rozenberg, G. (ed.): Handbook of Graph Grammars and Computing by Graph Transformation, vol. 1. World Scientific, Singapore (1999)

35. Ehrig, H., Ehrig, K., Prange, U., Taentzer, G.: Fundamentals of Algebraic Graph Transformation. Springer (2006)

36. Löwe, M., Korff, M., Wagner, A.: An algebraic framework for the transformation of attributed graphs, pp. 185–199. John Wiley and Sons Ltd., Chichester (1993)

37. Plump, D., Steinert, S.: Towards Graph Programs for Graph Algorithms. In: Ehrig, H., Engels, G., Parisi-Presicce, F., Rozenberg, G. (eds.) ICGT 2004. LNCS, vol. 3256, pp. 128–143. Springer, Heidelberg (2004)

38. Orejas, F., Lambers, L.: Delaying Constraint Solving in Symbolic Graph Transformation. In: Ehrig, H., Rensink, A., Rozenberg, G., Schürr, A. (eds.) ICGT 2010. LNCS, vol. 6372, pp. 43–58. Springer, Heidelberg (2010)

39. Bardohl, R., Ehrig, H., de Lara, J., Taentzer, G.: Integrating Meta-modelling Aspects with Graph Transformation for Efficient Visual Language Definition and Model Manipulation. In: Wermelinger, M., Margaria-Steffen, T. (eds.) FASE 2004. LNCS, vol. 2984, pp. 214–228. Springer, Heidelberg (2004)

40. Golas, U., Lambers, L., Ehrig, H., Orejas, F.: Attributed graph transformation with inheritance: Efficient conflict detection and local confluence analysis using abstract critical pairs. Theoretical Computer Science 424, 46–68 (2012)

41. Gorp, P.V., Mazanek, S., Rose, L. (eds.): Proceedings Fifth Transformation Tool Contest. EPTCS, vol. 74 (2011)

42. Ermel, C., Rudolf, M., Taentzer, G.: The AGG approach: language and environment. In: Ehrig, H., Engels, G., Rozenberg, G. (eds.) Handbook of Graph Grammars and Computing by Graph Transformation: Applications, Languages, and Tools, vol. 2, pp. 551–603. World Scientific Publishing Co., Inc., River Edge (1999)

43. Arendt, T., Biermann, E., Jurack, S., Krause, C., Taentzer, G.: Henshin: Advanced Concepts and Tools for In-Place EMF Model Transformations. In: Petriu, D.C., Rouquette, N., Haugen, Ø. (eds.) MoDELS 2010. LNCS, vol. 6394, pp. 121–135. Springer, Heidelberg (2010)

44. Schürr, A., Winter, A., Zündorf, A.: The PROGRES Approach: Language and Environment. In: Ehrig, H., Engels, G., Kreowski, H.J., Rozenberg, G. (eds.) Handbook of Graph Grammars and Computing by Graph Transformation: Application, Languages and Tools, vol. 2, pp. 487–546. World Scientific, Singapore (1999)

45. Giese, H., Hildebrandt, S., Seibel, A.: Improved Flexibility and Scalability by Interpreting Story Diagrams. In: Magaria, T., Padberg, J., Taentzer, G. (eds.) Proceedings of the Eighth International Workshop on Graph Transformation and Visual Modeling Techniques (GT-VMT 2009), Electronic Communications of the EASST, vol. 18 (2009)

46. Seibel, A., Neumann, S., Giese, H.: Dynamic hierarchical mega models: comprehensive traceability and its efficient maintenance. Software and System Modeling 9(4), 493–528 (2010), doi:10.1007/s10270-009-0146-z

47. Fischer, T., Niere, J., Torunski, L., Zündorf, A.: Story Diagrams: A New Graph Rewrite Language Based on the Unified Modeling Language and Java. In: Ehrig, H., Engels, G., Kreowski, H.-J., Rozenberg, G. (eds.) TAGT 1998. LNCS, vol. 1764, pp. 296–309. Springer, Heidelberg (2000)

48. Zündorf, A.: Rigorous Object Oriented Software Development with Fujaba. Draft Version 0.3. (2002), http://www.se.eecs.uni-kassel.de/ se/fileadmin/se/publications/Zuen02.pdf

49. Becker, B., Beyer, D., Giese, H., Klein, F., Schilling, D.: Symbolic Invariant Verification for Systems with Dynamic Structural Adaptation. In: Proc. of the 28th International Conference on Software Engineering (ICSE), Shanghai, China. ACM Press (2006)

50. Fowler, M.: Refactoring: Improving the Design of Existing Code. Addison-Wesley (1999)

51. Krasnogolowy, A., Hildebrandt, S., Wätzoldt, S.: Flexible Debugging of Behavior Models. In: Proceedings of 2012 IEEE International Conference on Industrial Technology (ICIT). IEEE (2011)

52. Stürmer, I., Kreuz, I., Schäfer, W., Schürr, A.: Enhanced Simulink/Stateflow Model Transformation: The MATE Approach. In: Proc. of MathWorks Automotive Conference (MAC 2007), Dearborn (MI), USA (2007)

53. Schafe, S.: Objektorientierte Entwurfsmethoden. Addison-Wesley (1994)

54. Giese, H., Hildebrandt, S., Lambers, L.: Toward Bridging the Gap Between Formal Semantics and Implementation of Triple Graph Grammars. In: Proceedings of MoDeVVa 2010, Models Workshop on Model-Driven Engineering, Verification and Validation, Oslo, Norway (2010)

55. Giese, H., Hildebrandt, S., Lambers, L.: Toward Bridging the Gap Between Formal Semantics and Implementation of Triple Graph Grammars. Technical Report 37, Hasso Plattner Institute at the University of Potsdam (2010)

56. Larchevêque, J.M.: Optimal incremental parsing. ACM Trans. Program. Lang. Syst. 17(1), 1–15 (1995)

57. Giese, H., Wagner, R.: Incremental Model Synchronization with Triple Graph Grammars. In: Nierstrasz, O., Whittle, J., Harel, D., Reggio, G. (eds.) MoDELS 2006. LNCS, vol. 4199, pp. 543–557. Springer, Heidelberg (2006)

58. Giese, H., Wagner, R.: From model transformation to incremental bidirectional model synchronization. Software and Systems Modeling (SoSyM) 8(1) (March 28, 2009)

59. Giese, H., Hildebrandt, S.: Incremental Model Synchronization for Multiple Updates. In: Proceedings of the 3rd International Workshop on Graph and Model Transformations, GraMoT 2008, Leipzig, Germany, May 12. ACM Press (2008)

60. Giese, H., Hildebrandt, S.: Efficient Model Synchronization of Large-Scale Models. Technical Report 28, Hasso Plattner Institute at the University of Potsdam (2009)

61. Giese, H., Hildebrandt, S., Neumann, S.: Model Synchronization at Work: Keeping SysML and AUTOSAR Models Consistent. In: Engels, G., Lewerentz, C., Schäfer, W., Schürr, A., Westfechtel, B. (eds.) Nagl Festschrift. LNCS, vol. 5765, pp. 555–579. Springer, Heidelberg (2010)

62. Vogel, T., Neumann, S., Hildebrandt, S., Giese, H., Becker, B.: Model-Driven Architectural Monitoring and Adaptation for Autonomic Systems. In: Proceedings of the 6th IEEE/ACM International Conference on Autonomic Computing and Communications (ICAC 2009), Barcelona, Spain. ACM (2009)

63. Vogel, T., Neumann, S., Hildebrandt, S., Giese, H., Becker, B.: Incremental Model Synchronization for Efficient Run-Time Monitoring. In: Ghosh, S. (ed.) MODELS 2009 Workshops. LNCS, vol. 6002, pp. 124–139. Springer, Heidelberg (2010)

64. Vogel, T., Giese, H.: Adaptation and Abstract Runtime Models. In: Proceedings of the 5th Workshop on Software Engineering for Adaptive and Self-Managing Systems (SEAMS 2010) at the 32nd IEEE/ACM International Conference on Software Engineering (ICSE 2010), Cape Town, South Africa, pp. 39–48. ACM (2010)

65. Vogel, T., Giese, H.: Requirements and Assessment of Languages and Frameworks for Adaptation Models. In: Kienzle, J. (ed.) MODELS 2011 Workshops. LNCS, vol. 7167, pp. 167–182. Springer, Heidelberg (2012)

66. Vogel, T., Seibel, A., Giese, H.: The Role of Models and Megamodels at Runtime. In: Dingel, J., Solberg, A. (eds.) MODELS 2010 Workshops. LNCS, vol. 6627, pp. 224–238. Springer, Heidelberg (2011)

67. Vogel, T., Giese, H.: A Language for Feedback Loops in Self-Adaptive Systems: Executable Runtime Megamodels. In: Proceedings of the 7th International Symposium on Software Engineering for Adaptive and Self-Managing Systems (SEAMS 2012). IEEE Computer Society (2012)

68. Hausmann, J., Heckel, R., Taentzer, G.: Detection of Conflicting Functional Requirements in a Use Case-Driven Approach. In: Proc. of Int. Conference on Software Engineering 2002, Orlando, USA, pp. 105–115. IEEE Computer Society (2002)

69. Engels, G., Güldali, B., Lohmann, M.: Towards Model-Driven Unit Testing. In: Kühne, T. (ed.) MODELS 2006 Workshops. LNCS, vol. 4364, pp. 182–192. Springer, Heidelberg (2007)

70. Ehrig, K., Küster, J., Taentzer, G., Winkelmann, J.: Generating Instance Models from Meta Models. In: Gorrieri, R., Wehrheim, H. (eds.) FMOODS 2006. LNCS, vol. 4037, pp. 156–170. Springer, Heidelberg (2006)

71. Heckel, R., Mariani, L.: Automatic Conformance Testing of Web Services. In: Cerioli, M. (ed.) FASE 2005. LNCS, vol. 3442, pp. 34–48. Springer, Heidelberg (2005)

72. Rensink, A., Schmidt, Á., Varró, D.: Model Checking Graph Transformations: A Comparison of Two Approaches. In: Ehrig, H., Engels, G., Parisi-Presicce, F., Rozenberg, G. (eds.) ICGT 2004. LNCS, vol. 3256, pp. 226–241. Springer, Heidelberg (2004)

73. Kastenberg, H., Rensink, A.: Model Checking Dynamic States in GROOVE. In: Valmari, A. (ed.) SPIN 2006. LNCS, vol. 3925, pp. 299–305. Springer, Heidelberg (2006)
74. Strecker, M.: Modeling and Verifying Graph Transformations in Proof Assistants. In: Mackie, I., Plump, D. (eds.) International Workshop on Computing with Terms and Graphs (TERMGRAPH), Braga, Portugal, March 31, 2007. Electronic Notes in Theoretical Computer Science, vol. 203, pp. 135–148. Elsevier Science (2008), http://www.elsevier.com
75. Pennemann, K.H.: Resolution-Like Theorem Proving for High-Level Conditions. In: Ehrig, H., Heckel, R., Rozenberg, G., Taentzer, G. (eds.) ICGT 2008. LNCS, vol. 5214, pp. 289–304. Springer, Heidelberg (2008)
76. Giese, H., Glesner, S., Leitner, J., Schäfer, W., Wagner, R.: Towards Verified Model Transformations. In: Hearnden, D., Süß, J., Baudry, B., Rapin, N. (eds.) Proc. of the 3rd International Workshop on Model Development, Validation and Verification (MoDeV^{2}a), Genova, Italy, Le Commissariat à l'Energie Atomique - CEA, pp. 78–93 (October 2006)
77. Baldan, P., Corradini, A., König, B.: A Static Analysis Technique for Graph Transformation Systems. In: Larsen, K.G., Nielsen, M. (eds.) CONCUR 2001. LNCS, vol. 2154, pp. 381–395. Springer, Heidelberg (2001)
78. Habel, A., Pennemann, K.-H., Rensink, A.: Weakest Preconditions for High-Level Programs. In: Corradini, A., Ehrig, H., Montanari, U., Ribeiro, L., Rozenberg, G. (eds.) ICGT 2006. LNCS, vol. 4178, pp. 445–460. Springer, Heidelberg (2006)
79. Poskitt, C.M., Plump, D.: A Hoare Calculus for Graph Programs. In: Ehrig, H., Rensink, A., Rozenberg, G., Schürr, A. (eds.) ICGT 2010. LNCS, vol. 6372, pp. 139–154. Springer, Heidelberg (2010)
80. Lambers, L.: Certifying Rule-Based Models using Graph Transformation. PhD thesis, Technische Universität Berlin (2010); Also as book available: Südwestdeutscher Verlag für Hochschulschriften, ISBN: 978-3-8381-1650-1
81. Becker, B., Giese, H.: On Safe Service-Oriented Real-Time Coordination for Autonomous Vehicles. In: Proc. of 11th International Symposium on Object/Component/Service-Oriented Real-time Distributed Computing (ISORC), May 5-7, pp. 203–210. IEEE Computer Society Press (2008)
82. Becker, B., Giese, H.: Incremental Verification of Inductive Invariants for the Run-Time Evolution of Self-Adaptive Software-Intensive Systems. In: Proc. 1st International Workshop on Automated engineeRing of Autonomous and run-tiMe evolvIng Systems (ARAMIS), pp. 33–40. IEEE Computer Society Press (2008)
83. Charpentier, M.: Composing Invariants. In: Araki, K., Gnesi, S., Mandrioli, D. (eds.) FME 2003. LNCS, vol. 2805, pp. 401–421. Springer, Heidelberg (2003)
84. Becker, B., Lambers, L., Dyck, J., Birth, S., Giese, H.: Iterative Development of Consistency-Preserving Rule-Based Refactorings. In: Cabot, J., Visser, E. (eds.) ICMT 2011. LNCS, vol. 6707, pp. 123–137. Springer, Heidelberg (2011)
85. Clarke, E.M., Grumberg, O., Peled, D.: Model Checking. MIT Press (2002)
86. Biere, A., Cimatti, A., Clarke, E., Strichman, O., Zhu, Y.: Bounded model checking. Advances in Computers 58 (2003)
87. Burch, J.R., Clarke, E.M., McMillan, K.L., Dill, D.L., Hwang, L.J.: Symbolic model checking: 10^{20} states and beyond. Inf. Comput. 98, 142–170 (1992)
88. Rensink, A.: Towards Model Checking Graph Grammars. In: Leuschel, M., Gruner, S., Presti, S.L. (eds.) 3rd Workshop on Automated Verification of Critical Systems (AVoCS), pp. 150–160. Technical Report DSSE–TR–2003–2, University of Southampton (2003)

89. Cicchetti, A., Ruscio, D.D., Eramo, R., Pierantonio, A.: Automating Co-evolution in Model-Driven Engineering. In: Proceedings of the 2008 12th International IEEE Enterprise Distributed Object Computing Conference, pp. 222–231. IEEE Computer Society, Washington, DC (2008)
90. Di Ruscio, D., Iovino, L., Pierantonio, A.: What is needed for managing co-evolution in MDE? In: Proceedings of the 2nd International Workshop on Model Comparison in Practice, IWMCP 2011, pp. 30–38. ACM, New York (2011)
91. Narayanan, A., Karsai, G.: Verifying Model Transformations by Structural Correspondence. Electronic Communications of the EASST: Graph Transformation and Visual Modeling Techniques 2008 10 (2008)
92. Varró, D., Pataricza, A.: Automated Formal Verification of Model Transformations. In: Jürjens, J., Rumpe, B., France, R., Fernandez, E.B. (eds.) CSDUML 2003: Critical Systems Development in UML; Proceedings of the UML 2003 Workshop. Number TUM-I0323 in Technical Report, Technische Universitat Munchen, pp. 63–78 (September 2003)
93. Hülsbusch, M., König, B., Rensink, A., Semenyak, M., Soltenborn, C., Wehrheim, H.: Showing Full Semantics Preservation in Model Transformation - A Comparison of Techniques. In: Méry, D., Merz, S. (eds.) IFM 2010. LNCS, vol. 6396, pp. 183–198. Springer, Heidelberg (2010)
94. Cabot, J., Clarisó, R., Guerra, E., Lara, J.: Verification and validation of declarative model-to-model transformations through invariants. J. Syst. Softw. 83(2), 283–302 (2010)
95. Rouvoy, R., Barone, P., Ding, Y., Eliassen, F., Hallsteinsen, S., Lorenzo, J., Mamelli, A., Scholz, U.: MUSIC: Middleware Support for Self-Adaptation in Ubiquitous and Service-Oriented Environments. In: Cheng, B.H.C., de Lemos, R., Giese, H., Inverardi, P., Magee, J. (eds.) Self-Adaptive Systems. LNCS, vol. 5525, pp. 164–182. Springer, Heidelberg (2009)
96. Bencomo, N., Blair, G.: Using Architecture Models to Support the Generation and Operation of Component-Based Adaptive Systems. In: Cheng, B.H.C., de Lemos, R., Giese, H., Inverardi, P., Magee, J. (eds.) Self-Adaptive Systems. LNCS, vol. 5525, pp. 183–200. Springer, Heidelberg (2009)
97. Burmester, S., Giese, H., Münch, E., Oberschelp, O., Klein, F., Scheideler, P.: Tool Support for the Design of Self-Optimizing Mechatronic Multi-Agent Systems. International Journal on Software Tools for Technology Transfer (STTT) 10(3), 207–222 (2008)
98. Giese, H.: Modeling and Verification of Cooperative Self-adaptive Mechatronic Systems. In: Kordon, F., Sztipanovits, J. (eds.) Monterey Workshop 2005. LNCS, vol. 4322, pp. 258–280. Springer, Heidelberg (2007)
99. Burmester, S., Giese, H.: Visual Integration of UML 2.0 and Block Diagrams for Flexible Reconfiguration in Mechatronic UML. In: Proc. of the IEEE Symposium on Visual Languages and Human-Centric Computing (VL/HCC 2005), Dallas, Texas, USA, pp. 109–116. IEEE Computer Society Press (2005)
100. Goldsby, H.J., Cheng, B.H.C., Zhang, J.: AMOEBA-RT: Run-time verification of adaptive software. In: Giese, H. (ed.) MODELS 2008 Workshops. LNCS, vol. 5002, pp. 212–224. Springer, Heidelberg (2008)
101. Zhang, J., Cheng, B.: Using temporal logic to specify adaptive program semantics. Journal of Systems and Software 79(10), 1361–1369 (2006); Architecting Dependable Systems
102. Zhang, J., Cheng, B.: Model-based development of dynamically adaptive software. In: ICSE 2006: Proceeding of the 28th International Conference on Software Engineering, pp. 371–380. ACM, New York (2006)

103. Zhang, J., Goldsby, H.J., Cheng, B.: Modular verification of dynamically adaptive systems. In: AOSD 2009: Proceedings of the 8th ACM International Conference on Aspect-oriented Software Development, pp. 161–172. ACM, New York (2009)

104. Adler, R., Schaefer, I., Trapp, M., Poetzsch-Heffter, A.: Component-based modeling and verification of dynamic adaptation in safety-critical embedded systems. ACM Transactions on Embedded Computing Systems 10, 20:1–20:39 (2011)

105. Ehrig, H., Ermel, C., Runge, O., Bucchiarone, A., Pelliccione, P.: Formal Analysis and Verification of Self-Healing Systems. In: Rosenblum, D.S., Taentzer, G. (eds.) FASE 2010. LNCS, vol. 6013, pp. 139–153. Springer, Heidelberg (2010)

106. Giese, H., Tichy, M., Burmester, S., Schäfer, W., Flake, S.: Towards the Compositional Verification of Real-Time UML Designs. In: Proc. of the European Software Engineering Conference (ESEC), Helsinki, Finland, Proc. of the 9th European Software Engineering Conference Held Jointly with 11th ACM SIGSOFT International Symposium on Foundations of Software Engineering (ESEC/FSE-11), pp. 38–47. ACM Press (2003)

107. Becker, B., Giese, H.: Modeling of Correct Self-Adaptive Systems: A Graph Transformation System Based Approach. In: CSTST 2008: Proc. 5th Intl. Conference on Soft Computing as Transdisciplinary Science and Technology, pp. 508–516. ACM Press (2008)

108. Song, H., Xiong, Y., Chauvel, F., Huang, G., Hu, Z., Mei, H.: Generating Synchronization Engines between Running Systems and Their Model-Based Views. In: Ghosh, S. (ed.) MODELS 2009 Workshops. LNCS, vol. 6002, pp. 140–154. Springer, Heidelberg (2010)

109. Morin, B., Fleurey, F., Bencomo, N., Jézéquel, J.-M., Solberg, A., Dehlen, V., Blair, G.S.: An Aspect-Oriented and Model-Driven Approach for Managing Dynamic Variability. In: Czarnecki, K., Ober, I., Bruel, J.-M., Uhl, A., Völter, M. (eds.) MoDELS 2008. LNCS, vol. 5301, pp. 782–796. Springer, Heidelberg (2008)

110. Morin, B., Barais, O., Jézéquel, J.M., Fleurey, F., Solberg, A.: Models@ Run.time to Support Dynamic Adaptation. Computer 42(10), 44–51 (2009)

111. Morin, B., Barais, O., Nain, G., Jézéquel, J.M.: Taming Dynamically Adaptive Systems using models and aspects. In: ICSE 2009: Proceedings of the 2009 IEEE 31st International Conference on Software Engineering, pp. 122–132. IEEE Computer Society, Washington, DC (2009)

112. Fleurey, F., Solberg, A.: A Domain Specific Modeling Language Supporting Specification, Simulation and Execution of Dynamic Adaptive Systems. In: Schürr, A., Selic, B. (eds.) MoDELS 2009. LNCS, vol. 5795, pp. 606–621. Springer, Heidelberg (2009)

113. Inverardi, P., Mori, M.: Model checking requirements at run-time in adaptive systems. In: Proceedings of the 8th Workshop on Assurances for Self-Adaptive Systems, ASAS 2011, pp. 5–9. ACM, New York (2011)

Abstractions for Validation in Action

Guido de Caso[1], Victor Braberman[1], Diego Garbervetsky[1],
and Sebastian Uchitel[1,2]

[1] Departamento de Computación, FCEyN, Universidad de Buenos Aires,
Buenos Aires, Argentina
{gdecaso,vbraber,diegog,suchitel}@dc.uba.ar
[2] Department of Computing, Imperial College,
London, UK
s.uchitel@doc.ic.ac.uk

Abstract. Many software engineering artefacts, such as source code or specifications, define a set of operations and impose restrictions to the ordering on which they have to be invoked. Enabledness Preserving Abstractions (EPAs) are concise representations of the behaviour space for such artefacts. In this paper, we exemplify how EPAs might be used for validation of software engineering artefacts by showing the use of EPAs to support some programming tasks on a simple C# class.

Keywords: Behaviour validation, enabledness-preserving abstractions.

1 Introduction

Verification and validation are artefact evaluation activities that are carried out by software engineers in multiple stages of software development projects. They come in many different guises: The artefacts under evaluation may be descriptions related to the problem domain (e.g. requirements) or the solution space (e.g. design) including the actual code. Furthermore, they can be written in languages with different degrees of formality (e.g. from mathematics to natural language). In addition, the evaluation itself can vary in terms of formality (e.g. from axiomatic proof, through structured argumentation, to human inspection) and exhaustiveness (e.g. from exhaustive search, through simulation, to selective scenario evaluation). All these characteristics lead to conclusions with very different degrees of certainty.

Verification and validation are related activities both of which aim to increase confidence regarding the quality of the software under construction. However, they are of very different nature.

1.1 Verification

Verification aims at determining whether an artefact satisfies specific properties [25]. For instance, if software requirements entail system goals, if the architecture satisfies its reliability requirements, if the code is structured according

M. Bernardo, V. Cortellessa, and A. Pierantonio (Eds.): SFM 2012, LNCS 7320, pp. 192–218, 2012.

to the static design, or the execution of a method never raises an array index out of bounds exception.

Verification is particularly prone to automated, rigorous and even sometimes exhaustive analysis. If both the artefact under evaluation and the properties are given in appropriate formal languages, it is plausible to apply a battery of tools such as model checkers [6], theorem provers [32], simulators [27] or symbolic executers [34]. There are, of course, both theoretical (indecidability results, e.g., [16]) and practical (e.g., state explosion [37]) limitations. However, automated verification techniques are tractable and have shown to be useful, specially when applying some restrictions on the artefact, the property, and/or the degree of certainty. Most notably, software testing, when the intended test results are provided (i.e., an oracle), is a widespread verification technique in industry.

1.2   Validation

Validation is, arguably, a much more complex task than verification as it aims to determine the degree to which an artefact is an accurate representation of the real world. At the requirements level, a typical example used to distinguish validation from verification is that validation evaluates if the requirements meet stakeholders needs, while verification is applied to check that the design and/or implementation has been built according to the requirements. In other words, validation ensures that you built the right thing while verification ensures that you built it right. Validation is indeed relevant in many software engineering settings. For instance, determining if an architectural description conforms to an architect's intent, if the deployment model is consistent with the actual hardware available at the client site, if assumptions on network traffic are reasonable, etc.

Validation, in industrial practice, is also a substitute for verification. The lack of explicit (formal or informal) intended property descriptions impedes verification and the only possibility is to validate if artefacts conform to the characteristics intended by the engineer. In other words, a comparison between the artefact and some mental model of what the artefact should comply to. Walkthroughs, inspections and reviews are common techniques that support validation.

When the artefact under validation is written in a formal language (be it code, or a well founded specification), a common strategy for validation is to apply an automated, semantics preserving, manipulation. The idea behind this strategy is that showing engineers alternative views of the artefact may exhibit elements that stand out as contradicting to what is expected by the engineers. Some examples of this strategy are the application of rewrite rules in specifications, minimisation of state machines, slicing techniques for code, or executions and simulations. Within the latter strategy, testing without oracles is a noteworthy technique.

Another common strategy for validation is to turn the validation problem into a verification one. More concretely, to produce a specification against which the artefact can be verified. The idea is that if the specification is simpler than the artefact, validation of the former is likely to be simpler and less error prone. This is an effective strategy that is commonly used in practice. For instance, sanity checks are used to filter out bugs in complex models (such as nonzenoness in real time system models [2], as well as internal consistency and satisfiability in requirements specifications [23]). However, this strategy has its downsides too. Since an alternative specification is required, we need to be sure that it has been validated appropriately. In other words, turning a validation problem into a verification problem creates a new (possibly simpler but of reduced scope) validation task, so eventually human intervention is required.

1.3   Abstraction

Abstraction is the act of withdrawing or removing something, the process of leaving out of consideration one or more properties of a complex artefact so as to attend to others. It is also used to refer to the simpler artefact that results from this process. The abstraction captures the original artefact's core or essence relative to a specific aspect of interest. Abstraction is central to computing [26], particularly to software engineering, and has been extensively applied to support verification and validation.

Abstraction reduces the complexity of the artefact under evaluation and consequently can reduce the cost and augment the effectiveness of verification and validation activities. However, abstraction comes at a price. Building abstractions can be costly, but perhaps more importantly, the loss of detail in the abstract artefact can impact the degrees of certainty of the evaluation outcome. Given a particular verification or validation task, analysing a carefully chosen abstraction will yield conservative (yet sound) results. On the other hand, an incorrect choice might lead to invalid conclusions. For instance, let's consider a language with automatic memory management. A garbage collector (GC) is in charge of reclaiming unreferenced objects. In order to make a decision whether an object o can be collected, the GC must ensure that no other object or variable points to o. If the GC makes the decision based on an abstraction that only considers elements in the program stack, it may collect objects that are still reachable from the heap.

Hence, given a validation or verification task, it is crucial to work with an appropriate abstraction. That is, carefully selecting which aspects to leave out of consideration and what mechanisms to use for representing the artefact's features relevant to the task at hand.

1.4   Abstractions for API Implementation Behaviour

We now set the scene for the rest of this paper. We first narrow the discussion by stating our interest in the behaviour of stateful API implementations: A collection of methods or procedures accessing a shared data structure. Such artefacts are commonplace and pose a number of challenges to verification and validation. It is insufficient to evaluate each method in isolation. We also need to consider their interaction via the shared data structure and the emergent behaviour of the combinations of method calls.

State machines or *behaviour models* constitute a natural abstraction to validate or verify an API implementation behaviour. Each abstract state in these models represents one or more possible concrete states of the shared data structure. Transitions in the abstraction represent changes of state related to the execution of one or more lines of code (including, for instance a whole method invocation).

Abstractions for Verification. There has been a significant amount of work in the use of abstractions for *verification*. Given an artefact a and a formalised property φ to be verified, the aim is to automatically come up with simplified versions $\hat{a}$ and $\hat{\varphi}$ of the artefact and property, respectively. Hopefully, verifying whether $\hat{a}$ satisfies $\hat{\varphi}$ will be more tractable, while still providing information about the initial verification problem regarding a and φ.

Applying abstraction to obtain a tractable behaviour model of the original artefact typically involves paying the cost of the omitted detail in terms of loss of precision. Abstracted behaviour models may be overapproximations (when $\hat{a}$ accepts all behaviour of a, but possibly more) or underapproximations (when $\hat{a}$ rejects all behaviour not in a, but possibly more) of the original artefact. Furthermore, some abstractions may neither be over nor underapproximations.

Given an API implementation, an overapproximation of its behaviour describes all legal invocation sequence that API clients can perform on the API. However, an overapproximation may include sequences which, if performed by clients, would result in illegal invocation chains. On the other hand, an underapproximation of the API implementation's behaviour forbids every illegal invocation sequence, which is why they are called *safe* from a client perspective. Underapproximated models may go too far and forbid behaviour which was permitted in the original artefact. For this reason, overaproximated models are sometimes referred to as *permissive*.

One common approach when applying abstraction for verification of API behaviour is to synthesise typestates [35,13,31,4] or interfaces [1,20,24]. The aim is to statically obtain finite state machine representing a *safe* model from a client perspective, using techniques such as automata learning [1,20,24] or abstract interpretation [31].

The safety requirement associated to these kind of models tends to make abstractions overly restrictive in terms of the model behaviour, sometimes leading to trivial abstractions (e.g. models in which very few or even no invocation sequences are allowed). In some cases, permissiveness is possible at the cost of assuming certain conditions over the artefacts. For instance, the algorithms in [20,24] guarantee permissiveness only when the library's internal state is finite.

Once inferred, safe typestates for an API can be used to effectively verify the absence of illegal invocations from clients (e.g., [7]). The cost of non-permissive typestates in this setting is that false-positives (client invocation sequences that are in fact legal) may be reported.

Another way of obtaining abstract behaviour models is by using predicate abstraction [36]. The idea is to define a set of predicates P and group concrete states according to the validity of those predicates. Concretely, each abstract state represents a set of concrete states that gives the same valuation to all the predicates in P.

There are techniques that use this approach to construct abstract state graphs from infinite state systems (e.g., [28,21,29,22]). For instance [21] builds an abstract state graph out of a guarded transition system and a set of input predicates. Concrete states are abstracted by using a lattice of monomials of abstract boolean variables representing the truth values of the input predicates.

For testing purposes, [29] proposes the use of user-provided parameterless boolean observers to quotient the state space of a class. The abstraction is not meant to represent behaviour (e.g., it does not define transitions between states) but to define goals for test coverage criteria (which may not be fulfilled due to the overapproximated nature of the abstraction) . These models are then fed to an algorithm that attempts to create a test suite that covers all of the states.

Another interesting approach is the mining of behaviour models out of execution traces (e.g., [11,19,18,30,12,5,33]). These techniques aim at inferring a specification which is used for test case generation or verification.

Mining techniques have a dynamic flavour, and thus heavily depend on the quality of the traces used as input. The inferred models tend to be underapproximations of the behaviour of the artefact under analysis, since some behaviour may not appear in the collected traces. However, in some cases, these approaches may also over-approximate due to the application of generalisation strategies.

For instance, [18] produces an automata by collecting information from the client's actual usage of a set of operations (underapproximation). ADABU [11] produces finite state machines whose states are determined by a fixed level of abstraction ranging over the return values of the inspectors in a class (e.g., integers are abstracted according to its sign), leading to both under and overappproximation of the concrete state. Another approaches [19,30], use invariant detection tools such as DAIKON [15] in order to generalise the set of traces and obtain more conservative models.

Abstractions for Validation. We are interested is studying the use of abstraction in the context of validation rather than verification. Since validation requires human intervention, the size and complexity of the models obtained are a key aspect at the moment of choosing the abstraction.

As we previously stated, most of the models used in the typestate and interface synthesis literature are used to feed machine-driven tasks such as automated verification and test-case generation. There are a few exceptions, though.

For instance, the approach followed in [5] uses logging mechanisms already in place and regular expressions to obtain behaviour models almost without user intervention. The logs are mined looking for invariants encoding simple temporal restrictions among operations. Then the authors build a behaviour model that satisfies every invariant found in the previous step. These models have been successfully used to guide human validation processes such as program understanding or bug confirmation.

Another example of synthesised models being used for human inspection is introduced in [14]. Authors present a technique to dynamically construct role transition diagrams (among other models), which have a resemblance to types-tates. These models are used, together with a powerful graphical user interface, to support program understanding tasks.

Even though these examples show the use of underapproximations for the validation of artefacts, we believe that in general overapproximations are bet-ter suited for validation since they are capable of exhibiting all the potential behaviour of the artefact.

In this paper we will study a particular abstraction level that we denominate *enabledness-based abstractions* [8] that focus the attention on the enabledness of a set of actions or method within a API. We have successfully evaluated the potential of these abstractions both for contract specifications validation [8] as well as for validating code implementing APIs [9].

This rest of this paper is structured as follows: Section 2 introduces enabledness-preserving abstractions (EPAs); Section 3 presents how the use of EPAs can aid software developers in various activities such as program under-standing or the implementation of new features; Section 4 provides a series of strategies and checklists to work with EPA-guided software validation; finally, Section 5 concludes our presentation.

2   Background

Enabledness-preserving abstractions (EPAs) are state machines that describe behaviour of API implementations by introducing abstraction in two different ways. Firstly, states reached by the implementation while executing API oper-ations are ignored; focus is on states of the implementation before and after operations are executed. Secondly, the actual values of the data structures of the implementation are abstracted; focus is what operations those values allow or disallow. Hence, states of an EPA represent sets of concrete implementation states which allow the same set of operations. Finally, parameters and return values of operations are also ignored; focus is on whether there exist values for parameters of an operation such that the execution of the operation will make the implementation transition from one abstract state to another.

We briefly define EPAs more formally utilising object oriented terminology. For a more detailed presentation see [9]. A *class* C can be seen as a structure $\langle M, F, R, inv, init \rangle$, where $M = \{m_1, \ldots, m_k\}$ is a finite set of *public method labels*, F is an M-indexed set of *method implementations*, R is an M-indexed set of *requires clauses*, *inv* is the *class invariant*, and *init* denotes the *initial conditions* given by the constructors. Given a class C and two instances c_1, c_2, we say that c_1 and c_2 are *enabledness equivalent* (noted $c_1 \equiv_e c_2$) iff for every $m \in M$: c_1 satisfies R_m iff c_2 satisfies R_m (i.e. if the two instances satisfy the same set of requires clauses).

The set of class instances, when quotiented by $\equiv_e$, results in a set of abstract states, such that each one is mapped to a (distinct) group of enabled methods. Each abstract state groups all the instances that share the same set of enabled methods, and can be characterized by a *state predicate*. Formally, the predicate for an abstract state given by a set of methods $ms \subseteq M$ is a function $pred_{ms}$ that takes an instance of C and returns a boolean. It is formally defined as:

$$pred_{ms}(c) \stackrel{\text{def}}{\Leftrightarrow} inv(c) \wedge \bigwedge_{m \in ms} c \text{ safisties } R_m \wedge \bigwedge_{m \notin ms} c \text{ does not satisfy } R_m$$

An abstract transition labeled with an action m between two abstract states exists if and only if a class instance in the target abstract state can be reached by executing m from a class instance in the source abstract state. Formally, let ms_1 and ms_2 be method sets (that is, abstract states) and $m \in ms_1$ an action. An m-labeled transition is added from ms_1 to ms_2 if there is a class instance c_1 in ms_1 that can execute m and evolve into a class instance c_2 in ms_2.

EPAs capture a superset of the concrete class' behaviour. In practice, this level of abstraction provides a good compromise: it is abstract enough to keep the EPAs concise, and it is precise enough so that it is still a valuable information source for humans to inspect.

2.1   EPA Construction

Enabledness-preserving abstractions can be statically and automatically built. While the details of the construction process are out of scope in this presentation, we present some brief notes and pointers to other articles.

The reader may notice that a class with k public methods has potentially 2^k reachable abstract states. A naïf construction algorithm would compute all the 2^k states and its transitions, only to later restrict the result to the reachable fragment. On the other hand, more sophisticated approaches such as parallelized BFS exploration strategies (e.g. [9]) can drastically reduce construction times.

We implemented a prototype tool[1] called CONTRACTOR which implements various EPA construction algorithms, together with several optimisations. In its current version, CONTRACTOR supports the construction of EPAs directly from pre/postcondition contracts [8], C code [9] and .NET code [38].

In the rest of this paper, we focus on constructing EPAs out of C# code, one of the most popular .NET languages. We leverage existing .NET infrastructure to let the programmer identify the requires clauses and the class invariant. More specifically, we use the CODE CONTRACTS [3] library calls Contract.Requires(...) and Contract.Invariant(...).

3   Developing with EPAs

In this section we describe some simple (and fictional) software development tasks supported by using enabledness-preserving abstractions as a visual aid. Although applied to a small class, we aim to exemplify how EPAs can aid in various tasks such as understanding someone else's source code, extending it

---

[1] Publicly available at http://lafhis.dc.uba.ar/contractor

```
1  public class Stack {              24      public bool isFull() {
2    private int[] elems;            25        return next == elems.Length;
3    private int next;               26      }
4                                    27
5    public Stack(int m) {           28      public void push(int k) {
6      next = 0;                     29        elems[next] = k;
7      elems = new int[m];           30        next++;
8    }                               31      }
9                                    32
10     public int top() {            33      public void pop() {
11       if (isEmpty())              34        if (isEmpty())
12         return -1;                35          return;
13       else                        36        next--;
14         return elems[next - 1];   37      }
15     }                             38
16                                   39      public void reset() {
17     public bool isEmpty() {       40        next = 0;
18       return next == 0;           41      }
19     }                             42  }
20
21     public int maxSize() {
22       return elems.Length;
23     }
```

Fig. 1. Train door controller

with a new feature, testing the new functionality, debugging the problems that may arise and fixing them. Interested readers are directed to [8,9] for a report on the application of EPAs on various real-life industrial scale software artefacts.

3.1   Understanding Code with EPAs

Tom, our fictional programmer hero, has just taken a job at DataXtructures Inc., a fictional software developing company specialized in implementing efficient data containers.

His first assignment is to extend the functionality of a Stack class with some new operations. The original code for the class that Tom has to extend is depicted in Figure 1.

After a brief code inspection, Tom soon realizes that this simple data structure was implemented using an underlying array. This imposes an upper bound on the number of elements that can be stored. He also discovers that the are a number of observer operations such as top(), isEmpty() or maxSize(). There are also mutator operations such as push(int k), pop() and reset().

While each method is at most a couple of lines long, understanding how these operations can be interleaved poses a much bigger challenge. For instance, it is reasonable to expect pop() to be an illegal operation on a freshly constructed Stack instance. Similarly, it would be awkward if that same operation was illegal after successfully pushing an element on any legal stack.

This restrictions and many others constitute a set of "common sense" behaviour that any programmer would expect from a stack. We refer to this set of informal (and often implicit) requirements as *mental model*.

The `Stack` class has been around in the company for a while, so Tom is quite confident that it behaves properly (this is, according to his mental model). Still, he wants to double-check this so he writes a couple of small programs such as the following.

```
1  public void Main(string[] args) {
2    Stack s = new Stack(10);
3    s.push(27); s.push(19);
4    System.Console.WriteLine(s.top());
5    s.pop();
6    System.Console.WriteLine(s.top());
7  }
```

Tom manually compares the output with his mental model, effectively confirming that 19 is printed first, followed by 27.

At this point Tom has a small positive piece of evidence that the `Stack` class behaviour is aligned with his mental model. The problem for Tom is how to confirm his hunch, how to know that he tested enough. In other words, he might wonder *"how do I know that this is indeed a correct stack implementation? When do I stop testing/inspecting?"*.

Fortunately, a colleague told Tom a little bit about enabledness-preserving abstractions and Tom is willing to give them a try. By statically constructing an EPA from the `Stack` source code, Tom will be able to compare his mental model with the graphical representation of the abstraction and decide if there are any inconsistencies between his understanding and the implementation.

As we mentioned before, in order to build an EPA for a class C we need to define its components: a set of methods names M, their implementations F, their requires clauses R, the class invariant *inv* and the class initial condition *init*.

The relevant operations that compose M are the mutators `push(int k)`, `pop()` and `reset()`. The constructor `Stack()` is used to define the initial condition *init*, and the rest of the operations are merely observers, which do not affect the internal state of the stack and which are excluded in the rest of the section to simplify presentation.

The implementation set F for the selected group of operations is given by the appropriate fragments of code in Figure 1. For instance, lines 28–31 define the implementation for the `push` operation.

Regarding the requires clauses, for each operation m Tom needs to identify (or explicitly add, if necessary) the adequate fragment of code that performs the parameter and/or fields validation. This code fragment is then converted to a boolean expression b that guarantees a safe invocation of m. Finally, Tom needs to prepend the code for m with Contract.Requires(b).

For instance, lines 34–35 of Figure 1 check that the stack is not empty while attempting to invoke the `pop` operation. Tom then rewrites this check as a Contract.Requires(...) invocation, which results in the following.

```
1 public void pop() {
2   Contract.Requires(!isEmpty());
3   next--;
4 }
```

When considering the **push** operation there are no explicit fragments of code that perform validation. However, this omission is actually a bug. The problem is that the stack is based on a fixed-size array and pushing infinitely would eventually produce an exception when the index goes beyond the limits of the array.

In order to fix this, Tom adds a Contract.**Requires(**...**)** check to the method as follows.

```
1 public void push(int k) {
2   Contract.Requires(!isFull());
3   elems[next] = k;
4   next++;
5 }
```

Finally, since it is safe to invoke the **reset** operation on any stack, there is no need to rewrite it.

Having fixed the requires clauses for the relevant operations, Tom still needs to define a class invariant *inv* and an initial condition *init*. As a first step, Tom decides to leave the invariant as **true**. In other words, any possible value assignment of the **Stack** class fields represents a valid stack.

Regarding the initial condition, it is straightforward to discover from the source code of the **Stack** constructor that initially **next == 0** and **elems** is a fresh integer array. The size of **elems** depends of the actual value of the constructor parameter m, but Tom realizes that empty arrays make no sense. He therefore decides to always leave room for at least 2 elements and adds a Contract.**Requires(**...**)** check to the constructor as follows.

```
1 public Stack(int m) {
2   Contract.Requires(m > 1);
3   next = 0;
4   elems = new int[m];
5 }
```

Having defined the action names, their implementations and requires clauses, as well the system invariant and initial condition, Tom is now ready to run CONTRACTOR and obtain an EPA for the **Stack** class. Notice that mining the requires clauses might seem an unnecessary burden (which could by lessened to some extent with dynamic inference and static code analysis techniques), but it actually led Tom to the discovery of a bug in the **push** operation.

Figure 2 presents the **Stack** EPA. As we mentioned, each abstract state is described by a set of operations and groups all concrete stacks that enable those operations only.

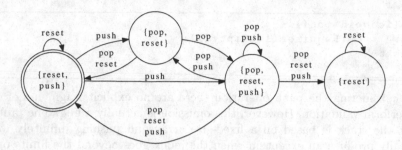

Fig. 2. Initial EPA for the Stack class

The initial abstract state is marked with a double circle and enables both the reset and push operations. This seems reasonable to Tom since reset is always enabled and a freshly constructed Stack always has room for at least one element, making push enabled as well. Furthermore, popping elements from a freshly constructed empty stack is illegal, which is also aligned with Tom's mental model.

Pushing from the initial state is a non-deterministic action. It can take the Stack instance to two possible destinations:

1. The {pop, reset} state, on which pushing is no longer enabled. This abstract states groups the full stacks.
2. The {pop, reset, push} state, on which pushing is still enabled. This is the abstract state that groups stacks that are 'half-full'.

Tom notices however, that since the minimum size for a Stack is 2, it is not possible to fill-up a freshly constructed instance after pushing a single element. The transition from the initial state to the full state is not feasible. Furthermore, while the initial abstract state and its outgoing transitions look rather good, there is a sink state {reset} on the right which seems suspicious. The presence of this abstract state indicates that eventually a Stack instance may be rendered virtually unusable, since both pushing and popping would never be enabled for the lifetime of that instance. Carefully reading the requires clauses for push and pop, Tom discovers that this could only happen if the Stack instance was full and empty at the same time. But this is not possible, so something is wrong.

These observations are not exhaustive, but even after a short inspection of the EPA Tom has discovered that stacks may present strange behaviour. However he feels pretty confident that it is impossible for a fresh Stack instance to get full after a single push operation. And it is as impossible for any Stack instance to be both empty and full at the same time.

Tom then remembers that he used an empty system invariant, and that might have affected the resulting EPA. He creates a refined invariant and adds it to the class as a new method as follows.

```
1 [ContractInvariantMethod]
2 private void Invariant()
3 {
4    Contract.Invariant(0 <= next);
5    Contract.Invariant(next <= elems.Length);
6    Contract.Invariant(elems.Length > 1);
7 }
```

The ContractInvariantMethod attribute in line 1 is a CODE CONTRACTS keyword that identifies the method as the class invariant. Lines 4 and 5 indicate the bounds for the variable that points to the next free element in the array (if any). Notice that since popping is disabled on empty stacks, next will never be negative; and since pushing is not allowed on full stacks, then next can not be larger than the size of the elems array. Following the decision made when redefining the constructor, the last line of the invariant states that there is always room for at least two elements.

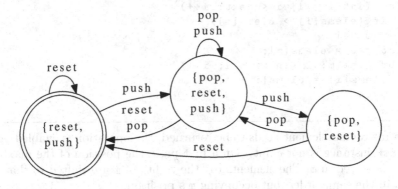

Fig. 3. EPA for the Stack class with proper invariant

Figure 3 presents the EPA that Tom gets when feeding CONTRACTOR with the newly defined invariant. Tom realizes that this EPA is very well aligned with his mental model. The suspicious sink state is now gone, and so is the push transition that connected empty stacks directly with full stacks. The remaining states and transitions are consistent with Tom's idea of how a Stack instance should behave. For instance, the reset operation always takes instances back to the initial state, pushing eventually leads to the full state and popping eventually takes instances back to the initial state.

However, not everything in Tom's mental model is covered in this EPA. For instance, the fact that the Stack shows actual LIFO (last in, first out) behaviour is not part of the abstraction. Likewise, the overapproximated nature of the EPA, implies it allows paths which are clearly illegal such as push⤳pop⤳pop. While EPAs convey a concise representation of a class state-space, the negative side-effect is that some aspects of the behaviour get lost in the way. More precise abstractions could capture some of these aspects that EPAs miss, but they would do so at the cost of larger representations that could get in the way when manually inspecting the abstraction.

3.2   Implementing and Debugging with EPAs

Now that Tom is confident with the `Stack` implementation being correct, he can proceed with his first assignment. Different projects inside DataXtructures Inc. make use of stacks, and some of them require the elements to be returned in an ordered fashion. In other words, Tom has to add a `popMax()` operation that returns the maximum integer on a `Stack` instance and removes it, leaving the rest of the elements untouched, preserving their relative order. Tom proceeds and produces the following implementation.

```
1  public int popMax()
2  {
3      Contract.Requires(!isEmpty());
4      int m = elems[0];
5      for (int i = 1; i < next; i++)
6          if (elems[i] > elems[m])
7              m = i;
8      int ret = elems[m];
9      for (i = m; i < next - 1; i++)
10         elems[i] = elems[i + 1];
11     return ret;
12 }
```

Since a maximum element needs to be returned, the operation is enabled only if the `Stack` instance is not empty. On a first pass, the position of the maximum element is stored in m. The elements to "the right" of m are shifted so that they remain in the same order, but occupying m's position.

Tom is confident with his implementation, but DataXtructures Inc. mandates that every new functionality needs to be subject to unit testing, so he writes the following test.

```
1  void testPopMax()
2  {
3      Stack s = new Stack(10);
4      s.push(3); s.push(42);
5      s.push(1); s.push(17);
6      int max = s.popMax();
7      Contract.Assert(max == 42);
8  }
```

This test is executed and fortunately it provides a 100% branch coverage on the `popMax` implementation. Furthermore, as Tom expected, the test passes and he can now focus on other assignments. At that point, Tom remembers that he can generate an new EPA that features the `popMax` operation.

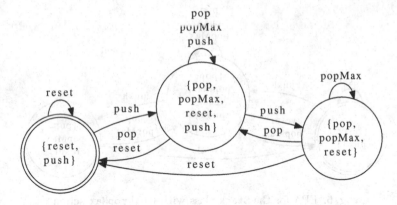

Fig. 4. EPA for the `Stack` class with `popMax` action

Tom then gets the EPA in Figure 4. As expected, the abstract states are similar to the ones in the previous EPA (see Figure 3). The `popMax` operation is enabled whenever the `pop` operation is enabled, since they indeed have the same requires clause.

After checking the abstract states, Tom decides to look at the transitions. Particularly, he is interested in the newly added `popMax` operation. He soon notices that there is a `popMax`-labeled transitions looping over the {`pop`, `popMax`, `reset`} abstract state. Since pushing is not allowed on this state, it represents full stacks. Popping elements with the standard `pop` operation on this state takes the stack back to the 'half-full' state. However, using the newer `popMax` operation leaves the stack full. The target of the `popMax` transition should be the 'half-full' state, so something looks suspicious. Similarly, there seems to be a missing `popMax`-labeled transition that takes a 'half-full' stack back to the initial empty state.

Tom figures out that since the `popMax` operation passed his test, the problem is not related to the returned element, but to the state in which the `Stack` structure is left after the operation. In particular, the fact that the only `popMax`-labeled transitions are loops indicates that the size of the structure appears to be unchanged by the operation, when it should be decreasing.

Tom reviews the implementation of `popMax` and discovers that the `next` variable is not altered and this is a bug! He then adds a `next--;` operation right before the end of the implementation in order to fix this.

CONTRACTOR is invoked once more after Tom has fixed the bug and the resulting EPA is shown in Figure 5. The set of abstract states remains the same, but the awkward `popMax` loop over the rightmost abstract state is now gone. Furthermore, Tom notices that the `popMax` operation presents the same (abstract) behaviour as `pop`.

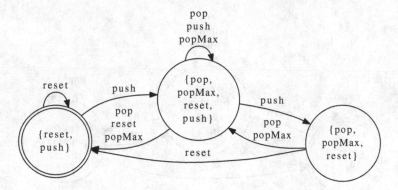

Fig. 5. EPA for the Stack class with fixed popMax action

3.3 Refining the EPA States

Tom is happy that he finished his first assignment, but his colleagues are concerned that the popMax operation is rather inefficient. Apparently, Stack instances are increasingly used in contexts on which the elements are orderly pushed in ascending order.

In such scenarios, going through all the elements looking for the maximum is unnecessary since returning the last element is sufficient. The problem is that returning the last element is not valid if the Stack instance is not ordered. Tom figures out a strategy to keep track of whether the elements are ordered or not by introducing an additional class field, as follows.

```
1  public class Stack {
2    private int[] elems;
3    private int next;
4    private int sorted;
5
6    [ContractInvariantMethod]
7    private void Invariant()
8    {
9      Contract.Invariant(0 <= next);
10     Contract.Invariant(next <= elems.Length);
11     Contract.Invariant(0 <= sorted);
12     Contract.Invariant(sorted <= next);
13     Contract.Invariant(elems.Length > 1);
14   }
15
16   // ...
17 }
```

The sorted field stores the length of the largest sorted prefix in the elems array. If sorted is equal to next then the Stack instance is sorted and returning the last element accounts for returning the maximum. Otherwise, a linear scan is still necessary.

Notice that the `Stack` invariant is extended to indicate that `sorted` is in range. The invariant could also be extended to indicate that `sorted` actually marks the size of the biggest sorted prefix, but this weaker invariant is enough for Tom's purposes.

The operations responsible of pushing and popping elements need to carefully update the new `sorted` field, as follows.

```
1  public void push(int k)
2  {
3    Contract.Requires(!isFull());
4    if (isEmpty() || sorted == next && k >= top())
5      sorted++;
6    elems[next] = k;
7    next++;
8  }
9
10 public void pop() {
11   Contract.Requires(!isEmpty());
12   if (sorted == next)
13     sorted--;
14   numberOfElements--;
15 }
```

Having extended the `Stack` representation and operations to work with the extra field, Tom re-implements the `popMax` operation with the optimisation.

```
1  public int popMax()
2  {
3    Contract.Requires(!isEmpty());
4    if (sorted == next) {
5      sorted--;
6      return elems[next];
7    } else {
8      int m = elems[0];
9      for (int i = 1; i < next; i++)
10       if (elems[i] > elems[m])
11         m = i;
12     int ret = elems[m];
13     for (i = m; i < next - 1; i++)
14       elems[i] = elems[i + 1];
15     next--;
16     return ret;
17   }
18 }
```

If the `Stack` instance is sorted, the last element is returned. Otherwise, the implementation is the same as before.

Tom first runs the unit test that he already had from the unoptimised version and it passes. He then runs CONTRACTOR to get a new EPA, which is shown in Figure 6.

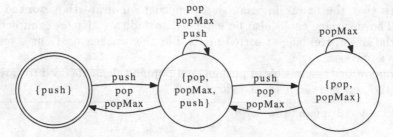

Fig. 6. EPA for the `Stack` class with optimized `popMax` action

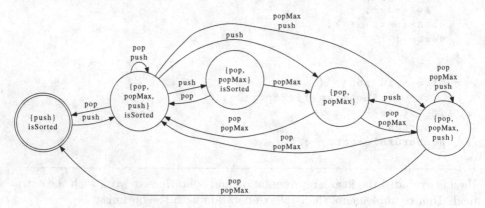

Fig. 7. Refined EPA for the `Stack` class with optimized `popMax` action

First of all, notice that for presentation purposes the `reset` operation is now not considered when building the EPA. The `popMax` operation appears to be doing its job since it is accompanying every `pop` transition. The problem is that there is an extra `popMax`-labeled transition looping over the full state.

Since the unoptimised version worked and the optimised seems to have a bug, Tom decides to get a finer-grained abstraction and check what is wrong with his code. Fortunately, CONTRACTOR provides the user with the ability to add additional predicates that can be used to refine the set of abstract states.

Tom adds the predicate `sorted == next`, which he names `isSorted`, for presentation purposes. The refined EPA that he gets is depicted in Figure 7.

There are now 5 abstract states, from left to right:

- The initial state, which is sorted. An empty array can not be unordered.
- The sorted 'half-full' state.
- The sorted full state.
- The unsorted full state.
- The unsorted 'half-full' state.

Pushing from the initial state takes the `Stack` instance to the sorted 'half-full' state; having a single element the elements have to be sorted.

Pushing from the sorted 'half-full' state is non-deterministic, as it can go to:

- Itself. In this case, the pushed element is higher than the top of the `Stack` instance, and therefore it remains sorted. There is also still room for more elements.
- The sorted full state. Similar to the previous case, but with no room for more elements.
- The unsorted full state. The pushed element is lower than the top of the `Stack` instance, so it is no longer sorted. There is no more room for new elements.
- The unsorted 'half-full' state. Similar to the previous case, but with extra room for other elements.

On the other hand, pushing a new element on the unsorted 'half-full' state (the one in the far right) is still non-deterministic, but it can never result in the `Stack` instance getting sorted.

The `pop` operation behaves dually. It can make an unsorted `Stack` become sorted. On sorted stacks, popping will never mangle the elements.

Tom expects the `popMax` operation to behave as `pop`. When the `Stack` is unsorted they share every transition. However, when the `Stack` is sorted, `popMax` behaves oddly. For instance, there is a missing `popMax`-labeled transition from the sorted 'half-full' state going back to the initial one. This manifestation is similar to the bug that Tom discovered in his original implementation.

On top of that, there are `popMax`-labeled transitions going out of any sorted abstract state to its unsorted counterpart. This is suspicious since taking elements out of an ordered array should never result in their elements getting unordered.

With this information in hand, Tom decides that his new implementation is working fine on unsorted stacks, but his optimisation to deal with sorted stacks is buggy. He then discovers that he forgot (again!) to update the `next` field in the case in which the elements are ordered (the `then` branch).

Tom then fixes the bug and runs CONTRACTOR once more to confirm that the suspicious elements in the original abstraction are now gone.

3.4 Refining the EPA Transitions

Having finished his previous assignment, Tom can now focus on his second task. Some `Stack` users need to remove several elements at once. Tom has to implement a `popN(int n)` operation, which takes an integer `n` and removes that amount of elements from the top of the `Stack` instance. If there are fewer than `n` elements, then the instance remains empty and the actual number of popped elements is returned.

Tom is eager to implement this new method, and in a couple of minutes he gets the following code.

```
1  public int popN(int n)
2  {
3     Contract.Requires(!isEmpty());
4     Contract.Requires(n >= 1);
5     for (int i = 0; i < n; i++) {
6        pop();
7        if (isEmpty())
8           break;
9     }
10    return i;
11 }
```

Similarly to the previous pop operations provided by the `Stack` class, `popN` requires the instance to have at least one element. Furthermore, the amount of elements to be popped has to be at least 1.

Tom decides to create a simple unit test to see what happens in two scenarios: *(a)* when the requested amount of pops can be fulfilled; and *(b)* when it is greater than the amount of elements in the stack.

```
1  void testPopN()
2  {
3     Stack s = new Stack(10);
4     s.push(99); s.push(89); s.push(79);
5     int n1 = s.popN(1);
6     Contract.Assert(n1 == 1);
7     int n2 = s.popN(3);
8     Contract.Assert(n2 == 2);
9  }
```

The `Assert` in line 6 checks for scenario *(a)*, while the one in line 8 checks for scenario *(b)*.

Fortunately, once again, the test achieves a 100% branch coverage over the added functionality. Furthermore, the first `Assert` passes correctly, so the operation seems to work properly when there are enough elements. Unfortunately, the test case fails to pass the second `Assert`. The amount of elements in the `Stack` instance at the time of the second `popN` operation is 2. However, when attempting to pop 3 elements, the `popN` operation returns 1 instead of 2.

As usual, Tom decides to construct an EPA of the `Stack`, which we can see in Figure 8. Unfortunately, the bug does not seem to be reflected in the abstraction. All the `popN`-labeled transitions behave like `pop`, with the exception that `popN` can also go directly from the full abstract state back to the initial one.

In his previous assignment, Tom used CONTRACTOR to refine the EPA states. Similarly, CONTRACTOR features the possibility to refine abstract transitions too. In order to do so, Tom needs to specify which label he wants to refine, and what conditions he wishes to use.

In this particular case, Tom needs to refine the `popN`-labeled transitions using two conditions:

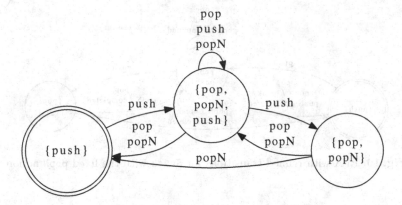

Fig. 8. EPA for the `Stack` class with `popN` action

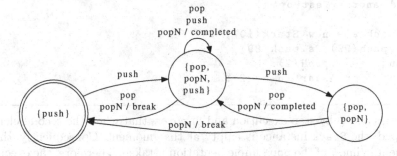

Fig. 9. EPA with refined transitions for the `Stack` class with `popN` action

completed. This is the case on which the amount of popped elements equals
  the amount that the user asked. Formally, `n == popN(n)`.
break. In this other case the operation has to stop early since there are no more
  elements to pop. Formally, `n < popN(n)`.

The refined EPA that Tom gets using this feature is depicted in Figure 9. Notice
that now the `popN` transitions show extra information indicating which of the
two conditions holds on each case.

The `popN / break` transitions always return to the initial abstract state. This
seems fine to Tom, since in those cases the operation had to stop early due to
lack of elements. On the other hand, the `popN / completed` transitions always
go to the 'half-full' abstract state. This is suspicious, since a user could ask `popN`
to return exactly the amount of elements currently in the stack, which should
empty the instance.

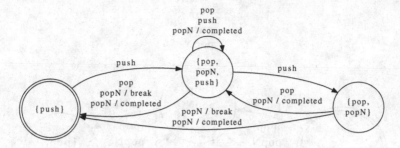

Fig. 10. EPA with refined transitions for `Stack` with the fixed `popN` action

Tom decides to write a new test case in order to figure out what is wrong with his implementation.

```
1  void anotherTestPopN ()
2  {
3      Stack s = new Stack(10);
4      s.push(99); s.push(89);
5      int n = s.popN(2);
6      Contract.Assert(n == 2);
7  }
```

Tom does a step-by-step execution and discovers that when the second element is popped, the `Stack` instance is empty at that moment. Consequently, the `if` statement in line 7 of the `popN` implementation is taken. Therefore, the execution of the `popN` operation is halted before the `i` variable is incremented.

The bug can be solved by using a `while`-loop instead of a `for`-loop, as follows.

```
1  public int popN(int n)
2  {
3      Contract.Requires(!isEmpty());
4      Contract.Requires(n >= 1);
5      int i = 0;
6      while (i < n) {
7          pop();
8          i++;
9          if (isEmpty())
10             break;
11     }
12     return i;
13 }
```

With this fixed version, the EPA in Figure 10 looks much better. Tom's job for the day is completed!

4   Validation Guidelines

The previous section showed a fictional story on which EPAs where used to identify and locate problems in a software artefact. Based on our experience in various real-life software artefacts [8,9], we now present a series of guidelines that developers can use as heuristics that aid identification of "suspicious behaviour" during the validation process.

We organise the heuristics into two categories. The first category is of a more semantic nature while the second is related to the structure of the EPA.

We hypothesise that one of the benefits of the approach presented is that the level of abstraction defined by the enabledness criterion is intuitive and modelers can interpret the different abstract states into the problem domain with relative ease. The first two heuristics we developed confirm, to some extent, this hypothesis.

- **Understanding states.** There are certain abstract states in the EPA that can be easily interpreted to particular situations of the system under analysis. Identifying empty, half-full and full abstract states in any of the `Stack` EPAs is an example of this.

    When it is not possible or not easy to associate a particular states with a declarative description of the set of instances that it abstracts, this may be an indication that there is a problem with the program under analysis. We have found that in these cases, it was often the case that the state should have been inconsistent (and hence should not have appeared in the EPA) but that the requires clauses of enabled actions or the system invariant were (incorrectly) too weak. This is the case in Figure 2, in which the invariant for the system was `true`.
- **Understanding action sequences.** On the other hand, states which can be declaratively traced to a meaningful set of instances are good candidates for analysing action sequences. Following fragments of traces from these states may lead to discovering a certain sequence of actions which should not be allowed by the program. Programmers should be aware that, given the approximate nature of the abstraction, the appearance of a (non singleton) trace is not a guarantee that it denotes a feasible action sequence.

    An example of this strategy is what led to the discovery that the EPA in Figure 8 lacks `popN` / `completed` transitions going back to the initial state.

We also identified the following *structural characteristics of an EPA* that can help pinpoint problems in the program under analysis:

- **Large state space.** A large state space in the EPA may be an indication of either a poorly designed set of operations. The intuition is that a set of operations that are intended to be used together to provide a more complex service (e.g., a protocol, a public API) will conceptually have a few modes that characterise the set operations available at a given moment. An unmanageable set of enabledness states is an indication that the protocol, class or API is either extremely complex to be used or that it is incorrectly implemented. More specifically, a large state space can be an indication of problems with requires clauses. A good strategy is to question why different states in the EPA differ in the actions that they enable.

An example of this problem is showcased in the MS-WINSRA case study in [8].

– **Deadlock states.** The presence (or absence) of a deadlock state is something that should be analysed in detail when validating a program using EPAs. By definition of EPA there can be only one deadlock state, the state whose action set is empty. The presence of an unintended deadlock state in an EPA is likely to be an indication of a bug in the actions that evolve into that state.

The MS-NSS case study in [8] presents a deadlock state which is studied and validated.

– **Sink states.** Similarly to deadlock states, states which only have outgoing transitions leading back to it can be indicators of problems. They are very similar to deadlock states since they indicate that once this "operation mode" is reached it can not be abandoned.

For instance, the `Stack` EPA in Figure 2 presents a suspicious sink state.

– **Missing action.** If a given specified action is not present in any of the EPA reachable states then this is an indication that something is not quite right. It may be the case that the requires clause for that action is inconsistent when combined with the system invariant. It might also be the case that none of the other actions leave the system in a state which enables the missing action.

– **High fan-in.** States in an EPA that have a large number of incoming transitions can be an indication of problems. In particular, they are typically undesirable since they cause history loss for all the paths that reach the state. These states can be an indication of problems in requires clauses that when corrected end up partitioning the high fan-in state into several states.

The MS-WINSRA case study in [8] presents this problem due to weak requires clauses.

– **Highly non-deterministic actions.** When a state has a large number of outgoing transitions labeled with the same action it is usually symptomatic of a problem. Such situations may be caused by two different scenarios. Firstly, it may be the case that the action is intrinsically non-deterministic. If this is the case, it can be a symptom that this action is a good candidate to be tested under different scenarios in order to trigger/cover all of its behaviour space.

Secondly, a highly non-deterministic action on an abstract state can also happen if the predicate for the state is weak. For instance, an action that updates the system following the formula $(A_1 \Rightarrow B_1) \wedge \ldots \wedge (A_n \Rightarrow B_n)$ may generate undesired non-deterministic behaviour in a state where A_i holds for several values of i. In these cases, it may be the case that a requires clause or the system invariant requires strengthening.

The {`pop`, `popMax`, `push`} `isSorted` abstract state in Figure 7 presents a highly non-deterministic `push` operation.

- **Mirrored actions.** If whenever there is a transition labeled with a given action a_1, there is another transition with the same origin and destination state labeled with action a_2, this is an indication that both actions were specified independently but are treated in the same way by the system. It may be the case that one action was copied from the other but the programmer forgot to modify the appropriate differences between the two (known as copy-paste bugs).

  This is the case with pop—popMax in Section 3.3, as well as pop—popN in Section 3.4.

Some of the heuristics presented in this section are straightforward to implement as a feature in our CONTRACTOR tool, and in fact some of them are already implemented. These include the detection of deadlock or sink states, mirrored or missing actions or enabled actions with missing transitions.

5   Closing Remarks

In this article we have shown how abstractions can play a key role in various development activities. More concretely, we presented enabledness-preserving abstractions and their application in a fictional development story involving code understanding, the addition of new functionality and the refactoring of parts of the implementation.

Even when this story is based on a toy stack implementation, EPAs have shown to provide useful information on various industrial scale software artifacts. For instance, in [8] we show the application of our CONTRACTOR tool to 2 Microsoft protocol descriptions in the form of pre/postcondition contracts with up to 33 actions. Our tool scaled well, keeping the construction time below 4 minutes in a standard desktop computer. More importantly, the resulting EPA led to the discovery of flaws in the descriptions. In [9] we apply CONTRACTOR directly on the Java Development Kit (JDK) 1.4 implementation of various standard classes such as ListItr (List iterator) or PipedOutputStream. The running times ranged from 8 seconds to 5 minutes, and the EPAs led to discoveries such as undocumented legal behaviour with respect to the official documentation.

Based on this experiences, this paper also presents a series of guidelines and checklists that can guide programmers in their use of EPAs as a visual aid to find suspicious elements in their programs.

While CONTRACTOR constructs EPAs statically and automatically, it requires the developer to identify and annotate important program elements such as requires clauses. The problem of tackling the annotation burden has been widely studied, and different approaches have been proposed which range from type inference or dataflow analysis (e.g., [17]) to carefully choosing default values [10]. More concretely, CODE CONTRACTS [3] presents an outstanding ability to infer requires clauses as the ones used in Section 3.

Enabledness-based abstractions constitute a good example of abstractions aimed at user inspection and validation. While we found EPAs useful in our experience, we believe that features such as state refinement via extra predicates (Section 3.3) or transitions refinement (Section 3.4) present a good opportunity to let developers "zoom in and out" the abstraction in order to fit their needs. That said, we envision that other carefully chosen non enabledness-based levels of abstraction could potentially help developers in their activities as well.

Acknowledgements. The work reported herein was partially supported by CONICET, UBACyT 2011-813 and 20020090300064, PIP112-200801-00955KA4, PICT-PAE 37279, ERC StG PBM-FIMBSE and PICT 2010-2351.

References

1. Alur, R., Černý, P., Madhusudan, P., Nam, W.: Synthesis of interface specifications for Java classes. In: POPL 2005, pp. 98–109 (2005)
2. Alur, R., Courcoubetis, C., Halbwachs, N., Henzinger, T., Ho, P., Nicollin, X., Olivero, A., Sifakis, J., Yovine, S.: The algorithmic analysis of hybrid systems. Theoretical Computer Science 138(1), 3–34 (1995)
3. Andersen, M., Barnett, M., Fahndrich, M., Grunkemeyer, B., King, K., Logozzo, F., Patel, V., Zuniga, D.: Code Contracts (2009), http://research.microsoft.com/en-us/projects/contracts/
4. Beckman, N., Nori, A.: Probabilistic, modular and scalable inference of typestate specifications. In: PLDI (2011)
5. Beschastnikh, I., Brun, Y., Sloan, S., Ernst, M.: Leveraging existing instrumentation to automatically infer invariant-constrained models. In: FSE 2011 (2011)
6. Beyer, D., Henzinger, T., Jhala, R., Majumdar, R.: The software model checker Blast. STTT 9, 505–525 (2007), http://www.springerlink.com/index/10.1007/s10009-007-0044-z
7. Bierhoff, K., Aldrich, J.: Plural: checking protocol compliance under aliasing. In: ICSE, pp. 971–972. ACM (2008)
8. de Caso, G., Braberman, V., Garbervetsky, D., Uchitel, S.: Automated abstractions for contract validation. IEEE Transactions on Software Engineering 38(1), 141–162 (2012)
9. de Caso, G., Braberman, V.A., Garbervetsky, D., Uchitel, S.: Program abstractions for behaviour validation. In: Proceedings of the 33rd International Conference on Software Engineering, ICSE 2011, Waikiki, Honolulu, HI, USA, May 21-28, pp. 381–390 (2011)
10. Chalin, P., James, P.R.: Non-null References by Default in Java: Alleviating the Nullity Annotation Burden. In: Bateni, M. (ed.) ECOOP 2007. LNCS, vol. 4609, pp. 227–247. Springer, Heidelberg (2007)
11. Dallmeier, V., Lindig, C., Wasylkowski, A., Zeller, A.: Mining object behavior with ADABU. In: Workshop on Dynamic Systems Analysis 2006 (2006)
12. Dallmeier, V., Knopp, N., Mallon, C., Hack, S., Zeller, A.: Generating test cases for specification mining. In: ISSTA 2010 (2010)
13. DeLine, R., Fahndrich, M.: Enforcing high-level protocols in low-level software. In: PLDI 2001, pp. 59–69 (2001)
14. Demsky, B., Rinard, M.: Automatic extraction of heap reference properties in object-oriented programs. IEEE Transactions on Software Engineering 35, 305–324 (2009)

15. Ernst, M., Perkins, J., Guo, P., McCamant, S., Pacheco, C., Tschantz, M., Xiao, C.:
    The Daikon system for dynamic detection of likely invariants. Science of Computer
    Programming 69, 35–45 (2007),
    http://linkinghub.elsevier.com/retrieve/pii/S016764230700161X
16. Esparza, J.: Decidability of model checking for infinite-state concurrent systems.
    Acta Informatica 34, 85–107 (1997),
    http://www.springerlink.com/
    openurl.asp?genre=article&id=doi:10.1007/s002360050074
17. Flanagan, C., Leino, K.: Houdini, an Annotation Assistant for ESC/Java. In:
    Oliveira, J.N., Zave, P. (eds.) FME 2001. LNCS, vol. 2021, pp. 500–517. Springer,
    Heidelberg (2001)
18. Gabel, M., Su, Z.: Symbolic mining of temporal specifications. In: ICSE 2008, pp.
    51–60 (2008), http://portal.acm.org/citation.cfm?id=1368096
19. Ghezzi, C., Mocci, A., Monga, M.: Synthesizing intensional behavior models by
    graph transformation. In: ICSE 2009, pp. 430–440 (2009)
20. Giannakopoulou, D., Păsăreanu, C.S.: Interface Generation and Compositional
    Verification in JavaPathfinder. In: Chechik, M., Wirsing, M. (eds.) FASE 2009.
    LNCS, vol. 5503, pp. 94–108. Springer, Heidelberg (2009)
21. Graf, S., Saïdi, H.: Construction of Abstract State Graphs with PVS. In: Grumberg,
    O. (ed.) CAV 1997. LNCS, vol. 1254, pp. 72–83. Springer, Heidelberg (1997)
22. Grieskamp, W., Kicillof, N., MacDonald, D., Nandan, A., Stobie, K., Wurden,
    F.: Model-based quality assurance of Windows protocol documentation. In: ICST
    2008, pp. 502–506 (2008),
    http://ieeexplore.ieee.org/lpdocs/epic03/wrapper.htm?arnumber=4539580
23. Heitmeyer, C.L., Jeffords, R.D., Labaw, B.G.: Automated consistency checking
    of requirements specifications. ACM Transactions on Software Engineering and
    Methodology (TOSEM) 5(3), 231–261 (1996)
24. Henzinger, T., Jhala, R., Majumdar, R.: Permissive interfaces. In: ESEC/FSE 2005,
    pp. 31–40 (2005)
25. IEEE: IEEE Standard Glossary of Software Engineering Terminology (September
    1990)
26. Kramer, J.: Is abstraction the key to computing? Commun. ACM 50, 36–42 (2007),
    http://doi.acm.org/10.1145/1232743.1232745
27. Kwiatkowska, M., Norman, G., Parker, D.: PRISM 4.0: Verification of Probabilistic
    Real-Time Systems. In: Gopalakrishnan, G., Qadeer, S. (eds.) CAV 2011. LNCS,
    vol. 6806, pp. 585–591. Springer, Heidelberg (2011)
28. Lee, D., Yannakakis, M.: Online minimization of transition systems (extended ab-
    stract). In: STOC 1992, pp. 264–274 (1992),
    http://portal.acm.org/citation.cfm?doid=129712.129738
29. Liu, L., Meyer, B., Schoeller, B.: Using Contracts and Boolean Queries to Improve
    the Quality of Automatic Test Generation. In: Gurevich, Y., Meyer, B. (eds.) TAP
    2007. LNCS, vol. 4454, pp. 114–130. Springer, Heidelberg (2007)
30. Lorenzoli, D., Mariani, L., Pezzè, M.: Automatic generation of software behavioral
    models. In: ICSE 2008, pp. 501–510 (2008)
31. Nanda, M., Grothoff, C., Chandra, S.: Deriving object typestates in the presence
    of inter-object references. ACM SIGPLAN Notices 40(10), 77–96 (2005)
32. Nipkow, T., Paulson, L.C., Wenzel, M.: Isabelle/HOL — A Proof Assistant for
    Higher-Order Logic. LNCS, vol. 2283. Springer, Heidelberg (2002)
33. Pradel, M., Gross, T.R.: Automatic Generation of Object Usage Specifications
    from Large Method Traces. In: ASE 2009, pp. 371–382. IEEE (November 2009),
    http://ieeexplore.ieee.org/lpdocs/epic03/wrapper.htm?arnumber=5431756

34. Sasnauskas, R., Dustmann, O.S., Kaminski, B.L., Wehrle, K., Weise, C., Kowalewski, S.: Scalable symbolic execution of distributed systems. In: Proceedings of the 2011 31st International Conference on Distributed Computing Systems, ICDCS 2011, pp. 333–342. IEEE Computer Society, Washington, DC (2011), http://dx.doi.org/10.1109/ICDCS.2011.28
35. Strom, R., Yemini, S.: Typestate: A programming language concept for enhancing software reliability. IEEE TSE 12(1), 157–171 (1986)
36. Uribe, T.: Abstraction-based Deductive-algorithmic Verification of Reactive Systems. Stanford University, Dept. of Computer Science (1999)
37. Valmari, A.: The State Explosion Problem. In: Reisig, W., Rozenberg, G. (eds.) APN 1998. LNCS, vol. 1491, pp. 429–528. Springer, Heidelberg (1998)
38. Zoppi, E., Braberman, V., de Caso, G., Garbervetsky, D., Uchitel, S.: Contractor.net: inferring typestate properties to enrich code contracts. In: Proceedings of the 1st Workshop on Developing Tools as Plug-ins, TOPI 2011, pp. 44–47. ACM, New York (2011), http://doi.acm.org/10.1145/1984708.1984721

Software Performance Modeling

Dorina C. Petriu, Mohammad Alhaj, and Rasha Tawhid

Carleton University, 1125 Colonel By Drive, Ottawa ON Canada, K1S 5B6
{petriu,malhaj}@sce.carleton.ca, rtawhid@connect.carleton.ca

Abstract. Ideally, a software development methodology should include both the ability to specify non-functional requirements and to analyze them starting early in the lifecycle; the goal is to verify whether the system under development would be able to meet such requirements. This chapter considers quantitative performance analysis of UML software models annotated with performance attributes according to the standard "UML Profile for Modeling and Analysis of Real-Time and Embedded Systems" (MARTE). The chapter describes a model transformation chain named PUMA (Performance by Unified Model Analysis) that enables the integration of performance analysis in a UML-based software development process, by automating the derivation of performance models from UML+MARTE software models, and by facilitating the interoperability of UML tools and performance tools. PUMA uses an intermediate model called "Core Scenario Model" (CSM) to bridge the gap between different kinds of software models accepted as input and different kinds of performance models generated as output. Transformation principles are described for transforming two kinds of UML behaviour representation (sequence and activity diagrams) into two kinds of performance models (Layered Queueing Networks and stochastic Petri nets). Next, PUMA extensions are described for two classes of software systems: service-oriented architecture (SOA) and software product lines (SPL).

1 Introduction

The quality of many software intensive systems, ranging from real-time embedded systems to web-based applications, is determined to a large extent by their performance characteristics, such as response time and throughput. The developers of such systems should be able to assess and understand the performance effects of various design decisions starting at an early stage and continuing throughout the software life cycle. Software Performance Engineering (SPE) is an approach introduced by Smith [37], which proposes to use quantitative methods and performance models in order to assess the performance effects of different design and implementation alternatives during the development of a system. SPE promotes the integration of performance analysis into the software development process from its earliest lifecycle stages, in order to insure that the system will meet its performance objectives.

The process of building a system's performance model before the system is completely implemented and can be measured begins with identifying a small set of key performance scenarios representative of the way in which the system will be used

M. Bernardo, V. Cortellessa, and A. Pierantonio (Eds.): SFM 2012, LNCS 7320, pp. 219–262, 2012.

[37]. The performance analysts must understand first the system behaviour for each scenario, following the execution path from component to component, identifying the quantitative demands for resources made by each component (such as CPU execution time and I/O operations), as well as the various reasons for queueing delays (such as competition for hardware and software resources). The scenario descriptions thus obtained can be mapped (manually or automatically) to a performance model, which can be used for By solving the model, the analyst will obtain performance results such as response times, throughput, utilization of different resources by different software components, etc. Trouble spots can be identified and alternative solutions for eliminating them can be assessed in a similar way. Many modeling formalisms have been developed over the years for software performance evaluation, such as queueing networks (QN), extended QN, Layered Queueing Networks (LQN) (a type of extended QN), stochastic Petri nets, stochastic process algebras and stochastic automata networks, as surveyed in [5][15].

Model-Driven Development (MDD) is an evolutionary step in the software field that changes the focus of software development from code to models. MDD uses *abstraction* to separate the model of the application under construction from underlying platform models and *automation* to generate code from models. The emphasis on models facilitates also the analysis of non-functional properties (NFP), by deriving analysis models for different NFPs from the software models. Ideally, analysis models should be generated automatically by model transformations from the software models used for development, and become part of the model suite which is maintained with the product. For brevity, we term the software models as *Smodels*, and the performance models as *Pmodels*.

To facilitate the generation of Pmodels, UML Smodels can be extended with standard performance annotations provided by the "UML Profile for Modeling and Analysis of Real-Time and Embedded Systems" (MARTE) [30] defined for UML 2.x or its predecessor, the "UML Profile for Schedulability, Performance and Time" (SPT) [31] defined for UML1.x. Using UML profiles provides the additional advantage that the extended models can be processed with standard UML editors, without any need to change the tools, as profiles are standard mechanisms for extending UML models.

This chapter addresses the problem of bridging the semantic gap between different kinds of software models and performance models. We present the PUMA (Performance by Unified Model Analysis) transformation chain, whose strategy [48] "unifies" performance evaluation in the sense that it can accept as input different types of source Smodels (from which the users choose the most suitable for their project) and it generate different types of Pmodels (also according to the user's choice). To permit a user to combine arbitrary Smodel and Pmodel types according to project needs (an N-by-M problem), PUMA employs an intermediate (or pivot) language called Core Scenario Model (CSM) [34]. Based around CSM, PUMA has an open architecture summarized in Figure 1 which shows the transformers (rounded rectangles) and the flow of artifacts (rectangles) between them. It exploits several standards: UML and its model-interchange XMI standard, MARTE, performance model standards [18] [31], and the CSM metamodel [24] [25]. With suitable translators, PUMA can support other design specification language defining scenarios and resources, and other performance models.

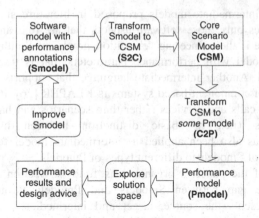

Fig. 1. PUMA transformation chain

Related Work. Many kinds of Pmodels (including queueing networks (QNs), extended QNs, stochastic Petri nets, process algebras and automata networks) can be used for performance analysis of software systems, as surveyed in [5]. The Pmodels are often constructed "by hand", based on the insight of the analysts and their interactions with the designers. To fit into MDD, the present purpose is to automate the derivation of Pmodels from the Smodels used for software development. A recent book [15] covers all the way from the basic concepts for performance analysis of software systems to describing the most representative methodologies from literature for annotating and transforming Smodels into Pmodels. For example, UML models with performance annotations (mostly SPT) containing some structural view and a certain kind of behavior diagrams have been used to generate different kinds of Pmodels: from sequence diagrams (SD) to simulation model [6], from SD and statecharts (SC) to stochastic Petri nets [11][12], from SD to QNs [16], from activity diagrams (AD) to stochastic process algebra (PEPA) [13], from SD to PEPA [44], from UML to an intermediate model called Performance Model Context (PCM) to stochastic Petri nets [20]. Many of these approaches transform from *one* kind of UML behaviour diagram plus architectural information to *one* kind of Pmodel. The difference of the PUMA strategy is that it *unifies* performance evaluation by accepting different types of source Smodels and generating multiple types of Pmodel, via the intermediate language Core Scenario Model (CSM), as described in more detail in the next sections.

Another model driven approach for development and evaluation of non-functional properties such as performance and reliability is based on the Palladio Component Model (PCM), which allows specifying component-based software architectures in a parametric way [27]. PCM captures the software architecture with respect to static structure, behaviour, deployment/allocation, resource environment/execution environment, and usage profile. Although its metamodel is completely different from UML, the Palladio Component Model has a UML-like graphical notation representing component diagrams, deployment and individual service behaviour models (similar to activity diagrams).

There are other intermediate models proposed in literature similar to PUMA's CSM, which captures only those software aspects that are relevant to performance models. An example is the pioneering "execution graph" of Smith [37], which is a kind of scenario model with performance parameters that is transformed into an extended QN model. Another intermediate language that supports performance and reliability analysis of component-based systems is KLAPER [26]. It is more oriented toward representing calls and services rather than scenarios and has a more limited view of resources (i.e., no basic distinction between hardware/software, active/passive). It has also been applied as intermediate model for transformation from different types of Smodels to different types of Pmodels.

The remaining of the paper is organized as follows: Section 2 describes how PUMA bridges the gap between Smodels and Pmodels through performance annotations and presents the source, target and intermediate models; Section 3 describes the transformations in the PUMA chain; Section 4 introduces PUMA extensions for handle service-oriented systems; Section 5 presents PUMA extensions needed to handle software product lines and Section 6 presents the conclusions and future work.

2   Source, Intermediate and Target Models

2.1   Bridging the Gap between Smodels and Pmodels

Time-related performance is a runtime property of a software system determined by how the software behaviour uses the system resources. Contention for resource creates queueing delays that directly affect the overall performance. System performance measures are closely connected with the use of the system as described by a subset of use cases with performance constraints, and more specifically by selected scenarios realizing such use cases. For instance, response time is usually defined as the end-to-end delay of a particular scenario, and throughput is the frequency of execution of a scenario or a set of related scenarios. Scenarios corresponding to online operations frequently required by customers who are waiting for the results have high priority for performance analysis, while scenarios doing housekeeping operations in the background may be less important.

The Smodel and Pmodel share similar concepts of *resources* and *scenarios*. In both, scenarios are composed of units of behaviour (called *steps*) which are using resources. Hierarchical definition of steps is possible: a step may represent an elementary operation or a whole sub-scenario. However an important difference between Smodel and Pmodel is that the first is function/data-centric, while the second is resource-centric. In other words, the Smodel scenario steps process data and implement algorithms, while the Pmodel steps care mostly about what resources are used, how and for what duration. This creates a semantic gap that needs to be bridged in the process of deriving a Pmodel from a Smodel by adding performance annotations to the latter.

Normally a Pmodel is generated from a Smodel subset containing the following:

- High-level software architecture describing the main system components instances and their interactions at a level of abstraction that captures certain characteristics relevant to performance, such as distribution, concurrency, parallelism, competition for software resources (such as software servers and critical sections), synchronization, serialization, etc.
- Allocation of high-level software components instances to hardware devices usually modeled as a deployment diagram.
- A set of key performance scenarios annotated with performance information (see section 2.3 for a concrete example).

In order to understand what kind of performance annotations need to be added to UML Smodels, we need to look at the basic concepts contained in the *performance domain model*. As already mentioned, performance is determined by how the system behaviour uses system resources. Scenarios define execution paths with externally visible end points. Performance requirements (such as response time, throughput, probability of meeting deadlines, etc.) can be placed on scenarios. In the "UML Profile for Schedulability, Performance and Time" (SPT), the performance domain model describes three main types of concepts: *resources*, *scenarios*, and *workloads* [31]. These concepts are also used in MARTE [30].

The resources used by the software can be active or passive, logical or physical software or hardware. Some of these resources belong to the software itself (e.g., critical section, software server, lock, buffer), others to the underlying platforms (e.g., process, thread, processor, disk, communication network).

Each scenario is composed from scenario steps joined by predecessor-successor relationships, which may include fork/join, branch/merge and loops. A step may represent an elementary operation or a whole sub-scenario. Quantitative resource demands for each step must be given in the performance annotations. Each scenario is executed by a workload, which may be open (i.e., requests arriving in some predetermined pattern) or closed (a fixed number of users or jobs in the system).

Another source for the gap between Smodels and Pmodels is the fact that performance is a system characteristic, affected not only by the application under development represented by the Smodel, but also by the underlying platforms on top of which the application will be running (such as middleware, operating system, communication network software, hardware). There are different ways to approach this problem: one is to add the missing platform information in performance annotations, as explained in the subsections 2.3 and 2.4. Another way is to take a MDA-like approach [33], by considering that the application Smodel is a Platform-Independent Model (PIM) which can be composed with platform models defined as aspect models; the result of the composition is a Platform Specific Model (PSM). Such an approach is presented in Section 4.

2.2   MARTE Performance Annotations

In the "UML Profile for Modeling and Analysis of Real-Time and Embedded Systems" (MARTE) [30], the foundation concepts and non-functional properties

(NFPs) shared by different quantitative analysis domains are joined in a single package called Generic Quantitative Analysis Model (GQAM), which is further specialized by the domain models for schedulability (SAM) and performance (PAM). Other domains for quantitative analyses, such as reliability, availability, safety, are currently being defined by specializing GQAM.

Core GQAM concepts describe how the system behavior uses resources over time, and contains the same three main categories of concepts presented at the beginning of the section: resources, behaviour and workloads.

GQAM Resource Concepts. A resource is based on the abstract *Resource* class defined in the General Resource Model and contains common features such as scheduling discipline, multiplicity, services. The following types of resources are important in GQAM: a) *ExecutionHost*: a processor or other computing device on which are running processes; b) *CommunicationsHost*: hardware link between devices; c) *SchedulableResource*: a software resource managed by the operating system, like a process or thread pool; and d) *CommunicationChannel*: a middleware or protocol layer that conveys messages.

Services are provided by resources and by subsystems. A subsystem service associated with an interface operation provided by a component may be identified as a *RequestedService*, which is in turn a subtype of *Step*, and may be refined by a *BehaviorScenario*.

GQAM Behaviour/Scenario Concepts. The class *BehaviorScenario* describes a behavior triggered by an event, composed of Steps related by predecessor-successor relationships. A specialized step, *CommunicationStep*, defines the conveyance of a message. Resource usage is attached to behaviour in different ways: a) a *Step* implicitly uses a *SchedulableResource* (process, thread or task); b) each primitive *Step* executes on a host processor; c) specialized steps, *AcquireStep* or *ReleaseStep*, explicitly acquire or release a *Resource*; and d) *BehaviorScenarios* and *Steps* may use other kind of resources, so *BehaviorScenario* inherits from *ResourceUsage* which links resources with concrete usage demands.

GQAM Workload Concepts. Different workloads correspond to different operating modes, such as takeoff, in-flight and landing of an aircraft or peak-load and average-load of an enterprise application. A workload is represented by a stream of triggering events, *WorkloadEvent*, generated in one of the following ways: a) by a timed event (e.g. a periodic stream with jitter); b) by a given arrival pattern (periodic, aperiodic, sporadic, burst, irregular, open, closed); c) by a generating mechanism named *WorkloadGenerator*; d) from a trace of events stored in a file.

As mentioned above, the Performance Analysis Model (PAM) specializes the GQAM domain model. It is important to mention that only a few new concepts were defined in PAM, while most of the concepts are reused from GQAM.

PAM specializes a *Step* to include more kinds of operation demands during a step. For instance, it allows for a non-synchronizing parallel operation, which is forked but never joins (*noSync* property). In addition to CPU execution, a *Step* can demand the execution of other *Scenarios*, *RequestedServices* offered by components at interfaces, and "external operations" (*ExtOp*) which are defined outside the Smodel. (ExtOp is one of the means of introducing platform resources in MARTE annotations). A new step subtype, *PassResource*, indicates the passing of a shared resource from one process to another.

In term of Resources, PAM reuses *ExecutionHost* for processor, *Schedulable Resources* for processes (or threads) and adds a *LogicalResource* defined by the software (such as semaphore, lock, buffer pool, critical section). A runtime object instance (*PaRunTInstance*) is an alias for a process or thread pool identified in behavior specifications by other entities (such as lifelines and swimlanes).

A UML model intended for performance analysis should contain a structural view representing the software architecture at the granularity level of concurrent runtime components and their allocation to hardware resources, as well as a behavioural view showing representative scenarios with their respective resource usage and workloads.

2.3   Source Model: UML+MARTE

This section presents an example of a UML+MARTE source model for two CORBA-based client-server systems selected from a performance case study published in [1]: one is called the Handle-driven ORB (H-ORB) and the other the Forwarding ORB (F-ORB). For each case, the authors have implemented a performance prototype based on a Commercial-Off-The-Shelf (COTS) middleware product and a synthetic workload running on a network of Sun workstations using Solaris 2.6; the prototypes were measured for a range of parameters.

We used the system description from [1] to build a UML+MARTE model of each system, which represents the source model for the PUMA transformation. The results of the LQN model generated by PUMA are compared with measurement results presented in [1].The synthetic application implemented in [1] contains two distinct services A and B; the clients connect to these services through the ORB. Each client executes a cycle repeatedly, making one request to Server A and one to Server B. Two copies of A, called A1 and A2, and two copies of B, called B1 and B2, are provided. The two copies of each server enable the system to handle more load and allow the investigation of the performance effects of load balancing that is provided by many commercial ORB products. The client performs a *bind* operation before every request. The client request path varies depending on the underlying ORB architecture. In the H-ORB, the client gets the address of the server from the agent and communicates with the server directly. In the F-ORB, the agent forwards the client request to the appropriate server, which returns the results of the computations directly to the client. When a service is requested form a particular server, the server process executes a loop and consumes a pre-determined amount of CPU time. The synthetic application is used because it provides flexibility in experimentation with various levels of different workload parameters, such as the service time at each server, and the inter-node delay.

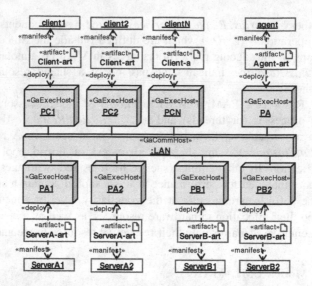

Fig. 2. The deployment of the H-ORD performance prototype

The synthetic application as considered here is characterized by the following parameters: number of clients N, service demands SA, SB representing the CPU execution time for each service, inter-node communication delay D and message length L. Since the experiments were performed on a local area network, the inter-node delay that would appear in a wide-area network was simulated by making a sender process sleeps for D units of time before sending a message. However, in the case of the H-ORB agent there was no access to the source code, so the inter-node delay for the handle returning operation was simulated by making the client sleep for D units of time before receiving the message.

Figure 2 shows the deployment diagram for the H-ORB performance prototype. The processing nodes are stereotyped as *«GaExecHost»* and the LAN communication network nodes as *«GaCommHost»*. Each client, each server and the ORB agent are allocated on their own processor.

Figure 3 represents the client request scenario in the form of a sequence diagram (SD), while Figure 4 represents the same scenario as an activity diagram (AD). Both the SD and the AD are stereotyped with *«GaAnalysisContext»* that indicate that the respective scenarios are to be considered for performance analysis. Each lifeline role stereotyped by *«PaRunTInstance»* is related to a runtime concurrent component instance, which is in turn allocated on a processor in the deployment diagram. The first step of the scenario has a workload stereotype *«GWorkloadEventt»* with an attribute pattern indicating that the scenario is used under a closed workload with a population of $N. ($N indicates a MARTE variable, to be substituted by a concrete value when the performance model is actually solved. By convention, the name of all MARTE variables in this work begin with "$" to distinguish them from other names). A *«PaStep»* stereotype is applied to each of the steps corresponding to the following messages: Get-Handle(), A1Work(), A2Work(), B1Work() and B2Work(). All scenario steps are characterized by a certain *hostDemand*, which represents the CPU execution time.

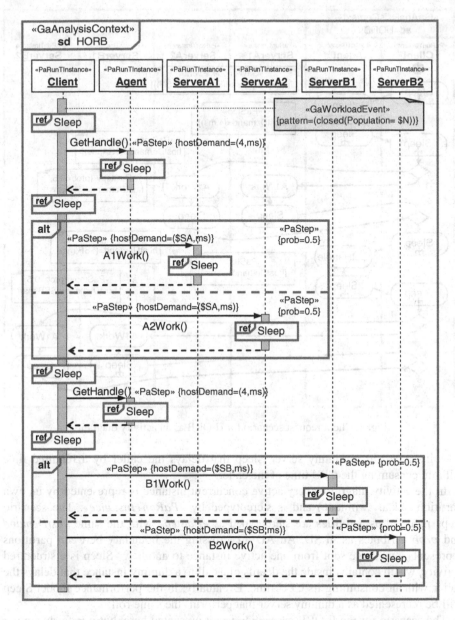

Fig. 3. Client request scenario for H-ORB as a sequence diagram

In the SD from Figure 3, the choice of which server instance to call (A1 or A2; B1 or B2) is modeled as two *alt* combined fragments respectively, with two operands each. An operand itself is a *«PaStep»* with the attribute *prob* indicating the probability of being chosen. The call to the Sleep() function in the SD is modeled by an interaction occurrence *ref* making reference to another SD not shown here, which

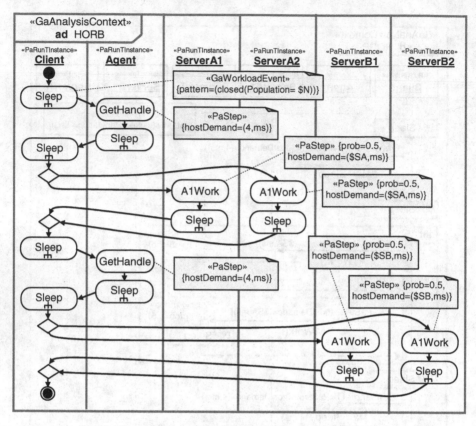

Fig. 4. Client request scenario for H-ORB as an activity diagram

contains a call to a dummy server Sleep that delays the caller by a required time without consuming the CPU time of the caller.

In the activity diagram, every active concurrent instance is represented by its own partition (a.k.a. swimlane) and is stereotyped by *«PaRunTInstance»*. The scenario steps modeled as activities are stereotyped as *«PaStep»* with the same *hostDemand* and *prob* attributes as in SD. An AD arc crossing the boundary between partitions represents a message sent from one active instance to another. Sleep is a structured activity, which contains inside the details of a call to a dummy instance that delays the caller without consuming its CPU time. Eventually, in the performance model Sleep will be represented as a dummy server that performs the same roll.

The scenario for the F-ORB case study is not presented here, but it is fairly similar with the H-ORB. In the F-ORB architecture the client sends the entire service request to the agent that locates the appropriate server and forwards the request to it. The server performs the desired service and sends a response back to the client.

After describing the UML source model extended with MARTE annotations, we will present the target performance model and then the intermediate model used in the PUMA transformation.

2.4   Target Performance Model: LQN

Many performance modeling formalisms have been developed over time, such as queueing networks (QN), extended QN, Layered Queueing Networks (LQN), stochastic Petri nets, stochastic process algebras and stochastic automata networks. Although PUMA can incorporate model transformations from CSM to nay performance modeling formalisms, in the paper we will consider one target performance model, the Layered Queueing Network (LQN) [46][36].

LQN was developed as an extension of the well-known Queueing Network model; the main difference is that LQN can easily represent nested services: a server may become in turn a client to other servers from which it requires nested services, while serving its own clients. The LQN toolset presented in [22][23] includes both simulation and analytical solvers.

A slightly simplified LQN metamodel is presented in Figure 5. Examples of LQN models are presented in Figures 5 and 18.

A LQN model is an acyclic graph, with nodes representing software entities and hardware devices (both known as *tasks*), and arcs denoting service requests. The software entities are drawn as rectangles with thick lines, and the hardware devices as ellipses. The nodes with outgoing but no incoming arcs play the role of clients, the intermediate nodes with both incoming and outgoing arcs are usually software servers and the leaf nodes are hardware servers (such as processors, I/O devices, communication network, etc.) A software or hardware server node can be either a single-server or a multi-server.

Each kind of service offered by a LQN task is modeled as an *entry*, drawn as a rectangle with thin lines attached to the task or other entries of the same task. Every entry has its own execution times and demands for other services (given as model parameters). Each software task is running on a processor shown as an ellipse. The communication network, disk devices and other I/O devices are also shown as ellipses. The word "layered" in the LQN name does not imply a strict layering of tasks (for example, tasks in a layer may call each other or skip over layers). The arcs with a filled arrow represent synchronous requests, where the sender is blocked until it receives a reply from the provider of service. It is possible to have also asynchronous request messages (shown as a stick arrow), where the sender does not block after sending a request and the server does reply back. Another communication style called *forwarding* (shown with a dotted line), allows for a client request to be processed by a chain of servers instead of a single server. The first server in the chain will forward the request to the second and become free; the second to the third, etc., and the last server in the chain will reply to the client. Although not explicitly illustrated in the LQN notation, every server, be it software or hardware, has an implicit message queue, where incoming requests are waiting their turn to be served. Servers with more then one entry have a single input queue where requests for different entries wait together.

A server entry may be decomposed in two or more sequential phases of service. Phase 1 is the portion of service during which the client is blocked waiting for a reply

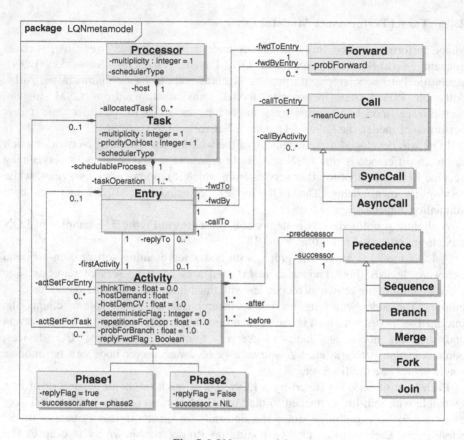

Fig. 5. LQN metamodel

from the server (it is assumed that the client has made a synchronous request). At the end of phase 1, the server will reply to the client, which will unblock and continue its execution. The remaining phases, if any, will be executed in parallel with the client. An extension to LQN [23] allows for an entry to be further decomposed into activities if more details are required to describe its execution (see Figure Y). The activities are connected together to form a directed graph that may branch into parallel threads of control, or may choose randomly between different branches. Just like phases, activities have execution time demands, and can make service requests to other tasks.

The parameters of a LQN model are as follows:

— customer (client) classes and their associated populations or arrival rates;
— for each phase (activity) of a software task entry: average execution time;
— for each phase (activity) making a request to a device: average service time at the device, and average number of visits;
— for each phase (activity) making a request to another task entry: average number of visits
— for each request arc: average communication delay;
— for each software and hardware server: scheduling discipline.

2.5   Intermediate Model: CSM

The Core Scenario Model [34] represents scenarios, which are implicit in many software specifications; they are useful for communicating partial behaviours among diverse stakeholders and provide the basis for defining performance characteristics. The CSM metamodel is similar to the SPT Performance Profile, describing three main types of concepts: *resources, scenarios,* and *workloads*. Each *Scenario* is a directed graph with *Steps* as nodes, and explicit *PathConnectors* which define *Sequence, Branch, Merge, Fork* and *Join*. A *Step* is owned by a *Component*, which may be a *ProcessResource*, and which in turn is associated to a *HostResource* (processor). *Logical resources* are acquired and released along the path by special subtypes of *Step* called *ResourceAcquire* and *ResourceRelease*. *External Resource* represents a resource not explicitly represented in the UML model required for executing external operations that have a performance impact (for example, a disk operation). The CSM metamodel is described in more detail in [34].

3   PUMA Transformation Chain

In this section we present the principles of the transformation used in PUMA: a) from source Smodel in UML extended with MARTE to the intermediate CSM; and b) from CSM to LQN Pmodel. The section also shows a few performance results obtained with the LQN model generated from the CORBA source model introduced in Section 2.3 and compares them with measurements.

3.1   Transformation from UML+MARTE to CSM

The general strategy is to identify the scenarios and structural diagrams to be considered by looking for MARTE stereotypes and then to generate structural CSM elements (*Resources* and *Components*) from the structure diagram (e.g., deployment),

Table 1. Mapping between MARTE stereotypes and CSM Elements

MARTE	CSM
«GaWorkloadEvent»	Closed/OpenWorkload
«GaScenario»	Scenario
«PaStep»	Step
«PaCommStep»	Step (for the message)
«GaResAcq»	ResourceAcquire
«GaResRel»	ResourceRelease
«PaResPass»	ResourcePass
«GaExecHost»	ProcessingResource
«PaCommHost»	ProcessingResource
«PaRunTInstance»	Component
«PaLogicalResource»	LogicalResource

and behavioural elements (*Scenarios*, *Steps* and *PathConnectors*) from the behaviour diagrams. The mapping between MARTE stereoptypes and CSM elements is presented in Table 1.

The transformation algorithm begins with generating the structural elements first. A UML Node from a deployment diagram stereotyped *«GaExecHost»* or *«PaCommHost»* is converted into a CSM *ProcessingResource*. A UML run-time component manifested by an artifact, which is in turn deployed on a node is converted into a CSM *Component*.

Scenarios Described by Sequence Diagrams. The transformation continues with the scenarios described by sequence diagrams stereotyped with *«GaAnalysisContext»*. For each scenario, a CSM *Start PathConnection* is generated first, and the workload information is attached to it. Each *Lifeline* from a sequence diagram describes the behaviour of a UML instance (be it active or passive) and corresponds in turn to a CSM *Component*. The *Lifelines* stereotyped as *«PaRunTInstance»* corresponds to an active runtime instance. We assume that the artifacts for all active UML instances are shown on the deployment diagram, so their corresponding CSM *Components* were already generated. However, it is possible that the sequence diagram contains lifelines for passive objects not shown in the deployment diagram. In such a case, the corresponding CSM *Passive Component* is generated, and its host is inferred to be the same as that of the active component in whose context it executes.

The translation follows the message flow of the scenario, generating the corresponding *Steps* and *PathConnections*. A simple *Step* corresponds to a UML *Execution Occurrence*, which is the execution of an operation as an effect of receiving a message. Complex CSM Steps with a nested scenario correspond to operand regions of UML *Combined Fragments* and *Interaction Occurrences*. A synchronous message will generate a CSM *Sequence PathConnection* between the step sending the message and the step executed as an effect. An asynchronous message spawns a parallel thread, and thus will generate a *Fork PathConnection* with two outgoing paths: one follows the sender's activity, and the other follows the path of the message. The two paths may rejoin later through a *Join PathConnection*. Fork/join of parallel paths may be also generated by a *par Combined Fragment*. Conditional execution of alternate paths is generated by *alt* and *opt Combined Fragments*.

Scenarios Described by Activity Diagrams. We consider all the scenarios described by activity diagrams stereotyped as *«GaAnalysisContext»*. For each scenario, the transformation starts with the *Initial ControNode,* which is converted into a CSM *Start PathConnection* and a *Resource Acquire* step for acquiring the component for the respective swimlane. Also, the scenario workload information described by a *«GaWorkloadEvent»* stereotype is used to generate a CSM *Workload* element attached to the *Start PathConnection*. (Note that in MARTE, the scenario workload information is associated by convention with the first step of a scenario, not with its *Initial ControlNode,* which cannot be stereotyped as *Step*). The translation follows the sequence of the scenario from start to finish, identifying the *Steps* and *PathConnections* (sequence, branch/merge, fork/join) from the context of the diagram. Each UML *ActivityNode* that represents a simple activity is converted into a CSM *Step*, one that represents an activity further refined by another diagram generates a CSM *Step* with a nested *Scenario*.

As mentioned before, we assume that each partition (a.k.a. swimlane) is associated with a *Component* through the *«PaRunTInstance»* stereotype. A special treatment is given to *ActivityEdges* that cross the partition boundary (named here cross-transition). A cross-transition represents a message (signal) between the corresponding components that implies releasing the sender (which is a *Component*, but also a *Resource*) and acquiring the receiver. Therefore, a cross-transition generates in CSM a *ResourceRelease* step, a *Sequence PathConnection* and *ResourceAcquire* step.

Figure 6 shows the CSM generated for the H-ORD source model from section 2.3.

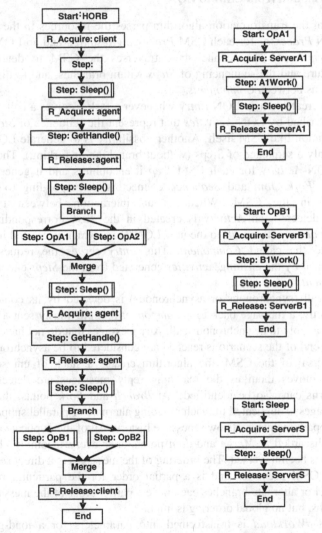

Fig. 6. CSM for the H-ORB system from Figures 2 and 3

The main CSM model represents the main flow of steps from the scenario represented in Figure 3 as SD and in Figure 4 as AD. Composite steps were generated for every *Interaction Occurrence* invoking Sleep() and for each operand of the *alt CombineFragments* making a choice of a server. The Composite steps are refined by CSM sub-scenarios on the right of the figure. (The fragment for the operand invoking A2 is not shown, being similar with the one invoking A1; the same is true for operand invoking B2, which is similar to B1).

3.2   Transformation from CSM to LQN

The first stage of the transformation algorithm parses the resources in the CSM and generates a LQN *Processor* for each CSM *ProcessingResource* and an LQN *Task* for each CSM *Component*. The second stage traverses the CSM to determine the branching structure and the sequencing of *Steps* within branches, and to discover the calling interactions between *Components*.

The traversal creates a new LQN *Entry* whenever a task receives a call. The entry internals are described by LQN *Activities* that represent the sequence of *Steps* for the call, using a notation like CSM itself. Another possibility is to generate LQN *Phases* when there is only a sequence of Steps (without branching or forking). The traversal generates an LQN *Activity* for each CSM *Step* it encounters and it generates LQN *Branch, Merge, Fork, Join* and *Sequence* connectors corresponding to the same *PathConnectors* in the CSM. Whenever an interaction between two CSM *Components* is detected, an *Activity* is created in the *Task* corresponding to the requesting *Component* with a *Call* to the new LQN *Entry* which is created in the *Task* corresponding to the called *Component*. This *Entry* serves the request and its workload is defined by the ensuing *Activities* generated from the *Steps* encountered in the new *Component*.

The type of call (synchronous or asynchronous) is detected by its context in the CSM. More exactly, a message back to a *Component* that previously sent a request is considered to be a reply to a synchronous call. Any messages that do not have matching replies when the end of the scenario is reached are considered to be asynchronous calls. During the traversal of the CSM, the algorithm creates a stack of unresolved call messages and removes them as the matching reply messages are detected (other interaction patterns can also be identified). At *Branch* and *Fork* points, the stack of unresolved messages is duplicated for each outgoing alternate or parallel subpath so that each ensuing subpath maintains its own message history. All of the duplicate call stacks except one are discarded at *Merge* and *Join* points after every incoming alternate or parallel branch has been traversed. The ordering of the messages is a direct result of the traversal of the CSM scenarios and is a partial order for the particular path being traversed. Parallel or alternate branches each have a partial order of the messages along their own subpaths, but no global ordering is implied.

A CSM *ClosedWorkload* is transformed into parameters for a load-generating *Reference Task*, and a CSM *OpenWorkload* into an open stream of requests made to the first entry. An *External Operation* by a CSM Step is represented by an activity which makes a call to a submodel that has to be provided by the analyst.

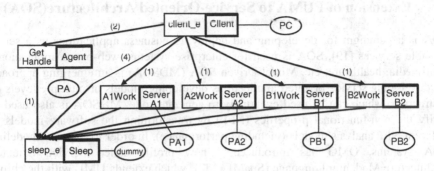

Fig. 7. LQN model for the H-ORB system

Figure 7 shows the LQN model generated from the CSM for the H-ORB given in Figure 6. As mentioned before, the Sleep task running on a dummy server implements the sleep function. All requests are synchronous calls in this example. The numbers in parentheses on the arcs represent the average number of calls. The service times (Not shown in the figure) are represented by the variables $A, $B, $D which are assigned concrete values doing the experiments.

The LQN model thus generated has been validated against measurements of the H-ORB and F-ORB performance prototypes that have been published in [1]. As it can be seen in Figure 8, the accuracy of the analytic model is fairly reasonable.

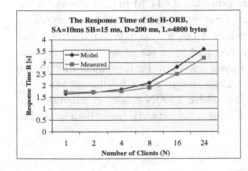
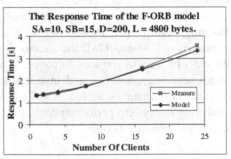

Fig. 8. Validation of the LQN results against measurements

In this section we have presented the PUMA transformations from a Smodel to the corresponding intermediate model to the Pmodel. According to the PUMA architecture from Figure 1, once the Pmodel has been generated, the next step is to use it for experiments that are exploring the parameter space in order to evaluate design changes such as execution in parallel, replication, modified concurrency, and reduced demands and delays. The Pmodel results evaluate the potential of these changes, which can then be mapped to possible software solutions [49].

In the next two sections we will present extensions to the PUMA transformation to specialize it for Service-Oriented Architecture and for Software Product lines.

4   Extension of PUMA to Service-Oriented Architecture(SOA)

SOA is a paradigm for developing and deploying business applications as a set of reusable services [19]. SOA is used for enterprise systems, web-based applications, multimedia, healthcare, etc. Model Driven SOA (MDSOA) is an emerging approach for developing service-oriented applications developing models at multiple levels of abstraction, which can be used eventually to generate code. MDSOA is also used to verify the non-functional properties (NFP) by transforming the software models to different NFP analysis models (including performance). In order to improve modeling SOA systems, OMG has introduced a new profile called Service Oriented Architecture Modeling Language (SoaML) [32], which extends UML with the ability to model the service structure and dependencies, to specify service capabilities and classification, and to define service consumers and providers.

The emergence of MDD in general and of MDSOA in particular has attracted a lot of interest in the research community in using software models to evaluate the non functional properties of service-based systems. A model transformation framework is proposed in [45] to automatically include the architectural impact and the performance overhead of the middleware layer in distributed systems. This allows one to model the application independent of the middleware and then obtain a platform specific model by composition. Another model-driven approach for development and evaluation of non-functional properties such as performance and reliability is based on the Palladio Component Model (PCM), which allows specifying component-based software architectures in a parametric way [27]. A parametric performance completion for message-oriented middleware proposed for PCM in [27] allows for the composition of platform components with application components. Other research on building performance models for web services takes a two layered user/provider approach in [18] and [28]: the user is a represented by a set of workflows and the provider by a set of services deployed on a physical system. Performance information about service capabilities and invocation mechanisms is given by the means of P-WSDL (Performance-enabled WSDL) in [18], where a LQN model is generated for analyzing the system performance. In [28] the queueing network formalism is used to derive performance bounds.

4.1   PUMA4SOA Transformation Chain

Performance by Unified Model Analysis for SOA (PUMA4SOA) is a modeling approach proposed first in [2] which extends the PUMA transformation, specializing it for service-based systems. The difference between the original PUMA and the extended one for SOA stems from: a) the kind of design models accepted as input, and b) the separation between Platform Independent Model (PIM) and Platform Specific Model (PSM) of the application and the use of platform models. Figure 4.1 illustrates the steps of PUMA4SOA; the top leftmost represents the main difference from PUMA (whose steps are shown in Figure 1). There are three input models to PUMA4SOA: a) application PIM, b) deployment model which describes the allocation of the artifacts to a deployment target, and c) platform aspect models.

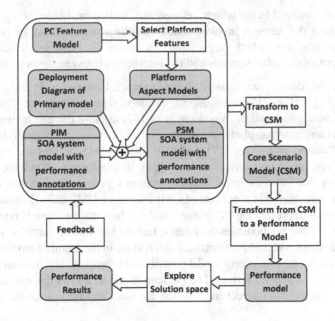

Fig. 9. The Steps of PUMA4SOA

The platform independent model of the application contains a UML software model with three levels of abstractions. The UML model is annotated with performance information using the standard UML profile MARTE. Each level represents a part of the system details that will be used together with the other parts to build the performance model. The three abstraction levels are as follows:

a) *Workflow Model* which represents a set of business processes. Each workflow contains a sequence of activities and actions controlled by conditions, iterations, and concurrency.

b) *Service Architecture Model* which describes the service capabilities arranged in a hierarchy showing anticipated usage dependencies. It also depicts the level of service granularity, which has a substantial effect on the system performance. Invoking services in heterogeneous and distributed environment produces message overheads due to marshalling/unmarshalling of the message data at the service platform. A coarser service granularity reduces the number of service invocations, which improves the performance, but produces unnecessary coupling between the components of the SOA system. However, a finer service granularity increases the number of service invocations, which reduces the performance but produces a loosely coupled system. Service Architecture Modeling helps the modeler to manage the tradeoff between the service granularity and performance.

c) *Service Behavior Model* which refines the workflow behavior, giving more details about the services invoked. Each workflow activity may be refined by a sequence diagram which represents its detailed behavior, including the invocations of the other services and the interaction between participants.

PUMA4SOA also defines two models: a) Performance Completion Feature model (PC feature model), and b) Platform aspect models. The concept of "performance completions" was introduced by Woodside et al. [47] to close the gap between abstract design models and external platform factors. The PC feature model, introduced in the work of the Palladio group (see [27]) and also used in [41], defines the variability in platform choices, execution environments, types of platform realizations, and other external factors that have an impact on the system's performance. Since the regular notation for feature diagrams is not part of UML, we use a UML class diagram extended with stereotypes to represent the PC feature model, where each feature is represented as a class element. Four relationships between a feature and its sub features are defined: Mandatory, Optional, Or, and Alternative. Each feature in the feature model represents a platform aspect. A platform aspect model describes the structure and the behavior of the service platform in a generic format. The PC feature model allows the modeler to select between different platform aspect models that are most appropriate for the application of interest.

The selected platform aspect models composed with the PIM generate the PSM. The Aspect Oriented Modeling (AOM) approach is used to generate the platform specific model (PSM) by weaving the selected platform aspect model behaviors into different locations of the platform independent model (PIM). The AOM approach requires two types of models: a) the primary model which describes the core design decisions, and b) a set of aspect models, each describing a concern that crosscuts the primary model [21]. PUMA4SOA considers the application PIM as the primary model. An aspect model can be seen as a template or pattern, independent of any primary model it may be composed with. For each composition with the primary model, the template is instantiated and its formal parameters are bound to concrete values using binding rules, to give a context-specific aspect model. The composed model is generated by weaving the context-specific aspect models into the primary model at different locations. In the next section, we will describe the PUMA4SOA approach with an example from the healthcare domain.

4.2   Platform Independent Model: Case Study

The platform independent model is illustrated with a healthcare case study, the Eligibility Referral System, which is introduced in [3]. A UML activity diagram is used to model the workflow in Figure 10. It is the top level model that describes the process of transferring a patient from one hospital to another. Three organizations are involved, the transferring and receiving hospitals and the insurance company. The workflow begins with the transferring hospital filling and processing the initial forms needed to transfer the patient. The next process is getting the physician and the payment approvals. The transferring hospital is then sending the forms and waits for

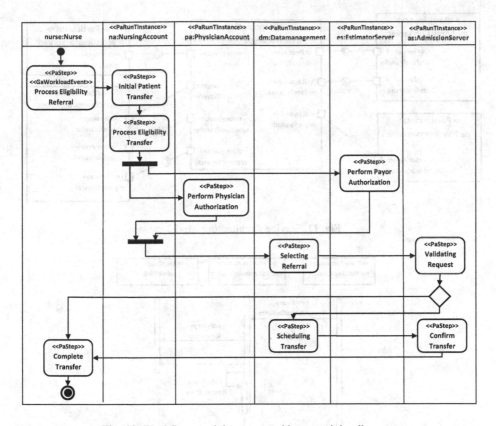

Fig. 10. Workflow model represented by an activity diagram

an acknowledgement from the receiving hospital. Finally, the transferring hospital schedules the transferring date and updates the transferring process. The workload of the system is described by the *«GaWorkloadEvent»* stereotype, which can be a closed arrival pattern defining a fixed populations of users or an open arrival pattern which defining a stream of requests that arrive at a given rate. A swimlane is stereotyped as *«PaRunTInstance»* to indicate that the activities are executed by a concurrent participant. This stereotype has a *poolsize* attribute to define the number of concurrent threads. An activity is stereotyped as *«PaStep»* to indicate a scenario step. It has a *hostDemand* attribute for the required execution time, a *prob* for its probability, and a *rep* for the number of repetitions. The communication between participants is described by *«PaCommStep»* to indicate the conveyance of a message. It has a *msgSize* attribute to indicate the amount of transmitted data.

The Service Architecture model, illustrated in Figure 11, is using a new OMG profile called the Service Oriented Architecture Modeling Language (SoaML) [32]. SoaML extends UML with the ability to define the service structure and dependencies to specify service capabilities, and to define service consumers and providers. The Eligibility Referral System defines five components stereotyped as *«participants»*:

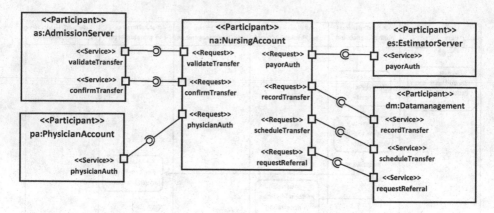

Fig. 11. Service Architecture Model

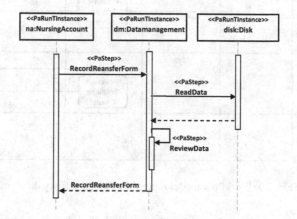

Fig. 12. Service behavior model for Initial Patient Transfer service

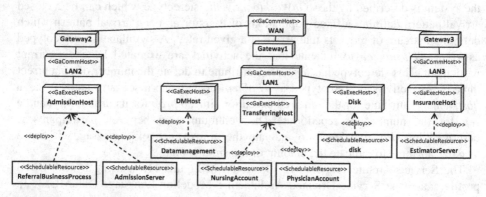

Fig. 13. Deployment of the Eligibility Referral System

NursingAccount, PhysicianAccount, AdmissionServer, EstimatorServer, and Data management. The model also presents different service contracts; each one of them defines service consumers (their ports are stereotyped with *«Request»*), and service providers (their ports are stereotyped with *«Service»*). UML sequence diagrams are used to model the behavior of each activity defined in the workflow model. Figure 12 shows an example of the service behavior model of "Initial Patient Transfer" activity. In this interaction, the nurse generates the patient transfer form by retrieving patient's data from the Database, and then reads and reviews it before sending it back to the form. Lifelines are stereotyped with *«PaRunTInstance»* to indicate a concurrent process, and messages are stereotyped with *«PaStep»* to indicate an action.

The UML Deployment diagram in Figure 12 shows the allocation of software to hardware. Physical communication nodes, such as WAN, LAN1, LAN2, and LAN3, are stereotyped with *«GaCommHost»* to indicate a physical communication link. Processors, such as *AdmissionHost, TransferringHost, InsuranceHost, DMHost,* and *Disk,* are stereotyped with *«GaExecHost»* to indicate the processor host. Artifacts, such as *NursingAccount, PhysicainAccount, AdmissionServer, EstimatorServer, Datamanagement,* and *disk,* are stereotyped with *«SchedulableResource»* to indicate a concurrent resource. The *ReferralBusinessProcess* component represents the execution engine which runs the business process of the system.

4.3   PC Feature Model

The PC feature model describes the variability in service platform which may affect the system's performance. Figure 13 describes the features which may affect the performance of our example, the Eligibility Referral System. There are three mandatory feature groups which are required by any service platform: the operation, message protocol and realization. There are also two optional feature groups: communication and data compression. The relationship between the feature groups and their sub-features are alternative with exactly-one-of feature selected. Although the dependencies between the sub-features are not shown in the model, some features, such as the operation feature, message protocol feature and realization feature, are dependent. As an example selecting one of the operation sub-features, such as invocation, requires selecting one of the message protocol (Http or SOAP) and the realization (WebService, REST, etc.)

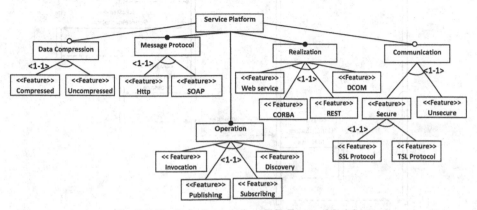

Fig. 14. Platform Completion (PC) Feature Model

4.4   Aspect Platform Model for Service Invocation

The aspect platform models define the middleware structure and behavior of the selected aspects from the PC feature model. In our example, we selected a service invocation aspect realized as a webservice with the message protocol SOAP. Figure 15 describes the generic deployment including the hosts and artifacts involved in the service invocation aspect model. As a naming convention the vertical bar 'l' indicate a generic role name as in [21]. Two hosts are involved in the service invocation operation, the l*Client* which consumes the service, and the l*Provider* which provides it.

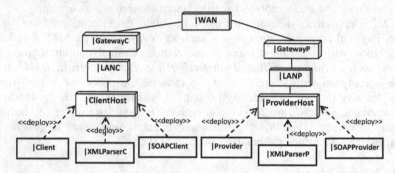

Fig. 15. Generic Invocation aspect: deployment view

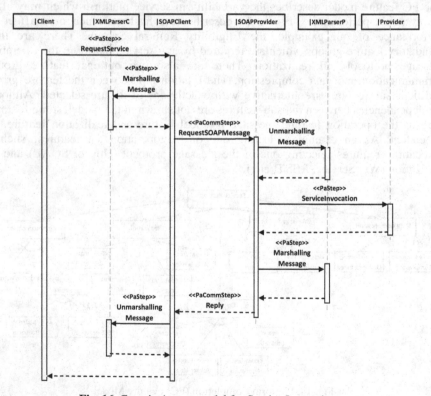

Fig. 16. Generic Aspect model for Service Invocation

The middleware on both sides contains an *XMLParser* to marshal/unmarshal the message, and a *SOAP* stub for message communication. Figure 16 describes the generic service request invocation and response behavior. A request message call is sent from a *Client* to a *Provider*. This message call differs from the regular operation call due to the heterogeneous environment it operates in, which require the message to be parsed in acceptable format at both *Client*, and *Provider* sides, before it is being sent or received.

In the AOM approach, the generic aspect model for the service invocation, illustrated in Figure 16, may be inserted in the PIM multiple times wherever there is a service invocation. For each insertion, the generic aspect model is instantiated and its formal parameters are bound to concrete values using binding rules to produce a context specific aspect model. Each context specific aspect model is then composed into the primary model, which in our case is the PIM. More details about AOM approach can be found in [2][48].

In PUMA4SOA the aspect composition can be performed at three modeling levels: the UML level, the CSM level or the LQN level. The complexity of the aspect composition may determine where to perform it. At the UML level, the aspect composition is more complex because the performance characteristics of the system are scattered between different views and diagrams, which may require many models to be used as input to the composition. On the contrary, performing aspect composition at the CSM or LQN level is simpler because only one view is used for modeling the system. In our example, we performed aspect composition at the CSM level which is discussed in the next section (see also [48]).

4.5   From Annotated UML to CSM

In PUMA4SOA, generating the Platform specific model can be delayed to the CSM level. The UML PIM and platform aspect models are first transformed to CSM models. The CSM PSM is then generated by composing the CSM platform aspect models with the CSM PIM. The generated CSM model is separated into two layers, the business layer representing the workflow model, and the component layer representing the service behavior model. The workflow model is transformed into the top level scenario model. The composite activities in the workflow are refined using multiple service behavior models, which are transformed into multiple sub-scenarios within the top level scenario. The CSM on the left in Figure 17 is the top level scenario representing the workflow model. It has a *Start*, and *End* elements for beginning and finishing the scenario. The *ResourseAcquire* and *ResourseRelease* indicate the usage of the resources. A *Step* element describes an operation or action. An atomic step is drawn as a box with a single line and a composite step as a box with double lines on the sides. The scenario on the right of Figure 17 illustrates the composed model which describes the PSM of the sub-scenario *InitialPatientTransfer*. The grayed parts originated from the context-specific aspect model which was composed with the PIM. Whenever a consumer requests a service in the workflow model, the generic service invocation aspect is instantiated using binding roles to generate the context specific service invocation aspect, which is then composed with the PIM to produce the PSM. Figure 10 shows seven service requests, which means that seven invocation aspect instances are composed within top level scenario.

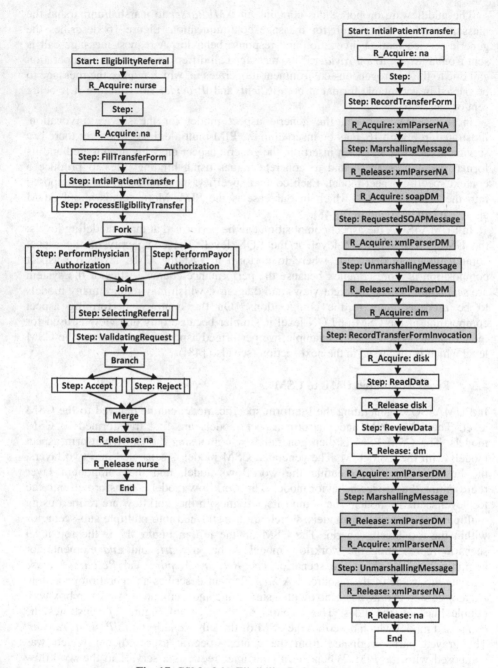

Fig. 17. CSM of the Eligibility Referral System

4.6   From CSM to LQN

Model transformation from CSM to LQN is performed by separating the workflow and service layer, as done in section 3.2. The workflow layer which represents the top level scenario is transformed into an LQN activity graph associated with a task called "workflow", and runs on its own processor. The service layer, which represents CSM sub-scenario containing services, is transformed into a set of tasks with their owned entries corresponding to services. Figure 18 shows the LQN performance model for the Eligibility Referral System. The top level of the LQN represents the workflow activity graph (in gray), while the underlying services are represented by the lower level tasks and entries. The middleware tasks are shown in darker gray.

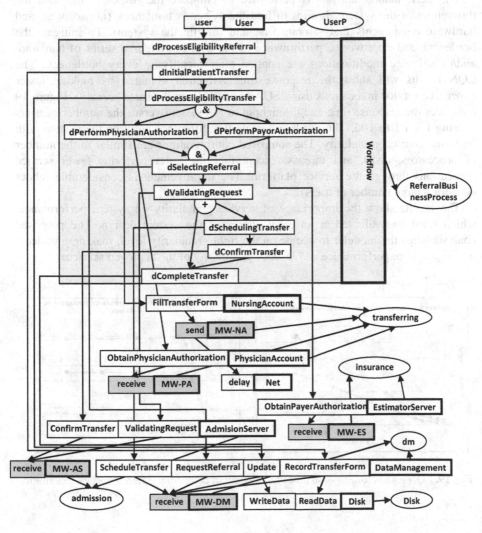

Fig. 18. LQN model

4.7   Performance Results

The performance of the Eligibility Referral System has been evaluated based on two design alternatives: a) with finer service granularity corresponding to service architecture from Figure 11; and b) with coarser service granularity, where the invocations of low level services for accessing the database DM are replaced with regular calls, avoiding the regular service invocation overhead. In the second solution, the functionality of the lower level services have been integrated within the higher level services provided by the NursingAccount component. Figure 18 shows the LQN model generated for the Eligibility Referral System for the first alternative only. The LQN model of the second alternative is not shown here.

The performance analysis is performed to compare the response time and the throughput of the system. It aims to find the system's bottleneck (i.e. software and hardware components that saturate first and throttle the system). To mitigate the bottleneck and improve the performance of the overall system, a series of hardware and/or software modifications are applied after identifying every bottleneck. The LQN results will show the response time reduction obtained by making fewer expensive service invocations using SOAP and XML in the same scenario. Figure 19 compares the response time and throughput of the system versus the number of users ranging from 1 to 100. The results illustrate the difference between the system with finer and coarser granularity. The compared configurations are similar in the number of processors, disks, and threads, except that the latter performs fewer service invocations through the service platform. The improvement is considerable (about 40% for a large number of users).

The results show the importance of service granularity on system performance, which must be evaluated at an early phases of the system design. The proposed analysis helps the modeler to decide on the right granularity level, making a tradeoff between system performance and level of granularity of the deployed services.

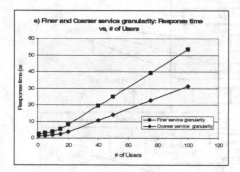
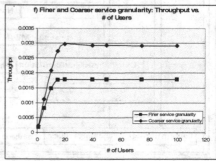

Fig. 19. LQN results for response time and throughput comparing different service granularity

5   Extension of PUMA to Software Product Lines (SPL)

A Software Product Line (SPL) is a set of similar software systems built from a shared set of assets, which are realizing common features satisfying a particular domain. Experience shows that by adopting a SPL development approach, organizations achieve increased quality and significant reductions in cost and time to market [14].

An emerging trend apparent in the recent literature is that the SPL development moves toward adopting a Model-Driven Development (MDD) paradigm. This means that models are increasingly used to represent SPL artifacts, which are building blocks for many different products with all kind of options and alternatives. We propose to integrate performance analysis in the early phases of the model-driven development process for Software Product Lines (SPL), with the goal of evaluating the performance characteristic of different products by generating and analyzing quantitative performance models [39]. Our starting point is the so-called SPL model, a multi-view UML model of the core family assets representing the commonality and variability between different products. We added another dimension to the SPL model, annotating it with generic performance specifications (i.e., using parameters instead of actual values) expressed in the standard UML profile MARTE [30]. Such parameters appear as variables and expression in the MARTE stereotype attributes. A model transformation realized in the Atlas Transformation Language (ATL) derives the UML model of a specific product with concrete MARTE performance annotations from the SPL model. The product derivation process binds the variability expressed in the SPL to a specific product, and also the generic SPL performance annotations to concrete values provided by the designer for this product. The proposed model transformation approach can be applied to any existing SPL model-driven development process using UML for modeling software.

Performance is a runtime property of the deployed system and depends on two types of factors: some are contained in the design model of the product (generated from the SPL model) while others characterize the underlying platforms and runtime environment. Performance models need to reflect both types of factors. Woodside et al. [47] proposed the concept of performance completions to close the gap between abstract design models and external platform factors. Since our goal is to automate the derivation of a performance model for a specific product from the SPL model, we propose to deal with performance completions in the early phases of the SPL development process by using a Performance Completion feature (PC-feature) model as described in the previous section. The PC-feature model explicitly captures the variability in platform choices, execution environments, different types of communication realizations, and other external factors that have an impact on performance, such as different protocols for secure communication channels and represents the dependencies and relationships between them [41]. Therefore, our approach uses two feature models for a SPL: 1) a regular feature model for expressing the variability between member products, and 2) a PC-feature model introduced for performance analysis reasons to capture platform-specific variability.

Dealing manually with a large number of performance parameters and with their mapping, by asking the developers to inspect every diagram in the model, to extract these annotations and to attach them to the corresponding PC-features, is an error-prone process. A model transformation approach is proposed in [43] to automate the collection of all the generic parameters that need to be bound to concrete variables from the annotated product model, presenting them to the user in a user-friendly format.

The automatic derivation of a specific product model based on a given feature configuration is enabled through the mapping between features from the feature model and their realizations in the design model. In this section, an efficient mapping technique is used, which aims to minimize the amount of explicit feature annotations in the UML design model of SPL. Implicit feature mapping is inferred during product derivation from the relationships between annotated and non-annotated model elements as defined in the UML metamodel [40].

In order to analyze the performance of a specific product running on a given platform, we need to generate a performance model for that product by model transformations from the SPL model with generic performance annotations. In our research, this is done in four big steps: a) instantiating a product platform independent model (PIM) with generic performance parameters from the SPL model; b) collecting all the generic parameters that need bounding from the automatically generated product PIM and presents them to the developer in a user-friendly spreadsheet format; c) performing the actual binding to concrete values provided by the developer to obtain a product platform specific model (PSM) and d) generating a performance model for the product from the model obtained in the previous step.

Related Work. To the best of our knowledge, no work has been done to evaluate and predict the performance of a given member of a SPL family by generating a formal performance model. Most of the work aims to model non-functional requirements (NFRs) in the same way as functional requirements. Some of the works are concerned with the interactions between selected features and the NFRs and propose different techniques to represent these interactions and dependencies. In [8], the MARTE profile is analyzed to identify the variability mechanisms of the profile in order to model variability in embedded SPL models. Although MARTE was not defined for product lines, the paper proposes to combine it with existing mechanisms for representing variability, but it does not explain how this can be achieved. A model analysis process for embedded SPL is presented in [9] to validate and verify quality attributes variability. The concept of multilevel and staged feature model is applied by introducing more than one feature models that represent different information at different abstraction levels; however, the traceability links between the multilevel models and the design model are not explained.

In [7], the authors propose an integrated tool-supported approach that considers both qualitative and quantitative quality attributes without imposing hierarchical structural constraints. The integration of SPL quality attributes is addressed by assigning quality attributes to software elements in the solution domain and linking these elements to features. An aggregation function is used to collect the quality attributes depending on the selected features for a given product.

A literature survey on approaches that analyze and design non-functional requirements in a systematic way for SPL is presented in [29]. The main concepts of the surveyed approaches are based on the interactions between the functional and non-functional features.

An approach called Svamp is proposed to model functional and quality variability at the architectural level of the SPL [35]. The approach integrates several models: a Kumbang model to represent the functional and structural variability in the architecture and to define components that are used by other models; a quality attribute model to specify the quality properties and a quality variability model for expressing variability within these quality attributes.

Reference [10] extends the feature model with so-called extra-functional features representing non-functional features. Constraint programming is used to reason on this extended feature model to answer some questions such as how many potential products the feature model contains.

The Product Line UML-Based Software Engineering (PLUS) method is extended in [38] to specify performance requirements by introducing several stereotypes specific to model performance requirements such as «optional» and «alternative performance feature».

5.1 Domain Engineering Process

The SPL development process is separated into two major phases: 1) *domain engineering* for creating and maintaining a set of reusable artifacts and introducing variability in these software artifacts, so that the next phase can make a specific decision according to the product's requirements; and 2) *application engineering* for building family member products from reusable artifacts created in the first phase instead of starting from scratch.

The domain engineering process is a development cycle *for* reuse and includes, but is not limited to, creating the requirement specifications, domain models, architecture, reusable software components [14]. The SPL assets created by the domain engineering process which are of interest for our research are represented by a multi-view UML design model of the family, called the *SPL model*, which represents a superimposition of all variant products. The creation of the SPL model employs two separate UML profiles: a *product line* profile based on [24] for specifying the commonality and variability between products, and the MARTE profile for performance annotations. Another important outcome of the domain engineering process is the feature model used to represent commonalities and variabilities between family members in a concise taxonomic form. Additionally, the PC-feature model is created to represent the variability space of the performance completions.

An e-commerce case study is used to illustrate the construction of the UML model for SPL that represents the source model of our model transformation approach. The e-commerce SPL is a web-based product line that can generate a distributed application that can handle either business-to-business (B2B) or business-to-consumer (B2C) systems. For instance, in B2B, a business customer can browse and select items through several catalogs. Each customer has a contract with a supplier for purchases, as well as bank accounts through which payments can be made. An operation fund is associated with each contract.

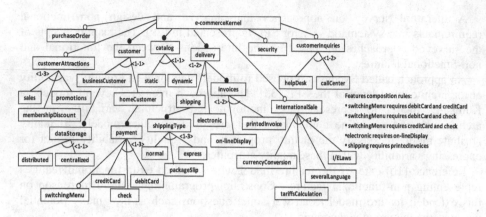

Fig. 20. Feature model of the e-commerce SPL

Feature Model. The feature models are used in our approach to represent two different variability spaces. The PC-feature model represents the variability in platform choices, execution environments, and other external factors that have an impact on performance as described in the previous section. This sub-section describes the regular feature model representing functional variabilities between products. An example of feature model of an e-commerce SPL is represented in Figure 20 in the extended FODA notation, Cardinality-Based Feature Model (CBFM) [17]. Since the FODA notation is not part of UML, the feature diagram is represented in the source model taken as input by our ATL transformation as an extended UML class diagram, where the features and feature groups are modeled as stereotyped classes and the dependencies and constraints between features as stereotyped associations. For instance, the two alternative features *Static* and *Dynamic* are mutually exclusive and so they are grouped into an *exactly-one-of* feature group called *Catalog*, while the three optional features CreditCard, DebitCard, and Check are grouped into an at-least-one-of feature group called Payment. Thus, an individual system can provide at least one of these features or any number of them. In the case of an individual system providing all of these features, the user can choose one of them during the run-time execution. In addition to functional features, we add to the diagram another type of features characterizing design decisions that have an impact on the non-functional requirements or properties. For example, the architectural decision related to the location of the data storage (centralized or distributed) affects performance, reliability and security, and is represented in the diagram by two mutually exclusive quality features. This type of feature related to a design decision is part of the design model, not just an additional PC-feature required only for performance analysis. This feature model represents the set of all possible combinations of features for the products of the family. It describes the way features can be combined within this SPL. A specific product is configured by selecting a valid feature combination from the feature model, producing a so-called feature configuration based on the product's requirements. To enable the automatic derivation of a given product model from the SPL model, the mapping between the features contained in the feature model and their realizations in a reusable SPL model needs to be specified, as shown in the next sub-section. Also, each stereotyped class in the feature model has a tagged value indicating whether it is selected in a given feature configuration or not.

SPL Model. The SPL model should contain, among other assets, structural and behavioural views which are essential for the derivation of performance models. It consists of: 1) structural description of the software showing the high-level classes or components, especially if they are distributed and/or concurrent; 2) deployment of software to hardware devices; 3) a set of key performance scenarios defining the main system functions frequently executed.

The functional requirements of the SPL are modeled as use cases. Use cases required by all family members are stereotyped as *«kernel»*. The variability distinguishing the members of a family from each other is explicitly modeled by use cases stereotyped as *«optional»* or *«alternative»*. In order to avoid polluting our model with extra annotations and to ensure the well-formedness of the derived product model, we propose to annotate explicitly the minimum number of model elements within each diagram of our SPL model. For instance, in the use case diagram, only the optional and alternative use cases are annotated with the name of the features requiring them (given as stereotype attributes); since a kernel use case represents commonality, it is sufficient to just stereotype it as «kernel». Other model elements, such as actors, associations, generalizations, properties, are mapped implicitly to feature through their relationship with the use cases, so there is no need to clutter the model with their annotations. The evaluation of implicit mapping during product derivation is explained in the following subsection.

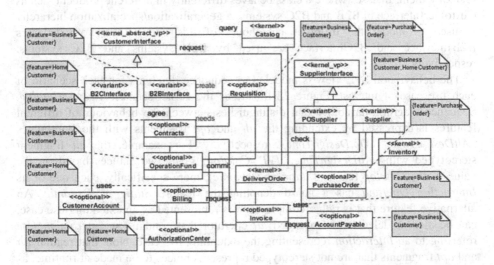

Fig. 21. A fragment of the class diagram of the e-commerce SPL

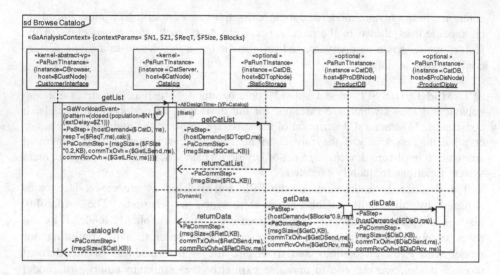

Fig. 22. SPL Scenario Browse Catalog

The structural view of the SPL is presented as a class diagram; Figure 21 depicts a small fragment. The classes that are common to all members of the SPL are stereotyped as *«kernel»*. The variability that distinguishes the members of a family from each other is explicitly modeled by classes stereotyped as *«optional»* or annotated with the name of the feature(s) requiring them (given as stereotype attributes). This is an example of mapping between features and the model elements realizing them. In cases where a class behaves differently in different product (such as CustomerInterface in B2B and B2C systems) a generalization/specialization hierarchy is used to model the different behaviours of this class. The two subclasses B2BInterface and B2CInterface are used by B2B systems and B2C systems, respectively.

The behavioural SPL view is modeled as sequence diagrams for each scenario of each use case of interest. Figure 22 illustrates the kernel scenario *BrowseCatalog*. Sequence diagram variability that distinguishes between the behaviour of different features is expressed by extending the *alt* and *opt* fragments with the stereotypes *«AltDesignTime»* *«OptDesignTime»*, respectively. For example, the *alt* fragment stereotyped with *«AltDesignTime»* *{VP=Catalog}* gives two choices based on the value of the *Catalog* feature (*Static* or *Dynamic*); more specifically, each one of its *Interaction Operand* has a guard denoting the feature *Static* or *Dynamic*. An alternative feature that is rather complex and is represented as an extending use case, can be also modeled as an extended *alt* operator that contains an *Interaction Use* referring to an *Interaction* representing the extending use case. Note that regular *alt* and *opt* fragments that are not stereotyped represent choices to be made at runtime, as defined in UML.

Since the SPL model is generic, covering many products and containing variation points with variants, the MARTE annotations need to be generic as well. We use

MARTE variables as a means of parameterizing the SPL performance annotations; such variables (parameters) will be assigned (bound to) concrete values during the product derivation process. For instance the message *getList* is stereotyped as a communication step (by convention, we use names starting with '$' for all MARTE variables to distinguish them from other identifiers and names):

$$«PaCommStep» \{ msgSize = (\$MReq, KB),$$
$$commTxOvh = (\$GetLSend, ms),$$
$$commRcvOvh = (\$GetLRcv, ms)\}\}$$

where the message size is the variable *$GetL* in KiloBytes. The overheads for sending and receiving this particular message are the variables *$GetLSend* and *$GetLRcv*, respectively, in milliseconds. We propose to annotate each communication step (which corresponds to a logical communication channel) with the CPU overheads for transferring the respective message: *commTxOvh* for transmitting (sending) the message and *commRcvOvh* for receiving it. Eventually, these overheads will be added in the performance model to the execution demands of the two execution hosts involved in the communication (one for sending and the other for receiving the respective message).

Performance Completions. In SPL, different members may vary from each other in terms of their functional requirements, quality attributes, platform choices, network connections, physical configurations, and middleware. Many details contained in the system that are not part of its design model but of the underlying platforms and environment, do affect the run-time performance and need to be represented in the performance model. *Performance completions*, as proposed by Woodside [47] and explained in the previous section, are a manner to close the gap between the high-level design model and its different implementations. Performance completions provide a general concept to include low-level details of execution environment/ platform in performance models

In this approach, we propose to include the performance impact of underlying platforms into the UML+MARTE model of a product as aggregated platform overheads, expressed in MARTE annotations attached to existing processing and communication resources in the generated product model. This will keep the model simple and still allow us to generate a performance model containing the performance effects of both the product and the platforms. Every possible PC-feature choice is mapped to certain MARTE annotations corresponding to UML model elements in the product model. This mapping is realized by the transformation generating the parameter spreadsheets, which is providing the user with mapping information in order to put the annotation parameters needing to be bound to concrete values into context.

Adding security solutions requires more resources and longer execution times, which in turn has a significant impact on system performance. The PC-feature group *Communication* shown in Figure 13 contains two alternative features *secured* and *unsecured*. The *secured* feature offers two security protocols, each with different overheads for sending and receiving secure messages. These overheads are mapped to the communication overheads through the attributes *commRcvOvh* and *commTxOvh*, which represent the host demand overheads for receiving and sending messages, respectively. Since not all the messages exchanged in a product need to have the same communication overheads, we propose to annotate each individual message stereotyped as *«PaCommStep»* with the processing overheads for the respective message: *commTxOvh* for transmitting (sending) it and *commRcvOvh* for receiving it. In fact, these overheads correspond to the logical communication channel that conveys the respective message. Eventually, the logical channel will be allocated to a physical communication channel (e.g., network or bus) and to two execution hosts, the sender and the receiver. The *commTxOvh* overhead will be eventually added in the performance model to the execution demands of the sender host and *commRcvOvh* to that of the receiver host.

Each feature from the PC-feature model shown in Figure 13 may affect one or more performance attributes. For instance, data compression reduces the message size and at the same time increases the processor communication overhead for compressing and decompressing the data. Thus, it is mapped to the performance attributes message size and communication overhead through the MARTE attributes *msgSize, commTxOvh* and *commRcvOvh*, respectively. The mapping here is between a PC-feature and the performance attribute(s) affected by it, which are represented as MARTE stereotype attributes associated to different model elements.

5.2   Model Transformation Approach

The derivation of a specific UML product model with concrete performance annotations from the SPL model with generic annotations requires three model transformations: a) transforming the SPL model to a product platform independent model (PIM) with generic performance annotations, b) generating spreadsheets for the user containing generic parameters and guiding information for the specific product, c) performing the actual binding by using the concrete values provided by the user to produce a product platform specific model (PSM). We have implemented these model transformations in the Atlas Transformation Language (ATL) [1]. We handle two kind of generic parametric annotations: a) product-specific (due to the variability expressed in the SPL model) and platform-specific (due to device choices, network connections, middleware, and runtime environment).

Product PIM Derivation. The derivation process is initiated by specifying a given product through its feature configuration (i.e., the legal combination of features characterizing the product). The selected features are checked for consistency against the feature dependencies and constraints in the feature model, in order to identify any inconsistencies. An example is checking to ensure that no two mutually exclusive features are chosen.

The second step in the derivation process is to select the use cases realizing the chosen features. All kernel use cases are copied to the product use case diagram, since they represent functionality provided by every member of the SPL. If a chosen feature is realized through extend or include relationships between use cases, both the base and the included or extending use cases have to be selected, as well. A use case containing in its scenario variation point(s) required to realize the selected feature(s) has to be chosen, too. The optional and alternative use cases are selected and copied to the target use case diagram if they are mapped to a feature from the feature configuration. The implicit mapping of other non-annotated elements is inferred from their relationships with annotated elements as defined in the UML metamodel and well-formedness rules. For example, Actor is a non-annotated element associated to one or more use cases, so its implicit mapping is evaluated through the attribute *memberEnd* owned by the *Association* connected it with a use case. The attribute *memberEnd* collects all the properties related to the association and since the *type* of the property refers to the end of the association, we can navigate to the use case and the corresponding actor through this attribute. Whenever, the use case is selected, the actor and the association are selected as well. Finally, the use case diagram for the product is developed after all the PL variability stereotypes were eliminated.

The third step is to derive the product class diagram by selecting first all kernel classes from the SPL class diagram. Optional and variant classes needed for the desired product are selected next (each is annotated with the feature(s) requiring it). Moreover, superclasses of the selected optional or variant classes have to be selected as well. The other non-annotated elements are selected based on their relationships with annotated elements as defined in the UML metamodel. For example, according to the UML metamodel, a binary association has to be attached to a classifier at each end. Therefore, the decision whether a binary association has to be copied or not to the target is based on the selection of both of its classifiers. If at least one of the classifiers is not selected, the association will not be created in the target model. In other words, the binary association is created in the target model if and only if both of its *memberEnd* properties have their classifiers already selected and created. At the same time, if only one of its classifier is selected, the property attached to this unselected association and owned by the selected classifier should not be created in the target model.

The final step of the product derivation is to generate the sequence diagrams corresponding to different scenarios of the chosen use cases. Each such scenario is modeled as a sequence diagram, which has to be selected from the SPL model and copied to the product one. The PL variability stereotypes are eliminated after binding the generic roles associated to the lifelines of each selected sequence diagram to specific roles corresponding to the chosen features. For instance, the sequence diagram *BrowseCatalog* has the generic alternate role *CustomerInterface* which has to be bound to a concrete role, either *B2BInterface* or *B2CInterface* to realize the features *BusinessCustomer* or *HomeCustomer*, respectively. However, the selection of the optional roles is based on the corresponding features. For instance, the generic optional role *StaticStorage* is selected if the feature *Static Catalog* is chosen. More details about the derivation approach and the mapping of functional features to model elements are presented in our previous work [40] [42].

The outcome of this model transformation is a product model where the variability related to SPL has been resolved based on the chosen feature configuration. However, the performance annotations are still generic and need to be bound to concrete values.

Generating User-Friendly Representation. The generic parameters of a product PIM derived from the SPL model are related to different kind of information: a) product-specific resource demands (such as execution times, number of repetitions and probabilities of different steps); b) software-to-hardware allocation (such as component instances to processors); and c) platform/environment-specific performance details (also called performance completions). The user (i.e., performance analyst) needs to provide concrete values for all generic parameters; this will transform the generic product model into a platform-specific model describing the run-time behaviour of the product for a specific run-time environment.

Choosing concrete values to be assigned to the generic performance parameters of type (a) is not a simple problem. In general, it is difficult to estimate quantitative resource demands for each step in the design phase, when an implementation does not exist and cannot be measured yet. Several approaches are used by performance analysts to come up with reasonable estimates in the early design stages: expert experience with previous versions or with similar software, understanding of the algorithm complexity, measurements of reused software, measurements of existing libraries, or using time budgets. As the project advances, early estimates can be replaced with measured values for the most critical parts. Therefore, it is helpful for the user of our approach to keep a clearly organized record for the concrete values used for binding in different stages of the project. For this reason, we proposed to automate the collection of the generic parameters from the model on spreadsheets, which will be provided to the user.

The parameters of type (b) are related to the allocation of software components to processors available for the application. The user has to decide for a product what the actual hardware configuration is and how to allocate the software to processing nodes. The MARTE stereotype *«RunTInstance»* annotating a lifeline in a sequence diagram provides an explicit connection between a role in the behaviour model and the corresponding runtime instance of a component. The attribute host of this stereotype indicates on which physical node from the deployment diagram the instance is running. Using parameters for the attribute host enable us to allocate each role (a software component) to an actual hardware resource. The transformation collects all these hardware resources and associates their list to each lifeline in the spreadsheets. The user decides on the actual allocation by choosing a processor from this list.

The performance effects of variations in the platform/environment factors (such as network connections, middleware, operating system and platform choices) are included into our model by aggregating the overheads caused by each factor and by attaching them via MARTE annotations to the affected model elements. As already mentioned, the variations in platform/environment factors are represented in our approach through the PC-feature model (as explained in the previous section). A specific run-time instance of a product is configured by selecting a valid PC-feature combination from the PC-feature model. We define a PC-feature configuration as a complete set of choices of PC-features for a specific model element.

It is interesting to note that a PC-feature has impact on a subset of model elements in the model, but not necessarily on all model elements of the same type. For instance, the PC-feature *Secured* affects only certain communication channels in a product

Element Type	Element Name	Stereotype Name	AttributeName	PC-Feature Group Name	PC-Feature Name	Guideline for Value	Generic Parameter	Concrete Value
Context Analysis Parameters ($N1, $Z1, $ReqT, $FSize, $Blocks)								
Message	getList	PaStep	hostDemand	application-annotation			$CatD (ms)	
		PaCommStep	msgSize	«exactly-one-of feature» DataCompression	Compressed	reduce by 10% ...30%		
					Uncompressed	No effect		
							$FSize *0.2 (KB)	
			commTxOverhead	«exactly-one-of feature» Communication	unsecured	No effect		
					secured			
					SSL	add (12.5+0.078*msgsize)		
					TLS	add (11.9+0.134*msgsize)		
				«exactly-one-of feature» DataCompression	compressed	increase by 2% ...5%		
					uncompressed	No effect		
							$GetL Send (ms)	
			commRcvOverhead	«exactly-one-of feature» Communication	unsecured	No effect		
					secured			
				«exactly-one-of feature» securityProtocol	SSL	add (12.5+0.078*msgsize)		
					TLS	add (11.9+0.134*msgsize)		
				«exactly-one-of feature» DataCompression	compressed	increase by 2% ...5%		
					uncompressed	No effect		
							$GetL.Rcv (ms)	

Fig. 23. Part of the generated Spreadsheet for the scenario Browse Catalog

model, not all of them. Hence, a PC-feature needs to be associated to certain model element(s), not to the entire product. This mapping is set up through the MARTE performance specifications annotating the affected model elements.

Dealing manually with a huge number of performance annotations by asking the developer to inspect every diagram in the generated product model, to extract the generic parameters and to match them with the PC-features is an error-prone process. We propose to automate the process of collecting all generic parameters that need to be bound to concrete values from the product model and to associate each PC-feature to the model element(s) it may affect, then present the information to the developer in a user-friendly format. We generate a spreadsheet per diagram, indicating for each generic parameter some guiding information that helps the user in providing concrete binding values.

The transformation handles differently the context analysis parameters, which are usually defined by the modeler to be carried without binding throughout the entire transformation process, from the SPL model to the performance model for a product. These parameters can be used to explore the performance analysis space. A list of the context analysis parameters are provided to the user, who will decide whether to bind them now to concrete values, or to use them unbound in MARTE expressions.

A part of the generated spreadsheet for the scenario *BrowseCatalog* is shown in Figure 23. For instance, the PC-feature *DataCompression* is mapped to the MARTE attribute *msgSize* annotating a model element of type message. As the value of the attribute *msgSize* is an expression *$FSize*0.2* in function of the context analysis parameter *$FSize*, it is the user's choice to bind it at this level or keep it as a parameter in the output it produces. The column titled Concrete Value is designated for the user to enter appropriate concrete value for each generic parameter, while the column Guideline for Value provides a typical range of values to guide the user. For instance, if the PC-selection features chosen are "secured" with "TLS", the concrete value entered by the user is obtained by evaluating the expression (11.9+0.134*msgsize), assuming that the user follows the provided guideline. Assuming that the choice for the PC-feature *DataCompression* is "compressed", the user may decide to increase by 4% the existing overhead due to compression features. In general, the guidelines can be adjusted by the performance analyst for a given SPL and a known execution environment. The generated spreadsheet presents a user-friendly format for the users of the transformation who have to provide appropriate concrete values for binding the generic performance annotations. Being automatically generated, they capture all the parameters that need to be bound and reduce the incidence of errors.

Performing the Actual Binding. After the user selects an actual processor for each lifeline role provided in the spreadsheets and enters concrete values for all the generic performance parameters, the next model transformation takes as input these spreadsheets along with its corresponding product model, and binds all the generic parameters to the actual values provided by the user. The outcome of the transformation is a specific product model with concrete performance annotations, which can be further transformed into a performance model.

In order to automate the actual binding process, the generated spreadsheets with concrete values are given as a mark model to the binding transformation. The mark model concept has been introduced in the OMG MDA guide [33] as a means of providing concrete parameter values to a transformation. This capability of allowing transformation parameterization through mark model instances makes the transformation generic and more reusable in different contexts.

6   Conclusions

In this chapter we presented the open PUMA tool architecture that can accept a variety of types of Smodels and generate a variety of types of Pmodels. The practicality of PUMA is demonstrated by different implemented transformations from UML 1.4 and UML 2.X to CSM for sequence and activity diagrams, and transformations from CSM to queueing networks, LQN and Petri nets. We are extending PUMA for SOA and SPL and are working on the final component of PUMA, to support the systematic use of performance models in order to generate feedback to the designers. PUMA promises a way out of the maze of possible evaluation techniques. From the point of view of practical adoption, this is of the utmost importance, as the software developer is not tied to an evaluation model whose limitations he or she does not understand. Performance modelers are similarly freed to generate a wide variety of forms of model, and explore their relative capabilities, without having to create the (quite difficult) interface to UML. As UML is constantly changing, this can also make maintenance of model-building easier. While PUMA is described for performance, CSM may be adapted to other evaluations based on behaviour.

In general, experience in conducting model-driven performance analysis and other non-functional properties (NFPs) in the context of model-driven development shows that the domain is still facing a number of challenges.

Human qualifications. Software developers are not trained in all the formalisms used for the analysis of performance and other kind of NFPs, which leads to the idea of hiding the analysis details from developers. However, the software models have to be annotated with extra information for each NFP and the analysis results have to be interpreted in order to improve the designs. A better balance needs to be made between what to be hidden and what to de exposed.

Abstraction level. The analysis of different NFPs may require source models at different levels of abstraction/detail. The challenge is to keep all the models consistent.

Tool interoperability. Experience shows that it is difficult to interface and to integrate seamlessly different tools, which were created at different times with different purposes and maybe running on different platforms or platform versions.

Software process. Integrating the analysis of different NFP raises process issues. For each NFP it is necessary to explore the state space for different design alternatives, configurations, workload parameters in order to diagnose problems and decide on improvement solutions. The challenge is how to compare different solution alternatives that may improve some NFPs and deteriorate others, and how to decide on trade-offs.

Change propagation through the model chain. Currently, every time the software design changes, a new analysis model is derived in order to redo the analysis. The challenge is to develop incremental transformation methods for keeping different model consistent instead of starting from scratch after every model improvement.

Acknowledgements. This work was partially supported by the Natural Sciences and Engineering Research Council (NSERC) and industrial and government partners, through the Healthcare Support through Information Technology Enhancements (hSITE) Strategic Research Network and through Discovery grants.

References

[1] Abdul Fatah, I., Majumdar, S.: Performance of CORBA-Based Client Server Architectures. IEEE Transactions on Parallel & Distributed Systems, 111–127 (February 2002)

[2] Alhaj, M., Petriu, D.C.: Approach for generating performance models from UML models of SOA systems. In: Proceedings of CASCON 2010, Toronto, November 1-4 (2010)

[3] Anyanwu, K., Sheth, A., Cardoso, J., Miller, J., Kochut, K.: Healthcare Enterprise Process Development and Integration. Journal of Research and Practice in Information Technology 35(2) (May 2003)

[4] Atlas Transformation Language (ATL), http://www.eclipse.org/m2m/atl

[5] Balsamo, S., DiMarco, A., Inverardi, P., Simeoni, M.: Model-based Performance Prediction in Software Development. IEEE Transactions on Software Eng. 30(5), 295–310 (2004)

[6] Balsamo, S., Marzolla, M.: Simulation Modeling of UML Software Architectures. In: Proc. ESM 2003, Nottingham, UK (June 2003)

[7] Bartholdt, J., Medak, M., Oberhauser, R.: Integrating Quality Modeling with Feature Modeling in Software Product Lines. In: Proc. of the 4th Int. Conference on Software Engineering Advances (ICSEA 2009), pp. 365–370 (2009)

[8] Belategi, L., Sagardui, G., Etxeberria, L.: MARTE Mechanisms to Model Variability When Analyzing Embedded Software Product Lines. In: Bosch, J., Lee, J. (eds.) SPLC 2010. LNCS, vol. 6287, pp. 466–470. Springer, Heidelberg (2010)

[9] Belategi, L., Sagardui, G., Etxeberria, L.: Model based analysis process for embedded software product lines. In: Proc. of 2011 Int. Conference on Software and Systems Process, ICSSP 2011 (2011)

[10] Benavides, D., Trinidad, P., Ruiz-Cortés, A.: Automated Reasoning on Feature Models. In: Pastor, Ó., Falcão e Cunha, J. (eds.) CAiSE 2005. LNCS, vol. 3520, pp. 491–503. Springer, Heidelberg (2005)

[11] Bernardi, S., Donatelli, S., Merseguer, J.: From UML sequence diagrams and statecharts to analysable Petri net models. In: Proc. 3rd Int. Workshop on Software and Performance, Rome, pp. 35–45 (July 2002)

[12] Bernardi, S., Merseguer, J.: Performance evaluation of UML design with Stochastic Well-formed Nets. Journal of Systems and Software 80(11), 1843–1865 (2007)

[13] Cavenet, C.G., Hillston, J., Kloul, L., Stevens, P.: Analysing UML 2.0 activity diagrams in the software performance engineering process. In: Proc. 4th Int. Workshop on Software and Performance, Redwood City, CA, pp. 74–83 (January 2004)

[14] Clements, P.C., Northrop, L.M.: Software Product Lines: Practice and Patterns, p. 608. Addison-Wesley (2001)

[15] Cortellessa, V., Di Marco, A., Inverardi, P.: Model-Based Software Performance Analysis. Springer (2011)

[16] Cortellessa, V., Mirandola, R.: Deriving a Queueing Network based Performance Model from UML Diagrams. In: Proc. Second Int. Workshop on Software and Performance, Ottawa, September 17-20, pp. 58–70 (2000)

[17] Czarnecki, K., Helsen, S., Eisenecker, U.: Formalizing cardinality-based feature models and their specialization. Software Process Improvement and Practice, 7–29 (2005)

[18] D'Ambrogio, A., Bocciarelli, P.: A Model-driven Approach to Describe and Predict the Performance of Composite Services. In: WOSP 2007, Buenos- Aires, Argentina (2007)

[19] Earl, T.: Service-Oriented Architecture: Concepts, Technology, and Design. Pearson Education (2005)

[20] DiStefano, S., Scarpa, M., Puliafito, A.: From UML to Petri Nets: The PCM-Based Methodology. IEEE Trans. on Software Engineering 37(1), 65–79 (2011)

[21] France, R., Ray, I., Georg, G., Ghosh, S.: An Aspect-Oriented Approach to Early Design Modeling. In: IEE Proceedings - Software, Special Issue on Early Aspects (2004)

[22] Franks, G., Hubbard, A., Majumdar, S., Petriu, D.C., Rolia, J., Woodside, C.M.: A toolset for Performance Engineering and Software Design of Client-Server Systems. Performance Evaluation 24(1-2), 117–135 (1995)

[23] Franks, G.: Performance Analysis of Distributed Server Systems, Report OCIEE-00-01, Ph.D. Thesis, Carleton University, Ottawa, Canada (2000)

[24] Gomaa, H.: Designing Software Product Lines with UML: From Use Cases to Pattern-based Software Architectures. Addison-Wesley Object Technology Series (July 2005)

[25] Gómez-Martínez, E., Merseguer, J.: Impact of SOAP Implementations in the Performance of a Web Service-Based Application. In: Min, G., Di Martino, B., Yang, L.T., Guo, M., Rünger, G. (eds.) ISPA Workshops 2006. LNCS, vol. 4331, pp. 884–896. Springer, Heidelberg (2006)

[26] Grassi, V., Mirandola, R., Randazzo, E., Sabetta, A.: KLAPER: An Intermediate Language for Model-Driven Predictive Analysis of Performance and Reliability. In: Rausch, A., Reussner, R., Mirandola, R., Plášil, F. (eds.) The Common Component Modeling Example. LNCS, vol. 5153, pp. 327–356. Springer, Heidelberg (2008)

[27] Happe, J., Becker, S., Rathfelder, C., Friedrich, H., Reussner, R.: Parametric performance completions for model-driven performance prediction. Performance Evaluation 67(8), 694–716 (2010)

[28] Marzolla, M., Mirandola, R.: Performance Prediction of Web Service Workflows. In: Overhage, S., Ren, X.-M., Reussner, R., Stafford, J.A. (eds.) QoSA 2007. LNCS, vol. 4880, pp. 127–144. Springer, Heidelberg (2008)

[29] Nguyen, Q.: Non-Functional Requirements Analysis Modeling for Software Product Lines. In: Proc. of Modeling in Software Engineering (MISE 2009), ICSE Workshop, pp. 56–61 (2009)

[30] Object Management Group, UML Profile for Modeling and Analysis of Real-Time and Embedded Systems (MARTE), Version 1.1, OMG document formal/2011-06-02 (2011)

[31] Object Management Group, UML Profile for Schedulability, Performance, and Time Specification, Version 1.1, OMG document formal/05-01-02 (January 2005)

[32] Object Management Group, Service oriented architecture Modeling Language (SoaML), ptc/2009-04-01 (April 2009)

[33] Object Management Group, MDA Guide Version 1.0.1, omg/03-06-01 (2003)

[34] Petriu, D.B., Woodside, C.M.: An intermediate metamodel with scenarios and resources for generating performance models from UML designs. Software and Systems Modeling 6(2), 163–184 (2007)

[35] Raatikainen, M., Niemelä, E., Myllärniemi, V., Männistö, T.: Svamp - An Integrated Approach for Modeling Functional and Quality Variability. In: 2nd Int Workshop on Variability Modeling of Software-intensive Systems, VaMoS (2008)

[36] Rolia, J.A., Sevcik, K.C.: The Method of Layers. IEEE Trans. on Software Engineering 21(8), 689–700 (1995)

[37] Smith, C.U.: Performance Engineering of Software Systems. Addison Wesley (1990)

[38] Street, J., Gomaa, H.: An Approach to Performance Modeling of Software Product Lines. In: Workshop on Modeling and Analysis of Real-Time and Embedded Systems, Genova, Italy (October 2006)

[39] Tawhid, R., Petriu, D.C.: Integrating Performance Analysis in the Model Driven Development of Software Product Lines. In: Czarnecki, K., Ober, I., Bruel, J.-M., Uhl, A., Völter, M. (eds.) MODELS 2008. LNCS, vol. 5301, pp. 490–504. Springer, Heidelberg (2008)

[40] Tawhid, R., Petriu, D.C.: Product Model Derivation by Model Transformation in Software Product Lines. In: Proc. of the 2nd IEEE Workshop on Model-based Engineering for Real-Time Embedded Systems (MoBE-RTES 2011), Newport Beach, CA, USA (2011)

[41] Tawhid, R., Petriu, D.C.: Automatic Derivation of a Product Performance Model from a Software Product Line Model. In: Proc. of the 15th International Conference on Software Product Line (SPLC 2011), Munich, Germany (2011)

[42] Tawhid, R., Petriu, D.C.: Integrating Performance Analysis in Software Product Line Development Process. In: Software Product Lines - The Automated Analysis. InTech - Open Access Publisher (2011)

[43] Tawhid, R., Petriu, D.C.: User-Friendly Approach for Handling Performance Parameters during Predictive Software Performance Engineering. In: Proc. of the 3rd ACM/SPEC International Conference on Performance Engineering (ICPE 2012), Boston, USA (2012)

[44] Tribastone, M., Gilmore, S.: Automatic Translation of UML Sequence Diagrams into PEPA Models. In: Proc. of 5th Int. Conference on Quantitative Evaluation of SysTems (QEST 2008), St Malo, France, pp. 205–214 (2008)

[45] Verdickt, T., Dhoedt, B., Gielen, F., Demeester, P.: Automatic Inclusion of Middleware Performance Attributes into Architectural UML Software Models. IEEE Trans. on Software Eng. 31(8), 695–711 (2005)

[46] Woodside, C.M., Neilson, J.E., Petriu, D.C., Majumdar, S.: The Stochastic Rendezvous Network Model for Performance of Synchronous Client-Server-like Distributed Software. IEEE Transactions on Computers 44(1), 20–34 (1995)

[47] Woodside, C.M., Petriu, D.C., Siddiqui, K.H.: Performance-related Completions for Software Specifications. In: Proc. of the 22nd Int. Conference on Software Engineering, ICSE 2002, Orlando, Florida, USA, pp. 22–32 (2002)

[48] Woodside, C.M., Petriu, D.C., Petriu, D.B., Xu, J., Israr, T., Georg, G., France, R., Houmb, S.H., Jürjens, J.: Performance Analysis of Security Aspects by Weaving Scenarios Extracted from UML Models. Journal of Systems and Software 82, 56–74 (2009)

[49] Xu, J.: Rule-based automatic software performance diagnosis and improvement. Performance Evaluation 67(8), 585–611 (2010)

Model Transformations
in Non-functional Analysis

Steffen Becker

Heinz Nixdorf Institute,
Department of Computer Science, University of Paderborn,
D-33102 Paderborn, Germany
steffen.becker@upb.de
http://www.cs.uni-paderborn.de/en/research-group/
software-engineering/people/steffen-becker.html

Abstract. The quality assessment of software design models in early
development phases can prevent wrong design decisions on the architectural level. As such wrong decisions are usually very cost-intensive to
revert in late testing phases, model-driven quality predictions offer early
quality estimates to prevent such erroneous decisions. By model-driven
quality predictions we refer to analyses which run fully automated based
on model-driven methods and tools. In this paper, we give an overview
on the process of model-driven quality analyses used today with a special
focus on issues that arise in fully automated approaches.

Keywords: Model-driven quality analyses, performance, reliability,
MARTE, Palladio Component Model.

1 Motivation

Dealing with non-functional requirements is still a major challenge in today's
software development processes. In the industrial state-of-the-art, non-functional
requirements are often not collected in a systematic manner or disregarded during the design and implementation phases. However, in testing phases or, even
worse, during final operation on the customer's side, systems often fail due to
insufficient performance or reliability characteristics.

Only few examples of insufficient quality have been reported in detail as they
are potentially hurtful to the image of the reporting companies. From the available case studies, we reference one from the area of performance problems. The
migration of SAP R3 to SAP's ByDesign SOA solution almost failed as the
legacy system architecture was unable to work properly in the new environment [34]. The consequence was that the performance was unacceptably low
and the system went through a costly redesign process deferring product release
by approximately 3 years.

During the last decade, model-based and model-driven quality analysis methods have been developed by the scientific community to prevent such issues.
These methods aim at early design time estimates of quality properties like

M. Bernardo, V. Cortellessa, and A. Pierantonio (Eds.): SFM 2012, LNCS 7320, pp. 263–289, 2012.

performance or reliability. Based on these estimates, system designs which are unable to fulfil their requirements can be ruled out and thus, costly failures at the end of the development process are prevented. For performance, most approaches are based on the initial idea of software performance engineering as introduced by Smith et al. [44]. Recently these efforts have been consolidated in the book by Cortellessa et al. [13]. For reliability, Gokhale [20] presents a survey on the recent trends.

In this article, we are going to present an overview of model-driven quality analysis approaches. These approaches are specialisations of model-based quality analysis methods. In model-driven quality analysis approaches, the idea is that the software model is the first-class entity under development and all other artefacts should be automatically derived from the model. Hence, activities like quality analyses should also be fully automated. In most cases, the automation requirement is realised by model transformations which automatically derive quality analyses models. This high degree of automation poses much higher requirements on the formalisation of the models involved in the process. Additionally, developers of the necessary transformations have to take difficult decisions on necessary abstractions both in the model's structural as well as for stochastic properties. We use the Palladio Component Model throughout this article as a running example of a model-driven quality analysis approach supporting multiple quality properties.

This article is structured as follows. The following section gives an overview of the process implemented in any model-driven quality analysis method discussed in this article. Subsequent sections then highlight specific aspects of this process. Section 3 explains the input models software architects have to create for quality analyses. Section 4 gives a brief overview of commonly used formal analysis models with a focus on performance and reliability predictions. For a model-driven quality analysis, automated transformations derive analysis models from input models as explained in Section 5. Section 6 illustrates how transformations can be used to automatically include performance overheads into analysis models as performance completions. The remaining sections address practical aspects in model-driven quality analyses. Section 7 illustrates how to use model transformations to bridge the differences between different modelling languages. Section 8 briefly surveys the use of reverse engineering techniques to generate input models for model-driven quality analyses. Section 9 gives a short introduction to architecture trade-offs on the basis of different model-driven quality analyses. To demonstrate the usefulness of model-driven quality analyses, Section 10 gives an overview on three different case studies. Finally, Section 11 summarises the topics presented in this article and gives pointers for further reading.

2   Process Overview

This section gives a high-level overview of the process which the software architect follows in the system's design phase to perform model-driven quality analyses. This process is illustrated in Figure 1. In the following we describe each of the steps in the order of execution followed by the software architect. We assume a classical web- or three tier business information system as system under study in our presentation. However, for other types of systems, the relevance of different aspects of the system model changes, while in general the process remains fixed.

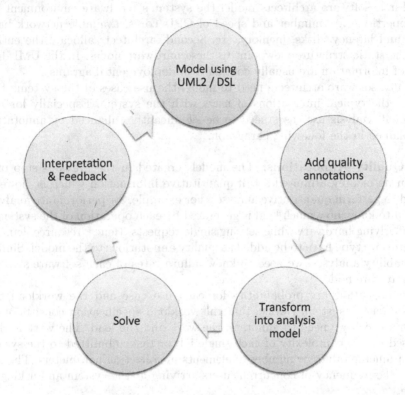

Fig. 1. Process for Model-Driven Quality Analyses

Modelling Using UML2/DSLs: In the first step, software architects needs to create a model of the system under study either using the UML or specific DSLs for software modelling. For most quality attributes this means to create a full model of the system's architecture, i.e., a model that covers a broad range of viewpoints of the system as explained in the following.

Commonly, software architects start by creating a model of the system's static structure, e.g., class or component diagrams. This viewpoint highlights the system's functional blocks and is guided by the functional decomposition of the system's requirements into software elements which realise specific parts of these requirements.

Based on the functional decomposition, software architects specify behavioural aspects of the system under study. Most processes rely on one of two options to represent behaviour: either they specify the behaviour of single entities as activities of these entities or they rely on the specification of the interaction between different entities by highlighting interaction scenarios, e.g., as sequence diagrams.

Having the system's software parts and their behaviour in place, software architects model the system's deployment. This covers two types of information. First, software architects model the system's hardware environment and its properties, e.g., number and speed of CPU cores, available network bandwidth and latency, disks, memory, etc. Second, architects allocate the entities from the static structure viewpoint to these hardware nodes. In the UML both kinds of information are usually contained in deployment diagrams.

Finally, software architects need to model the use cases of the system. They capture the typical interactions of users with the system. Especially for non-functional analysis use cases need to be significantly enhanced by annotations as explained in the following paragraph.

Add Quality Annotations: The models created in the previous step often contain no or only a limited set of quantitative information which is, however, needed to perform quantitative analyses. For example, for performance analyses, we need to know how much load is generated by each operation of the system on the underlying hardware while serving single requests. Hence, resource demands per hardware type have to be added as quality annotations to the model. Similar, for reliability analyses, we need to know failure rates of each software step and each hardware node.

Also important are probabilities for each use case and the workload they generate on the system. Notice, that the workload specification consists of two elements which we need to annotate: the work and the load. The work is characterised by the complexity of each single job or task submitted to the system, e.g., parameter values or number of elements in collection parameters. The load reflects the frequency of concurrent users arriving at the system and asking for service.

To realise quality annotations, modelling languages follow different approaches. UML2-based approaches rely on profiles. For approximately a decade the SPT profile was used, however, today it has been superseded by the MARTE profile. In case of special DSLs for quality analyses, e.g., the Palladio Component Model (PCM) [7], these languages usually provide build-in mechanisms to specify quality annotations (in the PCM this is the Stochastic Expression language). We provide a more detailed discussion of the quality annotation in Section 3.

Transform: The UML2 or domain specific models are transformed in the next step into analysis models. These models have formal semantics and allow the analysis of properties of interest. For performance, we use queueing networks, stochastic process algebras, or queued Petri-Nets in order to analyse response times, throughput, or utilisations. For reliability analyses, most approaches rely on discrete-time Markov chains. From them, reliability analyses derive for example the probability of failure on demand, i.e., the probability that a certain request issued returns an incorrect result or fails during request processing. For safety analyses, approaches rely on fault-trees or model checking techniques. For development cost estimates, transformations generate workflow models describing the necessary development tasks and do an estimate of the human resources needed.

To summarise, while the type of analysis model depends on the properties of interest, the overall workflow remains fixed. The software model and its annotations are transformed into formal models which are then solved in the next step.

Solve: After generating the formal analysis models, usually solving these models relies on existing solvers. These solvers are typically either analytical or simulation-based. Analytical methods rely on established mathematical rules which allow fast and accurate analyses of the models they solve. However, this comes at the cost of preconditions the models have to fulfil and limitations on the available result metrics. On the other hand, simulations usually imply no restrictions on the models to be simulated or the result metrics to be collected. However, simulating a model up to a certain level of accuracy takes time. As a rule of thumb, simulations are orders of magnitude slower than analytical methods to achieve the same level of accuracy.

For example, performance models can be solved efficiently with analytic methods if the resource demands or arrival rates are exponentially distributed. For the result metric, they are restricted for example to the mean response time, e.g., the average time a request takes to be handled by the system. If the response time distribution is needed, simulation-based approaches are used.

Interpretation and Feedback: In the last step of the model-driven analysis of a software system, the results collected from solving the analytical models need to be fed back into the initial software model. For example, the utilisation value of a formal representation of a hardware node in the analysis model, e.g., as queue in a queuing network, needs to be interpreted as the utilisation of a hardware node in the initial software model.

Additionally, after feeding the results of the analytical model back into the software model, a decision support step usually takes place which aims at giving recommendations on how to further improve the system's design (or, in case that the results were not satisfying at all, how to make the system's design feasible).

3   Input Models

In the following, we present an example of an input model. We intentionally present an instance of a DSL [18] for non-functional analyses as we assume that UML models with MARTE annotations have been used and discussed more often. We show the Palladio Component Model here as it addresses several requirements:

- Support for a distributed software development process based on a rigorous definition of software components and their functional and non-functional interfaces

- A specifically tailored language known as Stochastic Expression Language to denote QoS annotations
- Explicit support for Model-Driven Completions [2], i.e., in-place transformations of PCM models that automatically include platform specific performance overheads into PCM models (see Section 6)

3.1 Component-Based Quality Analyses

In component-based software development (and similarly in service-oriented development), the development task is split among several independent software developers which develop components or services. However, in software performance engineering, we assume the availability of models of the internal behaviour of the software including the resource demands caused by it according to the process outlined in Section 2. This is a contradiction to the idea that components are provided as black-boxes, i.e., software architects only have access to the component's binary code and its specification. Hence, in order to enable performance engineering in component-based software development processes, component developers have to provide specifications on the performance relevant behaviour of their components.

In the Palladio Component Model, component developers model components (either basic or composite), their interfaces, and their behaviour. For the latter, they use so called `ResourceDemanding-ServiceEffectSpecifications` (RD-SEFFs) [7]. RD-SEFFs model the externally observable behaviour of single component operations as a kind of activity diagram (cf. Figure 2). These activities contain so called `InternalActions`, `ExternalActions`, acquiring and releasing resources, and control flow constructs.

`InternalActions` model the observable resource requests a component issues while running. This includes for example CPU demands as a consequence of algorithmic computations, I/O demands to hard disks, or network accesses. `ExternalActions` model the call of an operation of a component connected to the required interface of the calling component. Modelling `ExternalCalls`, however, requires special attention. As the parameters passed to a called operation may have significant impact on the execution time of the operation, component developers also need to specify performance characteristics of the parameter values. To give an example, if a component operation executes an algorithm on items of a collection, component developers need to provide a specification of the number of elements in this collection (cf. Figure 2 and Section 3.2).

`Acquire-` and `ReleaseActions` model access to limited resources like semaphores, database connections or locks, etc. Control flow constructs model loops, branches, and fork-join blocks.

Most elements may be annotated using the Stochastic Expressions languages as explained in the following subsection.

3.2 Stochastic Expression Language

Stochastic Expressions [7] are used in the PCM as annotation language. Software architects use this language to provide quantitative stochastic information in

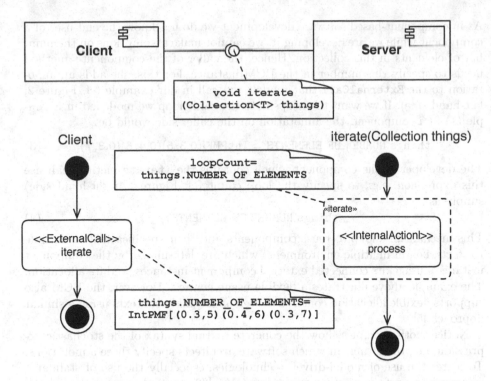

Fig. 2. Example of one component's SEFF calling another component's SEFF

order to characterise typical executions of the software systems they model. For example, software architects can annotate the number of loop iterations, resource demands caused by `InternalActions`, branch transition probabilities, or aspects of the data flow, e.g., how the size of collections changes during processing. An alternative language for a similar task is the value specification language (VSL) from the MARTE specification [39].

In the following, we discuss two examples of stochastic expressions. In the first example, we model the fact that a loop iterates in 30% of all cases 5 times, in 40% of all cases 6 times, and in the remaining 30% it loops 7 times. The corresponding stochastic expression is

$$\text{IntPMF}[(0.3, 5)(0.4, 6)(0.3, 7)] \tag{1}$$

`IntPMF` here indicates that the expression is of type Integer and PMF is an abbreviation for probability mass function, i.e., the expression characterises the distribution of a discrete random variable [10].

In the second example, we illustrate the use of stochastic expressions to model performance relevant aspects of the data flow as introduced by Koziolek in his PhD thesis [28]. Assume we model the performance of a component's method which iterates over a collection of items. The signature of the method is

$$\text{void iterate}(\text{Collection} < \text{T} > \text{things}) \tag{2}$$

As in component-based software development we do not know the end-user of a component while we are developing it, we cannot make assumptions on the number of elements in this collection. Hence, the caller of the component's method needs to specify this number in the PCM instance. For this, she adds an annotation to the `ExternalCall` that models the call in our example (cf. Figure 2, left-hand side). If we want to encapsulate the same loop we modelled in Example (1) in a component, the annotation on the caller side would be

$$things.NUMBER\_OF\_ELEMENTS = IntPMF[(0.3, 5)(0.4, 6)(0.3, 7)] \qquad (3)$$

The developer of the component which contains the `iterate` method can use this expression, e.g., to specify the loop count (cf. Figure 2, right-hand side) simply as

$$things.NUMBER\_OF\_ELEMENTS \qquad (4)$$

This mechanism allows to reuse components and their specification in multiple *contexts*, i.e., in multiple environments which are determined by the component instance's usage, its connected external component instances, and its allocation. The example above illustrates a flexible usage context. However, the PCM also supports flexible allocation contexts as well as assembly contexts using a similar approach [5].

Notice, both examples show the concrete textual syntax of the stochastic expression, i.e., the format in which software architects specify these annotations. To foster the use of model-driven technologies, especially the use of standardised model transformation languages like QVT [38], textual annotations like the stochastic expressions presented here, need to be parsed into an abstract syntax tree and not just stored as simple string values. In the PCM, this is done by a parser generated by the ANTLR framework [40]. This parser has been integrated with the PCM manually. However, today, model-driven approaches like the xText framework [17] are used more frequently to generate concrete textual syntaxes [21].

3.3   Completions

In this subsection, we introduce model-driven performance completions [23]. Performance completions have been introduced by Woodside et al. [46] as a mean to include the performance impact of underlying system layers into performance analyses, i.e, layers below the application layer itself. Examples of sources for such kinds of impact are internal database overheads, overheads of middleware platforms like resources needed to serialise messages, virtual machine layers, etc.

Model-driven performance completions extend the initial idea in situations where the application code is strictly corresponding to its model, e.g., when it is generated from the model. In such cases, model-driven completions are automatically added to the model in order to increase its accuracy. Most approaches use in-place model-transformations to enrich the analysis model automatically.

In this section, we focus on the input models needed for model-driven performance completions, while Section 6 explains the details of the technical realisation of these completions.

In the modelling phase, software architects need to specify their selection of layers they use for their implementation. As an example, consider Figure 3.

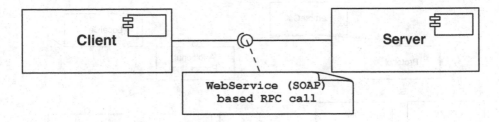

Fig. 3. Annotated component communication

In our example, we see again the `Client` and `Server` component used before. They are connected via an assembly connector. In the technical realisation of this architecture, the software architect has to decide how to realise the communication running over the assembly connector technically. For example, in Java she could select among an RPC realisation based on Java RMI, REST, or the SOAP protocol used in the WebService technology stack. Further options arise if the software architect intended a realisation based on message exchange, e.g., using the Java Messaging Standard (JMS).

If we now consider the performance overhead implied by each variant, we realise that this overhead differs significantly. For example, when we compare RMI and SOAP, SOAP has a much higher overhead due to the fact, that SOAP relies on XML technology. Hence, there is additional time required to process XML documents, send them over the network (as they usually need more bytes to encode their information), and to de-serialise and interpret them on the receiver's side.

For the input models of the quality analysis process, we assume that the software architect is well aware of such technical alternatives. However, as she is not an expert for performance or reliability modelling, she does not want to provide detailed specifications of the quality impact of her choice. Therefore, our model-driven performance completions require the software architect to annotate model elements of the application model (e.g., assembly connectors) with the technical details on their realisation in an abstract way.

In our approach, we selected feature diagrams [14] and their instances (known as configurations) as a well-known modelling formalism to express different variants in software product line engineering. To give an example, Figure 4 shows a feature diagram for the selection of the communication details.

The feature diagram first allows to differentiate between local and remote procedure calls (with local calls having almost no performance impact). For remote procedure calls, software architects can select among RMI and SOAP. Additionally, they can add features which impact the reliability, performance or security of the connector.

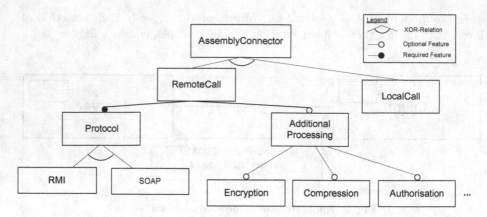

Fig. 4. Feature diagram showing different options to realise an assembly connector [3]

In order to create a valid input model for the model-driven quality analysis, a software architect needs to select a feature configuration for all connectors in the model.

4   Analyses Models

In the following we briefly introduce analysis models for performance and reliability. They are the output of the transformations discusses in the next Section. We can distinguish analysis models according to the quality properties they are able to analyse.

For **performance**, a large set of analysis models has been developed in the past - each of them having its own advantages and disadvantages. In general we aim for models which can be analytically solved which normally implies efficient solutions that can be solved quickly. However, if models become too complex, we have to simulate which is time intensive.

Among the often used models in analytical performance predictions are queuing networks [10]. They are intuitive to understand, and many networks can be solved analytically with a sufficient degree of accuracy with respect to mean response times, utilisation and throughput. However, their disadvantage is while they provide a good abstraction of shared resources like CPUs, HDDs, or network links, they fail in modelling the layered behaviour of software systems, i.e., blocking calls in client/server communications, or acquiring and releasing passive resources. On the tooling side, there is a variety of tools, for example, the Java Modelling Tools which both provide analytical and simulation based solvers.

To overcome these limits, Layered Queuing Networks have been introduced [42]. They allow to model systems in layers, where the behaviour of an upper layer is allowed to call the behaviour of lower layers. The lowest layers then contain the hardware resources as in standard queuing networks. LQNs have built-in support for performance relevant aspects of client/server systems like thread pools or clean up procedures on the server side that execute after sending the request's response. Heuristic and simulation-based solvers exist that can predict mean response times, utilisations and throughput of systems efficiently.

For concurrent systems, Queuing Petri nets extend standard stochastic Petri nets [1]. They introduce a new type of places that model queues, i.e., tokens get queued when they enter such places and can only leave the place after passing the queue. They provide an easily understandable modelling language. However, most Queuing Petri nets cannot be solved analytically but need to be simulated to derive response time distributions, utilisations of queuing places, and net throughput. Recent tools like the QPME tool rely on Eclipse technologies for modelling and analyses.

Finally, there are stochastic process algebras which model systems as a set of communicating processes. Among them, for example, PEPA [24] is a process algebra which has been applied in different projects successfully. The advantage of this formalism is that many systems are indeed implemented as a set of communicating systems. However, process algebras are often difficult to use for systems where you have to model a large set of identical processes, e.g., the user processes in business information systems. PEPA is supported by tools implemented on top of Eclipse technologies.

For **reliability** analyses, most approaches are built on top of Discrete Time Markov Chains (DTMCs) [10]. In DTMCs, time passes in discrete steps. The Markov chain itself is composed from states and probabilistic transitions. On each time step, the Markov chain proceeds to the next state according to the transition probabilities of all outgoing transitions of the current state. DTMCs can be solved efficiently by analytical means. Today, most approaches utilise the PRISM probabilistic model checker [25] to solve the DTMCs. PRISM reads the DTMC to be analysed in a textual language defined by the tool. It then can evaluate for example the steady state probability to reach a failure state from the DTMC's start state.

When taking the viewpoint of model-driven performance analyses, we notice, that most languages and tools discussed above have been developed before current model-driven methods and tools. Hence, most of them do not provide a MOF [37] compliant meta-model which is a pre-requisite for the use of most model-driven tools. The reason is that these tools have to rely on a common modelling foundation and data formats. As a consequence, we cannot simply transform our software models to analytical models via model-2-model transformations, but need an additional model-2-text transformation step that generates the corresponding performance model in a format readable by the solvers. However, such transformation and parsing steps incur additional performance overheads for solving the performance models. They are crucial at least in online methods [13], i.e., when we use performance predictions at run-time (cf. Section 11).

Second, we notice that transformations from software models to analytical model may need to make additional abstraction steps in order to keep the analytical models solvable in reasonable time. This may both include abstractions in the structure of the model as well as in the complexity of the annotations.

To give an example, in the PCM there is an additional transformation step involved (known as Dependency Solver [11,28]) that computes for each component instance its context and the impact of this context on the component's performance or reliability. This involves computing the convolution of probability distributions which is realised via Fourier transforms. They are computational complex. The same problem arises when having general MARTE annotations in the software model and generating analytical model with tighter constraints. For example, MARTE allows the use of generally distributed service time specifications while most analytical performance models are restricted to exponential distributions to ensure efficient analytical solutions.

5   Transformations

In this section, we give concrete examples for transformations for the performance and the reliability domain. We discuss on these examples which requirements they have to deal with. We use the transformations implemented in the Palladio Component Model for the discussion here as typical examples of transformations used in other approaches. For an overview, see Figure 5.

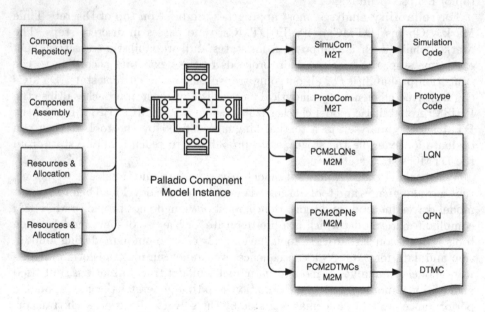

Fig. 5. Overview of PCM transformations

5.1   PCM2SimuCom

SimuCom (Simulation of Component Architectures) is the PCM's reference solver. It has been implemented as a simulation to define and evaluate the semantics of PCM models with respect to their performance properties. It relies on an extended queuing network simulation, where the PCM's active resources (CPUs, HDDs, LANs) are mapped to simulated queues. The behaviour as defined by the RD-SEFFs of the components is simulated directly. SimuCom also directly interprets Stochastic Expressions by drawing samples from the simulation framework's random number generator. Figure 6 gives an overview on the layers of a SimuCom simulation.

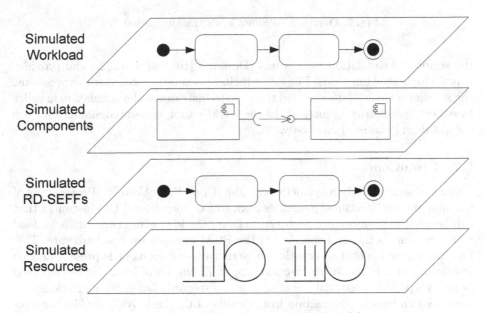

Fig. 6. Conceptual overview on SimuCom [3]

On the top layer, SimuCom simulates users accessing a component-based system. For each user, it simulates the user's behaviour. Each call to the simulated system then triggers a control flow thread that runs through the components and triggers their RD-SEFFs. Finally, `InternalActions` inside of RD-SEFFs cause resource loads which are then handled by the simulated resource queues.

In the context of this paper, we focus on the model-driven realisation of SimuCom. SimuCom simulations are generated by a model-driven tool chain as Java-based simulation code (cf. Figure 7). This tool chain is an instance of the Architecture Centric Model-Driven Software Development (AC-MDSD) paradigm introduced by Völter and Stahl [45]. In this paradigm, software is generated in a single model-2-text transformation step. This steps reads an instance of a DSL (here a PCM instance) and generates source code of it which makes use of generic library code (also known as platform code in AC-MDSD).

In SimuCom's transformation, we generate components as specified in the PCM instance. For a component, we use a set of implementing Java classes. The methods of these classes contain the code to simulate the component's RD-SEFF. SimuCom's platform contains generic simulation support code. It encapsulates

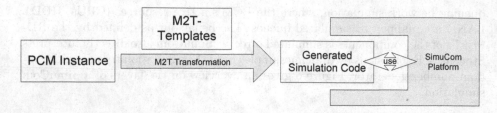

Fig. 7. Overview on SimuCom's transformation [3]

the supported simulation frameworks (Desmo-J [16] and SSJ [32]) and provides generic high-level functions. The latter include evaluating stochastic expressions, the simulation logic of queues, and the code to instrument the simulation in order to collect the metrics of interest. In the PCM's tool, generated simulations are compiled and executed on-the-fly.

5.2 ProtoCom

Using the same underlying principles as SimuCom, ProtoCom [4] (Prototyping of Component Architectures) generates Java source code from PCM instances that can be used as performance prototypes. Here, the idea is to create artificial load which represents the load specified in the PCM instance on real hardware. This has the advantage that a realistic infrastructure environment is present and no restrictions due to model abstractions apply. Examples of such abstraction used in today's performance analyses models are: disregard of memory limitations and memory bandwidth, abstraction from details of the underlying middleware, realistic operating system scheduling policies, hard-drive characteristics, etc. However, the major disadvantage of performance prototypes is that it takes a lot of time to configure and run them on realistic soft- and hardware environments.

Generating prototypes using model-driven techniques relieves developers from the burden to develop such prototypes by themselves. ProtoCom follows the same AC-MDSD process as SimuCom, i.e., again there is a single model-2-text transformation that generates the prototype based on a given PCM instance. However, the platform code now contains algorithms which can be used to mimic resource loads on CPUs and HDDs instead of the simulation code.

5.3 PCM2LQNs

PCM2LQN [29] allows the generation of LQN models from PCM instances. The layers provided by the LQNs are used in this transformation to reflect the layers implied by PCM models (cf. Figure 6). That is, there is a layer for user behaviours, for the system, and for each of the component instances. Like in the queuing network based SimuCom, hardware resources are again mapped to queues. For full details of the PCM2LQN mappings please consult [29].

From the model-driven perspective, PCM2LQN is a model-2-model transformation. It is implemented as a two step transformation. In the first step, the dependencies are resolved as explained in the beginning of Section 4. In the second step, the LQN model is created. Both transformations are implemented in Java and use the Visitor design pattern [19] to structurally [15] traverse the PCM instance and generate elements in the LQN.

5.4 PCM2QPNs

As a last example from the performance domain, we introduce PCM2QPN [36]. This transformation takes a PCM model and generates a Queuing Petri net. The central mapping ideas are as follows. User requests are represented as tokens in the Petri net. These tokens traverse through the network of places and transitions. Places represent single elements of PCM RD-SEFFs. In case of control flow elements of RD-SEFFs, transitions are aligned according to their RD-SEFF counterparts. For example, for a loop there is a place which models checking the loop condition and a network of places and transitions which models the loop's body behaviour.

Internal actions are represented by queued places in the QPN. Their scheduling discipline is set according to the scheduling discipline of the active resource referenced by the internal action.

Investigating the transition again from a model-driven perspective, it is similar to the PCM2LQN transformation. Again, there are two steps, where the first transformation step solves the dependencies of single component's quality annotations. The second step then generates the QPNs using the solved dependencies. It is implemented as a model-2-model transformation using the imperative QVT Operations [38] transformation language.

5.5 PCM2DTMCs

In the area of reliability predictions, we present the PCM2DTMC approach [11]. Conceptually, it generates DTMCs from a given PCM instance. In these DTMCs it takes both, hardware and software failures into account. For the hardware failures, a matrix is computed which contains the probabilities for all possible combinations of any hardware device from the PCM model being either in a working or in a failure state. For example, if we consider two hardware resources, e.g., two CPUs, we have four possible hardware states. Either both CPUs are working, both failed, CPU1 failed but CPU2 is working, or CPU1 is working but CPU2 failed.

For software failures, RD-SEFFs are interpreted as control flow graphs, where each action in the RD-SEFF can either succeed or fail - the latter either due to a software failure or due to a hardware failure. In case of hardware failures, only failures of hardware resources needed for a certain step in the RD-SEFF are taken into account. For all resources needed in a step, the transformation sums up the probabilities of all system states in which any needed resource is in a failure state.

Inside the DTMC, the control flow graph given by the RD-SEFFs is translated into a Markov chain where each state in the Markov chain models the fact, that the corresponding RD-SEFF is processing the corresponding action. Then for each of these states in the Markov chain, there is an additional transition to a single failure state. This transition has the combined probability of a software or hardware failure which would lead to a failure in the processing of this action. Figure 8 gives a simplified example of a RD-SEFF with failure probability annotations for software failures on the left hand side. The right hand side illustrates the resulting DTMC showing the two absorbing states for failure and success and the two transient states which represent the two RD-SEFF's `InternalActions`.

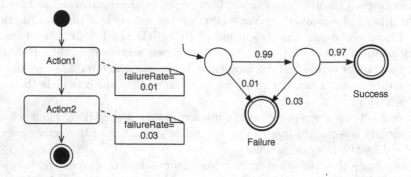

Fig. 8. Illustrating example of an RD-SEFF and its corresponding DTMC

PCM2DTMC generates a DTMC for each possible hardware state from the matrix of all hardware states. For each DTMC it computes the probability of failure on demand (PROFOD).

From the perspective of model transformations, the PCM2DTMC approach uses again a two step transformation approach. In the first step, component dependencies are solved and the hardware failure matrix is computed. In the second step for each hardware system state a DTMC is generated and solved. The transformation is a structural transformation written in Java.

6   Model-Driven Completions

As introduced in Section 3.3, model-driven completions enhance performance models with details which model performance overheads of underlying infrastructure services. In the following, we focus on connector completions and we restrict the discussion to performance as quality attribute.

Types of Completion Transformations: In principle, there is a general choice in designing model-driven completions. First, we can use a transformation to alter the software model in-place and then use standard transformations to create the analysis models from the extended software model. Second, we can enhance the transformation from the software model to the analysis model and create an extended analysis model. The advantage of the first alternative is that we can reuse all features of the software modelling language, e.g., the introduced stochastic expressions from the Palladio Component Model. Furthermore, the completion transformation often does not become too complex, as it can be split into a part that adds completions and a reused part that generates the analysis model. The advantage of the second alternative is that we have direct access to all features provided by the analysis model, i.e., we can utilise special modelling features like modelling resource demands which happen after sending the response in LQNs (cf. Section 4).

In the PCM, we use the first alternative as its advantages outweigh its disadvantages in our context. Especially the fact that PCM supports multiple analysis transformations which we all could reuse in the first approach is a strong argument.

Connector Completions in the PCM: In the following, we illustrate how the PCM's completion transformations include technical details of RPC connectors as an example. As input we expect PCM models which have been annotated by the software architect as illustrated in Figure 3 in Section 3.3. The aim is to include PCM components that model the performance overhead of the middleware platform which realises the annotated connectors.

To design the completion, we first need to understand the reasons for the performance overhead of RPC communication. First, the method call and all its parameters are sent to the server. For this, they are processed by a pipe-and-filter architecture [12], that takes the high level method call and generates its serialised form as byte stream. It first marshals the method call and all parameters which causes respective computational performance overheads. Depending on additional setting for the connector, subsequent filters in the pipe-and-filter chain encrypt the message, sign it, validate it, etc. Depending on the message size, this causes again a performance overhead. When the communication layer has produced the byte stream, it is send over the network which delays the processing according to network throughput and latency. Notice, that the size of the network package depends on the underlying RPC protocol and all applied processing steps. For example, SOAP messages are usually larger than RMI messages, causing an additional networking overhead. On the server side the whole process is executed in the other direction, i.e., the byte stream is converted back into a method call. Finally, after processing the method call, the whole RCP stack is used again to send back the server's response.

We now present the in-place transformation [15] we have created to model this processing chain as performance completion. In the first step, we remove the annotated connector and replace it with components which model the marshalling and demarshalling steps. The result is shown in Figure 9.

Figure 9 shows the connector completion component (as indicated by the component's stereotype) which now replaces the connector in Figure 3. It has the same provides and requires interface as the connector it replaces (IA in our example). This is needed to fit our completion in the place of the original connector and still create a valid PCM instance. The second aspect to notice are the interfaces starting with IMiddleware. They have been introduced to

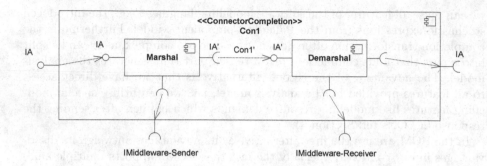

Fig. 9. First transformation step to include a connector completion [3]

make the completion more flexible. The underlying idea is that the `Marshal` and `Demarshal` components do not issue resource demands directly, but rather delegate their internal processing steps to the `IMiddleware` interfaces. These interfaces then are connected to a specific instance of a middleware component, e.g., a Sun Glassfish JavaEE server component. By exchanging this middleware component, we can model the different performance overheads of different server implementations. For example, exchanging the Glassfish component by a JBoss component we can include the performance overhead of this particular JavaEE server into our model. Also notice, that there are a client and a server variant of the middleware interface. Hence, we can also include different overheads on each communication side, depending on the real deployment setup.

In order to include the performance overhead of further processing steps, the transformation now executes further steps depending on the selected features in the connector's annotation. For example, assume the software architect in addition to the communication protocol also selected an encrypted communication channel. Then an additional step, as illustrated in Figure 10, includes the additional overhead into the completion component by adding another completion component, i.e., by applying the transformation idea illustrated in the previous paragraph again.

In Figure 10 we can again see the same structure we discussed before. However, notice that the interface has changed from `IA` to `IA'`. This was needed as the `IA'` interface now deals with the byte stream which represents the method call on the network instead of the method call itself. The interface `IA'` takes track of the size of the message stream as this size is important for the network overhead later (as stated in the description of the RPC protocol above). However, as the full details of the structure of the interface `IA'` would go into too much detail, we refer the reader to [3] where the full mechanics of the transformation are documented.

Figure 11 shows the resulting model after the execution of the completion transformation.

In Figure 11 we can see that the transformation has added a component realising the middleware on both, the client's and the server's, side. Which middleware

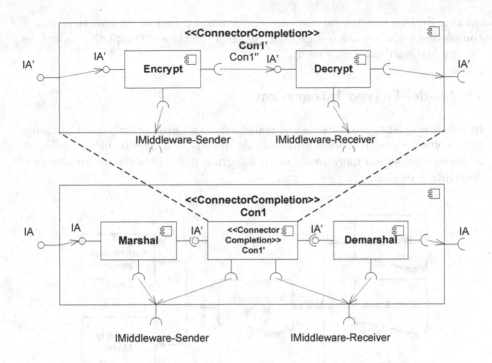

Fig. 10. Second transformation step to include a connector completion [3]

component gets added on which side is configurable in the system's deployment model. However, providers of middleware server's ideally need to provide a library of components which model their server's performance overhead. Today such libraries are not available. As an alternative, we used an automated benchmark for our experiments in [23] which created performance models of middleware servers. Our completion transformation then included these generated models. Additionally, we can see in Figure 11 that the completion transformation automatically deployed the created components to either the client's deployment node or the server's node.

To summarise, we have demonstrated in this section how a completion transformation transforms specially annotated software models to include middleware

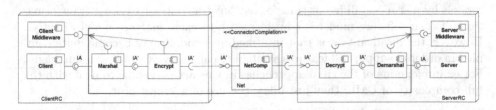

Fig. 11. PCM instance with connector completion [3]

details. Besides this special use case, the general principle on how to design a completion transformation is invariant of both the type of completion as well as the quality attribute under study.

7   Model-Driven Integration

In software quality analyses, model transformations are not only used to transform software design models into analysis models, but also to bridge different levels of abstraction more easily or to integrate different software architecture description models.

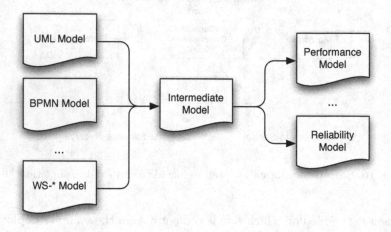

Fig. 12. Basic idea of intermediate models

Intermediate Models: There are approaches like KLAPER [22] or the Core Scenario Model (CSM) [41] which promote the use of intermediate models. These models aim at alleviating the creation of transformations into the analysis domain. To reach this goal, they favour a two-step transformation from the software model to the analysis model. First, a software model is transformed into the intermediate model which then is transformed into the analysis model.

Figure 12 outlines the idea of intermediate models. Their advantage is that they allow to transform n different software models into m different analysis models by just $n + m$ different transformations (in contrast to $m * n$ transformations if each software model is transformed into each analysis model directly). However, the disadvantage is that intermediate models may become quite complex in order to support all features available in all software modelling languages. For example, none of the cited approaches in this article is able to deal with the full complexity of UML, they just allow the use of a subset of it.

Integration of Software Models. There are also some approaches for using model transformations to integrate different types of software modelling languages. The DUALLy tool developed by Malavolta et al. [33] focuses on bridging different software architecture modelling languages. In the EU project Q-ImPrESS [6] we focused on bridging different component-based software modelling languages via a core model that takes quality aspects into account. Figure 13 provides an overview on the approach taken by Q-ImPrESS.

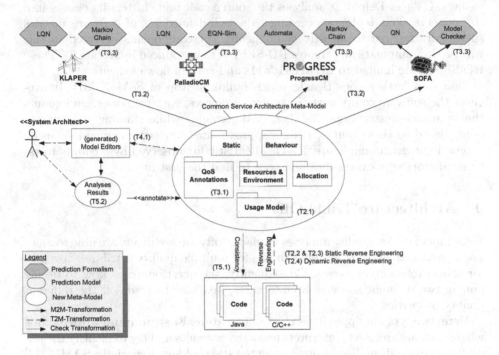

Fig. 13. Overview on Transformations in Q-ImPrESS [8]

There are different software architecture modelling languages on top of Figure 13. Each of these approaches has its own dedicated meta-model and support different types of analyses. To reuse as many of these analysis approaches, Q-ImPrESS promotes the use of a core meta-model, the Service Architecture Meta-Model (SAMM). Transformations exist from the SAMM into each of the software architecture models. This allows to perform different analyses with respect to different types of quality properties. This is useful for architecture trade-off analysis, i.e., finding the right trade-off among different quality attributes (see Section 9) for details.

On the bottom of Figure 13, it is also indicated that Q-ImPrESS also supports reverse engineering of source code to create initial instances of the SAMM. This step is discussed in the following Section.

8   Reverse Engineering of Models

In model-driven quality analyses, the most important step is to get to the models of the software under study. Hence, researches have proposed approaches in the past to create initial models from source code or execution traces. However, only a few of them support reverse engineering of models which can be used for quality analyses.

For Q-ImPrESS and the PCM, there is support via the SoMoX tool chain [30]. SoMoX creates instances of the SAMM from object-oriented source codes written in Java, C++ or Delphi. It analyses the source code and clusters its classes into components. This is done according to a well-defined set of software metrics specifically tailored to identify components. For components detected in this way SoMoX automatically creates RD-SEFFs (as introduced in Section 3). These RD-SEFFs are limited to `ExternalCalls` and control flow elements.

One step further goes Beagle which builds on top of SoMoX [31]. It executes the software components in typical use cases, e.g., test cases, and counts the byte code instructions the Java VM executes while running the component. Based on these counts, Beagle approximates stochastic expressions using a genetic programming heuristic. This heuristic fits observed byte counts to estimated stochastic expressions and tries to find the best fit.

9   Architecture Trade-Offs

With model-driven quality analyses in place, software architects are able to analyse a particular software system's model for multiple quality attributes like performance, reliability, or costs. Consequently, the question arises how to decide among two different software architectures, i.e., how to trade-off the different quality properties.

Here, two types of approaches exist in literature. First, **manual approaches** where software architects interpret the analyses results and try to identify the underlying trade-offs in discussions among the stakeholders. Especially, SAMM [27] and ATAM promoted by the SEI contain structured processes for this. Second, **quantitative methods** which are semi-automated and supported by tools try to quantify the preferences of the software architect for different quality properties and compute a ranking of alternative software designs according to these preferences. In the latter, the AHP method invented by Saaty has been used [43]. We describe this approach in the following.

In the AHP process, the decision problem is split into hierarchical subdecisions. For example, we could subdivide the overall quality goal into external quality goals (e.g., performance, reliability) on the same level as the goals for internal quality attributes (e.g., maintainability, understandability). For each hierarchy level, the AHP method determines weights that capture the decision makers preferences for all sub-goals. For example, if the decision maker states that internal and external quality goals are equally important, the weights would be 0.5 (50%) for each of the sub-goals. Finally, different software architecture alternatives are evaluated with respect to the leafs of the decision tree and AHP computes from this an overall ranking of the alternatives.

10   Case Studies

In this section, we report on case studies of model-driven quality analyses in practice. All case studies are based on Q-ImPrESS or PCM. The reason for this may be in the fact that Q-ImPrESS and PCM have mature tooling which allows their use in industry projects. Most other model-driven quality analysis approaches found in literature stay, in contrast, on the conceptual or prototype level.

We can evaluate model-driven approaches with two different evaluation goals. First, we can empirically evaluate whether software architects are able to create the necessary input model with sufficient degree of accuracy. Second, we can evaluate how prediction results help in realistic projects in making decisions.

10.1   Empirical Evaluation

We have performed a series of empirical experiments in which we evaluated the applicability of model-driven performance analysis with the PCM [35]. In one of the experiments we conducted, we compared modelling with PCM against modelling with the software performance engineering tool SPE [44].

In the experiment setup two sets of students performed performance analyses of two different systems in a cross-over experiment, i.e., the first group of students used PCM to model the first system and the second group used SPE. For the second system we switched the roles of the groups.

In the experiment, we evaluated both, the time it took the students to model the systems and make performance predictions as well as the correctness of their solution. It turned out that both approaches supported performance predictions to an extend in which the students were able to produce meaningful results. Modelling and analysing with the PCM revealed more issues related to tooling, e.g., issues with the model editors, while modelling with SPE revealed more problems on the conceptual level, especially with non-automated stochastic computations.

10.2   Industrial Case Studies

From the industrial case studies, we report here on a case study performed at IBM and another case study at ABB. We briefly characterise the analysis goal, the analysed system and the main findings. For additional details, please refer to the literature reference of each study. For smaller case studies visit the PCM homepage[1].

IBM Storage Modelling. In our case study performed with IBM Germany [26], we supported the design decision whether to implement the I/O layer of an IBM server system in a synchronous or asynchronous communication style. This layer's main responsibility is to communicate with the hard disks array of the server. Due to external requirements, this layer has to guarantee high throughput. While modelling the system in the PCM showed several obstacles in modelling the system with sufficient degree of accuracy, the results showed that from

---

[1] http://www.palladio-simulator.com

a performance perspective this decision did not have a significant impact. Both alternatives were comparable in their performance.

ABB Process Control System. In the course of the Q-ImPrESS project we evaluated a process control system at ABB with respect to performance and reliability [30]. The case study revealed good prediction results for performance as well as reliability. However, it also showed that collecting the required input data for the model-driven quality analyses is a non-trivial task and should be better supported in the future. Especially collecting failure rates for reliability models turned out to be a difficult task. Additionally, we also tried to use reverse engineering of models of the ABB PCS system. However, this failed to produce useful models due to the complexity and size of the system's code base.

11   Conclusions and Further Reading

In this article, we give an overview on model-driven analyses methods of non-functional properties. We illustrate a process which consists of the steps modelling the system, annotating the model, transforming the model, solving it, and interpreting the results. For each of the steps, this article gives details of the actions performed by the software architect. Furthermore, we presented brief discussions on practical aspects related to model-driven quality analyses, namely model-driven integration, reverse engineering of the input models from existing systems, and architecture trade-off analyses among several different quality attributes. Case studies show the practicability of the presented approaches in industrial settings.

Software architects use the presented methods to analyse the quality of their systems in various dimensions. They can make dedicated design decisions by taking their quality impacts into account. Also the evolution of existing systems under quality constraints is supported by quality analyses.

In the future, model-driven quality analyses have to deal with systems which are much more dynamic than the systems we modeled in the past. For example, cloud computing results in dynamic allocations where the amount of available hardware changes at run-time. Here, quality analyses at run-time can guide adaptation decisions in order to resolve quality problems of running systems [13]. For this, these approaces use quality models@run-time [9].

References

1. Bause, F.: Queueing petri nets-a formalism for the combined qualitative and quantitative analysis of systems. In: Proceedings of 5th International Workshop on Petri Nets and Performance Models, pp. 14–23 (October 1993)
2. Becker, S.: Coupled Model Transformations. In: WOSP 2008: Proceedings of the 7th International Workshop on Software and Performance, pp. 103–114. ACM, New York (2008)
3. Becker, S.: Coupled Model Transformations for QoS Enabled Component-Based Software Design. Karlsruhe Series on Software Quality, vol. 1. Universitätsverlag Karlsruhe (2008)

4. Becker, S., Dencker, T., Happe, J.: Model-Driven Generation of Performance Prototypes. In: Kounev, S., Gorton, I., Sachs, K. (eds.) SIPEW 2008. LNCS, vol. 5119, pp. 79–98. Springer, Heidelberg (2008),
http://www.springerlink.com/content/62t1277642tt8676/fulltext.pdf
5. Becker, S., Happe, J., Koziolek, H.: Putting Components into Context: Supporting QoS-Predictions with an explicit Context Model. In: Reussner, R., Szyperski, C., Weck, W. (eds.) Proc. 11th International Workshop on Component Oriented Programming (WCOP 2006), pp. 1–6 (July 2006),
http://research.microsoft.com/ cszypers/events/
WCOP2006/WCOP06-Becer.pdf
6. Becker, S., Hauck, M., Trifu, M., Krogmann, K., Kofron, J.: Reverse Engineering Component Models for Quality Predictions. In: Proceedings of the 14th European Conference on Software Maintenance and Reengineering, European Projects Track, pp. 199–202. IEEE (2010),
http://sdqweb.ipd.kit.edu/publications/pdfs/becker2010a.pdf
7. Becker, S., Koziolek, H., Reussner, R.: The Palladio component model for model-driven performance prediction. Journal of Systems and Software 82, 3–22 (2009),
http://dx.doi.org/10.1016/j.jss.2008.03.066
8. Becker, S., Trifu, M., Reussner, R.: Towards Supporting Evolution of Service Oriented Architectures through Quality Impact Prediction. In: 1st International Workshop on Automated Engineering of Autonomous and Run-time Evolving Systems (ARAMIS 2008) (September 2008)
9. Blair, G., Bencomo, N., France, R.: Models@ run.time. Computer 42(10), 22–27 (2009)
10. Bolch, G., Greiner, S., de Meer, H., Trivedi, K.S.: Queueing Networks and Markov Chains. John Wiley & Sons Inc. (1998)
11. Brosch, F., Koziolek, H., Buhnova, B., Reussner, R.: Parameterized Reliability Prediction for Component-Based Software Architectures. In: Heineman, G.T., Kofron, J., Plasil, F. (eds.) QoSA 2010. LNCS, vol. 6093, pp. 36–51. Springer, Heidelberg (2010)
12. Clements, P.C., Bachmann, F., Bass, L., Garlan, D., Ivers, J., Little, R., Nord, R., Stafford, J.: Documenting Software Architectures. SEI Series in Software Engineering. Addison-Wesley (2003)
13. Cortellessa, V., Marco, A.D., Inverardi, P.: Model-Based Software Performance Analysis. Springer, Berlin (2011)
14. Czarnecki, K., Eisenecker, U.W.: Generative Programming. Addison-Wesley, Reading (2000)
15. Czarnecki, K., Helsen, S.: Classification of Model Transformation Approaches. In: OOPSLA 2003 Workshop on Generative Techniques in the Context of Model Driven Architecture (October 2003),
http://www.softmetaware.com/oopsla2003/czarnecki.pdf
(last retrieved January 6, 2008)
16. The DESMO-J Homepage (2007),
http://asi-www.informatik.uni-hamburg.de/desmoj/ (last retrieved January 6, 2008)
17. Eclipse Foundation: xText website, http://www.xtext.org (last visited February 22, 2012)
18. Fowler, M., Parsons, R.: Domain Specific Languages. Addison-Wesley, Reading (2010)
19. Gamma, E., Helm, R., Johnson, R., Vlissides, J.: Design Patterns: Elements of Reusable Object-Oriented Software. Addison-Wesley, Reading (1995)

20. Gokhale, S.S.: Architecture-based software reliability analysis: Overview and limitations. IEEE Trans. on Dependable and Secure Computing 4(1), 32–40 (2007)
21. Goldschmidt, T., Becker, S., Uhl, A.: Classification of Concrete Textual Syntax Mapping Approaches. In: Schieferdecker, I., Hartman, A. (eds.) ECMDA-FA 2008. LNCS, vol. 5095, pp. 169–184. Springer, Heidelberg (2008), http://sdqweb.ipd.uka.de/publications/pdfs/goldschmidt2008b.pdf
22. Grassi, V., Mirandola, R., Sabetta, A.: From Design to Analysis Models: a Kernel Language for Performance and Reliability Analysis of Component-based Systems. In: WOSP 2005: Proceedings of the 5th International Workshop on Software and Performance, pp. 25–36. ACM Press, New York (2005)
23. Happe, J., Becker, S., Rathfelder, C., Friedrich, H., Reussner, R.H.: Parametric Performance Completions for Model-Driven Performance Prediction. Performance Evaluation 67(8), 694–716 (2010), http://sdqweb.ipd.uka.de/publications/pdfs/happe2009a.pdf
24. Hermanns, H., Herzog, U., Katoen, J.P.: Process algebra for performance evaluation. Theoretical Computer Science 274(1-2), 43–87 (2002), http://www.sciencedirect.com/science/article/B6V1G-4561J4H-3/2/21516ce76bb2e6adab1ffed4dbe0d24c
25. Hinton, A., Kwiatkowska, M., Norman, G., Parker, D.: PRISM: A Tool for Automatic Verification of Probabilistic Systems. In: Hermanns, H., Palsberg, J. (eds.) TACAS 2006. LNCS, vol. 3920, pp. 441–444. Springer, Heidelberg (2006)
26. Huber, N., Becker, S., Rathfelder, C., Schweflinghaus, J., Reussner, R.: Performance Modeling in Industry: A Case Study on Storage Virtualization. In: ACM/IEEE 32nd International Conference on Software Engineering, Software Engineering in Practice Track, Capetown, South Africa, pp. 1–10. ACM, New York (2010), http://sdqweb.ipd.uka.de/publications/pdfs/hubern2010.pdf
27. Kazman, R., Bass, L., Abowd, G., Webb, M.: SAAM: A method for analyzing the properties of software architectures. In: Fadini, B. (ed.) Proceedings of the 16th International Conference on Software Engineering, pp. 81–90. IEEE Computer Society Press, Sorrento (1994)
28. Koziolek, H.: Parameter Dependencies for Reusable Performance Specifications of Software Components. The Karlsruhe Series on Software Design and Quality, vol. 2. Universitätsverlag Karlsruhe (2008)
29. Koziolek, H., Reussner, R.: A Model Transformation from the Palladio Component Model to Layered Queueing Networks. In: Kounev, S., Gorton, I., Sachs, K. (eds.) SIPEW 2008. LNCS, vol. 5119, pp. 58–78. Springer, Heidelberg (2008), http://www.springerlink.com/content/w14m0g520u675x10/fulltext.pdf
30. Koziolek, H., Schlich, B., Bilich, C., Weiss, R., Becker, S., Krogmann, K., Trifu, M., Mirandola, R., Koziolek, A.: An industrial case study on quality impact prediction for evolving service-oriented software. In: Proceeding of the 33rd International Conference on Software Engineering, Software Engineering in Practice Track, ICSE 2011, pp. 776–785. ACM, New York (2011), http://doi.acm.org/10.1145/1985793.1985902
31. Krogmann, K., Kuperberg, M., Reussner, R.: Using Genetic Search for Reverse Engineering of Parametric Behaviour Models for Performance Prediction. IEEE Transactions on Software Engineering 36(6), 865–877 (2010), http://sdqweb.ipd.kit.edu/publications/pdfs/krogmann2009c.pdf
32. L'Ecuyer, P., Buist, E.: Simulation in Java with SSJ. In: WSC 2005: Proceedings of the 37th Conference on Winter Simulation, Winter Simulation Conference, pp. 611–620 (2005)

33. Malavolta, I., Muccini, H., Pelliccione, P., Tamburri, D.A.: Providing architectural languages and tools interoperability through model transformation technologies. IEEE Transactions of Software Engineering 36(1), 119–140 (2010)
34. Marshall, R.: SAP gives update on Business ByDesign plans (2009), http://www.v3.co.uk/v3-uk/news/1970547/sap-update-business-bydesign-plans (last visited November 22, 2009)
35. Martens, A., Koziolek, H., Prechelt, L., Reussner, R.: From monolithic to component-based performance evaluation of software architectures. Empirical Software Engineering 16(5), 587–622 (2011), http://dx.doi.org/10.1007/s10664-010-9142-8
36. Meier, P., Kounev, S., Koziolek, H.: Automated Transformation of Palladio Component Models to Queueing Petri Nets. In: 19th IEEE/ACM International Symposium on Modeling, Analysis and Simulation of Computer and Telecommunication Systems (MASCOTS 2011), Singapore, July 25-27 (2011)
37. Object Management Group (OMG): MOF 2.0 Core Specification (formal/2006-01-01) (2006), http://www.omg.org/cgi-bin/doc?formal/2006-01-01
38. Object Management Group (OMG): Meta Object Facility (MOF) 2.0 Query/View/Transformation Specification – Version 1.1 Beta 2 (December 2009), http://www.omg.org/spec/QVT/1.1/Beta2/
39. Object Management Group (OMG): UML Profile for MARTE: Modeling and Analysis of Real-Time Embedded Systems, version 1.0 (2009), http://www.omg.org/spec/MARTE/1.0/PDF
40. Parr, T.: The Definitive ANTLR Reference Guide: Building Domain-specific Languages (Pragmatic Programmers). Pragmatic Programmer (2007)
41. Petriu, D.B., Woodside, M.: An intermediate metamodel with scenarios and resources for generating performance models from UML designs. Software and Systems Modeling 6(2), 163–184 (2007)
42. Rolia, J.A., Sevcik, K.C.: The Method of Layers. IEEE Transactions on Software Engineering 21(8), 689–700 (1995)
43. Saaty, T.L.: The Analytic Hierarchy Process, Planning, Piority Setting, Resource Allocation. McGraw-Hill, New York (1980)
44. Smith, C.U., Williams, L.G.: Performance Solutions: A Practical Guide to Creating Responsive, Scalable Software. Addison-Wesley (2002)
45. Völter, M., Stahl, T.: Model-Driven Software Development. Wiley & Sons, New York (2006)
46. Woodside, M., Petriu, D.C., Siddiqui, K.H.: Performance-related Completions for Software Specifications. In: Proceedings of the 22nd International Conference on Software Engineering, ICSE 2002, Orlando, Florida, USA, May 19-25, pp. 22–32. ACM (2002)

Software Performance Antipatterns: Modeling and Analysis

Vittorio Cortellessa, Antinisca Di Marco, and Catia Trubiani

University of L'Aquila, Dipartimento di Informatica, Italy
{vittorio.cortellessa,antinisca.dimarco,
catia.trubiani}@univaq.it

Abstract. The problem of capturing performance problems is critical in the software design, mostly because the results of performance analysis (i.e. mean values, variances, and probability distributions) are difficult to be interpreted for providing feedback to software designers. Support to the interpretation of performance analysis results that helps to fill the gap between numbers and design alternatives is still lacking. The aim of this chapter is to present the work that has been done in the last few years on filling such gap. The work is centered on software performance antipatterns, that are recurring solutions to common mistakes (i.e. bad practices) affecting performance. Such antipatterns can play a key role in the software performance domain, since they can be used in the investigation of performance problems as well as in the formulation of solutions in terms of design alternatives.

Keywords: Software Architecture, Performance Evaluation, Antipatterns, Feedback Generation, Design Alternatives.

1 Introduction

In the software development domain there is a very high interest in the early validation of performance requirements because this ability avoids late and expensive fix to consolidated software artifacts.

Model-based approaches, pioneered under the name of Software Performance Engineering (SPE) by Smith [1–3], aim at producing performance models early in the development cycle and using quantitative results from model solutions to refactor the architecture and design [4] with the purpose of meeting performance requirements [5]. Advanced Model-Driven Engineering (MDE) techniques have successfully been used in the last few years to introduce automation in software performance modeling and analysis [6, 7].

Nevertheless, the problem of interpreting the performance analysis results is still quite critical. A large gap exists between the representation of performance analysis results and the feedback expected by software architects. Additionally, the former usually contains numbers (e.g. mean response time, throughput variance, etc.), whereas the latter should embed architectural suggestions, i.e. design

M. Bernardo, V. Cortellessa, and A. Pierantonio (Eds.): SFM 2012, LNCS 7320, pp. 290–335, 2012.

alternatives, useful to overcome performance problems (e.g. split a software component in two components and re-deploy one of them).

Such activities are today exclusively based on the analysts' experience, and therefore their effectiveness often suffers of lack of automation. MDE techniques represent very promising means on this scenario to tackle the problem.

Figure 1 schematically represents the typical steps that are executed at the architectural phase of the software lifecycle to conduct a model-based performance analysis process. Rounded boxes in the figure represent operational steps whereas square boxes represent input/output data. Vertical lines divide the process in three different phases: in the *modeling* phase, an (annotated) software architectural model is built; in the *performance analysis* phase, a performance model is obtained through model transformation, and such model is solved to obtain the performance results of interest; in the *refactoring* phase, the performance results are interpreted and, if necessary, feedback is generated as refactoring actions on the original software architectural model.

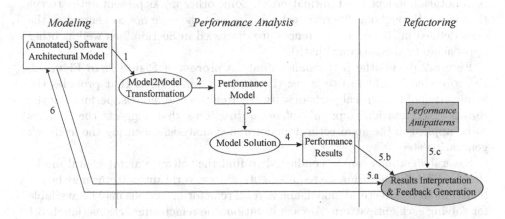

Fig. 1. Model-based software performance analysis process

The modeling and performance analysis phases (i.e. arrows numbered from 1 through 4) represent the forward path from an (annotated) software architectural model all the way through the production of performance indices of interest. As outlined above, while in this path well-founded model-driven approaches have been introduced for inducing automation in all steps (e.g. [6, 8, 9]), there is a clear lack of automation in the backward path that shall bring the analysis results back to the software architecture.

The core step of the backward path is the shaded rounded box of Figure 1. Here, the performance analysis results have to be interpreted in order to detect, if any, performance problems. Once performance problems have been detected (with a certain accuracy) somewhere in the architectural model, solutions have to be applied to remove those problems[1]. A performance problem originates from a set of unfulfilled requirement(s), such as "the estimated average response time of a service is higher than the required one". If all the requirements are satisfied then the feedback obviously suggests no changes.

In Figure 1 the (annotated) software architectural model (label 5.a) and the performance results (label 5.b) are both inputs to the core step that searches problems in the model. The third input of this step represents the most promising elements that can drive this search, i.e. *performance antipatterns* (label 5.c). The rationale of using performance antipatterns is two-fold: on one hand, a performance antipattern identifies a bad practice in the software architectural model that negatively affects the performance indices, thus it supports the *results interpretation* step; on the other hand, a performance antipattern definition includes a solution description that lets the software architect devise refactoring actions, thus it supports the *feedback generation* step.

The main reference we consider for performance antipatterns is the work done across the years by Smith and Williams [10] that have ultimately defined fourteen notation-independent antipatterns[2]. Some other works present antipatterns that occur throughout different technologies, but they are not as general as the ones defined in [10] (more references are discussed in Section 2 as well as other approaches to the backward path).

Figure 2 details the performance analysis process of Figure 1. In Figure 2, the core step is split in two steps: (i) *detecting antipatterns* that provides the localization of the critical parts of software architectural models, performing the results interpretation step; (ii) *solving antipatterns* that suggests the changes to be applied to the architectural model under analysis, executing the feedback generation step.

Several *iterations* can be conducted to find the software architectural model that best fits the performance requirements, since several antipatterns may be detected in an architectural model, and several refactoring actions may be available for solving each antipattern. At each iteration, the refactoring actions (labels 6.1 ... 6.h of Figure 2) aim at building a new software architectural model (namely *Candidate*) that replaces the analyzed one. For example, $Candidate_{i-j}$ denotes the j-th candidate generated at the i-th iteration. Then, the detection and solution approach can be iteratively applied to all newly generated candidates to further improve the system, when necessary.

---

[1] Note that this task very closely corresponds to the work of a physician: observing a sick patient (the model), studying the symptoms (some bad values of performance indices), making a diagnosis (performance problem), prescribing a treatment (performance solution through refactoring).

[2] From the original list of fourteen antipatterns [10] two antipatterns are not considered for the following reason: the *Falling Dominoes* antipattern refers to reliability and fault tolerance issues and it is out of interest; the *Unnecessary Processing* antipattern deals with the semantics of the processing by judging the importance of the application code that it is an abstraction level not included in software architectural models. Hence, twelve is the total number of the antipatterns we examine.

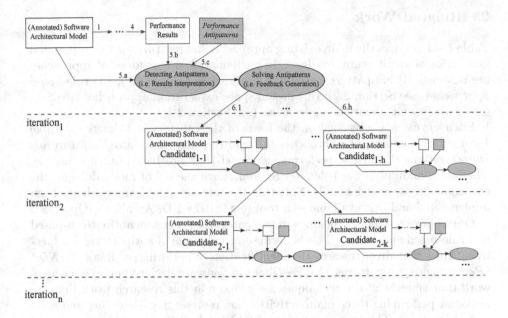

Fig. 2. Software performance analysis process across different iterations

Different termination criteria can be defined in the antipattern-based process: (i) *fulfilment* criterion, i.e. all requirements are satisfied and a suitable software architectural model is found; (ii) *no-actions* criterion, i.e. antipatterns are not detected in the software architectural models therefore no refactoring action can be experimented; (iii) *#iterations* criterion, i.e. the process can be terminated if a certain number of iterations have been completed.

It is worth to notice that the solution of one or more antipatterns does not a priori guarantee performance improvements, because the entire process is based on heuristic evaluations. However, an antipattern-based refactoring action is usually a correctness-preserving transformation that improves the quality of the software. For example, the interaction between two components might be refactored to improve performance by sending fewer messages with more data per message. This transformation does not alter the semantics of the application, but it may improve the overall performance.

The remainder of the chapter is organized as follows. Section 2 discusses existing work in this research area. Sections 3 and 4 present our approach to the representation, and detection/solution activities, needed to embed antipatterns in a software performance process. Section 5 describes a model-driven framework to widen the scope of antipatterns. Finally, Section 6 concludes the chapter by pointing out the pros and cons of using antipatterns in the software performance process and illustrating the most challenging research issues in this area.

2   Related Work

Table 1 summarizes the main existing approaches in literature for the automated generation of architectural feedback. In particular, four categories of approaches are outlined: (i) antipattern-based approaches (see Section 2.1); (ii) rule-based approaches (see Section 2.2); (iii) design space exploration approaches (see Section 2.3); (iv) metaheuristic approaches (see Section 2.4).

Each *approach* is classified on the basis of the category it belongs to. Table 1 compares the different approaches by reporting the *(annotated) software architectural model* and the *performance model* they are based on, if available. The last column of Table 1 denotes as *framework* the set of methodologies the corresponding approach entails. Note that in some cases the framework has been implemented and it is available as a tool (e.g. SPE • ED, ArchE, PerOpteryx).

Our approach somehow belongs to two categories, that are: antipattern-based and rule-based approaches. This is because it makes use of antipatterns for specifying rules that drive towards the identification of performance flaws. *PANDA* (*P*erformance *A*ntipatterns a*N*d Fee*D*back in Software *A*rchitectures) is a framework that embeds all the techniques we propose in this research work that are aimed at performing three main activities, i.e. representing, detecting and solving antipatterns. The implementation of PANDA is still a work in progress and we aim at developing it in the next future.

2.1   Antipattern-Based Approaches

Williams et al. in [11] introduced the PASA (Performance Assessment of Software Architectures) approach. It aims at achieving good performance results through a deep understanding of the architectural features. This is the approach that firstly introduces the concept of antipatterns as support to the identification of performance problems in software architectural models as well as in the formulation of architectural alternatives. However, this approach is based on the interactions between software architects and performance experts, therefore its level of automation is still low.

Cortellessa et al. in [12] introduced a first proposal of automated generation of feedback from the software performance analysis, where performance antipatterns play a key role in the detection of performance flaws. However, this approach considers a restricted set of antipatterns, and it uses informal interpretation matrices as support. The main limitation of this approach is that the interpretation of performance results is only demanded to the analysis of Layered Queue Networks (LQN) [28] performance model. Such knowledge is not enriched with the features coming from the software architectural models, thus to hide feasible refactoring actions.

Enterprise technologies and EJB performance antipatterns are analyzed by Parsons et al. in [13]: antipatterns are represented as sets of rules loaded into an engine. A rule-based performance diagnosis tool, named Performance Antipattern Detection (PAD), is presented. However, it deals with Component-Based Enterprise Systems, targeting only Enterprise Java Bean (EJB) applications.

Table 1. Summary of the approaches for the generation of architectural feedback

	Approach	(Annotated) Software Architectural Model	Performance Model	Framework
Antipattern-based	Williams et al. [11], 2002	Software execution model (Execution graphs)	System execution model (Queueing Network)	SPE • ED
	Cortellessa et al. [12], 2007	Unified Modeling Language (UML)	Layered Queueing Network (LQN)	GARFIELD (Generator of Architectural Feedback through Performance Antipatterns Revealed)
	Parsons et al. [13], 2008	JEE systems from which component level end-to-end run-time paths are collected	Reconstructed run-time design model	PAD (Performance Antipattern Detection)
	Our approach [14] [15], 2009-2011	Unified Modeling Language (UML), Palladio Component Model (PCM)	Queueing Network, Simulation Model	PANDA (Performance Antipatterns aNd FeeDback in Software Architectures)
Rule-based	Barber et al. [16], 2002	Domain Reference Architecture (DRA)	Simulation Model	RARE and ARCADE
	Dobrzanski et al. [17], 2006	Unified Modeling Language (UML)	-	Telelogic TAU (i.e. UML CASE tool)
	McGregor et al. [18], 2007	Attribute-Driven Design (ADD)	Simulation Model	ArchE
	Kavimandan et al. [19], 2009	Real-Time Component Middleware	-	extension of the LwCCM middleware [20]
	Xu [21], 2010	Unified Modeling Language (UML)	Layered Queueing Network (LQN)	PB (Performance Booster)
Design Exploration	Zheng et al. [22], 2003	Unified Modeling Language (UML)	Simulation Model	-
	Bondarev et al. [23], 2007	Robocop Component Model	Simulation model	DeepCompass (Design Exploration and Evaluation of Performance for Component Assemblies)
	Ipek et al. [24], 2008	Artificial Neural Network (ANN)	Simulation Model	-
Metaheuristic	Canfora et al. [25], 2005	Workflow Model	Workflow QoS Model	-
	Aleti et al. [26], 2009	Architecture Analysis and Description Language (AADL)	Markov Model	ArcheOpterix
	Martens et al. [27], 2010	Palladio Component Model (PCM)	Simulation Model	PerOpteryx

From the monitored data of running systems, it extracts the run-time system design and detects EJB antipatterns by applying the defined rules to it. Hence, the scope of [13] is restricted to such domain, and performance problems can neither be detected in other technology contexts nor in the early development stages.

2.2   Rule-Based Approaches

Barber et al. in [16] introduced heuristic algorithms that in presence of detected system bottlenecks provide alternative solutions to remove them. The heuristics are based on architectural metrics that help to compare different solutions. However, it basically identifies and solve only software bottlenecks, more complex problems are not recognized.

Dobrzanski et al. in [17] tackled the problem of refactoring UML models. In particular, *bad smells* are defined as structures that suggest possible problems in the system in terms of functional and non-functional aspects. Refactoring operations are suggested in the presence of bad smells. However, no specific performance issue is analyzed, and refactoring is not driven by unfulfilled requirements.

McGregor et al. in [18] proposed the ArchE framework to support the software designers in creating architectures that meet quality requirements. It embodies knowledge of quality attributes and the relation between the achievement of quality requirements and architectural design. However, the suggestions (or tactics) are not well explained, and it is not clear at which extent the approach can be applied.

Kavimandan et al. in [19] presented an approach to optimize deployment and configuration decisions in the context of distributed, real-time, and embedded component-based systems. Enhanced bin packing algorithms and schedulability analysis have been used to make fine-grained assignments of components to different middleware containers, since they are known to impact on the system performance and resource consumption. However, the scope of this approach is limited to deployment and configuration features.

Xu in [21] presented an approach to software performance diagnosis that identifies performance flaws before the software system implementation. It defines a set of *rules* detecting patterns of interaction between resources. The software architectural models are translated in a performance model, i.e. Layered Queueing Networks (LQNs) [28], and then analyzed. The approach limits the detection to bottlenecks and long execution paths identified and removed at the level of the LQN performance model. The overall approach applies only to LQN models, hence its portability to other notations is yet to be proven and it may be quite complex.

2.3   Design Space Exploration Approaches

Zheng et al. in [22] described an approach to find optimal deployment and scheduling priorities for tasks in a class of distributed real-time systems. In particular, it is intended to evaluate the deployment of such tasks by applying a heuristic search strategy to LQN models. However, its scope is restricted to adjust the priorities of tasks competing for a processor, and the only refactoring action is to change the allocation of tasks to processors.

Bondarev et al. in [23] presented a design space exploration framework for component-based software systems. It allows an architect to get insight into a space of possible design alternatives with further evaluation and comparison of these alternatives. However, it requires a manual definition of design alternatives of software and hardware architectures, and it is meant to only identify bottlenecks.

Ipek et al. in [24] described an approach to automatically explore the design space for hardware architectures, such as multiprocessors or memory hierarchies. The multiple design space points are simulated and the results are used to train a neural network. Such network can be solved quickly for different architecture candidates and delivers accurate results with a prediction error of less than 5%. However, the approach is limited to hardware properties, it is not suitable for the analysis of software architectural models that usually spread on a wide rage of features.

2.4 Metaheuristic Approaches

Canfora et al. in [25] used genetic algorithms for Quality of Service (QoS)-aware service composition, i.e. to determine a set of *concrete* services to be bound to the *abstract* ones in the workflow of a composite service. However, each basic service is considered as a black-box element, where performance metrics are fixed to certain units, and the genetic algorithms search the best solutions by evaluating the composition options. Hence, no real feedback is given to the designer with the exception of a pre-defined selection of basic services.

Aleti et al. in [26] presented a framework for the optimization of embedded system architectures. In particular, it uses the AADL (Architecture Analysis and Description Language) [29] as the underlying architecture description language and provides plug-in mechanisms to replace the optimization engine, the quality evaluation algorithms and the constraints checking. Architectural models are optimized with evolutionary algorithms considering multiple arbitrary quality criteria. However, the only refactoring action the framework currently allows is the component re-deployment.

Martens et al. in [27] used meta-heuristic search techniques for improving performance, reliability, and costs of component-based software systems. In particular, evolutionary algorithms search the architectural design space for optimal trade-offs by means of Pareto curves. However, this approach is quite time-consuming, because it uses random changes (spanning on all feasible solutions) of the architecture, and the optimality is not guaranteed.

3   Representation of Performance Antipatterns

Performance antipatterns were originally defined in natural language [10]. For sake of simplification, Table 2 reports some examples (i.e. the *Blob*, the *Concurrent Processing Systems*, and the *Empty Semi Trucks* antipatterns [10]) that will be used throughout this section as driving examples. In the table, the *problem* column identifies the system properties that define the antipattern and are useful for detecting it[3]; the *solution* column suggests the architectural changes for solving the antipattern.

Table 2. Some examples of Performance Antipatterns [10]

Antipattern	Problem	Solution
Blob	Occurs when a single class or component either 1) performs all of the work of an application or 2) holds all of the applications data. Either manifestation results in excessive message traffic that can degrade performance.	Refactor the design to distribute intelligence uniformly over the applications top-level classes, and to keep related data and behavior together.
Concurrent Processing Systems	Occurs when processing cannot make use of available processors.	Restructure software or change scheduling algorithms to enable concurrent execution.
Empty Semi Trucks	Occurs when an excessive number of requests is required to perform a task. It may be due to inefficient use of available bandwidth, an inefficient interface, or both.	The Batching performance pattern combines items into messages to make better use of available bandwidth. The Coupling performance pattern, Session Facade design pattern, and Aggregate Entity design pattern provide more efficient interfaces.

Starting from their textual description, in the following we provide a graphical representation of performance antipatterns (Section 3.1) in order to quickly convey their basic concepts. The graphical representation (here visualized in a UML-like notation) reflects our interpretation of the textual description of performance antipatterns [10]. It is conceived to capture one reasonable illustration of both the antipattern problem and solution, but it does not claim to be exhaustive. Either the problem or even more the solution description of antipatterns gives rise to a set of options that could be considered to refine the current interpretation.

An antipattern identifies unwanted software and/or hardware properties, thus an antipattern can be formulated as a (maybe complex) logical predicate on the software architectural model elements. In fact, from the informal representation of the *problem* (as reported in Table 2), a set of *basic predicates* (BP_i) is built, where each BP_i addresses part of the antipattern problem specification. The basic predicates are first described in a semi-formal natural language and then formalized by means of first-order logics (Section 3.2).

---

[3] Such properties refer to software and/or hardware architectural characteristics as well as to the performance indices obtained by the analysis.

3.1   Graphical Representation of Performance Antipatterns

In this section we present the graphical representation of some performance antipatterns, i.e. the *Blob*, the *Concurrent Processing Systems*, and the *Empty Semi Trucks*[4] [10].

We organize the software architectural model elements into views, each capturing a different aspect of the system. Similarly to the Three-View Model [31], we consider three different views representing three sources of information: the *Static View* that captures the software elements (e.g. classes, components) and the static relationships among them; the *Dynamic View* that represents the interaction (e.g. messages) that occurs between the software entities elements to provide the system functionalities; and finally the *Deployment View* that describes the hardware elements (e.g. processing nodes) and the mapping of the software entities onto the hardware platforms.

Blob Antipattern

Figures 3 and 4 provide a graphical representation of the *Blob* antipattern in its two forms, i.e. *Blob-controller* and *Blob-dataContainer* respectively.

The upper side of Figures 3 and 4 describes the properties of a *Software Model* S with a *BLOB* problem: (a) *Static View*, a complex software entity instance, i.e. S_x, is connected to other software instances, e.g. S_y and S_z, through *many* dependencies (e.g. *setData*, *getData*, etc.); (b) *Dynamic View*, the software instance S_x generates (see Figure 3) or receives (see Figure 4) *excessive* message traffic to elaborate data managed by other software instances such as S_y; (c) *Deployment View*, it includes two sub-cases: (c1) the centralized case, i.e. if the communicating software instances are deployed on the same processing node then a shared resource will show *high* utilization value, i.e. $util$; (c2) the distributed case, i.e. if the communicating software instances are deployed on different processing nodes then the network link will be a critical resource with a *high* utilization value, i.e. $utilNet$ [5]. The occurrence of such properties leads to assess that the software resource S_x originates an instance of the Blob antipattern.

The lower side of Figures 3 and 4 contains the design changes that can be applied according to the *BLOB solution*. The refactoring actions are: (a) the number of dependencies between the software instance S_x and the surrounding ones, like S_y and S_z, must be decreased by delegating some functionalities to the surrounding instances; (b) the number of messages sent (see Figure 3) or received (see Figure 4) by S_x must be decreased by moving the data management from S_x to the surrounding software instances. As consequence of previous actions: (c1) if the communicating software instances were deployed on the same hardware resource then the latter will not be a critical resource anymore, i.e. $util' \ll util$; (c2) if the communicating software instances are deployed on different

---

[4] Readers interested to the graphical representation of other antipatterns can refer to [30].

[5] The characterization of antipattern parameters related to system characteristics (e.g. *many* usage dependencies, *excessive* message traffic) or to performance results (e.g. *high*, *low* utilization) is based on thresholds values (see more details in Section 4).

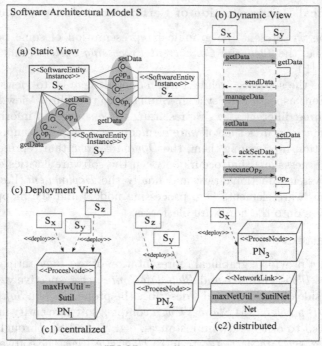

"BLOB-controller" problem

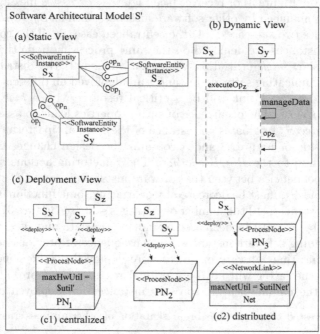

"BLOB-controller" solution

Fig. 3. A graphical representation of the *Blob-controller* Antipattern

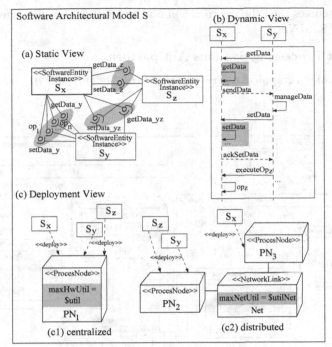

"BLOB-dataContainer" problem

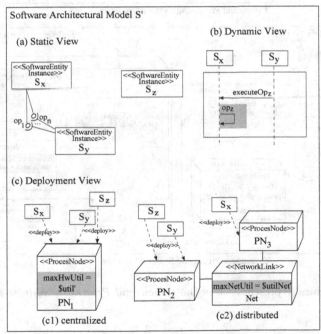

"BLOB-dataContainer" solution

Fig. 4. A graphical representation of the *Blob-dataContainer* Antipattern

hardware resources then the network will not be a critical resource anymore, i.e. $utilNet' \ll utilNet$.

Concurrent Processing Systems Antipattern

Figure 5 provides a graphical representation of the *Concurrent Processing Systems* antipattern.

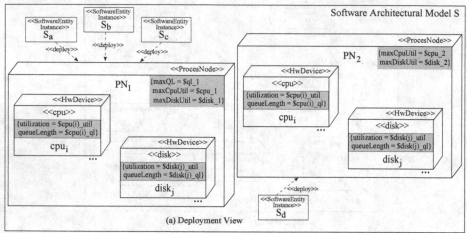

"Concurrent Processing Systems" problem

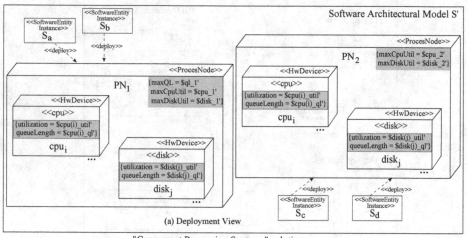

"Concurrent Processing Systems" solution

Fig. 5. A graphical representation of the *Concurrent Processing Systems* Antipattern

The upper side of Figure 5 describes the system properties of a *Software Model* S with a *Concurrent Processing Systems* problem: (a) *Deployment View*, there are two processing nodes, e.g. PN_1 and PN_2, with un unbalanced processing, i.e. many tasks are assigned to PN_1 whereas PN_2 is not so heavily used. The over used processing node will show *high* queue length value (ql_1, estimated as the maximum value overall its hardware devices, i.e. $cpu(i)\_ql$ and $disk(j)\_ql$), and a *high* utilization value among its hardware entities either for cpus (cpu_1, estimated as the maximum value overall its cpu devices, i.e. $cpu(i)\_util$), and disks ($disk\_1$, estimated as the maximum value overall its disk devices, i.e. $disk(j)\_util$). The less used PN_2 processing node will show *low* utilization value among its hardware entities either for cpus (cpu_2), and disks ($disk\_2$). The occurrence of such properties leads to assess that the processing nodes PN_1 and PN_2 originate an instance of the Concurrent Processing Systems antipattern.

The lower side of Figure 5 contains the design changes that can be applied according to the *Concurrent Processing Systems solution*. The refactoring actions are: (a) the software entity instances must be deployed in a better way, according to the available processing nodes. As consequences of the previous action, if the software instances are deployed in a balanced way then the processing node PN_1 will not be a critical resource anymore, hence ql_1', cpu_1', $disk\_1'$ values improves despite the cpu_2', $disk\_2'$ values.

Empty Semi Trucks Antipattern

Figure 6 provides a graphical representation of the *Empty Semi Trucks* antipattern.

The upper side of Figure 6 describes the system properties of a *Software Model S* with a *Empty Semi Trucks problem*: (a) *Static View*, there is a software entity instance, e.g. S_x, retrieving some information from several instances ($Srem_1$, ..., $Srem_n$); (b) *Dynamic View*, the software instance S_x generates an *excessive* message traffic by sending a big amount of messages of *low* sizes ($msgS$), much lower than the network bandwidth, hence the network link has a *low* utilization value ($utilNet$); (c) *Deployment View*, the processing node on which S_x is deployed, i.e. PN_1, reveals a *high* utilization value ($util$). The occurrence of such properties leads to assess that the software instance S_x originates an instance of the Empty Semi Trucks antipattern.

The lower side of Figure 6 contains the design changes that can be applied according to the *Empty Semi Trucks solution*. The refactoring action is: (a) the communication between S_x and the remote instances must be restructured, messages are merged in bigger ones ($msgS'$) to reduce the number of messages sent over the network. As consequences of the previous action, if the information is exchanged with a smarter organization of the communication, then the utilization of the processing node hosting S_x is expected to improve, i.e. $util' \ll util$.

3.2 Logic-Based Representation of Performance Antipatterns

Logical predicates for antipatterns are aimed at defining conditions on specific architectural model elements (e.g. number of interactions among software resources, hardware resources throughput) that we had originally organized in an XML Schema [30], and we here denote with the `typewriter font`.

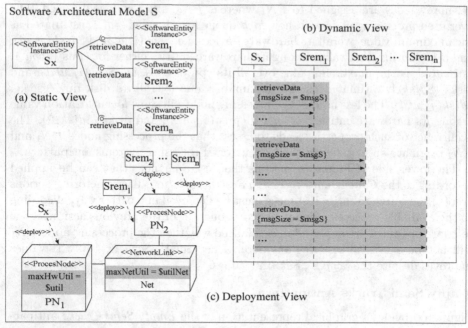

"Empty Semi Trucks" problem

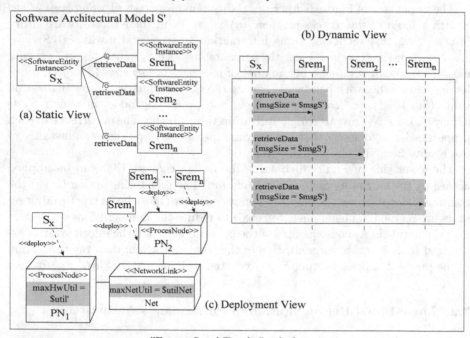

"Empty Semi Trucks" solution

Fig. 6. A graphical representation of the *Empty Semi Trucks* Antipattern

As shown in Section 3.1, the specification of *model elements* to describe antipatterns is a quite complex task, because such elements can be of different types: (i) elements of a software architectural model (e.g. software resource, message, hardware resource); (ii) performance results (e.g. utilization of a network resource); (iii) structured information that can be obtained by processing the previous ones (e.g. the number of messages sent by a software resource towards another one); (iv) bounds that give guidelines for the interpretation of the system features (e.g. the upper bound for the network utilization).

These two latter model elements, i.e. structured information and bounds, can be defined, respectively, by introducing supporting *functions* that elaborate certain sets of system elements (represented in the predicates as $F_{funcName}$), and *thresholds* that need to be compared with (observed) properties of the software system (represented in the predicates as $Th_{thresholdName}$).

In this section we present the logic-based representation of the performance antipatterns graphically introduced in Section 3.1, that are *Blob, Concurrent Processing Systems*, and *Empty Semi Trucks*[6] [10].

Blob Antipattern

The *Blob* (or "god" class/component) antipattern [10] has the following problem informal definition: *"occurs when a single class either 1) performs all of the work of an application or 2) holds all of the application's data. Excessive message traffic that can degrade performance"* (see Table 2).

Following the graphical representation of Figures 3 and 4, we formalize this sentence with four basic predicates: the BP_1 predicate whose elements belong to the Static View; the BP_2 predicate whose elements belong to the Dynamic View; and finally the BP_3 and BP_4 predicates whose elements belong to Deployment View.

BP_1- Two cases can be identified for the occurrence of the blob antipattern.

In the first case there is at least one SoftwareEntityInstance, e.g. swE_x, such that it *"performs all of the work of an application"*, while relegating other instances to minor and supporting roles. Let us define by $F_{numClientConnects}$ the function that counts how many times the software entity instance swE_x is in a Relationship with other software entity instances by assuming swE_x as client. The property of performing all the work of an application can be checked by comparing the output value of the $F_{numClientConnects}$ function with the $Th_{maxConnects}$ threshold:

$$F_{numClientConnects}(swE_x) \geq Th_{maxConnects} \tag{1}$$

In the second case there is at least one SoftwareEntityInstance, e.g. swE_x, such that it *"holds all of the application's data"*. Let us define the function $F_{numSupplierConnects}$ that counts how many times the software entity instance swE_x is in a Relationship with other software entity instances by assuming swE_x as supplier. The property of holding all of the application's data can be

---

[6] Readers interested to the logic-based representation of other antipatterns can refer to [30].

checked by comparing the output value of the $F_{numSupplierConnects}$ function with the $Th_{maxConnects}$ threshold:

$$F_{numSupplierConnects}(swE_x) \geq Th_{maxConnects} \tag{2}$$

BP_2 - swE_x performs most of the business logics in the system or holds all the application's data, thus it generates or receives excessive message traffic. Let us define by $F_{numMsgs}$ the function that takes in input a software entity instance with a `senderRole`, a software entity instance with a `receiverRole`, and a `Service` S, and returns the multiplicity of the exchanged `Messages`. The property of excessive message traffic can be checked by comparing the output value of the $F_{numMsgs}$ function with the $Th_{maxMsgs}$ threshold in both directions:

$$F_{numMsgs}(swE_x, swE_y, S) \geq Th_{maxMsgs} \tag{3a}$$

$$F_{numMsgs}(swE_y, swE_x, S) \geq Th_{maxMsgs} \tag{3b}$$

The performance impact of the excessive message traffic can be captured by considering two cases. The first case is the *centralized* one (modeled by the BP_3 predicate), i.e. the blob software entity instance and the surrounding ones are deployed on the same processing node, hence the performance issues due to the excessive load may come out by evaluating the utilization of such processing node. The second case is the *distributed* one (modeled by the BP_4 predicate), i.e. the Blob software entity instance and the surrounding ones are deployed on different processing nodes, hence the performance issues due to the excessive message traffic may come out by evaluating the utilization of the network links.

BP_3- The `ProcesNode` P_{xy} on which the software entity instances swE_x and swE_y are deployed shows heavy computation. That is, the `utilization` of a hardware entity of the `ProcesNode` P_{xy} exceeds a certain $Th_{maxHwUtil}$ threshold. For the formalization of this characteristic, we use the $F_{maxHwUtil}$ function that has two input parameters: the processing node, and the type of `HardwareEntity`, i.e. 'cpu', 'disk', or 'all' to denote no distinction between them. In this case the $F_{maxHwUtil}$ function is used to determine the maximum `Utilization` among 'all' the hardware entities of the processing node. We compare such value with the $Th_{maxHwUtil}$ threshold:

$$F_{maxHwUtil}(P_{xy}, all) \geq Th_{maxHwUtil} \tag{4}$$

BP_4- The `ProcesNode` P_{swE_x} on which the software entity instance swE_x is deployed, shows a high utilization of the network connection towards the `Proces Node` P_{swE_y} on which the software entity instance swE_y is deployed. Let us define by $F_{maxNetUtil}$ the function that provides the maximum value of the `usedBandwidth` overall the network links joining the processing nodes P_{swE_x} and P_{swE_y}. We must check if such value is higher than the $Th_{maxNetUtil}$ threshold:

$$F_{maxNetUtil}(P_{swE_x}, P_{swE_y}) \geq Th_{maxNetUtil} \tag{5}$$

Summarizing, the *Blob (or "god" class/component)* antipattern occurs when the following composed predicate is true:

$$\exists swE_x, swE_y \in \text{swE}, S \in \mathbb{S} \mid \boxed{((1) \vee (2)) \wedge ((3a) \vee (3b)) \wedge ((4) \vee (5))}$$

where swE represents the `SoftwareEntityInstances`, and $\mathbb{S}$ represents the `Services` in the software system. Each (swE_x, swE_y, S) instance satisfying the predicate must be pointed out to the designer for a deeper analysis, because it represents a Blob antipattern.

Concurrent Processing Systems Antipattern

The *Concurrent Processing Systems* antipattern [10] has the following problem informal definition: *"occurs when processing cannot make use of available processors"* (see Table 2).

Following the graphical representation of Figure 5, we formalize this sentence with three basic predicates: the BP_1, BP_2, BP_3 predicates whose elements belong to the Deployment View. In the following, we denote with $\mathbb{P}$ the set of the `ProcesNode` instances in the system.

BP_1 - There is at least one `ProcesNode` in $\mathbb{P}$, e.g. P_x, having a large `Queue-Length`. Let us define by F_{maxQL} the function providing the maximum `Queue-Length` among all the hardware entities of the processing node. The first condition for the antipattern occurrence is that the value obtained from F_{maxQL} is greater than the Th_{maxQL} threshold:

$$F_{maxQL}(P_x) \geq Th_{maxQL} \tag{6}$$

BP_2 - P_x has a heavy computation. This means that the utilizations of some hardware entities in P_x (i.e. cpu, disk) exceed predefined limits. We use the already defined $F_{maxHwUtil}$ to identify the highest `utilization` of cpu(s) and disk(s) in P_x, and then we compare such utilizations to the $Th_{maxCpuUtil}$ and $Th_{maxDiskUtil}$ thresholds:

$$F_{maxHwUtil}(P_x, cpu) \geq Th_{maxCpuUtil} \tag{7a}$$
$$F_{maxHwUtil}(P_x, disk) \geq Th_{maxDiskUtil} \tag{7b}$$

BP_3- The processing nodes are not used in a well-balanced way, as there is at least another instance of `ProcesNode` in $\mathbb{P}$, e.g. P_y, whose `Utilization` of the hardware entities, differentiated according to their type (i.e. cpu, disk), is smaller than the one in P_x. In particular two new thresholds, i.e. $Th_{minCpuUtil}$ and $Th_{minDiskUtil}$, are introduced:

$$F_{maxHwUtil}(P_y, cpu) < Th_{minCpuUtil} \tag{8a}$$
$$F_{maxHwUtil}(P_y, disk) < Th_{minDiskUtil} \tag{8b}$$

Summarizing, the *Concurrent Processing Systems* antipattern occurs when the following composed predicate is true:

$$\exists P_x, P_y \in \mathbb{P} \mid \boxed{(6) \wedge [((7a) \wedge (8a)) \vee ((7b) \wedge ((8b)))]}$$

where $\mathbb{P}$ represents the set of all the ProcesNodes in the software system. Each (P_x, P_y) instance satisfying the predicate must be pointed out to the designer for a deeper analysis, because it represents a Concurrent Processing Systems antipattern.

Empty Semi Trucks Antipattern

The *Empty Semi Trucks* antipattern [10] has the following problem informal definition: *"occurs when an excessive number of requests is required to perform a task. It may be due to inefficient use of available bandwidth, an inefficient interface, or both"* (see Table 2).

Following the graphical representation of Figure 6, we formalize this sentence with three basic predicates: the BP_1 predicate whose elements belong to the Dynamic View; the BP_2 and BP_3 predicates whose elements belong to the Deployment View.

BP_1 - There is at least one SoftwareEntityInstance swE_x that exchanges an excessive number of Messages with remote software entities. Let us define by $F_{numRemMsgs}$ the function that calculates the number of remote messages sent by swE_x in a Service S. The antipattern can occur when this function returns a value higher or equal than the $Th_{maxRemMsgs}$ threshold:

$$F_{numRemMsgs}(swE_x, S) \geq Th_{maxRemMsgs} \tag{9}$$

BP_2- The inefficient use of available bandwidth means that the SoftwareEntityInstance swE_x sends a high number of messages without optimizing the network capacity. Hence, the ProcesNode P_{swE_x}, on which the software entity instance swE_x is deployed, reveals an utilization of the network lower than the $Th_{minNetUtil}$ threshold. We focus on the NetworkLink(s) that connect P_{swE_x} to the whole system, i.e. the ones having P_{swE_x} as their EndNode. Since we are interested to the network links on which the software instance swE_x generates traffic, we restrict the whole set of network links to the ones on which the interactions of the software instance swE_x with other communicating entities take place:

$$F_{maxNetUtil}(P_{swE_x}, swE_x) < Th_{minNetUtil} \tag{10}$$

BP_3- The inefficient use of interface means that the software instance swE_x communicates with a certain number of remote instances, all deployed on the same remote processing node. Let us define by $F_{numRemInst}$ the function that provides the maximum number of remote instances with which swE_x communicates in the service S. The antipattern can occur when this function returns a value higher or equal than the $Th_{maxRemInst}$ threshold:

$$F_{numRemInst}(swE_x, S) \geq Th_{maxRemInst} \tag{11}$$

Summarizing, the *Empty Semi Trucks* antipattern occurs when the following composed predicate is true:

$$\exists swE_x \in swE, S \in \mathbb{S} \mid \boxed{(9) \wedge ((10) \vee (11))}$$

where swE represents the `SoftwareEntityInstances`, and $\mathbb{S}$ represents the `Services` in the software system. Each (swE_x, S) instance satisfying the predicate must be pointed out to the designer for a deeper analysis, because it represents an Empty Semi Trucks antipattern.

Finally, Table 3 lists the logic-based representation of all the performance antipatterns we consider. Each row represents a specific antipattern that is characterized by two attributes: *antipattern* name, and its *formula*, i.e. the first order logics predicate modeling the corresponding antipattern problem.

The list of performance antipatterns has been here enriched with an additional attribute. As shown in the leftmost part of Table 3, we have partitioned antipatterns in two different categories: antipatterns detectable by single values of performance indices (such as mean, max or min values), named as *Single-value* Performance Antipatterns, and antipatterns requiring the trend (or evolution) of the performance indices during the time to capture the performance problems in the software system, named as *Multiple-values* Performance Antipatterns. The mean, max or min values are not sufficient to define the latter category of antipatterns, unless these values refer to several observation time frames. Due to these characteristics, the performance indices needed to detect such antipatterns must be obtained via simulation or monitoring.

Note that the formalization of antipatterns is the result of multiple formulations and checks. This is a first attempt to formally define antipatterns and it may be subject to some refinements. However, the logic-based formalization was meant to demonstrate the potential for a machine-processable management of performance antipatterns.

4   Detection and Solution of Performance Antipatterns

In this section we apply the antipattern-based approach to an Electronic Commerce System (ECS) case study, modeled with the Unified Modeling Language (UML) [32]. Figure 7 customizes the approach of Figure 1 to the specific methodologies adopted for this case study.

ECS has been modeled with UML annotated with the MARTE profile[7] [33] that provides all the information we need for reasoning on performance issues. The transformation from the software architectural model to the performance model is performed with PRIMA-UML, i.e. a methodology that generates Queueing Network models from UML models [34]. Once the Queueing Network (QN) model is derived, classical QN solution techniques based on well-known methodologies [35], such as Mean Value Analysis (MVA), can be applied to solve it. The performance model is analyzed to obtain the performance indices of interest (i.e. response time, utilization, throughput, etc.).

The UML model and the performance indices are joined in an XML representation[8] of the ECS, parsed by a detection engine that provides the critical

---

[7] MARTE provides stereotypes and tags to annotate UML models with information required to perform performance analysis.

[8] The XML representation of the ECS can be viewed in
http://www.di.univaq.it/catia.trubiani/phDthesis/ECS.xml

Table 3. A logic-based representation of Performance Antipatterns

		Antipattern	Formula
Single-value		Blob (or god class/component)	$\exists swE_x, swE_y \in swE, S \in \mathbb{S} \mid (F_{numClientConnects}(swE_x) \geq Th_{maxConnects} \lor F_{numSupplierConnects}(swE_x) \geq Th_{maxConnects}) \land (F_{numMsgs}(swE_x, swE_y, S) \geq Th_{maxMsgs} \lor F_{numMsgs}(swE_y, swE_x, S) \geq Th_{maxMsgs}) \land (F_{maxHwUtil}(P_{xy}, all) \geq Th_{maxHwUtil} \lor F_{maxNetUtil}(P_{swE_x}, P_{swE_y}) \geq Th_{maxNetUtil})$
	Unbalanced Processing	Concurrent Processing Systems	$\exists P_x, P_y \in \mathbb{P} \mid F_{maxQL}(P_x) \geq Th_{maxQL} \land [(F_{maxHwUtil}(P_x, cpu) \geq Th_{maxCpuUtil} \land F_{maxHwUtil}(P_y, cpu) < Th_{minCpuUtil}) \lor (F_{maxHwUtil}(P_x, disk) \geq Th_{maxDiskUtil} \land (F_{maxHwUtil}(P_y, disk) < Th_{minDiskUtil}))]$
		"Pipe and Filter" Architectures	$\exists OpI \in \mathbb{O}, S \in \mathbb{S} \mid \forall i : F_{resDemand}(Op)[i] \geq Th_{resDemand}[i] \land F_{probExec}(S, OpI) = 1 \land (F_{maxHwUtil}(P_{swE_x}, all) \geq Th_{maxHwUtil} \lor F_T(S) < Th_{SthReq})$
		Extensive Processing	$\exists OpI_1, OpI_2 \in \mathbb{O}, S \in \mathbb{S} \mid \forall i : F_{resDemand}(Op_1)[i] \geq Th_{maxOpResDemand}[i] \land \forall i : F_{resDemand}(Op_2)[i] < Th_{minOpResDemand}[i] \land F_{probExec}(S, OpI_1) + F_{probExec}(S, OpI_2) = 1 \land (F_{maxHwUtil}(P_{swE_x}, all) \geq Th_{maxHwUtil} \lor F_{RT}(S) > Th_{SrtReq})$
		Circuitous Treasure Hunt	$\exists swE_x, swE_y \in swE, S \in \mathbb{S} \mid swE_y.isDB = true \land F_{numDBmsgs}(swE_x, swE_y, S) \geq Th_{maxDBmsgs} \land F_{maxHwUtil}(P_{swE_y}, all) \geq Th_{maxHwUtil} \land F_{maxHwUtil}(P_{swE_y}, disk) > F_{maxHwUtil}(P_{swE_y}, cpu)$
		Empty Semi Trucks	$\exists swE_x \in swE, S \in \mathbb{S} \mid F_{numRemMsgs}(swE_x, S) \geq Th_{maxRemMsgs} \land F_{maxNetUtil}(P_{swE_x}, swE_x) < Th_{minNetUtil} \lor F_{numRemInst}(swE_x, S) \geq Th_{maxRemInst})$
		Tower of Babel	$\exists swE_x \in swE, S \in \mathbb{S} \mid F_{numExF}(swE_x, S) \geq Th_{maxExF} \land F_{maxHwUtil}(P_{swE_x}, all) \geq Th_{maxHwUtil}$
		One-Lane Bridge	$\exists swE_x \in swE, S \in \mathbb{S} \mid F_{numSynchCalls}(swE_x, S) \gg F_{poolSize}(swE_x) \land F_{serviceTime}(P_{swE_x}) \ll F_{waitingTime}(P_{swE_x}) \land F_{RT}(S) > Th_{SrtReq}$
		Excessive Dynamic Allocation	$\exists S \in \mathbb{S} \mid (F_{numCreatedObj}(S) \geq Th_{maxCrObj} \lor F_{numDestroyedObj}(S) \geq Th_{maxDeObj}) \land F_{RT}(S) > Th_{SrtReq}$
Multiple-values		Traffic Jam	$\exists OpI \in \mathbb{O} \mid \frac{\sum_{1 \leq t \leq k}|(F_{RT}(OpI,t) - F_{RT}(OpI,t-1))|}{k-1} < Th_{OpRtVar} \land F_{RT}(OpI,k) - F_{RT}(OpI,k-1) > Th_{OpRtVar} \land \frac{\sum_{k \leq t \leq n}|(F_{RT}(OpI,t) - F_{RT}(OpI,t-1))|}{n-k} < Th_{OpRtVar}$
		The Ramp	$\exists Op \in \mathbb{O} \mid \frac{\sum_{1 \leq t \leq n}|(F_{RT}(OpI,t) - F_{RT}(OpI,t-1))|}{n} > Th_{OpRtVar} \land \frac{\sum_{1 \leq t \leq n}|(F_T(OpI,t) - F_T(OpI,t-1))|}{n} > Th_{OpThVar}$
		More is Less	$\exists P_x \in \mathbb{P} \mid \forall i : F_{par}(P_x)[i] \ll \frac{\sum_{1 \leq t \leq N}(F_{RTpar}(P_x,t)[i] - F_{RTpar}(P_x,t-1)[i])}{N}$

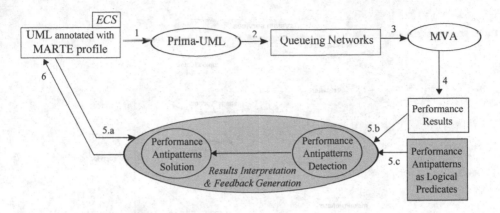

Fig. 7. ECS case study: customized software performance process

elements in architectural models representing the source of performance problems as well as a set of refactoring actions to overcome such issues.

The rest of this section is organized as follows. Section 4.1 describes the UML model of the system under analysis. Then, the stepwise application of our antipattern-based process is performed, i.e. the detection of antipatterns (see Section 4.2) and their solution (see Section 4.3). Finally, in Section 4.4 we briefly discuss a technique to optimize the antipatterns solution process.

4.1 Electronic Commerce System

Figure 8 shows an overview of the ECS software system. It is a web-based system that manages business data: customers browse catalogs and make selections of items that need to be purchased; at the same time, suppliers can upload their catalogs, change the prices and the availability of products, etc. The services we analyze here are *browseCatalog* and *makePurchase*. The former can be perfomance-critical because it is required by a large number of (registered and not registered) customers, whereas the latter can be perfomance-critical because it requires several database accesses that can drop the system performance.

In Figures 9 and 10 we report an excerpt of the ECS annotated software architectural model. We use UML 2.0 [32] as modeling language and MARTE [33] to annotate additional information for performance analysis (such as workload to the system, service demands, hardware characteristics). In particular, the UML Component Diagram in Figure 9 describes the software components and their interconnections, whereas the UML Deployment Diagram of Figure 10 shows the deployment of the software components on the hardware platform. The deployment is annotated with the characteristics of the hardware nodes to specify CPU attributes (*speedFactor* and *schedPolicy*) and network delay (*blockT*).

Performance requirements are defined for the ECS system on the response time of the main services of the system (i.e. *browseCatalog* and *makePurchase*) under a closed workload with a population of 200 requests/second, and thinking

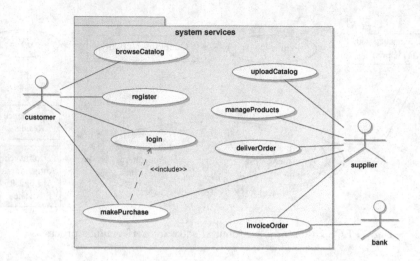

Fig. 8. ECS case study: UML Use Case Diagram

time of 0.01 seconds. The requirements are defined as follows: the *browseCatalog* service must be performed in 1.2 seconds, whereas the *makePurchase* in 2 seconds. These values represent the upper bound for the services they refer to.

The Prima-UML methodology requires the modeling of: (i) system requirements with a UML Use Case Diagram, (ii) the software dynamics with UML Sequence Diagrams, and (iii) the software-to-hardware mapping with a UML Deployment Diagram. The Use Case Diagram must be annotated with the operational profile, the Sequence Diagram with service demands and message size of each operation, and the Deployment Diagram with the characteristics of hardware nodes (see more details in [34]).

Figure 11 shows the Queueing Network model produced for ECS. It includes: (i) a set of queueing centers (e.g. *webServerNode*, *libraryNode*, etc.) representing the hardware resources of the system, a set of delay centers (e.g. *wan1*, *wan2*, etc.) representing the network communication delays; (ii) two classes of jobs, i.e. *browseCatalog* (*class A*, denoted with a star symbol in Figure 11) is invoked with a probability of 99%, and *makePurchase* (*class B*, denoted with a bullet point in Figure 11) is invoked with a probability of 1%.

The parametrization of the Queueing Network model for the ECS case study is summarized in Table 4. In particular the input parameters of the QN are reported: the first column contains the service center names, the second column shows their corresponding service rates for each class of job (i.e. *class A* and *class B*).

Table 5 summarizes the performance analysis results of the ECS Queueing Network model: the first column contains the names of requirements; the second column reports their *required values*; the third column shows their *predicted values*, as obtained from the QN solution. As it can be noticed both services have a response time that does not fulfill the required ones: the *browseCatalog*

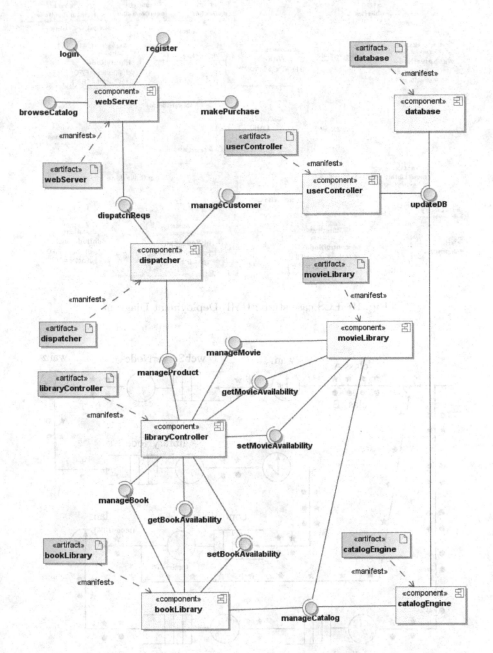

Fig. 9. ECS case study: UML Component Diagram

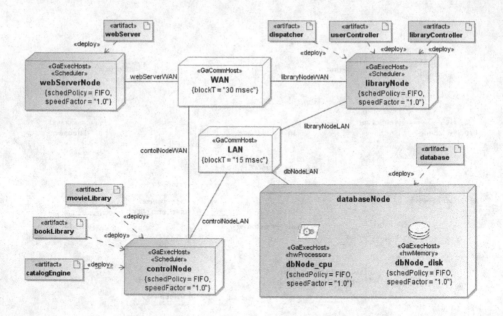

Fig. 10. ECS case study: UML Deployment Diagram

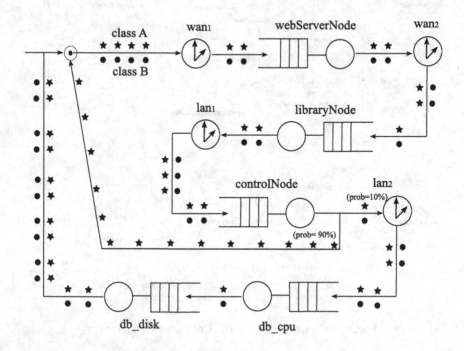

Fig. 11. ECS - Queueing Network model

Table 4. Input parameters for the queueing network model in the ECS system

Service Center	Input parameters ECS	
	$class_A$	$class_B$
lan	44 msec	44 msec
wan	208 msec	208 msec
webServerNode	2 msec	4 msec
libraryNode	7 msec	16 msec
controlNode	3 msec	3 msec
db_cpu	15 msec	30 msec
db_disk	30 msec	60 msec

Table 5. Response time requirements for the ECS software architectural model

Requirement	Required Value	Predicted Value ECS
RT(*browseCatalog*)	1.2 sec	1.5 sec
RT(*makePurchase*)	2 sec	2.77 sec

service has been predicted as 1.5 sec, whereas the *makePurchase* service has been predicted as 2.77 sec. Hence we apply our approach to detect performance antipatterns.

As said in Section 3.2, basic predicates contain boundaries that need to be actualized on each specific software architectural model. Table 6 reports the

Table 6. ECS- antipatterns boundaries binding

antipattern	parameter	value
Blob	$Th_{maxConnect}$	4
	$Th_{maxMsgs}$	18
	$Th_{maxHwUtil}$	0.75
	$Th_{maxNetUtil}$	0.85
CPS	$Th_{maxQueue}$	40
	$Th_{cpuMaxUtil}$	0.8
	$Th_{diskMaxUtil}$	0.7
	$Th_{cpuMinUtil}$	0.3
	$Th_{diskMinUtil}$	0.4
EST	$Th_{remMsgs}$	12
	$Th_{remInst}$	5
	$Th_{minNetUtil}$	0.3
...	...	...

binding of the performance *antipatterns boundaries* for the ECS system[9]. Such values allow to set the basic predicates, thus to proceed with the actual detection.

4.2 Detecting Antipatterns

The detection of antipatterns is performed by running a detection engine on the XML representation of the ECS software architectural model. This leaded to detect three antipatterns occurrences in the model, that are: Blob, Concurrent Processing Systems, and Empty Semi Trucks.

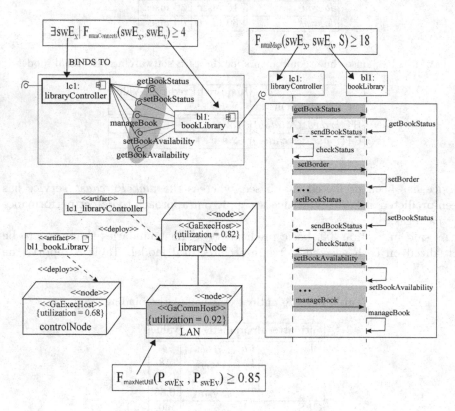

Fig. 12. ECS- the *Blob* antipattern occurrence

In Figure 12 we illustrate an excerpt of the ECS software architectural model where we highlight, in the shaded boxes, the parts of the model that give evidence to the Blob antipattern occurrence. Such antipattern is detected since the instance *lc1* of the component *libraryController* satisfies all the Blob logical predicates. In particular (see Table 6 and Figure 12): (a) it has more than

---

[9] Readers interested to the heuristics used to set antipatterns boundaries can refer to [30].

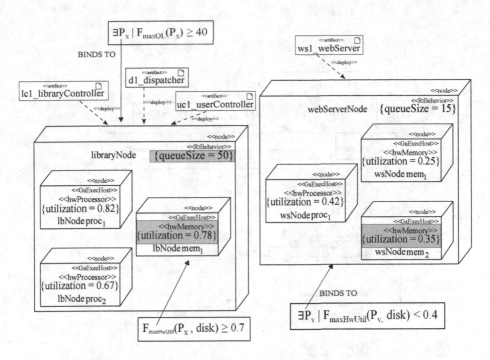

$\exists P_x \mid F_{maxQL}(P_x) \geq 40$

BINDS TO

<<artifact>> □
d1_dispatcher

<<artifact>> □
ws1_webServer
<<deploy>>

<<artifact>> □
lc1_libraryController
<<deploy>>

<<deploy>>

<<artifact>> □
uc1_userController
<<deploy>>

webServerNode   {queueSize = 15}
<<node>>   <<RtBehavior>>

libraryNode   {queueSize = 50}
<<node>>   <<RtBehavior>>

<<node>>
<<GaExecHost>>
<<hwMemory>>
{utilization = 0.25}
wsNode mem₁

<<node>>
<<GaExecHost>>
<<hwProcessor>>
{utilization = 0.82}
lbNode proc₁

<<node>>
<<GaExecHost>>
<<hwMemory>>
{utilization = 0.78}
lbNode mem₁

<<node>>
<<GaExecHost>>
<<hwProcessor>>
{utilization = 0.42}
wsNode proc₁

<<node>>
<<GaExecHost>>
<<hwMemory>>
{utilization = 0.35}
wsNode mem₂

<<node>>
<<GaExecHost>>
<<hwProcessor>>
{utilization = 0.67}
lbNode proc₂

$F_{maxHwUtil}(P_x, disk) \geq 0.7$

BINDS TO

$\exists P_v \mid F_{maxHwUtil}(P_v, disk) < 0.4$

Fig. 13. ECS- the *Concurrent Processing Systems* antipattern occurrence

4 usage dependencies towards the instance *bl1* of the component *bookLibrary*;
(b) it sends more than *18* messages (not shown in Figure 12 for sake of space);
(c) the component instances (i.e. *lc1* and *bl1*) are deployed on different nodes,
and the LAN communication host has an utilization (i.e. 0.92), higher than the
threshold value (*0.85*).

In Figure 13 we illustrate an excerpt of the ECS software architectural model
where we highlight, in the shaded boxes, the parts of the model that give evidence
to the CPS antipattern occurrence. Such antipattern is detected the instances
libraryNode and *webServerNode* satisfy all the CPS logical predeicates. In particular (see Table 6 and Figure 13): (a) the queue size of *libraryNode* (i.e. 50)
is higher than the threshold value of *40*; (b) an unbalanced load among CPUs
does not occur, because the maximum utilization of CPUs in *libraryNode* (i.e.
0.82 in the *lbNodeproc₁* instance) is higher than *0.8* threshold value, but the
maximum utilization of CPUs in *webServerNode* (i.e. 0.42 in the *wsNodeproc₁*
instance) is not lower than *0.3* threshold value; (c) an unbalanced load among
disks occurs, in fact the maximum utilization of disks in *libraryNode* (i.e. 0.78
in the *lbNodemem₁* instance), is higher than the threshold value of *0.7*, and the
maximum utilization of disks in *webServerNode* (i.e. 0.35 in the *wsNodemem₁*
instance), is lower than the threshold value of *0.4*.

In Figure 14 we illustrate an excerpt of the ECS software architectural model
where we highlight, in the shaded boxes, the parts of the model that give evidence

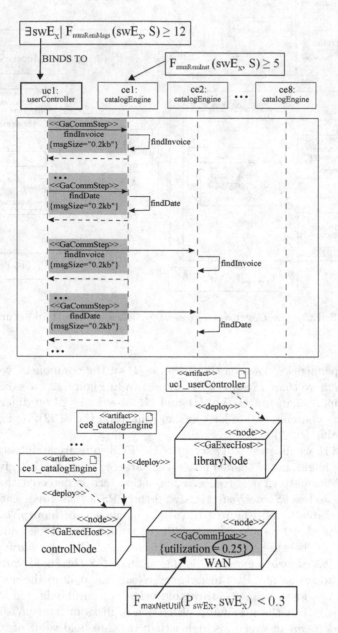

Fig. 14. ECS- the *Empty Semi Trucks* antipattern occurrence

to the EST antipattern occurrence. Such antipattern occurs since the instance *uc1* of the *userController* component satisfies all the EST logical predicates. In particular (see Table 6 and Figure 14): (a) it sends more than *12* remote messages (not shown in Figure 14 for sake of space); (b) the component instances are deployed on different nodes, and the communication host utilization (i.e. 0.25 in the *wan* instance) is lower than the *0.3* threshold value; (c) it communicates with more than *5* remote instances (*ce1*, . . . , *ce8*) of the *catalogEngine* component.

4.3 Solving Antipatterns

In Table 7 we have tailored the textual descriptions (see Table 2) on antipattern instances detected on ECS.

Table 7. ECS Performance Antipatterns: problem and solution

Antipattern	Problem	Solution
Blob	*libraryController* performs most of the work, it generates excessive message traffic.	Refactor the design to keep related data and behavior together. Delegate some work from *libraryController* to *bookLibrary*.
Concurrent Processing Systems	Processing cannot make use of the processor *webServerNode*.	Restructure software or change scheduling algorithms between processors *libraryNode* and *webServerNode*.
Empty Semi Trucks	An excessive number of requests is performed for the *makePurchase* service.	Combine items into messages to make better use of available bandwidth.

According to Table 7, we have refactored the ECS (annotated) software architectural model obtaining three new software architectural models, namely $ECS \setminus \{blob\}$, $ECS \setminus \{cps\}$, and $ECS \setminus \{est\}$, where the Blob, the Concurrent Processing Systems and the Empty Semi Trucks antipatterns have been solved, respectively.

Figure 15 shows the software model $ECS \setminus \{blob\}$ where the *Blob* antipattern is solved by modifying the inner behavior of the *libraryController* software component, thus it delegates some work to the *bookLibrary* component and the logical predicates are not valid anymore. The *Concurrent Processing Systems* antipattern is solved by re-deploying the software component *userController* from *libraryNode* to *webServerNode*. The *Empty Semi Trucks* antipattern is solved by modifying the inner behavior of the *userController* component in the communication with the *catalogEngine* component for the *makePurchase* service.

$ECS \setminus \{blob\}$, $ECS \setminus \{cps\}$, and $ECS \setminus \{est\}$ systems have been separately analyzed. Input parameters are reported in Table 8 where bold numbers represent the changes induced from the solution of the corresponding antipatterns.

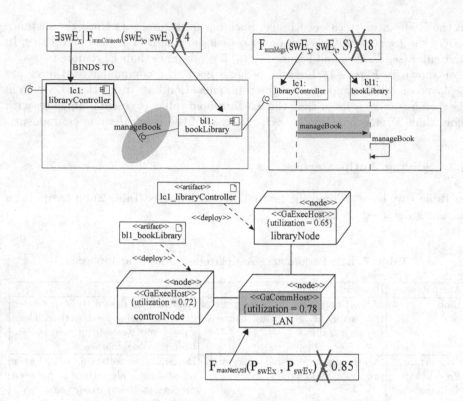

Fig. 15. $ECS \setminus \{blob\}$- the *Blob* antipattern refactoring

For example, in the column $ECS \setminus \{cps\}$ we can notice that the service centers *webServerNode* and *libraryNode* have different input values, since the re-deployment of the software component *userController* implies to move the load from *libraryNode* to *webServerNode*.

In case of *class A*, the load is estimated of 2 msec, in fact in *libraryNode* the initial value of 2 msec in ECS (see Table 4) is increased by 2 msec, thus to become 4 msec in $ECS \setminus \{cps\}$ (see Table 8), whereas in *webServerNode* the initial value of 7 msec in ECS (see Table 4) is decreased by 2 msec, thus to become 5 msec in $ECS \setminus \{cps\}$ (see Table 8). In case of *class B*, the load is estimated of 8 msec, in fact in *libraryNode* the initial value of 4 msec in ECS (see Table 4) is increased by 8 msec, thus to become 12 msec in $ECS \setminus \{cps\}$ (see Table 8), whereas in *webServerNode* the initial value of 16 msec in ECS (see Table 4) is decreased by 8 msec, thus to become 8 msec in $ECS \setminus \{cps\}$ (see Table 8).

Table 9 summarizes the performance analysis results obtained by solving the QN models of the new ECS systems (i.e. $ECS \setminus \{blob\}$, $ECS \setminus \{cps\}$, and $ECS \setminus \{est\}$ columns), and by comparing them with the results obtained from the analysis of the initial system (i.e. ECS column). The response time of the *browseCatalog* service is 1.14, 1.15, and 1.5 seconds, whereas the response time of the *makePurchase* service is 2.18, 1.6, and 2.24 seconds, across the different reconfigurations of the ECS architectural model.

Table 8. Input parameters for the queueing network model across different software architectural models

Service Center	Input parameters					
	$ECS \setminus \{cps\}$		$ECS \setminus \{est\}$		$ECS \setminus \{blob\}$	
	$class_A$	$class_B$	$class_A$	$class_B$	$class_A$	$class_B$
lan	44 msec	44 msec	44 msec	44 msec	44 msec	44 msec
wan	208 msec	208 msec	208 msec	208 msec	208 msec	208 msec
$webServerNode$	**4 msec**	**12 msec**	2 msec	4 msec	2 msec	4 msec
$libraryNode$	**5 msec**	**8 msec**	7 msec	**12 msec**	**5 msec**	**14 msec**
$controlNode$	3 msec	3 msec	3 msec	3 msec	3 msec	3 msec
db_cpu	15 msec	30 msec	15 msec	30 msec	15 msec	30 msec
db_disk	30 msec	60 msec	30 msec	60 msec	30 msec	60 msec

Table 9. Response time required and observed

Requirement	Required Value	Predicted Value			
		ECS	$ECS \setminus \{blob\}$	$ECS \setminus \{cps\}$	$ECS \setminus \{est\}$
RT($browseCatalog$)	1.2 sec	1.5 sec	1.14 sec	1.15 sec	1.5 sec
RT($makePurchase$)	2 sec	2.77 sec	2.18 sec	1.6 sec	2.24 sec

The solution of the Blob antipattern satisfies the first requirement, but not the second one. The solution of the Concurrent Processing System leads to satisfy both requirements. Finally, the Empty Semi Trucks solution was useless for the first requirement as no improvement was carried out, but it was quite beneficial for the second one, even if both of them were not fulfilled.

We can conclude that the software architectural model candidate that best fits with user needs is obtained by applying the following refactoring action: the *userController* software component is re-deployed from *libraryNode* to *webServerNode*, i.e. the solution of the Concurrent Processing Systems antipattern. In fact, as shown in Table 9 both requirements have been fulfilled by its solution, i.e. the *fulfilment* termination criterion (see Section 1). The experimental results are promising, and other decisions can be taken by looking at these results, as opposite to the common practice where software architects use to blindly act without this type of information.

4.4 A Step Ahead in the Antipatterns Solution

In this section the problem of identifying, among a set of detected performance antipattern instances, the ones that are the real causes of problems (i.e. the "guilty" ones) is tackled. In particular, it is introduced a process to elaborate the performance analysis results and to score performance requirements, model entities and performance antipattern instances. The cross observation of such scores allows to classify the level of guiltiness of each antipattern.

Figure 16 reports the process that we propose: the goal is to modify a software architectural model in order to produce a model *candidate* where the performance problems of the former have been removed. Shaded boxes of Figure 16 represent the *ranking step* that is object of this section.

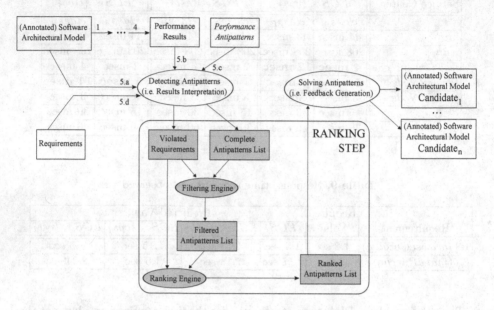

Fig. 16. A process to improve the performance analysis interpretation

The typical inputs of the detection engine are: the software architectural model, the performance results, and the performance antipatterns representation (see Figure 1). We here also report performance *requirements* (label 5.d) because they will be used in the ranking step. We obtain two types of outputs from the detection step: (i) a list of *violated requirements* as resulting from the analysis, and (ii) a *complete antipatterns list*. If no requirement is violated by the current software architectural model then the process terminates.

Then we compare the complete antipatterns list with the violated requirements and examine relationships between detected antipattern instances and each violated requirement through the system entities involved in them. We obtain a *filtered antipatterns list*, where instances that do not affect any violated requirement have been filtered out.

On the basis of relationships observed before, we estimate how guilty an antipattern instance is with respect to a violated requirement by calculating a guiltiness score. As a result, we obtain a *ranked antipatterns list* for each violated requirement. Finally, *candidates* software architectural model can be obtained by applying the solutions of one or more high-ranked antipattern instances to the current software architectural model for each violated requirement[10].

---

[10] For sake of space we do not detail this approach here, but interested readers can refer to [36].

5 Plugging Antipatterns in a Model-Driven Framework

In this section we discuss the problem of interpreting the performance analysis results and generating architectural feedback by means of a model-driven framework that supports the antipatterns management. The aim is to make use of all basic and advanced model-driven techniques.

We recall that the main activities performed within such framework are: (i) representing antipatterns (see Section 5.1), to define in a well-formed way the properties that lead the software system to reveal a bad practice, as well as the changes that provide a solution; (i) detecting and solving antipatterns (see Section 5.2), to actually locate and remove antipatterns in software models. Finally, Section 5.3 provides some afterthoughts about the model-driven framework.

5.1 Model-Driven Representation of Antipatterns

The activity of representing antipatterns is performed on this framework by introducing a metamodel (i.e. a neutral and a coherent set of interrelated concepts) to collect the system elements that occur in the definition of antipatterns (e.g. software entity, network resource utilization, etc.), which is meant to be the basis for a machine-processable definition of antipatterns.

This section briefly presents the metamodel, named Performance Antipattern Modeling Language (PAML), that collects all the system elements identified by analyzing the antipatterns definition in literature [10].

The PAML structure is shown in Figure 17. It is constituted of two main parts as delimited by the horizontal dashed line: (i) the *Antipattern Specification* collects the high-level features, such as the views of the system (i.e. static, dynamic, deployment) and their boolean relationships; (ii) the *Model Elements Specification* collects the concepts of the software architectural models and the performance results.

All the architectural model elements and the performance indices occurring in antipatterns' specifications are grouped in a metamodel called SML+ (see Figure 17). SML+ shares many concepts with existing Software Modeling Languages. However, it is not meant to be another modeling language, rather it is oriented to specify the basic elements of performance antipatterns[11].

An antipattern can be specified as a PAML-based model that is intended to formalize its textual description (similarly to what we have done with the logic-based representation of Section 3.2). For example, following the graphical representation of the Blob antipattern (see Figure 3), the corresponding PAML-based model will be constituted by an `AntipatternSpecification` with three `AntipatternViews`: (a) the `StaticView`, (b) the `DynamicView`, (c) the `DeploymentView` for which two `AntipatternSubViews` are defined, i.e. (c1) the centralized one and (c2) the distributed one. A `BooleanRestriction` can be defined

---

[11] For sake of space we do not detail SML+ here. However, a restricted set of model elements, such as software entity, processing node, etc., are shown in Figure 18, and readers interested to the whole language can refer to [30].

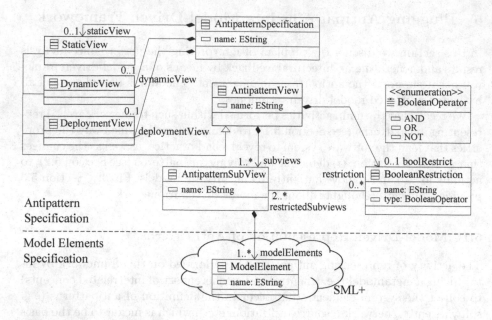

Fig. 17. The Performance Antipattern Modeling Language (PAML) structure

between these sub-views, and the *type* is set by the `BooleanOperator` equal to the *OR* value. Each subview will contain a set of `ModelElements`.

5.2   Model-Driven Detection and Solution of Antipatterns

The activities of detecting and solving antipatterns are performed on this framework by translating the antipatterns representation into concrete modeling notations. In fact, the modeling language used for the target system, i.e. the (annotated) software architectural model of Figure 1, is of crucial relevance, since the antipatterns neutral concepts must be translated into the actual concrete modeling language, if possible[12].

Our model-driven framework is currently considering two concrete notations: UML [32] plus MARTE profile [33]; and the Palladio Component Model (PCM) [37]. Note that the subset of target modeling languages is being enlarged (e.g. with an Architecture Description Language like Æmilia [38]) as far as the concepts for representing antipatterns are available.

Figure 18 shows how the neutral specification of performance antipatterns in PAML can be translated into concrete modeling languages. In fact, antipatterns are built on a set of model elements belonging to SML+, i.e. the infrastructure upon which constructing the semantic relations among different notations.

The semantic relations between a concrete modeling language and SML+ depend on the expressiveness of the target modeling language. For example, in

---

[12] It depends on the expressiveness of the target modeling language.

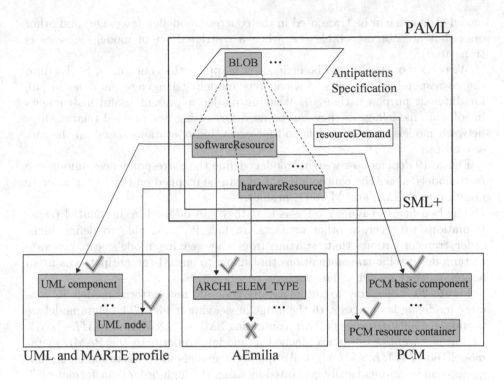

Fig. 18. Translating antipatterns into concrete modeling languages

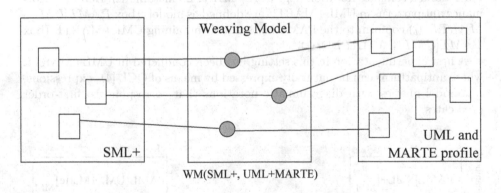

Fig. 19. Metamodel instantiation via weaving models

Figure 18 we can notice that a *SoftwareEntity* is respectively translated in a *UML Component*, a *PCM Basic Component*, and an *Æmilia ARCHI_ELEM_TYPE*. On the contrary, the *ProcesNode* translation is only possible to a *UML Node* and a *PCM Resource Container*, whereas in Æmilia this concept remains uncovered.

We can therefore assert that in a concrete modeling language there are antipatterns that can be automatically detected (i.e. when the entire set of SML+

model elements can be translated in the concrete modeling language) and other
ones that are not detectable (i.e. when a restricted set of model elements is
translated).

Weaving models [39] can be defined by mapping the concepts of SML+ into
the corresponding concepts of a concrete modeling language (as done in [40]
for different purposes, though). Weaving models represent useful instruments
in software modeling, as they can be used for setting fine-grained relationships
between models or metamodels and for executing operations based on the link
semantics.

Figure 19 depicts how weaving models define the correspondences among two
metamodels, hence the concepts in SML+ can be mapped on those of a concrete
notation (e.g. UML and MARTE profile).

The benefit of weaving models is that they can be used in automated transformations to generate other artifacts. In fact it is possible to define high-
order transformations that, starting from the weaving models, can generate
metamodel-specific transformations that allow to embed the antipatterns in an
actual concrete modeling language.

Figure 20 shows how to automatically generate antipatterns models in concrete modeling languages with the usage of weaving models. The metamodel we
propose for antipatterns is PAML containing SML+ (box $PAML[SML+]_{MM}$).
Performance antipatterns are defined as models conform to the PAML metamodel (box $PAML[SML+]_M$). Antipatterns models in concrete modeling languages can be automatically generated by using the high-order transformation T
that takes as input the weaving model WM specifying correspondences between
$SML+$ and a concrete notation (e.g. $UML+MARTE$) metamodel. Hence, performance antipatterns in UML+MARTE are defined as models (box $PAML[UML+$
$MARTE]_M$) conform to the PAML metamodel containing UML+MARTE (box
$PAML[UML + MARTE]_{MM}$).

A first experimentation in this setting has been conducted in UML+MARTE
where antipatterns can be naturally expressed by means of OCL [41] expressions,
i.e. model queries with diagrammatic notations that correspond to first-order
predicates.

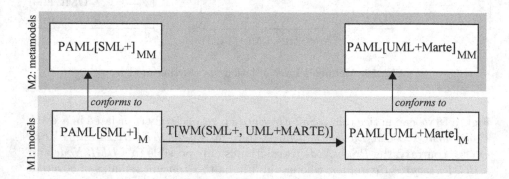

Fig. 20. Weaving model over different software modeling languages

Figure 21 shows the process that gives to each antipattern model an OCL-based semantics, in a similar way to [42], and OCL detection code can be automatically generated from the antipattern specification. The leftmost part of the Figure 21 reports again the PAML metamodel (box $PAML[UML + MARTE]_{MM}$) and antipatterns models (box $PAML[UML + MARTE]_M$) defined in the UML+MARTE concrete modeling notation. Firstly, antipatterns models are translated into intermediate models (box OCL_M) conforming to the OCL metamodel (box OCL_{MM}) with a model-to-model transformation. The *OCL code* is generated by using a model-to-text transformation, and it is used to check software model elements, thus to actually perform the antipattern detection. Note that the PAML metamodel provides semantics in terms of OCL: a semantic anchoring [43] is realized by means of automated transformations that map each antipattern model to an OCL expression.

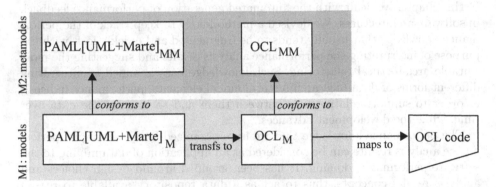

Fig. 21. Tranforming PAML-based models in OCL code

5.3 Afterthoughts

The benefits of introducing a metamodel for representing antipatterns are manifold: (i) *expressiveness*, as it currently contains all the concepts needed to specify performance antipatterns introduced in [10]; (ii) *usability*, as it allows a user-friendly representation of (existing and upcoming) performance antipatterns; (iii) *extensibility*, i.e., if new antipatterns are based on additional concepts the metamodel can be extended to introduce such concepts.

Note that the set of the antipatterns can be enlarged as far as the concepts for representing new ones are available. Technology-specific antipatterns, such as EJB and J2EE antipatterns [44] [45], can be also suited to check if the current metamodel is reusable in domain-specific fields. For example, we retain that the EJB Bloated Session Bean Antipattern [44] can be currently specified as a PAML-based model, since it describes a situation in EJB systems where a session bean has become too bulky, thus it is very similar to the Blob antipattern in the Smith-Williams' classification.

Currently PAML only formalizes the performance problems captured by antipatterns. As future work we plan to complete PAML with a Refactoring Modeling Language (RML) for formalizing the solutions in terms of refactorings, i.e. changes of the original software architectural model. Such formalization may be supported by high order transformations (similarly to what done for problems) that express the refactoring in concrete modeling languages.

The problem of refactoring architectural models is intrinsically complex and requires specialized algorithms and notations to match the abstraction level of models [46]. Recently, in [47, 48] two similar techniques have been introduced to represent refactorings as difference models. Interestingly these proposals combine the advantages of declarative difference representations and enable the reconstruction of the final model by means of automated transformations which are inherently defined in the approaches.

6   Discussion and Conclusions

In this chapter we dealt with the automated generation of performance feedback in software architectures. We devised a methodology to keep track of the performance knowledge that usually tends to be fragmented and quickly lost, with the purpose of interpreting the performance analysis results and suggesting the most suitable architectural refactoring. Such knowledge base is aimed at integrating different forms of data (e.g. architectural model elements, performance indices), in order to support relationships between them and to manage the data over time, while the development advances.

The performance knowledge that we have organized for reasoning on performance analysis results can be considered as an application of data mining to the software performance domain. It has been grouped around design choices and analysis results concepts, thus to act as a data repository available to reason on the performance of a software system. Performance antipatterns have been of crucial relevance in this context since they represent the source of the concepts to identify performance flaws as well as to provide refactorings in terms of architectural alternatives.

6.1   Summary of Contributions

A list of the main scientific contributions is given in the following.

Specifying Performance Antipatterns. The activity of *specifying antipatterns* has been addressed in [15]: a structured description of the system elements that occur in the definition of antipatterns has been provided, and performance antipatterns have been modeled as logical predicates. Additionally, in [15] the operational counterpart of the antipattern declarative definitions as logical predicates has been implemented with a java rule-engine application. Such engine was able to detect performance antipatterns in an XML representation of the software system that grouped the software architectural model and the performance results data.

A Model-Driven Approach for Antipatterns. A Performance Antipattern Modeling Language (PAML), i.e. a metamodel specifically tailored to describe antipatterns, has been introduced in [14]. Antipatterns are represented as PAML-based models allows to manipulate their (neutral) specification. In fact in [14, 49] it has been also discussed a vision on how model-driven techniques (e.g. weaving models [39], difference models [47]) can be used to build a notation-independent approach that addresses the problem of embedding antipatterns knowledge across different modeling notations.

Detecting and Solving Antipatterns in UML and PCM. The activities of *detecting* and *solving antipatterns* have been currently implemented by defining the antipattern rules and actions into two modeling languages: (i) the UML and MARTE profile notation in [50]; (ii) the PCM notation in [51]. In [50] performance antipatterns have been automatically detected in UML models using OCL [41] queries, but we have not yet automated their solution. In [51] a limited set of antipatterns has been automatically detected and solved in PCM models through a benchmark tool. These experiences led us to investigate the expressiveness of UML and PCM modeling languages by classifying the antipatterns in three categories: (i) detectable and solvable; (ii) semi-solvable (i.e. the antipattern solution is only achieved with refactoring actions to be manually performed); (iii) neither detectable nor solvable.

A Step Ahead in the Antipatterns Solution. Instead of blindly moving among the antipattern solutions without eventually achieving the desired results, a technique to rank the antipatterns on the basis of their guiltiness for violated requirements has been defined in [52] [36], thus to decide how many antipatterns to solve, which ones and in what order. Experimental results demonstrated the benefits of introducing ranking techniques to support the activity of solving antipatterns.

6.2 Open Issues and Future Work

There are several open issues in the current version of the framework and many directions can be identified for future work.

6.2.1 Short/Medium Term Issues

Further Validation. The approach has to be more extensively validated in order to determine the extent to which it can offer support to user activities. The validation of the approach includes two dimensions: (i) it has to be exposed to a set of target users, such as graduate students in a software engineering course, model-driven developers, more or less experienced software architects, in order to analyze its scope and usability; (ii) it has to be applied to complex case studies by involving industry partners, in order to analyze its scalability. Such experimentation is of worth interest because the final purpose is to integrate the framework in the daily practices of the software development process.

Both the detection and the solution of antipatterns generate some pending issues that give rise to short term goals.

The detection of antipatterns presents the following open issues:

Accuracy of Antipatterns Instances. The detection process may introduce false positive/negative instances of antipatterns. We outlined some sources to suitably tune the values of antipatterns boundaries, such as: (i) the system requirements; (ii) the domain expert's knowledge; (iii) the evaluation of the system under analysis. However, threshold values inevitably introduce a degree of uncertainty and extensive experimentation must be done in this direction. Some fuzziness can be introduced for the evaluation of the threshold values [53]. It might be useful to make antipattern detection rules more flexible, and to detect the performance flaws with higher/lower accuracy.

Some metrics are usually used to estimate the efficiency of design patterns detection, such as *precision* (i.e. measuring what fraction of detected pattern occurrences are real) and *recall* (i.e. measuring what fraction of real occurrences are detected). Such metrics do not apply for antipatterns because usually negative patterns are not explicitly documented in projects' specifications, due to their nature of revealing bad practices. A confidence value can be associated to an antipattern to quantify the probability that the formula occurrence corresponds to the antipattern presence.

Relationship between Antipatterns Instances. The detected instances might be related to each other, e.g. one instance can be the generalization or the specialization of another instance. A dependence value can be associated to an antipattern to quantify the probability that its occurrence is dependent from other antipatterns presence.

The solution of antipatterns presents the following open issues:

No Guarantee of Performance Improvements. The solution of one or more antipatterns does not guarantee performance improvements in advance: the entire process is based on heuristics evaluations. Applying a refactoring action results in a new software architectural model, i.e. a candidate whose performance analysis will reveal if the action has been actually beneficial for the system under study. However, an antipattern-based refactoring action is usually a correctness-preserving transformation that does not alter the semantics of the application, but it may improve the overall performance.

Dependencies of Performance Requirements. The application of antipattern solutions leads the system to (probably) satisfy the performance requirements covered by such solutions. However, it may happen that a certain number of other requirements get worse. Hence, the new candidate architectural model must take into account at each stage of the process all the requirements, also the previously satisfied ones.

Conflict between Antipattern Solutions. The solution of a certain number of antipatterns cannot be unambiguously applied due to incoherencies among their solutions. It may happen that the solution of one antipattern suggests to split a component into three finer grain components, while another antipattern at the same time suggests to merge the original component with another one.

These two actions obviously contradict each other, although no pre-existing requirement limits their application. Even in cases of no explicit conflict between antipattern solutions, coherency problems can be raised from the order of application of solutions. In fact the result of the sequential application of two (or more) antipattern solutions is not guaranteed to be invariant with respect to the application order. Criteria must be introduced to drive the application order of solutions in these cases. An interesting possibility may be represented by the *critical pairs analysis* [54] that provides a mean to avoid conflicting and divergent refactorings.

6.2.2   Long Term Issues

Lack of Model Parameters. The application of the antipattern-based approach is not limited (in principle) along the software lifecycle, but it is obvious that an early usage is subject to lack of information because the system knowledge improves while the development process progresses. Both the architectural and the performance models may lack of parameters needed to apply the process. For example, internal indices of subsystems that are not yet designed in details cannot be collected. Lack of information, or even uncertainty, about model parameter values can be tackled by analyzing the model piecewise, starting from sub-models, thus to bring insight on the missing parameters.

Influence of Domain Features. Different cross-cutting concerns such as the workload, the operational profile, etc. usually give rise to different performance analysis results that, in turn, may result in different antipatterns identified in the system. This is a critical issue and, as usually in performance analysis experiments, the choice of the workload(s) and operational profile(s) must be carefully conducted.

Influence of Other Software Layers. We assume that the performance model only takes into account the (annotated) software architectural model that usually contains information on the software application and hardware platform. Between these two layers there are other components, such as different middlewares and operating systems, that can embed performance antipatterns. The approach shall be extended to these layers for a more accurate analysis of the system. An option can be to integrate benchmarks or models suitable for these layers in our framework.

Limitations from Requirements. The application of antipattern solutions can be restricted by functional or non-functional requirements. Example of functional requirements may be legacy components that cannot be split and redeployed whereas the antipattern solution consists of these actions. Example of non-functional requirements may be budget limitations that do not allow to adopt an antipattern solution due to its extremely high cost. Many other examples can be provided of requirements that (implicitly or explicitly) may affect the antipattern solution activity. For sake of automation such requirements should be pre-defined so that the whole process can take into account them and preventively excluding infeasible solutions.

Consolidated Formalization of Performance Antipatterns. The Performance Antipatterns Modeling Language (PAML) currently only formalizes the performance problems captured by antipatterns. As future work we plan to complete PAML with a Refactoring Modeling Language (RML) for formalizing the solutions in terms of refactorings, i.e. changes of the original software architectural model.

Note that the formalization of antipatterns reflects our interpretation of the informal literature. Different formalizations of antipatterns can be originated by laying on different interpretations. This unavoidable gap is an open issue in this domain, and certainly requires a wider investigation to consolidate the formal definition of antipatterns. Logical predicates of antipatterns can be further refined by looking at probabilistic model checking techniques, as experimented in [55].

Architectural Description Languages. The framework is currently considering two modeling notations: UML and PCM. In general, the subset of target modeling languages can be enlarged as far as the concepts for representing antipatterns are available; for example, architectural description languages such as AADL [56] can be also suited to validate the approach. A first investigation has been already conducted on how to specify, detect, and solve performance antipatterns in the Æmilia architectural language [38], however it still requires a deep experimentation.

Multi-objective Goals. The framework currently considers only the performance goals of software systems. It can be extended to other quantitative quality criteria of software architectures such as reliability, security, etc., thus to support trade-off decisions between multiple quality criteria.

Acknowledgments. This work has been partially supported by VISION ERC project (ERC-240555).

References

1. Smith, C.U., Millsap, C.V.: Software performance engineering for oracle applications: Measurements and models. In: Int. CMG Conference, Computer Measurement Group, pp. 331–342 (2008)
2. Williams, L.G., Smith, C.U.: Software performance engineering: A tutorial introduction. In: Int. CMG Conference, Computer Measurement Group, pp. 387–398 (2007)
3. Smith, C.U.: Introduction to Software Performance Engineering: Origins and Outstanding Problems. In: Bernardo, M., Hillston, J. (eds.) SFM 2007. LNCS, vol. 4486, pp. 395–428. Springer, Heidelberg (2007)
4. Mens, T., Tourwé, T.: A survey of software refactoring. IEEE Trans. Software Eng. 30, 126–139 (2004)

5. Woodside, C.M., Franks, G., Petriu, D.C.: The Future of Software Performance Engineering. In: Briand, L.C., Wolf, A.L. (eds.) FOSE, pp. 171–187 (2007)
6. Balsamo, S., Di Marco, A., Inverardi, P., Simeoni, M.: Model-Based Performance Prediction in Software Development: A Survey. IEEE Trans. Software Eng. 30, 295–310 (2004)
7. Cortellessa, V., Di Marco, A., Inverardi, P.: Model-Based Software Performance Analysis. Springer (2011)
8. Koziolek, H.: Performance evaluation of component-based software systems: A survey. Perform. Eval. 67, 634–658 (2010)
9. Woodside, C.M., Petriu, D.C., Petriu, D.B., Shen, H., Israr, T., Merseguer, J.: Performance by unified model analysis (PUMA). In: WOSP, pp. 1–12. ACM (2005)
10. Smith, C.U., Williams, L.G.: More New Software Antipatterns: Even More Ways to Shoot Yourself in the Foot. In: International Computer Measurement Group Conference, pp. 717–725 (2003)
11. Williams, L.G., Smith, C.U.: PASA(SM): An Architectural Approach to Fixing Software Performance Problems. In: International Computer Measurement Group Conference, Computer Measurement Group, pp. 307–320 (2002)
12. Cortellessa, V., Frittella, L.: A Framework for Automated Generation of Architectural Feedback from Software Performance Analysis. In: Wolter, K. (ed.) EPEW 2007. LNCS, vol. 4748, pp. 171–185. Springer, Heidelberg (2007)
13. Parsons, T., Murphy, J.: Detecting Performance Antipatterns in Component Based Enterprise Systems. Journal of Object Technology 7, 55–91 (2008)
14. Cortellessa, V., Di Marco, A., Eramo, R., Pierantonio, A., Trubiani, C.: Approaching the Model-Driven Generation of Feedback to Remove Software Performance Flaws. In: EUROMICRO-SEAA, pp. 162–169. IEEE Computer Society (2009)
15. Cortellessa, V., Di Marco, A., Trubiani, C.: Performance Antipatterns as Logical Predicates. In: Calinescu, R., Paige, R.F., Kwiatkowska, M.Z. (eds.) ICECCS, pp. 146–156. IEEE Computer Society (2010)
16. Barber, K.S., Graser, T.J., Holt, J.: Enabling Iterative Software Architecture Derivation Using Early Non-Functional Property Evaluation. In: ASE, pp. 172–182. IEEE Computer Society (2002)
17. Dobrzanski, L., Kuzniarz, L.: An approach to refactoring of executable UML models. In: Haddad, H. (ed.) ACM Symposium on Applied Computing (SAC), pp. 1273–1279. ACM (2006)
18. McGregor, J.D., Bachmann, F., Bass, L., Bianco, P., Klein, M.: Using arche in the classroom: One experience. Technical Report CMU/SEI-2007-TN-001, Software Engineering Institute, Carnegie Mellon University (2007)
19. Kavimandan, A., Gokhale, A.: Applying Model Transformations to Optimizing Real-Time QoS Configurations in DRE Systems. In: Mirandola, R., Gorton, I., Hofmeister, C. (eds.) QoSA 2009. LNCS, vol. 5581, pp. 18–35. Springer, Heidelberg (2009)
20. Object Management Group (OMG): Lightweight CCM RFP. OMG Document realtime/02-11-27 (2002)
21. Xu, J.: Rule-based automatic software performance diagnosis and improvement. Perform. Eval. 67, 585–611 (2010)
22. Zheng, T., Woodside, M.: Heuristic Optimization of Scheduling and Allocation for Distributed Systems with Soft Deadlines. In: Kemper, P., Sanders, W.H. (eds.) TOOLS 2003. LNCS, vol. 2794, pp. 169–181. Springer, Heidelberg (2003)
23. Bondarev, E., Chaudron, M.R.V., de Kock, E.A.: Exploring performance trade-offs of a JPEG decoder using the deepcompass framework. In: International Workshop on Software and Performance, pp. 153–163 (2007)

24. Ipek, E., McKee, S.A., Singh, K., Caruana, R., de Supinski, B.R., Schulz, M.: Efficient architectural design space exploration via predictive modeling. ACM Transactions on Architecture and Code Optimization (TACO) 4 (2008)
25. Canfora, G., Penta, M.D., Esposito, R., Villani, M.L.: An approach for QoS-aware service composition based on genetic algorithms. In: Beyer, H.G., O'Reilly, U.M. (eds.) GECCO, pp. 1069–1075. ACM (2005)
26. Aleti, A., Björnander, S., Grunske, L., Meedeniya, I.: ArcheOpterix: An extendable tool for architecture optimization of AADL models. In: ICSE Workshop on Model-Based Methodologies for Pervasive and Embedded Software, pp. 61–71 (2009)
27. Martens, A., Koziolek, H., Becker, S., Reussner, R.: Automatically improve software architecture models for performance, reliability, and cost using evolutionary algorithms. In: WOSP/SIPEW International Conference on Performance Engineering, pp. 105–116 (2010)
28. Petriu, D.C., Shen, H.: Applying the UML Performance Profile: Graph Grammar-Based Derivation of LQN Models from UML Specifications. In: Field, T., Harrison, P.G., Bradley, J., Harder, U. (eds.) TOOLS 2002. LNCS, vol. 2324, pp. 159–177. Springer, Heidelberg (2002)
29. Feiler, P.H., Gluch, D.P., Hudak, J.J.: The Architecture Analysis and Design Language (AADL): An Introduction. Technical Report CMU/SEI-2006-TN-001, Software Engineering Institute, Carnegie Mellon University (2006)
30. Trubiani, C.: Automated generation of architectural feedback from software performance analysis results. PhD thesis, University of L'Aquila (2011)
31. Woodside, C.M.: A Three-View Model for Performance Engineering of Concurrent Software. IEEE Transactions on Software Engineering (TSE) 21, 754–767 (1995)
32. Object Management Group (OMG): UML 2.0 Superstructure Specification. OMG Document formal/05-07-04 (2005)
33. Object Management Group (OMG): UML Profile for MARTE. OMG Document formal/08-06-09 (2009)
34. Cortellessa, V., Mirandola, R.: PRIMA-UML: a performance validation incremental methodology on early UML diagrams. Sci. Comput. Program. 44, 101–129 (2002)
35. Jain, R.: The Art of Computer Systems Performance Analysis: Techniques for Experimental Design, Measurement, Simulation, and Modeling. SIGMETRICS Performance Evaluation Review 19, 5–11 (1991)
36. Cortellessa, V., Martens, A., Reussner, R., Trubiani, C.: A Process to Effectively Identify "Guilty" Performance Antipatterns. In: Rosenblum, D.S., Taentzer, G. (eds.) FASE 2010. LNCS, vol. 6013, pp. 368–382. Springer, Heidelberg (2010)
37. Becker, S., Koziolek, H., Reussner, R.: The Palladio component model for model-driven performance prediction. Journal of Systems and Software 82, 3–22 (2009)
38. Bernardo, M., Donatiello, L., Ciancarini, P.: Stochastic Process Algebra: From an Algebraic Formalism to an Architectural Description Language. In: Calzarossa, M.C., Tucci, S. (eds.) Performance 2002. LNCS, vol. 2459, pp. 236–260. Springer, Heidelberg (2002)
39. Bézivin, J.: On the unification power of models. Software and System Modeling 4, 171–188 (2005)
40. Malavolta, I., Muccini, H., Pelliccione, P., Tamburri, D.A.: Providing Architectural Languages and Tools Interoperability through Model Transformation Technologies. IEEE Trans. Software Eng. 36, 119–140 (2010)
41. Object Management Group (OMG): OCL 2.0 Specification. OMG Document formal/2006-05-01 (2006)

42. Stein, D., Hanenberg, S., Unland, R.: A Graphical Notation to Specify Model Queries for MDA Transformations on UML Models. In: Aßmann, U., Aksit, M., Rensink, A. (eds.) MDAFA 2003. LNCS, vol. 3599, pp. 77–92. Springer, Heidelberg (2005)
43. Chen, K., Sztipanovits, J., Abdelwalhed, S., Jackson, E.: Semantic Anchoring with Model Transformations. In: Hartman, A., Kreische, D. (eds.) ECMDA-FA 2005. LNCS, vol. 3748, pp. 115–129. Springer, Heidelberg (2005)
44. Dudney, B., Asbury, S., Krozak, J.K., Wittkopf, K.: J2EE Antipatterns (2003)
45. Tate, B., Clark, M., Lee, B., Linskey, P.: Bitter EJB (2003)
46. Lin, Y., Zhang, J., Gray, J.: Model Comparison: A Key Challenge for Transformation Testing and Version Control in Model Driven Software Development. In: OOPSLA Workshop on Best Practices for Model-Driven Software Development (2004)
47. Cicchetti, A., Di Ruscio, D., Pierantonio, A.: A Metamodel Independent Approach to Difference Representation. Journal of Object Technology 6, 165–185 (2007)
48. Rivera, J.E., Vallecillo, A.: Representing and Operating with Model Differences. In: International Conference on TOOLS, pp. 141–160 (2008)
49. Trubiani, C.: A Model-Based Framework for Software Performance Feedback. In: Dingel, J., Solberg, A. (eds.) MODELS 2010 Workshops. LNCS, vol. 6627, pp. 19–34. Springer, Heidelberg (2011)
50. Cortellessa, V., Di Marco, A., Eramo, R., Pierantonio, A., Trubiani, C.: Digging into UML models to remove performance antipatterns. In: ICSE Workshop Quovadis, pp. 9–16 (2010)
51. Trubiani, C., Koziolek, A.: Detection and solution of software performance antipatterns in palladio architectural models. In: International Conference on Performance Engineering (ICPE), pp. 19–30 (2011)
52. Cortellessa, V., Martens, A., Reussner, R., Trubiani, C.: Towards the identification of "Guilty" performance antipatterns. In: WOSP/SIPEW International Conference on Performance Engineering, pp. 245–246 (2010)
53. So, S.S., Cha, S.D., Kwon, Y.R.: Empirical evaluation of a fuzzy logic-based software quality prediction model. Fuzzy Sets and Systems 127, 199–208 (2002)
54. Mens, T., Taentzer, G., Runge, O.: Detecting Structural Refactoring Conflicts Using Critical Pair Analysis. Electr. Notes Theor. Comput. Sci. 127, 113–128 (2005)
55. Grunske, L.: Specification patterns for probabilistic quality properties. In: Schäfer, W., Dwyer, M.B., Gruhn, V. (eds.) ICSE, pp. 31–40. ACM (2008)
56. Feiler, P.H., Lewis, B.A., Vestal, S.: SAE, Architecture Analysis and Design Language (AADL), as5506/1 (2006), http://www.sae.org

An Introduction to Model Versioning*

Petra Brosch[1], Gerti Kappel[1], Philip Langer[1],
Martina Seidl[2], Konrad Wieland[3], and Manuel Wimmer[4]

[1] Vienna University of Technology, Austria
{brosch,gerti,langer}@big.tuwien.ac.at
[2] Johannes Kepler University Linz, Austria
martina.seidl@jku.at
[3] LieberLieber Software GmbH, Austria
konrad.wieland@lieberlieber.com
[4] Universidad de Málaga, Spain
mw@lcc.uma.es

Abstract. With the emergence of model-driven engineering (MDE), *software models* are considered as central artifacts in the software engineering process, going beyond their traditional use as sketches. In MDE, models rather act as the single source of information for automatically generating executable software. This shift poses several new research challenges. One of these challenges constitutes *model versioning*, which targets at enabling efficient team-based development of models. This compelling challenge induced a very active research community, who yielded remarkable methods and techniques ranging from model differencing to merging of models.

In this tutorial, we give an introduction to the foundations of model versioning, the underlying technologies for processing models and their evolution, as well as the state of the art in model versioning. Thereby, we aim at equipping students and researchers alike that are new to this domain with enough information for commencing to contribute to this challenging research area.

1 Introduction

Since the emergence of *software engineering* [72,94], researchers and practitioners have been struggling to cope with the ever growing *complexity* and *size* of the developed systems. One way of coping with the complexity of a system has been raising the level of abstraction in the languages used to specify a system. Besides dealing with the complexity of software systems under development, also managing the size of software systems constitutes a major challenge. As stated by Ghezzi et al., "software engineering deals with the building of software systems that are so large or so complex that they are built by teams of engineers" [37].

---

* This work has been funded by the Vienna Science and Technology Fund (WWTF) through project ICT10-018, by the Austrian Science Fund (FWF) under grant J 3159-N23, and by the fFORTE WIT Program of the Vienna University of Technology and the Austrian Federal Ministry of Science and Research.

M. Bernardo, V. Cortellessa, and A. Pierantonio (Eds.): SFM 2012, LNCS 7320, pp. 336–398, 2012.

Orthogonal to the challenge entailed by the complexity and size of software systems, dealing with the demand to constantly *evolve* a system in order to meet ever changing requirements constitutes an additional major challenge. To summarize, Parnas defines software engineering as the "multi-person construction of multi-version software" [92].

Model-driven engineering (MDE) has been proposed as a new paradigm for raising the level of abstraction [7,38,98]. In MDE, softare models are considered as central artifacts in the software engineering process, going beyond their traditional use as sketches and blueprints. Models constitute the basis and the single source of information to specify and automatically generate an executable system. Thereby, developers may build models that are less bound to an underlying implementation technology and are much closer to the problem domain [103]. However, the emergence of this shift from code to models poses several new research challenges. One of these challenges is to cope with the ever growing *size* of systems being built in practice [34]. Developing a large system entails the need for a large number of developers who collaborate to succeed in creating a large system. Thus, adequate support for *team-based development of models* is a crucial prerequisite for the success of MDE. Therefore, as in traditional code-centric software engineering, *versioning systems* [18,66] are required, which allow for concurrent modification of the same model by several developers and which are capable of merging the operations applied by all developers to obtain ultimately one consolidated version of a model again.

In traditional code-centric software engineering, text-based versioning systems, such as Git[1], Subversion[2], and CVS[3], have been successfully deployed to allow for collaborative development of large software systems. To enable *collaborative modeling* among several team members, such text-based versioning systems have been reused for models. Unfortunately, it turned out quickly that applying text-based versioning is inadequate for models and leads to unsatisfactory results [2]. This is because such versioning systems consider only text lines in a text-based representation of a model as, for instance, the XMI serializations [81]. As a result, the information stemming from the model's graph-based structure is destroyed and associated syntactic information is lost. To overcome these drawbacks of text-based versioning systems used for models, dedicated *model versioning* approaches have been proposed recently. Such approaches do not operate on the textual representation; instead, they work directly on the model's graph-based structure.

Especially *optimistic versioning systems* gained remarkable popularity because they enable several developers to work concurrently on the same artifacts instead of pessimistically locking each artifact for the time it is changed by one developer. The price to pay for being able to work in parallel is that the concurrently applied operations of all developers have to be merged again. Therefore, the *versioning process* depicted in Fig. 1 is applied, which is referred to

---

[1] http://git-scm.com

[2] http://subversion.tigris.org

[3] http://cvs.nongnu.org

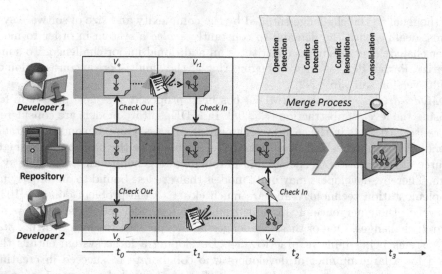

Fig. 1. Versioning Process

as *check-out/check-in protocol* [30]. Developers may concurrently check-out the latest version V_o of a model from a common repository at the time of t_0 (cf. Fig. 1). Thereby, a local working copy of V_o is created. Both developers may independently modify their working copies in parallel. As soon as one developer completes the work, assume this is developer 1, she performs a check-in at t_1. Because no other developer performed a check-in in the meanwhile, her working copy can be saved directly as a new revised version V_{r1} in the repository. Whenever developer 2 completes his task and performs the check-in, the versioning system recognizes that a new version has been created since the check-out. Therefore, the merge process is triggered at t_2 in order to merge the new version V_{r1} in the repository with the version V_{r2} by developer 2. Once the merge is carried out, the resulting merged version incorporating the operations of developer 1 and developer 2 is saved in the repository.

In this tutorial, we give an introduction to the underlying technologies for realizing this versioning process to allow for merging concurrently modified models. Therefore, we discuss the foundations of versioning in Section 2 and introduce the prerequisites for building a model versioning system in Section 3. Subsequently, we review the state of the art in model versioning in Section 4 and present our own model versioning system AMOR in Section 5. Finally, we conclude this tutorial with some challenging topics for future research in the domain of model versioning in Section 6.

2   Foundations of Versioning

The history of versioning in software engineering goes back to the early 1970s. Since then, software versioning was constantly an active research topic. As stated by Estublier et al. in [30], the goal of software versioning systems is twofold. First, such systems are concerned with maintaining a historical archive of a set of artifacts as they undergo a series of operations and form the fundamental building block for the entire field of Source Configuration Management (SCM), which deals with controlling change in large and complex software systems. Second, versioning systems aim at managing the evolution of software artifacts performed by a distributed team of developers.

In that long history of research on software versioning, diverse formalisms and technologies emerged. To categorize this variety of different approaches, Conradi and Westfechtel [18] proposed *version models* describing the diverse characteristics of existing versioning approaches. A version model specifies the objects to be versioned, version identification and organization, as well as operations for retrieving existing versions and constructing new versions. Conradi and Westfechtel distinguish between the *product space* and the *version space* within version models. The product space describes the structure of a software product and its artifacts without taking versions into account. In contrast, the version space is agnostic of the artifacts' structure and copes with the artifacts' evolution by introducing versions and relationships between versions of an artifact, such as, for instance, their differences (deltas). Further, Conradi and Westfechtel distinguish between extensional and intentional versioning. *Extensional versioning* deals with the reconstruction of previously created versions and, therefore, concerns version identification, immutability, and efficient storage. All versions are explicit and have been checked in once before. *Intentional versioning* deals with flexible automatic construction of consistent versions from a version space. In other words, intentional versioning allows for annotating properties to specific versions and querying the version space for these properties in order to derive a new product consisting of a specific combination of different versions.

In this paper, we only consider extensional versioning in terms of having explicit versions, because this kind of versioning is predominantly applied in practice nowadays. Furthermore, we focus on the *merge phase* in the optimistic versioning process (cf. Fig. 1). In this section, we outline the fundamental design dimensions of versioning systems and elaborate on the consequences of different design decisions concerning the quality of the merge based on an example.

2.1 Fundamental Design Dimensions for Versioning Systems

Current approaches to merging two versions of one software artifact (software models or source code) can be categorized according to two basic dimensions. The first dimension concerns the product space, in particular, the *artifact representation*. This dimension denotes the representation of a software artifact, on which the merge approach operates. The used representation may either be *text-based* or *graph-based*. Some merge approaches operate on a tree-based representation. However, we consider a tree as a special kind of graph in this categorization. The second dimension is orthogonal to the first one and concerns how deltas are *identified*, *represented*, and *merged* in order to create a consolidated version. Existing merge approaches either operate on the *states*; that is, the versions of an artifact, or on identified operations that have been applied between a common origin model (cf. V_o in Fig. 1) and the two successors (cf. V_{r1} and V_{r2} in Fig. 1).

When merging two concurrently modified versions of a software artifact, conflicts might inevitably occur. The most basic types of conflicts are *update-update* and *delete-update* conflicts. Update-update conflicts occur if two elements have been updated in both versions whereas delete-update conflicts are raised if an element has been updated in one version and deleted in the other (cf. [66] for more information on software merging in general).

Text-based merge approaches operate solely on the textual representation of a software artifact in terms of text files. Within a text file, the atomic unit of the versioned text file may either be a paragraph, a line, a word, or even an arbitrary set of characters. The major advantage of such approaches is their independence of the programming languages used in the versioned artifacts. Since a solely text-based approach does not require language-specific knowledge it may be adopted for all flat text files. This advantage is probably, besides simplicity and efficiency, the reason for the widespread adoption of pure text-based approaches in practice. However, when merging flat files—agnostic of the syntax and semantics of a programming language—both compile-time and run-time errors might be introduced during the merge. Therefore, graph-based approaches emerged, which take syntax and semantics into account.

Graph-based merge approaches operate on a graph-based representation of a software artifact for achieving more precise conflict detection and merging. Such approaches de-serialize or translate the versioned software artifact into a specific structure before merging. Mens [66] categorized these approaches in *syntactic* and *semantic merge approaches*. Syntactic merge approaches consider the syntax of a programming language by, for instance, translating the text file into the abstract syntax tree and, subsequently, performing the merge in a syntax-aware manner. Consequently, unimportant textual conflicts, which are, for instance, caused by reformatting the text file, may be avoided. Furthermore, such approaches may also avoid syntactically erroneous merge results. However, the textual formatting intended by the developers might be obfuscated by syntactic merging because only a graph-based representation of the syntax is merged and has to be translated back to text eventually. Westfechtel was among the first to propose a merging algorithm that operates on the abstract syntax tree of a software artifact [116]. Semantic merge approaches go one step further and consider also the static and/or dynamic semantics of a programming language. Therefore, these approaches may also detect issues, such as undeclared variables or even infinite loops by using complex formalisms like program dependency graphs and program slicing. Naturally, these advantages over flat textual merging have the disadvantage of the inherent language dependence (cf. [66]) and their increased computational complexity.

The second dimension for categorizing versioning systems is orthogonal to the first one and considers *how deltas are identified and merged* in order to create a consolidated version. This dimension is agnostic of the unit of versioning.

Therefore, a versioned element might be a line in a flat text file, a node in a graph, or whatsoever constitutes the representation used for merging.

State-based merging compares the states (i.e., versions) of a software artifact to identify the differences (deltas) between these versions and merge all differences that are not contradicting with each other. Such approaches may either be applied to two states (V_{r1} and V_{r2} in Fig. 1), called two-way merging, or to three states (including their common ancestor V_o in Fig. 1), called three-way merging. Two-way merging cannot identify deletions since the common original state is unknown. A state-based comparison requires a match function which determines whether two elements of the compared artifact correspond to each other. The easiest way to match two elements is to search for completely equivalent elements. However, the quality of the match function is crucial for the overall quality of the merge approach. Therefore, especially graph-based merge approaches often use more sophisticated matching techniques based on identifiers and heuristics (cf. [47] for an overview of matching techniques). Model matching, or more generally the graph isomorphism problem is NP-hard [46] and, therefore, very computation intensive. If the match function is capable of matching also partially different elements, a difference function is additionally required to determine the fine-grained differences between two corresponding elements. Having these two functions, two states of the same artifact may be merged by using the following process. For each element in the common origin version V_o of a software artifact, the corresponding elements from the two modified versions V_{r1} and V_{r2} are retrieved. If in both versions V_{r1} and V_{r2} a corresponding element is available, the algorithm checks whether the matching element has been modified in the versions V_{r1} and V_{r2}. If this is true in one and only one of the two versions V_{r1} and V_{r2}, the modified element is used for creating the merged version. If, however, the matching element is different in *both versions*, an update-update conflict is raised by the algorithm. If the matching element has not been modified at all, the original element can be left as it is in the merged version. In case there is no corresponding element in one of the two modified versions (i.e., it has been removed), it is checked whether it has been concurrently modified in the opposite revision and raises, in this case, a delete-update conflict. If the element has not been concurrently modified, it is removed from the merged version. The element is also removed, if there is no corresponding element in both modified versions (i.e., it has been deleted in both versions). Finally, the algorithm adds all elements from V_{r1} and V_{r2} that have no corresponding element in the original version V_o, as they have been added in V_{r1} or V_{r2}.

Operation-based merging does not operate on the states of an artifact. Instead, the operation sequences which have been concurrently applied to the original version are recorded and analyzed. Since the operations are directly recorded by the applied editor, operation-based approaches may support, besides recording atomic operations, also to record composite operations, such as refactorings (e.g., [48]). The knowledge on applied refactorings may significantly increase the quality of the merge as stated by Dig et al. [22]. The downside of operation recording is the strong dependency on the applied editor, since it has to record each performed operation and it has to provide this operation sequence in a format which the merge approach is able to process. The directly recorded operation sequence might include obsolete operations, such as updates to an element which will be removed later on. Therefore, many operation-based approaches apply a cleansing algorithm to the recorded operation sequence for more efficient merging. The operations within the operation sequence might be interdependent because some of the operations cannot be applied until other operations have been applied. As soon as the operation sequences are available, operation-based approaches check parallel operation sequences (V_o to V_{r1} and V_o to V_{r2}) for commutativity to reveal conflicts [60]. Consequently, a decision procedure for commutativity is required. Such decision procedures are not necessarily trivial. In the simplest yet least efficient form, each pair of operations within the cross product of all atomic operations in both sequences are applied in both possible orders to the artifact and both results are checked for equality. If they are not equivalent, the operations are not commutative. After checking for commutativity, operation-based merge approaches apply all non-conflicting (commutative) operations of both sides to the common ancestor in order to obtain a merged model.

In comparison to state-based approaches, the recorded operation sequences are, in general, more precise and potentially allow for gathering more information (e.g., change order and refactorings), than state-based differencing; especially if the state-based approach does not rely on a precise matching technique. Moreover, state-based comparison approaches are—due to complex comparison algorithms—very expensive regarding their run-time in contrast to operation-based change recording. However, these advantages come at the price of strong editor-dependence. Nevertheless, operation-based approaches scale for large models from a conceptual point of view because their computational effort mainly depends on the length of the operation sequences and—in contrast to state-based approaches—not on the size of the models [48].

Anyhow, the border between state-based and operation-based merging is sometimes blurry. Indeed, we can clearly distinguish whether the operations are recorded or differences are derived from the states, nevertheless, some *state-based approaches* derive the *applied operations* from the states and use operation-based conflict detection techniques. However, this is only reasonable if a reliable matching function is available, for instance, using unique identifiers. On the contrary, some *operation-based approaches* derive the *states* from their operation sequences to check for potentially inconsistent states after merging. Such an inconsistent state might for instance be a violation of the syntactic rules of a language. Detecting such conflicts is often not possible by solely analyzing the operation sequences. Eventually, the conflict detection strategies conducted in state-based and operation-based approaches are very similar from a conceptual point of view. Both check for direct or indirect concurrent modifications to the same element and try to identify illegal states after merging, whether the modifications are explicitly given in terms of operations or whether they are implicitly derived from a match between two states.

2.2   Consequences of Design Decisions

To highlight the benefits and drawbacks of the four possible combinations of the
versioning approaches (text-based vs. graph-based and state-based vs. operation-
based), we present a small versioning example depicted in Fig. 2 and conceptually
apply each approach for analyzing its quality in terms of the detected conflicts
and derived merged version.

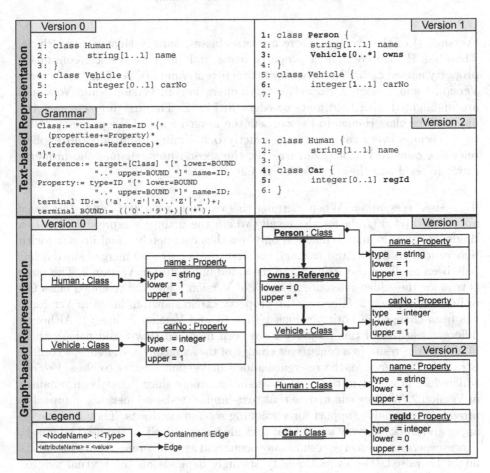

Fig. 2. Versioning Example

Consider a small language for specifying *classes*, its *properties*, and *references*
linking two classes. The textual representation of this language is depicted in the
upper left area of Fig. 2 and defined by the EBNF-like Xtext[4] grammar specified
in the box labeled *Grammar*. The same language and the same examples are
depicted in terms of graphs in the lower part of Fig. 2. In the initial version

---

[4] http://www.eclipse.org/Xtext

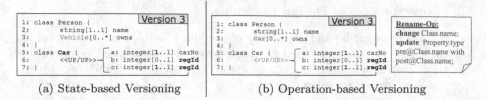

(a) State-based Versioning   (b) Operation-based Versioning

Fig. 3. Text-based Versioning Example

(Version 0) of the example, there are two classes, namely Human and Vehicle. The class Human contains a property name and the class Vehicle contains a property named carNo. Now, two users concurrently modify Version 0 and create Version 1 and Version 2, respectively. All operations in Version 1 and Version 2 are highlighted with bold fonts or edges in Fig. 2. The first user changes the name of the class Human to Person, sets the lower bound of the property carNo to 1 (because every car must have exactly one number) and adds an explicit reference owns to Person. Concurrently, the second user renames the property carNo to regId and the class Vehicle to Car.

Text-based versioning. When merging this example with *text- and state-based* approaches (cf. Fig. 3a for the result) where the artifact's representation is a single line and the match function only matches completely equal lines (as with Subversion, CVS, Git, and bazaar), the first line is correctly merged since it has only been modified in Version 1 and remained untouched in Version 2. The same is true for the added reference in line 3 of Version 1 and the renamed class Car in line 4 of Version 2. However, the property carNo shown in line 5 in Version 0 has been changed in both Versions 1 (line 6) and Version 2 (line 5). Although different features of this property have been modified (lower and name), these modifications result in a concurrent change of the same line and, hence, a conflict is raised. Furthermore, the reference added in Version 1 refers to class *Vehicle*, which does not exist in the merged version anymore since it has been renamed in Version 2. We may summarize that text- and state-based merging approaches provide a reasonable support for versioning software artifacts. They are easy to apply and work for every kind of flat text file irrespectively of the used language. However, erroneous merge results may occur and several "unnecessary" conflicts might be raised. The overall quality strongly depends on the textual syntax. Merging textual languages with a strict syntactic structure (such as XML) might be more appropriate than merging languages which mix several properties of potentially independent concepts into one line. The latter might cause tedious manual conflict and error resolution.

One major problem in the merged example resulting from text-based and state-based approaches is the wrong reference target (line 3 in Version 1) caused by the concurrent rename of Vehicle. *Operation-based approaches* (such as MolhadoRef) solve such an issue by incorporating knowledge on applied refactorings in the merge. Since a *rename* is a refactoring, MolhadoRef would be aware of

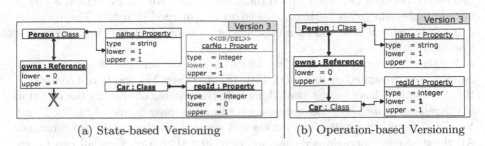

(a) State-based Versioning | (b) Operation-based Versioning

Fig. 4. Graph-based Versioning Example

the rename and resolve the issue by re-applying the rename after a traditional merge is done. The result of this merge is shown in Fig. 3b.

Graph-based versioning. Applying the merge on top of the *graph-based representation* depicted in Fig. 2 may also significantly improve the merge result because the representation used for merging is a node in a graph which more precisely represents the versioned software artifact. However, as already mentioned, this advantage comes at the price of language dependence because merging operates either on the language specific graph-based representation or a translation of a language to a generic graph-based structure must be available. *Graph- and state-based approaches* additionally require a match function for finding corresponding nodes and a difference function for explicating the differences between matched nodes. The preciseness of the match function significantly influences the quality of the overall merge. Assume matching is based on name and structure heuristics for the example in Fig. 2. Given this assumption, the class Human may be matched since it contains an unchanged property name. Therefore, renaming the class Human to Person can be merged without user intervention. However, heuristically matching the class Vehicle might be more challenging because both the class and its contained property have been renamed. If the match does not identify the correspondence between Vehicle and Car, Vehicle and its contained property carNo is considered to be removed and Car is assumed to be added in Version 2. Consequently, a delete-update conflict is reported for the change of the lower bound of the property carNo in Version 1. Also the added reference owns refers to a removed class which might be reported as conflict. This type of conflict is referred to as *delete-use* or *delete-reference* in literature [110,117]. If, in contrast, the match relies on unique identifiers, the nodes can soundly be matched. Based on this precise match, the state-based merge component can resolve this issue and the added reference owns correctly refers to the renamed class Car in the merged version. However, the concurrent modification of the property carNo (name and lower) might still be a problem because purely state-based approaches usually take either the entire element from either the left or the right version to construct the merged version. Some state-based approaches solve this issue by conducting a more fine-grained difference function to identify the detailed differences between two elements. If these differences are not overlapping—as in our example—they can both be applied to the merged element. The result of a graph-based and state-based merge without taking identifiers into account is visualized in Fig. 4a.

Purely *graph- and operation-based approaches* are capable of automatically merging the presented example (cf. Fig. 4b). Between Version 0 and Version 1, three operations have been recorded, namely the rename of Human, the addition of the reference owns and the update concerning the lower bound of carNo. To get Version 2 from Version 0, class Vehicle and property carNo have been renamed. All these atomic operations do not interfere and therefore, they all can be re-applied to Version 0 to obtain a correctly merged version.

In summary, a lot of research activity during the last decades in the domain of traditional source code versioning has lead to significant results. Approaches for merging *software models* draw a lot of inspiration from previous works in the area of *source code* merging. Especially graph-based approaches for source code merging form the foundation for model versioning. However, one major challenge still remains an open problem. The same trade-off as in traditional source code merging has to be made regarding editor- and language-independence versus preciseness and completeness. Model matching, comparison and merging, as discussed above, can significantly be improved by incorporating knowledge on the used modeling language, as well as language-specific composite operations, such as refactorings. On the other hand, model versioning approaches are also forced to support several languages at the same time, because even in small MDE projects several modeling languages are usually combined.

3   Five Steps towards Model Versioning

In this section, we survey the fundamental techniques for stepwise establishing versioning support for software models. Therefore, we introduce the basics of model-driven engineering, model transformations, model differencing, conflicts, and merging in the following.

3.1   Model-Driven Engineering

The idea of MDE is to automate the repetitive task of translating model based blueprints to code and enable developers to concentrate on creative and non-trivial tasks which computers cannot do, i.e., creating those blueprints [10]. Several techniques are indispensable for putting MDE into practice. In the following, we introduce a common framework for creating domain-specific modeling languages and models called *metamodeling*.

An early attempt towards MDE was made in the 1980s with computer-aided software engineering (CASE) tools, already following the goal to directly generate executable systems based on graphical domain-specific models [98]. As CASE tools were (1) costly to develop, and (2) only appropriate to certain domains, it was soon realized that the development of domain-specific environments was

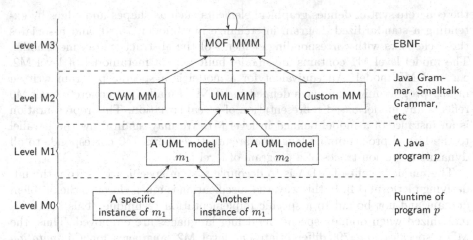

Fig. 5. Metamodeling Layers; adapted from [9]

itself a domain and metamodeling environments to create domain-specific environments were established [58,106,71]. In fact, the term *meta* denotes that an operation is applied on itself, e.g., a discussion about conducting a discussion is called meta-discussion [53]. In a similar vein, metamodeling is referred to modeling modeling languages.

In an endeavor to establish a commonly accepted set of key concepts and to preserve interoperability between the rapidly growing number of domain-specific development environments, the Object Management Group (OMG) released the specification for *Model Driven Architecture* (MDA) [79], standardizing the definition and usage of (meta-)metamodels as driving factor of software development. To this end, the OMG proposes a layered organization of the metamodeling stack similar to the architecture of formal programming languages [9], as depicted in Fig. 5. The meta-metamodel level M3 manifests the role of the *Meta-Object Facility* (MOF) [77] as the unique and self-defined metamodel for building metamodels, i.e., the meta-metamodel ensuring interoperability of any metamodel defined therewith. Every metamodel defined according OMG's proposed MDA standard share the same metatypes and may be reflectively analyzed. MOF may be compared to the Extended Backus-Naur Form (EBNF) [42], the metagrammar for expressing programming languages. The metamodel level M2 contains any metamodel defined with MOF, including the Unified Modeling Language (UML) [86], the Common Warehouse Metamodel (CWM) [76] also specified by the OMG, and any custom domain-specific metamodel. A metamodel at this level conforms to a definition of a programming language with EBNF, such as the Smalltalk grammar or the Java grammar. A metamodel defines the abstract syntax of the modeling language and is usually supplemented with one or more concrete syntactics. Though textual concrete syntactics get more and more popular, graphical concrete syntactics are more common. To leverage MOF's interoperability power also for the graphical visualization of models, a graphical concrete syntax is again defined as metamodel at level M2. The metamodel for the concrete syntax defines graphical elements such as shapes and edges by extending a standardized diagram interchange metamodel [75,80] and associates those elements with corresponding elements of the abstract syntax metamodel. The model level M1 contains any model built with a metamodel of level M2, e.g., a UML model. An equivalent for a model is a specific program written in any programming language defined in EBNF. Finally, the concrete level M0 reflects any model based representation of a real situation. This representation is an instance of a model defined in level M1. We may again draw the parallel to the formal programming language architecture. Level M0 corresponds to all dynamic execution traces of a program of level M1.

The major benefit of MDA is to decouple system specifications from the underlying platform [14]. In this way, the specification is much closer to the problem domain and not bound to a specific implementation technique. This benefit is maximized when domain-specific modeling languages are employed. Thus, the MDA specification [79] differentiates at level M2 languages for *Computation Independent Model* (CIM), *Platform Independent Model* (PIM), and *Platform Specific Model* (PSM) to quantify the abstraction quality of a model. While a CIM provides a fully computation independent viewpoint close to the domain in question, a PIM approximates the system description in a technology neutral manner. A PSM eventually unifies the PIM with the specifics of the underlying platform to be used as specification for code generation.

To bridge metamodeling and programming languages, and to justify MOF as interoperability standard, the OMG provides a standardized way for exchanging MOF based artifacts. OMG's standard for *XML Metadata Interchange* (XMI) [81] defines a mapping of any (meta)model expressed in MOF to the *Extensible Markup Language* (XML) [114]. The specification of MOF itself is divided into the kernel metamodel *Essential MOF* (EMOF) and the more expressive *Complete MOF* (CMOF) [77]. EMOF is closely related to object-oriented programming languages, such as Java, which allows a straightforward mapping, as implemented in [91,23]. Especially the Eclipse Modeling Framework (EMF) with its reference implementations for EMOF [23] and UML [24] fosters several adjacent subprojects for arbitrary MDA tasks, such as querying and comparing models, building textual and graphical modeling editors, etc. leading to increasing adoption in academia and in practice.

3.2   Model Transformation

In modern software engineering practice employing the MDE paradigm, a vast amount of interrelated models accrues. Those models are in the first place utilized to gain abstraction of the technical realization of a system, such that developers may completely concentrate on a specific matter of the problem domain and serve finally as construction plan for implementation. To free developers from the burden of repetitive and error-prone tasks such as translating models into source code and propagating changes throughout dependent models, a mechanism to transform and synchronize models is demanded. The field of *model transformation* accepts to play this central role and is thus noticed as the heart and soul of MDE [104]. To embrace the diversity of domain-specific modeling languages the transformable models conform to, a model transformation language usually makes use of the flexible type-system gained by metamodeling and defines a fixed syntax for defining transformation rules only. The metamodels holding the actual types of elements to be transformed are bound not until a specific model transformation is specified [8]. Reflecting the plethora of application areas of models, model transformation tasks cover all sorts of activities, such as updating, synchronizing, translating models to other models, or translating models to code. To support these activities, a multitude of either general or specifically tailored model transformation languages and approaches emerged.

In the following, we briefly present distinguishing characteristics of current model transformation approaches. However, those approaches may not only be adopted for one specific task. As shown in [27], exogenous model transformations may be also achieved with tools primarily built for endogenous model transformations. Conversely, tools for exogenous model transformations may perform endogenous model transformations by defining transformations with equal input metamodel and output metamodel. Even bidirectional model transformations may be achieved by defining one transformation for each direction. Although this interchange is possible, defining transformations is much easier and safer with the right tool.

Endogenous model transformation. Endogenous model transformation describes transformations where source and target model conform to the same metamodel. In case that the source and target models are one and the same artifact, i.e., the source model is directly refined, this kind of transformation is also called *in-place transformation*. If a new target model based on the source model's properties is created, the transformation is called *out-place*, even if both models conform to the same metamodel [67].

Outstanding approaches realizing endogenous model transformations are among others the graph transformation tool AGG [29], the model transformation by-demonstration approach EMF Modeling Operations (EMO) [13], and the reflective API of Eclipse's Modeling Framework EMF allowing direct programmatic manipulation of models as, e.g., employed in graphical modeling editors [23]. This kind of model transformation frames the basis for model versioning, as it describes the evolution of a model. More precisely, the original version is considered as input model for an endogenous model transformation—either for a predefined transformation or for a manual transformation performed in a modeling editor—and the output model shapes the revised version.

Exogenous model transformation. An exogenous model transformation denotes a model transformation between models conforming to different metamodels, i.e., it takes one or more models of any modeling language as input and generates one or more new models of another modeling language from scratch. A special case of exogenous model transformation is *bidirectional model transformation*, which provides a synchronous framework, i.e., the transformation definition may be executed in both directions. Based on this definition, bidirectional model transformation further enables incremental change propagation from one model to another model, triggering an in-place transformation to recover a consistent state. The unidirectional exogenous model transformation approach is implemented in, e.g., the Atlas Transformation Language (ATL) [43]. One representatives for the bidirectional model transformation approach is OMG's standard for model transformation Query/View/Transformation (QVT) [78].

Model-to-text transformation. Model-to-text transformations address the generation of code or any other text representation (e.g., configuration files and reports) from an input model. Such transformation languages employ usually a template-based approach, where the expected output text is parameterized with model elements conforming the input metamodel. Acceleo[5] implementing OMG's MOF Model-to-Text Transformation Language standard (Mof2Text) [82], JET[6], and Xpand[7] are well-known representatives for this category.

3.3   Model Differencing

One major task of model versioning is to obtain the operations that have been applied between two versions of a model (e.g., between V_o and V_{r1} in Fig. 1). As already discussed in Section 2, obtaining the applied operations can be accomplished using two alternatives: *operation recording* [41,48,60,101], which is often referred to as operation-based versioning, and *model differencing* [1,14,45,54,59], which is also referred to as state-based versioning. As operation recording is largely straightforward and depends on the interfaces of the modeling editor heavily, we will focus on the state of the art in model differencing in the following.

Model differencing is usually realized as follows. First, a *match* is computed, which describes the correspondences between two versions of a model. Second, the actual *differences* are obtained by a fine-grained comparison of all corresponding model elements based on the beforehand computed match. After the differences have been obtained, they have to be represented in some way for their further usage, such as conflict detection and merging. In the following, we will elaborate on the state of the art of these three tasks, matching, differencing, and representing differences in more detail.

Model Matching. The problem of matching two model elements is to find the *identity* of the model elements to be matched. Once the identity is explicit, model elements with equal identities are considered as a match. Thereby, the identity is computed by a match function. The characteristics a model element that are incorporated to compute the identity of a model element within the match function, however, varies among approaches, scenarios, and objectives of performing model matching. The predecessors of model matching approaches stem from schema matching in the data base research domain [95] and from ontology matching in the knowledge representation research domain [115]. Therefore, we first highlight remarkable categorizations of matching techniques from these two

---

[5] http://www.eclipse.org/acceleo
[6] http://www.eclipse.org/modeling/m2t/?project=jet#jet
[7] http://wiki.eclipse.org/Xpand

research domains and, subsequently, proceed with surveying recent approaches to model matching.

Schema matching and ontology matching. The problem of matching database schema gained much attention among researchers for addressing various research topics, such as schema integration, data extraction for data warehouses and e-commerce, as well as semantic query processing. To reconcile the structure and terminology used in the emerged approaches from these research topics, Rahm and Bernstein [95] proposed a remarkable classification of existing approaches. On the most upper layer, Rahm and Bernstein distinguish between *individual matcher approaches* and *combining matchers*. Individual matchers are further classified according to the following largely orthogonal criteria. First of all, they consider whether matching approaches also incorporate instance data (i.e., data contents) or only the schema for deriving correspondences among schema elements. Further, they distinguish between approaches that perform the match only on single schema elements (i.e., they operate on *element level*) or on combinations of multiple elements to also regard complex schema structures (i.e., *structure level*). Another distinction is made upon approaches that uses either *linguistic-based matching* (e.g., based on names or descriptions) or *constraint-based matching* (e.g., unique key properties or data types). Matching approaches may also be characterized according to the match cardinality; that is, whether they return one-to-one correspondences or also one-to-n or even n-to-m correspondences. Finally, there are approaches that not only take a schema as input, but also exploit auxiliary information (e.g., dictionaries, global schemata, previous matching decisions, or user input). On the other side, among combining matchers, Rahm and Bernstein identified *hybrid matchers* that directly combine several matching approaches to determine match candidates based on multiple criteria or information sources. They also identified *composite matchers*, which combine the results of several *independently executed* matchers. The composition of matchers is either done automatically or manually by the user.

With the rise of the semantic web [6], the problem of integrating, aligning, and synchronizing different *ontologies* into one reconciled knowledge representation induced an active research area. Therefore, several ontology matching approaches have been proposed (cf. [115] for a survey). As argued by Shvaiko and Euzenat [105], schema matching and ontology matching are largely the same problem because schemata and ontologies both provide a vocabulary of terms that describes a domain of interest and both constrain the meaning of terms used in the vocabulary [105].

Model matching. The aforementioned categorizations and terminologies also can be used for characterizing model matching approaches. However, the distinction between schema-only and instance-based approaches only applies to approaches specifically tailored to match *metamodels*, because models on the $M1$ level in the metamodeling stack (cf. Section 3.1) have no instances to be used for matching. Furthermore, in the context of model matching, the only constraint-based similarity measure that can be used across all meta levels is the type information (i.e., the respective metaclass) of a model element. Besides applying the categorization coming from schema and ontology matching, Kolovos et al. [52] further proposed a categorization specifically dedicated to model matching approaches. In particular, they distinguish between static identity-based matching, signature-based matching, similarity-based matching, and custom language-specific matching. Static identity-based matching relies on immutable UUIDs attached to each model element, whereas signature-based matching compares model elements based on a computed combination of feature values (i.e., its signature) of the respective model elements. Which features should be incorporated for computing this signature strongly depends on the modeling language. Whereas approaches of these two categories, identity- and signature-based matching, treat the problem of model matching as a true/false identity (i.e., two model elements are either a match or not), similarity-based matching computes an aggregated similarity measure between two model elements based on their feature values. As not all feature values of a model element are always significant for matching, they often can be configured in terms of weights attached to the respective features. Finally, custom language-specific matching enables its users to specify dedicated match rules in order to also respect the underlying semantics of the respective modeling language for matching.

In the following, we discuss existing approaches in the domain of model matching. Many existing approaches in this domain are integrated in *model versioning* tools. In the following, however, we focus on their model matching capabilities only, and discuss the respective approaches concerning their model versioning support again in Section 4.

One of the first model matching approaches has been proposed alongside their model comparison algorithm by Alanen and Porres [93]. Although their approach only supports UML models and, thereby, they easily could have incorporated language-specific match rules, the proposed match function relies on static identifiers only. Also, specifically tailored for a specific modeling language is UMLDiff [119], which is, however, not based on static identifiers. Instead, UMLDiff computes similarity metrics based on a model element's name and structure. In terms of the aforementioned categorizations, UMLDiff applies string-based matching at the element level as well as graph-based matching at the structure level and internally combines the obtained similarity measures; thus, UMLDiff is a hybrid matching approach. The same is true for the approach by Nejati et al. [73], which is specifically tailored for matching UML state machines. Their matching approach uses static similarity measures, such as typographic, linguistic, and depth properties of model elements, but also behavioural similarity measures. Also specifically tailored to UML models is ADAMS [20], which uses a hybrid matcher that first applies a static identity-based matcher and matches all remaining (not matched) model elements using a simple static signature-based approach based on model element names. In contrast to language-specific matching approaches, also several generic approaches have been proposed such as DSMDiff [59] and EMF Compare [14]. DSMDiff first compares elements based on a computed signature (incorporating the element name and type) and, subsequently, considers the relationship among model elements previously matched by signature. Largely similar to DSMDiff, EMF Compare computes four different metrics and combines them to obtain a final similarity measure. In particular, EMF Compare regards the name of an element, its content, its type and the relations to other elements. EMF Compare also offers a static identity-based comparison mode, which works similarly to the approach by Alanen and Porres [93]. However, EMF Compare only allows for either similarity-based or static-identity based matching; both strategies cannot be combined. The similarity-based matching approach applied in EMF Compare heavily exploits the tree-based containment structure when comparing models. Rivera and Vallecillo [97] argue that this leads to issues concerning the detection of, for instance, elements that have been moved to new container elements. Therefore, Rivera and Vallecillo [97] propose to compare model elements independently of their depth in the containment tree. Besides this difference, the exploited information on model elements for matching is largely similar to DSMDiff and EMF Compare. DSMDiff and EMF Compare aim at obtaining an optimal result, whereas no language-specific information or configuration is necessary; in contrast, the goal of SiDiff [99] is to provide an adaptable model comparison framework, which may be fine-tuned for specific modeling languages by configuring the actual characteristics of model elements to be considered in the comparison process and attaching weights to these characteristics. DSMDiff, EMF Compare, and SiDiff are hybrid matching approaches. On the contrary, Barret et al. recently presented Mirador [5], which is a composite matching approach. That is, several matching strategies are independently applied and presented in a consolidated view of all match results. Using this view, users may interactively refine the computed match by attaching weights and manually discarding or adding matches. Thereby, the goal is to offer a wide assortment of model comparison algorithms and matching strategies under control of the user. Yet another approach is taken by Kolovos with the Epsilon Comparison Language (ECL) [50]. Instead of providing a set of predefined and configurable matching strategies, ECL is a hybrid rule-based language, which enables users to implement comparison algorithms at a high level of abstraction and execute them for identifying matches. Although it indeed requires some dedicated knowledge to create language-specific match rules with ECL, it facilitates highly specialized matching algorithms, which may also incorporate external knowledge, such as lexicons and thesauri.

In summary, during the last years several notable yet diverse approaches for model matching have been proposed. The set of available matchers ranges from generic to language-specific and from hybrid to composite approaches, whereas some are adaptable and some are not. Nearly all operate on the structure level regarding the importance of a model element's context. In contrast to ontology matching approaches, the approaches for model matching are mainly syntactic and do not incorporate external knowledge. Only ECL explicitly enables matchers that take advantage of external knowledge or even formal semantics.

Computing and Representing Differences. The differences among models may be computed based on three orthogonal levels: the *abstract syntax*, the *concrete syntax*, and the *semantics* of the models. The abstract syntax describes a model in terms of a tree (or more generally, a graph), whereas nodes represent model elements and edges represent references among them. Each node may further be described by a set of features values (i.e., attribute values). Thus, abstract syntax differencing approaches are only capable of detecting differences in the *syntactic data* that is carried in the compared models. Differencing approaches that also take the concrete syntax of a model into account are further capable of detecting changes of the *diagramming layout* visualizing of a model (e.g., [20,65,87,88]). More recently, Maoz et al. [62] introduce *semantic model differencing*, which aims at comparing the meaning [39] of models rather than their syntactic representation. For instance, Maoz et al. propose an algorithm to compute the differences between two UML activity diagrams regarding their possible execution traces, as well as the differences concerning the instantiability of UML class diagrams [63,64]. In the context of model versioning, the comparison of models is largely based on the abstract syntax currently, which is why we focus on such differencing approaches in the remainder of this section.

Model differencing based on the abstract syntax. Existing work in the area of differencing based on the abstract syntax mainly differ regarding the used approach for matching model elements across two versions of a model, which has been discussed above already, and they vary concerning the detectable types of differences. Most of the existing model differencing approaches are only capable of detecting the applied *atomic operations* (i.e., add, delete, move, and update). The computation of such applied operations works largely similar in existing approaches. That is, the differencing algorithms perform a fine-grained comparison of two model elements that correspond to each other (as indicated by the applied match function). If two corresponding model elements differ in some way (i.e., an update has been applied), a description of the update is created and saved to the list of differences. If a model element has no corresponding model element on the opposite side, an element insertion or deletion is noted.

Besides such atomic operations, developers may also apply *composite operations*. A composite operation is a set of cohesive atomic operations that are applied within one transaction to achieve ultimately one common goal. The most prominent class of such composite operations are *refactorings* as introduced by Opdyke [90] and further elaborated by Fowler et al. [33]. The composite operations that have been applied between two versions of a model represents a valuable source of information for several model management tasks [68]. Furthermore, this information helps other developers significantly to better understand the evolution of a software artifact [49]. Three approaches have been proposed for detecting applied composite operations from two states of a model. First, Xing and Stroulia [120] presented an extension of UMLDiff for detecting refactorings. In their approach, refactorings are expressed in terms of change pattern queries that are used to query a set of atomic differences obtained from the UMLDiff model differencing algorithm. If a query returns a match, an application of a refactoring is reported.

A very similar approach has been proposed by Vermolen et al. [113] to allow for a higher automation in model migration. Both approaches are restricted to a specific modeling language and use hard-coded refactoring detection rules. In contrast to these approaches, Kehrer et al. [44] propose to derive the detection rules from graph transformation units realizing the composite operations. The derived detection rules may then be matched with generic difference models containing the atomic operations that have been applied between two versions of a model.

Representation of differences. For assessing different approaches for representing differences between two versions of a model, Cicchetti et al. [16] identified a number of properties a representation of operations should fulfill. Most importantly, they mention the properties indicating whether a representation is *model-based* (i.e., conforming to a dedicated difference metamodel), *transformative* (i.e., applicable to the compared models), and *metamodel independent* (i.e., agnostic of the metamodel the compared models conform to). Besides these properties, it is also important how explicit the detected operations are represented, or whether important information (such as the index at which a value has been added to an ordered feature) is hidden in the context of a detected operation's representation.

In several research papers addressing the topic of model differences, such as [5,20,65], it is not explicitly mentioned how the detected differences are represented. Many others at least define the types of differences they aim to detect. For instance, DSMDiff [59] marks model elements to be *added*, *deleted*, or *changed*. Alanen & Porres [93] explicitly represent, besides added and deleted model elements, *updates* of single-valued features, *insertions* and *deletions* of values in multi-valued features as well as *ordered* features. SiDiff [99] distinguishes among *structural differences*, *attribute differences*, *reference differences*, and *move differences*. Several language-specific approaches, in particular, Gerth et al. [35], UMLDiff [119], and Ohst et al. [88], introduce operations that are tailored to the specific modeling language they support; thus, they use a metamodel dependent representation of applied operations. For instance, Gerth et al. defines the operations, such as *move activity* and *delete fragment*, for state machines and UMLDiff presents a fine-grained definition of UML class diagram operations, such as *new inheritance relationship* (for UML classes).

All of the approaches mentioned above do not represent the detected differences in terms of a model that conforms to a dedicated difference metamodel; at least, it is not explicitly mentioned in their research papers. Nevertheless, the difference representations by Alanen & Porres and Gerth et al. are transformative; that is, detected differences can be applied to the compared models in order to create a merged version. To the best of our knowledge, the only approaches that use a model-based representation of differences are EMF Compare [14], Herrmannsdoerfer & Koegel [41], and Cicchetti et al. [16]. All of these approaches are designed to be independent from the metamodel. Whereas EMF Compare and Herrmannsdoerfer & Koegel use a generic metamodel, Cicchetti et al. *generate* a dedicated difference metamodel for specific modeling languages. Thereby, in the approach by Cicchetti et al., a dedicated metaclass for indicating insertions, deletions, and changes for every metaclass in the respective modeling language's metamodel is generated. For instance, for UML class diagrams, difference metaclasses, such as AddedClass and ChangedAttribute are generated, whereas Class and Attribute are metaclasses in the modeling language's metamodel. In contrast, EMF Compare and Herrmannsdoerfer & Koegel make use of the reflective power of EMF and refer to the modeling language's metaclasses to indicate, for instance, a modification of a specific feature of a model element. EMF Compare refers to the affected model element by a generic reference to EObject, which is the abstract type of all objects within EMF. In contrast, Herrmannsdoerfer & Koegel foresee a more flexible model referencing technique to also enable, for instance, persistent ID-based model element references.

3.4   Conflicts in Versioning

Whenever an artifact is modified concurrently by two or more developers, conflicts may occur. In the following, we survey existing definitions of the term *conflict* and discuss proposed conflict categorizations.

The term conflict has been used in the area of versioning to refer to interfering operations in the parallel evolution of software artifacts. However, the term conflict is heavily overloaded and differently co-notated. Besides using the term conflict, also the terms *interference* and *inconsistency* have been applied synonymously in the literature as, for instance, in [32,112] and [66], respectively. The term conflict usually refers to directly contradicting operations; that is, two operations, which do not commute [60]. Nevertheless, there is a multitude of further problems that might occur, especially when taking syntax and semantics of the versioned artifact's language into account. Therefore, in order to better understand the notion of conflict, different categories have been created to group specific merge issues as surveyed in the following.

In the field of software merging, Mens [66] introduces *textual*, *syntactic*, *semantic*, and *structural* conflicts. Whereas *textual* conflicts concern contradicting operations applied to text lines as detected by a line-based comparison of a program's source code, *syntactic* conflicts denote issues concerning the contradicting modification of the parse tree or the abstract syntax graph; thus, syntactic merging takes the programming language's syntax into account and may also report operations that cause parse errors when merged (cf. line-based versus graph-based versioning in Section 2). *Semantic* merging goes one step further and also considers the semantic annotation of the parse tree, as done in the semantic analysis phase of a compiler. In this context, static semantic conflicts denote issues in the merged artifact such as undeclared variables or incompatible types. Besides static semantic conflicts, Mens also introduced the notion of *behavioral* conflicts, which denote unexpected behavior in the merged result. Such conflicts can only be detected by applying even more sophisticated semantic merge techniques that rely on the runtime semantics. Finally, Mens introduces the notion of *structural* conflicts, which arise when one of the applied operations to be merged is a "restructuring" (i.e., a refactoring) and the merge algorithm cannot uniquely decide in which way the merged result should be restructured.

Also the notion of conflict in the domain of graph transformation theory serves as a valuable source of knowledge in this matter. As defined by Heckel et al. [40], two direct graph transformations are in conflict, if they are *not parallel independent*. Two direct graph transformations are parallel independent, if they preserve all elements that are in the match of the other transformation; otherwise we encounter a *delete-use* conflict. Another manifestation of such a case is a *delete-delete* conflict. Although both transformations delete the same element anyway, this is still considered a conflict because one transformation deletes an element that is indeed in the match of the other transformation. If the graph transformations comprise negative application conditions, they also must not create elements that are prohibited by negative application conditions of the other transformation; otherwise an *add-forbid* conflict occurs. To summarize, two direct graph transformations are in conflict, if one of both disables the other. Furthermore, as shown in [26], based on the local Church-Rosser theorem [15], we may further conclude that two parallel independent direct transformations can be executed in any order with the same final result.

In the domain of model versioning, no widely accepted categorization of different types of merge conflicts has been established yet. Nevertheless, two detailed categorizations have been proposed by Westfechtel [117] and Taentzer et al. [110,111]; these categorizations concern *generic* conflicts between *atomic* operations only. In the following, we summarize these definitions briefly.

The conflict categorization by Westfechtel [117] is defined using set-theoretical rules and distinguishes between *context-free conflicts* and *context-sensitive conflicts*. Context-free conflicts denote contradicting modifications of the same feature value at the same model element; thus, such conflicts are independent of the context of the model element. Context-sensitive conflicts take also the context of a concurrently modified model element into account. With the term "context", Westfechtel refers to the neighbor elements of a model elements, such as its container or referenced model elements. Context-sensitive conflicts are again classified into *(i) containment conflicts*, which occur, for instance, if both developers move the same model element to different containers so that no unique container can be chosen automatically, *(ii) delete conflicts*, which denote deletions of elements that have been updated or moved concurrently, and *(iii) reference conflicts*, which concern contradicting changes to bi-directional references.

Taentzer et al. [110,111] present a fundamental categorization of conflicts based on graph theory. Thus, models are represented in terms of graphs, and changes applied to the models are formalized using graph modifications. On the most general level of this categorization, Taentzer et al. distinguish between *operation-based conflicts* and *state-based conflicts*. Operation-based conflicts are caused by two directly interfering graph modifications. More precisely, two graph modifications are conflicting, if either the source or the target node of an edge that has been inserted in one graph modification has been deleted concurrently in the other graph modification. State-based conflicts denote inconsistencies concerning the consistency rules of the respective modeling language in the merged graph; that is, the final *state* of the graph after applying the concurrent graph

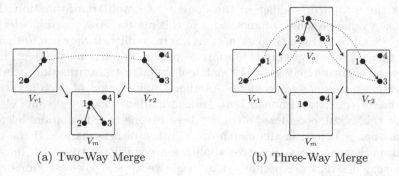

(a) Two-Way Merge   (b) Three-Way Merge

Fig. 6. Two-Way and Three-Way Merge Strategies

modifications to the common ancestor graph violates graph constraints stemming from the definition of the modeling language. In [111], Taentzer et al. refine this fundamental categorization for conflicts in EMF-based models. Thus, also the additional modeling features of EMF-based models are taken into account, such as containment references, feature multiplicities, and ordered features. Therefore, conflict patterns are introduced, which indicate combinations of concurrently applied operations leading to a conflict when applied to common model elements. In particular, they define *delete-use*, *delete-move*, *delete-update*, *update-update*, *move-move*, and *insert-insert* conflicts.

3.5   Merging

When only non-conflicting changes are detected between two versions of an artifact, merging is a straightforward task. In case of two-way merging, only the revised versions V_{r1} and V_{r2} are compared [18]. As deletions cannot be determined (cf. Section 2.1), the merged version V_m is constructed as joint union of both input artifacts, as depicted in Fig. 6a. In case of three-way merging, the merge is more reliable, as it takes the common ancestor V_o of both artifacts into account and is thus able to consider deleted elements [18]. The merge is performed by applying the union of all changes detected between the common ancestor and both revised versions to the common ancestor version. Consider the example in Fig. 6b. Element 3 is deleted in V_{r1}, while in V_{r2} element 2 is deleted and element 4 is added. Consequently, the merged version V_m is constructed by deleting elements 2 and 3 from the ancestor version V_o and adding the new element 4 resulting in a version consisting of elements 1 and 4. As the more powerful three-way merging approach is the preferred strategy in almost all versioning systems [66], we neglect two-way merging in the following. However, whenever conflicting changes are detected between the two revised versions V_{r1} and V_{r2}, the merged version cannot be uniquely determined, regardless whether two-way or three-way merging is employed.

Manual conflict resolution. The most pragmatic solution is to shift the responsibility of merging to the user, whenever it comes to conflicting changes. Versioning systems for code like Subversion typically employ a manual merge strategy. Then, the two parallel evolved versions are shown to the user side by side. Conflicting and non-conflicting changes are highlighted. The user has to analyze the evolution of the artifact and to decide which changes shall be integrated into the merged version. This approach works satisfactory well for line-oriented artifacts like source code and is thus employed in most model versioning systems too. However, the graph based structure of models impedes manual merging, as dependent changes are not located close together in a sequence, but may be scattered across the model. Considering visual models with their dual representation manifested in the abstract syntax and the graphical concrete syntax, renders manual merging even harder. If these representations are merged separately, the user's perception is completely destroyed. Even if graphical comparison of both versions side by side mitigates the representational gap, the manual effort for identifying corresponding elements on the two-dimensional canvas increases with the model's size. Recently, Gerth et al. [36] propose to support manual merging of process models by guiding the modeler through conflict resolution. They apply non-conflicting changes automatically and suggest one of three strategies depending on the conflict type at hand.

Automatic conflict resolution. As manual conflict resolution is error-prone and cumbersome, it seems naturally, that avoiding conflicts by automatic merge strategies is a preferable goal. Munson and Dewan present a flexible framework for merging arbitrary objects, which may be configured in terms of merge policies [69]. Merge policies may be tailored by users to their specific needs and include rules for conflict detection and rules for automatic conflict resolution. Actions for automatic conflict resolution are defined in merge matrices and incorporate the kinds of changes made to the object and the users who performed those changes. Thus, it may be configured, e.g., that changes of specific users always dominate changes of others, or that updates outpace deletions. Edwards [25] proposes further strategies for conflict management in collaborative applications and allows to distinguish manual and automatic resolution in his merge policies. Automatic conflict resolution is achieved by calculating all possible combinations of parallel performed operations leading to a valid version. Alanen & Porres [1] use a fixed policy in their merge algorithm for MOF based models to interleave the differences performed in V_{r2} with the differences of V_{r1}. Cicchetti et al. [17] allow to adapt conflict detection and merging by defining conflict patterns describing specific difference patterns, which are not allowed to occur in V_{r1} and V_{r2} together. These conflict patterns are supplemented with a reconciliation strategy, stating which side should be preferred in the merge process. While policy based approaches require user intervention in certain conflict cases where no policy is at hand, Ehrig et al. [28] present a formal merge approach based on graph transformation theory, yielding a merged model by construction.

Conflict tolerance. In contrast to automatic merging, nearly as long as collaborative systems exist, several works have been published, arguing that inconsistencies are not always a negative result of collaborative development. They propose to tolerate inconsistencies at least temporarily for several reasons [74]. Inconsistencies may identify areas of a system, where the developers' common understanding has broken down, and where further analysis is necessary. Another reason for tolerable inconsistencies arise when changes to the system are so large, that not all dependent changes can be performed at once. Further, fixing inconsistencies may be more expensive than their impact and risk costs. Tolerating inconsistencies requires the knowledge of their existence and careful management. Undetected inconsistencies in contrast, should be avoided. Schwanke and Kaiser [102] propose an adapted programming environment for identifying, tracking, tolerating, and periodically resolving inconsistencies. Similarly, Balzer [4] allows to tolerate inconsistencies in programming environments and database systems by relaxing consistency constraints and annotating inconsistent parts with so called *pollution markers*.

To summarize, existing merge strategies are manifold. Manual merge approaches provide on the one hand most user control, but require on the other hand high effort and bear the risk of loosing changes. Automatic merge approaches in contrast, accelerate merging and reduce manual intervention. However, this benefit comes at the cost of loss of control. Conflict tolerance reveals a completely different strategy and allows to temporarily tolerate an inconsistent state of the merged artifact instead of immediately rolling back conflicting changes. The drawback of conflict tolerance is the need for dedicated editors and that the attached pollution markers may violate the grammar of highly structured artifacts like models. However, the variety of existing merge approaches reflects the pivotal role of the merge process.

4   State-of-the-art Model Versioning Systems

In the previous section, we discussed underlying concepts and existing fundamental techniques acting as a basis for building a model versioning system. In this section, we present the current state-of-the-art in model versioning and evaluate the features of existing solutions stemming from industry and academia.

4.1   Features of Model Versioning Approaches

Before we survey the state-of-the-art model versioning systems, we first discuss the particular features of model versioning systems that we have investigated in this survey.

Operation recording versus model differencing. As already introduced in Section 2, we may distinguish between approaches that obtain operations performed between two versions of a model by applying *operation recording* or by *model differencing.* If an approach applies model differencing, which is, in general, more flexible concerning the adopted modeling editors, it is substantial to consider the techniques conducted in the match function for identifying corresponding model elements because the quality of the match is crucial for an accurate subsequent operation detection. We may distinguish between match functions that rely on universally unique IDs (*UUIDs*), and those applying heuristics based on the model element's *content* (i.e., feature values and contained child elements).

Composite operation detection. The knowledge on applied composite operations is the prerequisite for considering them in the merge process. Therefore, it is a distinguished feature whether an operation detection component is also capable of detecting applications of composite operations besides only identifying atomic operations. It is worth noting that, in case of model differencing, the state-based a posteriori detection of composite operation applications is highly challenging as stated in Section 6 of [21].

Adaptability of the operation detection. Obviously, generic operation detection approaches are, in general, more flexible than language-specific approaches because it is very likely that several modeling languages are concurrently applied even within one project and, therefore, should be supported by one model versioning system. However, neglecting language-specific aspects in the operation detection phase might lead to a lower quality of the detected set of applied operations. Therefore, we investigate whether generic operation detection approaches are adaptable to language-specific aspects. In particular, we consider the adaptability concerning language-specific match rules, as well as the capability to extend the detectable set of language-specific composite operations.

Detection of conflicts between atomic operations. One key feature of model versioning systems is, of course, their ability to detect conflicts arising from contradictory operations applied by two developers in parallel. Consequently, we first investigate whether the approaches under consideration are capable of detecting conflicts between contradictory atomic operations. In this survey, we do not precisely examine *which* types of conflicts are supported. We rather investigate whether conflicts among atomic operations are considered at all.

Detection of conflicts caused by composite operations. Besides conflicts caused by contradicting atomic operations, conflicts might also occur if a composite operation applied by one developer is not applicable anymore, after the concurrent operations of another developer have been performed. Such a conflict occurs, if a concurrent operation causes the preconditions of an applied composite operation to fail. Therefore, we investigate whether the model versioning approaches adequately consider composite operations in their conflict detection phase.

Detection of inconsistencies. Besides conflicts caused by operations (atomic operations and composite operations), a conflict might also occur if the merged model contains errors in terms of the modeling language's well-formedness and validation rules. Consequently, we examine model versioning approaches under consideration whether they perform a validation of the resulting merged model.

Adaptability of the conflict detection. With this feature, we review the adaptability to language-specific aspects of the conflict detection approach. This involves techniques to configure language-specific conflict types that cannot be detected by analyzing of the applied operations only generically.

Graphical visualization of conflicts. Developers largely create and modify models using a graphical diagramming editor. Thus, also the occurred conflicts should be visualized and resolved graphically on top of the model's concrete syntax. Hence, we investigate whether developers have to cope with switching the visualization for understanding and resolving conflicts, or whether they are allowed to stick with their familiar way of working with their models.

Adaptable resolution strategies. If a model versioning system offers techniques for resolving certain types of conflicts automatically, the correct resolution strategy is key. However, the correct resolution strategy may depend strongly on the modeling language, the aim of the models, the project culture, etc. Thus, it is important to allow users to adapt the offered resolution strategies to their needs.

Flexibility concerning the modeling language. This feature indicates whether model versioning systems are tailored to a specific modeling language and, therefore, are only usable for one modeling language, or whether they are generic and, therefore, support all modeling languages defined by a common meta-metamodel.

Flexibility concerning the modeling editor. Model versioning systems may be designed to work only in combination with a specific editor or modeling environment. This usually applies to approaches using operation recording. In contrast, model versioning systems may avoid such a dependency and refrain from relying on specific modeling environments by only operating on the evolved models put under version control.

4.2   Evaluation Results

In this section, we introduce current state-of-the-art model versioning systems and evaluate them on the basis of the features discussed in the previous section. The considered systems and the findings of this survey are summarized in Table 1 and discussed in the following. Please note that the order in which we introduce the considered systems is alphabetically and has no further meaning.

ADAMS. The "Advanced Artifact Management System" (ADAMS) offers process management functionality, supports cooperation among multiple developers, and provides artifact versioning [19]. ADAMS can be integrated via specific plug-ins into modeling environments to realize versioning support for models. In [20], De Lucia et al. present an ADAMS plug-in for ArgoEclipse[8] to enable version support for ArgoUML models. Because artifacts are stored in a proprietary ADAMS-specific format to be handled by the central repository, models have to be converted into that format before they are sent to the server and translated back to the original format, whenever the model is checked out again. ADAMS applies state-based model differencing based on UUIDs. Added model elements, which, as a consequence, have no comparable UUIDs, are matched using simple heuristics based on the element names to find corresponding elements concurrently added by another developer. The differences are computed at the client and sent to the ADAMS server, which finally performs the merge.

---

[8] http://argoeclipse.tigris.org

Table 1. Evaluation of State-of-the-art Model Versioning Systems

	Operation Detection						Conflict Detection				Resolution		Flexibility	
	Operation Recording	Model Differencing		Composite Operations	Adaptability		Operation-based Conflicts		Inconsistencies	Adaptability	Graphical Visualization	Adaptable Resolution Strategies	Modeling Language	Modeling Editor
		UUID	Content		Match	Operations	Atomic	Composite						
ADAMS	-	✓	✓	-	-	-	✓	-	-	~	-	-	-	✓
Alanen and Porres	-	✓	-	-	-	-	✓	-	✓	-	-	-	-	✓
Cicchetti et al.	n/a	n/a	n/a	n/a	n/a	n/a	✓	✓	-	✓	-	✓	✓	✓
CoObRA	✓	-	-	✓	-	-	✓	-	~	-	✓	-	-	-
EMF Compare	-	✓	✓	~	-	~	✓	-	-	~	-	-	✓	✓
EMFStore	✓	-	-	✓	-	~	✓	~	✓	-	-	-	✓	~
Gerth et al.	-	✓	-	✓	-	-	✓	✓	✓	-	-	-	-	✓
Mehra et al.	-	✓	-	-	-	-	✓	-	-	-	✓	-	✓	✓
Oda and Saeki	✓	-	-	-	-	-	~	-	✓	-	-	-	✓	-
Odyssey-VCS 2	-	✓	-	-	-	-	✓	-	?	~	-	-	✓	✓
Ohst, Welle, Kelter	-	✓	-	-	-	-	✓	-	-	-	✓	-	-	✓
RSA	-	✓	✓	-	-	-	✓	-	✓	-	✓	-	-	✓
SMOVER	-	✓	-	-	-	-	~	-	-	~	-	-	✓	✓
Westfechtel	-	n/a	n/a	-	-	-	✓	-	~	-	-	-	✓	✓

Legend	
✓	Feature applies.
~	Feature partially applies.
-	Feature does not apply.
n/a	Not applicable or unknown.

The ADAMS plug-in supports ArgoUML models only. Interestingly, ADAMS can be customized to a certain extent. For instance, it is possible to customize the unit of comparison; that is, the smallest unit, for which, if concurrently modified, a conflict is raised. In [20], it is also mention that the conflict detection algorithm may be customized for specific model types with user-defined *correlation rules*, which specify when two operations should be considered as conflicting. However, it remains unclear, how these rules are exactly specified and how these rules influence the conflict detection. The implementation promoted in this publication is not available to further review this interesting customization feature. Composite operations and state-based conflicts are not supported.

Approach by Alanen and Porres. One of the earliest works on versioning UML models was published by Alanen and Porres [1], who present metamodel-independent algorithms for difference calculation, model merging, as well as conflict resolution. They identified seven elementary operation types a developer may perform to modify a model. For calculating the differences between the original version and the modified version, a match between model elements is computed based on UUIDs first. Subsequently, the created, deleted, and changed elements are identified based on the match computed before; composite operations are, however, not considered. Alanen and Porres provide an algorithm to compute a union of two sets of operations, whereas also an automatic merging for values of ordered features is presented. Furthermore, Alanen and Porres also popose to validate the merged result and envision a semi-automatic resolution process. Their work serves as a fundamental contribution to the model versioning domain and influenced many other researchers strongly.

Approach by Cicchetti, Di Ruscio, and Pierantonio. Cicchetti et al. [17] present an approach to specify and detect language-specific conflicts arising from parallel modifications. Their work does not address the issue of obtaining differences, but proposes a model-based way of representing them. Howsoever the differences are computed, they are represented by instantiating an automatically generated language-specific difference metamodel (cf. Section 3.3). Conflicts are specified by manually created conflict patterns. Language-specific conflict patterns are represented in terms of forbidden difference patterns. Thereby, the realization of a customizable conflict detection component is possible. Although the authors do not discuss how differences and applications of composite operations are obtained, their approach supports also conflicts caused by composite operations. The authors also allow to specify reconciliation strategies (i.e., automatic resolution strategies) to specific conflict patterns. It seems to be a great deal of work to establish a complete set of conflict patterns and resolution patterns for a specific language; nevertheless, in the end, a highly customized model versioning system can be achieved.

CoObRA. The Concurrent Object Replication framework CoObRA developed by Schneider et al. [101] realizes optimistic versioning for the UML case tool Fujaba[9]. CoObRA records the operations performed on the model elements and stores them in a central repository. Whenever other developers update their local models, these operations are fetched from this repository and replayed locally. To identify equal model elements, UUIDs are used. Conflicting operations are not applied (also the corresponding local change is undone) and finally presented to the user, who has to resolve these conflicts manually. In [100], the authors also shortly discuss state-based conflicts (i.e., inconsistencies). CoObRA is capable of detecting a small subset of such conflicts when the underlying modeling framework rejects the execution of a certain operation. For example, a class cannot be instantiated anymore if the respective class has been concurrently deleted. However, for instance, concurrent additions of an equally named class is not reported as conflict. The authors also shortly mention composite operations in terms of a set of atomic operations grouped into commands. The operation recording component seems to be capable of grouping atomic operations into commands to

---

[9] http://www.fujaba.de

allow for a more comprehensible undo mechanism. In particular, one command in the modeling editor might cause several atomic operations in the log; if the user aims to undo the last change, the complete command is undone and not only the latest atomic change. In their papers, however, no special treatment of these commands in the merge process is mentioned.

EMF Compare. The open-source model comparison framework EMF Compare [14], which is part of the Eclipse Modeling Framework Technology project, supports generic model comparison and model merging. EMF Compare provides two-way and three-way model comparison algorithms for EMF-based models. EMF Compare's model comparison algorithm consists of two phases, a matching phase and a differencing phase (cf. Section 3.3). EMF Compare provides a merge service, which is capable of applying difference elements in a difference model to allow for merging models. It also offers basic conflict detection capabilities and user interfaces for displaying match and difference models. All these features of EMF Compare are generic; consequently, they can be applied to any EMF-based model irrespectively of the modeling language these models conform to. However, EMF Compare can be extended programmatically for language-specific matching and differencing. Thus, it is not adaptable in the sense that it can be easily configured for a specific language, but it constitutes a programmatically extensible framework for all tasks related to model comparison.

EMFStore. The model repository EMFStore, presented by Koegel et al. [48], has been initially developed as part of the Unicase[10] project and provides a dedicated framework for model versioning of EMF models. After a copy of a model is checked out, all operations applied to this copy are tracked by the modeling environment. Once all modifications are done, the recorded operations are committed to a central repository. For recording the operations, a framework called *Operation Recorder* [41] is used, which allows to track any modifications performed in an EMF-based editor. Also transactions (i.e., a series of dependent operations) can be tracked and grouped accordingly. Having two lists of the recorded operations, in particular, the list of uncommitted local operations and the list of new operations on the server since the last update, the relationships the *requires relationship* and the *conflicts relationship* are established among the operations. The former relationship expresses dependencies between operations, the later indicates contradicting modifications. As the exact calculation of these relationships requires expensive computations, heuristics are applied to obtain an approximation for setting up those relationships. The conflict detection component classifies two operations as conflicting, if the same attribute or the same reference is modified. Furthermore, the authors introduce levels of severity to classify conflicts. They distinguish between hard conflicts and soft conflicts referring to the amount of user support necessary for their resolution. Whereas hard conflicts do not allow including both conflicting operations within the merged model, for soft conflicts this is possible (with the danger of obtaining

---

[10] http://www.unicase.org

an inconsistent model). Summarizing, EMFStore is completely operation-based; that is, the actual model states are never considered for detecting conflicts. This also entails that a removed and subsequently re-added model element is treated as a new model element so that all concurrent operations to the previously re-moved element are reported as conflict. Composite operations can be recorded and saved accordingly. In the conflict detection, however, composite operations are not specifically treated. If an atomic change within a composite operation conflicts with another change, the complete transaction is indeed marked as conflicting; the intentions behind composite operations, as well as potentially violated preconditions of composite operations are not specifically considered.

Approach by Gerth et al. Gerth et al. [35] propose a conflict detection approach specifically tailored to the business process modeling language (BPMN) [83]. To identify the differences between two process models (cf. [54]), in a first step, a mapping between corresponding elements across two versions of a process model is computed based on UUIDs which are attached to each element. In the next step, for each element that has no corresponding counterpart in the opposite version, a operation is created representing the addition or deletion. The result-ing operations are specific to the type of the added or deleted element (e.g., InsertAction or DeleteFragment). Finally, this list of operations is hierarchically structured according to the fragment hierarchy of the process model in order to group those atomic operations into so-called compound operations. Conse-quently, these compound changes group several atomic operations into composite additions or deletions. Having identified all differences in terms of operations be-tween two process models, syntactic, as well as semantic conflicts among those concurrent operations can be identified using a term formalization of process models. According to their definitions, a syntactic conflict occurs if an opera-tion is not applicable after another operation has been performed. A semantic conflict is at hand whenever two operations modify the same elements so that the process models are not "trace equivalent"; that is, all possible traces of a process model are not exactly equal. Obviously, rich knowledge on the opera-tional semantics of process models has to be encoded in the conflict detection to be able to reveal semantic conflicts. Although the authors presented an efficient way of detecting such conflicts, no possibility to adapt the operation detection and conflict detection mechanisms to other languages is foreseen.

Approach by Mehra, Grundy, and Hosking. The publication by Mehra et al. [65] mainly focuses on the graphical visualization of differences between versions of a diagram. Therefore, they provide a plug-in for the meta-CASE tool *Pounamu,* a tool for the specification and generation of multi-view design editors. The di-agrams created with this tool are serialized in XMI and are converted into an object graph for comparison. In their proposed comparison algorithm, the dif-ferences are obtained by applying a state-based model differencing algorithm, which uses UUIDs to map corresponding model elements. The obtained differ-ences are translated to Pounamu editing events, which are events corresponding to the actions performed by users within the modeling environment. Differences cover not only modifications performed on the model, but also modifications performed on the graphical visualization. The differences between various versions are visualized in the concrete syntax so that developers may directly accept or reject modifications on top of the graphical representation developers are familiar with. In their works, also conflict detection facilities are shortly mentioned, however, not discussed in detail.

Approach by Oda and Saeki. Oda and Saeki [87] propose to also generate versioning features along with the modeling editor generated from a specified metamodel as known from metamodeling tools. The generated *versioning-aware* modeling editors are capable of recording all operations applied by the users. In particular, the generated tool records operations to the logical model (i.e., the abstract syntax tree of a model), as well as the diagram's layout information (i.e., the concrete syntax). Besides recording, the generated modeling tool includes check in, check out, and update operations to interact with a central model repository. It is worth noting that only the change sequences are sent to the repository and not the complete model state. In case a model has been concurrently modified and, therefore, needs to be merged, conflicts are identified by re-applying all recorded operations to the common ancestor version. Before each change is performed in the course of merging, its precondition is checked. In particular, the precondition of each change is that the modified model element must exist. Thereby, delete-update conflicts can be identified. Update-update conflicts, however, remain unrevealed and, consequently, the values in the resulting merged model might depend on the order in which the recorded updates are applied because one update might overwrite another previous update. Composite operations and their specific preconditions are not particularly regarded while merging. The approach also does not enable to specify additional language-specific conflicts. Although metamodel violations can, in general, be checked in their tool, they are not particularly considered in the merge process. As the versioning tool is generated from a specific metamodel, the generated tool is language dependent; the approach in general, however, is independent from the modeling language. However, the approach obviously forces users to use the generated modeling editor to be able to use their versioning system.

Odyssey-VCS 2. The version control system Odyssey-VCS by Oliveira et al. [89] is dedicated to versioning UML models. Operations between two versions of a model are identified by applying state-based model differencing relying on UUIDs for finding corresponding model elements. Language-specific heuristics for the match functions may not be used. Also language-specific composite operations are neglected. Interestingly, however, for each project, so-called behavior descriptors may be specified, which define how each model element should be treated during the versioning process. Consequently, the conflict detection component of Odyssey-VCS is adaptable, in particular, it may be specified which model elements should be considered to be atomic. If an atomic element is changed in two different ways at the same time, a conflict is raised. These behavior descriptors (i.e., adaptations) are expressed in XML configuration files. Thus, Odyssey-VCS is customizable for different projects concerning the unit of comparison, as well as whether to apply pessimistic or optimistic versioning. Conflicts coming from language-specific operations, as well as additional language-specific conflicts, however, may not be configured. More recently, Odyssey-VCS 2 [70] has been published, which is capable of processing any EMF-based models and not only UML models. A validation of the resulting merged model is not considered.

Approach by Ohst, Welle, and Kelter. Within the proposed merge algorithm, also Ohst et al. [88] put special emphasis on the visualization of the differences. Therefore, differences between the model as well as the layout of the diagram are computed by applying a state-based model differencing algorithm relying on UUIDs. Conflict detection, however, is not discussed in detail; only update-update and delete-update conflicts are shortly considered. After obtaining the differences, a preview is provided to the user, which visualizes all modifications, even if they are conflicting. The preview diagram can also be modified and, therefore, allows users to resolve conflicts easily using the concrete syntax of a diagram. For indicating the modifications, the different model versions are shown in a unified document containing the common parts, the automatically merged parts, as well as the conflicts. For distinguishing the different model versions, coloring techniques are used. In the case of delete-update conflicts, the deleted model element is crossed out and decorated with a warning symbol to indicate the modification.

IBM Rational Software Architect (RSA). The Eclipse-based modeling environment RSA [11] is a UML modeling environment built upon the Eclipse Modeling Framework. Under the surface, it uses an adapted version of EMF Compare for UML models offering more sophisticated views on the match and difference models for merging. These views show the differences and conflicts in the graphical syntax of the models. The differencing and conflict detection capabilities are, however, equal to those of EMF Compare, besides that RSA additionally runs a model validation against the merged version and, in case an validation rule is violated, the invalid parts of the model are graphically indicated.

SMOVER. The semantically-enhanced model versioning system by Reiter et al. [96], called SMOVER, aims at reducing the number of falsely detected conflicts resulting from syntactic variations of semantically equal modeling concepts. Furthermore, additional conflicts shall be identified by incorporating knowledge on the modeling language's semantics. This knowledge is encoded by the means of model transformations, which rewrite a given model to so-called semantic views. These semantic views provide a canonical representations of the model, which makes certain aspects of the modeling language more explicit. Consequently, also potential semantic conflicts might be identified when the semantic view representations of two concurrently evolved versions are compared. It is worth noting that the system itself is independent from the modeling language and language-specific semantic views can be configured to adapt the system to

---

[11] http://www.ibm.com/developerworks/rational/library/05/712_comp/
index.html

a specific modeling language. The differences are identified using a state-based model differencing algorithm based on UUIDs. Therefore, the system is independent of the used modeling editor. However, this differencing can not be adapted to specific modeling languages and only works in a generic manner. SMOVER also only addresses detecting conflicts regarding the semantics of a model and does not cover syntactic operation-based conflicts.

Approach by Westfechtel. Recently, Westfechtel [117] presented a formal approach for merging EMF models. Although no implementation of his work is available, it provides well-defined conflict rules based on set-theoretical conflict definitions. In [117], Westfechtel does not address the issue of identifying differences between model versions and rather focuses on conflict detection only and assumes the presence of change-based differences that can be obtained by, for instance, EMF Compare. Westfechtel's approach is directly tailored to EMF models and defines *context-free merge rules* and *context-sensitive merge rules*. Context-free merge rules determine "the set of objects that should be included into the merged versions and consider each feature of each object without taking the context [i.e., relationships to other objects] into account" [117]. The presented algorithm also supports merging of ordered features and specifies when to raise update-update conflicts. The conflict types defined by Westfechtel have been discussed in Section 3.4 already. Besides these operation-based conflicts, Westfechtel also addresses conflicts arising from the well-formedness rules of EMF. However, no techniques that enable further language-specific constraints are discussed. Moreover, he only addresses conflicts among atomic operations and is not adaptable to language-specific knowledge.

4.3 Summary

After surveying existing model versioning approaches, we may conclude that the predominant strategy is to apply state-based model differencing and generic model versioning. The majority of model differencing approaches rely on UUIDs for matching. However, only ADAMS combines UUIDs and (very simple) content-based heuristics. The detection of applications of composite operations is only supported by approaches applying operation recording. The only approach that is capable of detecting composite operations by using a state-based model comparison approach is Gerth et al.; however, their approach is specifically tailored to process models and the supported composite operations are limited to compound additions and deletions. Consequently, none of the surveyed generic approaches is capable of detecting applications of more complex composite operations having well-defined pre- and postconditions without directly recording their application in the editor. Furthermore, none of the approaches are adaptable in terms of additional match rules or composite operation specifications. EMF Compare and EMFStore foresee at least an interface to be implemented in order to extend the set of detectable applications of composite operations. In EMF Compare, however, the detection algorithm has to be provided by an own implementation.

In EMFStore, additional commands may be plugged into the modeling editor programmatically for enabling EMFStore to record them.

Obviously, all model versioning approaches provide detection capabilities for conflicts caused by two concurrent atomic operations. Unfortunately, most of them lack a detailed definition or at least a publicly available implementation. Therefore, we could not evaluate which types of conflicts can actually be detected by the respective approaches. In this regard, we may highlight Alanen and Porres, EMF Compare, EMFStore, Gerth et al., and Westfechtel. These either clearly specify their conflict detection rules in their publications or publish their detection capabilities in terms of a publicly available implementation.

Only Cicchetti et al. and Gerth et al. truly consider composite operations in their conflict detection components. However, in the case of Cicchetti et al., all potentially occurring conflict patterns in the context of composite operations have to specified manually. It is not possible to derive automatically the conflict detection capabilities regarding composite operations from the specifications of such operations. The approach by Gerth et al. is limited to specific modeling language and supports only rather simple composite operations. EMFStore partially respects composite operations: if a conflict between two atomic operations is revealed and one atomic operation is part of a composite operation, the complete composite operation is reverted. However, additional preconditions of composite operations are not considered. None of the surveyed approaches aims at respecting the original intention behind the composite operation; that is, incorporating concurrently changed or added elements in the re-application of the composite operation when creating the merged version.

Several of the surveyed approaches take inconsistent merge results into account. CoObRA is capable of detecting at least a subset of all potentially occurring violations of the modeling language's rules. Westfechtel only addresses the basic well-formedness rules coming from EMF, such as spanning containment tree. The approaches proposed by Alanen and Porres, EMFStore, Gerth et al., Oda and Saeki, and the RSA perform a full validation after merging.

Most of the proposed conflict detection approaches are not adaptable. ADAMS and Odyssey-VCS provide some basic configuration possibilities such as changing the unit of comparison. EMF Compare can be programmatically extended to attach additional conflict detection implementations. Only Cicchetti et al. and SMOVER allow to plug in language-specific artifacts to enable revealing additional conflicts. However, in the approach by Cicchetti et al., the conflict patterns have to be manually created in terms of object models, which seems to be a great deal of work requiring deep understanding of the underlying metamodel. Due to the lack of a public implementation, it is hard to evaluate the ease of use and the scalability of this approach. SMOVER allows to provide a mapping of a model to a semantic view in order to enable the detection of semantically equivalent or contradicting parts of a model. The comparison and conflict detection algorithm that is applied to the semantic views, however, is not adaptable. Consequently, SMOVER only aims to detect a very specific subset of conflicts only.

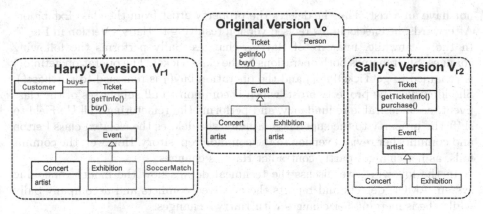

Fig. 7. Model Versioning Example

Conflict resolution has not gained much attention among existing approaches yet. Only four of the 15 surveyed approaches, namely CoObRA, Mehra et al., Ohst et al., and the RSA provide dedicated views for visualizing conflicts adequately to help developers to understand and resolve conflicts. Most notably concerning conflict resolution is the approach by Cicchetti et al., which allows to specify dedicated conflict resolution strategies for certain conflict patterns.

5   An Introduction to AMOR

In this section, we introduce the *adaptable model versioning system* AMOR[12], which has been jointly developed at the Vienna University of Technology[13], the Johannes Kepler University Linz[14], and SparxSystems[15]. Therefore, we first present a model versioning scenario in Section 5.1 serving as running example throughout the remainder of this section. Next, we discuss the goals of AMOR and give an overview of the AMOR merge process in Section 5.2. Subsequently, we describe each step in the merge process in more detail in the sections 5.3 to 5.6.

5.1   Running Example

Consider the following example. The modelers Harry and Sally work together on a project, where an event managing system has to be developed. Both modelers check out the latest version of the common repository (cf. Original Version V_o in Fig. 7) and start with their changes. Harry renames the class Person to Customer and adds an association buys from Customer to Ticket. He further renames the operation getInfo() in class Ticket to getTInfo(). In Harry's opinion exhibitions do

---

[12] http://www.modelversioning.org
[13] http://www.tuwien.ac.at
[14] http://www.jku.at
[15] http://www.sparxsystems.eu

not have an artist. Thus he deletes the property artist from the class Exhibition. Afterwards, he checks in his revised version resulting in Harry's Version in Fig. 7. In the meanwhile, unaware of Harry's changes, Sally performs the following changes. She renames both operations in the class Ticket. The operation getInfo() is renamed to getTicketInfo() and the operation buy() is renamed to purchase(). She identifies the property artist, which is common to all subclasses of the class Event, as undesirable redundancy, and performs the refactoring Pull Up Field to shift the property to the superclass. Finally, she deletes the isolated class Person and commits her revised version to the common repository. However, the commit fails, as her changes partly contradict Harry's changes.

In the following, we discuss the technical details how the model versioning system AMOR detects and reports the occurred conflicts and accompany Sally while she is merging her changes with Harry's changes.

5.2   AMOR at a Glance

The main goal of AMOR is to combine the advantages of both generic and language-specific model versioning by providing a generic, yet adaptable model versioning framework. The generic framework offers versioning support for all modeling languages conforming to a common meta-metamodel out of the box and enables users to enhance the quality of the versioning capabilities by adapting the framework to specific modeling languages using well-defined adaptation points. Thereby, developers are empowered to balance flexibly between reasonable adaptation efforts and the required level for versioning support. For realizing this goal, we aligned the development of each component according to the following design principles.

Flexibility concerning modeling language and editor. In traditional, code-centric versioning, mainly language-independent systems that do not pose any restrictions concerning the used editor gained significant adoption in practice. Thus, we may draw the conclusion that a versioning system that only supports a restricted set of languages and that has an inherent dependency on the used editor might not find broad adoption in practice. Also, when taking into consideration that domain-specific modeling languages are becoming more and more popular, language-specific systems seem to be an unfavorable choice.

Therefore, AMOR is designed to provide generic versioning support irrespective of the used modeling languages and modeling editors. Generic versioning is accomplished by using the reflective interfaces of the Eclipse Modeling Framework [107] (EMF) serving as reference implementation of OMG's MOF standard [77] (cf. Section 3.1). Thereby, all modeling languages can be handled immediately for which an EMF-based metamodel is available.

AMOR is also independent of the used modeling editor and does not rely on specific features on the editor side. Therefore, we may not apply editor-specific operation recording to obtain the applied operations. Instead, AMOR works only with the states of a model before and after it has been changed and derives the applied operations using state-based model differencing.

Easy adaptation by users. Generic versioning systems are very flexible, but they lack in precision in comparison to language-specific versioning systems because no language-specific knowledge is considered. Therefore, AMOR is adaptable with language-specific knowledge whenever this is needed. Some existing model versioning approaches are adaptable in terms of programming interfaces. Hence, it is possible to implement specific behavior to adapt the system according to their needs. Especially with domain-specific modeling languages, a plethora of different modeling languages exists, which often are not even publicly available. Bearing that in mind, it is hardly possible for versioning system vendors to pre-specify the required adaptations to incorporate language-specific knowledge for all existing modeling languages. Thus, users of the versioning system should be enabled to create and maintain those adaptation artifacts by themselves. This, however, entails that these adaptation artifacts do not require deep knowledge on the implementation of the versioning system and programming skills. Therefore, AMOR is designed to be adapted by providing descriptive adaptation artifacts and uses, as far as possible, well-known languages to specify the required language-specific knowledge. No programming effort is necessary to enhance AMOR's versioning capabilities with respect to language-specific aspects. Besides aiming at the highest possible adaptability, the *ease of adaptation* is one major goal of AMOR.

AMOR Merge Process. The merge process of AMOR is depicted in Fig. 8. This figure presents a more fine-grained view on the same merge process that is depicted in Fig. 1. Furthermore, we now illustrate explicitly the artifacts that are exchanged between the steps of this process. The input of this merge process are three models: the common original model V_o and two concurrently changed models, V_{r1} and V_{r2}.

The first phase of the merge process concerns the operation detection. The goal of this phase of the process is to detect precisely which operations have been applied in between V_o and V_{r1}, as well as between V_o and V_{r2}. As argued above, AMOR aims to be independent from the modeling editor. Hence, a state-based model comparison is performed, which is carried out in three steps in AMOR. First, the revised models are each *matched* with the common original model V_o. Therefrom, two *match models* are obtained, which describe the correspondences among the original model and the revised models. Next, the applied *atomic operations* are computed. Besides these atomic operations, AMOR also provides techniques for detecting *composite operations*, such as model refactorings [109], among the applied atomic operations. The output of this phase of the process are two difference models $D_{V_o,V_{r1}}$ and $D_{V_o,V_{r2}}$, which describe all operations performed in the concurrent modifications. The operation detection is discussed more precisely in Section 5.3.

Based on the two difference models computed in the previous phase of the process, the next phase of the process aims to detect *conflicts* among the concurrently applied operations. Thereby not only *atomic operation conflicts* (e.g., delete-update conflicts), but also conflicts among *composite operations* are revealed in the respective steps of this phase. All detected conflicts are saved into

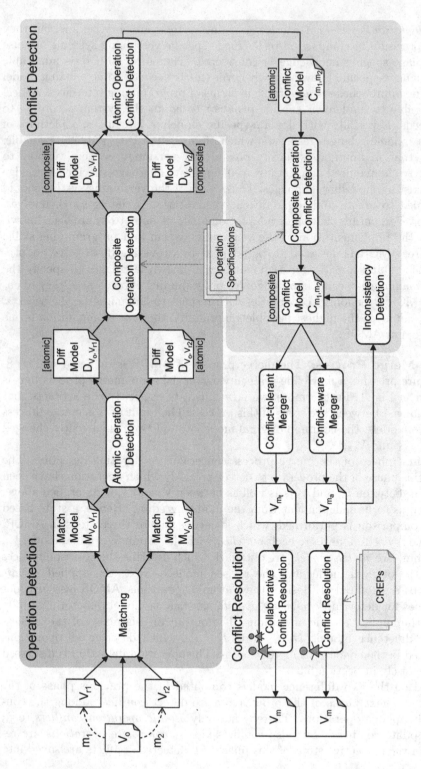

Fig. 8. AMOR Merge Process

a *conflict model* called C_{m_1,m_2} in Fig. 8. More information on how conflicts are detetected in AMOR is provided in Section 5.4.

The computed differences and detected conflicts serve then as input for the *conflict resolution* phase. AMOR's conflict resolution process may be adapted and provides two interchangeable strategies. Both strategies combine the strength of automatic merging and inconsistency toleration and calculate a *tentative merge*, which is discussed in Section 5.5. The tentative merge acts as base for either *collaborative* conflict resolution or for *recommendation supported* conflict resolution, as elaborated in Section 5.6.

5.3   Operation Detection

The first phase of the merge process is the operation detection with the goal to detect precisely which operations have been applied in between V_o and V_{r1}, as well as V_o and V_{r2}. This phase consists of three steps, model *matching*, *atomic operation detection*, and *composite operation detection* (cf. Fig. 8), which are discussed in the following.

Model Matching. AMOR aims to be independent from the modeling editor. Hence, state-based model differencing is applied. The first step of model differencing is model matching, which computes the corresponding model elements between the original model V_o and the revised models V_{r1} and V_{r2}. The computed correspondences are saved in two distinct match models $M_{V_o,V_{r1}}$ and $M_{V_o,V_{r2}}$. Therein, one correspondence connects a model element in the original model V_o with its corresponding revised model in V_{r1} or V_{r2}, respectively.

Computing correspondences between model elements. Even if UUID-based matching is probably the most efficient and straightforward technique for obtaining the actual model changes, there are some drawbacks of this approach. In particular, if model elements loose their UUID, they cannot be matched anymore. Unfortunately, such a scenario is happening quite frequently; not only because the developer deletes and re-creates a similar model element subsequently, but also because of improperly implemented copy & paste or move actions in certain modeling editors causing the model elements' UUIDs to be lost (e.g., in the tree-based Ecore editor).

To address these drawbacks, we apply a two-step matching process: first, a UUID-based matching is applied to obtain a base match, which is improved subsequently by applying user-specified language-specific match rules to the pairs of model elements that could not be matched based on their UUIDs. Thereby, the advantages of UUID-based matching is retained and its drawbacks are reduced significantly. As the comparatively slow rule-based matching is kept at a minimum with this approach, the additional execution time of the model matching phase should still be reasonable.

Representing correspondences. Having obtained the model element correspondences between the original model V_o and a revised model, called V_r to refer

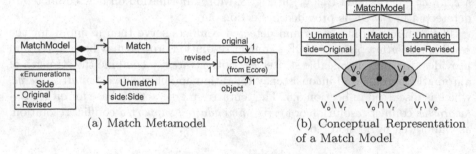

(a) Match Metamodel

(b) Conceptual Representation of a Match Model

Fig. 9. Representing Model Correspondences

to both V_{r1} and V_{r2}, they have to be represented in some way for their further usage. Therefore, we introduce the match metamodel depicted in Fig. 9a. Please note that this match metamodel is largely equivalent to the one used in EMF Compare [14]. Basically, a match model is a so-called *weaving model* [31], which adds additional information to two existing models by introducing new model elements that refer to the model elements in the original and the revised model. In particular, a match model comprises an instance of the class MatchModel, which contains, for each pair of matching model elements, an instance of the class Match. This instance refers to the corresponding model element in the original version through the reference original and the revised version through the reference revised. If a model element, either in the original model and in the revised model, could not be matched, an instance of the class Unmatch is created, which refers to the unmatched model element in the respective model. The attribute side indicates whether the unmatched model element resides in the original or the revised model.

A match model groups the model elements in V_o and V_r into three distinct sets (cf. Fig. 9b). The first set constitutes all model elements that are contained in the original version, but not in the revised version (i.e., $V_o \backslash V_r$). The second set contains all model elements that are contained in both models (i.e., $V_o \cap V_r$) and the third set comprises all model elements that are contained in the revised model but not in the original model (i.e., $V_r \backslash V_o$). In EMF, attribute and reference values of a model element are possessed by the respective model element. Thus, they are considered as being a property of the model element rather than being treated as its own entity. Consequently, in the match model only corresponding *model elements* are linked by Match instances.

Atomic Operation Detection. Having obtained the correspondences among model elements in an original model V_o and a revised model V_r, we may now proceed with deriving the atomic operations that have been applied by the user to V_o in order to create V_r. As already mentioned, match models only indicate the corresponding model elements and those model elements that only exist either in V_o or in V_r. Corresponding model elements, however, might not be entirely equal as their attribute values or reference value might have been modified. Therefore,

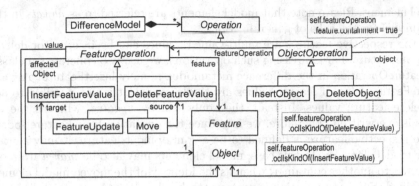

Fig. 10. Difference Metamodel

we further derive a *diff model* from the match model to also represent operations affecting attribute values and reference values before we may search for conflicts among concurrently performed operations. To put the detection of atomic operations in the context of a model versioning scenario, recall that we have two modifications, m_1 and m_2, and one match model comprising the correspondences for each side, $M_{V_o,V_{r1}}$ and $M_{V_o,V_{r2}}$. Therefore, we also have two *diff models* (cf. Fig. 8). In particular, $D_{V_o,V_{r1}}$, which is computed from $M_{V_o,V_{r1}}$, represents the operations applied in m_1 and $D_{V_o,V_{r2}}$, derived from $M_{V_o,V_{r2}}$, represents the operations applied in m_2.

Computing operations from corresponding model elements. Starting from a match model, the detection of applied operations is largely straightforward. In particular, the atomic operation detection component first iterates through all Match instances of this match model and performs a fine-grained feature-wise comparison of the two corresponding model elements. Thereby, the feature values of each feature of both corresponding model elements are checked for equality. If a feature value of one model element differs from the respective value of the corresponding model element, the respective feature of the model element has been subjected to a modification in the revision. After all Match instances have been processed, we proceed with iterating through all Unmatch instances. Depending on its value at the attribute side, we either encounter an *addition* of a new model element if the side is Revised, or a *deletion* if the side is Original.

Representing operations. To represent the applied operations, we introduce a difference model, which is depicted in Fig. 10. Due to space limitations, we only present the *kernel* of the difference metamodel in this paper, which does not reflect more advanced modeling features of EMF models, such as ordered features. For a complete specification of differences between EMF models, we kindly refer to Section 5.2.2 in [56]. In this kernel difference model, we distinguish between two types of operations: FeatureOperation, which modifies the value of a feature, and ObjectOperation, which represent the insertion or deletion of a model element. Please note that model elements are referred to as *objects* in this metamodel for the sake of generalization.

If the respective features are multi-valued, values can be inserted or deleted from the feature. For expressing such operations, we use two concrete subclasses of FeatureOperation in the difference metamodel, namely InsertFeatureValue and DeleteFeatureValue. If feature values are single-valued, it is not possible to add or delete feature values. Instead, they only can be *updated*, whereas the old value is overwritten. Therefore, we introduce the operation type FeatureUpdate. If the respective feature is defined to be a containment feature, it may contain other model elements. In this case, model elements may also be *moved* from one container to another container, whereas the identity of the moved model element is retained. Such an operation is represented by the class Move, which links the deletion of it in the source feature and the insertion of it in the target feature. All types of feature operations refer to the object that has been changed using the reference affectedObject, to the affected feature in the modeling language's metamodel (reference affectedFeature), and to the inserted or deleted feature value (reference value). In case of a reference, this value is a model element and in case of an attribute, the value is a simple data type such as String, or Boolean, etc. However, we omitted to distinguish explicitly between model elements and simply typed data values in Fig. 10 for the sake of readability. It is worth noting that, in case of a InsertFeatureValue, the reference value refers to the inserted value in the revised model (V_{r1} or V_{r2}) and, in case of a DeleteFeatureValue, it refers to the deleted value in the original model V_o.

Besides modifying feature values in existing objects, users may also insert and delete entire objects (i.e., model elements). Therefore, the metamodel contains the two classes InsertObject and DeleteObject, which are subclasses of Object-Operation. Except for root objects, objects are always contained by another object through a *containment feature*. Consequently, inserting and removing an object is realized by a feature operation affecting the respective containment feature. Thus, object operations are further specified by a reference to the respective instance of a FeatureOperation, which gives information on the inserted or deleted object (reference value), the container of the inserted or removed object (reference affectedObject), and the containment feature through which the object is or originally was contained (reference affectedFeature). Certainly, as defined by the invariants in Fig. 10, a valid instance of InsertObject must refer to an instance of InsertFeatureValue and a valid instance of DeleteObject must refer to an instance of DeleteFeatureValue, whereas the affected feature has to be a containment feature.

Example of a difference model. To exemplify the difference metamodel, a concrete instance is depicted in terms of an object diagram in Fig. 11, which represents a subset of the operations applied by Sally in the example introduced in Section 5.1. Please note that we depicted the object diagrams representing the original and the revised model in gray for the sake of readability. This figure depicts an excerpt of the original UML class diagram V_o and Sally's revision V_{r2}, the respective difference model $D_{V_o, V_{r2}}$, as well as an excerpt of the metamodel

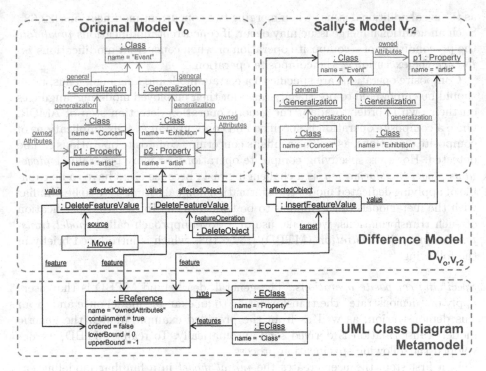

Fig. 11. Example of a Difference Model

for UML class diagrams. Sally moved the attribute artist from the class Concert to its superclass Event and deleted the equally named attribute artist from the class Exhibition. As a result, the difference model contains five operations. First of all, there is an instance of Move, which represents the shift of the attribute artist. As a move is realized by a deletion and a subsequent insertion of a feature value, the instance of Move refers to an instance of DeleteFeatureValue via the reference source and an instance of InsertFeatureValue with the reference target. Besides, Sally deleted the second attribute artist from the class Exhibition, which is represented by an instance of DeleteObject. This deletion is realized by another instance of DeleteFeatureValue referring to the deleted value (i.e., the deleted attribute artist), the affected object (i.e., the containing class Exhibition), as well as the UML metamodel feature the deleted value originally resided in (i.e., the feature ownedAttributes).

Composite Operation Detection. Having represented the applied atomic operations, we proceed with detecting applications of composite operations. Composite operations, such as model refactorings [109], pose specific pre- and postconditions and consist of a set of atomic operations that are executed in a transaction in order to fulfill one common goal. Thus, the knowledge on applications of composite operations between two versions of a model significantly helps in many scenarios to better respect the original intention of a developer, as well as to reveal additional issues when merging two concurrent modifications [22,68]. Such an additional merge issue may occur, if concurrent modifications *invalidate* the preconditions of a composite operation or when concurrent modifications *influence* the execution of the composite operation.

Composite operations are specific to a certain modeling language. Thus, users should be empowered to pre-specify them for their employed modeling languages on their own in order to adapt the generic operation detection step of AMOR. Once a composite operation is specified and configured in AMOR, applications of composite operations, as well as conflicts concerning composite operations can be detected. However, specifying composite operations, or more generally, *endogenous model transformation*, is a challenging task, because users have to be capable of applying dedicated model transformation languages and have to be familiar with the metamodels of the models to be transformed. To ease the specification of such transformations, we make use of a novel approach called *model transformation by demonstration* (MTBD) [13,56,108], which is introduced briefly in the following.

Specifying composite operations. The general idea behind MTBD is that users apply or "demonstrate" the transformation to an example model once and, from this demonstration, as well as from the provided example model, the generic model transformation is derived semi-automatically. To realize MTBD, we developed the following specification process.

In a first step, the user creates the *initial model* in a familiar modeling environment. This initial model contains all model elements that are required in order to apply the composite operation. Next, each element of the initial model is annotated automatically with an ID, and a so-called *working model* (i.e., a copy of the initial model for demonstrating the composite operation by applying its atomic operations) is created. Subsequently, the user performs the complete composite operation on the working model by applying all necessary atomic operations. The output of this step is the *revised model*, which is together with the initial model the input for the following steps of the operation specification process. Due to the unique IDs, which preserve the relationship among model elements in the initial model and their corresponding model elements in the revised model, the atomic operations of the composite operation may be obtained precisely using our model comparison approach presented above. The obtained operations are saved in a *difference model*. Subsequently, an initial version of *pre-* and *postconditions* of the composite operation is inferred by analyzing the initial model and the revised model, respectively. The automatically generated conditions from the example might not always entirely express the intended pre- and postconditions of the composite operation. They only act as a basis for accelerating the operation specification process and may be refined by the user. In particular, parts of the conditions may be activated, deactivated, or modified within a dedicated environment. If needed, additional conditions may be added. After the configuration of the conditions, an operation specification is generated, which is a model-based representation of the composite operation consisting of the diff model and the revised pre- and postconditions, as well as the initial and

Excerpt of the Preconditions	Excerpt of the Postconditions

•**Class_0** [Event]
•**Class_1** [Concert]
  • generalisations->includes(Generalisation_0)
  • ownedAttributes->includes(Property_0)
•**Generalisation_0**
  • general = Class_0
• **Property_0** [artist] ⟳
•**Class_2** [Exhibition] ⟳
  • generalisations->includes(Generalisation_1)
  • ownedAttributes->includes(Property_1)
• **Generalisation_1**
  • general = Class_0
• **Property_1** [artist] ⟳
  • name = Property_0.name
	•**Class_0** [Event]
	  • **Property_0** [artist]
	•**Class_1** [Concert]
	  • generalisations->includes(Generalisation_0)
	  • ownedAttributes->includes(Property_0)
	•**Generalisation_0**
	  • general = Class_0
	•**Class_2** [Exhibition]
	  • generalisations->includes(Generalisation_1)
	•**Generalisation_1**
	  • general = Class_0

Legend: ⟳ ... iteration

Fig. 12. Excerpt of the Pre- and Postconditions of "Pull Up Field"

revised example model. Thus, this model contains all necessary information for executing the composite operation, as well as for detecting applications of it. For more information on the specification process, and how these specifications can be executed automatically to arbitrary models, we kindly refer to [13,56,108].

Example for specifying "Pull Up Field". To provide a better understanding of how composite operations can be specified, we discuss the specification process for developing the composite operation "Pull Up Field". In the first step, the user creates the initial model, which contains all model elements that are necessary to apply the composite operation. The resulting initial model is equivalent to the original model depicted in Fig. 11. Now, a copy of this initial model is created automatically, to which the user now applies all atomic operations, which leads to the revised model again shown in Fig. 11. From these two models, we now compute the applied atomic operations using the previously discussed model comparison resulting in the difference model of our previous example presented in Fig. 11. Besides for computing the atomic operations, these two models also act as input for the automatic derivation of the pre- and postconditions in the form of OCL expressions [84], which may now be fine-tuned by the user. The resulting conditions, after the refinement by the user, are illustrated in Fig. 12. The pre- and postconditions are structured according to the model elements in the initial and revised model, respectively, and my refer to each other using a model element identifier (e.g., Class_0), which is comparable to a variable. The user only has to refine the precondition name = Property_0.name in order to restrict the names of the properties that are pulled up to the common superclass to be equal. In other words, the property Property_1, which resides in the second subclass Class_2 must have the same name as the other property Property_0, which is contained by the class Class_1, for acting as a valid property in this composite operation. Without satisfying this condition, the execution of the refactoring would lead to a change of the semantics of the model, because Class_2 would inherit a differently named property from its superclass after the refactoring has been applied. Besides fine-tuning this precondition, the user may also attach *iterations*, which has been done for Property_0, Class_1, and Property_1. With these iterations, the user specifies that all atomic operations that have been applied to these model elements in the demonstration have to be repeated *for all* model elements that match the respective preconditions when applied to an arbitrary model.

Detecting composite operations. After the difference models are computed, we may proceed with the next step in the merge process, which aims at detecting applications of composite operations (cf. Fig. 8). The composite operation detection step relies on a set of composite operation specification. As mentioned above, an operation specification contains a description of the atomic operations applied during the demonstration of the composite operation, which can be thought of as the *difference pattern* of the composite operation. Besides this difference pattern, an operation specification also contains the composite operation's pre- and postconditions.

For detecting applications of composite operations, it is searched for occurrences of the composite operations' difference pattern in each of the difference models $D_{V_o,V_{r1}}$ and $D_{V_o,V_{r2}}$. If a difference pattern could be found, the respective parts of the original model V_o are evaluated concerning the composite operation's preconditions. If also these preconditions are fulfilled in the original model, also the postconditions of the composite operation are verified for the corresponding model elements in the respective revised model. In case also the postconditions can be evaluated positively in the revised model, an application of the respective composite operation is reported and annotated in the difference model. For more information on how composite operations are detected in AMOR, we kindly refer to Section 5.3 in [56].

5.4   Conflict Detection

Having obtained the operations that have been applied concurrently to the common original model, we may now proceed with detecting conflicts among them. As discussed in Section 3.4, a conflict occurs if two operations do not commute or if one operation is not applicable anymore after the other operation has been performed. The conflict detection in AMOR takes two difference models, $D_{V_o,V_{r1}}$ and $D_{V_o,V_{r2}}$, as input and is realized by two subsequent steps: the *atomic operation conflict detection* and the *composite operation conflict detection*.

Atomic operation conflict detection. The goal of the first step, the atomic operation conflict detection, is to find concurrent *atomic operations* that interfere with each other. This step is completely generic and does not demand for language-specific information. Also composite operations remain unconsidered in this step; however, the atomic operations that realize the composite operation applications are still included in the conflict detection mechanisms.

We define the types of atomic operation conflicts by so-called generic *conflict patterns*. These conflict patterns serve, on the one hand, as a clear specification of the existing conflict types, and, on the other hand, they can be used for

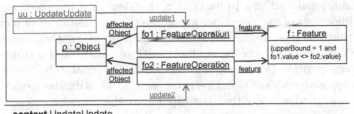

context UpdateUpdate
inv: self.update1.affectedObject = self.update2.affectedObject **and**
self.update1.feature = self.update2.feature **and**
(self.update1.feature.upperBound = 1 **and**
self.update1.value <> self.update2.value)

Fig. 13. Update-update Conflict Pattern

detecting conflicts. More precisely, if such a conflict pattern matches with two operations in the difference models, $D_{V_o,V_{r1}}$ and $D_{V_o,V_{r2}}$, a conflict of the respective type occurred. However, for the sake of efficiency, we refrain from checking the complete crossproduct of all operation combinations among all operations of both difference models. In contrast, both difference models are translated in a first step into an optimized view grouping all operations according to their type into potentially conflicting combinations. Secondly, all combinations are filtered out if they do not spatially affect overlapping parts of the original model. Finally, all remaining combinations are checked in detail by evaluating the conflict rules.

An example for such a conflict pattern is provided in Fig. 13, which defines an *update-update conflict* in terms of an object diagram, as well as an OCL constraint. As already mentioned, if a single-valued feature is concurrently modified in EMF models a conflict occurs, because the merged model may not contain both values and one value overwrites the other; thus, two updates of the same feature value do not commute. Therefore, as illustrated in the conflict pattern in Fig. 13, an *update-update* conflict is raised, if an object o has been concurrently updated at the same feature f by two instances of FeatureOperation, fo1 and fo2, unless both operations set the same new value such that fo1.value = fo2.value. In our running example presented in Section 5.1, we encounter such a conflict. Harry and Sally both renamed the UML operation getInfo(). Since the name of UML operations is a single-valued feature and the new values for the name of the UML operation are different (getTInfo() vs. getTicketInfo()), an update-update conflict is raised.

All detected conflicts are saved into a conflict model called C_{m_1,m_2}, which is a model-based description of the occurred conflicts. Such a description provides the necessary information concerning the type of the conflict and the involved atomic operations. The complete set of all conflict patterns, as well as the conflict metamodel is discussed more profoundly in Section 6.1 of [56].

Composite operation conflict detection. The next step in the conflict detection phase is the composite operation conflict detection, which takes the knowledge on the ingredients of composite operations, such as preconditions, into account for revealing additional conflicts. In particular, this step aims to detect scenarios in which modifications of one developer invalidate the preconditions of a composite operation that has been applied in a parallel revision by another developer.

To detect composite operation conflicts, each application of a composite operation in one revision (let us assume this is V_{r1}) is separately checked at the respective opposite revision V_{r2}. Therefore, we first identify the model elements of the opposite revision V_{r2} that correspond to the model elements in V_o to which the composite operation has been applied originally. Next, we evaluated the preconditions of the composite operation with the identified model elements of V_{r2}. If the preconditions are not fulfilled, the composite operation cannot be applied after the concurrent operations have been performed; thus, a conflict is raised and added to the conflict model C_{m_1,m_2}.

Such a conflict is illustrated in the running example presented in Section 5.1. Sally applied the refactoring "Pull Up Field" by moving the property artist from the classes Concert and Exhibition to their common superclass Event. As discussed in Section 5.3, a precondition of this composite operation is that each subclass must contain a property having the same name as the property that is moved to the common superclass. However, in the concurrent revision, Harry deleted the property artist and added another subclass named SoccerMatch without having a property named artist. Thus, the composite operation is not applicable to the revised version of Harry, because no valid match could be found for the preconditions of the refactoring. Consequently, a composite operation conflict, which is also referred to as *composite operation contract violation*, is added to the conflict model C_{m_1,m_2}.

5.5   Merging

With the conflict model C_{m_1,m_2} at hand, we may now proceed with merging the parallel evolved models. Merging is the intricate task of usually one developer, i.e., the developer who performs the later check-in, of integrating all changes into one consolidated version of the model. However, several strategies exist how merging may be realized, as discussed in Section 3.5. To justify AMOR's claim for adaptability not only with respect to supported modeling languages and detectable conflicts, also the merge process may be configured. The overall goal is to support the developer in understanding the evolution of the other developer's version as well as how this version contradicts her own changes to the model. In fact, AMOR provides two interchangeable merge strategies, each tailored to specific needs of a project's stage.

Conflict-tolerant merging is adopted in the early phases of a project, i.e., analysis phase and design phase, where a common perception of the system under study is not yet established. These phases are considered critical, as mistakes are likely to happen and the costs of fixing such errors are high, when detected in later phases [37]. Thus, in order to keep all viewpoints on the system, conflicts are not resolved immediately after each commit, but are tolerated until a specified milestone is reached. Then, to minimize the risk of losing any modifications, all developers may resolve conflicts together in a meeting or with the help of a tool-supported collaborative setting as proposed in [118,12].

Conflict-aware merging is primary designed to support merging of a single developer after each commit. If conflicts are not collaboratively resolved, it is even more important, that the developer in charge of merging is supported to effectually understand the model's evolution. In a manual merge process, the developer has to navigate through several artifacts to collect information necessary to comprehend the intentions behind all operations and the reasons of occurred conflicts. To support this process, we combine automatic merge strategies with the benefits of pollution markers known from the field of tolerating inconsistencies [4,74,102]. We therefore calculate an automatically merged version which reveals all operations and conflicts at a single glance by introducing dedicated annotations. This automatically merged version acts as basis for conflict resolution and is thus denoted *tentative merge*.

In the remainder of this section, we present details how the tentative merge is calculated employing the conflict-aware merge strategy of AMOR.

Design Rationale. In order to fully exploit the abstraction power of models, modeling languages, such as UML, are usually complemented with a graphical concrete syntax to hide the complexity of the abstract syntax. As developers are mostly used to the graphical concrete syntax only, merging shall also be performed directly using the concrete syntax of models. The major goal of conflict-aware merging is to provide the model's evolution in a single graphical view without losing any model elements or modifications. Our design rationale is based on the following requirements.

- *User-friendly visualization.* Information about performed operations and resulting merge conflicts shall be presented in the concrete syntax of the model retaining the original diagram layout.
- *Integrated view.* All information necessary for the merge shall be visualized within a single diagram to provide a complete view on the models evolution.
- *Standard conform models.* The models incorporating the merge information shall be conform to the corresponding metamodel without requiring heavy-weight modifications.
- *Model-based representation.* The merge information shall be explicitly represented as model elements to facilitate model exchange between modeling tools, as well as postponing the resolution of certain conflicts.
- *No editor modifications.* The visualization of the merge information shall be possible without modifying the graphical editors of modeling tools.

In the following, we elaborate on the technical details of the conflict-aware merge strategy with respect to the mentioned requirements.

Model Versioning Profile. As mentioned above, we use annotations to mark conflicting or inconsistent parts of the merged model. Those conflicts are tolerated to a certain extent and eventually corrected. In our case, conflicts are tolerated during the merge phase.

Annotations extend the model and carry information. Hence, annotations need an appropriate representation in the modeling language's abstract and concrete syntaxes. However, creating new modeling languages goes hand in hand with building new editors and code generators, as well as preparing documentation and teaching materials, among others. Further, several modeling languages have already matured and may not be neglected when setting up versioning support. Thus, mechanisms are needed to *customize existing languages*. When directly *modifying existing languages*, the aforementioned issues remain unsolved, as newly introduced metamodel elements cannot be parsed by existing editors. According to [3], a lightweight language customization approach is desirable. For customizing immutable modeling languages like UML, *UML profiles* are the means of choice. UML profiles provide a language-inherent, non-intrusive mechanism for dynamically adapting the existing language to specific needs. As UML profiles are not only part of UML, but defined in the infrastructure specification [85], various modeling languages, which are defined as instance of the common core may be profiled and thus dynamically tailored. UML profiles define a lightweight extension to the UML metamodel and allow for customizing UML to a specific domain. UML profiles typically comprise *stereotypes*, *tagged values*, and additional *constraints* stating how profiled UML models shall be built. Stereotypes are used to introduce additional modeling concepts which extend standard UML metaclasses. Once a stereotype is specified for a metaclass, the stereotype may be applied to instances of the extended metaclass to provide further semantics. With tagged values, additional properties may be defined for stereotypes. These tagged values may then be set on the modeling level for applied stereotypes. Furthermore, syntactic sugar in terms of icons for defined stereotypes may be configured to improve the visualization of profiled UML models. The major benefit of UML profiles is, reflected by the fact that profiled models are still conforming to UML, that they are naturally handled by current UML tools. Recently, in an endeavor to broaden the idea of UML profiles to modeling languages based on implementations of Essential MOF [77], such as Ecore [23], several works have been published [51,57,61]. The profiling mechanism inherently reflects our design rationale and is thus our means of choice. UML profiles are standardized by the OMG and act as conceptual role model for Ecore based implementations. Thus, we discuss the annotations for the conflict-aware merge based on UML profiles in the following.

The information on detected operations and conflicts is already available in the difference models $D_{V_o,V_{r1}}$ and $D_{V_o,V_{r2}}$, as well as the conflict model C_{m_1,m_2}, as described in Section 5.3 and Section 5.4, respectively. However, we assemble the difference and conflict models and generate a dedicated *model versioning profile* to realize the gluing of the available information into the model. Thus, the versioning profile reflects the separation on changes and conflicts and explicates additional information on the respective users, which was only implicitly available beforehand. An excerpt of the versioning profile is depicted in Fig. 14. Detailed information on the versioning profile may be found in Section 5.3 in [11].

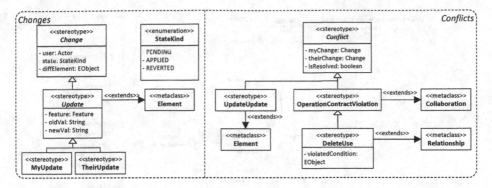

Fig. 14. Excerpt of the Model Versioning Profile

Changes. The versioning profile provides stereotypes for each kind of atomic operation, i.e., ≪Add≫, ≪Delete≫, ≪Update≫, ≪Move≫, and a stereotype for composite operations, i.e., ≪CompositeChange≫. Each change stereotype is specialized as ≪MyChange≫ and ≪TheirChange≫ to explicate the user who performed the change. An atomic change is always performed on a single UML element, i.e., Class, Generalization, Property, etc., and thus, is defined to extend Element, the root metaclass of the UML metamodel (cf. stereotype ≪Update≫ in the left part of Fig. 14). In contrast, a composite change incorporates a set of indivisible atomic operations. Therefore, we introduce a new UML Collaboration interlinking the involved elements, which is annotated with a ≪CompositeChange≫ stereotype. Further metadata regarding the respective users, the application state of the change, and the affected feature of the changed element including its old and new value in case of updates is stored in tagged values.

Conflicts. The conflict part of the versioning profile defines stereotypes for all conflict patterns subsumed in the conflict metamodel. Again, stereotypes for overlapping operations regarding a single element, such as ≪UpdateUpdate≫ in the right part of Fig. 14, extend the metaclass Element, while violations, like an ≪OperationContractViolation≫ comprise different modeling elements and are thus annotated on newly introduced Collaboration elements. In case of an ≪OperationContractViolation≫, the UML relationships interlinking the involved elements to the UML collaboration, are annotated with stereotypes (inspired from graph transformation theory [55]) indicating how the contract is violated by the model element. The stereotype ≪DeleteUse≫ are applied on model elements already existing in the original model, which are involved in a composite operation and deleted by the other user, respectively. ≪AddForbid≫ indicates the addition of a new model element which invalidates the precondition of a composite operation. Finally, all conflict stereotypes refer via tagged values to the underlying change stereotypes, what makes understanding and reproducing the conflicts possible.

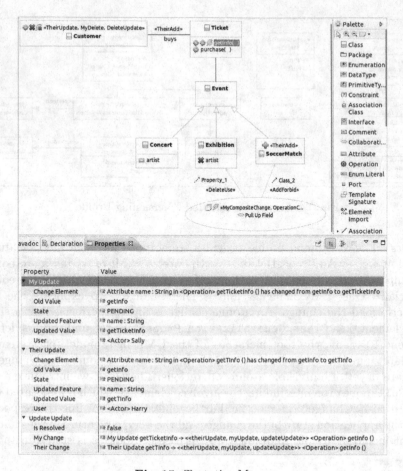

Fig. 15. Tentative Merge

Merge Algorithm. With the versioning profile at hand, we may now proceed with merging the parallel evolved versions V_{r1} and V_{r2}. The conflict-aware merge strategy automatically calculates a tentatively merged version V_{m_a}, by embracing all non-conflicting operations in an element preserving manner. Additionally, conflicting operations are not ignored, but integrated via dedicated stereotypes of the versioning profile. The merge algorithm takes the common original model V_o, the difference models $D_{V_o,V_{r1}}$ and $D_{V_o,V_{r2}}$, and the conflict model C_{m_1,m_2} as input and produces a tentative merge, as depicted in Fig. 15. Details on merging the concrete syntax of the models may be found in Chapter 5 in [11]. The algorithm for merging the abstract syntax proceeds as follows. In order to keep the original model V_o untouched, it is initially copied to the output model V_{m_a}.

1. *Merge atomic operations.* For each atomic change of $D_{V_o,V_{r1}}$ and $D_{V_o,V_{r2}}$, it is checked, whether the change is involved in a conflict pattern described in the conflict model C_{m_1,m_2}, or whether it is considered non-conflicting. If

the change is non-conflicting and non-deleting, it is applied to the tentative merge V_{m_a} and annotated with the respective stereotype. In the running example of Fig. 7, the renaming of the operation buy() to purchase() performed by Sally is executed and annotated as ≪MyUpdate≫, as Sally did the later check-in and the merge is performed reflecting her viewpoint. The corresponding metadata of the difference model is stored in tagged values of the stereotype. Additionally, the tagged value user is set to Sally and the state value is set to APPLIED. Even if deletions are non-conflicting, they are not yet executed, as they otherwise cannot be annotated and information would get lost. Similarly, conflicting operations are annotated with state value set to PENDING without applying them to the tentative merge. Thus, the class Person deleted by Sally and renamed to Customer by Harry is annotated with the stereotypes ≪TheirUpdate≫ and ≪MyDelete≫ in this step.

2. *Annotate overlapping operations.* After processing all atomic operations, conflicts due to overlapping atomic operations are annotated. In the running example, the operation getInfo() of class Ticket is concurrently renamed resulting in an update-update conflict. Thus, the operation is annotated with an ≪UpdateUpdate≫ stereotype, which links to the respective change stereotypes via tagged values. Further, it the tagged value indicating the resolution state is set to `false`, as depicted in Fig. 15.

3. *Merge composite operations.* To express that composite operations consists of an indivisible unit of atomic operations, a UML `Collaboration` is added to the tentative merge, which links to the involved elements and is annotated with a ≪CompositeChange≫ stereotype. If no composite operation conflict is reported in the conflict model C_{m_1,m_2}, the composite change is replayed to the tentative merge and set to APPLIED. Otherwise, it is still PENDING.

4. *Annotate operation contract violations.* If a composite operation conflict is at hand, a ≪CompositeOperationConflict≫ stereotype is attached to the collaboration. Further, the relationships linking to the affected model elements of conflicting operations are named according to the the operation specification's template names and subsequently annotated. In the running example, the deletion of the property artist in class Exhibition (cf. Property_1 in Fig. 12) and the added class SoccerMatch (Class_2) violate the precondition of the refactoring Pull Up Field. Thus, the relationships are annotated with ≪DeleteUse≫ and ≪AddForbid≫, respectively.

5. *Validate model.* Next, the tentative merge is then validated and, if constraints are violated, the violation is added to the conflict report C_{m_1,m_2}.

6. *Annotate constraint violations.* Finally, the detected violations are annotated in the tentative merge, by again introducing UML `Collaboration` elements linking to the model elements involved in the violation.

5.6   Conflict Resolution

In AMOR, conflict resolution is performed on top of the tentative merge. The stereotypes included in the tentative merge may be further exploited to provide dedicated tooling support for conflict resolution. For example, resolution actions in form of "take my change", "take their change", or "revert this change" may be easily implemented, as the link to the difference model is retained. However, as the same kind of conflicts are likely to reoccur, AMOR provides a recommender system for conflict resolution, which suggests even Conflict Resolution Patterns going beyond a combination of applied changes. These patterns are stored in AMOR's conflict resolution pattern repository and are currently predefined in the same manner as composite operations (cf. Section 5.3).

Coming back to the running example, Sally has to resolve several conflicts, which are annotated in the tentative merge. She starts resolving the delete-update conflict annotated in the class Customer. As there is currently no conflict resolution pattern stored in the conflict resolution recommender system for the resolution of delete-update conflicts, only the choices of applying one of the respective changes is available. Sally decides to revert her delete operation. The application states stored in the tagged values of the overlapping delete and update operations are automatically set to REVERTED and APPLIED, respectively. Further, the tagged value isResolved of the ≪DeleteUpdate≫ stereotype is set to true. She continues with the update-update conflict of the operation get-Info(), where she prefers her change. Now, only the composite operation conflict remains left. Sally disagrees with Harry's opinion that exhibitions do not have an artist, and she reverts his change, resulting in a removal of the delete-use conflict. The conflict resolution recommender system announces, that a conflict resolution pattern is found for the remaining add-forbid conflict. The resolution is performed by introducing a new class into the inheritance hierarchy. The new class gets subclass of the class Event and superclass of the classes Concert and Exhibition. In this way, it displaces the original superclass as target for the Pull Up Field refactoring. Sally has only to provide a name for the new class and is confident with this solution. Finally, she commits the resolved version to the repository.

6   Open Challenges

In this paper, we introduced the fundamental technologies in the area of model versioning and surveyed existing approaches in this research domain. Besides, we gave an overview on the model versioning system AMOR and showcased its techniques based on a model versioning example. Although the active research community accomplished remarkable achievements in the area of model versioning in the last years, this research field still poses a multitude of interesting open challenges to be addressed in future, which we outline in the following.

Intention-aware model versioning. When merging two concurrently modified versions, ideally the merged version represents a combination of *all intentions* each developer had in mind when performing their operations. Merging intentions is usually more than just naively combining all non-conflicting atomic operations of both sides. When a developer modifies a model, this is done in order to realize a certain goal rather than simply modifying some parts of it. However, capturing the developer's intention from a set of operations is a major challenge.

A first step in this direction is respecting the original intention of composite operations, such as model refactorings, in the merge process. Composite operations constitute a set of cohesive atomic operations that are applied in order to fulfill one common goal. Therefore, detecting applications of well-defined composite operations and regarding their conditions and intention during the merge is a first valuable step towards intention-aware versioning [22,56,68].

However, further means for capturing and respecting the intention of applied operations may be investigated, such as allowing developers to annotate his/her intention for a set of applied operations in a structured and automatically verifyable manner. For instance, a developer might want to change a metamodel in order to limit its instatiability. Thus, an "issue witness" in terms of an instance model that should not be valid anymore can be annotated to give the set of applied operations more meaning. After merging concurrent operations, the versioning system may verify whether the original intention (i.e., the noninstatiability of the issue witness) is still fulfilled.

Semantics-aware model versioning. Current model versioning systems mainly facilitate matching and differencing algorithms operating on the syntactic level only. However, syntactical operations that are not conflicting may still cause semantic issues and unexpected properties (e.g., deadlocks in behavior diagrams). Thus, a combination of syntactic and semantic conflict detection is highly valuable but very challenging to achieve, because currently no commonly agreed formal semantics exists for widespread employed modeling languages, such as UML. First approaches for performing semantic differencing are very promising [62,63,64,73]. As these approaches focus only on two-way comparison and operate on a restricted set of modeling languages and constructs, the application of semantic differencing techniques in model versioning systems is not directly possible yet and the definition of a formal semantics for a comprehensive set of the UML, including intra-model dependencies, is a challenge on its own. Furthermore, as models may be used as sketch in the early phases of software development, as well as for specifying systems precisely to generate code, a satisfactory compromise has to be found to do justice to the multifaceted application fields of modeling.

Overall, we conclude this tutorial with the observation that the research area of model versioning still offers a multitude of tough challenges despite the many achievements which have been made until today. These challenges must be overcome in order to obtain solutions which ease the work of the developers in practice. The final aim is to establish methods which are so well integrated in the development process that the developers themselves do not have to care about versioning tasks and that they are not distracted from their actual work by time consuming management activities. Therefore, different facets of the modeling process itself have to be reviewed to gain a better understanding of the inherent dynamic. Versioning is about supporting team work, i.e., about the management of people who work together in order to achieve a common goal. Consequently, versioning solutions require not only the handling of technical issues like adequate differencing and conflict detection algorithms or adequate visualization approaches, but also the consideration of social and organizational aspects. Especially in the context of modeling, the current versioning approaches have to be questioned and eventually revised. Here the requirements posed on the versioning systems may depend on the intended usage of the models.

References

1. Alanen, M., Porres, I.: Difference and Union of Models. In: Stevens, P., Whittle, J., Booch, G. (eds.) UML 2003. LNCS, vol. 2863, pp. 2–17. Springer, Heidelberg (2003)
2. Altmanninger, K., Brosch, P., Kappel, G., Langer, P., Seidl, M., Wieland, K., Wimmer, M.: Why Model Versioning Research is Needed!? An Experience Report. In: Proceedings of the MoDSE-MCCM 2009 Workshop @ MoDELS 2009 (2009)
3. Atkinson, C., Kühne, T.: A Tour of Language Customization Concepts. Advances in Computers 70, 105–161 (2007)
4. Balzer, R.: Tolerating Inconsistency. In: Proceedings of the 13th International Conference on Software Engineering (ICSE 1991), pp. 158–165. IEEE (1991)
5. Barrett, S., Butler, G., Chalin, P.: Mirador: A Synthesis of Model Matching Strategies. In: Proceedings of the International Workshop on Model Comparison in Practice (IWMCP 2010), pp. 2–10. ACM (2010)
6. Berners-Lee, T., Hendler, J.: Scientific Publishing on the Semantic Web. Nature 410, 1023–1024 (2001)
7. Bézivin, J.: On the Unification Power of Models. Software and Systems Modeling 4(2), 171–188 (2005)
8. Bézivin, J.: From Object Composition to Model Transformation with the MDA. In: Proceedings of the 39th International Conference and Exhibition on Technology of Object-Oriented Languages and Systems (TOOLS 2001), pp. 350–355. IEEE (2001)
9. Bézivin, J., Gerbé, O.: Towards a Precise Definition of the OMG/MDA Framework. In: Proceedings of the 16th Annual International Conference on Automated Software Engineering, ASE 2001, pp. 273–280 (2001)
10. Booch, G., Brown, A.W., Iyengar, S., Rumbaugh, J., Selic, B.: An MDA Manifesto. MDA Journal (5) (2004)
11. Brosch, P.: Conflict Resolution in Model Versioning. Ph.D. thesis, Vienna University of Technology (2012)
12. Brosch, P., Langer, P., Seidl, M., Wieland, K., Wimmer, M., Kappel, G.: Concurrent Modeling in Early Phases of the Software Development Life Cycle. In: Kolfschoten, G., Herrmann, T., Lukosch, S. (eds.) CRIWG 2010. LNCS, vol. 6257, pp. 129–144. Springer, Heidelberg (2010)
13. Brosch, P., Langer, P., Seidl, M., Wieland, K., Wimmer, M., Kappel, G., Retschitzegger, W., Schwinger, W.: An Example Is Worth a Thousand Words: Composite Operation Modeling By-Example. In: Schürr, A., Selic, B. (eds.) MoDELS 2009. LNCS, vol. 5795, pp. 271–285. Springer, Heidelberg (2009)
14. Brun, C., Pierantonio, A.: Model Differences in the Eclipse Modeling Framework. UPGRADE, The European Journal for the Informatics Professional 9(2), 29–34 (2008)
15. Church, A., Rosser, J.: Some Properties of Conversion. Transactions of the American Mathematical Society, 472–482 (1936)

16. Cicchetti, A., Di Ruscio, D., Pierantonio, A.: A Metamodel Independent Approach to Difference Representation. Journal of Object Technology 6(9), 165–185 (2007)
17. Cicchetti, A., Di Ruscio, D., Pierantonio, A.: Managing Model Conflicts in Distributed Development. In: Czarnecki, K., Ober, I., Bruel, J.-M., Uhl, A., Völter, M. (eds.) MoDELS 2008. LNCS, vol. 5301, pp. 311–325. Springer, Heidelberg (2008)
18. Conradi, R., Westfechtel, B.: Version Models for Software Configuration Management. ACM Computing Surveys 30(2), 232 (1998)
19. De Lucia, A., Fasano, F., Oliveto, R., Tortora, G.: ADAMS: Advanced Artefact Management System. In: Proceedings of the European Conference on Software Maintenance and Reengineering (CSMR 2006), pp. 349–350. IEEE (2006)
20. De Lucia, A., Fasano, F., Scanniello, G., Tortora, G.: Concurrent Fine-Grained Versioning of UML Models. In: Proceedings of the European Conference on Software Maintenance and Reengineering, pp. 89–98. IEEE (2009)
21. Dig, D., Comertoglu, C., Marinov, D., Johnson, R.: Automated Detection of Refactorings in Evolving Components. In: Hu, Q. (ed.) ECOOP 2006. LNCS, vol. 4067, pp. 404–428. Springer, Heidelberg (2006)
22. Dig, D., Manzoor, K., Johnson, R., Nguyen, T.: Effective Software Merging in the Presence of Object-Oriented Refactorings. IEEE Transactions on Software Engineering 34(3), 321–335 (2008)
23. Eclipse: Eclipse Modeling Framework Project (EMF), http://www.eclipse.org/modeling/emf (accessed November 04, 2011)
24. Eclipse: EMF UML2, http://www.eclipse.org/modeling/mdt/?project=uml2 (accessed December 05, 2011)
25. Edwards, W.K.: Flexible Conflict Detection and Management in Collaborative Applications. In: Proceedings of the 10th Annual ACM Symposium on User Interface Software and Technology, UIST 1997, pp. 139–148. ACM (1997)
26. Ehrig, H.: Introduction to the Algebraic Theory of Graph Grammars (A Survey). In: Ng, E.W., Ehrig, H., Rozenberg, G. (eds.) Graph Grammars 1978. LNCS, vol. 73, pp. 1–69. Springer, Heidelberg (1979)
27. Ehrig, H., Ehrig, K.: Overview of Formal Concepts for Model Transformations Based on Typed Attributed Graph Transformation. Electronic Notes in Theoretical Computer Science 152, 3–22 (2006)
28. Ehrig, H., Ermel, C., Taentzer, G.: A Formal Resolution Strategy for Operation-Based Conflicts in Model Versioning Using Graph Modifications. In: Giannakopoulou, D., Orejas, F. (eds.) FASE 2011. LNCS, vol. 6603, pp. 202–216. Springer, Heidelberg (2011)
29. Ermel, C., Rudolf, M., Taentzer, G.: The AGG Approach: Language and Environment. In: Handbook of Graph Grammars and Computing by Graph Transformation: Applications, Languages and Tools, ch. 14, vol. 2, pp. 551–603. World Scientific Publishing Co., Inc. (1999)
30. Estublier, J., Leblang, D., Hoek, A., Conradi, R., Clemm, G., Tichy, W., Wiborg-Weber, D.: Impact of Software Engineering Research on the Practice of Software Configuration Management. ACM Transactions on Software Engineering and Methodology (TOSEM) 14(4), 383–430 (2005)
31. Fabro, M., Bézivin, J., Jouault, F., Breton, E., Gueltas, G.: AMW: A Generic Model Weaver. In: Proceedings of the 1re Journe sur l'Ingnierie Dirige par les Modles, IDM 2005 (2005)

32. Feather, M.: Detecting Interference When Merging Specification Evolutions. In: Proceedings of the International Workshop on Software Specification and Design (IWSSD 1989), pp. 169–176. ACM (1989)

33. Fowler, M., Beck, K., Brant, J., Opdyke, W., Roberts, D.: Refactoring: Improving the Design of Existing Code. Addison-Wesley (1999)

34. France, R., Rumpe, B.: Model-driven Development of Complex Software: A Research Roadmap. In: Proceedings of Future of Software Engineering @ ICSE 2007, pp. 37–54 (2007)

35. Gerth, C., Küster, J.M., Luckey, M., Engels, G.: Precise Detection of Conflicting Change Operations Using Process Model Terms. In: Petriu, D.C., Rouquette, N., Haugen, Ø. (eds.) MoDELS 2010. LNCS, vol. 6395, pp. 93–107. Springer, Heidelberg (2010)

36. Gerth, C., Küster, J., Luckey, M., Engels, G.: Detection and Resolution of Conflicting Change Operations in Version Management of Process Models. Software and Systems Modeling, pp. 1–19 (Online First)

37. Ghezzi, C., Jazayeri, M., Mandrioli, D.: Fundamentals of Software Engineering, 2nd edn. Prentice Hall PTR, Upper Saddle River (2002)

38. Greenfield, J., Short, K.: Software Factories: Assembling Applications With Patterns, Models, Frameworks and Tools. In: Proceedings of the Conference on Object-oriented Programming, Systems, Languages, and Applications (OOPSLA 2003), pp. 16–27. ACM (2003)

39. Harel, D., Rumpe, B.: Meaningful Modeling: What's the Semantics of Semantics? Computer 37(10), 64–72 (2004)

40. Heckel, R., Küster, J., Taentzer, G.: Confluence of Typed Attributed Graph Transformation Systems. In: Corradini, A., Ehrig, H., Kreowski, H.-J., Rozenberg, G. (eds.) ICGT 2002. LNCS, vol. 2505, pp. 161–176. Springer, Heidelberg (2002)

41. Herrmannsdoerfer, M., Koegel, M.: Towards a Generic Operation Recorder for Model Evolution. In: Proceedings of the International Workshop on Model Comparison in Practice @ TOOLS 2010. ACM (2010)

42. International Organization for Standardization and International Electrotechnical Comission: Information Technology—Syntactic Metalanguage—Extended BNF 1.0 (December 1996), http://standards.iso.org/ittf/ PubliclyAvailableStandards/s026153_ISO_IEC_14977_1996(E).zip

43. Jouault, F., Kurtev, I.: Transforming Models with ATL. In: Bruel, J.-M. (ed.) MoDELS 2005. LNCS, vol. 3844, pp. 128–138. Springer, Heidelberg (2006)

44. Kehrer, T., Kelter, U., Taentzer, G.: A rule-based approach to the semantic lifting of model differences in the context of model versioning. In: Proceedings of the International Conference on Automated Software Engineering (ASE 2011). IEEE (2011)

45. Kelter, U., Wehren, J., Niere, J.: A Generic Difference Algorithm for UML Models. In: Software Engineering, pp. 105–116. LNI, GI (2005)

46. Khuller, S., Raghavachari, B.: Graph and network algorithms. ACM Computing Surveys 28(1), 43–45 (1996)

47. Kim, M., Notkin, D.: Program Element Matching for Multi-version Program Analyses. In: Proceedings of the International Workshop on Mining Software Repositories (MSR 2006). ACM (2006)

48. Koegel, M., Herrmannsdoerfer, M., Wesendonk, O., Helming, J.: Operation-based Conflict Detection on Models. In: Proceedings of the International Workshop on Model Comparison in Practice @ TOOLS 2010. ACM (2010)

49. Koegel, M., Herrmannsdoerfer, M., von Wesendonk, O., Helming, J., Bruegge, B.: Merging Model Refactorings – An Empirical Study. In: Proceedings of the Workshop on Model Evolution @ MoDELS 2010 (2010)

50. Kolovos, D.S.: Establishing Correspondences between Models with the Epsilon Comparison Language. In: Paige, R.F., Hartman, A., Rensink, A. (eds.) ECMDA-FA 2009. LNCS, vol. 5562, pp. 146–157. Springer, Heidelberg (2009)

51. Kolovos, D.S., Rose, L.M., Drivalos Matragkas, N., Paige, R.F., Polack, F.A.C., Fernandes, K.J.: Constructing and Navigating Non-invasive Model Decorations. In: Tratt, L., Gogolla, M. (eds.) ICMT 2010. LNCS, vol. 6142, pp. 138–152. Springer, Heidelberg (2010)

52. Kolovos, D., Di Ruscio, D., Pierantonio, A., Paige, R.: Different Models for Model Matching: An Analysis of Approaches to Support Model Differencing. In: Proceedings of the International Workshop on Comparison and Versioning of Software Models @ ICSE 2009. IEEE (2009)

53. Kühne, T.: Matters of (Meta-) Modeling. Software and Systems Modeling 5, 369–385 (2006)

54. Küster, J.M., Gerth, C., Förster, A., Engels, G.: Detecting and Resolving Process Model Differences in the Absence of a Change Log. In: Dumas, M., Reichert, M., Shan, M.-C. (eds.) BPM 2008. LNCS, vol. 5240, pp. 244–260. Springer, Heidelberg (2008)

55. Lambers, L., Ehrig, H., Orejas, F.: Conflict Detection for Graph Transformation with Negative Application Conditions. In: Corradini, A., Ehrig, H., Montanari, U., Ribeiro, L., Rozenberg, G. (eds.) ICGT 2006. LNCS, vol. 4178, pp. 61–76. Springer, Heidelberg (2006)

56. Langer, P.: Adaptable Model Versioning based on Model Transformation by Demonstration. Ph.D. thesis, Vienna University of Technology (2011)

57. Langer, P., Wieland, K., Wimmer, M., Cabot, J.: From UML Profiles to EMF Profiles and Beyond. In: Bishop, J., Vallecillo, A. (eds.) TOOLS 2011. LNCS, vol. 6705, pp. 52–67. Springer, Heidelberg (2011)

58. Ledeczi, A., Maroti, M., Karsai, G., Nordstrom, G.: Metaprogrammable Toolkit for Model-Integrated Computing. In: Proceedings of the IEEE Conference and Workshop on Engineering of Computer-Based Systems, ECBS 1999, pp. 311–317 (March 1999)

59. Lin, Y., Gray, J., Jouault, F.: DSMDiff: A Differentiation Tool for Domain-specific Models. European Journal of Information Systems 16(4), 349–361 (2007)

60. Lippe, E., van Oosterom, N.: Operation-Based Merging. In: ACM SIGSOFT Symposium on Software Development Environment, pp. 78–87. ACM (1992)

61. Madiot, F., Dup, G.: EMF Facet Website (November 2010), http://www.eclipse.org/modeling/emft/facet/

62. Maoz, S., Ringert, J.O., Rumpe, B.: A Manifesto for Semantic Model Differencing. In: Dingel, J., Solberg, A. (eds.) MoDELS 2010 Workshops. LNCS, vol. 6627, pp. 194–203. Springer, Heidelberg (2011)

63. Maoz, S., Ringert, J., Rumpe, B.: ADDiff: Semantic Differencing for Activity Diagrams. In: Proceedings of the ACM SIGSOFT Symposium on the Foundations of Software Engineering (FSE 2011), pp. 179–189. ACM (2011)

64. Maoz, S., Ringert, J.O., Rumpe, B.: CDDiff: Semantic Differencing for Class Diagrams. In: Mezini, M. (ed.) ECOOP 2011. LNCS, vol. 6813, pp. 230–254. Springer, Heidelberg (2011)

65. Mehra, A., Grundy, J., Hosking, J.: A Generic Approach to Supporting Diagram Differencing and Merging for Collaborative Design. In: Proceedings of the International Conference on Automated Software Engineering (ASE 2005), pp. 204–213. ACM (2005)
66. Mens, T.: A State-of-the-Art Survey on Software Merging. IEEE Transactions on Software Engineering 28(5), 449–462 (2002)
67. Mens, T., Gorp, P.V.: A Taxonomy of Model Transformation. Electronic Notes in Theoretical Computer Science 152, 125–142 (2006)
68. Mens, T., Taentzer, G., Runge, O.: Detecting Structural Refactoring Conflicts Using Critical Pair Analysis. Electronic Notes in Theoretical Computer Science 127(3), 113–128 (2005)
69. Munson, J.P., Dewan, P.: A Flexible Object Merging Framework. In: Proceedings of the 1994 ACM Conference on Computer Supported Cooperative Work, CSCW 1994, pp. 231–242. ACM (1994), http://doi.acm.org/10.1145/192844.193016
70. Murta, L., Corrêa, C., Prudêncio, J., Werner, C.: Towards Odyssey-VCS 2: Improvements Over a UML-based Version Control System. In: Proceedings of the International Workshop on Comparison and Versioning of Software Models @ MoDELS 2008, pp. 25–30. ACM (2008)
71. Nagl, M. (ed.): Building Tightly Integrated Software Development Environments: The IPSEN Approach. LNCS, vol. 1170. Springer, Heidelberg (1996)
72. Naur, P., Randell, B., Bauer, F.: Software Engineering: Report on a Conference Sponsored by the NATO SCIENCE COMMITTEE, Garmisch, Germany, October 7-11, 1968. Scientific Affairs Division, NATO (1969)
73. Nejati, S., Sabetzadeh, M., Chechik, M., Easterbrook, S., Zave, P.: Matching and Merging of Statecharts Specifications. In: Proceedings of the International Conference on Software Engineering (ICSE 2007), pp. 54–64. IEEE (2007)
74. Nuseibeh, B., Easterbrook, S.M., Russo, A.: Making Inconsistency Respectable in Software Development. Journal of Systems and Software 58(2), 171–180 (2001)
75. Object Management Group: Diagram Definition (DD), http://www.omg.org/spec/DD/1.0/Beta2/ (accessed: February 21, 2012)
76. Object Management Group: Common Warehouse Metamodel (CWM) Specification V1.1. (March 2003), http://www.omg.org/spec/CWM/1.1/
77. Object Management Group: Meta-Object Facility 2.0 (MOF) (October 2004), http://www.omg.org/cgi-bin/doc?ptc/03-10-04
78. Object Management Group: Meta Object Facility (MOF) 2.0 Query/View/-Transformation Specification. Final Adopted Specification (November 2005), http://www.omg.org/docs/ptc/07-07-07.pdf
79. Object Management Group: Model-driven Architecture (MDA) (April 2005), http://www.omg.org/mda/specs.html
80. Object Management Group: UML Diagram Interchange, Version 1.0. (April 2006), http://www.omg.org/spec/UMLDI/1.0/
81. Object Management Group: XML Metadata Interchange 2.1.1 (XMI) (December 2007), http://www.omg.org/spec/XMI/2.1.1
82. Object Management Group: MOF Model to Text Transformation Language (MOFM2T) (January 2008), http://www.omg.org/spec/MOFM2T/1.0/
83. Object Management Group: Business Process Modeling Notation (BPMN), Version 1.2 (January 2009), http://www.omg.org/spec/BPMN/1.2
84. Object Management Group: Object Constraint Language (OCL), Version 2.2 (February 2010), http://www.omg.org/spec/OCL/2.2
85. Object Management Group: OMG Unified Modeling Language (OMG UML), Infrastructure V2.4.1 (August 2011), http://www.omg.org/spec/UML/2.4.1/

86. Object Management Group: OMG Unified Modeling Language (OMG UML), Superstructure V2.4.1 (July 2011), http://www.omg.org/spoc/UML/2.4.1/

87. Oda, T., Saeki, M.: Generative Technique of Version Control Systems for Software Diagrams. In: Proceedings of the IEEE International Conference on Software Maintenance (ICSM 2005), pp. 515–524. IEEE (2005)

88. Ohst, D., Welle, M., Kelter, U.: Differences Between Versions of UML Diagrams. ACM SIGSOFT Software Engineering Notes 28(5), 227–236 (2003)

89. Oliveira, H., Murta, L., Werner, C.: Odyssey-VCS: A Flexible Version Control System for UML Model Elements. In: Proceedings of the International Workshop on Software Configuration Management, pp. 1–16. ACM (2005)

90. Opdyke, W.: Refactoring Object-oriented Frameworks. Ph.D. thesis, University of Illinois at Urbana-Champaign (1992)

91. Oracle: Java Metadata Interface (JMI) (June 2002), http://java.sun.com/products/jmi/

92. Parnas, D.: Software Engineering or Methods for the Multi-person Construction of Multi-version Programs. In: Hackl, C.E. (ed.) IBM 1974. LNCS, vol. 23, pp. 225–235. Springer, Heidelberg (1975)

93. Porres, I.: Rule-based Update Transformations and their Application to Model Refactorings. Software and System Modeling 4(4), 368–385 (2005)

94. Pressman, R., Ince, D.: Software Engineering: A Practitioner's Approach. McGraw-Hill, New York (1982)

95. Rahm, E., Bernstein, P.: A Survey of Approaches to Automatic Schema Matching. The VLDB Journal 10(4), 334–350 (2001)

96. Reiter, T., Altmanninger, K., Bergmayr, A., Schwinger, W., Kotsis, G.: Models in Conflict – Detection of Semantic Conflicts in Model-based Development. In: Proceedings of International Workshop on Model-Driven Enterprise Information Systems @ ICEIS 2007, pp. 29–40 (2007)

97. Rivera, J., Vallecillo, A.: Representing and Operating With Model Differences. In: Paige, R.F., Meyer, B. (eds.) TOOLS EUROPE 2008. LNBIP, vol. 11, pp. 141–160. Springer, Heidelberg (2008)

98. Schmidt, D.: Guest Editor's Introduction: Model-driven Engineering. Computer 39(2), 25–31 (2006)

99. Schmidt, M., Gloetzner, T.: Constructing Difference Tools for Models Using the SiDiff Framework. In: Companion of the International Conference on Software Engineering, pp. 947–948. ACM (2008)

100. Schneider, C., Zündorf, A.: Experiences in using Optimisitic Locking in Fujaba. Softwaretechnik Trends 27(2) (2007)

101. Schneider, C., Zündorf, A., Niere, J.: CoObRA – A Small Step for Development Tools to Collaborative Environments. In: Proceedings of the Workshop on Directions in Software Engineering Environments (2004)

102. Schwanke, R.W., Kaiser, G.E.: Living With Inconsistency in Large Systems. In: Proceedings of the International Workshop on Software Version and Configuration Control, pp. 98–118. Teubner B.G. GmbH (1988)

103. Selic, B.: The Pragmatics of Model-driven Development. IEEE Software 20(5), 19–25 (2003)

104. Sendall, S., Kozaczynski, W.: Model Transformation: The Heart and Soul of Model-Driven Software Development. IEEE Software 20, 42–45 (2003)

105. Shvaiko, P., Euzenat, J.: A Survey of Schema-Based Matching Approaches. In: Spaccapietra, S. (ed.) Journal on Data Semantics IV. LNCS, vol. 3730, pp. 146–171. Springer, Heidelberg (2005)

106. Sprinkle, J.: Model-integrated Computing. IEEE Potentials 23(1), 28–30 (2004)
107. Steinberg, D., Budinsky, F., Paternostro, M., Merks, E.: Eclipse Modeling Framework 2.0. Addison-Wesley Professional (2008)
108. Sun, Y., White, J., Gray, J.: Model Transformation by Demonstration. In: Schürr, A., Selic, B. (eds.) MoDELS 2009. LNCS, vol. 5795, pp. 712–726. Springer, Heidelberg (2009)
109. Sunyé, G., Pollet, D., Le Traon, Y., Jézéquel, J.-M.: Refactoring UML Models. In: Gogolla, M., Kobryn, C. (eds.) UML 2001. LNCS, vol. 2185, pp. 134–148. Springer, Heidelberg (2001)
110. Taentzer, G., Ermel, C., Langer, P., Wimmer, M.: Conflict Detection for Model Versioning Based on Graph Modifications. In: Ehrig, H., Rensink, A., Rozenberg, G., Schürr, A. (eds.) ICGT 2010. LNCS, vol. 6372, pp. 171–186. Springer, Heidelberg (2010)
111. Taentzer, G., Ermel, C., Langer, P., Wimmer, M.: A Fundamental Approach to Model Versioning Based on Graph Modifications. Accepted for Publication in Software and System Modeling (2012)
112. Thione, G., Perry, D.: Parallel Changes: Detecting Semantic Interferences. In: Proceedings of the International Computer Software and Applications Conference, pp. 47–56. IEEE (2005)
113. Vermolen, S., Wachsmuth, G., Visser, E.: Reconstructing Complex Metamodel Evolution. Tech. Rep. TUD-SERG-2011-026, Delft University of Technology (2011)
114. W3C: Extensible Markup Language (XML), Version 1.0 (2008), http://www.w3.org/TR/REC-xml
115. Wache, H., Voegele, T., Visser, U., Stuckenschmidt, H., Schuster, G., Neumann, H., Hübner, S.: Ontology-based Integration of Information — A Survey of Existing Approaches. In: Proceedings of the Workshop on Ontologies and Information Sharing (IJCAI 2001), pp. 108–117 (2001)
116. Westfechtel, B.: Structure-oriented Merging of Revisions of Software Documents. In: Proceedings of the International Workshop on Software Configuration Management, pp. 68–79. ACM (1991)
117. Westfechtel, B.: A Formal Approach to Three-way Merging of EMF Models. In: Proceedings of the International Workshop on Model Comparison in Practice @ TOOLS 2010, pp. 31–41. ACM (2010)
118. Wieland, K.: Conflict-tolerant Model Versioning. Ph.D. thesis, Vienna University of Technology (2011)
119. Xing, Z., Stroulia, E.: UMLDiff: An Algorithm for Object-oriented Design Differencing. In: Proceedings of the International Conference on Automated Software Engineering (ASE 2005), pp. 54–65. ACM (2005)
120. Xing, Z., Stroulia, E.: Refactoring Detection based on UMLDiff Change-Facts Queries. In: Proceedings of the 13th Working Conference on Reverse Engineering (WCRE 2006), pp. 263–274. IEEE (2006)

Formal Specification and Testing
of Model Transformations

Antonio Vallecillo[1], Martin Gogolla[2], Loli Burgueño[1], Manuel Wimmer[1],
and Lars Hamann[2]

[1] GISUM/Atenea Research Group, Universidad de Málaga, Spain
[2] Database Systems Group, University of Bremen, Germany
{av,loli,mw}@lcc.uma.es, {gogolla,lhamann}@informatik.uni-bremen.de

Abstract. In this paper we present some of the key issues involved
in model transformation specification and testing, discuss and classify
some of the existing approaches, and introduce the concept of *Tract*, a
generalization of model transformation contracts. We show how Tracts
can be used for model transformation specification and black-box testing,
and the kinds of analyses they allow. Some representative examples are
used to illustrate this approach.

1 Introduction

Model transformations are key elements of Model-driven Engineering (MDE).
They allow querying, synthesizing and transforming models into other models
or into code, and can also be composed in chains for building new and more
powerful model transformations.

As the size and complexity of model transformations grow, there is an increasing need to count on mechanisms and tools for testing their correctness. This
is specially important in case of transformations with hundreds or thousands
of rules, which are becoming commonplace in most MDE applications, and for
which manual debugging is no longer possible. Being now critical elements in
the software development process, their correctness becomes essential for ensuring that the produced software applications work as expected and are free from
errors and deficiencies. In particular, we do need to check whether the produced
models conform to the target metamodel, or whether some essential properties
are preserved by the transformation.

In general, correctness is not an absolute property. Correctness needs to be
checked against a *contract*, or *specification*, which determines the expected behaviour, the context whether such a behaviour needs to be guaranteed, as well
as some other properties of interest to any of the stakeholders of the system (in
this case, the users of a model transformation and their implementors). A specification normally states *what* should be done, but without determining *how*. An
additional benefit of some forms of specifications is that they can also be used
for testing that a given implementation of the system (which describes the *how*,
in a particular platform) conforms to that contract.

M. Bernardo, V. Cortellessa, and A. Pierantonio (Eds.): SFM 2012, LNCS 7320, pp. 399–437, 2012.

In general, the specification and testing of model transformations are not easy tasks and present numerous challenges [1–4]. Besides, the kinds of tests depend on the specification language and vice-versa. Thus, in the literature there are two main approaches to model transformation specification and testing (see also Section 3). In the first place we have the works that aim at fully *validating* the behaviour of the transformation and its associated properties (confluence of the rules, termination, etc.) using formal methods and their associated toolkits (see, e.g., [5–11]). The potential limitations of these proposals lie in their inherent computational complexity, which makes them inappropriate for fully specifying and testing large and complex model transformations. An alternative approach (proposed in, e.g., [12–15, 8]) consists using declarative notations for the specification, and then trying to *certify* that a transformation works for a selected set of test input models, without trying to validate it for the full input space. Although such a certification approach cannot fully prove correctness, it can be very useful for identifying bugs in a very cost-effective manner and can deal with industrial-size transformations without having to abstract away any of the structural or behavioural properties of the transformations.

In this paper we show a proposal that follows this latter approach, making use of some of the concepts, languages and tools that have proved to be very useful in the case of model specification and validation [16]. In particular, we generalize *model transformation contracts* [2, 17] for the specification of the properties that need to be checked for a transformation, and then apply the ASSL language [18] to generate input test models, which are then automatically transformed into output models and checked against the set of contracts defined for the transformation, using the USE tool [19].

In the following we will assume that readers are familiar with basic Software Engineering techniques such as program specification (using, in particular, pre- and postconditions [20]) and program testing (using, e.g., JUnit); with modeling techniques using UML [21] and OCL [22]; and have basic knowledge of model transformations [23].

This paper is organized as follows. After this introduction, Section 2 describes the context of our work and Section 3 presents existing related works. Then, Section 4 presents our proposal and Section 5 discusses the kinds of tests and analysis that can be conducted and how to perform them. Tracts are illustrated in Section 6 with several application examples. Finally, Section 7 draws the final conclusions and outlines some future research lines.

2 Context

2.1 Models and Metamodels

In MDE, models are defined in the language of their metamodels. In this paper we consider that metamodels are defined by a set of classes, binary associations between them, and a set of integrity constraints.

Figure 1 shows our first running example as handled by the tool USE [19]. The aim of the example is to transform a `Person` source metamodel shown in

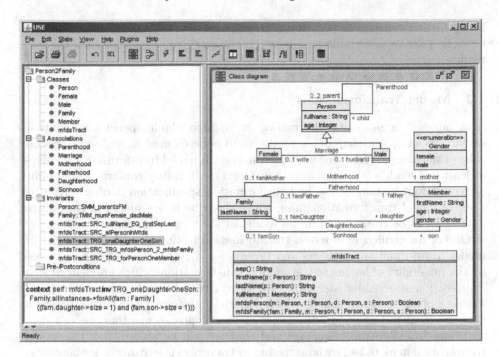

Fig. 1. USE Screenshot with the `Families2Person` example

the upper part of the class diagram into a `Family` target metamodel displayed in the middle part. The source permits representing people and their relations (marriage, parents, children) while the target focuses on families and their members. (This example is just the opposite to the typical `Families2Person` model transformation example [24, 25], that we shall also discuss later in Section 6.1.)

Some integrity constraints are expressed as multiplicity constraints in the metamodels, such as the ones that state that a family always has to have one mother and one father, or that a person (either female or male) can be married to at most one person.

There are other constraints that require specialized notations because they imply more complex expressions. In this paper we will use OCL [26] as the language for stating constraints. In order to keep matters simple, we have decided to include only one source metamodel constraint (`SMM`) and one target metamodel constraint (`TMM`). On the `Person` side (source), we require that, if two parents are present, they must have different gender (`SMM_parentsFM`). On the `Family` side (target), we require an analogous condition (`TMM_mumFemale_dadMale`).

```
context Person inv SMM_parentsFM:
  parent->size()=2 implies
    parent->select(oclIsTypeOf(Female))->size()=1 and
    parent->select(oclIsTypeOf(Male))->size()=1

context Family inv TMM_mumFemale_dadMale:
  mother.gender = #female and father.gender = #male
```

Many further constraints (like acyclicity of parenthood or exclusion of marriage between parents and children or between siblings) could be stated for the two models.

2.2   Model Transformations

In a nutshell, a model transformation is an algorithmic specification (either declarative or operational) of the relationship between models, and more specifically of the mapping from one model to another. A model transformation involves at least two models (the source and the target), which may conform to the same or to different metamodels. The transformation specification is often given by a set of model transformation rules, which describe how a model in the source language can be transformed into a model in the target language.

One of the challenges of model transformation testing is the heterogeneity of model transformation languages and techniques [4]. This problem is aggravated by the possibility of having to test model transformations which are defined as a composition of several model transformations chained together. In our proposal we use a black-box approach, by which a model transformation is just a program that we invoke. The main advantages of this approach are that we can deal with any transformation language and that we will be able to test the model transformation *as-is*, i.e., without having to transform it into any other language, represent it using any formalism, or abstract away any of its features.

To illustrate one example of model transformation, we asked some students to write the model transformation that, given a `Family` model, creates a `Person` model described in the example above. The resulting code of the `Persons2Family` transformation is shown below. It is written in ATL [27], a hybrid model transformation language containing a mixture of declarative and imperative constructs which is widely used in industry and academia. There are of course other model transformation languages, such as for instance QVT [28], RubyTL [29] or JTL [30], that we could have also used. Nevertheless, in this paper we will mainly focus on ATL for illustration purposes.

This transformation is defined in terms of four basic rules, each one responsible for building the corresponding target model elements depending on the four kinds of role a source person can play in a family: father, mother, son or daughter. The attributes and references of every target element are calculated using the information of the source elements. Target elements that represent families are created with the last name of the father (in rule `Father2Family`).

```
module Persons2Families;
create OUT : Families from IN : Persons;

rule Father2Family{
 from f : Persons!Male (not f.child -> isEmpty())
 to fam : Families!Family (
     lastName <-f.name.substring(f.name.lastIndexOf(' ')+2,
                                 f.name.size()) ),
    mb : Families!Member (
     firstName <- f.name.substring(1,f.name.lastIndexOf(' ')),
     age <- f.age, gender <- #male, famFather <- fam )
}
```

```
rule Mother2Family{
 from m : Persons!Female (not m.child -> isEmpty())
 to mb : Families!Member (
     firstName <- m.name.substring(1,m.name.lastIndexOf(' ')),
     age <- m.age, gender <- #female, famMother <- m.husband )
}
rule Son2Family{
 from s : Persons!Male (s.child -> isEmpty())
 to mb : Families!Member (
     firstName <- s.name.substring(1,s.name.lastIndexOf(' ')),
     age <- s.age, gender <- #male,
     famSon <-s.parent->select(e|e.oclIsTypeOf(Persons!Male)) )
}
rule Daughter2Family{
 from d : Persons!Female (d.child -> isEmpty())
 to mb : Families!Member (
     firstName <-d.name.substring(1,d.name.lastIndexOf(' ')),
     age <- d.age, gender <- #female,
     famDaughter <- d.parent->select(e|e.oclIsTypeOf(Persons!Male)) )
}
```

The question is whether this transformation is *correct*. For that we need to determine first which is expected behaviour (i.e., its specification) and then test whether the provided implementation conforms to such a specification.

3 Related Work

The need for systematic verification of model transformations has been documented by the research community by several publications outlining the challenges to be tackled [31–33, 4]. As a response, a plethora of approaches ranging from lightweight certification to full verification have been proposed to reason about different kinds of properties of model transformations [34]. Before specification and testing approaches for model transformations are discussed in more detail, the broader landscape of transformation properties is spanned first.

3.1 Categories of Model Transformation Properties

The right hand side of figure 2 (column *model transformation (MT) implementation*) aligns different kinds of properties for model transformations with the well-known model transformation pattern [35]. The transformation pattern gives an overview of the main concepts involved in model transformation. A model transformation is represented by a transformation model (*TM* in the *description* layer) has to conform to a model transformation language (described by a metamodel, *TMM* in the *language* layer) and analogously, the execution of the model transformation (*TM Ex* in the *execution* layer) has to conform to the description layer for producing from a source model (*SoM*) a corresponding target model (*TaM*).

Having this model transformation pattern as a framework for classifying model transformation properties which have been discussed in literature, the first discriminator for classifying them is the level on which they are introduced. In particular, two kinds of properties may be distinguished: (i) *general transformation properties* defined on the *language layer* allow to make statements about

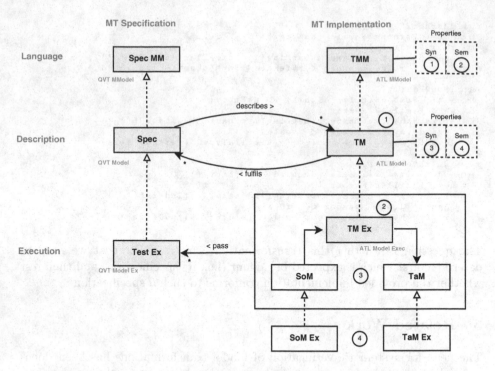

Fig. 2. Specification and testing of model transformations at a glance

transformations themselves and (ii) *specific transformation properties* defined on the *description layer* allow to make statements about pairs of *source* and *target models* of a transformation execution. Properties of the first kind abstract from the specifics of a transformation problem and are therefore usable for every transformation defined in a transformation language offering such properties. Properties of the second kind are always specific to a transformation problem, and thus, have to be defined for each transformation individually.

Orthogonal to the distinction between general and specific, is the distinction if properties are related to syntax or semantics. Thus, properties may be partitioned into *syntactic* and *semantic* properties. While syntactic properties are stated and checked based on the information provided by the next lower layer, for specifying semantic properties two steps down the stack have to be made. To be more concrete, for general transformation properties (defined on the *language* layer), the syntactic properties are calculated based on the transformation (defined on the *description* layer). However, the semantic properties have to be verified by taking the knowledge of the execution of the transformation into account (available on the *execution layer*, defined by the transformation execution engine). Analogously, for specific transformation properties, syntactical properties of the source and target model as well as their relationships are directly calculated using the models. For semantic properties, again the execution of the models has to be considered. This means, knowledge on the model execution engines used for the source and target models is needed to reason about their semantic properties.

General properties. General properties may be calculated based solely on the knowledge of the transformation language. It has to be emphasized that these properties are about the transformation, i.e., only statements about the transformation itself can be made, but not about the source and target models of the transformation.

An example for a basic general syntactic property is conformance of the transformation to the transformation language. A transformation language may be either *generic* or *specific* to a transformation problem, i.e., in the second case, the metamodels of the source and target models are considered to form an important part of the transformation language. This allows to provide enhanced syntactic checks compared to just using a generic transformation language. Approaches how to build specific transformation languages are presented in [36] for graphical modeling languages and in [37] for textual ones.

Several general semantic properties have been proposed for model transformation languages such as confluence [6, 8], applicability [38], and termination [39] of a set of graph transformation rules. Other group of works aim at fully validating the behavior of the transformation using formal methods and their associated toolkits. For example, in [11] model transformations defined in ATL are translated to Maude for analyzing them using out-of-the-box verification techniques.

Specific properties. In addition to general properties, there are properties that are specific for a certain transformation. In particular, this means that it is not enough to reason about the transformation itself: statements about the source and target models are also needed. In particular, this is a must when one has to reason about the correctness of the translation of the source model into a target model. As models comprise syntax as well as semantics, both aspects have to be considered.

Concerning syntactic properties, one may reason about if for each source element of a certain type a corresponding target element of a certain type is produced by the transformation. Such concerns are naturally formulated as contracts by using specification languages which allow to state the requirements which have to be fulfilled by a transformation implementation. Contracts [20] are a well-established technique in software engineering in general and in particular for verifying object-oriented programs by providing pre- and post-conditions as well as invariants for operations. Inspired by this work, contracts have also been applied for model transformations. In particular, as is explained in the next subsection in more detail, contracts allow for several benefits such as they can be used as oracle functions for testing model transformations by using a set of test source models. Oracle functions give an approximation of the target models which should be produced by the transformation.

For dealing with semantic properties which have to be fulfilled by the source and target models, their execution have to be taken into account. Thus, the operational semantics of the source and target languages are needed as a prerequisite.

Reasoning about semantic properties of models ranges from reasoning about some selected behavioral property such as liveness or deadlock freeness to a more complete notion of behavioral equivalence, e.g., based on bi-similarity. For example, if liveness is guaranteed by a source model, one may be interested in a transformation which generates from such models always target models guaranteing liveness as well. Furthermore, one may reason about bi-similarity of the source and target model pairs, i.e., an observer should not be able to differentiate the state-transition systems generated by the source and target models. For instance, [40] describes such an approach where each execution of the transformation is verified by checking whether the target model bi-simulates the source model. Another similar approach is presented in [41] where a model checker is used to check dynamic properties of the source and target models. It has to be noted that semantic properties are not limited to behavioral models, but may also be verified for structural models. For example, in [42] an approach is presented for reasoning about semantic differences between class diagrams by comparing all possible instantiations of them.

This chapter is dedicated to the *specification* and *testing* of *transformation specific* and *syntax related* properties of model transformations. Thus, in the following subsection, approaches going in this direction are elaborated in more detail. For a more in-depth discussion of approaches supporting the verification of other kind of properties, we kindly refer the interested reader to [34].

3.2   Specification and Testing Approaches for Model Transformations

The left hand side of figure 2 (column *model transformation (MT) specification*) focusses on the specification of specific syntactic properties and their verification. The relationships between the left hand side and the right hand side of figure 2 illustrates how transformation specifications are related to transformation implementations. As mentioned before, these properties are naturally defined in terms of contracts which form the specification for a transformation implementation. One of the advantages of contracts is that they allow defining *what* a piece of software does but not *how* it is done. In the context of model transformations, basic syntactic contracts are specified by the source and target metamodels since source and target models must conform to them. However, further restrictions on the source and target models as well as on their relationships are needed [14]. First, contracts can be used to precisely specify the constraints (going beyond metamodel constraints) to be satisfied by source models such that the transformation is applicable, i.e., *preconditions* of the transformations. Second, they can be used to express constraints on the target models, i.e., *postconditions* of the transformation. Finally, they can be used to specify constraints that need to be satisfied by any pair of source/target models of a correct transformation. Thus, a specification language should allow to formulate these three kinds of contracts.

Model transformation contracts may be used for several scenarios [17]. (i) Contracts are useful information for the transformation designer in the development and maintenance phase. (ii) They can be used to check the compatibility of transformations in a model transformation chain, e.g., the postconditions of a preceding transformation have to be compatible with the preconditions of a succeeding transformation. (iii) Contracts may be used as oracle functions to approximate the expected output for a given source model.

Especially, this latter aspect has been the subject of several kinds of works that apply contracts for model transformation testing using different notations for defining the contracts. In the following, we elaborate on these approaches which are divided into the two main categories. First, contracts may be defined on the *model level* by either giving (i) complete examples of source and target model pairs, or (ii) giving only model fragments which should be included in the produced target models for given source models. Second, contracts may be defined on the *metamodel level* either by using (iii) graph constraint languages or (iv) textual constraint languages such as OCL.

Contracts at Model Level

Model Examples. A straight-forward approach is to define the expected target model for a given source model which acts as a reference model for analyzing the actual produced target model of a transformation as proposed in [43, 1, 44, 45]. Model comparison frameworks are employed for computing a difference model between the expected and the actual target models. If there are differences then there is considered to be an error either in the transformation or in the source/target model pair. The advantage of this approach is its simplicity, e.g., as specification language, the source and target metamodels are sufficient. However, reasoning about the cause for the mismatch between the expected and actual target model solely based on the difference model is challenging. Even more aggravating, several elements in the difference model may be caused by the same error, however, the transformation engineer has the burden to cluster the differences by herself.

Fragments. A special form of verification by contract was presented in [46]. The authors propose to use model fragments (introduced in [47]) which are expected to be included in a target model which is produced from a specific source model. For verifying these properties, the model fragments are matched on the produced target model. Using fragments as contracts is different from using examples as contracts. Examples require an equivalence relationship between the expected model and actual target model, while fragments require an inclusion relationship between the expected fragments and the actual target model. As for examples, the source and target metamodels are sufficient to define the specifications; but as before, this benefit comes with the price that the contracts are described at the model level. Thus, they have to be defined for each particular test source model again and again.

Contracts at Metamodel Level

Graph constraints. In [48], the authors propose to use the graph patterns supported by the VIATRA2 tool to specify contracts for model transformations at the metamodel level. However, the patterns cannot define contracts crossing the borders of one metamodel, being therefore usable to specify pre- and postconditions, but not the relations between the source and target models.

In [49] a declarative language for the specification of visual contracts is introduced for defining pre- and post-conditions as well as invariants for model transformations. For evaluating the contracts on test models, the specifications are translated to QVT Relations which are executed in check-only mode. In particular, QVT Relations are executed before the transformation under test is executed to check the preconditions on the source models and afterwards to check relationships between the source and target models as well as postconditions on the target models.

Textual constraints. The first approach using contracts for model transformations was proposed by Cariou et al. [50, 17]. The authors suggest implementing transformations with OCL. In this way, the source metamodel classes are provided with operations, which may comprise preconditions, postconditions, and invariants. Although OCL natively supports design-by-contract, OCL is not intended to specify transformations and relationships between models. Thus, the authors propose an extension for OCL that allows defining mappings between input and output model elements.

The work in [2] also proposes OCL for defining transformation contracts. Their ideas are also close to [17], but in their paper they just provide a general view of what they think that could be done with model transformation contracts, but without delving into the details about how to achieve it. A similar approach for defining contracts with OCL has been proposed in [14]. Kuester et al. [8] also proposes to use OCL for the definition of transformation constraints.

In [51, 45], the Epsilon Unit Testing Language for testing model management operations is presented. The language permits defining, as already mentioned, expected target models, but in addition, test operations where post-conditions for the target models can be specified. Giner and Pelechano [52] propose a test-driven development approach for model transformations. Test cases comprising an input model together with output fragments and OCL assertions are defined before the actual transformation implementation is developed.

Finally, formal notations to specify and test model transformations may be employed. For instance, Anastasakis et al [10] convert the model transformation under test into Alloy to perform the analysis if given assertions that have to hold for a transformation. If no target model is found by Alloy for a given source model, means that the transformation does not fulfill the assertions. Similarly, ATL transformations are translated into Maude in [11] for defining their formal semantics and for conducting different kinds of formal analyses.

4   Tracts for Model Transformations

4.1   Model Transformation Contracts

One of the problems of the previous specification approaches of Model Transformations lies on its complexity. The specifications of a model transformation can

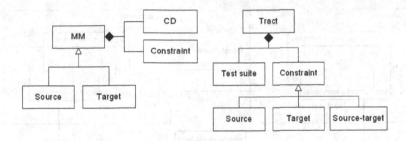

Fig. 3. Concepts in a Tract

become monstrously large as far as the transformation is not trivial (even far more complex than the transformation itself). The reasons are, among others, the lack of modularity, having to deal with too many details at the same time, and the excessive size. Because the specifications try to capture all the model transformation behaviour in one huge set of constraints, they become hard to write, debug and maintain. In addition, tests become quite cumbersome, very complex, and computationally prohibitive to prove.

In order to deal with these problems, tracts were introduced in [53] as a specification and black-box testing mechanism for model transformations. They provide modular pieces of specification, each one focusing on a particular scenario or *context of use*. Thus every model transformation can be specified by means of a set of tracts, each one covering a particular use case—which is defined in terms of particular input and output models and how they should be related by the transformation. In this way, tracts allow to partition the full input space of the transformation into smaller, more focused behavioural units, and to define specific tests for them. Basically, what we do with the tracts is to identify the scenarios of interest to the user of the transformation (each one defined by a tract) and check whether the transformation behaves as expected in these scenarios. Another characteristic of our proposal is that we not require complete proofs, just to check that the transformation works for the tract test suites, hence providing a *light-weight* form of verification.

In a nutshell, a tract defines a set of constraints on the *source* and *target* metamodels, a set of *source-target* constraints, and a tract *test suite*, i.e., a collection of source models satisfying the source constraints. The constraints serve as "contracts" (in the sense of contract-based design [20]) for the transformation in some particular scenarios, and are expressed by means of OCL invariants. The provide the *specification* of the transformation. Figure 3 gives an overview on the used concepts and their connection.

Additionally, every tract provides a *test suite* that allows to operationalize the conformance tests. We do not provide the full behavioral specification of a model transformation, but just a set of tracts that defines how the transformation should behave in certain particular scenarios (or use cases) which are the ones of interest to the user. We do not care how the transformation works in the rest of the cases. In this respect, this approach is a form of *Duck typing*: "If it

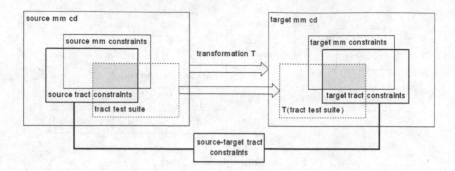

Fig. 4. Building Blocks of a Tract

looks like a duck, swims like a duck, and quacks like a duck, then it probably is a duck" [54]. Tracts are composed by conjunction, similarly to the modular specification of an operation using several pre- and post-conditions, each one defining a specific situation or use case of the operation.

In figure 4 we have displayed the central ingredients of our approach for transformation testing: a source and target metamodel, the transformation T under test, and a transformation contract, for short *tract*, which consists of a tract test suite and a set of tract constraints. The test suite and its transformation result are shown with dashed lines and the different tract constraints with thick lines. Five different kinds of constraints are present: the source and target class diagrams are restricted by source and target metamodels constraints, and the tract imposes source, target, and source-target tract constraints. Such constraints are expressed by means of OCL invariants. The context of these invariants is a class representing a transformation tract, a so-called tract class. An example of a tract class called mfdsTract is shown in figure 1.

Assume a source model m being an element of the test suite and satisfying the metamodel source and the tract source constraints is given. Then, the tract essentially requires that the result $T(m)$ of applying transformation T satisfies the target metamodel and the target tract constraints and the pair $(m, T(m))$ satisfies the source-target tract constraints. The source-target tract constraints are crucial insofar that they can establish a correspondence between a source element and a target element in a declarative way by means of a formula. In technical terms, a source tract constraint is basically an OCL expression with free variables over source elements, a target tract constraint has free variables over target elements, and a source-target tract constraint possesses free variables over source and target elements.

In figure 4, the rectangles indicate possible overlap (resp. disjointness) of source and target models. Basically, the tract—consisting of the test suite and the three kinds of constraints—checks for the correctness of the transformation in the sense that correct source models from the test suite are transformed to correct target models, i.e., our approach checks that in figure 4 the grey source section is transformed into the grey target section. In general, there will be more than one tract for a single transformation because particular source models are constructed in the test suite which then induce particular tract constraints.

Although this approach to testing does not guarantee full correctness, it provides very interesting benefits. In particular, it can be useful for identifying bugs in a cost-effective manner. Moreover, it allows dealing with industrial-size transformations without having to transform them into any other formalism or to abstract away any of its features. Tracts also provide a modular approach to specification and testing, allowing to focus on particular scenarios of use, and to define precise specifications for them. These are important advantages over other approaches that prove full correctness but at a higher computational cost.

To test a transformation T against a tract t, the input test suite models can be automatically generated using languages like ASSL [18], and then transformed into their corresponding target models. These models can also be automatically checked with the USE tool [19] against the constraints defined for the transformation. The checking process can be automated, allowing the model transformation tester to process a large number of models in a mechanical way.

Let us go back to our example in figure 1. The lower part of the class diagram pictures the tract metamodel represented by the class mfdsTract where mfds is a shortcut for mother-father-daughter-son expressing that our tract and our testing (for demonstration purposes) concentrates on conventional families with exactly one person in the respective role. The operations in class mfdsTract are helper operations for formulating the tract constraints which are shown as invariants on the left in the project browser. The five different kinds of constraints are reflected by different prefixes for invariant names: SMM for source metamodel constraints, TMM for target metamodel constraints, SRC for source tract constraints, TRG for target tract constraints, and SRC_TRG for source-target tract constraints.

Note that concepts like father or mother are not explicitly present in the Person metamodel (through attributes or association ends). Besides, please be warned: both metamodels and their transformation seem simple, but intricate complications live under the surface. Roughly speaking, the transformation must (a) split one source attribute into two target attributes in different target classes; (b) merge two source associations into one target class and four target associations; (c) map a source generalization hierarchy into a target attribute. The following listing details the five OCL invariants that constitute the mfdsTract.

```
inv SRC_fullName_EQ_firstSepLast:
  Person.allInstances->forAll(p|
    p.fullName=firstName(p).concat(sep()).concat(lastName(p)))
inv SRC_allPersonInMfds:
  let allFs=Female.allInstances in let allMs=Male.allInstances in
  Person.allInstances->forAll(p|
    Bag{allFs->exists(d  | allMs->exists(f,s| mfdsPerson(p,f,d,s))),
        allFs->exists(m,d| allMs->exists(s  | mfdsPerson(m,p,d,s))),
        allFs->exists(m  | allMs->exists(f,s| mfdsPerson(m,f,p,s))),
        allFs->exists(m,d| allMs->exists(f  | mfdsPerson(m,f,d,p)))} =
    Bag{true,false,false,false})
inv TRG_oneDaughterOneSon:
  Family.allInstances->forAll(fam |
    fam.daughter->size()=1 and fam.son->size()=1)
inv SRC_TRG_mfdsPerson_2_mfdsFamily:
  Female.allInstances->forAll(m,d| Male.allInstances->forAll(f,s|
    mfdsPerson(m,f,d,s) implies
```

```
    Family.allInstances->exists(fam|mfdsFamily(fam,m,f,d,s))))
inv SRC_TRG_forPersonOneMember:
  Female.allInstances->forAll(p| Member.allInstances->one(m|
    p.fullName=fullName(m) and p.age=m.age and m.gender = #female and
    (p.child->notEmpty() implies (let fam=m.famMother in
      p.child->size()=fam.daughter->union(fam.son)->size())) and
    (p.parent->notEmpty() implies m.famDaughter.isDefined()) and
    (p.husband.isDefined() implies m.famMother.isDefined()) )) and
  Male.allInstances->forAll(p| Member.allInstances->one(m|
    p.fullName=fullName(m) and p.age=m.age and m.gender = #male and
    (p.child->notEmpty() implies (let fam=m.famFather in
      p.child->size()=fam.daughter->union(fam.son)->size())) and
    (p.parent->notEmpty() implies m.famSon.isDefined()) and
    (p.wife.isDefined() implies m.famFather.isDefined()) ))
```

There are two source, one target, and two source-target tract constraints. The source constraint SRC_fullName_EQ_firstSepLast guarantees that one can decompose the fullName into a firstName, a separator, and a lastName. The source constraint SRC_allPersonInMfds requires that every Person appears exactly once in a mfdsPerson pattern. mfdsPerson patterns are described by the boolean operation mfdsPerson which characterizes an isolated mother-father-daughter-son pattern having no further links to other persons.

The constraint SRC_allPersonInMfds is universally quantified on Person objects. Each Person must appear either as a mother or as a father or as a daughter or as a son. This exclusive-or requirement is formulated as a comparison between bags of Boolean values. From the four possible cases, exactly one case must be true. Technically this is realized by requiring that the bag of truth values, which arises from the evaluation of the respective sub-formulas, contains exactly once the Boolean value true and three times the Boolean value false.

```
mfdsTract::mfdsPerson(m:Person,f:Person,d:Person,s:Person):Boolean=
  Set{m,f,d,s}->excluding(null)->size()=4 and
  m.oclIsTypeOf(Female) and f.oclIsTypeOf(Male) and
  m.oclAsType(Female).husband=f and
  d.oclIsTypeOf(Female) and s.oclIsTypeOf(Male) and
  m.child=Set{d,s} and f.child=Set{d,s} and
  d.parent=Set{m,f} and s.parent=Set{m,f}
mfdsTract::
  mfdsFamily(fam:Family,m:Person,f:Person,d:Person,s:Person):Boolean=
  fam.lastName=lastName(m) and fam.lastName=lastName(f) and
  fam.lastName=lastName(d) and fam.lastName=lastName(s) and
  fam.mother.firstName=firstName(m) and
  fam.father.firstName=firstName(f) and
  fam.daughter.firstName=Bag{firstName(d)} and
  fam.son.firstName=Bag{firstName(s)}
```

Both source constraints reduce the range of source models to be tested. The target tract constraint TRG_oneDaughterOneSon basically focusses the target on models in which the multiplicity "*" on the daughter and son roles are changed to the multiplicity 1. The first central source-target constraint SRC_TRG_mfds-Person_2_mfdsFamily demands that a mfdsPerson pattern must be found in transformed form as a mfds Family pattern in the resulting target model. The second central source-target constraint SRC_TRG_forPersonOneMember requires that a Person must be transformed into exactly one Member having comparable attribute values and roles as the originating Person. Both source-target tract constraints are central insofar that they establish a correspondence between a Person (from the source) and a `Family Member` (from the target) in a declarative way by means of a formula.

4.2   Generating Test Input Models

The generation of source models for testing purposes is done by means of the language ASSL (A Snapshot Sequence Language) [18]. ASSL was developed to generate object diagrams for a given class diagram in a flexible way. Positive and negative test cases can be built, i.e., object diagrams satisfying all constraints or violating at least one constraint. ASSL is basically an imperative programming language with features for randomly choosing attribute values or association ends. Furthermore ASSL supports backtracking for finding object diagrams with particular properties.

For the example, we concentrate on the generation of (possibly) isolated mfds patterns representing families with exactly one mother, father, daughter, and son in the respective role. The procedure `genMfdsPerson` shown below is parameterized by the number of mfds patterns to be generated. It creates four `Person` objects for the respective roles, assigns attribute values to the objects, links the generated objects in order to build a family, and finally links two generated mfds patterns by either two parenthood links or one parenthood link or no parenthood link at all. The decision is taken in a random way. For example, for a call to `genMfdsPerson(2)` a generated model could look like one of the three possibilities shown in figure 5. Marriage links are always displayed horizontally, whereas parenthood links are shown vertically or diagonally.

```
procedure genMfdsPerson(numMFDS:Integer)        -- number of mfds patterns
  var lastNames:Sequence(String), m:Person ... -- further variables
begin
-------------------------------------------------- variable initialization
lastNames:=[Sequence{'Kennedy' ... 'Obama'}];            -- more
firstFemales:=[Sequence{'Jacqueline' ... 'Michelle'}];   -- constants
firstMales:=[Sequence{'John' ... 'Barrack'}];            -- instead
ages:=[Sequence{30,36,42,48,54,60,66,72,78}];            -- of ...
mums:=[Sequence{}]; dads:=[Sequence{}];


---------------------------------------------------- creation of objects
for i:Integer in [Sequence{1..numMFDS}] begin
  m:=Create(Female); f:=Create(Male);                    -- mother father
  d:=Create(Female); s:=Create(Male);                    -- daughter son
  mums:=[mums->append(m)]; dads:=[dads->append(f)];


-- - - - - - - - - - - - - - - - - - - - - - - - assignment of attributes
lastN:=Any([lastNames]); firstN:=Any([firstFemales]);
[m].fullName:=[firstN.concat(' ').concat(lastN)];[m].age:=Any([ages]);
firstN:=Any([firstMales]);
[f].fullName:=[firstN.concat(' ').concat(lastN)];[f].age:=Any([ages]);
...                        -- analogous handling of daughter d and son s


-- - - - - - - - - - - - - - - - - - - - - - - - creation of mfds links
Insert(Marriage ,[m],[f]);
Insert(Parenthood ,[m],[d]); Insert(Parenthood ,[f],[d]);
Insert(Parenthood ,[m],[s]); Insert(Parenthood ,[f],[s]);
--------- random generation of additional links between mfds patterns
------------------------------ such links lead to negative test cases
flagA:=Any([Sequence{0,1,2,3}]); -- 0 none, 1 mother, 2 father, 3 both
if [i>1 and flagA >0] then begin
  if [flagA=1 or flagA=3] then begin
```

```
    flagB:=Any([Sequence{0,1}]);          -- 1 give daughter, 0 give son
    if [flagB=1] then begin
      Insert(Parenthood,[mums->at(i-1)],[mums->at(i)]); end
    else begin
      Insert(Parenthood,[mums->at(i-1)],[dads->at(i)]); end;
    end; ...
end; end;
```

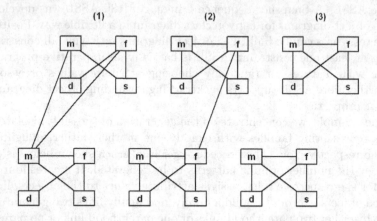

Fig. 5. Three Possibilities for Linking Two mfds Patterns

5   Analysis

Counting on mechanisms for specifying tract invariants on the source and target metamodels, and on the relationship that should be established between them, has proved to be beneficial when combined with the testing process defined above.

Transformation Code Errors: In the first place, we can look for errors due to either bugs in the transformation code that lead to misbehaviours, or to hidden assumptions made by the developers due to some vagueness in the (verbal) specification of the transformation. These errors are normally detected by observing how valid input models (i.e., belonging to the grey area in the left hand side of figure 1) are transformed into target models that break either the target metamodel constraints or the source-target constraints. This is the normal kind of errors pursued by most MT testing approaches.

Transformation Tract Errors: The second kind of errors can be due to the tract specifications themselves. Writing the OCL invariants that comprise a given tract can be as complex as writing the transformation code itself (sometimes even more). This is similar to what happens with the specification of the contract for a program: there are cases in which the detailed description of the expected behaviour of a program can be as complex as the program itself. However, counting on a high-level specification of what the transformation should do at the tract level (independently of how it actually implements it) becomes beneficial because both descriptions provide

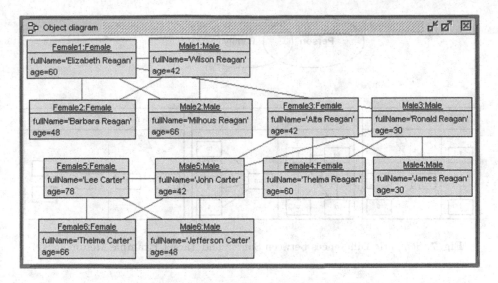

Fig. 6. Generated Negative Test Case with Linked mfds Patterns

two complementary views (specifications) of the behaviour of the transformation. In addition, during the checking process the tract specifications and the code help testing each other. In this sense, we believe in an incremental and iterative approach to model transformation testing, where tracts are progressively specified and the transformation checked against them. The errors found during the testing process are carefully analyzed and either the tract or the transformation refined accordingly.

Issues due to Source-Target Semantic Mismatch: This process also helps revealing a third kind of issues, probably the most difficult problems to cope with. They are due neither to the transformation code nor the tract invariant specifications, but to the semantic gap between the source and target metamodels. We already mentioned that the metamodels used to illustrate our proposal look simple but hide some subtle complications. For example, one of the tracts we tried to specify was for input source models that represented three-generation families, i.e., mfds patterns linked together by parenthood relations (see figure 6 representing a generated negative test case failing to fulfill SRC_allPersonInMfds; without the links ('Elizabeth Reagan', 'Ronald Reagan'), ('Alta Reagan', 'John Carter'), and ('Ronald Reagan', 'John Carter') we would obtain a valid mfds source model). This revealed the fact that valid source models do not admit in general persons with grandchildren. More precisely, after careful examination of the problem we discovered that such patterns are valid inputs for the transformation only if the last name of all persons in the family is the same. This is because the transformed model will consist of three families, where one of the members should end up, for example, playing the role of a daughter in one family and the role of mother in the other. Since all members of a family should share the same

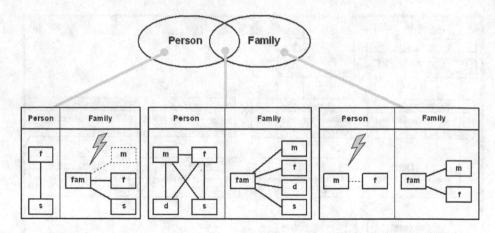

Fig. 7. Semantic Differences between Source and Target Example Metamodels

last name, and due to the fact that a person should belong to two families, the last names of the two families should coincide.

Examples of these problems can also happen because of more restrictive constraints in the target metamodel. For instance a family in the target metamodel should have both a father and a mother, and they should share the same last name. This significantly restricts the set of source models that can be transformed by *any* transformation because it does not allow unmarried couples to be transformed, nor families with a single father or mother. Married couples whose members have maintained their last names cannot be transformed, either. Another problem happens with persons with only a single name (i.e., neither a first nor last name, but a name only), because they cannot be transformed. These are good examples of semantic mismatches between the two metamodels that we try to relate through the transformation. How to deal with (and solve) this latter kind of problems is out of the scope of this paper, here we are concerned only with the detection of such problems. A visual representation of some semantic differences between the example metamodels is shown in figure 7.

Being able to select particular patterns of source models (the ones defined for a tract test suite) offers a fine-grained mechanism for specifying the behaviour of the transformation, and allows the MT tester to concentrate on specific behaviours. In this way we are able to partition the full input space of the transformation into smaller, more focused behavioural units, and to define specific tests for them. By selecting particular patterns we can traverse the full input space, checking specific spots. This is how we discovered that the size of the grey area in figure 1 was much smaller than we initially thought, as mentioned above.

It is also worth pointing out that tracts open the possibility of testing the transformation with invalid inputs, to check its behaviour. For example, we defined a tract where people could have two male parents, being able to check whether the transformation produced output models that violated the target metamodel constraints or not, or just hanged. In this way we can easily define both positive and negative tests for the transformation.

5.1 Model Transformation Typing Using Tracts

Tracts can also be used for "typing" model transformations. Let us explain how (sub-)typing works for tracts.

As mentioned at the beginning, what we basically do with the tracts is to identify the scenarios of interest to the user of the transformation (each one defined by a tract) and check whether the transformation behaves as expected in these scenarios. We do not care how the transformation works in the rest of the cases. This is why we consider this approach to typing is a form of "Duck" typing.

In Fig. 8 we see that TractG transforms metamodel SourceG into metamodel TargetG. 'G' and 'S' stand for 'general' (resp. 'special'). SourceS is a specialization of SourceG in the the sense that it extends SourceG by adding new elements (classes, attributes, associations) and possibly more restricting constraints.

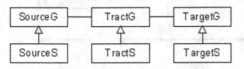

Fig. 8. Tract subtyping

Analogously this is the case for TargetS. TractS is a specialization of TractG and inherits from TractG its connecting associations. Constraints must guarantee that the tract TractS connects SourceS and TargetS elements. Both, TractG and TractS are established with a test suite generating a set of SourceG models (resp. a set of SourceS models).

In order to illustrate our typing approach, Fig. 9 shows an example for tract subtyping, using a different case study. The first source metamodel is the plain Entity-Relationship (ER) model with entities, relationships and attributes only. An ER model is identified by an object of class ErSchema. The second source metamodel is a specialization of the Entity-Relationship model which adds cardinality constraints for the relationship ends. Objects of class ErSchemaC are associated with ER models which additionally possess cardinality constraints.

The first target metamodel is the relational data model allowing primary keys to be specified for relational schemas. Objects of class RelDBSchema identify relational database schemas with primary keys. The second target metamodel describes relational database schemas with primary keys and additional foreign keys. The upper part of the diagram shows the principal structure with respective source and target as well as general and special elements. The lower part shows the details. Please note that the four source and target metamodels have a common part, namely the class Attribute.

It would also be possible to have disjoint source and target models by introducing classes ErAttribute and ErDataType for the ER model as well as RelAttribute and RelDataType for the relational model. The association class ForeignKey belongs exclusively to the relational database metamodel with foreign keys. This

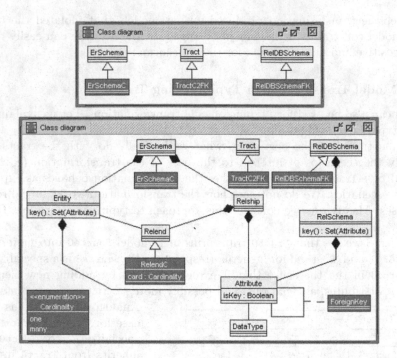

Fig. 9. An example of tract subtyping

could be made explicit by establishing a component relationship, a black diamond, from class RelDBSchemaFK to ForeignKey. The central class Tract specifies the transformation contract and has access, through associations, to both the source and target metamodel. Tract subtyping is expressed through the fact that class TractC2FK is a subtype of class Tract.

The scenario Town-liesIn-Country depicted in Fig. 10 shows informally what will be represented further down as a formal instantiation of the metamodels. Three transformations are shown. The first one ER_2_Rel transforms a plain ER schema (without cardinalities) into a relational database schema with primary keys only. The second one ERC_2_Rel goes from an ER schema with cardinalities into a relational database schema with only primary keys. The third transformation ERC_2_RelFK takes the ER schema with cardinalities and yields a relational database schema with primary keys and foreign keys. Please note that the three relational database schemas can be distinguished by their use of primary keys and foreign keys.

The informal scenario Town-liesIn-Country is formally presented in Fig. 11 with object diagrams instantiating the metamodel class diagrams. The most interesting parts which handle the primary and foreign keys are pictured in a white-on-black style. Please pay attention to the typing of the source, target, and tract objects which are different in each of the three cases and which formally reflect the chosen names of the transformations (trafo_GG, trafo_SG, trafo_SS).

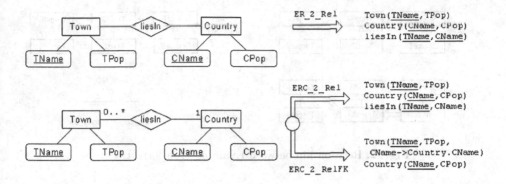

Fig. 10. Town-liesIn-Country scenario

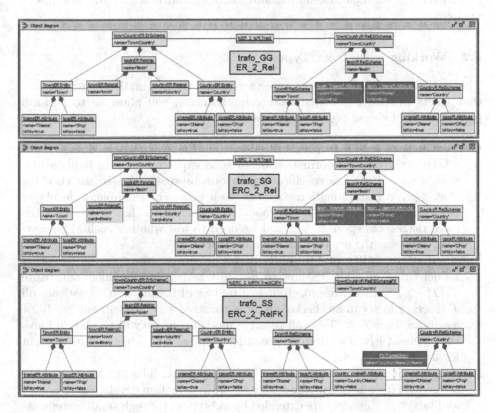

Fig. 11. Town-liesIn-Country object diagram

As shown in Fig. 12, in the ER and relational database metamodel example we see three different transformations: trafo_GG, trafo_SS, and trafo_SG. trafo_GG and trafo_SS are the transformations directly obtained from the respective tracts. Another transformation is trafo_SG, which takes SourceS models, builds TargetG

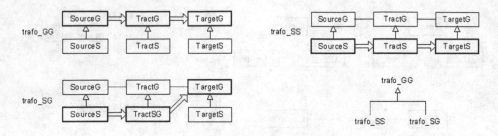

Fig. 12. Relationship between Example Transformations

models and checks them against the `TargetG` constraints. As shown in the right lower part, the example transformations `trafo_SS` and `trafo_SG` are subtypes of `trafo_GG`.

5.2 Working with Tract Types

The fact of considering tracts as types for model transformations, and the fact that tracts provide automated testing mechanisms, will allow us to perform several kinds of checks over model transformations.

Correctness of a MT Implementation. The first thing we can do is to check whether a given transformation behaves as expected, i.e., its implementation is correct w.r.t. a specification. In our approach, this is just checking that a given transformation conforms to a type. For example, a developer can come up with an ATL [27] model transformation that implements the `Families2Person` specification, and we need to test whether such MT is correct. This was the original intention of Tracts [53].

Safe Substitutability of Model Transformations. Now, given another model transformation T', how to decide whether T' can safely substitute T ($T' <: T$)? In our approach, it is a matter of testing that T' satisfies all T tracts, which can be checked in an automated way. We will not get 100% assurance that $T' <: T$ for all possible models, but we will be able to know that at least it will work in all scenarios that we have identified as relevant for us with the tracts.

Incrementality of Transformation Development. The `ERC_2_RelFK` example uses an incremental methodology for transformation development. Source and target metamodels are extended by subtyping through small increments which are accompanied by corresponding tracts including test suites. The tract test suites can give direct feedback on the correctness of the increment.

Declarative vs Imperative Tracts. Tracts may have a descriptive nature when only the relationship between source and target elements is characterized. Tracts may also be described in an operational way when the tract includes operations that map source elements to target elements. Operational tracts may be understood as implementations of descriptive ones and their correctness can be checked against the descriptive tract by employing the descriptive test suite for the operational tract.

Pros and Cons. In general, we have found that typing model transformations using tracts provides interesting advantages, such as modularity, usability, and cost-effectiveness, but at the cost of sacrificing completeness and full verification. Furthermore, having a high-level specification of what the transformation should do at the tract level (independently of how it actually implements it) becomes beneficial because both descriptions provide two complementary views (specifications) of the behaviour of the transformation. Then, during the checking process the tract specifications and the code help testing each other.

5.3 Tool Support

The approach we have presented in this paper allows modellers to check the behaviour of a transformation by specifying a set of tracts that should be fulfilled. For each of these tracts we generate the tract test suite mentioned in the previous section, i.e. the sample input models for the tract, and then we check that the corresponding output models (i.e., the ones produced by the transformation) fulfil the tract invariants.

As a proof-of-concept of our proposal we have built a prototype that allows testing a transformation in an automated way, chaining three tools. In the first place, the tract classes and their associated invariants are specified using USE. The ASSL program that generates the tract test suite is also specified within the USE environment, and then executed within it. The second tool is a script that takes the input models generated by the ASSL procedure (which are in the textual format that both ASSL and USE understand, .cmd), converts them into the Ecore format so that they can be manipulated by ATL, invokes the ATL transformation under test, and converts the resulting target model into the USE .cmd format again (using an ATL query). Finally, the correctness of these output models is checked against the OCL invariants specified in the transformation tract using USE.

6 Further Application Examples

This sections presents two further case studies, showing their specification using tracts.

6.1 Families2Person

This section presents a set of *tracts* for the Families2Person model transformation, one of the simplest examples of model transformations used in the literature to explain model transformation concepts and mechanisms—it is even mentioned in the ATL documentation as some kind of ATL "hello world" example [24, 25]. Despite its apparent simplicity, the formalization of this example using tracts

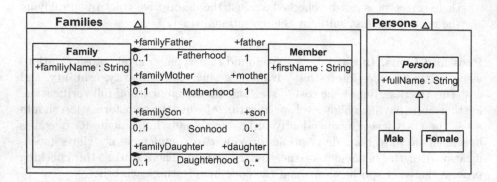

Fig. 13. Families and Persons Metamodels

has allowed us to reveal several critical problems of this transformation, which ends up being by no means *simple*.

This transformation takes models conforming to the Families metamodel and transforms them into models that conform to the Persons metamodel. Figure 13 shows these input and output metamodels. The first one describes families, which are composed of members: a father, a mother, several sons and several daughters. Each family member has a first name. In the Persons metamodel, a person has a full name (first name and surname), and is either a male or a female. This example follows the original specification by Freddy Allilaire and Frédéric Jouault in 2007, described in [25]. Cardinality constraints, as well as black diamonds, impose some restrictions on the relationships: for example, a family should have exactly one father and one mother. Other significant constraints are also implicitly imposed by black diamonds, as we shall later see.

The ATL transformation that implements the conversion is shown in figure 14, also taken from [25]. It has two helpers, one to decide whether a member is female or not, and other to compute the full name of members. The transformation comprises two rules, for producing male and female persons.

Tracts for the Families2Person Transformation. The Families2Persons transformation has been extensively used in many tutorials and papers to show a simple ATL model transformation. We therefore assume it is perfectly correct. Our aim in this section is to specify it using tracts. As mentioned earlier, tracts allow a modular specification of a model transformation whereby each tract concentrates on a set of input models (intensionally defined by the *source tract constraints*), the corresponding set of output models (intensionally defined by the *target tract constraints*), and the relationships between them as (should be) realized by the transformation (intensionally defined by the *source-target tract constraints*). In addition, every tract defines a *tract test suite* which is a collection of sample input models that are used to test the actual behaviour of the transformation.

```
module Families2Persons;
create OUT: Persons from IN: Families;

helper context Families!Member def: isFemale(): Boolean =
  if not self.familyMother.oclIsUndefined() then true
  else
    if not self.familyDaughter.oclIsUndefined() then true
    else false
    endif
  endif;

helper context Families!Member def: familyName: String =
  if not self.familyFather.oclIsUndefined() then
    self.familyFather.lastName
  else
    if not self.familyMother.oclIsUndefined() then
      self.familyMother.lastName
    else
      if not self.familySon.oclIsUndefined() then
        self.familySon.lastName
      else
        self.familyDaughter.lastName
      endif
    endif
  endif;

rule Member2Male {
  from
    s: Families!Member (not s.isFemale())
  to
    t: Persons!Male ( fullName <- s.firstName + '␣' + s.familyName )
}
rule Member2Female {
  from
    s: Families!Member (s.isFemale())
  to
    t: Persons!Female (fullName <- s.firstName + '␣' + s.familyName)
}
```

Fig. 14. ATL transformation `Families2Persons` (from [24])

Every tract is formally specified in terms of a class, that serves as context for all the OCL invariants that describe the different tract constraints.

Members Only Tract. The first tract (specified by class `MembersOnlyTract`) focuses on the simplest elements that can be used as input of the transformation: just members. According to the `Families` metamodel, a valid model may contain members associated to no family. An example of such model is shown in figure 15.

The *tract source constraint* that specifies such models is defined by OCL invariant `SCR_MembersOnly`:

```
context MembersOnlyTract
inv SCR_MembersOnly:
  Member.allInstances->forAll (m |
    m.familyFather->size() + m.familyMother->size() +
    m.familySon->size() + m.familyDaugther->size() = 0)
```

We need to decide what the transformation should do when these models are used as input models. In the first place, there is no restriction on the kind of persons that can be produced. So no *tract target constraint* is needed. Regarding

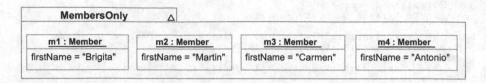

Fig. 15. A *source test model* for the `MembersOnly` tract

the *source-target constraints*, in this case there is no family to get the last name from, and there is no indication about the sex of the members. We can then decide that their full names will coincide with their first names, and that they all will be female. This is expressed by the following constraint:

```
context MembersOnlyTract
inv SRC_TRG_MembersOnly :
  Member.allInstances->forAll (m |
    Female.allInstances->one (p | p.fullName=m.firstName))
  and Member.allInstances->size () = Person.allInstances->size ()
```

Now it comes to checking what the transformation does, and (with horror) we find that the transformation does not work. In fact, it aborts execution with the following error message:

```
An internal error occurred during: "Launching Families2Persons".
java.lang.ClassCastException :
  org.eclipse.m2m.atl.engine.emfvm.lib.OclUndefined cannot be cast to
    org.eclipse.m2m.atl.engine.emfvm.lib.HasFields
```

After investigating, it is due to the fact that the `familyName` attribute of variable `s` in the transformation rule is not defined. And what is worse, even if the transformation did not abort its execution, we realized that it would convert all members into male persons. And then, it would add a blank space to their names. So the exemplar transformation have not even passed our most simple test... What is wrong with all this?

In the first place, our decisions above may seem arbitrary. Why should they all become female persons and not male? In fact, it may be not fair to make any decision at all, it really does not make any sense to have no families in the `Families` model, only members. So the best option in this case is to rule out the possibility of having members with no associated families in any valid `Families` model. This is expressed by OCL constraint `NoIsolatedMembers` that provides an invariant for class `Member` in the `Families` metamodel:

```
context Member
inv NoIsolatedMembers :
  Member.allInstances->forAll (m |
    m.familyFather->size () + m.familyMother->size () +
    m.familySon->size () + m.familyDaugther->size () > 0)
```

From this moment on, we will suppose that this constraint forms an integral part of the `Families` metamodel.

No Children Tract. The second tract (specified by class `NoChildrenTract`) focuses on simple families composed of two members: a father and a mother.

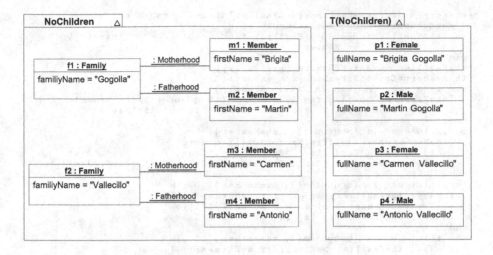

Fig. 16. Test model for the `NoChildren` tract and its corresponding transformed model

An example of such model is shown on the left hand side of figure 16. The *tract source constraint* that specifies such models is defined by OCL invariant `SCR_NoChildren`:

```
context NoChildrenTract
inv SCR_NoChildren:
  Family. allInstances->forAll(f | f.son->size()+f.daughter->size() = 0)
```

We need to decide what the transformation should do when these models are used as input models. In the first place, there is no restriction on the kind of persons that can be produced. So no *tract target constraint* is needed.

Regarding the *source-target constraints*, in this case we need to check that for every member there is one person that is either male or female depending on the role he or she plays in the family, and whose full name corresponds to the first name of the member and the family name of the family. This is expressed by the following constraint:

```
context NoChildrenTract inv SRC_TRG_NoChildren:
  Member. allInstances->forAll (m |
   m.familyMother->size()=1 implies Female. allInstances->exists(p |
   p.fullName=m. firstName.concat('␣').concat(m.familyMother.familyName)))
 and
  Member. allInstances->forAll (m |
   m.familyFather->size()=1 implies Male. allInstances->exists(p |
   p.fullName=m. firstName.concat('␣').concat(m.familyFather.familyName)))
 and
  Member. allInstances->size() = Person. allInstances->size()
```

The test suite for this tract is defined by the following ASSL procedure, which generates sample input models that conform to the `Families` metamodel to be transformed by the transformation.

```
procedure mkSourceNoChildren(numFamily:Integer, numMember:Integer,
    numMother:Integer, numFather:Integer)
  var theFamilies: Sequence(Family), theMember: Sequence(Member),
        f: Family, m: Member;
begin
  theFamilies:=CreateN(Family,[numFamily]);
  theMember:=CreateN(Member,[numMember]);
  for i:Integer in [Sequence{1..numFamily}] begin
    [theFamilies->at(i)].familyName:=Any([Sequence{'Red','Green',
            'Blue','Black','White','Brown','Amber','Yellow'}]);
  end;
  for i:Integer in [Sequence{1..numMember}] begin
    [theMember->at(i)].firstName:=Any([Sequence{
      'Ada','Bel','Cam','Day','Eva','Flo','Gen','Hao','Ina','Jen',
      'Ali','Bob','Cyd','Dan','Eli','Fox','Gil','Hal','Ike','Jan'}]);
  end;
  for i:Integer in [Sequence{1..numMother}] begin
    f:=Try([theFamilies->select(f|f.noMother())]);
    m:=Try([theMember->select(m|m.noFamily())]);
    Insert(Motherhood,[f],[m]);
  end;
  for i:Integer in [Sequence{1..numFather}] begin
    f:=Try([theFamilies->select(f|f.noFather())]);
    m:=Try([theMember->select(m|m.noFamily())]);
    Insert(Fatherhood,[f],[m]);
  end; end;
```

The following Ecore model shows an example of the models constructed in this
way (also shown in figure 16), ready to serve as input to the model transformation
under study:

```
<?xml version="1.0" encoding="ISO-8859-1"?>
<xmi:XMI xmi:version="2.0" xmlns:xmi="http://www.omg.org/XMI"
        xmlns="Families">
  <Family lastName="Gogolla">
    <mother firstName="Brigita"/>
    <father firstName="Martin"/>
  </Family>
  <Family lastName="Vallecillo">
    <mother firstName="Carmen"/>
    <father firstName="Antonio"/>
  </Family>
</xmi:XMI>
```

MFDS Tract. This tract (specified by class MFDS) focuses on families composed
of exactly four members: one father, one mother, one son and one daughter. An
example of such model is shown in figure 17. The *tract constraint* that specifies
such models is defined by the next OCL invariants:

```
context MFDS inv SRC_OneDaughterOneSon:
  Family.allInstances->forAll(f|f.daughter->size=1 and f.son->size()=1)
context MFDS inv SRC_TRG_MotherDaughter2Female:
  Family.allInstances->forAll(fam|Female.allInstances->exists(m|
    fam.mother.firstName.concat('ω').concat(fam.familyName)=m.fullName))
  and
  Family.allInstances->forAll(fam|Female.allInstances->exists(d|
    fam.daughter->any(true).firstName.concat('ω').concat(fam.familyName)
    =d.fullName))

context MFDS inv SRC_TRG_FatherSon2Male:
  Family.allInstances->forAll(fam|Male.allInstances->exists(f|
    fam.father.firstName.concat('ω').concat(fam.familyName)
    =f.fullName))
    and
```

```
      Family.allInstances->forAll(fam|Male.allInstances->exists(s|
        fam.son->any(true).firstName.concat('␣').concat(fam.familyName)=
        s.fullName))

context MFDS inv SRC_TRG_Female2MotherDaughter:
  Female.allInstances->forAll(f|Family.allInstances->exists(fam|
    fam.mother.firstName.concat('␣').concat(fam.familyName)=f.fullName
    or
    fam.daughter->any(true).firstName.concat('␣').concat(fam.familyName)
      =f.fullName))

context MFDS inv SRC_TRG_Male2FatherSon:
  Male.allInstances->forAll(m|Family.allInstances->exists(fam|
    fam.father.firstName.concat('␣').concat(fam.familyName)=m.fullName
    or
    fam.son->any(true).firstName.concat('␣').concat(fam.familyName)
      =m.fullName))

context MFDS inv SRC_TRG_MemberSize_EQ_PersonSize:
  Member.allInstances->size=Person.allInstances->size
```

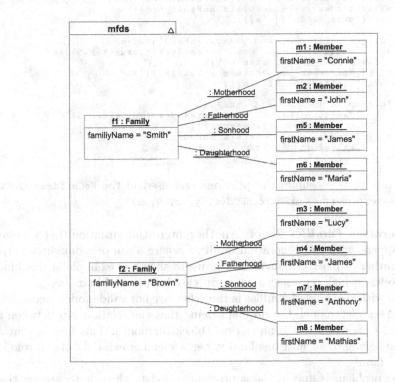

Fig. 17. A test model for the MFDS tract

And the ASSL code is:

```
procedure mkSourceMFDS(numFamily:Integer, numMember:Integer, numMother:
    Integer, numFather:Integer, numDaughter:Integer, numSon:Integer)
    var theFamilies: Sequence(Family), theMember: Sequence(Member),
        f: Family, m: Member;
begin
    theFamilies:=CreateN(Family,[numFamily]);
    theMember:=CreateN(Member,[numMember]);
    for i:Integer in [Sequence{1..numFamily}] begin
        [theFamilies->at(i)].familyName:=Any([Sequence{'Red','Green',
            'Blue','Black','White','Brown','Amber','Yellow'}]);
    end;
    for i:Integer in [Sequence{1..numMember}] begin
        [theMember->at(i)].firstName:=Any([Sequence{
            'Ada','Bel','Cam','Day','Eva','Flo','Gen','Hao','Ina','Jen',
            'Ali','Bob','Cyd','Dan','Eli','Fox','Gil','Hal','Ike','Jan'}]);
    end;
    for i:Integer in [Sequence{1..numMother}] begin
        f:=Try([theFamilies->select(f|f.noMother())]);
        m:=Try([theMember->select(m|m.noFamily())]);
        Insert(Motherhood,[f],[m]);
    end;
    for i:Integer in [Sequence{1..numFather}] begin
        f:=Try([theFamilies->select(f|f.noFather())]);
        m:=Try([theMember->select(m|m.noFamily())]);
        Insert(Fatherhood,[f],[m]);
    end;
    for i:Integer in [Sequence{1..numDaughter}] begin
        f:=Try([Family.allInstances->sortedBy(f|f.daughter->size()+
            f.son->size)->asSequence()]);
        m:=Try([theMember->select(m|m.noFamily())]);
        Insert(Daughterhood,[f],[m]);
    end;
    for i:Integer in [Sequence{1..numSon}] begin
        f:=Try([Family.allInstances->sortedBy(f|f.daughter->size+
            f.son->size())->asSequence()]);
        m:=Try([theMember->select(m|m.noFamily())]);
        Insert(Sonhood,[f],[m]);
    end; end;
```

Note that this code subsumes the previous one used in the NoChildren tract, which can be expressed as mkSourceMFDS(x, y, z, 0, 0).

Two Generation Families Tract. Another interesting situation that we may think of happens with two-generation families, where a son or a daughter plays the role of father or mother in another. Figure 18 shows an example of this kind of input models, which represent a common case in real-world families.

The issue with this kind of families is that they are not valid models according to the Families metamodel, the problem being that the relationship between a family and its members is a composition (black diamond). This means that a member can belong to at most one family, i.e., a member can only play a role in at most one family.

Here, the problem is due to the source metamodel, which is too restrictive and does not allow this kind of families. A possible solution would be to change the source metamodel, relaxing it, but this is outside our hands. We wanted to respect the source and target metamodels, as well as the transformation itself, as much as possible. At most we could add some constraints if the transformation is ill-defined, to avoid problematic source models (as we have done with

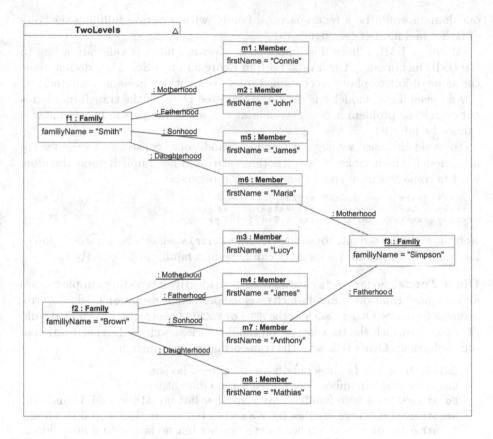

Fig. 18. A two-generations model

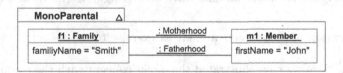

Fig. 19. A test model for the Monoparental tract

the first tract). But relaxing the original constraints may not be appropriate. Besides, making this kind of changes to any of the metamodels can produce undesirable effects, because the developers of the example may have made use of these constraints.

Monoparental Tract. Although a composition relation forbids an element to play two roles in two different containers, it is not so clear whether a contained element can play two different roles in the same container or not. An example in our domain would be a mono-parental family, with a person fulfilling the roles of father and mother (see figure 19).

Although UML allows this model to be drawn, and it is valid according to the UML metamodel, it is invalid both in Ecore and in USE. They do not allow the same object to play two contained roles even within the same container.

And even if this model was valid, the expected result of the transformation is not clear. The problem here is determining the sex of the person because now it cannot be inferred.

To avoid this case we suggest to add an additional constraint to the Family metamodel, which makes this restriction clear, and not implicit (and therefore valid in some technical spaces, and invalid in others):

```
context Member inv BlackDiamonds:
 familyMother->size() + familyFather->size() +
 familyDaughter->size() + familySon->size() <= 1
```

Note how this invariant, together with the NoIsolatedMembers invariant, forces the number of roles that a member can have in a family to be exactly 1.

Other Tracts. So far tracts have allowed us to identify interesting sample models for the transformation, some of which revealed problematic source models and erroneous behaviours. Others, such as the MFDS or NoChildren tracts, determined valid use cases for which the transformation should work as well as the specification of such behaviour. Other tracts for the transformation may include:

- OnlyGirls where families only have daughters, no sons.
- OnlyBoys where families only have sons, no daughters.
- NoFather3Kids where families have a mother but no father, and 3 children.
- NoMother3Kids where families have a father but no mother, and 3 children.
- NoFatherNoKids where families have a mother but no father, and no children.
- NoMotherNoKids where families have a father but no mother, and no children.
- OrphanSons where families have only sons (no father, mother or daughters).
- OrphanDaughthers where families have only daughters (no father, mother or sons).

The specification of these tracts are left as exercise to the reader.

Summary. Here we have illustrated the *Tract* concept with the example of the Families2Person transformation. It has allowed us to discover that even such a simple example is by no means trivial. In particular, the specification of this transformation using *Tracts* has uncovered one case where the transformation fails (MembersOnly), and has also allowed us to explore the input and output spaces of the transformation, discovering that its scope is much more reduced that we intuitively thought: only individual families are allowed, with no shared members. This rules out, for instance, most common cases of two-generation families (grandparent-parent-children) or families whose children marry members of other families. We have also discovered that the implicit restrictions imposed by some modeling constructs, such as black diamonds, are treated differently in several modeling tools. In these cases, the explicit expression of these constraints may be helpful.

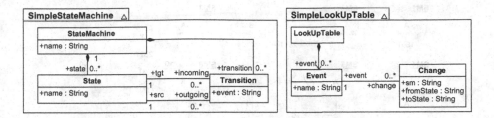

Fig. 20. Source and Target Metamodels of transformation SM2T

6.2 StateMachineTo LookUp Tables

As a second example, let us consider a model transformation SM2T between simple state machines and a lookup table that lists the events and their associated transitions [55]. The source and target metamodels of this transformation are shown in figure 20. In this case, we want only one lookup table to be built, whose entries are all the events of all the state machines in the source model. In addition to the (multiplicity) constraints shown in these class diagrams, we need to add uniqueness on names of the state machines, and uniqueness of names of states within the same state machine:

```
context StateMachine inv uniqueNames:
    self.state->isUnique(name) and
    StateMachine.allInstances->isUnique(name)
```

To specify the SM2T transformation we can define the following six tracts, whose test suite models are illustrated in figure 21 (literals SM1...SM6 represent the names of the state machines):

- 1S0T: state machines with single states and no transitions.
- 2S1T: state machines with two states and one transition between them. In this case the entries of the resulting lookup table will have the form $\{x \mapsto (SM2, A, B)\}$.
- 2S2T: state machines with two states and two transition between them. In this case the entries of the resulting lookup table will be of the form $\{x \mapsto (SM3, A, B), y \mapsto (SM3, B, A)\}$.
- 1S1T: state machines with single states and one transition. In this case the entries of the resulting lookup table will have the form $\{x \mapsto (SM4, A, A)\}$.
- 3S3T: state machines with three states and three transitions, forming a cycle. In this case the entries of the resulting lookup table will be of the form $\{x \mapsto (SM5, A, B), y \mapsto (SM5, B, C), z \mapsto (SM5, C, A)\}$.
- 3S9T: state machines with three states and 9 transitions (see figure 21). In this case the entries of the resulting lookup table will have the form $\{x0 \mapsto (SM6, A, A), x1 \mapsto (SM6, A, B), x2 \mapsto (SM6, B, A), y0 \mapsto (SM6, B, B), y1 \mapsto (SM6, B, C), y2 \mapsto (SM6, C, B), z0 \mapsto (SM6, C, C), z1 \mapsto (SM6, C, A), z2 \mapsto (SM6, A, C)\}$.

Let us show here one of this tracts, 2S1T, for illustration purposes. The rest follow similar patters. In the first place, the *tract source constraint* that specifies the source models is defined by OCL invariant SCR_2S1T:

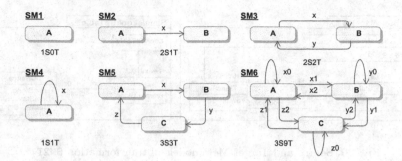

Fig. 21. Test suites samples for the 6 tracts defined for model transformation SM2T

```
context 2S1T−Tract
inv SCR_2S1T:
   StateMachine.allInstances−>forAll (sm |
      (sm.state−>size() = 2)  and (sm.transition−>size() = 1)
      (sm.transition.src <> sm.transition.tgt)
```

We need to decide what the transformation should do when these models are used as input models. There is no restriction on the kinds of entries that can be produced in the lookup table, but we need to state that only one lookup table is produced. This is expressed by the following OCL constraint:

```
context 2S1T−Tract
inv TRG_2S1T: LookUpTable.allInstances−>size() = 1
```

Regarding the *source-target constraints*, given that every state machine has only one transition, there should be one change in the lookup table for every state machine, and the attributes should match with the events and states related by the corresponding transition in the state machine. This is expressed by the following source-target constraint:

```
context 2S1T−Tract
inv SRC_TRG_2S1T:
   StateMachine.allInstances−>size() = LookUpTable.change−>size() and
   LookUpTable.change−>forAll (c |
      StateMachine.allInstances−>one(sm | (sm.name = c.sm) and
         (sm.transition.src−>collect(name) = c.fromState.asSet()) and
         (sm.transition.tgt−>collect(name) = c.toState.asSet()) and
         (sm.transition.event = c.event.name) )
```

Finally, the test suite for this tract is defined by an ASSL procedure that generates the input models.

```
procedure mk2S1T(numSM:Integer)
   var theStateMachines: Sequence(StateMachine),
      theStates: Sequence(State),
      theTransitions: Sequence(Transition);
begin
   theStateMachines:=CreateN(StateMachine,[numSM]);
   theStates:=CreateN(State,[2*numSM]);
   theTransitions:=CreateN(Transition,[numSM]);
   for i:Integer in [Sequence{1..numSM}] begin
      [theStateMachines−>at(i)].name:= ['SM'.concat(i.toString())];
         [theTransitions−>at(i)].event:= ['E'.concat(i.toString())];
         [theStates−>at(2*i−1)].name:= ['ST'.concat((2*i−1).toString())];
         [theStates−>at(2*i)].name:= ['ST'.concat((2*i).toString())];
```

```
        Insert(States,[theStateMachines->at(i)],[theStates->at(2*i-1)]);
        Insert(States,[theStateMachines->at(i)],[theStates->at(2*i)]);
  Insert(Transition,[theStateMachines->at(i)],[theTransitions->at(i)]);
  Insert(Cause,[theTransitions->at(i)],[theStates->at(2*i-1)]);
        Insert(Effect,[theTransitions->at(i)],[theStates->at(2*i)]);
  end;
end;
```

In the example above, the type of the SM2T transformation is given by the six
tracts defined for it: SM2T $\models$ 1S0T $\wedge$ 2S1T $\wedge$ 2S2T $\wedge$ 1S1T $\wedge$ 3S3T $\wedge$ 3S9T. Of course,
other tracts could have been defined for this transformation if the user requires
to include further contexts of use.

7 Conclusion

In this paper we have presented the issues involved in model transformation
specification and testing, and introduced the concept of *Tract*, a generalization of model transformation contracts. We have showed how it can be used
for model transformation specification and black-box testing. A tract defines a
set of constraints on the source and target metamodels, a set of source-target
constraints, and a tract test suite, i.e., a collection of source models satisfying
the source constraints. To test a transformation T we automatically generate
the input test suite models using the ASSL language, and then transform them
into their corresponding target models. These models are checked with the USE
tool against the constraints defined for the transformation. The checking process
can be automated, allowing the model transformation tester to process a large
number of models in a mechanical way. Although this approach to testing does
not guarantee full correctness, it provides very interesting advantages over other
approaches, as we have discussed above.

There are other issues that we have not covered in this paper, such as the generation of source models (test suites) to optimize metamodel coverage or transformation code coverage (in case of white-box testing). In this respect, there are
several lines of work that we plan to address next. In particular, we would like to
study how to improve our proposal by incorporating some of the existing works on
the effective generation of input test cases. We expect this to help us enhance the
definition of our tract test suites. Larger case studies will be carried out in order
to stress the applicability of our approach and to obtain more extensive feedback.
We would also like to conduct some empirical studies on the effects of the use
of tracts in the lifecycle of model transformations. Concerning the tracts, we also
plan to investigate some of their properties, such as their composability, subsump-
tion, refinement or coverage. Finally, we plan to improve the current tool support
for tracts, incorporating the creation and maintenance of libraries of tracts, and
the concurrent execution of the tests using sets of distributed machines.

Acknowledgements. The authors would like to thank the volume editors,
Marco Bernardo, Vittorio Cortellessa and Alfonso Pierantonio for their invitation
to present our ideas on model transformation specification and testing, and to
Mirco Kuhlmann, Fernando López and Javier Troya for their help and support

during the preparation of the paper. This work is supported by Research Projects TIN2008-03107 and TIN2011-23795 and by the Austrian Science Fund (FWF) under grant J 3159-N23.

References

1. Lin, Y., Zhang, J., Gray, J.: Model comparison: A key challenge for transformation testing and version control in model driven software development. In: Control in Model Driven Software Development. OOPSLA/GPCE: Best Practices for Model-Driven Software Development, pp. 219–236. Springer (2004)
2. Baudry, B., Dinh-Trong, T., Mottu, J.M., Simmonds, D., France, R., Ghosh, S., Fleurey, F., Traon, Y.L.: Model transformation testing challenges. In: Proc. of IMDD-MDT 2006 (2006)
3. Stevens, P.: A Landscape of Bidirectional Model Transformations. In: Lämmel, R., Visser, J., Saraiva, J. (eds.) GTTSE 2008. LNCS, vol. 5235, pp. 408–424. Springer, Heidelberg (2008)
4. Baudry, B., Ghosh, S., Fleurey, F., France, R., Traon, Y.L., Mottu, J.M.: Barriers to systematic model transformation testing. Communications of the ACM 53(6), 139–143 (2010)
5. Baresi, L., Ehrig, K., Heckel, R.: Verification of Model Transformations: A Case Study with BPEL. In: Montanari, U., Sannella, D., Bruni, R. (eds.) TGC 2006. LNCS, vol. 4661, pp. 183–199. Springer, Heidelberg (2007)
6. Ehrig, H., Ehrig, K., de Lara, J., Taentzer, G., Varró, D., Varró-Gyapay, S.: Termination Criteria for Model Transformation. In: Cerioli, M. (ed.) FASE 2005. LNCS, vol. 3442, pp. 49–63. Springer, Heidelberg (2005)
7. Ehrig, K., Küster, J.M., Taentzer, G.: Generating instance models from meta models. Software and Systems Modeling 8, 479–500 (2009)
8. Küster, J.M.: Definition and validation of model transformations. Software and Systems Modeling 5(3), 233–259 (2006)
9. Cabot, J., Clarisó, R., Guerra, E., de Lara, J.: Verification and validation of declarative model-to-model transformations through invariants. Journal of Systems and Software 83(2), 283–302 (2010)
10. Anastasakis, K., Bordbar, B., Küster, J.M.: Analysis of model transformations via Alloy. In: Proc. of MODEVVA (2007),
    http://www.cs.bham.ac.uk/~bxb/Papres/Modevva07.pdf
11. Troya, J., Vallecillo, A.: A rewriting logic semantics for ATL. Journal of Object Technology 10(5), 1–29 (2011)
12. Brottier, E., Fleurey, F., Steel, J., Baudry, B., Traon, Y.L.: Metamodel-based test generation for model transformations: an algorithm and a tool. In: Proc. of ISSRE 2006, pp. 85–94 (2006)
13. Solberg, A., Reddy, R., Simmonds, D., France, R., Ghosh, S.: Developing distributed services using an aspect-oriented model driven framework. International Journal of Cooperative Information Systems 15(4), 535–564 (2006)
14. Mottu, J.-M., Baudry, B., Le Traon, Y.: Reusable MDA Components: A Testing-for-Trust Approach. In: Wang, J., Whittle, J., Harel, D., Reggio, G. (eds.) MoDELS 2006. LNCS, vol. 4199, pp. 589–603. Springer, Heidelberg (2006)
15. Fleurey, F., Baudry, B., Muller, P.A., Traon, Y.L.: Qualifying input test data for model transformations. Software and Systems Modeling 8(2), 185–203 (2009)

16. Gogolla, M., Hamann, L., Kuhlmann, M.: Proving and Visualizing OCL Invariant Independence by Automatically Generated Test Cases. In: Fraser, G., Gargantini, A. (eds.) TAP 2010. LNCS, vol. 6143, pp. 38–54. Springer, Heidelberg (2010)

17. Cariou, E., Marvie, R., Seinturier, L., Duchien, L.: OCL for the specification of model transformation contracts. In: Proc. of the OCL and Model Driven Engineering Workshop (2004)

18. Gogolla, M., Bohling, J., Richters, M.: Validating UML and OCL Models in USE by Automatic Snapshot Generation. Software and Systems Modeling 4(4), 386–398 (2005)

19. Gogolla, M., Büttner, F., Richters, M.: USE: A UML-based specification environment for validating UML and OCL. Science of Computer Programming 69, 27–34 (2007)

20. Meyer, B.: Applying design by contract. IEEE Computer 25(10), 40–51 (1992)

21. Andova, S., van den Brand, M.G.J., Engelen, L.J.P., Verhoeff, T.: MDE Basics with a DSL Focus. In: Bernardo, M., Cortellessa, V., Pierantonio, A. (eds.) SFM 2012. LNCS, vol. 7320, pp. 21–57. Springer, Heidelberg (2012)

22. Cabot, J., Gogolla, M.: Object Constraint Language (OCL): A Definitive Guide. In: Bernardo, M., Cortellessa, V., Pierantonio, A. (eds.) SFM 2012. LNCS, vol. 7320, pp. 58–90. Springer, Heidelberg (2012)

23. Di Ruscio, D., Eramo, R., Pierantonio, A.: Model Transformations. In: Bernardo, M., Cortellessa, V., Pierantonio, A. (eds.) SFM 2012. LNCS, vol. 7320, pp. 91–136. Springer, Heidelberg (2012)

24. Eclipse: ATL Tutorials – A simple ATL transformation (2007), http://wiki.eclipse.org/ATL/ Tutorials_Create_a_simple_ATL_transformation

25. Eclipse: Basic ATL examples (2007), http://www.eclipse.org/m2m/atl/basicExamples_Patterns/

26. Object Management Group: Object Constraint Language (OCL) Specification. Version 2.2. OMG Document formal/2010-02-01 (2010)

27. Jouault, F., Allilaire, F., Bézivin, J., Kurtev, I.: ATL: A model transformation tool. Science of Computer Programming 72(1-2), 31–39 (2008)

28. OMG: MOF QVT Final Adopted Specification. Object Management Group. OMG doc. ptc/05-11-01 (2005)

29. Cuadrado, J.S., Molina, J.G., Tortosa, M.M.: RubyTL: A Practical, Extensible Transformation Language. In: Rensink, A., Warmer, J. (eds.) ECMDA-FA 2006. LNCS, vol. 4066, pp. 158–172. Springer, Heidelberg (2006), http://rubytl.rubyforge.org/

30. Cicchetti, A., Di Ruscio, D., Eramo, R., Pierantonio, A.: JTL: A Bidirectional and Change Propagating Transformation Language. In: Malloy, B., Staab, S., van den Brand, M. (eds.) SLE 2010. LNCS, vol. 6563, pp. 183–202. Springer, Heidelberg (2011), http://jtl.di.univaq.it/

31. Baudry, B., Dinh-Trong, T., Mottu, J., Simmonds, D., France, R., Ghosh, S., Fleurey, F., Le Traon, Y.: Model transformation testing challenges. In: ECMDA Workshop on Integration of MDD and Model Driven Testing (2006)

32. France, R.B., Rumpe, B.: Model-driven development of complex software: A research roadmap. In: Proc. of ISCE 2007, pp. 37–54 (2007)

33. Van Der Straeten, R., Mens, T., Van Baelen, S.: Challenges in Model-Driven Software Engineering. In: Chaudron, M.R.V. (ed.) MoDELS 2008. LNCS, vol. 5421, pp. 35–47. Springer, Heidelberg (2009)

34. Amrani, M., Lúcio, L., Selim, G., Combemale, B., Dingel, J., Vangheluwe, H., Traon, Y.L., Cordy, J.R.: A tridimensional approach for studying the formal verification of model transformations. In: Proc. of the 1st International Workshop on Verification and Validation of Model Transformations, VOLT 2012 (2012)
35. Czarnecki, K., Helsen, S.: Feature-based survey of model transformation approaches. IBM Systems Journal 45(3), 621–646 (2006)
36. Kühne, T., Mezei, G., Syriani, E., Vangheluwe, H., Wimmer, M.: Systematic transformation development. ECEASST 21 (2009)
37. Weisemoeller, I., Rumpe, B.: A domain specific transformation language. In: Models and Evolution Workshop @ MoDELS 2011 (2011)
38. Cabot, J., Clarisó, R., Guerra, E., de Lara, J.: An Invariant-Based Method for the Analysis of Declarative Model-to-Model Transformations. In: Czarnecki, K., Ober, I., Bruel, J.-M., Uhl, A., Völter, M. (eds.) MODELS 2008. LNCS, vol. 5301, pp. 37–52. Springer, Heidelberg (2008)
39. Varró, D., Varró–Gyapay, S., Ehrig, H., Prange, U., Taentzer, G.: Termination Analysis of Model Transformations by Petri Nets. In: Corradini, A., Ehrig, H., Montanari, U., Ribeiro, L., Rozenberg, G. (eds.) ICGT 2006. LNCS, vol. 4178, pp. 260–274. Springer, Heidelberg (2006)
40. Narayanan, A., Karsai, G.: Towards verifying model transformations. Electr. Notes Theor. Comput. Sci. 211, 191–200 (2008)
41. Varró, D.: Automated formal verification of visual modeling languages by model checking. Software and System Modeling 3(2), 85–113 (2004)
42. Maoz, S., Ringert, J.O., Rumpe, B.: CDDiff: Semantic Differencing for Class Diagrams. In: Mezini, M. (ed.) ECOOP 2011. LNCS, vol. 6813, pp. 230–254. Springer, Heidelberg (2011)
43. Kolovos, D.S., Paige, R.F., Polack, F.A.: Model comparison: a foundation for model composition and model transformation testing. In: GaMMa 2006, pp. 13–20. ACM (2006)
44. Lin, Y., Zhang, J., Gray, J.: A testing framework for model transformations. Model-Driven Software Development, 219–236 (2005)
45. García-Domínguez, A., Kolovos, D.S., Rose, L.M., Paige, R.F., Medina-Bulo, I.: EUnit: A Unit Testing Framework for Model Management Tasks. In: Whittle, J., Clark, T., Kühne, T. (eds.) MoDELS 2011. LNCS, vol. 6981, pp. 395–409. Springer, Heidelberg (2011)
46. Mottu, J.M., Baudry, B., Traon, Y.L.: Model transformation testing: oracle issue. In: ICSTW 2008, pp. 105–112. IEEE (2008)
47. Ramos, R., Barais, O., Jézéquel, J.-M.: Matching Model-Snippets. In: Engels, G., Opdyke, B., Schmidt, D.C., Weil, F. (eds.) MoDELS 2007. LNCS, vol. 4735, pp. 121–135. Springer, Heidelberg (2007)
48. Balogh, A., Bergmann, G., Csertán, G., Gönczy, L., Horváth, Á., Majzik, I., Pataricza, A., Polgár, B., Ráth, I., Varró, D., Varró, G.: Workflow-Driven Tool Integration Using Model Transformations. In: Engels, G., Lewerentz, C., Schäfer, W., Schürr, A., Westfechtel, B. (eds.) Nagl Festschrift. LNCS, vol. 5765, pp. 224–248. Springer, Heidelberg (2010)
49. Guerra, E., de Lara, J., Wimmer, M., Kappel, G., Kusel, A., Retschitzegger, W., Schönböck, J., Schwinger, W.: Automated verification of model transformations based on visual contracts. Autom. Softw. Eng. (accepted for publication) (2012)
50. Cariou, E., Belloir, N., Barbier, F., Djemam, N.: OCL contracts for the verification of model transformations. ECEASST 24 (2009)
51. Kolovos, D., Paige, R., Rose, L., Polack, F.: Unit testing model management operations. In: ICSTW 2008, pp. 97–104. IEEE (2008)

52. Giner, P., Pelechano, V.: Test-Driven Development of Model Transformations. In: Schürr, A., Selic, B. (eds.) MoDELS 2009. LNCS, vol. 5795, pp. 748–752. Springer, Heidelberg (2009)
53. Gogolla, M., Vallecillo, A.: Tractable Model Transformation Testing. In: France, R.B., Kuester, J.M., Bordbar, B., Paige, R.F. (eds.) ECMFA 2011. LNCS, vol. 6698, pp. 221–235. Springer, Heidelberg (2011)
54. Heim, M.: Exploring Indiana Highways: Trip Trivia. Exploring America's Highway. Travel Organization Network (2007), http://en.wikipedia.org/wiki/Duck_test
55. Steel, J., Jézéquel, J.M.: On model typing. Software and Systems Modeling 6(4), 401–413 (2007)

Author Index